COPPER MOUNTAIN COLLEGE
GREENLEAF LIBRARY
3 0193 0002 3192 5

Y0-DCH-341

	DATE DUE	

Principles of Business: Management

Principles of Business: Management

Edited by
Richard Wilson, Ph.D.
The University of Tennessee at Chattanooga

SALEM PRESS

A Division of EBSCO Information Services, Inc.
Ipswich, Massachusetts

GREY HOUSE PUBLISHING

Cover photo: iStock

For information contact Grey House Publishing/Salem Press, 4919 Route 22, PO Box 56, Amenia, NY 12501

Principles of Business: Management, published by Grey House Publishing, Inc., Amenia, NY, under exclusive license from EBSCO Publishing, Inc.

∞ *The paper used in these volumes conforms to the American National Standard for Permanence of Paper for Printed Library Materials, Z39.48 1992 (R2009).*

Publisher's Cataloging-In-Publication Data
(Prepared by The Donohue Group, Inc.)

Names: Wilson, Richard L., 1944- editor.
Title: Principles of business. Management / edited by Richard Wilson, Ph.D., the University of Tennessee at Chattanooga.
Other Titles: Management
Description: [First edition]. | Ipswich, Massachusetts : Salem Press, a division of EBSCO Information Services, Inc. ; Amenia, NY : Grey House Publishing, [2017] | Includes bibliographical references and index.
Identifiers: ISBN 978-1-68217-330-5 (hardcover)
Subjects: LCSH: Management.
Classification: LCC HD31.2 .P75 2017 | DDC 658--dc23

First Printing
Printed in the United States of America

Contents

PUBLISHER'S NOTE

Management is the second of a new six-volume series with the title *Principles of Business.* The first volume, *Principles of Business: Finance,* has already appeared, and future volumes on Marketing, Entrepreneurship, Accounting, and International Business will be published into 2018. This resource is intended to introduce students and researchers to the fundamentals of business topics using easy-to-understand language. We hope that these books will become a go-to resource for interested readers seeking understanding of these important and far-reaching business topics.

The entries in this volume are arranged in an A to Z order, from "Behavioral Economics" to "Types of Business Organizations," making it easy to find the topic of interest. Each entry includes the following:

- An Abstract that provides a brief, concrete introduction to the topic and how the entry is organized;
- An Overview that offers a clear presentation of the topic;
- Multiple subheads that anchor the reader to the various concepts being discussed;
- Suggested Reading list that relates to the entry;
- A detailed Bibliography.

The book begins with an introduction to business management that discusses, in particular, the impact of technological innovations in business data management and supply chain management. The evolution of technology and thus, the workplace, has allowed organizations to offer benefits such as telecommuting, job-sharing, traditional flextime, and compressed work weeks. In order to remain competitive, businesses must continue to be flexible and above all else, have excellent management in place for organizational sustainability.

Added features include numerous illustrations and helpful diagrams of relevant topics.

The back matter in *Principles of Business: Management* is another valuable resource and includes:

- Detailed Glossary with more than 600 terms;
- Subject Index.

Salem Press extends its appreciation to all involved in the development and production of this work. The signed entries have all been written by scholars and experts in business. Without these expert contributions, a project of this nature would not be possible. A full list of contributor's names and affiliations follows this Publisher's Note. *Principles of Business: Management* is available in print and as an e-book.

Introduction

The functions and activities of management have remained broadly the same since modern firms first began engaging in commercial activities. Managers have always had to develop strategy, plan actions, organize functions, control processes, and lead others—all in a manner that successfully drives business. What has changed over time is how managers have viewed and executed these functions in response to evolving business conditions and new technologies.

This volume provides an arsenal of essential business management knowledge and practices. This knowledge is what enables managers and executives to function effectively in a complex world of change. These management practices provide managers and executives with proven means to transform management knowledge into action steps and initiatives that help organizations function more smoothly and achieve and maintain long term sustainability. The ability of managers and executives to guide their organization is especially critical in turbulent times, such as the current business climate that many businesses find themselves in.

Entrepreneurs who shun traditional business careers to pursue their unique and creative ideas, with little regard for formalized knowledge, may find that they can take their ideas only so far before the kinds of management knowledge and practices described in this work are needed to move the enterprise forward. Investors and venture capitalists may be attracted to an innovative idea, but they understand the need to adequately manage business functions and operations in order to achieve long-term growth of a new company. Many such investors, in fact, implant seasoned managers into a start up in which they have invested. It's not unusual for the original founders of a start up to be relegated to symbolic roles in their company as more experienced managers take over. The bottom line is that there is no escaping from the study of management knowledge and practices if a business is to succeed.

The Impact of Technology on Business Management

Business data management has become a core activity for all businesses, supporting a wide array of activities that include financial management, accounting, purchasing, sales, human resource management, facilities management, product planning, manufacturing, and strategic planning. The activities of virtually every employee in every organization are dependent on business data management (Moynihan, Tony 1990).

The ways in which information technology (IT) is used in an organization have also changed. Over the last few decades the technology that supports business data communications has been moving away from networks built solely with cables and wires to wireless systems. Cell phones provide access to e-mail, apps, web pages, and text messages. Laptops and tablets connect to the Internet from almost anywhere in the world and can be used in the same way, for the same work, as a desktop computer connected to an office network with a cable.

Implementation of IT-based supply chain management systems has been shown to have a positive effect on procurement of materials for production as well as on distribution, marketing, and sales after production (Richardson 2006). The integration associated with these processes is achieved through a variety of initiatives that may require expertise spanning the business process domain, partnership context, IT, and data communications (Rai, Patnayakuni and Seth 2006).

Information systems must be effectively managed to assure that business data processing is performed correctly and that the outcomes of data processing operations (reports, records, analysis, etc.) are accurate and reliable. During the last two decades the importance of information system (IS) controls has grown. What might have begun as a process for maintaining the internal integrity of business data processing can now be used to help assure compliance with various complex laws regarding the accuracy of corporate financial data or the protection of data regarding individuals. An information systems audit often include tests of transactions and outputs in order to provide reasonable assurance that security standards and controls are properly designed and implemented (ISACA 2001).

Because firms are so thoroughly dependent on business data management and the technologies that support data management, contingency planning has also become an essential business function. Contingency planners must be able to identify critical systems and critical data. They are tasked with developing alternative means to provide systems and data so that disruptions in operations and the potential loss of revenue can be avoided. Contingency plans must also be updated to reflect changes in an organization's needs.

Changes in the Workplace

Management of the 21st-century workplace faces several challenges. In a number of sectors, employers are expected to face a serious labor shortage. While baby boomers continue to retire, an insufficient number of younger people are entering the workforce to replace them. Those who do will certainly not have comparable experience. Recent estimates put the U.S. labor shortfall between 3 and 10 million workers.

In addition, the demographics of the workforce are changing in interesting ways. Women in the workforce have increased from 43 percent to 60 percent in the last three decades. Today, nearly three-quarters of mothers with children under age 18 are in the workforce, and most married couples live in two income households (Clark and Reed, 2004).

Thanks to increasing choices and opportunities, women today are more likely to hold more than one job or to attend a night program for graduate school, and in general to work both harder and longer, than their counterparts 50 years ago. Because women have a greater interest in work/family balance, they are also more likely to negotiate flexible arrangements, including flextime and compressed work weeks, telecommuting, job sharing, part-time employment, shorter work hours, or to leave the workforce altogether, when affordable (Piscione, 2004).

Management is adapting to this changing world by offering family-friendly benefits, including dependent care flexible spending accounts, job-sharing, child care, daily and traditional flextime, compensatory time off, family leave above the legal requirements, part-time telecommuting, the option to work at satellite sites or off-site locations, compressed work weeks, domestic partner benefits, and paid time-off banks. They may also offer family- or employee-friendly benefits such as wellness programs, home buying assistance, scholarship programs for the children of employees, tuition reimbursement, flexible or cafeteria style benefits plans, volunteer release time, phased retirement, and concierge services (Clark and Reed 2004).

Conclusion

Organizations take many things into consideration when developing their competitiveness. Success is the result of numerous factors, and excellent management is always essential for organizational sustainability. Employees possess expertise and experience, for example, and human resource management and development is required to improve and leverage this into a competitive advantage.

Principles of Business: Management addresses important aspects of business management ranging from strategy development to planning to project management. Familiarity with these topics is necessary for anyone who wants to lead an organization towards its corporate goals. Of course, it will take time to develop a productive understanding of all of the areas covered in this work, but successful business executives know that learning is a life-long process. Keep in mind, too, that what matters is not what an education can do for you; what matters is what you do with your education.

Michael Erbschloe, M.A.

Bibliography

Clark, S., and Reed, P. "Win-Win Workplace Practices: Improved Organizational Results and Improved Quality of Life." United States Department of Labor Women's Bureau. (September 2004)

"Employment and Earnings." United States Department of Labor, Bureau of Labor Statistics. (January 2006)

Fox, S. "Sleazy Scammers Push Unrelenting Assaults." *PC World*, p. 7. (2009, April)

Hill, C. & McShane, S. *Principles of Management.* McGraw-Hill, 2008.

"IS Auditing Guideline." Application Systems Review Document G14. Information Systems Audit and Control Association (ISACA) (2001).

Karygiannis, T., & Owens, L. "Wireless Network Security: 802.11, Bluetooth and Handheld Devices." *NIST Special Publication 800-48.* Computer Security Division. Information Technology Laboratory, National Institute of Standards and Technology. Gaithersburg, MD (2002).

Moynihan, Tony. "What Chief Executives and Senior Managers Want From Their IT Departments." *MIS Quarterly*, Mar 90, Vol. 14 Issue 1, p15-25. Retrieved

June 25, 2007 from EBSCO Online Database Academic Source Premier http://search.ebscohost.com/login.aspx?direct=true&db=aph&AN=9604086230&site=ehost-live

Piscione, D. "The Many Faces of 21st Century Working Women: A Report to the Women's Bureau of the United States Department of Labor." (1990, March)

Provos, N., Rajab, M., & Mavrommatis, P. "Cybercrime 2.0: When the Cloud Turns Dark." *Communications of the ACM, 52*(4), 42-47. (2009, April)

Rai, A., Patnayakuni, R., & Seth, N. "Firm Performance Impacts Of Digitally Enabled Supply Chain Integration Capabilities." *MIS Quarterly, 30(2)*, 225-246. Retrieved July 16, 2007, from Academic Search Premier database. http://search.ebscohost.com/login.aspx?direct=true&db=aph&AN=21145595&site=ehost-live

Stansky, L. (2009, February). "Internet law and cyber crime: the future is here." *Student Lawyer, 37*(6), 8-10. Retrieved April 20, 2009, from Academic Search Complete database. http://search.ebscohost.com/login.aspx?direct=true&db=a9h&AN=36888641&site=ehost-live

Contributors

Michael P. Auerbach
Michael P. Auerbach holds a Bachelor's degree from Wittenberg University and a Master's degree from Boston College. Mr. Auerbach has extensive private and public sector experience in a wide range of arenas including political science, business and economic development, tax policy, international development, defense, public administration and tourism.

Seth M. Azria
Mr. Azria earned his J.D., magna cum laude, from New York Law School where he was an editor of the Law Review and a research assistant. He has written appellate briefs and other memoranda of law on a variety of legal topics for submission to state and federal courts. He is a practicing attorney in Syracuse, New York.

John D. Benson
Mr. Benson is currently completing his doctoral degree in Management from the University of Phoenix, where his dissertation research is focused on the effect of emotional intelligence on employee empowerment. Mr. Benson is an organizational consultant specializing in leadership and behavior. He received his M.B.A. in 1994 from the University of Connecticut, and his B.S. in Mechanical Engineering in 1986 from Worcester Polytechnic Institute.

Edwin D. Davison
Mr. Davison is a licensed attorney from Dayton, OH and holds a Master of Business Administration degree and a Doctor of Law degree from the University of Wisconsin Madison. He has also acquired professional management training at the University of Michigan Ross School of Business, the UCLA Anderson School of Management, and the University of South Carolina Moore School of Business. He has over twenty years of experience as a management consultant, business professor (most recently UCLA Online Extension), entrepreneur, and U.S. Navy JAG attorney. Edwin Davison has presented and published research on multinational human resource practices.

Marlanda English
Dr. Marlanda English is president of ECS Consulting Associates which provides executive coaching and management consulting services. ECS also provides online professional development content. Dr. English was previously employed in various engineering, marketing and management positions with IBM, American Airlines, Borg-Warner Automotive and Johnson & Johnson. Dr. English holds a doctorate in business with a major in organization and management and a specialization in e-business.

Michael Erbschloe
Michael Erbschloe is an information technology consultant, educator, and author. He has taught graduate level courses and developed technology-related curriculum for several universities, and he speaks at conferences and industry events around the world. Michael holds a Master's degree in Sociology from Kent State University. He has authored hundreds of articles and several books on technology.

Simone I. Flynn
Dr. Simone I. Flynn earned her Doctorate in Cultural Anthropology from Yale University, where she wrote a dissertation on Internet communities. She is a writer, researcher, and teacher in Amherst, Massachusetts.

Marie Gould
Marie Gould is an Associate Professor and the Faculty Chair of the Business Administration Department at Peirce College in Philadelphia, Pennsylvania. She teaches in the areas of management, entrepreneurship, and international business. Although Ms. Gould has spent her career in both academia and corporate, she enjoys helping people learn new things — whether it's by teaching, developing or mentoring.

Steven R. Hoagland
Dr. Hoagland holds Bachelor and Master degrees in Economics, a Master of Urban Studies, and a Doctorate in Urban Services Management with a cognate in Education, all from Old Dominion University. His background includes service as senior-level university administrator responsible for planning, assessment, and research. He has consulted in the health care, information technology, and education sectors and taught as an adjunct professor of economics.

SHERYL D. MCCLINTON

Sheryl D. McClinton holds an M.A. in Management with concentrations in General Management and Conflict Resolution Management from Dallas Baptist University. She is a business professional with extensive knowledge and experience in leadership and business concepts.

SARA ROGERS

Sara Rogers is a lawyer and professor for several major universities. She earned two Master's degrees in Education from City University in Seattle Washington, and her Juris Doctor from Franklin Pierce Law Center in Concord, New Hampshire. Dr. Rogers resides in Phoenix, Arizona, where she teaches, serves as a legal consultant, and writes extensively on current legal issues and policies.

CAROLYN SPRAGUE

Carolyn Sprague holds a B.A. degree from the University of New Hampshire and a Master's degree in Library Science from Simmons College. Carolyn gained valuable business experience as owner of her own restaurant which she operated for 10 years. She has worked in numerous library/information settings within the academic, corporate and consulting worlds. Her operational experience as a manger at a global high tech firm and more recent work as a web content researcher have afforded Carolyn insights into many aspects of today's challenging and fast-changing business climate.

VANESSA A. TETTEH

Dr. Tetteh earned her doctorate from the University of Buckingham in England, U.K., where she wrote a dissertation on tourism policy, education, and training. She is a teacher, writer and management consultant based in Ghana, West Africa. Her work has appeared in journals such as *International Journal of Contemporary Hospitality Management*, *The Consortium Journal*, and *Ghana Review International*.

RICHA S. TIWARY

Dr. Richa S. Tiwary holds a doctorate in Marketing Management with a specialization in consumer behavior from Banaras Hindu University in India. She also holds a Master's in Library Sciences with dual concentration in Information Science & Technology, and, Library Information Services, from the Department of Information Studies, University at Albany-SUNY.

FRED WESTMARK

Mr. Westmark holds a doctorate in Business Management. Professionally, he has worked with a number of international consulting firms in the areas of finance, accounting, human resources, and management. He holds a number of patents for internet software. More recently, Dr. Westmark has devoted most of his time to writing. Besides business articles, he has written six film scripts, three novels, and over twenty five short stories.

RUTH A. WIENCLAW

Dr. Ruth A. Wienclaw holds a Ph.D. in industrial/organizational psychology with a specialization in organization development from the University of Memphis. She is the owner of a small business that works with organizations in both the public and private sectors, consulting on matters of strategic planning, training, and human/systems integration.

SCOTT ZIMMER

Mr. Scott Zimmer has earned a Master of Library Science degree, a Master's degree in computer science, and a Juris Doctor degree. He is both an attorney and the University Librarian at Alliant International University.

B

BEHAVIORAL ECONOMICS & FINANCE

ABSTRACT

A burgeoning field within the economics discipline concerns itself with consumer psychology. As such, the field of behavioral economics and finance employs a broad array of tools and methods to create a substantial composite of the consumer. Such an illustration is critical as it aids economists, financial professionals and policymakers to implement effective approaches and responses to problems within a system. This paper takes an in-depth look at the growing field of behavioral economics and finance and its significance for the overall study of economics.

OVERVIEW

The esteemed political economist and writer Peter Drucker once said "A business exists because the consumer is willing to pay you his money. You run a business to satisfy the consumer. That isn't marketing. That goes way beyond marketing" ("Building brands," 2009).

The most significant "x-factor" in an economic system is the behavior of the consumer. How he or she acts or reacts in a given situation is arguably the key to determining a business's best course of action. It is for this reason that economics looks to understand consumer behavior as part of its pursuits.

For generations, the approach to understanding consumer behavior in economics has been somewhat limited, due scientific dependence upon modeling and "real time" assessments. Such a conservative approach has led to a lack of information regarding consumer mindsets and also on how consumer behavior impacts the economic system in question.

The Development of a New Sub-Discipline

Behavioral economics and behavioral finance are terms that apply to a field of study that involves the application of social and human cognitive and emotional patterns for the purposes of understanding economic decisions and how they impact market prices, returns and resource allocation ("What is behavioral economics?", 2005). Behavioral economics is combines the disciplines of psychology and sociology within an economic framework.

Because it entails the application of varying degrees of other scientific fields, a great deal of debate continues regarding the origins of behavioral economics. In the view of many observers, iconic economist Adam Smith was perhaps the first to see "psychology as part of decision-making," according to business professor Nava Ashraf, adding, "He saw a conflict between the passions and an impartial spectator" (Lambert, 2006). Regardless of the founder of this increasingly relevant field, the fact that many applications of behavioral economics in recent history have coincided with major changes in economic conditions is undeniable.

In the mid-19th century, for example, the introduction of the concept of social insurance (like Social Security) in Chancellor Otto von Bismarck's Germany represented a major change in economic systems. Such programs were implemented in large part to counter the growing socialist and communist movements in Europe. They also heralded a new order of government-managed financial assistance programs which transformed bureaucratic institutions and administrative budgets. At the same time that Bismarck introduced these programs, Germany saw an increase in the number of university departments and research institutions that were dedicated to studying the social aspects of economics. It was believed that the idea of social insurance programs originated not in economic policymaking circles but by non-academic social activists. Therefore, the study of the forces that created such programs would require methodologies and disciplinary applications from outside of the economic sphere, such as sociology, political science and psychology (Shiller, 2005).

Prospect Theory

The application of psychology and other non-economic disciplines to the study of economics has continued to develop for more than a century. One of the most prominent manifestations of this field of study came in 1979, when psychologists Daniel Kahneman and Amos Tversky introduced the "Prospect Theory." With this theory, Kahneman and Tversky offered a critique on the inability of mainstream economic analysis to accurately account for consumer decision-making behavior. Specifically, they noted that people tend to underweigh outcomes that are based on probability (as opposed to certain outcomes) in risk situations. In this capacity, value was assigned to gains and losses, rather than the conventional approach, which assigned value in terms of final assets ("Prospect theory," 2008). Their theory represented a milestone in the burgeoning field of behavioral economics and finance.

The evolution of behavioral economics and finance has indeed progressed alongside the ever-changing economic landscape; it is to the fundamental elements of this growing field of economics that this paper will next turns attention.

Heuristics

At the center of behavioral economics is the notion that neoclassical economics falls short of fully explaining consumer behavior. Neoclassical economics has long dominated microeconomics, focusing on supply and demand frameworks (such as pricing, output, profits and income distribution). However, it also relies heavily on assumptions that the actors involved in a given study are going to act in a rational manner in order to create the maximum utility (value derived from choice). Such themes are evident in utility theory, which is often used to explain decision-making in situations with risk and explicitly outlined probabilities ("Utility theory," 2009).

Behavioral economics does not necessarily dismiss utility theory — rather, it compliments it with an additional perspective. By adding the psychological concept of heuristics (a method used to rapidly come to a conclusion based on the probability of an optimal solution), behavioral economists believe a more comprehensive picture of the consumer's decision-making may be presented. In essence, heuristics involves so-called "rules of thumb" rather than in-depth, case-by-case analysis.

Heuristic decision-making processes entail biased judgments. In other words, past experiences or conditions that are either familiar or imaginable to the individual are seen as influences on the decision being made. In fact, people often overestimate the likelihood that past events and experiences will occur again (or have occurred prior to the decision), which will in turn create more biases in the decision-making process. In financial investments, such judgments may be critical to how the individual proceeds with his or her money.

Heuristic decision-making also often involves "representativeness." This term applies to judgments by individuals of conditional probabilities that are based on how the data or sample represents the existing hypothesis or classification (Camerer & Lowenstein, 2002). For example, an individual who is operating from the hypothesis that a student fits the profile to attend a certain class might glean a set of generalities about that class and affix them to the student's profile.

Like other forms of heuristics, representativeness does not necessarily provide wholly accurate information about a concept — however, what is important for the purposes of this paper is the fact that such a thought-process creates a short-cut methodology for individuals to make decisions on how they might proceed in a given economic situation. These "short-cuts" may in fact diverge from rational consumer behavior and create inconsistencies in terms of the outcome of a given transaction or series thereof.

Framing

In an ideal situation, an individual bases his or her decisions on the information that is manifest. In other words, the individual simply takes account of the data presented and acts based on that information. Of course, such ideal situations are rarely part of reality. Instead, data and information is both presented and perceived — this latter term suggests that the individual making the financial decision may experience bias due to the way in which the information is presented. This fact is demonstrative of another element of behavioral economics and finance, one that often proves integral in the manner by which individuals make their financial decisions: Framing.

In economic terms, framing can be defined as the manner by which a rational choice problem is presented. Framing looks beyond the rational and seeks to understand the perception of the individual, providing once again a more comprehensive illustration of the mindset of the consumer.

In retirement planning, for example, framing appears to play a role in individual savings. In a recent study, two approaches to an employee retirement plan were examined. On one hand, employees were told that they would have to make a "positive election" to join the company's 401(k) plan. On the other hand, employees were automatically signed up for the plan at a given participation rate with the ability to opt out of the program. The two ways by which this plan was presented showed a significant difference in terms of the amounts participants saved. Those who were told that they were required to opt into the program saved very little for the program. However, those who were simply enrolled at the company rate invested significantly more. One company saw plan participation rates skyrocket from 37 percent to 86 percent among new hires under the automatic enrollment. The clear divide in response between this framing suggests that workers are not particularly firm in their retirement planning behavior, and that the way in which options are presented may make a difference in how much an individual saves (Mitchell & Utkus, 2006).

By understanding the impact framing has on the consumer, the economist develops a better grasp of the individual's decision-making process. Indeed, framing is neither a fully rational nor logical type of behavior — in fact, it may be argued that it is largely based on sensitivity or emotion rather than rationality. However, taking framing into account helps an economist to better develop a profile of the consumer and aids businesses and leaders in the implementation of effective policies.

Market Anomalies

As stated earlier, behavioral economics and finance was borne of the view that the traditional notion of economics — a system that operates based on rational behavior — was too rigid to account for an assessment of certain anomalies. Thus far, this paper has focused on one side of the equation regarding such behavioral anomalies — the consumer. However, behavioral finance and economics concurrently reviews the economic system which is built, maintained and even undone as a result of consumer behavior: The market. It is to this area of the economy that this paper next turns attention in order to illustrate the field of behavioral economics.

Behavioral economics and finance has evolved as a response to irrational behavior among economic players. However, there are anomalies that occur in the marketplace that would suggest irrational behavior within the system itself. In the late 1970s and early 1980s, several scholarly works pointed to apparent inconsistencies between market prices and economic conditions. One suggested that an apparent illusion of inflation resulted in the undervaluation of the stock market. A similar claim was made regarding bond prices, suggesting that the realities of the economic landscape simply did not correspond with the resulting price.

The imbalance between the climate and market conditions has led to a reinvestigation of the traditional concepts of market efficiency. Some economists assert that this imbalance is caused by investors who take advantage of market inefficiencies so as to yield higher returns. These traditionalists suggest reviewing the returns as a method for pinpointing and correcting market inefficiencies. However, a 1993 study concluded that while this approach may remove some irrational behavior from the markets, it will not correct fundamental inconsistencies (Summers, 1993).

Prospect Theory

A useful analytical tool in this arena is the aforementioned Prospect Theory. Whereas traditional utility in economics has been measured by market returns, Prospect Theory focuses on the separation of gains and losses as definitive of utility. This practice provides a more comprehensive illustration of the consumer's trading behavior which permits investors to make decisions concerning risk on a case-by-case basis. In addition, Prospect Theory allows investors to combine high- and low-risk situations and assess the overall portfolio before proceeding.

In terms of market anomalies, Prospect Theory is of particular use in analyzing the behavior of market agents (those who make market transactions on behalf of the investors). According to a 1998 study on stock market trading and a 2001 study on housing transactions (both of which employed Prospect Theory in their evaluative approaches), investors treat each asset on a separate basis, weighing losses and gains and making decisions on risk aversion and acceptance appropriately. The resulting profile of investor behavior within the marketplace is therefore more complex than the traditional, return-based analysis of investor behavior (Pesendorfer, 2006).

Prospect Theory has come under some criticism, however, due to the sheer complexity of the profiles it creates. For example, the reference point by which utility is determined is somewhat nebulous, since it focuses on a set of gains and losses rather than a final, fixed figure. Still, in light of ongoing market inconsistencies in an era of economic flux, more careful analyses of how investor behavior affects markets (and vice versa) continue to generate interest in economics and finance.

Behavioral vs. Neoclassical Economics

Behavioral economics and finance developed from a perceived need to provide greater answers about consumer decision-making and how it affects the overall economy. However, there remains a debate as to the usefulness of applying psychological concepts to the field of economics.

The example of market anomalies described earlier in this paper provides one such area of controversy. The fact that much of this growing field focuses not on the outcomes of such decision-making but rather the risks and gains makes the process and its assessment somewhat difficult. Without conclusive evidence that such a focus provides insight on neoclassical utility analysis, traditionalists suggest that behavioral economics may not be of value in dealing with systemic inefficiencies.

This debate may not be concluded without mentioning the successful application of behavioral finance and economic tenets to fiscal policy. Behavioral concepts have been useful for the development of legal business contracts, as they allow consumer mindsets to be better understood and supported. As one study indicates, "the success or failure of the behavioral challenge will be judged by its ability to improve upon neoclassical economics — both descriptively and prescriptively — in specific legal applications" (Bar-Gill & Epstein, 2007-2008). Until greater clarity can be applied to the conclusions of behavioral economics as a compliment to neoclassical finance, the debate for or against its utility will likely continue.

CONCLUSION

The American author Dale Carnegie once advised, "When dealing with people, remember you are not dealing with creatures of logic, but creatures of emotion" ("Dale Carnegie quotes," 2009). Indeed, in virtually every facet of life, humans demonstrate the propensity to behave both logically and emotionally. Quite often, however, these two types of behavior are significantly divergent from one another.

Throughout its long history, the science of economics has proceeded from the standpoint that the system it studies adheres to a logical, rational mentality. Within this framework, economists conclude that markets and systems operate based on rational behavior that pursues maximum utility. This assumption in many ways discounts consumer behavior because it is not always manifested in this logical manner.

Since the late 19th century, as market economies have developed and flourished, it has become increasingly clear that the consumer is a more complex element than previously assumed. Although Adam Smith would make such assertions more than a century prior, interest in consumer decision-making and behavior became more relevant as social welfare programs became more commonplace. Kahneman and Tversky's Prospect Theory of the late 1970s was arguably one of the most significant contributors to the development of the subdiscipline known as behavioral economics and finance.

As this paper has demonstrated, behavioral economics and finance has evolved not as a replacement of neo-classical economics but as a complement thereto. By employing psychological techniques to the study of economic and financial systems, behavioral economics helps cast a light on irrational consumer decision-making and behavior.

Shown above, the study of heuristics, framing and market anomalies can help the economist create a more complete profile of consumer behavior. Adherents to the field of behavioral economics assert that understanding the basis of irrational consumer behavior not only aids business development but government policymaking as well; particularly during times of economic recession and/or market flux.

Debate continues as to the relevance of the application of behavioral economics in the study of economic systems. In particular, while the field does raise interesting questions about irrational consumer decision-making, it often falls short of contradicting the conclusions of neo-classical economic analysis. Nevertheless, behavioral economics and finance does provide important insight into the mechanics of economic systems; analyzing the relationship between the market and the rational and irrational human elements that play a major role therein.

Bibliography

Altman, M. (2006). *Handbook of contemporary behavioral economics.* Armonk, NY: M.E. Sharpe. Retrieved April 3, 2009, from Google Books. http://books.google.com/books?id=yw4CgjEnx2AC&printsec=frontcover

Bar-Gill, O. & Epstein, R.A. (2007). Consumer contracts: Behavioral economics vs. neoclassical economics. *Minnesota Law Review, 92.* Retrieved April 6, 2009, from http://papers.ssrn.com/sol3/papers.cfm?abstract_id=982527

Bubb, R., & Pildes, R. H. (2014). How behavioral economics trims its sails and why. *Harvard Law Review, 127*(6), 1594–678. Retrieved November 17, 2014, from EBSCO Online Database Business Source Complete. http://search.ebscohost.com/login.aspx?direct=true&db=bth&AN=95587073

Building brands. (2009). 'Quotes' newsletter archives. Retrieved April 1, 2009, from http://www.buildingbrands.com/members/newsletters_archives.php

Camerer, C. F. & Loewenstein, G. (2002, October 25). Behavioral economics: Past, present and future. Retrieved April 2, 2009, from Caltech. http://www.hss.caltech.edu/~camerer/ribe239.pdf

Cottingham, P. (2013). We need to talk. *Money Marketing,* 33. Retrieved November 15, 2013, from EBSCO Online Database Business Source Complete. http://search.ebscohost.com/login.aspx?direct=true&db=bth&AN=88324201&site=ehost-live

Dale Carnegie quotes. (2009). Retrieved April 8, 2009, from BrainyQuote.com. http://www.brainyquote.com/quotes/quotes/d/dalecarneg130727.html

Gounaris, K.M., & Prout, M.F. (2009). Repairing relationships and restoring trust: Behavioral finance and the economic crisis. *Journal of Financial Service Professionals, 63*(4), 75-84. Retrieved November 15, 2013, from EBSCO Online Database Business Source Complete. http://search.ebscohost.com/login.aspx?direct=true&db=bth&AN=42999230&site=ehost-live

Gradinaru, A. (2014). Behavioral economics and the need of psychology in economic research. *USV Annals of Economics and Public Administration, 14*(1), 85–91. Retrieved November 17, 2014, from EBSCO Online Database Business Source Complete. http://search.ebscohost.com/login.aspx?direct=true&db=bth&AN=99046927

Lambert, C. (2006, March/April). The marketplace of perceptions. *Harvard Magazine.* Retrieved April 4, 2009, from http://harvardmagazine.com/2006/03/the-marketplace-of-perce.html

Mitchell, O.S. & Utkus, S.P. (2006). How behavioral finance can inform retirement plan design. *Journal of Applied Corporate Finance, 18(1),* 82-94.

Pesendorfer, W. (2006). Behavioral economics comes of age. *Journal of Economic Literature, 44(3),* 712-721. Retrieved April 6, 2009, from EBSCO Online Database Business Source Complete. http://search.ebscohost.com/login.aspx?direct=true&db=bth&AN=22285123&site=ehost-live

Prospect theory. (2008). Retrieved April 2, 2009, from BehaviouralFinance.net. http://prospect-theory.behaviouralfinance.net/

Raines, J., & Leathers, C.G. (2011). Behavioral finance and post Keynesian-institutionalist theories of financial markets. *Journal of Post Keynesian Economics, 33*(4), 539-554. Retrieved November 15, 2013, from EBSCO Online Database Business Source Complete. http://search.ebscohost.com/login.aspx?direct=true&db=bth&AN=63968074&site=ehost-live

Shiller, R.J. (2005, January). Behavioral economics and institutional innovation. Cowles Foundation for Research in Economics, Yale University. Retrieved April 2, 2009, from http://cowles.econ.yale.edu/P/cd/d14b/d1499.pdf

Summers, L. (1993). Does the stock market rationally reflect fundamental values? In Richard Thaler (ed.), *Advances in behavioral finance* (153-167). New York, NY: Russell Sage Foundation. Retrieved April 3, 2009, from Google Books. http://books.google.com/books?id=kAtba1WxkKkC&printsec=frontcover

Thaler, R.H. (1999, November/December). The end of behavioral finance. *Financial Analysts Journal.* Retrieved April 4, 2009, from http://faculty.chicagobooth.edu/richard.thaler/research/end.pdf

Utility theory. (2009). *Decision consortium.* Retrieved April 4, 2009, from the University of Michigan. http://www.lsa.umich.edu/psych/decision-consortium/Tutorials/utility_theory.htm

What is behavioral economics? (2005, April 17). *Decision Science News.* Retrieved April 1, 2009, from http://www.dangoldstein.com/dsn/archives/2005/04/what_is_behavio.html

SUGGESTED READING

Chuvakhin, N. (2002). Efficient market hypothesis and behavioral finance — is a compromise in sight? *Graziadio Business Report, 22.* Retrieved April 8, 2009, from http://ncbase.com/papers/EMH-BF.pdf

Driscoll, J. C., & Holden, S. (2014). Behavioral economics and macroeconomic models. *Journal of Macroeconomics, 41,* 133–47. Retrieved November 17, 2014, from EBSCO Online Database Business Source Complete. http://search.ebscohost.com/login.aspx?direct=true&db=bth&AN=97335499

Hoje, J. & Kim, Dong Man. (2008). Recent development of behavioral finance. *International Journal of Business Research, 8*(2), 89-101. Retrieved April 8, 2009, from EBSCO Online Database Business Source Complete. http://search.ebscohost.com/login.aspx?direct=true&db=bth&AN=35793508&site=ehost-live

Michaud, R.O. (2001, September). The behavioral finance hoax. Inquire UK. Retrieved April 8, 2009, from http://www.behaviouralfinance.net/introduction/Mich01.pdf

Ritter, J.R. (2003). Behavioral finance. *Pacific-Basin Finance Journal, 11*(4), 429-437. Retrieved April 8, 2009, from EBSCO Online Database Business Source Complete. http://search.ebscohost.com/login.aspx?direct=true&db=bth&AN=10571083&site=ehost-live

Shefrin, H. (2002). *Beyond greed and fear.* Oxford: Oxford University Press. Retrieved April 8, 2009, from Google Books. http://books.google.com/books?id=hX18tBx3VPsC&printsec=frontcover

Shleifer, A. (2000). *Inefficient markets.* Oxford: Oxford University Press. Retrieved April 8, 2009, from Google Books. http://books.google.com/books?id=mGjStFEi2kQC&printsec=frontcover

Special report: The behavioral economy. (2008, October 23). *Gallup Poll Briefing,* 1. Retrieved April 8, 2009, from EBSCO Online Database Business Source Complete. http://search.ebscohost.com/login.aspx?direct=true&db=bth&AN=35118452&site=ehost-live

Michael P. Auerbach, M.A.

BEHAVIORAL FOUNDATIONS OF MANAGEMENT

ABSTRACT

Management is the process of efficiently and effectively accomplishing work through the coordination and supervision of others. To do this effectively requires an understanding of human behavior in the workplace; in particular, how to lead employees, motivate them to do what needs to be done, and provide an environment that facilitates them in achieving team and organizational objectives. Regardless of one's theoretical approach to leadership, certain practical behaviors have been found to characterize successful leaders. In addition, good management depends not only on understanding the behavior of the manager but also on understanding the behavior of the subordinate. Managers need to be able to motivate their employees to contribute to the success of the organization.

OVERVIEW

Although there are many aspects to management, including administration, decision making, and supervising, at its heart, management is the process of efficiently and effectively accomplishing work through the coordination and supervision of others. To do this effectively requires an understanding of human behavior in the workplace—in particular, how to lead employees, motivate them to do what needs to be done, and provide an environment that facilitates them in achieving team and organizational objectives. Leadership is not a characteristic or quality that automatically induces other people to follow the leader. It is a process: a series of actions, changes, or functions that bring about the desired result. Leadership is also an intentional act. Although leaders' behavior may inspire others to action or to follow in their footsteps, they are not leaders unless they are conscious of the attempt to modify the behavior of others.

Levels of Leadership

As shown in Figure 1, there are three levels of leadership.

Attempted Leadership
The first level is attempted leadership, where Harvey attempts to modify the behavior of other people in order to do what he wants them to do. This can be done with one of three orientations.

- Task orientation is an approach to leadership where the would-be leader focuses on the thing to be done (such as meeting a quarterly sales goal, designing a new widget, or producing gizmos with fewer defects). People who have a task orientation to leadership tend to be good managers or executives and focus on organizational goals.
- The interaction orientation to leadership is one in which the would-be leader is cognizant of the needs, abilities, and personalities of the followers. The primary goal of the interaction oriented leader is to maintain group harmony. This is an important orientation for group leadership and necessary for facilitating efficient group interactions. In fact, in many group situations, there are two *de facto* leaders: One who is task oriented and one who is interaction oriented.
- In addition, there is a third approach to attempted leadership — the self orientation. The person who attempts to lead by this approach tends to be a day dreamer or underachiever who sees the world as a stage on which to act. Self-oriented leaders think more about themselves than about the task at hand or about the people who are accomplishing that task.

Successful/Effective Leadership
If the people whom Harvey is trying to influence actually change their behavior as a result of his attempt at leadership, he is a successful leader. If, on the other hand, they do not change their behavior as a result of his efforts, Harvey's attempts at leadership have not been successful.

Styles of Leadership
There are three general styles of leadership that are based on some combination of power and ability. Without one or both of these characteristics, the attempted leadership will not be successful.

- The coercive leadership style is based strictly on power. Within the organization, this is typically organizational power (such as one's position as a supervisor or manager), but it can also be any other type of power to reward or hurt the followers. This style of leadership is frequently seen in organizations with supervisors or managers who invite neither discussion nor participation on the part of the employees but use their organizational standing and concomitant power (e.g., promote or fire; give or withhold raises) to get employees to do what they want them to do.
- On the other end of the spectrum is the persuasive leader who leads purely on ability. This type of leader can be seen in organizations in the form of the expert on a work team who is followed because of his or her level of technical expertise, ability to organize and facilitate work, or other skill. Strictly persuasive leaders do not have any power and must lead solely by their ability.
- Some leaders, however, use both power and ability to lead others using a permissive style of leadership. People using this type of leadership style use both their power and ability to bring about the desired actions of the part of their followers. For example, many persuasive leaders within organizations use their abilities to lead their followers in most circumstances and rely on brute use of organizational power only in extreme circumstances.

A leader can be said to be effective if his or her efforts bring about a change in the behavior of others and they do what the leader wanted them to do. This, however, does not necessarily mean that the leader was effective. The effectiveness of Harvey's leadership lies in the perceptions of those he was leading, specifically whether or not they were rewarded for following Harvey. Reward can be monetary or social — such as a bonus or praise — but it can also take more subtle forms, such as getting the task accomplished on time

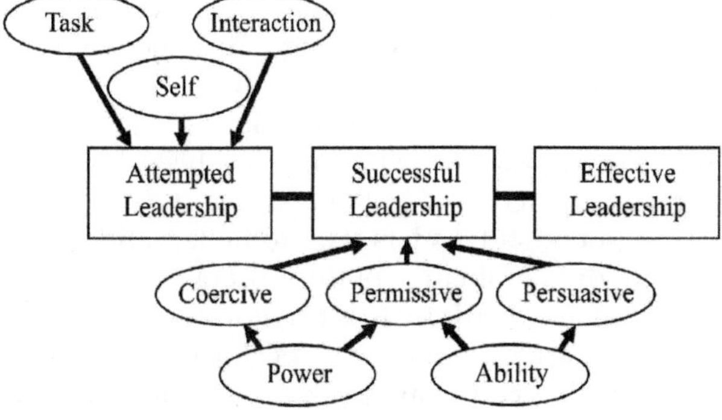

Figure 1: Three Levels of Leadership

and within budget. Those who have been effective leaders in the past will typically attempt to lead in other situations in the future.

Traits & Behaviors Common to Successful Leaders

Leadership theorists have examined the traits and behaviors of successful leaders for decades in order to help determine what distinguishes an effective leader from one who is not. Although many theories have been posited over the years, one enduring theme is that leaders need to change their behaviors depending on the characteristics of the situation such as the motivation and abilities of the people that they are leading. In some situations, a good leader needs to focus on concern for the task, while in other situations a good leader needs to focus on having concern for people. For example, a leader may be both successful and effective with a hands-off approach in a situation in which the people who are being led are experienced and trained in the task that they need to perform. In such situations, a good leader is often well-advised to provide the environment that the employees need to do their job and to support them rather than actively trying to be "in charge." On the other hand, in a situation where the leader has knowledge and experience not possessed by the followers, he or she may have to be more directive as a leader in order to get the task accomplished. In the situational approach to leadership, theorists state that effective leaders change the style of their leadership depending on the ability and even the personality of the people they are trying to lead. Similarly, the contingency model of leadership suggests that effective leadership depends on whether or not the leader's style is appropriate to the situation. For example, a leader who prefers to wade into a situation and tell people what to do will not be successful in a situation where a team works best through synergy, piggybacking ideas off each other, and developing a product or idea greater than they could have done alone.

No matter one's theoretical approach to leadership, certain practical behaviors have been found to characterize successful leaders.

- First, successful leaders tend to be fair and objective in their evaluation of the work of others. Organizational rewards such as promotions, raises, and bonuses are often linked to performance in high performing companies, so it is essential that performance appraisals be fair.
- Second, it is also important that a leader treat all employees fairly and equally. Lack of fair treatment or perceptions of favoritism can lead to job dissatisfaction among employees.
- Third, good leaders need to be available to all the employees and be willing to discuss the employees' problems with them. This observation stems from the need to be concerned both with the task as well as with the interactions of a work group and the individual needs of the employees.
- Finally, good leaders tend to delegate responsibility as appropriate to their subordinates. This allows the employees to learn new skills, helps them prepare for even more responsibility, and lets them feel as if they are making a valued contribution to the organization.

APPLICATIONS

Understanding the Employee

Good management depends not only on understanding the behavior of the manager but also on understanding the behavior of the subordinate. In addition to good leadership skills, managers need to be able to motivate their employees to contribute to the success of the organization. Too much emphasis on the task at hand and not enough concern with the needs of the individual employee can easily result in a situation in which the employees are dissatisfied and do not contribute to helping the organization maximize its performance. Too much emphasis on the needs of the individual without concern for the task, on the other hand, may end with employees who are satisfied with their jobs but still do not contribute to helping the organization maximize its performance.

One of the ways that a manager can help reach the proper balance between these two extremes is through an understanding of motivation theory and application in the work place. Motivation is the study of the needs and thought processes that determine a person's behavior. By understanding what motivates employees, a manager can better reward them for behavior that contributes to achieving the objectives of the organization. For example, a worker who is motivated by money can often be motivated through the possibility of raises or bonuses. For an employee who is motivated by status or power, the possibility of a promotion or corner office may offer a greater incentive for desired behavior.

Motivation

Although part of the role of the manager is to clearly specify what kind of behavior is expected in the organization and to encourage employees to meet or exceed these standards by providing feedback, most employees need more from the organization than to know that they are helping it succeed. To motivate employees to perform at a consistently high level, the organization must give them what they want or need. Good managers tend to try to determine what motivates their employees and offer these things within the confines of the organization in order to encourage them to contribute to the success of the organization. High performing organizations in particular frequently motivate employees to contribute to the company's high performance by linking desired performance to rewards.

Different people are motivated by different things. While Harvey may want security to save for the future, Mathilde may have what she needs for a secure future and want, instead, more time to spend with her family. Harvey is more likely to be motivated to work to earn more money, whereas Mathilde is more likely to work if she is promised more time off. Some motivation theorists try to reduce motivation to an equation that connects the probability of increased performance with such things as the employee's perceived expectancy of obtaining a reward for doing so. Others, however, posit that different people are motivated by different things, from having one's physical needs met (e.g., food on the table and a roof over one's head) to having the esteem of others or some other internal incentive. However, most motivation theorists recognize that people working in organizations both need and expect remuneration. Money means different things to different people and can act as a motivator for various needs. For example, some people are motivated by money to meet basic physical needs or to have the security of knowing that those needs will continue to be met for the foreseeable future. Others see pay incentives in the form of bonuses, raises, or promotions as recognition from the organization for a job well done.

The Hierarchy of Needs

One of the most enduring theories of motivation that has been applied to the understanding of employee behavior is Abraham Maslow's hierarchy of needs (Figure 2). Maslow hypothesizes that people are motivated by different things at different times in their lives depending on what needs have or have not been met. The hierarchy also hypothesizes that needs lower on the hierarchy must have been satisfied before higher level needs can be satisfied.

Physiological Needs

According to Maslow, the most basic level of needs is the physiological needs, including the needs to satisfy hunger and thirst, sleep, and sex. From an employee motivation point of view, this means that a manager is unlikely to motivate an employee who cannot put food on the table by offering him or her the possibility of a promotion without a pay raise; the need to eat in this case is more important than the need to impress others with a fancy new title.

Safety Needs

Once the physiological level of needs has been met, people become more concerned with safety needs, including the need to feel safe, secure, and stable in life (e.g., having a job so that one not only has food for today but also can buy food for the foreseeable future). People who are at this level of Maslow's hierarchy want to feel that their world is organized and predictable. From an employee motivation point of view, this might mean that people at this level of need would be willing to work without a raise for a given period of time if they were assured that there would not be a layoff during that period.

Belongingness Needs

Once the security and safety needs of the individual are satisfied, the next level of needs is for belongingness. People at this level of need are motivated by such factors as the need to feel accepted and part of a group, to love or feel affection and be loved in return,

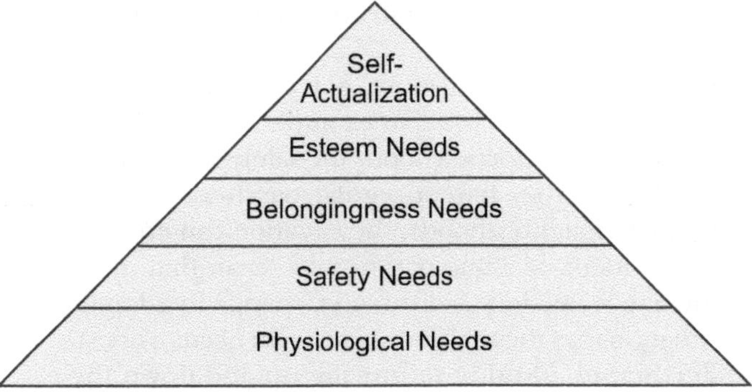

Figure 2: Maslow's Hierarchy of Needs

and to avoid loneliness and alienation. Someone at this level of need may be motivated by being given the opportunity to work on a special team to solve an organizational problem, thus allowing him or her to feel part of a group.

Esteem Needs

The next level of needs in Maslow's hierarchy is the esteem needs, including such things as the need to achieve, be competent, and be independent. Other needs at this level of the hierarchy include the needs for self-respect and a sense of self-worth as well as the need for recognition and respect from others. From an employee motivation point of view, someone at this level of need might be motivated by the offer to be part of a special team not because it was an opportunity to be part of a group but because it was a respected position that showed his or her importance or expertise.

Self-Actualization

The final level on Maslow's hierarchy of needs is self-actualization. This is a complex concept that basically means the need to live up to one's full and unique potential and is associated with such concepts as wholeness, perfection, or completion; a divestiture of "things" in preference to simplicity, aliveness, goodness, and beauty; and a search for meaning in life. Employees at this level in the hierarchy would be less interested in the things that motivated at lower levels on the hierarchy unless they enabled them to reach other goals, such as learning, spiritual development, or enjoying the wonders of nature.

Other Points of Interest

In addition to the fact that different people are motivated by different things, there are several other things that can be learned from Maslow's hierarchy of needs that have direct application to good management.

- First, employees can move not only up the hierarchy, but down as well. For example, although most adults are not worried about the safety and security needs (i.e., they have a regular paycheck and live in a safe neighborhood), the situation can change. An accident or ailing parent may mean that more income is needed. A divorce or change in a family situation may mean that one's esteem needs a boost.
- Further, in addition to moving up and down the hierarchy, people can experience multiple needs at once. For example, in negotiating a strike settlement, a manager will understand that although the workers need more money, they also need to have the assurance that they will continue to have jobs. Sometimes settlements can be negotiated that take such considerations into account by giving a token or low level raise in the short term for the security of a continuing job with the promise of reevaluation of the situation after a given period of time.

CONCLUSION

To be a good manager requires an understanding of organizational behavior. In particular, it is important to understand the behaviors necessary to be a good leader and how these behaviors may change depending on the individual situation. In addition, good managers need to understand the motivations for the behavior of their subordinates so that appropriate rewards can be tied with performance that contributes to the objectives of the organization.

Bibliography

Alfes, K., Truss, C., Soane, E. C., Rees, C., & Gatenby, M. (2013). The relationship between line manager behavior, perceived HRM practices, and individual performance: Examining the mediating role of engagement. *Human Resource Management, 52*(6), 839–859. Retrieved December 2, 2013, from EBSCO Online Database Business Source Complete. http://search.ebscohost.com/login.aspx?direct=true&db=bth&AN=92038571

Dessler, G. (2005). *Human resource management* (10th ed.). Upper Saddle River, NJ: Pearson/Prentice Hall.

Landy, F. J. & Conte, J. M. (2004). *Work in the 21st Century: An introduction to industrial and organizational psychology.* Boston: McGraw Hill.

Lorinkova, N. M., Pearsall, M. J., & Sims Jr., H. P. (2013). Examining the differential longitudinal performance of directive versus empowering leadership in teams. *Academy of Management Journal, 56*(2), 573–596. Retrieved December 2, 2013, from EBSCO Online Database Business Source Complete. http://search.ebscohost.com/login.aspx?direct=true&db=bth&AN=87563907

McShane, S. L. & Von Glinow, M. A. (2003). *Organizational behavior: Emerging realities for the workplace revolution* (2nd ed). Boston: McGraw-Hill/Irwin.

Myers, D. G. (2001). *Psychology* (6th ed.). New York: Worth Publishers.

Schaubroeck, J. M., Hannah, S. T., Avolio, B. J., Kozlowski, S. W., Lord, R. G., Trevinño, L. K., & Peng, A. C. (2012). Embedding ethical leadership within and across organization levels. *Academy of Management Journal, 55*(5), 1053–1078. Retrieved December 2, 2013, from EBSCO Online Database Business Source Complete. http://search.ebscohost.com/login.aspx?direct=true&db=bth&AN=82571469

Suggested Reading

Ilies, R., Judge, T., & Wagner, D. (2006). Making sense of motivational leadership: The trail from transformational leaders to motivated followers. *Journal of Leadership and Organizational Studies, 13*(1), 1–22. Retrieved September 29, 2007, from EBSCO Online Database Business Source Complete. http://search.ebscohost.com/login.aspx?direct=true&db=bth&AN=21955772&site=bsi-live

Mohd Soieb, A., Othman, J., & D'Silva, J. (2013). The effects of perceived leadership styles and organizational citizenship behaviour on employee engagement: The mediating role of conflict management. *International Journal of Business & Management, 8*(8), 91–99. Retrieved December 2, 2013, from EBSCO Online Database Business Source Complete. http://search.ebscohost.com/login.aspx?direct=true&db=bth&AN=87080476

Pless, N. (2007). Understanding responsible leadership: Role identity and motivational drivers. *Journal of Business Ethics, 74*(4), 437–456. Retrieved September 29, 2007, from EBSCO Online Database Business Source Complete. http://search.ebscohost.com/login.aspx?direct=true&db=bth&AN=26210805&site=bsi-live

Toegel, G., Kilduff, M., & Anand, N. N. (2013). Emotion helping by managers: An emergent understanding of discrepant role expectations and outcomes. *Academy of Management Journal, 56*(2), 334–357. Retrieved December 2, 2013, from EBSCO Online Database Business Source Complete. http://search.ebscohost.com/login.aspx?direct=true&db=bth&AN=87562952

US General Accounting Office. (2001). Human capital: Practices that empowered and involved employees. (GAO-01-1070). Retrieved March 27, 2007, from EBSCO Online Database Business Source Complete. http://search.ebscohost.com/login.aspx?direct=true&db=bth&AN=18203790&site=bsi-live

Ruth A. Wienclaw, Ph.D.

Business Data Management

ABSTRACT

Business data management is an essential activity in all types of companies. This article explains the four basic steps in business data processing: Data creation, data storage, data processing, and data analysis. Various methods to accomplish the four steps are examined along with changes in technology that have impacted how the steps are being accomplished in a modern enterprise. As business practices have changed over the last few decades so have business data management methods. The emerging supply chain business model is explained along with its implications for business data management. The necessity for contingency planning for business data management is examined and the basic steps to contingency planning are explained.

OVERVIEW

Over the last two decades corporations have been placing increased emphasis on the management of data (Goodhue, Quillard & Rockart, 1988). Business data management is a core activity for all businesses and supports a wide array of activities including financial management, accounting, purchasing, sales, human resource management, facilities management, product planning, manufacturing, and strategic planning. The activities of virtually every employee in every organization are dependent on business data management. There are four basic steps to business data management: Data creation, data storage, data processing, and data analysis.

Generally, it is the central Management Information Systems (MIS) department that designs, implements, and maintains the computer systems, networks, and applications software that support the four basic steps of business data management. The director of the MIS department, or Chief Information Officer (CIO) often participates in business decision making at the highest management level in the organization (Moynihan, 1990). This participation helps to align the activities of the MIS department with the strategic business goals of an organization (Grant, 2003). The strategic alignment of MIS activities and business goals can provide a company with a competitive edge as well as reduce overhead by avoiding expenditure for less than useful management information systems.

Trained information technology professionals staff the MIS department. MIS staff specialize in the many different disciplines necessary to create and maintain systems to support business data processing. These include operations specialists that support the data centers that house computer and storage systems, network staff that maintain the data communications systems that link systems together, and applications programmers who design and maintain software. Other specialties include database administrators who are responsible for database software and applications, systems analysts who keep large systems up-to-date and operational, and helpdesk staff that support end-users throughout the company.

The Creation of Data

Data is created through every-day business processes such as the production of items, the consumption of supplies or resources, the sale of goods or services, and customer service activities. In a consumer goods retailer, for example, data is created when inventory is ordered, sales are made in stores, employees clock in and out for work, and when accounts are paid or collected. The larger the retail operation the more data that is created on a daily basis, and the more important it is for data to be accurate and readily available to support business processes.

Achieving good data management requires an understanding of data, data management systems, and data management software (Chalfant, 1998). This means that the staff in the MIS department must understand the data needs of the organization in order for them to best apply their skills to business problems. But this requires that managers and data users throughout the orgnization understand their data and how they use it. Interdepartmental teams can be established to address business information needs. These teams can identify the organization's data management needs, what data is needed to meet those needs, where the data will come from, how it will get into a database, and what can be done with it after it is stored.

One of the most important steps in creating and maintaining good data is the establishment of a data dictionary (DD). A DD is a database of descriptors for each piece of data used in an organization's data management activities. A wide assortment of DD software packages is available. In general, a DD system will hold data that describes data along with its associated structures, processes, users, applications, and equipment (Vanecek, Solomon & Mannino, 1983).

The Storage of Data

Data storage has three major elements: The software used to manage stored data (most often database software); the technology used to store data (disk drives); and the networks which connect computers and computer users to data storage systems. The importance of database software has increased over the last three decades and has enabled banks, retailers, and manufacturers to grow beyond small local operations into global giants. Disk drive technology has also dramatically changed with increases in storage capacity, manageability, reliability, and accessibility. Data communications networks have become like the nervous system of an organization; allowing data to be instantly collected from locations across the country or around the world. The networks also allow data to be utilized by managers and decision-makers in offices far from where data is created or stored.

The primary tool for managing large amounts of data is database software. IBM, Oracle, Microsoft, and other software companies offer a wide variety of database software packages. The packages are capable of managing several thousand up to billions of pieces of data. Database software can operate on desktop and laptop computers as well as on servers and giant mainframe complexes. Database software is used in virtually all industries especially those that are transaction focused and need to track large quantities of items or activities.

Organizations with large amounts of data are turning to data warehousing models of data storage. The five basic steps required to build a data warehouse is planning, design, implementation, support, and enhancement. In the planning and design phases, metadata is created. In data warehousing, "metadata refers to anything that defines a data warehouse object, such as a table, a column, a query, a report, a business rule, or a transformation algorithm. Building a data warehouse is a complex process requiring careful planning between the IT department and business users" (Gardner, 1998, p. 59).

Data storage technology has rapidly evolved over the last two decades. In large organizations there are still what many refer to as disk farms, which are vast conglomerations of high-density disk drives, capable of storing billions and billions of business records. New approaches to storage technology include the storage area network (SAN), which is a "specialized, high-speed network attaching servers and storage devices. A SAN allows any-to-any connection across the network, using interconnect devices such as routers, gateways, hubs, and switches. It eliminates the traditional dedicated connection between a server and storage. It also eliminates any restriction to the amount of data that a server can access, usually limited by the number of storage devices attached to the individual server" (Tate, Lucchese & Moore, 2004, p. 1.1).

The Processing of Data

There are two major components required for data processing: The software used for processing data and the computer systems on which data is processed. The goals of data processing procedures are to take large amounts of data and make it useful to the personnel responsible for operations, managers that oversee various business functions, and planners who rely on data to forecast business activity. Data is processed for day-to-day operations in many ways using several different types of software ranging from accounting software to inventory control or payroll. In addition to helping to manage the storage of data, database software can also be used to generate planned reports or on-the-spot queries necessary to make business decisions.

The second essential element in processing data is the computer system on which the data is processed. These systems can range from servers capable of supporting small organizations to large complexes of mainframe systems capable of processing billions of pieces of data in a few hours or in many cases just a few minutes.

IBM has dominated the business data processing field for several decades. Ever since computing started to be used commercially, IBM has been a key player in providing businesses with information technology. Historically, the mainframe has performed the role of a central data server for many large enterprises and has typically provided high data throughput, scalability and strong security capabilities. However, over time business computing has evolved and now most companies have a multi-tier hardware infrastructure with various types of servers spread throughout the enterprise.

For decades, mainframes have been viewed as large and very expensive systems. However, over the last ten years are so, mainframe technology has become more scalable and systems are available to support the largest global companies as well as small companies. The new age mainframe can have from one to 54 processors in a single system. In addition to flexibility in the number of processors, the new mainframe provides scalability in memory and in input/output capabilities.

The Analysis of Data

Complex data analysis, beyond what database software provides, has become essential to manage large organizations. This type of data analysis can be performed with a variety data mining, statistical analysis, and decision support software packages. This software helps managers and analysts compile or create statistics on millions of business transactions. These statistics can support business forecasting and planning efforts enabling a company to maintain a competitive edge in a competitive global marketplace.

Data analysis software has evolved over the last 60 years. For several years, such software was rather cumbersome and required custom programming. In the 1970s decision support systems (DSS) were introduced that provided assistance for specific decision-making tasks. While DSSs can be developed for and used by personnel throughout the organization, they are most commonly employed by line staff or middle and lower managers. Among the latest developments are expert systems, which capture the expertise of highly trained, experienced professionals in specific problem domains.

In the 1990s, executive information systems (EIS) or executive support systems (ESS) were being developed in large organizations (Main, 1989). At first these systems were cumbersome and most were stand alone systems requiring time consuming data entry processes. As expected, the technology for EIS has evolved rapidly, and new systems are more integrated with other applications like the DDS or Enterprise Resource Planning (ERP) systems (Watson, Rainer & Koh, 1991).

Data warehouses can also serve as analytical tools and in some cases data warehouses are developed specifically for data analysis purposes. According to Jukic (2006), there are "two main reasons that could necessitate the creation of a data warehouse as a separate analytical data store. The first reason is that the performance of operational queries can be severely diminished if they must compete for computing resources with analytical queries. The second reason lies in the fact that, even if the performance is not an issue, it is often not possible to structure a database that can be used (queried) in a straightforward manner for both operational and analytical purposes" (p. 84).

APPLICATIONS

Supply Chains Extend the Scope of Business Data Management

A supply chain is a network of organizations with specialized activities that work together, usually in a sequential manner, to produce, distribute, sell, and service goods. According to Kumar (2001), "Supply chain systems support entire networks of manufacturers and distributors, transportation and logistics firms, banks, insurance companies, brokers, warehouses and freight forwarders, all directly or indirectly attempting to make sure the right goods and services are available at the right price, where and when the customers want them.

Having delivered the goods or services, the chain does not terminate. At the front end, through delivery, installation, customer education, help desks, maintenance, or repair, the goods or services are made useful to the customer. At the end of the product life, reverse logistics can ensure that used and discarded products are disassembled, brought back, and where possible, recycled. The scope of the supply chain, thus, extends from "dirt to dirt," from the upstream sources of supply, down to the point of consumption, and finally retirement and recycling" (p. 58).

Conventional strategic thinking relied on the individual firm as the basic unit of competition in a given industry. The individual company created, stored, processed, and analyzed data all produced within the company itself. In a supply chain environment, "the competitive success of a firm is no longer a function of its individual efforts-it depends, to a great extent, on how well the entire supply chain, as compared to competing supply chains, is able to deliver value to the ultimate consumers" (Kumar, 2001, p. 58). Consequently, business data management has evolved from focusing on data produced by the individual entity to that of data created by companies up and down the supply chain (Kumar, 2001).

Information technology plays a key role in the modern supply chain system by supporting business-to-business (B2B) applications. Supply chain management (SCM) is a digitally enabled interfirm process that integrates information flow, physical flow, and financial flow. Research indicates that a firm's IT-based platform capabilities have a substantial effect on supply chain process integration. This capability is deeply embedded into the structure of interfirm operational processes, such as order processing, inventory management, logistics, and distribution; financial processes, such as billing and receivables management; and information processes, such as demand planning and forecasting.

Implementation of IT-based supply chain management systems has been shown to have a positive effect on procurement of materials for production as well as distribution, marketing, and sales after production (Richardson, 2006). The integration associated with these processes is achieved through a variety of initiatives that may include trading partner agreements and supply chain partnerships and even deeply embedded IT capabilities. The development of process integration capability based on an IT infrastructure requires expertise that spans the business process domain, partnership context, and IT (Rai, Patnayakuni & Seth, 2006).

ISSUES

Contingency Planning for Business Data Management

Many types of incidents can disrupt computer operations, and thus critical mission and business functions. These incidents can include a power outage, hardware failure, fire, or storm. To prevent disruption, many organizations have contingency plans that directly support the "goal of continued operations. Organizations practice contingency planning because it makes good business sense" (NIST, 2004,

p. 121). The U.S. National Institute of Standards and Technology (NIST) has worked to develop a model for contingency planning. NIST breaks the contingency planning process into six basic steps:

Step 1: Identify the Mission- or Business-Critical Function

In government organizations, the focus is normally on performing a mission, such as providing citizen benefits. In private organizations, the focus is normally on conducting a business, such as manufacturing widgets. Protecting the continuity of an organization is very difficult if the mission or business is not clearly identified. The definition of an organization's critical mission or business functions is often identified in detailed business plans.

Step 2: Identify the Resources That Support Critical Functions

After identifying critical missions and business functions, it is necessary to identify the supporting resources, the time frames in which each resource is used and the effect on the mission or business if the resource is unavailable. Contingency planning should address all the resources needed to perform a function, regardless of whether or not they directly relate to a computer. The analysis of needed resources should be conducted by those who understand how the function is performed and the dependencies of various resources on other resources and other critical relationships.

Step 3: Anticipate Potential Contingencies

Although it is impossible to think of all the things that can go wrong, the next step is to identify a likely range of problems. The development of scenarios will help an organization to develop a plan to address the wide range of things that can go wrong. Scenarios should include small and large contingencies. The contingency scenarios should address each of the resources described above.

Step 4: Select Contingency Planning Strategies

A contingency planning strategy normally consists of three parts: Emergency response, recovery, and resumption. Emergency response encompasses the initial actions taken to protect lives and limit damage. Recovery refers to the steps that are taken to continue support for critical functions. Resumption is the return to normal operations. Strategies for processing capability are normally grouped into five categories: Hot site; cold site; redundancy; reciprocal agreements; and hybrids. These terms originated with recovery strategies for data centers but can be applied to other platforms.

Step 5: Implement the Contingency Strategies

Once contingency planning strategies have been selected, it is necessary to make appropriate preparations, document the strategies, and train employees. Much preparation is needed to implement the strategies for protecting critical functions and their supporting resources. For example, one common preparation is to establish procedures for backing up computer data files and applications. Another is to establish contracts and agreements, if the contingency strategy calls for them; or if necessary, renegotiate existing service contracts to add contingency services. Backing up data files and applications software is a critical part of virtually every contingency plan. Backups are used, for example, to restore files after a computer virus corrupts the files or after a hurricane destroys a data processing center.

Step 6: Test & Revise

A contingency plan should be tested periodically because the plan will become outdated as time passes and as the resources used to support critical functions change. Responsibility for keeping the contingency plan current should be specifically assigned. The extent and frequency of testing will vary between organizations and among systems. There are several types of testing, including reviews, analyses, and simulations of disasters (NIST, 2004, p. 122-132).

A review can be a simple test to check the accuracy of contingency plan documentation. For instance, a reviewer could check if individuals listed are still in the organization and still have the responsibilities that cause them to be included in the plan. This test can check home and work telephone numbers, organizational codes, and building and room numbers. The review can determine if files can be restored from backup tapes or if employees know emergency procedures.

CONCLUSION

There are four basic steps to business data management: Data creation, data storage, data processing, and data analysis. Business data management supports the day-to-day operations of an organization and provides managers and executives with the analytical support necessary to direct activities and plan for the future. As the global market place has become more competitive and information technology (IT) and telecommunications have evolved, IT enabled supply chain systems have become a widely used competitive business tool.

The dependence on business data management and the technology that supports data management efforts has made contingency planning an essential business function. To be effective, contingency planners must be able to identify critical systems and data and develop alternative means to provide systems and data in order to avoid disruptions in operations and the potential loss of revenue. Contingency plans must also be updated to reflect changes in an organization's needs.

Bibliography

Bartram, P. (2013). The value of data. *Financial Management (14719185), 42*(2), 26-31. Retrieved November 15, 2013, from EBSCO Online Database Business Source Complete. http://search.ebscohost.com/login.aspx?direct=true&db=bth&AN=86054116&site=ehost-live

Chalfant, C. (1998). Achieving good data management. *Water Engineering & Management, 145(7)*, 14. Retrieved July 11, 2007, from EBSCO Online Database Academic Search Premier. http://search.ebscohost.com/login.aspx?direct=true&db=aph&AN=8856620&site=ehost-live

Gardner, S. (1998). Building the data warehouse. *Communications of the ACM, 41(9)*, 52-60. Retrieved July 13, 2007, from EBSCO Online Database Academic Search Premier. http://search.ebscohost.com/login.aspx?direct=true&db=aph&AN=11950998&site=ehost-live

Goodhue, D., Kirsch, L., Quillard, J., & Wybo, M. (1992). Strategic data planning: Lessons from the field. *MIS Quarterly, 16(1)*, 11. Retrieved July 11, 2007, from EBSCO Online Database Academic Search Premier. http://search.ebscohost.com/login.aspx?direct=true&db=aph&AN=9604010620&site=ehost-live

Goodhue, D., Quillard, J., & Rockart, J. (1988). Managing the data resource: A contingency perspective. *MIS Quarterly, 12(3)*, 372. Retrieved July 11, 2007, from EBSCO Online Database Academic Search Premier. http://search.ebscohost.com/login.aspx?direct=true&db=aph&AN=4679308&site=ehost-live

Grant, G. (2003). Strategic alignment and enterprise systems implementation: The case of Metalco. *Journal of Information Technology, 18*(3), 159-175. Retrieved June 25, 2007, from EBSCO Online Database Academic Search Premier. http://search.ebscohost.com/login.aspx?direct=true&db=aph&AN=11291699&site=ehost-live

Jukic, N. (2006). Modeling strategies and alternatives for data warehousing projects. *Communications of the ACM, 49*(4), 83-88. Retrieved July 16, 2007, from EBSCO Online Database Academic Search Premier. http://search.ebscohost.com/login.aspx?direct=true&db=aph&AN=20371679&site=ehost-live

Kumar, K. (2001). Technology for supporting supply chain management. *Communications of the ACM, 44*(6), 58-61. Retrieved July 16, 2007, from EBSCO Online Database Academic Search Premier. http://search.ebscohost.com/login.aspx?direct=true&db=aph&AN=4771986&site=ehost-live

Lock, T. (2013). Manage data for business benefits. *Computer Weekly*, 15. Retrieved November 15, 2013, from EBSCO Online Database Business Source Complete. http://search.ebscohost.com/login.aspx?direct=true&db=bth&AN=91871344&site=ehost-live

Moynihan, T. (1990). What chief executives and senior managers want from their IT departments. *MIS Quarterly, 14*(1), 15-25. Retrieved June 25, 2007, from EBSCO Online Database Business Source Complete. http://search.ebscohost.com/login.aspx?direct=true&db=aph&AN=9604086230&site=ehost-live

National Institute of Standards & Technology (NIST). (2004). Preparing for contingencies and disasters. *An Introduction to Computer Security — The NIST Handbook. Special Publication 800-12.*. Retrieved from http://csrc.nist.gov/publications/nistpubs/800-12/800-12-html/chapter11.html

Rai, A., Patnayakuni, R., & Seth, N. (2006). Firm performance impacts of digitally enabled supply chain integration capabilities. *MIS Quarterly, 30*(2), 225-246. Retrieved July 16, 2007, from EBSCO Online Database Academic Search Premier. http://search.ebscohost.com/login.aspx?direct=true&db=aph&AN=21145595&site=ehost-live

Raymond, A.H. (2013). Data management regulation: Your company needs an up-to-date data/information management policy. *Business Horizons.* 513-520. Retrieved November 15, 2013, from EBSCO Online Database Business Source Complete. http://search.ebscohost.com/login.aspx?direct=true&db=bth&AN=89121977&site=ehost-live

Richardson, V. (2006). Supply chain IT enables coordination. *Industrial Engineer: IE, 38*(11), 10-10. Retrieved July 16, 2007, from EBSCO Online Database Academic Search Premier. http://search.ebscohost.com/login.aspx?direct=true&db=aph&AN=25170345&site=ehost-live

Tate, J., Lucchese, F. & Moore, R. (2006). *Introduction to Storage Area Networks,* 4th ed. Poughkeepsie, NY: IBM Corp./Redbooks. Retrieved from IBM.com http://www.redbooks.ibm.com/redbooks/SG245470/wwhelp/wwhimpl/js/html/wwhelp.htm?href=19-4.htm

Vanecek, M., Solomon, I., & Mannino, M. (1983). The Data Dictionary: An evaluation from the EDP audit perspective. *MIS Quarterly, 7*(1), 15-27. Retrieved July 11, 2007, from EBSCO Online Database Academic Search Premier. http://search.ebscohost.com/login.aspx?direct=true&db=aph&AN=4679333&site=ehost-live

Watson, H., Rainer Jr., R., & Koh, C. (1991). Executive information systems: A framework for development and a survey of current practices. *MIS Quarterly, 15*(1), 13. Retrieved July 13, 2007, from EBSCO Online Database Academic Search Premier. http://search.ebscohost.com/login.aspx?direct=true&db=aph&AN=9604086246&site=ehost-live

Suggested Reading

Behera, J., Bhuta, C., & Thorpe, G. (2000). Management information systems: An overview of practices at Marine Container Terminals in Australia and Asia. *Transportation Quarterly, 54*(4), 59-73.

Booth, M., & Philip, G. (2005). Information systems management: Role of planning, alignment and leadership. *Behaviour & Information Technology, 24*(5), 391-404. Retrieved June 27, 2007, from EBSCO Online Database Academic Search Premier. http://search.ebscohost.com/login.aspx?direct=true&db=aph&AN=18406091&site=ehost-live

Giraud-Carrier, C., & Povel, O. (2003). Characterising data mining software. *Intelligent Data Analysis, 7*(3), 181-192. Retrieved July 2, 2007, from EBSCO Online Database Academic Search Premier. http://search.ebscohost.com/login.aspx?direct=true&db=aph&AN=10388834&site=ehost-live

Miller, D., & Toulouse, J. (1998) Quasi-rational organizational responses: Functional and cognitive sources of strategic simplicity. *Canadian Journal of Administrative Sciences, 15*(3), 230-244. Retrieved June 25, 2007, from EBSCO Online Database Business Source Complete. http://search.ebscohost.com/login.aspx?direct=true&db=bth&AN=1170310&site=ehost-live

Nicolaou, A. (2004). Firm performance effects in relation to the implementation and use of Enterprise Resource Planning Systems. *Journal of Information Systems, 18*(2), 79-105. Retrieved June 27, 2007, from EBSCO Online Database Academic Search Premier. http://search.ebscohost.com/login.aspx?direct=true&db=aph&AN=15672357&site=ehost-live

Kettinger, W. J.; Grover, V.; Guha, S.& Segars, A. H.. Strategic information systems revisited: A study in sustainability and performance. *MIS Quarterly, 18*(1), 31-58. Retrieved June 25, 2007, from EBSCO Online Database Academic Search Premier. http://search.ebscohost.com/login.aspx?direct=true&db=aph&AN=9503310355&site=ehost-live

Michael Erbschloe, M.A.

BUSINESS IMPACT ANALYSIS

ABSTRACT

As recent disasters such as 9/11 and Hurricane Katrina have demonstrated, it is important for organizations to plan for unexpected interruptions to their business processes and to develop plans for dealing with such situations. This is particularly important in today's businesses that rely heavily on information that would be difficult if not impossible to recreate. Preparation for interruptions is done through the development of a business continuity that describes how an organization will recover and restore interrupted critical function(s) after an extended disruption due to disaster or other causes. An essential step in developing an appropriate business continuity plan is to perform a business impact analysis. This process helps identify the risk of exposure to specific threats to the organization and assesses their impact on the organization's functioning if a disaster should occur. The Federal Emergency Management Agency (FEMA) suggests a number of considerations for a business impact analysis.

OVERVIEW

There is a story of a doctoral candidate who had just finished his dissertation and put it in the back of the car so that he could take it to the university in order to have the final copy signed before being submitted to the graduate school for completion of his doctorate. It was a beautiful spring day and the man was full of the joys of knowing that one has just completed a major milestone in one's life and the that future is rosy. So, he carefully placed the requisite three copies of the dissertation in the back seat and proceeded down the road. However, the day was so beautiful that he decided to roll down the windows. As he pressed the accelerator toward the floor and felt the rush of the wind blowing on his face, his joy soon changed to horror as he watched helplessly as the clean white pages flew out the window and blew down the road.

The worst could have been avoided had the doctoral candidate avoided taking such risks. The candidate could have kept the windows of his car rolled up tightly and kept backup copies (digital and hardcopy) at several different (safe) locations.

The loss of information is not only of concern to poor graduate students without the means or time to recreate their dissertations. As anyone who has ever experienced a computer crash knows, the loss of data and information can be devastating. Without backups of data and information, as well as application software and operating systems, it can be extremely difficult if not impossible to recreate the information stored on one's computer. If this happens to a business, the problem can be multiplied untold times to the point where it is impossible to recover. For this reason, not only data but entire computer systems and their concomitant software programs are regularly backed up.

Sometimes, however, conveniently available backups are insufficient to recover from a disaster. As the tragedies of September 11, 2001, and Hurricane Katrina should have taught us, it is not always sufficient to have a backup disk in the computer lab or even elsewhere in the building. In fact, sometimes it is not sufficient to have a backup disk on the same block or even in the same area of town. By definition, disaster is widespread. By definition, also, disasters are unexpected. In order to face disaster and recover from it, therefore, one must plan for the unexpected and prepare for it.

The Importance of Backup Systems

Of course, in many (if not most) situations, it is impossible to backup everything. From a purely software point of view, one could conceivably backup all data as well as all application and operating systems programs. However, having these things available to recover after a disaster may not be sufficient. For example, if the building in which the business resided was destroyed by a fire, the hardware would also have to be replaced. In some situations, this might only mean that a new computer system would have to be obtained using expedited delivery and new facilities leased in order for the business to be up and running within the week.

In other cases, however, these actions might be insufficient. Getting the power grid, telephone system, or emergency services up and running after a disaster can be of paramount importance. In such cases, waiting a week may not be an option not only for the success of the business, but more importantly from the standpoint of the potential in lives lost if such services could not be quickly restored. This is why there are extensive backup systems and facilities for many such organizations. Although most business organizations do not provide critical lifeline services, interruption of business processes for an extended period of time can be devastating to an organization. Therefore, every business is well-advised to develop a business continuity plan. Particularly in many of today's businesses that rely so heavily on information as their stock in trade, it is essential that data and concomitant systems be backed up and a plan put in place to recover in case of a disaster.

Business Continuity Plans

A business continuity plan (also referred to as a disaster recovery plan or a business process contingency plan) is a logistical plan that describes how an organization will recover and reestablish interrupted critical function(s) after an extended disruption due to disaster or other causes. Business continuity plans are written to address the possibility of loss of an organization's facility or access to it, loss of information technology, loss of people, or loss of one or more elements of the supply chain. A business continuity plan comprises the actions and procedures necessary to restore any data lost when a system stops functioning. The plan should include both consideration of how to minimize the negative impact of a potential disaster and as well as how to maintain or quickly regain normal operations after a disaster occurs. Business impact analysis is the process of identifying the risk of exposure to specific threats to the organization and assessing the impact of these threats should a disaster occur. The three phases of developing a business continuity plan are shown in Figure 1.

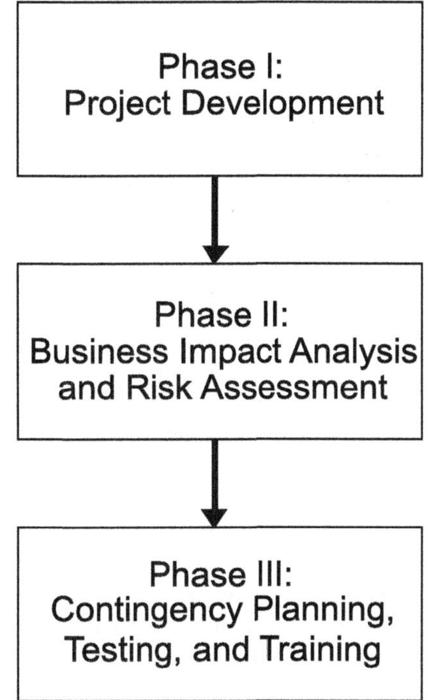

Figure 1: The Three Phases of Developing a Business Continuity Plan

Risk Assessment

Part of the task of developing a business continuity plan is to assess the degree of an organization's risk that is associated with various potential disasters. Risk assessment is the process of determining the potential loss, probability of loss of the organization's objectives, and the concomitant impact on the business. Risk assessment will help the organization perform risk management by analyzing the tasks and activities of the organization, planning ways to reduce the impact if the predicted normal course of events does not occur, and implementing reporting procedures so that project problems are discovered earlier in the process rather than later.

During risk assessment, the various risks that could affect the organization are defined and the probability of their occurrence is estimated. However, not all risks are equally pressing, so their relative impact needs to be estimated. For example, for a business located in Washington, DC, it is more important to plan for recovery after a terrorist attack, fire, or tornado than it is to plan for recovery after an elephant stampede. Similarly, without additional information that changes the probability of occurrence, it would be unsound practice to spend a large amount of money to prepare for the possibility of a flood in a desert area. However, no matter how one tries to quantify risk, the perception of risk is always a subjective thing. In addition, risk assessment must also take into account the severity of the impact if the risk is incurred. For example, the planning for a high impact but low probability risk does not eliminate the need to plan for a lesser impact, high probability risk. In addition, there are things that one can do to reduce the probability that a fire will occur. Similarly, in many organizations although the loss of data could be disastrous, the loss of the hardware would be less so since hardware can be more easily replaced. Business impact analysis is a type of risk assessment.

Business Impact Analysis

During business impact analysis, data and information are collected from each business unit in the organization to determine what standards or regulations must be upheld in an emergency situation. The analysis describes and prioritizes the tasks within each unit, and identifies the resources necessary to perform the critical tasks (without which essential business processes cannot proceed). These tasks are usually evaluated on the basis of the recovery time objective — the time goal for reestablishing and recovering the business functions and resources. The recovery time objective should be prioritized and take into account any interdependencies between processes and functions as well as any possible economies of scale. All processes and functions within a business unit or department may not have the same recovery time objective. For example, although it might be necessary to recover telephone technical support of the customer service department within minutes of interruption, other functions within the department (e.g., development work) could be delayed significantly longer without impacting the organization's effectiveness. Although it might be possible to recover many or all of the processes or functions in the organization quickly, in most cases this would also entail excessive expense. A properly conducted business impact analysis can help cut down on unnecessary expenses during the recovery period.

In addition to analyzing the impact to effectiveness of the various internal business processes, it is also important to analyze the impact of interruption of processes external to the business as well. The inability to obtain raw materials, supplies, or component parts from one's supply chain could bring a business process to a halt if there is not a continuity plan. This is particularly true if there is only one source for the input. Similarly, one must also continue the other side of the supply chain, including the transportation of products to warehouses or retail outlets or of an interruption in those facilities. Although some business interruptions may affect only the organization or one of its facilities, other interruptions may be caused by area-wide disasters. The business recovery plan should plan for such contingencies.

APPLICATIONS

Considerations When Performing Business Impact Analyses

Critical Products, Services & Operations

The United States government Federal Emergency Management Agency (FEMA) suggests a number of considerations for a business impact analysis. Before a business continuity plan can be developed and implemented, an organization must first identify its critical products, services, and operations. The areas considered in this part of the analysis should include such things as the products and services offered by the organization as well as the facilities and equipment needed to produce them; the products and services that are provided by suppliers or vendors (particularly if these are sole source); "lifeline" services such as electricity, water, sewer, gas, telecommunications, and transportation; and which operations, equipment, and personnel are vital to the continued functioning of the facility or organization. In addition to the primary systems that are necessary to keep the organization functioning, one must also consider support functions that also need backup. These include payroll, communications, customer service, shipping and receiving, and information systems support (Disaster, n.d.).

Potential Disasters

The next step in determining the impact of various disasters on a business is to determine what potential disasters may befall and to assess the probability of occurrence and the potential impact of each. Disasters to be considered include not only those that could occur within the organization (e.g., a fire), but also those that could affect the entire community (e.g., a hurricane). The latter type of disaster could affect lifeline services as well as make other resources more difficult to obtain than would a disaster that only affected the organization's facility.

It is, of course, very difficult to consider all the possible emergencies with which an organization could be faced. However, there are several categories that should be considered and that can help guide this part of the analysis (Disaster, n.d.).

- Historical emergencies comprise those things that have happened in the past in the community in which the organization is situated or at the organization's facility or at other facilities in the area. Examples of this kind of emergency include fires, severe weather conditions (e.g., hurricanes, tornadoes), hazardous material spills, transportation accidents, earthquakes, terrorism, and utility outages.
- Potential geographic disasters include those that can happen as a result of the facility's physical location. These include such factors as proximity to flood plains, seismic faults, or dams; proximity to facilities that produce, store, use, or transport hazardous materials; proximity to major transportation routes and airports; and proximity to nuclear power plants.
- Technological disasters are those that could arise from a process or system failure. Examples include fire, explosion, or hazardous materials accident; failure of a safety system; failure of telecommunications systems (e.g., for networks); failure of a computer system; power failure; heating/cooling system failure; or emergency notification system failure.
- Another general type of disaster results from human error. The probability of this type of disaster can be reduced through proper training in job tasks and in emergency procedures. Examples of human error that can have disastrous effects on an organization's functioning include lack of adequate training for personnel; poor equipment maintenance (due to poor training of maintenance technicians, inadequate procedures, or failure to follow procedures); and carelessness, misconduct, fatigue, or substance abuse.
- Disasters can also result from the physical design or construction of the facility. Things to be considered include the construction of the facility, any hazardous processes or byproducts, safety of the facilities for the storage of combustible materials, layout and location of the equipment, lighting, availability of evacuation routes and exits, and the proximity of shelter areas. The analysis should also consider any potential emergencies or hazards that the business is regulated to consider.

Estimation of Likelihood & Impact

Once a list of potential causes of emergency situations or disasters has been developed, the next step necessary to determine their impact on the business is to estimate their likeliness of occurrence. Although the resultant number is subjective, this task is an important part of risk analysis and necessary to determine the potential impact of each cause to the business.

Once probabilities have been assigned to each of the potential disaster causes, one can assess the potential impact of each on the business. This step involves the estimation of the impact of the various types of disasters on the organization's market share. Considerations during this part of the analysis should include such items as loss due to an interruption of the business, inability of the employees to report to work, inability of customers to reach the organization's facility, impact due to inability to meet contractual requirements (including loss of future business and imposition of fines, penalties, or legal costs), interruption of the supply chain (both of parts and supplies to the facility and products from the facility). A sample form for performing these estimates is shown in Figure 2.

CONCLUSION

A business continuity plan is a logistical plan that describes how an organization will recover and reestablish interrupted critical function(s) after an extended disruption due to natural disaster, sabotage or terrorism, or other cause. Particularly in businesses that rely heavily on information, it is essential that data and concomitant systems be backed up and a plan put in place to recover in case of a disaster or other type of business interruption. Otherwise, the organization may not only lose short-term profits, but long-term market share as well. Business impact analysis is an essential part of developing a business continuity plan. This process includes identifying the risk of exposure to specific organizational threats and assessing the impact of these threats should the unthinkable occur.

Type of Emergency	Probability	Human Impact	Property Impact	Business Impact	Internal Resources	External Resources	Total*
	High ⟷ Low 5 1	Weak Resources ⟷ Strong Resources 5 1			High Impact ⟷ Low Impact 5 1		

* *The lower the score the better.*

Figure 2: Vulnerability Analysis Chart (Adapted from Wahle & Beatty, p. 67)

Bibliography

Henry, A. (2006). Developing a business continuity plan. *Rural Telecommunications, 25*(6), 14–20. Retrieved October 11, 2007, from EBSCO Online Database Business Source Complete. http://search.ebscohost.com/login.aspx?direct=true&db=bth&AN=23337414&site=bsi-live

Disaster information. FEMA. Retrieved 26 July 2010, from http://www.fema.gov/hazard/index.shtm

Mazouz, A., Crane, K., & Gambrel, P. A. (2012). The impact of cash flow on business failure analysis and prediction. *International Journal of Business, Accounting, & Finance, 6* (2), 68–83. Retrieved November 26, 2013 from EBSCO Online Database Business Source Complete. http://search.ebscohost.com/login.aspx?direct=true&db=bth&AN=83173535&site=ehost-live

Sikdar, P. (2011). Alternate approaches to business impact analysis. *Information Security Journal: A Global Perspective, 20* (3), 128–134. Retrieved November 26, 2013 from EBSCO Online Database Business Source Complete. http://search.ebscohost.com/login.aspx?direct=true&db=bth&AN=60900178&site=ehost-live

Wahle, T. & Beatty, G. (1993). *Emergency management guide for business and industry: A step-by-step approach to emergency planning, response and recovery for companies of all sizes* (FEMA 141). Retrieved 26 November, 2013, from FEMA Website. http://www.fema.gov/pdf/business/guide/bizindst.pdf

Wright, T. (2011). Can business impact analysis play a meaningful role in planning a cost-saving programme?. *Journal of Business Continuity & Emergency Planning, 5* (1), 400–408. Retrieved November 26, 2013 from EBSCO Online Database Business Source Complete. http://search.ebscohost.com/login.aspx?direct=true&db=bth&AN=61819907&site=ehost-live

Suggested Reading

Anderson, J. D. (2007). How's your disaster recovery plan? *CPA Technology Advisor, 17*(4), 58–59. Retrieved October 11, 2007, from EBSCO Online Database Business Source Complete. http://search.ebscohost.com/login.aspx?direct=true&db=bth&AN=26379774&site=bsi-live

Fitzpatrick, G. (2007). Risk intelligent enterprises business impact analysis benefits. *Accountancy Ireland, 39*(1), 38–41. Retrieved October 8, 2007, from EBSCO Online Database Business Source Complete. http://search.ebscohost.com/login.aspx?direct=true&db=bth&AN=24040967&site=bsi-live

Hudson, R. (2000). Business continuation demands planning. *Business Insurance, 34*(25), 17–18. Retrieved October 11, 2007, from EBSCO Online Database Business Source Complete. http://search.ebscohost.com/login.aspx?direct=true&db=bth&AN=3571817&site=bsi-live

Semer, L. J. (1998). Disaster recovery planning for the distributed environment. *Internal Auditor, 55*(6), 40–46.Retrieved October 11, 2007, from EBSCO Online Database Business Source Complete. http://search.ebscohost.com/login.aspx?direct=true&db=bth&AN=1401195&site=bsi-live

Smith, J. (2013). Strategic continuity planning: The first critical step. *Journal of Business Continuity & Emergency Planning, 7* (1), 6–12. Retrieved November 26, 2013 from EBSCO Online Database Business Source Complete. http://search.ebscohost.com/login.aspx?direct=true&db=bth&AN=91896038&site=ehost-live

Vozar, R. (2013). Disaster preparedness. *Smart Business St. Louis, 6* (6), 20. Retrieved November 26, 2013 from EBSCO Online Database Business Source Complete. http://search.ebscohost.com/login.aspx?direct=true&db=bth&AN=88179354&site=ehost-live

Ruth A. Wienclaw, Ph.D.

Business Information Systems & Technologies

Abstract

The influx of data enabled by the technologies of the Information Age has literally transformed many businesses. Most businesses today use information technology in some form to create, store, and distribute information. There are three interdependent components of information systems: Computers, communications and expertise. These components must work together in order for an information system to effectively support the organization in its activities and mission. Information systems have several basic functions, including the capture, processing, generation, storage, retrieval, and transmission of data.

OVERVIEW

The influx of data enabled by the technologies of the Information Age and with which we are bombarded every day has literally transformed many businesses. At a basic level, much correspondence today is not sent by mail or even faxed, but is transmitted nearly instantaneously around the world via e-mail. Accounting and project management tasks that used to be labor intensive jobs done by hand have benefited from spreadsheet application software that allows quick and easy manipulation of data, checking of calculations, and monitoring of tasks. Huge databases improve the ability of organizations to perform customer relationship management to better serve the customer as well as data mining to determine previously unknown relationships that help the organization better market its products and services. Information technology is the use of technology from computers, communications networks, and electronics to create, store, and disperse information and knowledge. Various technology components are put together in an information system that facilitates the flow of data (i.e., raw facts, figures, or details) and information (i.e., organized, meaningful, interpreted data) between people or departments.

There are several characteristics of the information age that set it apart from other periods in history. First, the proliferation of information technology has led to a situation where society in many countries today is information-based, with more people dealing with information than with agriculture or manufacturing. As the number and range of available information technologies increase, a concomitant number of businesses depend on information technology to accomplish their work. This dependence is on both the computer technologies that enable organizations to gather, store, manipulate, and analyze data, and also on the communication technologies that allow them to interconnect more quickly and efficiently than ever before. In fact, the understanding of information technology and information systems is so important in the information age, that in many situations it is difficult if not impossible to be successful in the business world without it. Information technology has become so much a part of our lives today that it is often embedded in other products and services that we take for granted. For example, the phone call one makes for technical support may be enabled by network technology and wireless communications systems so that the call can be answered by a technician working halfway around the world. The prevalence of information technology does not mean that an organization needs to implement information technology to be successful, however. Like the manufacturing technology that came before it and the agricultural technology before that, information technology is only a tool and must be understood in order to optimize its usefulness in the organization.

Information technology does more than support our work. In many cases it also transforms the way that we accomplish our tasks and even allows us to do things that we would never have been able to accomplish before. Work processes are constantly being transformed through the application of information technology in order to improve productivity and free humans from many repetitive tasks. For example, typewriters have given way to word processors which, in turn, have given way to multitasking computers that allow us to view, create, edit, and interact with not just documents but images, audio, animation, movies, websites, and more. However, information technology not only allows humans to perform existing processes more quickly or efficiently than ever before, in many cases it also allows us to rethink and reengineer the way that we do things in the workplace. Business process reengineering helps organizations and managers rethink their practices and processes and introduce radical improvements that benefit both the organization and its customers. For example, the division of labor necessary to the industrial age is frequently being replaced by teamwork, information sharing, and other ways of increasing the interconnectedness of workers.

Three Components of Information Technology

As shown in Figure 1, information technology comprises three interdependent components: computers, communications and expertise. The computer component of an information technology system can be any electronic system that can be instructed to accept, process, store, and present data. Although most people are familiar with desktop computers for work and home, many other devices meet this definition, including the microwave oven in the kitchen, the timer for the front door lights, the autofocus digital

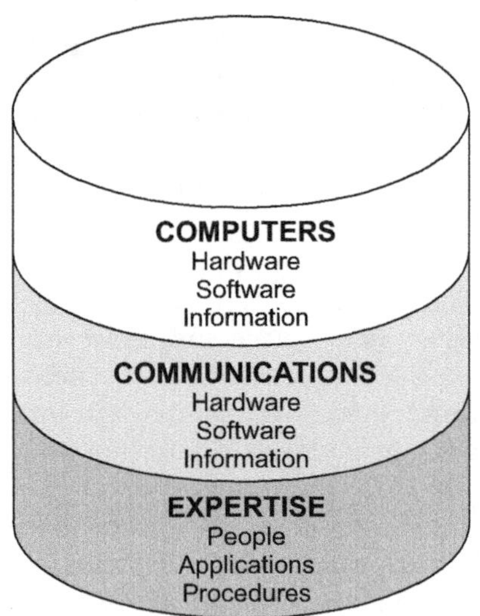

Figure 1: The Three Components of Information Technology
(Adapted from Senn, p. 15)

camera, the ATM machine outside the bank, and the automatic ticket kiosk at the cinema.

Computers

In general, computers can be classified into four size categories. Microcomputers or personal computers are relatively compact. This category of computers includes desktop computers that comprise a display unit and keyboard which sit easily on a desk or table with the processing unit fitting on or under the desk. Notebook or laptop computers are smaller versions of the desktop computer and are designed for portability. The keyboard, display, and processing unit are all part of one unit, and weigh an average of three to nine pounds, making them easy to transport from site to site. Tablet personal computers range in weight from just over half a pound to just over two pounds (ConsumerReports.org, 2013). Tablet personal computers are available in a variety of shapes and sizes depending on their purpose. For example, many police departments use tablet computers for writing tickets while insurance agents often use other models to sketch details of situations or prepare damage claims in the field. Smart phones are not just phones but are small computers that weigh ounces, yet are both fast and powerful, with a wide and growing range of applications.

Personal computers are prevalent in most businesses. In addition, many medium to large sized business also may have midrange or mainframe computers. Midrange computers (sometimes called minicomputers) are used to interconnect people and large sets of information. Midrange computers can be used across the entire organization (i.e., enterprise-wide) or within a specific department. Midrange computers typically are dedicated to performing specific functions. In addition, mainframe computers — which are typically larger, faster, and more expensive than midrange computers — allow the interconnection of larger numbers of people or processing of larger amounts of data. As opposed to midrange computers, mainframe computers typically perform several functions at once. In addition to these classifications of computers, supercomputers are available to solve problems comprising long and difficult calculations. Supercomputers run various complex applications including scientific research and real-world simulations for the design of complex equipment such as new aircraft.

In order for a computer to do the work it is intended to do, it needs software as well as hardware. Computer software is a set of instructions that controls the computer or communications network and that manages the hardware in the system. Operating systems are sets of software programs that coordinate the actions of the computer and its peripheral devices (e.g., printer). Application software performs functions not directly related to the running of the actual computer. Application software packages focus on particular types of tasks such as desktop publishing, graphic design, or database management.

Communications Networks

In addition to computer systems, information technology also includes various communications networks. These are sets of locations (or nodes) with concomitant hardware, software, and information that are linked together to form a system that transmits and receives information and data. Communications networks include local area networks (LANs) that comprise multiple computers that are located near each other and linked into a network that allows the users to share files and peripheral devices such as printers, fax machines, and storage devices; metropolitan area networks (MANs) that transmit data and information citywide and at greater speeds than a local area network; and wide area networks (WANs) that comprise multiple computers that are widely dispersed and are linked into a network. Wide area networks typically use high speed, long distance communications networks or satellites to connect the computers within the network.

Organizations, by definition, involve groups of people working together to accomplish work. Information technology can aid organizations in their tasks by linking together multiple computers to share files and peripheral devices such as printers. This capability allows multiple people to work on the same document (e.g., inputting data, commenting on a document, creating reports from a database). Wide area networks — which typically use high speed, long distance communications networks or satellites to connect the computers within the network — can also allow employees to communicate and cooperate not only with colleagues in the next office, but across the globe.

Expertise

Just as computer hardware and software are useless without each other, both require the additional input of the user's expertise in order to be able to optimize the work that they can do. This expertise includes familiarity with the tools of information technology, the skills needed to use these tools, and an understanding of how and where information technology can best be implemented. When all three of these components of information technology are working together, they can create an information system that facilitates and optimizes the flow of information and data between people or departments. Information technology and systems can support the organization in its processes and help it to maximize the use of its other resources and be more effective.

Basic Functions of Information Technology

As shown in Figure 2, information technology has several basic functions. These functions may occur sequentially or simultaneously. First, information technology captures data, that is, it compiles detailed records of activities for later analysis or processing. Examples of data capture include the collection of patron information and book information when a book is checked out of the library; the assignment of seats on an airplane or in a theatre; and the collection of customer information for orders taken over the Internet. Captured data are processed (i.e., converted, analyzed, or synthesized) into information that can be used by the organization and its employees. Data processing comprises the handling and

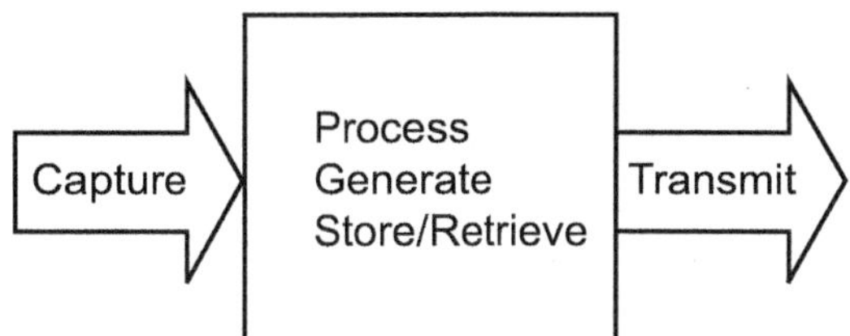

Figure 2: The functions of Information Technology

transformation of data into information. Information processing involves the transformation of collected data from one form into another. Word processing allows users to create documents and other text-based documents. Image processing converts visual information such as graphics and photographs into a format that can be stored or manipulated in the information system and/or transmitted across the network. Voice processing systems transform and transmit spoken information to enable virtual meetings and other applications. Information technology can also be used to generate data through processing. The generation function organizes data and information into a useful form such as in the generation of a document or multimedia presentation. Data and information are also stored so that they can be retrieved and processed at a later time. Finally, data and information can also be transmitted by information systems and distributed to other parties via a communications network.

APPLICATIONS

Linking computers into networks can enhance the productivity and effectiveness of the entire enterprise. A common example of this can be seen in the information systems used in many modern retail stores. Computerized cash registers in a retail store or other point of sale can be linked together so that sales clerks can search across the network to see what other store may have a particular item in stock. In addition, the computers at the point of sale can be linked directly to the corporate headquarters so that the store's closing data each evening can be directly and immediately shared with corporate management. Information technology can also help individual stores keep track of their inventories including what items they have in stock, what products are most in demand, when it is time to reorder, and even assist in automatically ordering stock. Information technology can also be used to automatically invoice customers and do other billing tasks.

It is not just the enterprise that uses computers to improve the effectiveness and efficiency of its processes. Individual employees, too, increasingly turn to information technology to help them in their tasks. For example, application software can help people keep track of their calendars, including scheduling of appointments, meetings, and tasks to be done. Other application software is available for project management to help employees keep track not only of their own tasks but the tasks and processes of large projects. These software applications allow project managers to track and control schedules for complex projects and to communicate status, risks, and other information about the project to customers and team members.

Another important use of information technology for businesses is database management systems. These systems are computer software application programs that allow the user to create, change, and manage a collection of data items that are related to each other. Databases are distinguished from other collections of data by the fact that their data are used for multiple purposes. In a database management system, data are placed into a series of tables that are keyed to each other and that can be manipulated into a variety of reports that display only that portion of the database in which the user is currently interested. The data in the system are managed through inputting data into the database, updating the data, and representing all or part of the data in various reports that meet the user's specific needs. Information technology enables the creation and manipulation of large databases that could not be managed through another medium.

Database management systems have a wide range of applications for business. Inventory control systems in retail stores or chains are one example of a database management system. Similarly, medical records management systems in hospitals can help a hospital or physician's office control, organize, and manage a wide range of demographic information about their patients and their medical histories, information about their medical insurance coverage, and other data that are important to the healthcare system. These systems can allow users to pull together the information in a variety of ways for various forms and records.

Database management systems are also used in marketing. Database systems can help marketers better understand their target market, collect and analyze data on prospective customers, keep track of current customers' buying histories, needs, and other characteristics. Database management systems can be used to develop targeted mailing lists for new products based on customer demographics or buying history or track customer purchases so that better solutions can be offered or new products developed to better meet their needs.

Another way that organizations are meeting the increasing demands for communication and information exchange is through communications networks. These networks can be used for a number of purposes. One of the most common uses of this application of information technology is the electronic transmission of messages and documents. These capabilities include e-mail, voice mail, electronic document exchange, electronic funds transfer, and access to the Internet or other networks. Communications networks can also be used for purposes of e-commerce to buy and sell goods or services — including products and information retrieval services — electronically rather than through conventional means. Networks can also be used to support group activities such as the ability to hold meetings with participants at geographically dispersed sites. Audio and videoconferencing capabilities combined with electronic document exchange capabilities can often obviate the need for extensive travel to meetings.

Bibliography

ConsumerReports.org (2013). Tablets: Tablet ratings & reliability. Retrieved December 4, 2013 from http://www.consumerreports.org/cro/electronics-computers/computers-internet/tablets/tablet-ratings/ratings-overview.htm

Drnevich, P. L., & Croson, D. C. (2013). Information technology and business-level strategy: Toward an integrated theoretical perspective. *MIS Quarterly, 37*(2), 483-509. Retrieved December 4, 2013 from EBSCO Online Database Business Source Premier. http://search.ebscohost.com/login.aspx?direct=true&db=buh&AN=87371536

Lucas, H. C. Jr. (2005). *Information technology: Strategic decision making for managers.* New York: John Wiley and Sons.

Otim, S., Dow, K. E., Grover, V., & Wong, J. A. (2012). The impact of information technology investments on downside risk of the firm: Alternative measurement of the business value of IT. *Journal of Management Information Systems, 29*(1), 159-194. Retrieved December 4, 2013 from EBSCO Online Database Business Source Premier. http://search.ebscohost.com/login.aspx?direct=true&db=buh&AN=79629592

Senn, J. A. (2004). *Information technology: Principles, practices, opportunities* (3rd ed.). Upper Saddle River, NJ: Pearson/Prentice Hall.

Wang, N., Liang, H., Zhong, W., Xue, Y., & Xiao, J. (2012). Resource structuring or capability building? An empirical study of the business value of information technology. *Journal of Management Information Systems, 29*(2), 325-367. Retrieved December 4, 2013 from EBSCO Online Database Business Source Premier. http://search.ebscohost.com/login.aspx?direct=true&db=buh&AN=83778602

SUGGESTED READING

DeJarnett, L. R. (2000). Knock, knock!...Who's there?...The twenty-first century century! *Information Strategy: The Executive's Journal, 16*(2), 3-5. Retrieved June 20, 2007, from EBSCO Online Database Business Source Complete. http://search.ebscohost.com/login.aspx?direct=true&db=bth&AN=2510654&site=ehost-live

Lu, Y., & Ramamurthy, K. (2011). Understanding the link between information technology capability and organizational agility: An empirical examination. *MIS Quarterly, 35*(4), 931-954. Retrieved December 4, 2013 from EBSCO Online Database Business Source Premier. http://search.ebscohost.com/login.aspx?direct=true&db=buh&AN=67129445

Mohamed, A. (2007, 6 Feb). How to get it right when shopping for a database management system. *Computer Weekly*, 30-32. Retrieved May 12, 2007, from EBSCO Online Database Business Source Complete. http://search.ebscohost.com/login.aspx?direct=true&db=bth&AN=24344224&site=ehost-live

Peterson, K. (2007). Organizing business staff for greater productivity. *Kitchen & Bath Design News, 25*(4), 40. Retrieved May 11, 2007, from EBSCO Online Database Business Source Complete. http://search.ebscohost.com/login.aspx?direct=true&db=bth&AN=24791674&site=ehost-live

Tallon, P. P., & Pinsonneault, A. (2011). Competing perspectives on the link between strategic information technology alignment and organizational agility: Insights from a mediation model. *MIS Quarterly, 35*(2), 463-486. Retrieved December 4, 2013 from EBSCO Online Database Business Source Premier. http://search.ebscohost.com/login.aspx?direct=true&db=buh&AN=60461965

Ruth A. Wienclaw, Ph.D.

BUSINESS STATISTICS

ABSTRACT

Business statistics is the application of mathematical statistical techniques to the real problems of the business world. In addition to helping the business analyst to organize and describe data, business statistics allows meaningful comparisons to be made between and among complex sets of data. Business statistics can be applied to a wide range of business problems including marketing, operations, quality control, and forecasting. The usefulness of statistical analysis, however, depends on the quality of the hypothesis being tested. There are a number of considerations for developing a testable hypothesis that will yield meaningful results when analyzed and for designing a research study that will control extraneous variables while emulating the real world situation to which the results will be extrapolated.

OVERVIEW

Every day, business persons are faced with a multitude of questions the answers to which can determine not only the course but the very success of the business. Will the new logo design better connect our product in the customer's mind than the current logo does? Will the new widget design attract people's attention and make them want to buy it? Are men or women more likely to buy a gizmo, and how do we best advertise it to them? How do we turn prospective customers into established customers? Will oil prices continue to rise and will people be open to alternative fuel sources? If the business answers these questions correctly, it can be on the leading edge of its industry. However, if the business answers these questions incorrectly, it can potentially lose money, its market share, or even its viability.

Mathematical statistics is a branch of mathematics that deals with the analysis and interpretation of data. Mathematical statistics provides the theoretical underpinnings for various applied statistical disciplines, including business statistics, in which data are analyzed to find answers to quantifiable questions. Business statistics is the application of these tools and techniques to the analysis of real world problems for the purpose of business decision making.

There are two general classes of statistics that are used by the business analyst. Descriptive statistics are used to describe and summarize data so that they can be more easily comprehended and studied. Among the tools of descriptive statistics are various graphing techniques, measures of central tendency, and measures of variability. Graphing techniques help the analyst aggregate and visually portray data so that they can be better understood. Included in this category are histograms, frequency distributions, and stem and leaf plots. Measures of central tendency estimate the midpoint of a distribution. These measures include the median (the number in the middle of the distribution), the mode (the number occurring most often in the distribution), and the mean (a mathematically derived measure in which the sum of all data in the distribution is divided by the number of data points in the distribution). Measures of variability summarize how widely dispersed the data are over the distribution. The range is the difference between the highest and lowest scores in the distribution. The standard deviation is a mathematically derived index of the degree to which scores differ from the mean of the distribution.

Descriptive statistics are helpful for taking large amounts of data and describing them in ways that are easily comprehendible. Pie charts, histograms, and frequency polygons are frequently used in business presentations and are all examples of ways that descriptive statistics can be used in business. Although such descriptive statistics are useful in summarizing and describing data, business statistics is an applied form of mathematics and is a valuable tool for helping analyze and interpret data. This can be done through the use of inferential statistics, a collection of techniques that allow one to make inferences about the data, including drawing conclusions about a population from a sample.

In general, inferential statistics are used to test hypotheses to determine if the results of a study occur at a rate that is unlikely to be due to chance (i.e., have statistical significance). A hypothesis is an empirically testable declarative statement that the independent and dependent variables and their corresponding measures are related to in a specific way as proposed by the theory. The independent variable is the variable that is being manipulated by the researcher. For example, a market researcher might be trying to determine which new breakfast cereal the organization should bring to market. The independent variable is the type of breakfast cereal. The dependent variable (so called because its value depends on which level of the independent variable the subject received) is the subject's response to the independent variable (e.g., whether or not the people like the breakfast cereal they are given to try). Examples of hypotheses include "the new red widget logo is better remembered than the old blue logo," "grade school children prefer the taste of new, improved Super Crunchies to original Crunchies cereal," or "Widget Corporation stores in the western states are more profitable than those in the East."

For purposes of statistical tests, the hypothesis is stated in two ways. The null hypothesis (H0) is the statement that there is no statistical difference between the status quo and the experimental condition. In other words, the treatment being studied made no difference on the end result. For example, a null hypothesis about the effectiveness of the two possible logos for Widget Corporation would be that there is no difference in the way that people react to the old logo versus the new logo. This null hypothesis states that there is no relationship between the variables of old/new logo (independent variable) and whether or not people like it (dependent variable). The alternative hypothesis (H1) states that there is a relationship between the two variables (e.g., people prefer the new logo).

Following the formulation of the null hypothesis, an experimental design is developed that allows the researcher to empirically test the hypothesis. Typically, this design will have a control group that

that does not receive the experimental conditions (e.g., the group sees only the old logo) and an experimental group that does receive the experimental condition (e.g., the group sees the new logo). The analyst then collects data from people in the study to determine whether or not the experimental condition had any effect on the outcome. After the data have been collected, they are statistically analyzed to determine whether the null hypothesis should be accepted (i.e., there is no difference between the control and experimental groups) or rejected (i.e., there is a difference between the two groups). As shown in Figure 1, accepting the null hypothesis means that if the data in the population are normally distributed, the results are more than likely due to chance. This is illustrated in the figure as the unshaded portion of the distribution. By accepting the null hypothesis, the analyst is concluding that it is likely that people do not react any differently to the red logo than they do to the blue logo. For the null hypothesis to be rejected and the alternative hypothesis to be accepted, the results must lie in the shaded portion of the graph. This means that there is a statistical significance that the difference observed between the two groups is probably not due to chance but to a real underlying difference in people's attitudes toward the two logos.

Part of the process of designing an experiment is determining how the data will be analyzed. There are a number of different statistical methods for testing hypotheses, each of which is appropriate to a different type of experimental design. One class of statistical tests is the *t-tests.* This type of statistical technique is used to analyze the mean of a population or compare the means of two different populations. In other situations where one wishes to compare the means of two populations, a *z* statistic may be used.

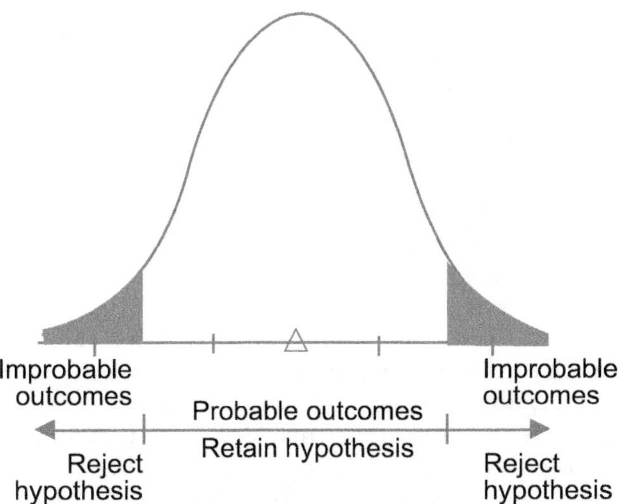

Figure 1: Hypothesized Sampling Distribution of the Mean Showing Areas of Acceptance and Rejection of the Null Hypothesis
(adapted from Witte, p. 118)

Another frequently used technique for analyzing data in applied settings is analysis of variance (ANOVA). This family of techniques is used to analyze the joint and separate effects of multiple independent variables on a single dependent variable and to determine the statistical significance of the effect. For example, analysis of variance might be used if one wished to determine the relative profitability of an organization's operations in three different countries. Multivariate analysis of variance (MANOVA) is an extension of this set of techniques that allows the business analyst to test hypotheses on more complex problems involving the simultaneous effects of multiple independent variables on multiple dependent variables.

Other types of applied statistics allow the business analyst to predict one variable from the knowledge of another variable. If one were launching a new cereal in marketplace, it might be helpful to know the demographics of the people who prefer the cereal so that it could be introduced into the correct market. For example, if the new cereal appealed primarily to children but not to adults, it would not be a prudent strategy to put it in the grocery store in an all-adult community. One way to answer this question is by determining the relationship between the two variables (e.g., age of consumer and attitude toward the new cereal). Correlation coefficients allow analysts to determine whether the two variables are positively correlated (e.g., the older people become, the more they like the new cereal), negatively correlated (e.g., the older people become, the less they like the new cereal), or not correlated at all.

However, real world problems do not always have easy answers involving only two variables. For example, consumers' attitudes toward the new cereal may depend not only on their age, but on other factors as well. If, for example, the new cereal is presweetened, consumer's preferences may be based also on such factors as what type of cereal they usually eat, how much sugar they usually consume in their diet, what cereal they ate when they were children, or whether or not they have a medical condition that requires them to reduce the amount of sugar in their diets. Multiple regression analysis is a family of statistical techniques that allow one to predict the score on the dependent variable when given the scores on one more independent variables. This statistical technique analyzes the effects of multiple predictors on behavior so that the business analyst has a better understanding of their relative contributions as well as the factors that make up a consumer's preference or other question of interest.

These are only a few of the statistical techniques that can be used in the analysis of business data. Statistical techniques can be applied to the gamut of business problems from marketing research, quality control, prediction of marketplace trends or sales volume, or comparing the relative efficiency of the various operations in a multinational organization.

APPLICATIONS

As opposed to mathematical statistics, the field of business statistics is an applied field used to help make practical decisions about real world problems. This is done through a variety of types of research studies.

In general, the goal of research is to describe, explain, and predict behavior. For example, a marketer may want to know which of two proposed new company logos will be most memorable and will have the most positive image in the minds of prospective customers. Another example of applied research is when the engineering department seeks to determine which of two graphical user interfaces is more user friendly. Designing a good research study depends in part on two factors: controlling the situation so that the research is only measuring what it is supposed to measure and including as many of the relevant factors as possible so that the research fairly emulates the real world experience.

In the simplest research design, a stimulus (e.g., a new company logo) is presented to the research subjects (e.g., potential customers) and a response is observed and recorded (e.g., which logo they liked better and why). There are three types of variables that are important in research. As discussed above, the variables of most concern in the design of a research study are the independent variable, which is the stimulus or experimental condition that is hypothesized to affect behavior, and the dependent variable, which is the observed effect on behavior caused by the independent variable. As shown in Figure 2, however, these are not the only variables that need to be controlled during a study. There are also extraneous variables — variables that affect the outcome of the experiment (e.g., their response to the cereal) that have nothing to do with the independent variable itself. For example, if the subject is tired and hungry after a long day at work and looking forward to going home and having a steak for dinner, no breakfast cereal is likely to taste good. Similarly, if a subject has a cold and is asked to rate the difference between the two breakfast cereals, s/he might not be able to do so because s/he cannot taste well at the time. There are any number of such variables that are extraneous to the research question being asked but that still affect the outcome of the research. As much as possible, these need to be controlled. In this example, the analyst could hold all the tastings of the breakfast cereal first thing in the morning when no one has eaten yet. Similarly, the researcher could make sure that subjects in the experiment do not have a cold or allergies before they taste the cereal. Although it is impossible to control literally every possible extraneous variable, the more of these that are accounted for and controlled in the experimental design, the more meaningful the results will be.

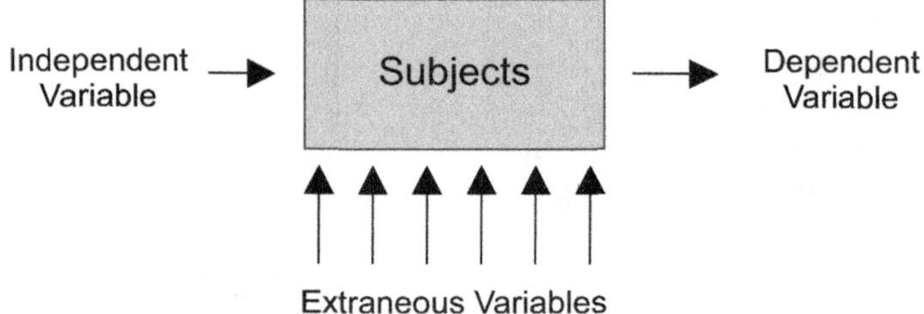

Figure 2: Research Variables

As shown in Figure 3, research design starts with a theory based on real world observation. For example, from personal experience with two types of cereal and observations of how other people react to the cereals, a researcher may develop a preliminary theory that "Super Crunchies" is more likely to be successful in the target market than "Very Flakies." From these observations, s/he forms an empirically testable hypothesis concerning the relative attractiveness of the two kinds of cereal. For example, the

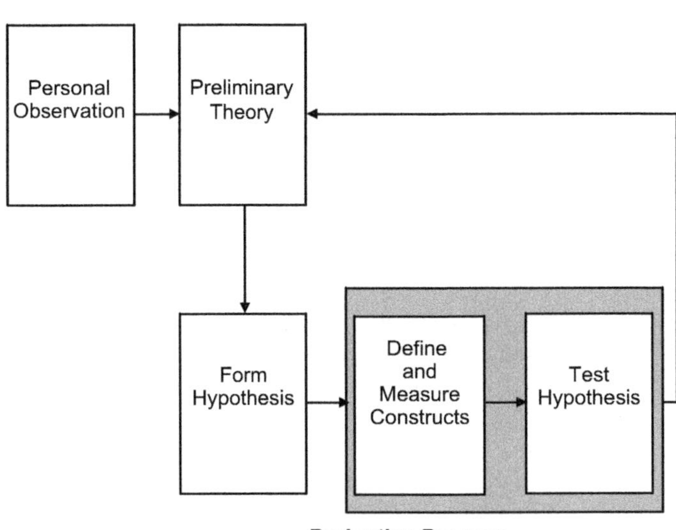

Figure 3: The Theory Building Process

hypothesis may be that "People like Super Crunchies better than Very Flakies." To find out if this hypothesis is true, the researcher next needs to operationally define the various terms (i.e., constructs) in the hypothesis. Specifically, s/he needs to determine what the components of "like better" are. To do this, s/he might develop a series of rating scales that measure the various components of whether someone buys a cereal (e.g., prefers it to the current brand, likes the taste, likes the mouth feel, likes the price). The researcher would then run the experiment, letting people try both cereals in a controlled setting, statistically analyzing the resulting data using inferential statistics, and — based on the statistical significance of the answer — determine whether it is likely to be cost effective to put one of the two cereals on the market.

Not all research is done in the laboratory, however. As stated above, it is important not only to control as many variables as one can when designing an experiment, but also to have the experimental situation emulate the real-world situation as much as possible. For example, although Super Crunchies may taste fine in a taste test in a laboratory, when the potential consumer is faced with the reality of feeding it to fussy children while simultaneously checking homework, making lunches, and driving the carpool, waiting for the cereal to lose a little of its crunch may be more than time allows.

There are a number of common research techniques that can be used to investigate business problems. The laboratory experiment allows the researcher the most control over extraneous variables. So, for example, the cereal tasting could always be held at the same time of day in a room with no distractions and allow people to eat as much of each cereal as they want at their leisure. However, this situation is far removed from the reality of how most people eat their breakfast. A second approach to research is to use a simulation. This can allow the researcher to bring in more real world variables but still control many of the extraneous variables. For example, people could be given only a limited time to eat the cereals while simultaneously being given other morning tasks to do. Alternatively, the research could be run as a field experiment in which people are given the cereal to try at home under the normal conditions in which they typically eat breakfast. This has the advantage of being more realistic, but it also has the disadvantage of giving the researcher less control over extraneous variables.

In addition to these research techniques in which the experimenter has some control over the variables, there are other approaches to studying business problems as well. The field study is an examination of how people behave in the real world. For example, if both cereals are already on the market, the researcher could observe what type of people bought each variety to determine whether the brands appealed to families with children or only to adults. This could be combined with another research technique called survey research. In survey research, subjects are interviewed by a member of the research team or asked to fill out a questionnaire regarding their preferences, reactions, habits, or other questions of interest to the researcher. For example, the researcher could ask each person buying the new cereal a list of questions such as how often they bought that particular variety of cereal, what other cereals they had tried before, what they liked about this brand, etc. However, although a very thorough interview or survey instrument can be written that would hypothetically gather all the data needed for the researcher to make decisions about the cereals, such instruments are often more lengthy than the potential research subject's attention span. In addition, as opposed to the other research techniques, surveys and interviews are not based on observation.

Therefore, there is no way to know whether the subject is telling the truth.

Finally, the analyst does not necessarily have to do new research in order to statistically analyze data for decision making. Meta analysis and other secondary analysis techniques allow researchers to analyze multiple previous research studies to look for trends or general findings. Statistical analysis can also be applied to existing data that the business has collected for other purposes or that are publicly available. Although these approaches do not give the researcher control over the way that the data are collected, these approaches often yield interesting results that can add to the body of knowledge about a topic or that can inform business decisions.

Bibliography

Black, K. (2006). *Business statistics for contemporary decision making* (4th ed.). New York: John Wiley & Sons.

Jance, M. L. (2012). Statistics and the entrepreneur. *Academy of Business Research Journal, 1* 33–37. Retrieved November 20, 2013 from EBSCO Online Database Business Source Complete. http://search.ebscohost.com/login.aspx?direct=true&db=bth&AN=85672206&site=ehost-live

Larwin, K. H., & Larwin, D. A. (2011). Evaluating the use of random distribution theory to introduce statistical inference concepts to business students. *Journal of Education For Business, 86* (1), 1–9. Retrieved November 20, 2013 from EBSCO Online Database Business Source Complete. http://search.ebscohost.com/login.aspx?direct=true&db=bth&AN=54533309&site=ehost-live

Levine, D. M., & Stephan, D. F. (2011). Teaching introductory business statistics using the DCOVA framework. *Decision Sciences Journal of Innovative Education, 9* (3), 395–400. Retrieved November 20, 2013 from EBSCO Online Database Business Source Complete. http://search.ebscohost.com/login.aspx?direct=true&db=bth&AN=65833386&site=ehost-live

Witte, R. S. (1980). *Statistics.* New York: Holt, Rinehart and Winston.

Suggested Reading

Bowerman, B. L. O'Connel, R. T., & Murphree, E. S. (2014). *Business statistics in practice* (7th ed.) New York, NY: McGraw-Hill.

Groebner, D. F., Shannon, P. W., Fry, P. C., & and Smith, K. D. (2011). *Business statistics: A decision-making approach* (8th ed.). Upper Saddle River, NJ: Prentice Hall/Pearson.

Kohli, A. S., Peng, C., & Mittal, P. (2011). Predictors of student success in undergraduate business statistics course. *Journal of the Academy of Business & Economics, 11* (4), 32–42. Retrieved November 20, 2013 from EBSCO Online Database Business Source Complete. http://search.ebscohost.com/login.aspx?direct=true&db=bth&AN=76503842&site=ehost-live

Levine, D. M., Krehbiel, T. C., & Berenson, M. L. (2013). *Business statistics: A first course* (6th ed.). Upper Saddle River, NJ: Prentice Hall/Pearson.

Witte, R. S., & Witte, J. S. (2013). *Statistics.* 10th ed. Hoboken, NJ: John Wiley & Sons.

Ruth A. Wienclaw, Ph.D.

C

Commercial Bank Management

ABSTRACT

Commercial banks have undergone great changes during the 20th and early 21st centuries, paralleling the ongoing evolution of the new ways in which business and commerce are conducted. This paper will provide an in-depth analysis of how such institutions are managed as well as the role commercial banks play in the 21st century economy. By understanding the many types of services such institutions offer, the reader will glean a better understanding of the vital contributions commercial banks provide for today's entrepreneurial environments.

OVERVIEW

Background

On April 18, 1906, the city of San Francisco experienced one of the most significant natural events in its storied history as a magnitude 7.8 earthquake violently razed much of the city. Amadeo Peter Giannini, who only two years earlier had founded the Bank of Italy in that city, immediately put on his clothes and rushed a horse-drawn produce cart to his bank. Picking through the rubble of his fledgling banking institution, he removed and secreted away about $2 million in gold, coins and securities. He brought the cart to the North Beach docks, where he set up two wooden barrels with a plank across them as a makeshift desk. Using the money from his leveled bank, he began to offer businesses credit based on informal agreements, helping to bring about the redevelopment of San Francisco.

Giannini's acts after the great earthquake were extraordinary measures taken during extraordinary times. However banks have long played a role, albeit somewhat understated during "normal" times, in the development and redevelopment of businesses and economies. Business is, after all, essential to the strength of an economic system — it provides jobs, produces goods and services, and generates tax revenues. For these reasons, banks — and in particular, commercial banks — have become the artery by which businesses receive their lifeblood at their earliest stages.

Commercial banks are also critical for the individual. Simple savings accounts, into which people have long deposited their personal funds, have expanded explosively into a tremendous range of options for individuals to see financial security and investment returns. Still, security is perhaps the most invaluable requirement in an individual's asset management endeavors, and the protections offered by commercial banks are not just anticipated but expected, as such institutions have long provided the most secure of financial management protocols.

A Brief History of Commercial Banks

In the earliest civilizations, those with wealth entrusted the storage of their gold and priceless items to an institution few dared to pillage, for it was one of the most fortified buildings in the city, was constantly crowded and was by reputation protected by the most powerful entities known: the gods. In fact, the first monetary depository was not a bank, government building or fortress, but a temple, a place whose sacredness was often enough of a deterrent for any would-be thief.

Of course, during these ancient times, temples did little with people's wealth except store it, where it would neither appreciate nor depreciate in value nor serve as the basis for any financial transaction. It was not until the 18th century BC, when the Code of Hammurabi was written, when priests in the temple also served as financial managers, administering loans and other financial arrangements with the people of the community.

Banks have evolved and diversified significantly since Hammurabi's era. People continued to put their pay and other personal financial wealth into savings banks, but others have used land banks to purchase their own real estate and investment banks to pursue growth via the markets. At the earliest stages of the formation of the United States, such diversity led a large percentage of the population to seek "one-stop" banking, creating a strong evolution of the commercial bank. Those seeking liquidity in their assets simply deposited their funds into a savings account, but a growing number of businesses and entrepreneurs sought loans and mortgages in order to strengthen their business position, yet they also sought liquidity. While they had the fortune of having access to a number of banking institutions, the majority of the early American banking customers used commercial banks, which were increasingly offering a wide range of services (Wright, 2001).

By definition, a commercial bank is an institution that provides banking services for businesses. Commercial banks provide savings and checking accounts for customers, but they also provide loans, lines of credit, foreign exchange and payment and transactions (Pritchard, 2009). While commercial banks' primary focus is on the business customer, a large percentage of the customers they attract are private individuals as well.

The growing use of commercial banks among business and individual customers alike has created issues for this form of banking. In the early 20th century, commercial banking had begun to expand into investing as well. Some leaders at the time of the Great Depression saw this trend as one of the contributions to the collapse of the stock market, as commercial banks were providing margin loans, underwriting stock purchases and even trading on stocks. When the market collapsed in 1929, commercial banks' attachment to the markets meant that the banks would suffer, exacerbating the situation. When President Franklin Roosevelt sought to reinvigorate the economy, he and his colleagues in Congress introduced the Glass-Steagall Act. Under this law, commercial banks and investment banks were given a definitive divorce, saying that the two should mesh no longer, in light of what Roosevelt saw as dangerous practices by a type of institution that should have been focused on financial security, not gains — a condition that is largely believed to have contributed to the epic collapse of Wall Street.

Glass-Steagall was functionally repealed in 1998 (the law's formal repeal occurred one year later), when investment giant Travelers (who owned Salomon Smith Barney) purchased commercial banking icon Citicorp. In fact, the failure of three of the five largest investment banks during the recession that began in 2007 has ignited interest in revisiting the pre-*Glass-Steagall* era (Gross, 2008), when commercial banks were heavily involved in investments.

Commercial banks, which were initially created for the purpose of business development and support, have become very diverse in terms of the services they provide. At the same time, they are increasingly seen as more trustworthy institutions for financial security than more limited-service banks or larger investment banks. It is important to understand how commercial banks manage this broad scope of services.

APPLICATIONS

Loans

One of the most important services a commercial bank offers is the loan. Lending funds to any customer will indubitably help that party in pursuing an immediate and critical goal. Commercial banks have proven to be important resources for such pursuits.

Commercial lending may be seen in two general forms:

- Intermediate-term Loans
- Long-term Financing

Intermediate term loans are an arrangement that has a life of between one and three years. Consumers use such shorter-term loans in order to finance working capital needs, purchase equipment such as computers and small machinery, using the hardware that is purchased as the basis for the repayment of the loan. In long-term financing, monies are issued primarily for larger companies (rather than small businesses), who use the loan to purchase real estate or a facility. In the case of long-term loans, up to 80 percent of the target asset's value is typically paid, with the remainder of that property's value serving as the collateral (Peavler, 2009).

Loans are one of the most important services a bank may offer its customers, particularly when they seek funds to support their pursuits of vital assets, such as new home, office space, or new inventory and equipment. Bank loans, therefore, may be considered the lifeblood of new and small (as well as large) businesses. One of the key individuals at a commercial institution, therefore, is the loan officer, whose job is to seek out and secure clients for loans. Loan officers are also charged with reviewing the client's credit history and assets in order to ensure that the client will be able to repay the loan. Furthermore, loan officers are expected to pursue delinquent loan recipients, assisting them in repayment plans if the original terms of the arrangement are not met (US Bureau of Labor Statistics, 2009).

The issue that arises when business customers demonstrate an inability to repay their loans to a commercial bank underscores an important point about the risks of the business of commercial lending. Even in times of relative economic stability, the notion of lending to new or expanding businesses represents a significant risk. If the economy turns sour and business falls, the commercial bank also stands to lose on repayment of loans. In the recession that began in 2007, the number of US commercial bank loans dropped more than 1 percent in 2009, a significant drop from the previous year. Large banks saw the biggest drop, 1.5 percent, at that time (Wagner, 2009). This trend exemplifies the risks involved in commercial lending — if the consumer experiences the challenges of a faltering economy (or marketplace), the commercial bank may be saddled with the debt, rendering it not just unable to collect on the single loan but unlikely to issue loans to others as freely as in previous cases.

Commercial banks have taken the lead on issuing loans for all sizes of business as they have increasingly among individuals. However, lending is not the only commercial banking activity seeing increased attention in the 21st century economy. Another strengthening area falling under the purview of commercial banks is investment practices.

Investments

It may be said that one of the major contributing factors to the depth and longevity of the Great Depression was assumption (Whipps, 2008). There were many investment banks in 1929, but most individuals also had their own personal accounts in commercial banks, which offered them a wide range of services. It was assumed that the stock market, which had shown great growth previously, would continue to grow and deliver returns for investors.

Commercial banks were all too willing to take part in the expanding markets. Investment banks, after all, were considered too expensive for anyone without strong corporate backing or were otherwise not wealthy. Commercial banks offered similar services, and at far more affordable rates. However, such banks failed to monitor the risks involved, and placed depositors' money into what were falsely believed to be safe investments. When the markets crashed, investors rushed to their banks in the hope of retrieving any and all of their monies, but the money simply was not there. Thus, the collapse of the country's economy was worsened exponentially by the fact that consumers did not have any protection from the investment practices of the commercial banks.

Lessons of the Great Depression

Glass-Steagall went a long way to separate investment banking from the traditional services of commercial banks. The law identified the risks involved with investments, particularly when such investments are made on the basis of a bank's securities. In 1933, one of Roosevelt's other actions to restore order to the finance industry, however, went far to create a backing system for banks, known as the Federal Deposit Insurance Corporation (FDIC). The FDIC would help prop up the existing banking system, which was still lying in ruins, as well as provide future banks with protection from similar collapses. Still, the establishment of the FDIC would not contradict the actions of Glass-Steagall, since the act operated under the impression that any "safety nets" offered by the federal government would not be expanded more than necessary ("Understanding how," 1998). In other words, although the FDIC and other government-initiated protections would be in place to insure the bank from failed accounts, such insurance did not open the door for future investments by commercial banks.

Since the repeal of *Glass-Steagall,* however, the idea of commercial banks acting in part as investment banks has captured the attention of observers, particularly in the wake of the virtual collapse of many of the largest investment banks in the world at the start of the 2007 recession. At the end of the Great Depression, the fear remained that commercial banks would return to the reckless practice of using customer assets to play the often volatile market. The Federal Reserve, which is responsible for regulation of the financial industry, has imposed a myriad of regulations on the investment banking industry. With the security created by the FDIC and the sizable volume of commercial banks' deposit and capital bases, some argue that commercial banks may (with the application of the same Federal Reserve regulations imposed on investment banks) be able to expand once again into Wall Street with less risk of collapse than their investment counterparts (Berman, 2008).

Then again, the collapse of the investment banking industry did not leave the commercial banking industry unscathed. Bank of America's purchase of investment giant Merrill Lynch led to headaches as the commercial bank inherited a public relations nightmare regarding executive bonuses. Executive incentives were later blamed for much of the high-risk activity of financial institutions that resulted in the global financial crisis in 2008 (DeYoung, Peng & Yan, 2013). Investment bank Wells Fargo purchased (and later absorbed) troubled commercial bank Wachovia during the crisis, but came under fire because of its mortgage lending practices (Flitter, 2009). Wachovia had inherited a "timebomb" of subprime mortgages as a result of its own acquistion of Golden West bank, but it was not alone in sinking under the burden of bad loans (Cole & White, 2012). Large banks had adopted the risky but profitable practice of securitizing real estate loans rather than holding them, which resulted in cavalier lending to home buyers who were uncreditworthy or unlikely to be able to continue making mortgage payments that would "balloon" sometime in the life of the mortgage. Small banks departed from their historic model and took on large commercial real estate loans. Easy lending drove up real estate values and created an unsustainable "bubble" that would burst, resulting in mass (and massive) defaults (Kyle, 2012). Mortgage Backed Securities (MBS) were sold to investors, including investment banks. As long as the real estate market was rising, investing in MBS and MBS derivatives was profitable, but when it crashed these instruments lost their value. In 2009, 117 commercial banks failed (Armbrister, 2013). Amid the ongoing interest in allowing commercial banks to invest once again is a vocal counter-argument that suggests a return to separation between the two types of institutions.

The continuing debate over the expansion of commercial bank services, which already include a myriad of offerings such as loans, savings and checking and money management, to include investment opportunities is reflective of an important point. The shortcomings of a great number of investment firms that contributed to the ongoing recession highlighted the apparent strength of commercial banks. This strength is based upon the popularity of commercial banks among businesses and individuals alike, as the large volume of deposits bolsters the banks' assets. Commercial banks, which long offered more services than savings and investment banks, may continue to enjoy the faith of consumers and businesses in stable and troubled economies alike.

CONCLUSIONS

In 1964, a *Chicago Tribune* article proclaimed, "David Rockefeller, President of Chase Manhattan Bank, briefed President [Lyndon] Johnson today on his recent meeting with Premier Nikita Khruschev of Russia" (www.Liberty-Tree.ca). The event illustrates the high regard people have for the institutions they charge with the management of their money: Johnson, the leader of the free world, would not be the one to meet with the leader of the Soviet Union. Instead, the head of the one of the largest banks in the world had the honor to represent the United States before the country's greatest adversary at the time.

In addition to the basic services commercial banks provide, such as deposit, checking and savings programs, they enable businesses and individuals to gain access to funds that may be used to either create, expand or maintain their corporate operations. During recessions, this aspect of commercial bank management can be both a challenge, due to the scarcity of lending funds, and a great benefit, because the generation of business means jobs, tax revenues and other business.

Commercial banks were the target of increased attention throughout the 20th century and are even more so in the 21st century. They have proven invaluable for businesses and individuals alike, providing a myriad of services that foster business and maintain the economy. The people's faith in commercial banks has led to a call for these institutions to expand their services to include investing, particularly in light of the stability they have due to government regulations and a broad base of securities.

How the management of commercial banks continues to evolve to meet the needs of an ever-changing global economy will demonstrate the relevance of commercial banking in the US and elsewhere. With the benefit of precedent, however, the trend of commercial bank expansions into investment arenas offers a strong indication that such practices, proposed and current, will continue.

Bibliography

Armbrister, M. (2013). Rules targeting risky loans spark worry. *Northern Colorado Business Report, 18*(22), 3-8. Retrieved November 15, 2013, from EBSCO Online Database Business Source Complete. http://search.ebscohost.com/login.aspx?direct=true&db=bth&AN=89334819&site=ehost-live

Bank of Italy. (2009). Retrieved August 15, 2009 from Anecdotage.com. http://www.anecdotage.com/index.php?aid=13764.

Berman, D. K. (2008, June 24). Maybe it's time to put the banks and Wall Street dealers back together. *Wall Street Journal — Eastern Edition, 251*(147).

Chicago Tribune. (1964, September). Banking quotes. Retrieved August 22, 2009 from Liberty-Tree.ca. http://quotes.liberty-tree.ca/quote/chicago%5ftribune%5fquote%5f5043.

Cole, R., & White, L. (2012). Déjà vu all over again: the causes of U.S. commercial bank failures this time around. *Journal of Financial Services Research, 42*(1/2), 5-29. Retrieved November 15, 2013, from EBSCO Online Database Business Source Complete. http://search.ebscohost.com/login.aspx?direct=true&db=bth&AN=77837086&site=ehost-live

DeYoung, R., Peng, E. Y., & Yan, M. (2013). Executive compensation and business policy choices at u.s. commercial banks. *Journal of Financial & Quantitative Analysis, 48*(1), 165-196. Retrieved November 15, 2013, from EBSCO Online Database Business Source Complete. http://search.ebscohost.com/login.aspx?direct=true&db=bth&AN=87775044&site=ehost-live

Flitter, E. (2009, August 11). It's *Glass-Steagall,* with a twist. *BankThink.* Retrieved August 20, 2009 from American Banker.com http://www.americanbanker.com/bankthink/image%5fwar-1000884-1.html.

Gross, D. (2008, September 15). Shattering the Glass-Steagall: The rise of the commercial banks. *Moneybox.* Retrieved August 17, 2009 from Slate.com http://www.slate.com/id/2200148/.

Kyle, A. (2012). A commentary on 'déjà vu all over again: The causes of U.S. commercial bank failures this time around'. *Journal of Financial Services Research, 42*(1/2), 31-34. Retrieved November 15, 2013, from EBSCO Online Database Business Source Complete. http://search.ebscohost.com/login.aspx?direct=true&db=bth&AN=77837081&site=ehost-live

Peavler, R. (2009). Commercial bank term loans. Retrieved August 17, 2009 from http://bizfinance.about.com/od/generalinformation/a/termloans.htm.

Pritchard, J. (2009). What is a commercial bank? Retrieved August 15, 2009 from http://banking.about.com/od/businessbanking/a/commercialbank.htm.

Understanding how *Glass-Steagall* Act impacts investment banking and the role of commercial banks. (1998, April 12). *Special Reports.* Retrieved August 20, 2009 from CoolFire Technology http://www.cftech.com/BrainBank/SPECIALREPORTS/GlassSteagall.html.

US Bureau of Labor Statistics. (2009). Occupational outlook handbook. Retrieved August 18, 2009 from http://www.bls.gov/oco/ocos018.htm.

Wagner, D. (2009, June 1). Bailed-out banks lent less money in March. *Associated Press.* Retrieved August 20, 2009 from ABCnews.com http://abcnews.go.com/Business/wireStory?id=7726276

Whipps, H. (2008, September 19). The long history of the 2008 financial mess. Retrieved August 20, 2009 from LiveScience.com http://www.livescience.com/history/080919- history-banking-industry.html.

Wright, R. (2001). *The Origins of Commercial Banking in America.* London and New York: Rowman & Littlefield Publishers.

Suggested Reading

Are bank deposits safe? (2008, March 19). *BusinessWeek Online.* Retrieved August 23, 2009 from EBSCO Online Database Academic Search Complete. http://search.ebscohost.com/login.aspx?direct=true&db=a9h&AN=31410654&site=ehost-live.

Bank credit at all commercial banks. (1993, October). *Economic Indicators.* 28.

Frame, W. S., Hancock, D. & Passmore, W. (2007). Federal home loan bank advances and commercial bank portfolio composition. *Working Paper Series — Federal Reserve Bank of Atlanta, 17,* 1-32. Retrieved August 23, 2009 from EBSCO Online Database Academic Search Complete. http://search.ebscohost.com/login.aspx?direct=true&db=a9h&AN=26073231&site=ehost-live.

Klee, E. & Natalucci, F. (2005). Profits and balance sheets at US commercial banks in 2004. *Federal Reserve Bulletin, 91*(2), 143-174. Retrieved August 23, 2009 from EBSCO Online Database Academic Search Complete. http://search.ebscohost.com/login.aspx?direct=true&db=a9h&AN=17659929&site=ehost-live.

McNulty, J., Murdock, M., & Richie, N. (2013). Are commercial bank lending propensities useful in understanding small firm finance?. *Journal of Economics & Finance, 37*(4), 511-527. Retrieved November 15, 2013, from EBSCO Online Database Business Source Complete. http://search.ebscohost.com/login.aspx?direct=true&db=bth&AN=90053001&site=ehost-live

Yunfeng, Z., Junwen, F. & Xiaoyang, L. (2008). Summarization and analysis on commercial bank risk management. *Canadian Social Science, 4*(1), 30-36. Retrieved August 23, 2009 from EBSCO Online Database Academic Search Complete. http://search.ebscohost.com/login.aspx?direct=true&db=a9h&AN=32753473&site=ehost-live.

Michael P. Auerbach, M.A.

Communications in the Workplace

ABSTRACT

Good communication skills are essential for success in virtually any organization. No matter how good one's technical skills or how innovative one's ideas, if not communicated clearly to others, they are irrelevant. Employees today need to be able to effectively communicate within the organization to each other, their bosses, and their subordinates as well outside the organization to customers or clients and vendors. Clear communication that unambiguously conveys one's meaning, however, is not a simple task and can be hampered by numerous barriers including different perceptions of a situation, filtering, language, jargon and ambiguity. In addition, cultural and gender differences can compound the process, making communication even more difficult. However, through such techniques as active listening, disclosure, and feedback, employees can learn to become better communicators and improve their own effectiveness and that of the organization.

OVERVIEW

I once worked on a project that required me to use a technical manual written for Japanese fax repair technicians that had been translated very literally (and badly) into English. "Imagine," it started, "two giants standing on opposite mountaintops in the fog." The illustration went on to describe a scenario in which the giants wished to communicate, but were having difficulty because the mountaintops were too far away to allow them to be heard by each other and the fog obscured their view so they could not signal each other. Eventually, the two giants threw boulders through the fog in an attempt to attract each other's attention. The story sounds strange and unprofessional to Western ears, but the point is that communication can be a complex process between sender and receiver, and requires that each party is paying attention and that the "fog" of distortion is cleared away no matter where in the world occurs. Even the very strangeness of the story illustrates how cultural expectations can color what we anticipate to hear.

Communication is the process of transmitting information between two or more parties. Although communication is often thought of as a verbal process, transmissions can also be written or even nonverbal; with our actions or body language communicating our message. Communication can be intentional (the interoffice memo describing a new implementation policy) or unintentional (the boss receives the message — correct or not — that the employee is not a hard worker when s/he never gets assignments in on time).

Good communication skills are essential for success in business. No matter how innovative one's idea is, no matter how skilled the service one offers, no matter how much the marketplace needs the product or service, if the business cannot articulate what it can do for potential customers or clients, it will not be successful. Good communication skills, however, are not only necessary for successful marketing. Employees must be able to communicate with each other and management must be able to communicate with employees. A boss who expects employees to be mind-readers will not be a boss for long. A team whose members cannot communicate their ideas to each other will not be able to achieve the synergy that is the goal of such work groups. The technical expert who cannot communicate his/her flash of insight will not be able to use it to help the organization. In short, communication is key to success not only on an organizational level, but on a personal level as well.

A study of entry-level job requirements listed in the job advertisements from newspapers in 10 large metropolitan areas found that "interpersonal skills" were mentioned most frequently. Even for jobs such as accounting where it would be reasonable to assume that mathematical ability was more important than communication skills, it has been found that up to 80% of work time is actually spent in communication rather than in working with numbers. Despite the importance of good communication skills in the workplace, however, research has found that employees often do not possess adequate communication skills for success. As a result, 89% of US companies give communication training to employees in areas such as team building; public speaking and presentation skills; interviewing skills; and business and technical writing.

At its simplest, communication starts when the sender decides to transmit a message to the receiver. S/he decides what message to communicate and how best to express this message (words, gestures, body language, intonation). This message is then sent to the receiver. This person then decodes the message and forms the appropriate feedback, be it a nod of the head, a smile, or other body language; an action such as doing what the sender requested; or forming another verbal or nonverbal reply to show that the message was understood or not understood. This message is then transmitted to the original sender who, in turn, receives and decodes the response, and forms a return message.

This is a simple enough process. However, communication is more than the sender transmitting a message and the receiver responding. There are numerous places during the process where barriers to communication can keep the receiver from correctly understanding the message sent in the way that the sender intended it. When this happens, miscommunication can occur. There are a number of different types of barriers to communication that can lead to miscommunication by hindering the unambiguous transmission and reception of a message between parties trying to communicate. Communication barriers include different perceptions of a situation, filtering, language, jargon, and ambiguity. Other sources of miscommunication include the degree to which the vocabulary (professional, technical, or general) of the two persons is shared, differences in their assumptions and expectations, and their relative skill at forming and decoding messages.

For example, Harvey may wish to tell George that the budget report that he had turned in was acceptable. So, Harvey forms a message: "Good job." However, George may consider the budget report to have been his best work to date or a significant improvement over his previous attempts, and is looking for more effusive praise. The terse "good job" may not carry with it sufficient information to supply George with the feedback he is seeking. As a result, George may think that Harvey did not appreciate his work or that Harvey did not think that George had done an outstanding job. Therefore, even though Harvey may have been trying to praise George, the message that George receives is that the work was neither extraordinary nor noteworthy. Such a situation can result in resentment or discouragement and may damage the relationship between the two co-workers.

Everyone comes to a situation with his/her own unique perspective, including assumptions and expectations. This perspective helps determine how an individual will react to what the other person says or does. For example, in the illustration of Harvey and George above, if George has entered the situation with the perception that Harvey is less than pleased with his previous work, then the off-hand "good work" could make him doubt his competence in other areas or lower his self-esteem. On the other hand, if his perception is that Harvey is pleased with his work in general, then the off-hand "good work" could be a confirmation even if Harvey was condemning the report with faint praise. On a small scale, this could cause needless friction in the workplace. However, if the miscommunication is between George and a customer, it could potentially lead to lost contracts or

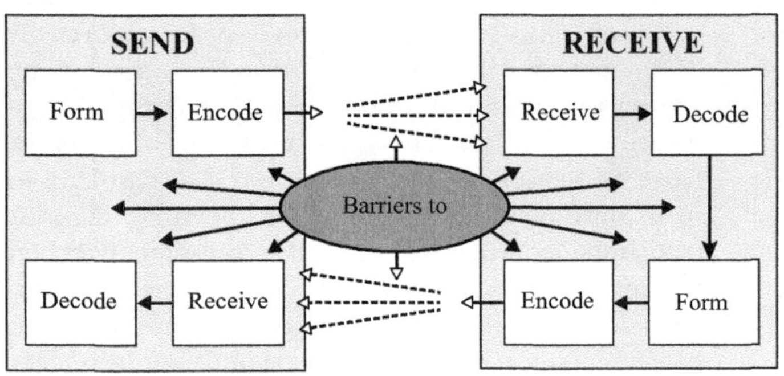

Figure 1: The Communication Process Model (adapted from McShane & von Glinow (2003), p. 324)

hours spent focusing on the wrong thing because an off-hand remark was misunderstood.

Different perceptions, however, are not the only reason for miscommunication in the workplace. Because the nature of workplace communication is often more formal than social, communications are often filtered to remove unwanted messages. For example, the culture in some organizations rewards good news but punishes bad news. In such cases, employees may tell only the good news ("we can put on a demonstration for the customer next week") but filters out the bad news ("but only if we get needed input from a vendor on time"). Similarly, when delivering performance feedback, supervisors may try to phrase negative feedback in a positive manner in the hope that it will be encouraging ("you may want to try to make your reports a little longer in the future") rather than giving the employee the entire message ("this report had none of the needed information in it and is totally unacceptable"). In the first example, if the needed input does not come from the vendor, not only does the employee look bad for not having delivered what was promised, but the supervisor looks bad to the customer or executives because the needed demonstration was a failure. In the second example, the employee's feelings were not hurt in the short-term. However, in the long-term, s/he will be left confused and bitter because raises, promotions, or other rewards that were reasonably expected on the basis of a perceived positive performance appraisal did not materialize.

To communicate effectively, both parties need to speak the same language and use words that clearly say what is meant. This does not just mean the difference between English and German, but the words chosen within the same language. One such language barrier is the use of jargon. This is any technical language, acronyms, specialized language, or other words or phrases that are unique — or uniquely interpreted — to a given group or organization but that are not in wide acceptance outside of that group. For example, the following message might not make sense to many people:

I've kluged a POC for the demo next week, but I need to stay down in the weeds so you'll have to pretty it up for the big boys.

However, to an engineer, it means that the sender has pulled together ("kluged") a proof-of-concept ("POC") to demonstrate that a theory will work. However, the sender of the message needs to work on other details ("stay down in the weeds") so the receiver will have to fine-tune it so that it looks viable ("pretty it up") when shown to the company executives ("big boys"). Although such short hand may enable communication between parties who both understand the jargon, it prevents communication when one or more parties do not.

Similarly, text messaging and other byproducts of today's high tech society have brought with them a language all their own. For example, the message "c u here @ 445 on 4/5" may mean to meet the sender at 4:45 on the 5th of April at his/her office. However, unless the organizational culture supports the use of such abbreviations, they are best left for less formal, social occasions. Using established rules of communication and grammar, however, apply not only to the abbreviations one might use in e-mails, but to any written — or oral — communication. One's professionalism is judged in part by the way that s/he expresses him/herself. The inability to write a coherent sentence using the established rules of English can prevent one from advancement within the organization or in one's career. There are social boundaries to language and its use. What is an acceptable way to speak or write to one's friend or in a social situation is not necessarily acceptable in a business setting.

Another language barrier to communication regarding the use of language is ambiguity. For example, Harvey asks George if he would like to redo the report, it could be taken in several ways: (1) a polite response to George's concern that the report might not be acceptable, but which is assumed George will not do, (2) an option that can be taken at George's discretion, or (3) a polite way of telling George that the report needs to be redone. If Harvey is merely making a polite response but George interprets it as a mandate to redo the report, much time is wasted. If Harvey is demanding that the report be redone but George interprets it as a polite response not requiring action, the miscommunication can lead to a strained working relationship.

APPLICATIONS

The current trend toward cultural diversity in the workplace makes communication an interesting proposition. Each individual comes with his/her own set of values, assumptions, and communication styles, yet needs to be able to communicate with others who have an entirely different set of communication rules. Further, the communication pattern that is effective in one work group may actually hamper communication between groups because of differing jargon or other barriers to communication. However, good communication skills are not only necessary but essential to the success of the organization. Fortunately, there are methods to improve communication skills both within the organization and between the organization and other parties so that work gets done more efficiently.

Cross-Cultural & Gender Communications

Culture is defined as the basic shared assumptions, beliefs, norms, and values held consciously or unconsciously by a group of people. In today's diverse workplaces, cultures often collide, causing miscommunications as a result of differing assumptions or differing ways of expressing oneself. For example, in Japan it is considered important that neither party in a transaction "lose face." As a result, communication tends to be much more formal and even ritualistic than is usually the case in the West. Telling a Japanese businessperson negative information in a blunt way would be considered a terrible breach of etiquette because it would cause him/her to lose face. Similarly, a Japanese businessperson would be considerate of the other person's feelings even when delivering bad news. Therefore, s/he might say that serious consideration would be given to the other person's idea but use body language that — to the knowledgeable observer — would indicate just the opposite.

One does not have to travel half way around the world to encounter different communication styles, however. Even within a culture, men and women frequently (although not universally) have different communication styles. While men, for example, tend to feel comfortable communicating in larger groups, women often prefer one-on-one communication or small group communication. Men also tend to multitask (doing two or more things at once such as looking for or even reading a report while talking), while women tend to make eye contact and focus on only the conversation at hand. Men often jump from topic to topic in their conversations, while most women prefer to talk about one topic at length. Although these may seem like little differences, they can cause significant problems. For example, a woman in conversation with a man might interpret his multitasking as a lack of concern or that he is not taking her seriously. If differences in communication style are not understood, such misunderstandings can lead to serious problems in the workplace.

To help employees become better communicators and better understand the text and subtext of the communications between people from different cultures, many organizations offer diversity training. This type of training is designed to help employees deal with persons from different cultures more effectively by helping them gain an understanding of the assumptions, values, and communication styles of the people that they may encounter in the workplace. With this understanding, employees are better prepared to be effective communicators in the workplace and both understand the message of others and get their own message across.

Improving Communication

Although good communication can be a complex process with many potential barriers that can distort the message that one is trying to send, it is also a skill that can be learned and improved. In addition to diversity training, many organizations offer training courses that help employees learn how to improve their communication skills with each other as well as with customers and clients in order to improve their effectiveness and the organization's success. Such skills relate not only to being a better sender of messages, but also to being a better receiver. There are many techniques that can help improve communication. Two of these are active listening — a way to improve one's skills as a receiver of messages and communication — and the Johari Window — a model used to explain techniques for improving communication effectiveness.

Active listening is an approach to improving communication through techniques to help better decode the message received from the sender, clarify the message, and respond appropriately. To listen actively, one must receive and process all the signals being transmitted by the sender. This includes not only the actual words that are said, but the body language and other nonverbal cues that accompany the verbal message. For example, if Harvey smiles and pats George on the back while telling him that his report shows that he is ready for a promotion, the message is quite different than if Harvey says that same thing with his arms crossed and in a sarcastic tone. Active listening skills include receiving and processing all the signals that the sender receives. This means that the receiver needs to postpone evaluation of what the sender is saying until all the information has been received. To further this process, the receiver should avoid interrupting, postpone evaluating what the sender says until s/he is finished and maintain interest. These skills help the receiver obtain sufficient data to accurately decode the message and form appropriate feedback.

After the information has been received, the receiver needs to evaluate the information s/he has received, organize it, and form an appropriate response. Part of this process includes showing the receiver that s/he has been understood and that his/her thoughts and feelings have been taken into account. Such displays of empathy are critical to showing the sender that both verbal and nonverbal cues have been received and understood. In addition, the receiver needs to organize the information that s/he has received. Human beings tend to process what they hear over three times faster than the average rate of speech. The active listener uses this opportunity to organize the information received into key points rather than becoming distracted while the sender completes transmission of the message. In complicated communications, it can also be helpful to summarize this information when the sender is finished to make sure that both parties understand the message in the same way. Similarly, active listeners take the opportunity to clarify any ambiguity in the transmission to avoid misunderstandings.

In most communication, each party is both a sender and receiver and each needs to be aware of the potential barriers to communication and how these can be avoided. One approach to helping people improve their communication through mutual understanding is called the Johari Window. In this model, it is posited that true communication occurs in the "arena"; that area where both the sender and receiver strive for open, honest communication. This area can be increased through disclosure and feedback. Disclosure in the workplace would include making sure that all parties to the communication understand the assumptions and preconceptions of each other. For example, when trying to communicate on a technical matter, it is helpful to know at what level to talk to the other person. Two engineers talking to each other, for example, would share many assumptions and knowledge in common, so could use professional jargon and talk at a higher level than if one person did not have a technical background. Disclosure can also apply to other areas in the person's life, too.

Feedback is when one party gives the other party information about how the communication is received. As in active listening, this could include information about how well the message was received by paraphrasing or summarizing it to make sure that it was correctly received. Feedback could also include information about the nonverbal portion of the communication: "When you say that in that way, I am not sure if you are kidding or not." Such comments — when considerately and empathetically expressed — can help both parties better understand both the text and subtext of the conversation.

When disclosure and feedback are not used to increase the openness of communication, miscommunication is more likely to arise. Sometimes this is intentional: the hidden area or façade that everyone uses from time to time to keep the communication on a profession level by not revealing likes and dislikes, personal experiences, or other attitudes that are not appropriate or relevant to the situation. Increasing the area of the arena through feedback also improves communication effectiveness by helping the person understand things that s/he does not know about him/herself (Harvey frequently says "um" while giving a presentation, which is distracting to the listener). The combination of disclosure and feedback can also help the person discover more of his/her hidden potential; that unknown area that neither party understands in isolation.

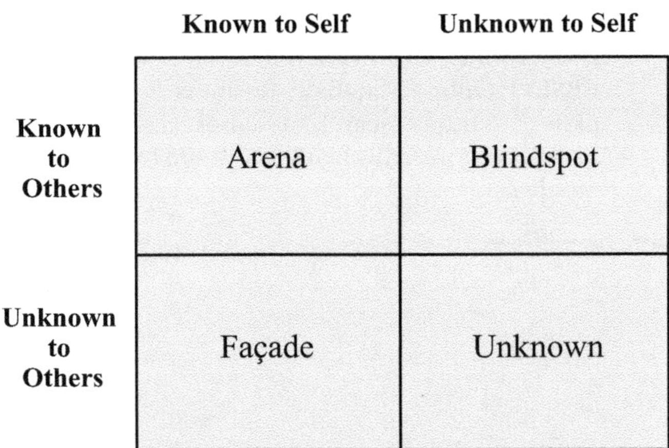

Figure 2: The Johari Window
(based on Hall, J. (1973, Spr). Communication revisited, California Management Review, 15, 56-57.)

Information and Communication Technologies

A strong social network has been shown to improve employee performance in that a worker who is able to seek timely advice from colleagues will benefit from a broad knowledge pool. One's reputation within such a network motivates a worker to defend perceptions of his/her competence, and feedback stimulates innovative problem solving. These dynamics have transferred to online social networking. Much face-to-face interaction has given way to technology-based modes of communication. The office memo has been almost entirely replaced by email, and employees can access forms and policy statements from the company Web site rather than encounter someone from human resources. Internal "ticketing" systems allow queries to find those best able to respond without the query poster having to personally track down the right parties. Online communications provide documentation of conversations, which is more reliable than memory or notetaking. Such documentation, however, has also been problemmatic for employees who regard their conversations as private and do not practice discretion. Companies in litigation may have their email records subpoenaed.

BIBLIOGRAPHY

Chaffee, J. (2000). *Thinking critically* (6th ed). Boston: Houghton Mifflin.

Gil, B. (2013). E-Mail: Not Dead, Evolving. Harvard Business Review, 91(6), 32-33. Retrieved October 31, 2013, from EBSCO Online Database Business Source Complete. http://search.ebscohost.com/login.aspx?direct=true&db=bth&AN=87715789&site=ehost-live

Keyton, J., Caputo, J., Ford, E., Fu, R., Leibowitz, S. A., Liu, T., & ... Wu, C. (2013). Investigating verbal workplace communication behaviors. *Journal of Business Communication, 50*(2), 152-169. Retrieved October 31, 2013, from EBSCO Online Database Business Source Complete. http://search.ebscohost.com/login.aspx?direct=true&db=bth&AN=86002071&site=ehost-live

Kinnick, K. N. & Parton, S. R. (2005). Workplace communication. *Business Communication, 68* (4), 429-456. Retrieved April 5, 2007, from EBSCO Online Database Business Source Complete. http://search.ebscohost.com/login.aspx?direct=true&db=bth&AN=18805319&site=bsi-live

Landy, F. J. & Conte, J. M. (2004). *Work in the 21st century: An introduction to industrial and organizational psychology.* Boston: McGraw Hill.

McShane, S. L. & Von Glinow, M. A.. (2003). *Organizational behavior: Emerging realities for the workplace revolution* (2nd ed). Boston: McGraw-Hill/Irwin.

Xiaojun, Z., & Venkatesh, V. (2013). Explaining employee job performance: The role of online and offline workplace communication networks. *MIS Quarterly, 37*(3), 695-A3. Retrieved October 31, 2013, from EBSCO Online Database Business Source Complete. http://search.ebscohost.com/login.aspx?direct=true&db=bth&AN=89477785&site=ehost-live

SUGGESTED READING

Couzins, M. & Beagrie, S. (2004, Nov 30). How to... produce powerful business writing. *Personnel Today,* 21. Retrieved April 5, 2007, from EBSCO Online Database Business Source Complete. http://search.ebscohost.com/login.aspx?direct=true&db=bth&AN=15414237&site=bsi-live

Dulye, L. (2004). "De-functionalizing" communication. *Strategic Communication Management, 8*(2), 6-7. Retrieved April 5, 2007, from EBSCO Online Database Business Source Complete http://search.ebscohost.com/login.aspx?direct=true&db=bth&AN=13108194&site=bsi-live

Gorman, Bob. (2003). Communicating to engage, not just to inform. *Strategic HR Review, 2*(2), 14-17. Retrieved April 5, 2007, from EBSCO Online Database Business Source Complete. http://search.

ebscohost.com/login.aspx?direct=true&db=bth&AN=8964925&site=bsi-live

Nicoll, D. C. (1994). Acknowledge and use your grapevine. *Management Decision, 32*(6), 25-30. Retrieved April 5, 2007, from EBSCO Online Database Business Source Complete. http://search.ebscohost.com/login.aspx?direct=true&db=bth&AN=9605301399&site=bsi-live

Schonfeld, E. (1994). Communication goes flat. *Fortune, 130*(5), 16. Retrieved April 5, 2007, from EBSCO Online Database Business Source Complete. http://search.ebscohost.com/login.aspx?direct=true&db=bth&AN=9408187524&site=bsi-live

Ruth A. Wienclaw, Ph.D.

COMPARATIVE MANAGEMENT

ABSTRACT

Many theorists believe that management style loses its effectiveness when applied in a different culture. With the increasing trend toward globalization in many organizations, therefore, there is a concomitant increase in the study of management practices in different countries and how they relate to organizational effectiveness. Cultural norms, assumptions, and values need to be understood by a manager who desires to be effective in a cross-cultural situation. This understanding can be helped through cross-cultural training for expatriate managers as well as by ensuring that the management team in an offshore operation includes members who understand the local culture and its implications.

OVERVIEW

Practitioners and theorists alike spend significant time examining organizations to determine what differentiates those organizations that succeed from those organizations that fail. Significant time and energy is expended to determine the best practices and how these practices can be generalized or extrapolated to become universal truths that help other organizations to succeed. This impetus led to the Industrial Revolution and to the development of novel ways to mass produce goods. As a result, contemporary businesses are able to produce goods more effectively and efficiently than ever before. This impetus also led to the Technological Revolution with its burst of new technologies and their application to both the home and workplace. As a result, many tiresome or routine tasks have been eliminated, and employees are better supported in the design and development of even more and better goods and services. What such technological innovations cannot change, however, is the human factor.

No matter how high tech or automated a contemporary organization is, it still is dependent on the inputs and work of human beings. Human beings are necessary not only to run the machines on which a business relies, but to design, develop, and repair them. Wherever there are human beings in an organization, their activities need to be coordinated and supervised to optimize their performance and increase the success of the organization. Management is the process of efficiently and effectively accomplishing work through the coordination and supervision of others.

When management first became a recognized field of study, the goal was to reduce the empirical observations of successful practices in isolated cases to simple lists of practices a manager should or should not do in order to be effective. When these practices were unsuccessfully applied in another organization, a new list was promulgated. Leadership theories were developed that described the differences between successful leaders and unsuccessful leaders and posited the characteristics or practices that differentiated between the two. However, human behavior is a complex and multifaceted thing, and it was found that such universal truths were apt to be neither universal nor truths.

Eventually, this discrepancy was recognized and the study of management became a multidisciplinary effort; drawing on the insights from scientific research rather than isolated or casual observation and incorporating the insights and practices of other fields of study including psychology, sociology, and anthropology. Insights gained from empirical research eventually led to the conclusion that there is not one best way to lead. Rather, effective management requires the consideration of numerous factors including the nature of the job to be done (routine, mechanized vs. creative, artistic), the readiness of the workers to do their jobs (experience, degree of training), personality and work style of the workers, as well as the ability and personality of the manager. Further, it was found that as some of these variables changed (the workers became more experienced as they learned on the job), the most appropriate management style also changed (experienced workers require less close supervision than those who are new to the job).

The effectiveness of a management style is also based on the type of organization in which it is used. The large organizations that came into being following the Industrial Revolution were often production facilities where a military command and control model was effective. Many of today's organizations, on the other hand, do not follow this model. Today, more organizations offer services rather than goods and the educational levels of employees are rising in many fields. Each type of organization and its concomitant workers requires a different type of management in order to be effective. An engineering organization, for example, where workers are hired to develop new ideas or products, cannot be managed on a piecework philosophy as can be done in some production facilities. Rather, different types of organizations require different styles of management in order to be effective.

The changing landscape of organizations today is made even more complex by the increasing globalization in many industries. In particular, the practice of offshoring — relocating part of an organization's business to another country with lower costs — can present significant challenges to an organization as it works in a foreign culture with different assumptions, practices, and laws. In particular, culture can play a significant role in the expectations on managers and the effectiveness of management practices. Cultural differences also can affect how people communicate, what assumptions they make, and how they perceive the world in general. For example, many cultures — including both Germany and Japan — tend to be more formal than US culture. If a manager acts without sensitivity to this fact, s/he can appear to local workers as rude, and can quickly lose effectiveness.

Comparative management is the study of management practices in different countries and how they relate to organizational effectiveness. To do this, comparative management theorists look at how managerial practices are similar and how they differ in order to accommodate the needs of the local culture. By looking at management styles and techniques that work well in different venues, it is possible to gain insight into which management issues are universal and how local culture and conditions require adaptation of management practices. Specifically, the field of comparative management seeks to help organizations and their managers to better understand the impact of local culture — the consciously or unconsciously held shared assumptions, beliefs, norms, and values held by a group of people — on the way that people and processes need to be managed.

There are several different theoretical approaches to studying comparative management. The socio-economic approach primarily examines variations in economic development between two or more countries and how these variations affect what constitutes effective managerial practice. Unfortunately, this approach is not easy to test empirically. In addition, this approach cannot account for differences in management style or effectiveness within a given country because it rests in part on the assumption that organizations operating at the same level of industrialization would have similar management practices. This assumption, however, is not borne out in fact.

Another approach to the study of comparative management is the environmental approach. This approach emphasizes the external factors — environmental factors and constraints — under which the organization must operate. As with the socio-economic approach, however, the environmental approach cannot explain differences between organizations operating within the same environment. This is due in part because both approaches fail to take into account the internal factors that can affect managerial effectiveness.

On the other end of the spectrum is the behavioral approach which focuses on the psychological factors (beliefs, values, attitudes, assumptions) that affect individual and group behavior within organizations. Although this approach rectifies the major shortcoming of the socio-economic and environmental approaches, it fails to consider the external factors that can also affect organizational and managerial effectiveness.

To make up for these shortcomings, various eclectic models have been proposed that take into consideration both the broad societal issues that affect organizational effectiveness as well as the organizational factors. Some of these models also consider the possible interaction between the two sets of variables.

APPLICATIONS

The comparison of international differences in effective management is of more than heuristic interest. The trend toward globalization spurred on by the search for lower personnel and production costs means that increasing numbers of organizations are offshoring parts of their operations. To be able to do this successfully, both executives and managers need to understand the differences in culture and how these differences affect management styles.

Cross-Cultural Comparisons

Comparative management is an emerging field, and models for predicting the success of managers in foreign operations are works in progress. However, theorists and practitioners have been observing the cultural differences and concomitant managerial imperatives associated with different cultures for years. These observations are not only helping to form newer and better models of comparative management, but are also providing clues for how to manage more effectively in a foreign culture.

One of the reasons that it is important for the manager to understand the culture in which s/he works is to better understand what motivates the employees. This understanding can help a manager achieve the objectives of the organization by being better able to reward the employee for desired behavior. Workers tend to be motivated by rewards that support their cultural patterns. For example, in sub-Saharan Africa, cultural values include respect for elders and for authority, family orientation (including the extended family), and collectivism. These traits have significant implications for how sub-Saharan Africans can most effectively be managed. Although African cultures tend to support absolute obedience to authority, the manager cannot count on this alone to force local employees into a foreign way of thinking. The collectivist nature of the sub-Saharan African culture means that local employees tend to be more comfortable working in a group than working alone. So, the incentive of a private office as a reward for high performance may not have the effect expected by a Western manager. The family orientation of these cultures may help bond work groups together, but it may also mean that it is difficult to reach agreement between teams or work groups. Further, motivating employees to work overtime or to not take time off for family obligations may be difficult. Such considerations tend to be more important to African workers than meeting organizational goals. It is perhaps for this reason that sub-Saharan African organizations rarely implement formal performance appraisal systems.

Another cultural pattern affecting sub-Saharan African organizations is resistance to change and aversion to risk taking. As a result of these patterns, managerial insistences on new techniques such as reengineering, just-in-time practices, or total quality management that are successful in Western organizations are unlikely to be met with enthusiasm or success. In fact, the respect for tradition prevalent in African cultures may result in a workforce that is neither flexible nor easily adaptable. Although workers ascribing to these cultural patterns can be managed effectively, they are unlikely to respond well to American independence or rugged individuality. To be effective, managers need to understand these cultural values and reward and encourage employees within those parameters.

East Asia also has cultural patterns that vary widely from those in the West. Chinese culture, for example, is also collectivistic in nature and emphasizes social interests and downplays personal goals and accomplishments. In fact, in China there tends to be an emphasis on harmony and conformity that governs all interpersonal relations. These cultural patterns can result in disagreement with Western management styles where conflict is taken as a matter of course. In Japan, the organization's goals are widely shared throughout the company, leaving top executives free from day-to-day management while middle managers carry out both operational and strategic activities. Although to the Japanese mind this management approach is a tribute to the competence of the middle managers, to the American mind it is indecisive and incompetent. This also means that the Japanese organizational chart is often little more than a listing of job titles rather than a formal definition of roles and responsibilities. As in the other cultures described above, Japanese management style also relies heavily on consensus resulting from extensive verbal consultation, a concept foreign in most US businesses. In addition, cultural norms in Japan do not accept the unpleasant face-to-face confrontations that Americans frequently think are a normal part of any interpersonal relationship. This means that the façade of the organization as a "happy family" is important in Japan. As a result, communication patterns rely much more heavily on nonverbal messages so that the façade can be maintained. Since an organization is dependent upon good communication for success, it is essential that this fact be recognized for a Western manager working in the Japanese culture.

Practical Concerns for Expatriates

Understanding of the cross-cultural considerations associated with management in foreign countries arises from two sources: the intellectual knowledge of cultural and managerial differences and the practical knowledge of these things that can only be acquired through immersion in the culture. There are a number of things that the organization can do on a micro level to help make the transition for expatriates — employees who are not citizens of the country in which they are working — easier. Language training alone is insufficient: Expatriates also need to be sensitive to the culture in which they work so that they can interpret situations and events in the same way as persons native to the culture in which they take place. This will prepare them to make better and more effective management decisions.

Fortunately, intercultural sensitivity is a learned process. Therefore, it is important that the organization provide cross-cultural training to help orient the prospective expatriate manager to the conditions that will be encountered as a manager in the foreign operation as well as more general orientation to the assumptions, values, and norms of the local population in general. Cross-cultural training programs are designed to help employees deal effectively with persons from a different culture by familiarizing them with various cultural differences including values, assumptions, and communication styles. In this way, cross-cultural training attempts to reduce potential misunderstandings that might arise. For example, the unacceptability of direct confrontation in Japan could be inadvertently breached by an American not used to this norm. Similarly, ignorance of the comparatively high level of formality in communication (using formal pronouns and titles for those one does not know well, particularly when higher in the organizational hierarchy) that one encounters in Germany could lead not only to misunderstandings, but to a larger inability to be effective in one's job.

There are several general objectives to most cross-cultural training programs. First, potential expatriates are taught about the reality of cultural differences and how these differences can impact managerial effectiveness or other business outcomes. Trainees are also familiarized with the process by which attitudes and stereotypes — both positive and negative — are formed and how such assumptions can unconsciously influence how a person interacts with those from a different culture. In addition, cross-cultural training usually provides specific information about the country in which the person will work, including any skills needed for business success. Cross-cultural training may also include intensive or advanced language skills training or other cultural adjustment skills.

In addition to helping expatriate managers acquire an intellectual appreciation for and empathy with both the general culture and the managerial culture in which they will work, comparative management theorists have also noted a number of practical actions that can be taken on an organizational level to help increase the managerial effectiveness of expatriates working in offshore operations. Many of the problems that arise in cross-cultural management situations can be resolved simply and do not require changes in corporate policy. For example, although it may be tempting to put a person from the home country in charge of the foreign subsidiary, it is more important that the foreign subsidiary be run by someone who understands the needs and assumptions of the local culture. This will not only enable the subsidiary to better deal with any cultural clashes that may occur, but will help prevent them from occurring in the first place. In addition, because of the relatively smaller size of offshore operations in relation to corporate headquarters, it must be remembered that the person in charge of a foreign subsidiary will more than likely need to run the entire local operation and will not have the same infrastructure available as when running a part of a larger operation. Top management in foreign operations, therefore, also needs to have an entrepreneurial spirit and the psychological ability to adapt to the new culture.

There are other practical steps that can be taken to help ensure the effectiveness of expatriates. Due to the prevalence of culture shock for expatriate employees and their families, many find themselves living in enclaves within the larger culture. Although this may seem like a good idea, it does not help one to understand the new culture better and also tends to reinforce an "us-them" attitude that is counterproductive to being a good manager. In addition, performance appraisal of the expatriate should be done by the local supervisor rather than by the corporate supervisor. This is because the local supervisor will be better able to understand how effective the expatriate manager is in working within the norms of the new culture and whether or not his/her outcomes are within the expected outcomes for that locality.

Bibliography

Beugré, C. D. & Offodile, O. F. (2001). Managing for organizational effectiveness in sub-Saharan Africa: A culture-fit model. *International Journal of Human Resources Management, 12*(4), 535-550. Retrieved April 5, 2007, from EBSCO Online Database Business Source Complete. http://search.ebscohost.com/login.aspx?direct=true&db=bth&AN=4480300&site=bsi-live

Campbell, J. P., Dunnette, M. D., Lawler, E. E. III, & Weick, K. E. (1970). *Managerial behavior, performance, and effectiveness.* New York: McGraw-Hill Book Company.

Dessler, G. (2005). *Human resource management* (10th ed.). Upper Saddle River, NJ: Pearson/Prentice Hall.

Endenich, C., Brandau, M., & Hoffjan, A. (2011). Two decades of research on comparative management accounting - achievements and future directions. *Australian Accounting Review, 21*(4), 365-382. Retrieved October 31, 2013, from EBSCO Online Database Business Source Complete. http://search.ebscohost.com/login.aspx?direct=true&db=bth&AN=69662939&site=ehost-live

Landy, F. J. & Conte, J. M. (2004). *Work in the 21st century: An introduction to industrial and organizational psychology.* Boston: McGraw Hill.

McShane, S. L. & Von Glinow, M. A. (2003). *Organizational behavior: Emerging realities for the workplace revolution* (2nd ed). Boston: McGraw-Hill/Irwin.

Neelankavil, J. P. (2001). Determinants of managerial performance: A cross-cultural comparison of the perceptions of middle-level managers in four countries. *Journal of International Studies, 31*(1), 121-40. Retrieved April 5, 2007, from EBSCO Online Database Business Source Complete. http://search.ebscohost.com/login.aspx?direct=true&db=bth&AN=3188515&site=bsi-live

Newman, W. H. (1978). Comparative management: A resource for improving managerial adaptability. *Columbia Journal of World Business, 13*(2), 5-6. Retrieved April 5, 2007, from EBSCO Online Database Business Source Complete. http://search.ebscohost.com/login.aspx?direct=true&db=bth&AN=5543643&site=bsi-live

Tsurumi, Y. (1978). The best of times and the worst of times: Japanese management in America. *Columbia Journal of World Business, 13*(2), 56-61. Retrieved April 11, 2007, from EBSCO Online Database Business Source Complete. http://search.ebscohost.com/login.aspx?direct=true&db=bth&AN=5544507&site=bsi-live

Tung, R. L. (1978). The use of the organizational climate construct in comparative management models. *Academy of Management Proceedings,* 292-296. Retrieved April 5, 2007, from EBSCO Online Database Business Source Complete. http://search.ebscohost.com/login.aspx?direct=true&db=bth&AN=4977143&site=bsi-live

Suggested Reading

Hattori, I. (1978). A proposition on efficient decision-making in the Japanese corporation. *Columbia Journal of World Business, 13*(2), 7-15. Retrieved April 5, 2007, from EBSCO Online Database Business Source Complete. http://web.ebscohost.com/ehost/pdf?vid=31&hid=14&sid=b1bfaefe-52b9-4923-83e7-bb423ac4c490%40SRCSM2.

Jackson, G. & Moerke, A. (2005). Continuity and change in corporate governance: Comparing Germany and Japan. *Corporate Governance, 13*(3), 351-361. Retrieved April 5, 2007, from EBSCO Online Database Business Source Complete http://search.ebscohost.com/login.aspx?direct=true&db=bth&AN=17065349&site=bsi-live

Teagarden, M. B. & von Glinow, M. A. (1995). Toward a theory of comparative management research: An idiographic case study of the best international human resources management project. *Academy* of *Management Journal, 39*(5), 261-287. Retrieved April 5, 2007, from EBSCO Online Database Business Source Complete http://search.ebscohost.com/login.aspx?direct=true&db=bth&AN=9512044534&site=bsi-live

Thomson, A. (2001, Jul). The case for management history. *Accounting, Business & Financial History, 11*(2), 99-115. Retrieved April 5, 2007, from EBSCO Online Database Business Source Complete. http://search.ebscohost.com/login.aspx?direct=true&db=bth&AN=5180418&site=bsi-live

Ruth A. Wienclaw, Ph.D.

Conflict Management

ABSTRACT

Conflict frequently arises in the workplace. Goal incompatibility between groups or individuals, differentiation, task interdependence, scarce resources, ambiguity, and communication problems can all lead to a situation that promotes conflict. There are a number of conflict management styles that can be used to effectively resolve such conflicts: competing, collaborating, compromising, avoiding, and accommodating. However, although each individual has his/her own preferred conflict management style, not every style is optimally effective in every conflict situation. To maximize the effectiveness of conflict management efforts, management and parties to the conflict need to be aware of their shortand longterm goals and strategies for both the task and the people involved, their personal involvement and emotions in the conflict, their personal conflict management style, and which styles work best in which situations.

OVERVIEW

It often seems as if whenever two or more parties attempt to work together there are at least three opinions. Although sometimes this situation can lead to synergy and a more creative final product, in many cases it leads to conflict. Although the most common view of conflict is that it is by its very nature dysfunctional and needs to be resolved, in many cases — if it is properly managed — it can be both functional and help the conflicting parties work together better or to produce a better product than if the conflict had not arisen in the first place. Conflict between groups may also improve team dynamics, cohesiveness, and task orientation. However, if the conflict becomes too emotionally charged, a winlose mentality can arise, with negative results such as groupthink, frustration, job dissatisfaction, and stress.

Very few people have the option to work in complete isolation of others. Even those who telecommute or work independently frequently find themselves in a position in which they need to interact with others: clients, suppliers, editors, etc. In virtually any situation in which there is more than one party with interests in the outcome, conflicts are likely to arise. In this context, conflict refers to any situation "in which one party perceives that its interests are being opposed or negatively affected by" the interests or actions of another party (McShane & Von Glinow, 2003). Conflict can manifest in any number of ways ranging from a mild disagreement between individuals to an allout war between nations.

In the workplace, conflict typically begins with a situation that is conducive to conflict, such as the need to share a single piece of equipment or other scarce resource. For example, Group A needs the copier to reproduce a proposal for a tight deadline for a potential client and Group B needs to use the copier to produce a deliverable to an equally tight — and incompatible — deadline for a current client. As the parties come to believe that conflict exists, the situation usually next manifests itself in actions that outwardly demonstrate that an underlying conflict exists (e.g., a member of Group A tries to monopolize the copier so that it cannot be used by Group B). Conflict need not lead to a dysfunctional workplace, however. Through appropriate conflict management techniques — either actions taken by one or more parties to the conflict or by an objective outside party in the attempt to deescalate the conflict — the severity and form of the conflict can be altered to maximize its benefits and minimize its negative consequences of the situation.

Types of Workplace Conflict Goal Incompatibility & Differentiation

As shown in Figure 1, conflict can arise from any one or more general sources in the workplace (McShane & Von Glinow, 2003). First, conflict can arise in the workplace due to incompatible goals between individuals or groups. For example, if two individuals are competing for the same promotion, it is likely that conflict will arise unless more than one position is available. Goal incompatibility becomes an even stronger source for potential conflict in situations in which there are financial rewards for achieving one's goals since, in such situations, employees tend to be more motivated to achieve their own goals at the expense of others. A second source of conflict in organizations is differentiation. This occurs when individuals or groups of employees hold divergent beliefs and attitudes as a result of their different backgrounds, experiences, or training. For example, differentiation often leads to conflict situations following business mergers and acquisitions. In such situations, the cultures, practices, and shared experiences of the formerly separate entities lead to an "usthem" situation.

Interdependence

A third source of potential conflict in organizations is task interdependence. This is the degree to which individuals or groups must share common inputs, interact during the course of performing their separate tasks, or receive outcomes that are partly determined by the mutual performance of both parties. There are three basic types of task independence:

- Pooled interdependence,
- Sequential interdependence, and
- Reciprocal interdependence

The lowest level of interdependence is pooled interdependence. Under this condition, individuals or teams work independently of each other except for their common reliance on a resource or authority. An example of pooled interdependence is the common reliance on a single copy machine, cited above. Sequential interdependence is a situation in which the output of one person or group becomes the direct input for another person or group. This situation frequently arises in assemblyline situations where the output of one process becomes the input to another process (McShane & Von Glinow, 2003). For example, the packing department cannot complete its task unless the department that makes the boxes or packing materials first completes its task. The third type of interdependence in organizations is reciprocal interdependence. This is the highest level of interdependence and occurs in situations in which work outputs are exchanged back and forth among individuals or groups. An example of this type of interdependence would be the relationship between bus drivers and maintenance crews. The drivers cannot drive the buses unless the maintenance crews maintain them, and the maintenance crews cannot maintain the buses unless the drivers bring them into the depot.

Scarce Resources, Ambiguity, Communication

A fourth type of situation that can lead to conflict in the workplace occurs when there are scarce resources. For example, if multiple technicians need the same laboratory equipment and there is insufficient equipment for each to have his or her own, conflict is likely to arise. Ambiguity in the workplace can also lead to conflict because such a situation increases the risk that one party may interfere with the achievement of the other party's goals. Situations of ambiguity in the workplace often lead to increased office politics. Another problem that can lead to conflict in the workplace is the lack of opportunity, ability, or motivation to communicate effectively.

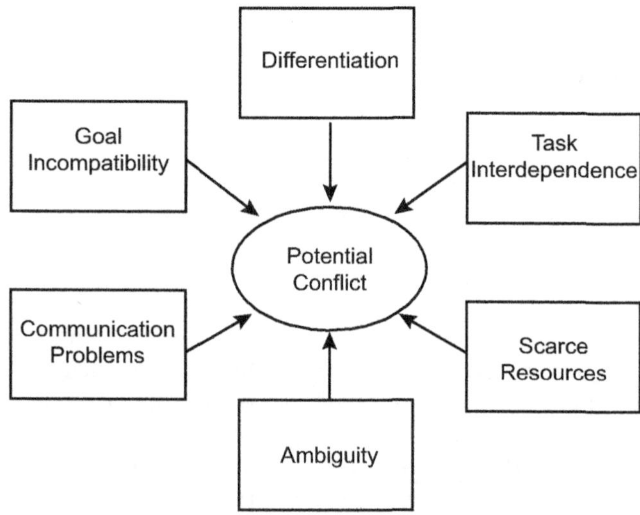

Figure 1: Sources of Conflict in Organizations (adapted from McShane & Von Glinow, 2003)

When effective communication does not exist, the likelihood that stereotypes will develop and conflict escalates. Good communication skills are necessary in order to communicate with other parties in a diplomatic, nonconfrontational manner. The lack of necessary skills for diplomatic communication can escalate a conflict situation and result in less motivation for effective communication in the future. Lack of communication skills is a common problem that occurs in crosscultural conflicts.

APPLICATIONS

Resolving Conflict

As shown in Figure 2, there are a number of ways to deal with conflict (Ruble & Thomas, 1976). Although sometimes it is assumed that there is only one best way to manage conflict, research has show that one conflict management style is best modified to fit the needs of the specific situation. These approaches to conflict management vary on the degree the party is cooperative — or motivated to satisfy the interests of the other party in the conflict (e.g., allow the other group to use the copier) — and assertive — or motivated to satisfy its own interests (e.g., make sure that it is able to use the copier whenever it needs it).

Collaboration

In collaboration, the parties attempt to resolve their conflict by finding a mutually beneficial solution through problem solving. Collaborative solutions are high in both cooperativeness and assertiveness. In the collaborative style of conflict management, information is shared among the parties to the conflict so that all parties can help identify solutions that will potentially satisfy the needs or interests of all parties. Collaboration is the preferred method for conflict management when the parties do not have perfectly opposing interests and when there is sufficient trust and openness between the parties so that information can be shared.

Avoidance

On the opposite side of the conflict management style grid is avoidance, an approach that is low in both assertiveness and cooperativeness. Avoidance is an approach to conflict management in which the parties attempt to manage their differences by smoothing them over or avoiding or minimizing the situations in which conflict might arise. Although avoidance is not a functional longterm solution to conflict situations, it can be useful in the shortterm as a way to temporarily cool down heated disputes or for situations where the issue causing conflict is trivial. For example, sometimes it is better to leave the room and cool off rather than to continue to unproductively try to resolve conflict. In such situations, avoidance can not only prevent a conflict situation from escalating, but may actually help it de-escalate.

Competition

A third approach to conflict management is competition. In this approach to conflict management, one party attempts to "win" at the other party's expense. Competition tends to be a win-lose situation characterized by high assertiveness and low cooperativeness. The underlying assumption in such an approach is that there is a fixed pool of resources from which to draw (e.g., hours during which the copier can be used) and that a gain on one side means a loss on the other side. Competitive solutions to conflict situations can be appropriate if the party knows that its solution is correct and a quick solution is needed or where the other party would take advantage of a more cooperative approach.

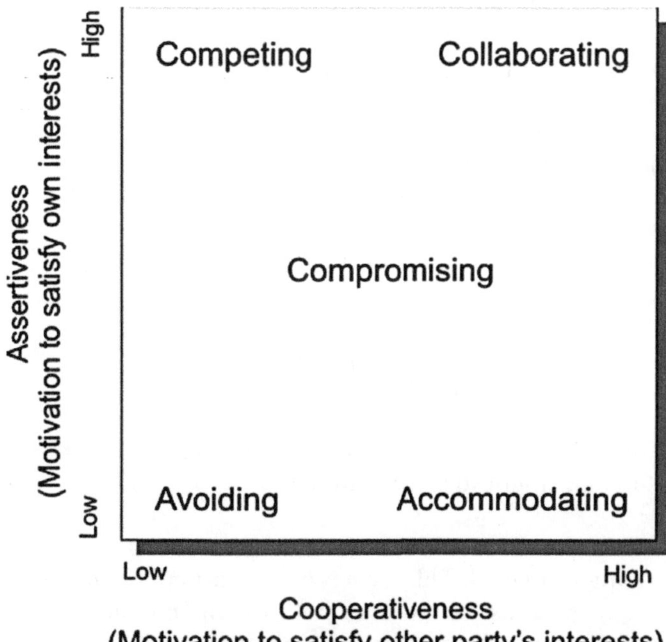

Figure 2: Interpersonal Conflict Management Styles (Ruble & Thomas, 1976)

Accommodation

On the opposite side of the grid is the accommodation style of conflict management, which is low on assertiveness and high on cooperativeness. In this approach, one party completely gives in to the position of the party or acts with little or no attention to its own interests. Accommodation can be a functional conflict management approach if the opposing party has substantially more power or if the issue is not as important to the first party as it is to the opposing party.

Compromise

Finally, compromise is an approach to conflict management in which one party attempts to reach a middle ground with the opposing party. Compromise positions tend to have moderate levels of assertiveness and cooperativeness. When attempting to compromise, parties typically look for solutions in which losses are offset by equally valued gains. Compromise tends to work best in situations in which there is little possibility of mutual gain through problem solving, both parties have equal power, and there are time pressures to settle the conflict (Ruble & Thomas, 1976).

ISSUE

Adapting Styles for Optimal Outcome

Although most people have a preferred conflict management style, it can be useful to apply a different approach to managing conflict to better meet the needs of each situation. Shetach (2009) expanded on the twodimensional model of interpersonal conflict management styles and developed a four dimensions model (see Figure 3). The model considers four critical factors that need to be taken into account in managerial attempts to increase the effectiveness of their conflict management skills:

1. "Northern star,"
2. "Conflict evolvement map,"
3. Awareness of available response options (see Figure 2), and
4. Awareness of one's preferred personal conflict management style from among these options.

"Northern star" is Shetach's metaphor for strategy or long-term goal. This term is used to articulate that a manager must be aware of both the main goal for communication in the current situation as well as the longterm, future objectives regarding the working relationship. By being aware of both the task at hand and the people involved, Shetach posits that it is possible to increase the likelihood that conflict can be constructively managed in order not only to meet a specific goal, but also to better manage the situation to advance one's longterm strategy. Further, by defining clear goals both for the task at hand and the people involved in the situation, one can better prioritize the variables, leading to a more constructive outcome. In addition to understanding the desired outcome for the situation, the four dimensions model also aims to help managers recognize their level of personal involvement in the conflict as well as any emotional responses so that these may be controlled and the conflict management approach be kept on a professional, not personal, level.

The four dimensions model also takes into account the various conflict management strategies discussed above and shown in Figure 2. Effective conflict management is often situational, and a manager needs to be aware of what options are available for resolving issues. In addition, it is helpful to know one's preferred personal conflict management style from among the five available options. Each approach to conflict management can lead to either a constructive or destructive conclusion, depending on the specifics of the situation. In order to maximize the effectiveness of conflict management efforts and help arrive at a win-win resolution, managers and others involved in conflict situations need to be aware of the specifics of the situation and their own personal styles, and be flexible enough to change their preferred style in order to resolve the conflict.

CONCLUSION

Wherever two or more people need to work together, share resources, or compete for scarce rewards, conflict is almost ensured to arise. There are a number of ways to deal with conflict, varying from concern about one's own needs to concern about the needs of the other party. Frequently, the desired outcome is a winwin situation in which the interests of both parties are met. However, depending on the circumstances, the best approach to conflict management will strive for a different outcome. No matter the approach used, however, it is important to realize that conflict situations can easily become personalized, and the original source of conflict forgotten, remaining unresolved. To

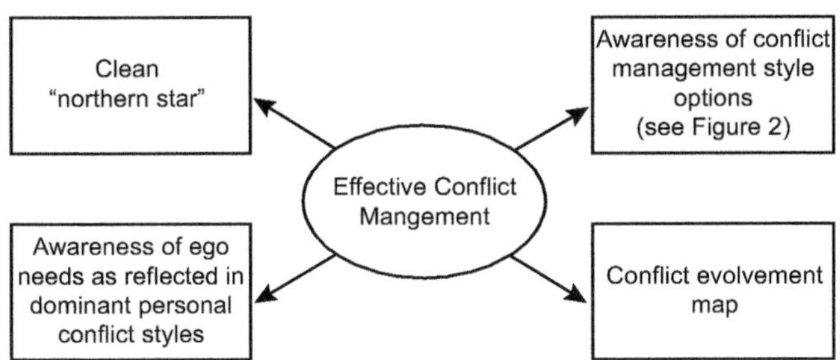

Figure 3: The Four Dimensions Model (adapted from Shetach, 2009)

avoid this possibility, it is important not only to know the various conflict management options available and where they are best applied, but also to be aware of personal emotions and involvement, as well as short-term and longterm goals in resolving the conflict.

Bibliography

Carlson, J. (2013). Rockpaper scissors: Strategies in conflict situations. *Baylor Business Review, 31* (2), 4849. Retrieved November 27, 2013 from EBSCO online database Business Source Premier. http://search.ebscohost.com/login.aspx?direct=true&db=buh&AN=86952171

Coleman, P. T., & Kugler, K. G. (2014). Tracking managerial conflict adaptivity: Introducing a dynamic measure of adaptive conflict management in organizations. *Journal of Organizational Behavior, 35*(7), 945–68. Retrieved November 14, 2014, from EBSCO Online Database Business Source Complete. http://search.ebscohost.com/login.aspx?direct=true&db=bth&AN=98352669

McShane, S. L., & Von Glinow, M. A. (2003). *Organizational behavior (2nd ed.).* Boston, MA: McGrawHill/Irwin.

Ruble, T. L., & Thomas, K. W. (1976). Support for a two-dimensional model of conflict behavior. *Organizational Behavior and Human Performance, 16* (1), 143155.

Sadri, G. (2013). Choosing conflict resolution by culture. *Industrial Management, 55* (5), 1015. Retrieved November 27, 2013 from EBSCO online database Business Source Premier. http://search.ebscohost.com/login.aspx?direct=true&db=buh&AN=90447258

Saeed, T., et al. (2014). Leadership styles: Relationship with conflict management styles. *International Journal of Conflict Management, 25*(3), 214–25. Retrieved November 14, 2014, from EBSCO Online Database Business Source Complete. http://search.ebscohost.com/login.aspx?direct=true&db=bth&AN=99126040

Sinha, A. (2011). Conflict management: Making life easier. *IUP Journal of Soft Skills, 5* (4), 3142. Retrieved November 27, 2013 from EBSCO online database Business Source Premier. http://search.ebscohost.com/login.aspx?direct=true&db=buh&AN=78153520

Shetach, A. (2009). The fourdimension model: A tool for effective conflict management. *International Studies of Management and Organization, 39* (3), 82106. Retrieved April 27, 2010 from EBSCO Online Database Business Source Complete http://search.ebscohost.com/login.aspx?direct=true&db=bth&AN=44505816&site=ehostlive

Suggested Reading

Atteya, N. (2012). The conflict management grid: A selection and development tool to resolve the conflict between the marketing and sales organizations. *International Journal of Business & Management, 7*(13), 2839. Retrieved November 27, 2013 from EBSCO online database Business Source Premier. http://search.ebscohost.com/login.aspx?direct=true&db=buh&AN=77935209

Busby, D. M., & Holman, T. B. (2009, December). Perceived match or mismatch on the Gottman conflict styles: Associations with relationship outcome variables. *Family Process, 48*(4), 531545. Retrieved April 27, 2010 from EBSCO Online Database Academic Search Complete http://search.ebscohost.com/login.aspx?direct=true&db=a9h&AN=45393409&site=ehostlive

Ergeneli, A., Camgoz, S. M., & Karapinar, P. B. (2010). The relationship between selfefficacy and conflicthandling styles in terms of relative authority positions of the two parties. *Social Behavior and Personality, 38*(1), 1328. Retrieved April 27, 2010 from EBSCO Online Database Academic Search Complete http://search.ebscohost.com/login.aspx?direct=true&db=a9h&AN=48096582&site=ehostlive

Eunson, B. (2012). *Conflict management.* Hoboken, NJ: John Wiley & Sons. Retrieved November 27, 2013 from EBSCO online database eBook Collection (EBSCOhost). http://search.ebscohost.com/login.aspx?direct=true&db=nlebk&AN=451596&site=ehostlive

Furumo, K. (2009). The impact of conflict and conflict management style on deadbeats and deserters in virtual teams. *Journal of Computer Information Systems, 49*(4), 6673. Retrieved April 27, 2010 from EBSCO Online Database Business Source Complete http://search.ebscohost.com/login.aspx?direct=true&db=bth&AN=43278847&site=ehostlive

Godse, A. S., & Thingujam, N. S. (2010). Perceived emotional intelligence and conflict resolution styles among information technology professionals: Testing the mediating role of personality. *Singapore Management Review, 32*(1), 6983. Retrieved April 27, 2010 from EBSCO Online Database Business Source Complete http://search.ebscohost.com/login.aspx?direct=true&db=bth&AN=45566340&site=ehostlive

Liberman, E., Levy, Y. F., & Segal, P. (2009). Designing and internal organizational system for conflict management. *Dispute Resolution Journal, 64*(2), 6274. Retrieved April 27, 2010 from EBSCO Online Database Business Source Complete http://search.ebscohost.com/login.aspx?direct=true&db=bth&AN=43582432&site=ehostlive

Salami, S. O. (2010). Conflict resolution strategies and organizational citizenship behavior: The moderating role of trait emotional intelligence. *Social Behavior and Personality, 38*(1), 7586. Retrieved April 27, 2010 from EBSCO Online Database Academic Search Complete http://search.ebscohost.com/login.aspx?direct=true&db=a9h&AN=48096588&site=ehostlive

Somech, A., Desivilya, H. S., & Lidogoster, H. (2009). Team conflict management and team effectiveness: The effects of task interdependence and team identification. *Journal of Organizational Behavior, 30*(3), 359378. Retrieved April 27, 2010 from EBSCO Online Database Business Source Complete http://search.ebscohost.com/login.aspx?d irect=true&db=bth&AN=36868134&site=ehostlive

Way, K. A., Jimmieson, N. L., & Bordia, P. (2014). Supervisor conflict management, justice, and strain: Multilevel relationships. *Journal of Managerial Psychology, 29*(8), 1044–63. Retrieved November 14, 2014, from EBSCO Online Database Business Source Complete. http://search.ebscohost.com/login.aspx?direct=true&db=bth&AN=99047371

Ruth A. Wienclaw, Ph.D.

Corporate Development: Mergers & Acquisitions

ABSTRACT

This article focuses on the corporate development practice of mergers and acquisitions. It provides a description and analysis of the main types of mergers and acquisitions including vertical mergers, horizontal mergers, and conglomerate mergers. Antitrust regulations, corporate procedures, and government guidelines overseeing mergers and acquisitions will be addressed. In addition, this article summarizes the human resource issues that result from corporate mergers and acquisitions.

OVERVIEW

Corporations create growth through organic or inorganic business activities. Growth refers to economic expansion as measured by any number of indicators such as increased revenue, staffing, and market share. Investors and economists debate the relative strengths and weaknesses of organic and inorganic business growth. Inorganic and organic business growth each move in and out of favor depending on the strength of the economy, political environment, and government regulations. Organic growth is created by expanding existing business resources rather than through mergers and acquisitions. Inorganic growth is created by corporate development practices. Corporate development refers to the activities that companies undertake to grow through inorganic means such as mergers and acquisitions, strategic alliances, and joint ventures.

Mergers and acquisitions are business methods that legally unify ownership of corporate assets that were formerly subject to separate controls. Mergers and acquisitions are considered to be one of the most important business tools for achieving competitive advantage and growth. In the merger and acquisition process, one corporation is completely absorbed by and into another corporation. The acquiring company usually maintains its identity and name. Mergers and acquisitions vary from corporate consolidation, the process through which two corporations join and form a wholly new corporation. Mergers and acquisitions were one of the main engines of business growth in the 1990s. For example, during the 1990s, the telecommunications industry grew from the merger and acquisitions activity of large companies such as AT & T and British Telecom. In the twenty-first century, business trends are moving more toward organic business growth and away from mergers and acquisitions as an engine of growth (Shin, 2005).

In the United States, mergers and acquisitions are regulated by the federal government to control anti-competitive practices. Mergers and acquisitions can potentially limit competition in the marketplace, reduce output, and raise prices for consumers. As a result of anti-competitive practices, the federal government has developed formal merger and acquisition regulations, procedures, and guidelines commonly referred to as antitrust regulation or law. Antitrust regulations operate to prohibit mergers and acquisitions that have more negative than positive consequences for society. Despite the problems associated with anti-competitive practices, mergers and acquisitions, when successful, have the potential to produce numerous benefits for business, government, and society. Common benefits of successful mergers and acquisitions include more effective management within a business organization; optimization of underused assets; reduced costs for corporations and consumers; improved product quality; and increased output.

The following section provides a description and analysis of the main elements of the merger and acquisition process: Choosing growth through mergers and acquisitions; types of mergers and acquisitions; managing mergers and acquisitions; and merger and acquisition regulations, procedures, and guidelines. This section will serve as a foundation for later discussion of human resource management of the problems that result from mergers and acquisitions.

APPLICATIONS

The merger and acquisition process, across businesses and industries, shares similar trajectories, timelines, management concerns, regulations, procedures, and guidelines. The following sections discuss these elements and variables of the merger and acquisition process.

Choosing Growth through Mergers & Acquisitions

The decision to create growth by merging with or acquiring another company is a form of corporate development and strategic planning. All successful business organizations engage in corporate development and strategic planning. Strategic planning, indistinguishable from corporate development in most instances, refers to the way an organization defines its future direction and makes decisions on allocating its human and capital resources in a way that will achieve these established goals. Corporate development and strategic planning require companies to accurately predict future needs and potential opportunities so to choose the appropriate course of action and time frame for growth. Once a corporation chooses its growth objective as a development strategy, corporations must choose the most effective course of action to achieve this goal. Corporations that choose merger and acquisition as their path or engine for growth must make decisions regarding what mode of merger or acquisition to choose based on their resources, industry, and goals (Lu, 2006).

Types of Mergers & Acquisitions

There are three main types of mergers and acquisitions: Horizontal merger, vertical merger, and conglomerate merger. Horizontal merger refers to the business act in which a firm acquires another firm in the same industrial and geographical area that sells a similar product. Horizontal mergers are a way companies eliminate competition. Vertical merger refers to the business act in which one firm acquires one of their customers or suppliers. Conglomerate mergers refer to all non-vertical and non-horizontal mergers and acquisitions. Examples of common conglomerate mergers and acquisitions include pure conglomerate transactions, geographic extension mergers, and product-extension mergers.

The nature of the competition between parties involved in the potential merger is the main factor influencing the choice of merger type. The federal government has different concerns about each type of merger and acquisition. Areas of concern surrounding horizontal mergers and acquisitions include the possibility that the merger will eliminate competition, raise prices, and reduce product output and availability. Areas of concern surrounding vertical mergers and acquisitions include the possibility that mergers will limit the competitions' access to sources of supply or to customers and impede new businesses from entering the market. Areas of concern surrounding conglomerate mergers and acquisitions include the possibility that mergers will transition a large firm into a dominant firm with a decisive competitive advantage and keep other companies from successfully entering the market.

Corporations decide what type of merger or acquisition to pursue based on their resources and objectives. Corporations with significant capital resources may choose to pursue the purchase of assets. In the purchase of assets scenario, the buyer purchases another company's assets and, in some instances, its debts. Corporations may choose to pursue the purchase of stock. In the purchase of stock scenario, the buyer buys some amount of the seller's stockholdings and inherits the seller's responsibilities and rights, including debt, relative to the amount bought. Corporations may choose to pursue a statutory merger. In the statutory merger scenario, the merger allows the merging companies to continue existing as one legal entity. Ultimately, there are numerous different types of mergers and acquisitions that correspond to varying business needs and business models (Lu, 2006).

Managing Mergers & Acquisitions

Common problems and issues experienced during and after mergers and acquisitions include strategic, moral, organizational, legal, financial and human resource issues. Mergers and acquisitions, throughout their lifecycle from the first proposed idea to post-merger, require careful oversight and management. Corporations are increasingly implementing ongoing merger and acquisition policies to guide merger and acquisition activities. From 1994 to 1995, the number of corporations in the United States with merger and acquisition policies in place grew from 35 to 65 percent. Corporate merger and acquisition policy ranges from very simple to very complex. Simple corporate merger and acquisition policy generally includes the mandate that any merger and acquisition transaction over a certain dollar amount must go to the board of directors for approval. Complex merger and acquisition policy may include, for example, rules and strategies for strategic plan approval, sale of company assets, reporting of inquiries, and formulation of a takeover defense. Corporate development officers are generally in charge of developing merger and acquisition policy as well as overseeing all merger and acquisition proposals. Corporate development officers are also increasingly proactive in seeking approval from the company's board before undertaking any merger or acquisition regardless of scale (Liebs, 1999).

Mergers and acquisitions of all types follow a somewhat similar trajectory. Ideally, mergers and acquisitions are implemented over a six to nine month period. This period, sufficient to address organizational issues, includes the following management duties: "pick the right people for a dedicated integration management team; orient employees to the new organization and the vision of the future quickly and directly; establish a clear sense of urgency to act; build an enthusiasm for a successful merger completion; set clear objectives and hold individuals and teams accountable for achieving them; communicate clearly, honestly, and frequently; clearly explain decisions once they are made; keep senior management on both sides highly visible; and change plans if conditions change" (Walker, 2000).

Regulations, Procedures, & Guidelines for Mergers & Acquisitions

In the United States, state governments, with government direction, oversee corporate mergers and acquisitions. Antitrust regulation, which is sometimes called competition policy, refers to legislation that regulates and forbids the consolidation of business power into industry monopolies. Although one of the benefits of a free-market economy is supposed to be competition between businesses, the reality of today's global market is often reduced competition due to corporate monopolies. In the United States, the electorate supports government regulation of mergers and acquisitions.

The procedure for a corporate merger and acquisition is, on the surface, a simple process. Corporations are required, in most states, to submit a plan of merger that explicitly describes the names of the corporations involved in the merger, any proposed change in the name of the acquiring corporation, the plan for converting and joining shares of both corporations, and the response of shareholders to the proposed merger. If the state and local governments approve the merger, the Secretary of State issues a certificate of merger that authorizes and officially recognizes the merger. Mergers and acquisitions between states and countries are often complicated by the need to meet the regulations and procedures of multiple state or national governments.

For example, in 1997, the companies of Boeing and McDonnell Douglas merged into a single company. The number of major aircraft manufacturers was reduced from three (Boeing, Airbus, and McDonnell Douglas) to two (Boeing/McDonnell Douglas and Airbus). This large merger fell within the scope and jurisdiction of the antitrust authorities of several nations, and, as a result, was evaluated by both the Federal Trade Commission (FTC) and the European Commission (EUC). The FTC ruled the merger lawful, but the EUC found the merger unlawful and required numerous concessions from the merging parties before approving the deal. The EUC's ruling was based on its desire to protect Airbus, a European Union-based corporation, which is Boeing/McDonnell Douglas's only real industry competition (Gifford, 2000).

Corporate mergers and acquisitions follow government procedures and guidelines established by the Federal Trade Commission in 1968, dramatically changed in 1982, modified slightly in 1984, and reworked and updated in 1992 to reflect the needs of business and society. The 1982 and 1992 versions of the Merger Guidelines are the most influential on current merger and acquisition activity and enforcement. In 1982, the Federal Trade Commission developed new Merger Guidelines to help corporations engage in lawful merger and acquisition activities. The Merger Guidelines are not law themselves but are the guides that state courts use in determining whether or not a merger is lawful. The Merger Guidelines are based on the Justice Department's interpretation of the merger provisions of the Clayton Act and the Sherman Act. The Clayton Act (1890) and the Sherman Act (1914) are the foundation laws of the federal government's antitrust policy. In 1992, the Federal Trade Commission joined with the Department of Justice to update the merger regulations, now called Horizontal Merger Guidelines, to include more focus on horizontal mergers.

The Horizontal Merger Guidelines, as described by the Federal Trade Commission, are founded on the principle that strict enforcement of merger regulations is a critical element of the free enterprise system. The federal government argues that sound merger enforcements are believed to benefit American firms through ensuring free competition and the welfare of the American consumer. The main goal of the Horizontal Merger Guidelines is to keep mergers that adversely affect competition from occurring while allowing competitively neutral mergers to happen freely. The Federal Trade Commission and the Department of Justice view the 1992 Horizontal Merger Guidelines as a framework for the evaluation of mergers by the public and private sectors.

Issues

Human Resource Management of the Merger & Acquisition Process

The mergers and acquisitions process, across businesses and industries, shares similar human resource problems including human resource management, ethical management of the merger and acquisition process, and post-merger management. The following sections discuss the human resource problems and solutions related to the merger and acquisition process.

Human Resource Management

Successful mergers and acquisitions require careful management to ensure that mergers and acquisitions are well-conceived, planned, and executed. Human resource leaders play a vital role in the merger and acquisition process as they function to integrate the staff of two distinct businesses. Common human resource problems created by mergers and acquisitions include the following: "retirement, pension, or other liabilities; executive contracts or other constraining compensation arrangements; employee relations risks, including union relationships, contracts, and issues; legal actions or compliance issues; availability of capable management talent for key roles; and employee commitment vital for the retention of talent and sustained high performance" (Price, 2000).

Human resource managers work to ensure that key talent of both businesses is integrated and retained and that the people-related systems, processes, and organization correspond to the new company's objectives. Human resource managers assess the merger and develop their strategy based on the answer to the following questions: "Does the merger make sense? What are the people-related issues? How will we integrate and retain talent? How will we integrate cultures and transfer knowledge? How will we maintain commitment and performance during the merger process? How will we implement the merger quickly and effectively?" (Price, 2000, ¶3).

Human resource managers are often responsible for the company-wide merger announcement. Managers evaluate and announce assumptions regarding potential costs, risks, and benefits. Human resource managers will do the following to integrate and retain key talent in the new business organization: "define the future roles of executives in both merger partners; define the management capabilities required for the future success of the business; identify the individuals who will be critical and any capability gaps that will need to be filled; determine the actions required to retain key individuals through the merger; and establish ways to share knowledge and learn from each other" (Price, 2000).

Choosing managers for the new, merged organization is one of the most important post-merger human resource decisions. If the merger occurs between equal companies, the new company generally includes management representation from both companies. The management representation decisions in acquisitions vary by business (Walker, 2000).

Ethical Management of Personnel during Mergers & Acquisitions

Mergers and acquisitions transform the cultures and structures of both businesses. As a result of the transition, the staff of each business may feel stressed, angry, disoriented, frustrated, confused, or frightened. Work-related manifestations may include lowered productivity, lowered commitment, increased dissatisfaction, disloyalty, high-turnover, leadership, power struggles, sabotage, and other dysfunctional behavior. Mergers and acquisitions have periods of waiting, frenzied activity, conflict, and rising tensions. Human resource problems associated with merger and acquisition are common. Managers can positively influence the integration process. For example, managers may strategize to alleviate the difficulties related to large-scale transformations including grief, loss, staff reduction, and termination.

Human resource managers should keep the following ethical principles in mind as they assess and plan the new human resources structure: Mergers and acquisitions involve multiple parties with separate interests, agendas, and needs; tensions can often arise from miscommunication and obfuscation of information; mergers and acquisitions often force people into certain work situations; grief, loss, and termination management effect employee attitudes; and managerial respect for organizational members as individuals influences the commitment that organizational members feel toward their work and the company (Buono, 1990).

Post-Merger Human Resource Management

The success of mergers and acquisitions, as measured by profitable and sustainable growth, is significantly influenced by post-merger management decisions. There are five management skills that are associated with successful post-merger business integration. These skills include: Early action regarding financial and physical integration of businesses, reengineering of products and processes, valuing and reshaping business culture, maintaining valued customers, and capitalizing strategic merger options such as new markets and new products.

Managers are rarely able to perform an in-depth human resources audit before the merger and acquisition. As a result, management is responsible for working quickly once the merger is in place to identify key talent and leaders. Issues include identifying key talent, resolving job-overlap, and resolving culture clash. Ideally, post-merger managers will create an explicitly transitional culture and job assignments to ease employee stress and upset over organizational changes. Management during the post-merger phase of the merger or acquisition should focus on key areas such as managing organizational stress; establishing performance criteria; identifying who will stay and who will go; creating a new organizational structure; and assuming the leadership of the emerging organization (Corwin, 1991).

CONCLUSION

Mergers and acquisitions are, for some countries, one of the most effective corporate development tools or tactics. Mergers and acquisitions are a key means of fast growth, increased market share, entry into new markets, expanded product offerings, strengthened supply chain, and optimized cost efficiencies (Walker, 2000). Companies that reject the quick growth and profit of mergers and acquisitions instead embrace organic growth and alliances. Companies that prioritize organic growth and alliances over mergers and acquisitions believe that organic growth is more profitable and more sustainable than mergers and acquisitions. In addition, financial markets tend to favor the stability of organic growth over growth created through mergers and acquisitions. Ultimately, individual companies planning their corporate development prospects must analyze their market, their resources, and their objectives and decide what tools are most appropriate to help the company grow (Dalton, 2006).

Bibliography

Barros, R., & Domínguez, I. (2013). Integration strategies for the success of mergers and acquisitions in financial services companies. *Journal of Business Economics & Management, 14*(5), 979-992. Retrieved November 15, 2013, from EBSCO Online Database Business Source Complete. http://search.ebscohost.com/login.aspx?direct=true&db=bth&AN=91840515&site=ehost-live

Buono, A., & Bowditch, J. (1990). Ethical considerations in merger and acquisition: a human resource perspective. *SAM Advanced Management Journal (07497075), 55*(4), 18. Retrieved June 12, 2007, from EBSCO Online Database Business Source Complete. http://search.ebscohost.com/login.aspx?direct=true&db=bth&AN=4614497&site=ehost-live

Corwin, S., Weinstein, H., & Sweeney, P. (1991). Facing the people issues of M & As. *Management Review, 80*(4), 47. Retrieved June 12, 2007, from EBSCO Online Database Business Source Complete. http://search.ebscohost.com/login.aspx?direct=true&db=bth&AN=6139615&site=ehost-live

Dalton, D., & Dalton, C. (2006). Corporate growth. *Journal of Business Strategy, 27*(1), 5-7. Retrieved June 12, 2007, from EBSCO Online Database Business Source Complete. http://search.ebscohost.com/login.aspx?direct=true&db=bth&AN=21350177&site=ehost-live

Davidson, A. (2004). Merging HP and Compaq. *Strategic Leadership, 32*(2), 49-52.

Dilshad, M. (2013). Profitability analysis of mergers and acquisitions: An event study approach. *Business & Economic Research (BER), 3*(1), 89-125. Retrieved November 15, 2013, from EBSCO Online Database Business Source Complete. http://search.ebscohost.com/login.aspx?direct=true&db=bth&AN=90222617&site=ehost-live

Gifford, D. (2000). Can international antitrust be saved for the post-Boeing merger world? A proposal to minimize international conflict and to rescue antitrust from misuse. *Antitrust Bulletin, 45*(1), 55-119.

Groob, J. (1997). The art of the deal. *Civil Engineering (08857024), 67*(5), 64. Retrieved June 12, 2007, from EBSCO Online Database Business Source Complete. http://search.ebscohost.com/login.aspx?direct=true&db=bth&AN=9705194785&site=ehost-live

Growth through acquisition. (1996). *Management Decision, 34*(5), 28-30.

Harrison, J. (2005). Why alliances are gaining momentum. *Mergers & Acquisitions: The Dealermaker's Journal, 40*(6), 28-31. Retrieved June 12, 2007, from EBSCO Online Database Business Source Complete. http://search.ebscohost.com/login.aspx?direct=true&db=bth&AN=19680400&site=ehost-live

Liebs, A. (1999). More U.S. companies have corporate development on their minds. *Mergers & Acquisitions Report, 12*(24), 3. Retrieved June 12, 2007, from EBSCO Online Database Business Source Complete. http://search.ebscohost.com/login.aspx?direct=true&db=bth&AN=1971973&site=ehost-live

Lu, C. (2006). Growth strategies and merger patterns among small and medium-sized enterprises: An empirical study. *International Journal of Management, 23*(3), 529-547. Retrieved June 12, 2007, from EBSCO Online Database Business Source Complete. http://search.ebscohost.com/login.aspx?direct=true&db=bth&AN=22433919&site=ehost-live

Lynch, J. (2002). Escaping merger and acquisition madness. *Strategy & Leadership, 30*(2), 5-13.

Managing merger madness. (2002). *Strategic Direction, 18*(11), 15-18.

Mergers and Acquisitions. (2007). *American Law Library*. Retrieved June 12, 2007, from http://law.jrank.org/pages/8550/Mergers-Acquisitions.html

Price, K. (2000). Why do mergers go right? Retrieved August 9, 2010 from http://www.allbusiness.com/human-resources/employee-development/636051-1.html

Shin, B. (2005). A comparison of the business strategies of two telecommunication service providers. *The Journal of Information Technology Case and Application Research, 7*(2), 19-31.

Walker, J., & Price, K. (2000). Perspectives: why do mergers go right? *Human Resource Planning, 23*(2), 6-9. 1992 Horizontal merger guidelines. (2007). The Federal Trade Commission. Retrieved June 12, 2007, from http://www.ftc.gov/bc/docs/horizmer.shtm

Xiaotian, Z., & Shuoyi, L. (2013). Earnings management through real activities manipulation before mergers and acquisitions. *Journal of Finance & Accountancy,* 131-17. Retrieved November 15, 2013, from EBSCO Online Database Business Source Complete. http://search.ebscohost.com/login.aspx?direct=true&db=bth&AN=90437033&site=ehost-live

Suggested Reading

Audretsch, D. (1989). The determinants of conglomerate mergers. *American Economist, 33*(1). Retrieved June 12, 2007, from EBSCO Online Database Business Source Complete. http://search.ebscohost.com/login.aspx?direct=true&db=bth&AN=4524508&site=ehost-live

Ettorre, B. (1997). Too much of a bad thing? *Management Review, 86*(11), 9. Retrieved June 12, 2007, from EBSCO Online Database Business Source Complete. http://search.ebscohost.com/login.aspx?direct=true&db=bth&AN=9712126577&site=ehost-live

Kreitl, G., & Oberndorfer, W. (2004). Motives for acquisitions among engineering consulting firms. *Construction Management & Economics, 22*(7), 691-700. Retrieved June 12, 2007, from EBSCO Online Database Business Source Complete. http://search.ebscohost.com/login.aspx?direct=true&db=bth&AN=14795126&site=ehost-live

Simone I. Flynn, Ph.D.

Corporate Strategy

ABSTRACT

This paper explores the topic of corporate strategy and how it fits within the strategic management process. Specifically, we'll examine the various types of corporate strategy, providing a framework to recognize when a given strategy is most appropriate. Also, we'll provide real-life examples of corporate strategy in action, along with an overview of corporate portfolio tools used in corporate strategy formulation.

OVERVIEW

Strategy is defined as "the art of devising or employing plans or stratagems toward a goal" (Merriam-Webster online, 2007). Within a broad business context, strategy is an integrated set of plans for achieving long-term organizational goals. Multi-unit corporations have three levels of organizational strategy: corporate strategy, business strategy, and functional strategy. "Corporate strategy concerns two different questions: what businesses should the company be in and how the corporate office should manage the array of business units" (Porter, 1987). In a broad sense, corporate strategy establishes the overall direction of the firm. Also, corporate strategy is a smaller part of a larger and distinct process known as the strategic management process, consisting of several interrelated stages, of which corporate strategy development falls within the strategy formulation stage. (There are four fundamental stages of strategic management: environmental scanning, strategy formulation, strategy implementation, evaluation and control.) Strategy formulation exists on a three-level hierarchy (see Figure 1 below). Typically, the strategy formulation process is an interactive top-down process beginning with corporate-level strategy developed by top management, followed by the business and functional levels of strategy. Yet, depending on the organization, managers at the functional and business levels provide varying degrees of input throughout the entire strategy formulation process.

Business Strategy — Once corporate strategies are developed, the focus is upon formulating business-level strategies. Business strategy is sometimes referred to as *competitive strategy*(Porter, 1980), i.e., strategy that gives the firm a competitive advantage. Business strategy development occurs within a multi-unit firm's divisions and subsidiaries, sometimes referred to as strategic business units or *SBUs*. A firm's internal strengths are sources of competitive advantage and are collectively defined as a firm's core competency. Porter (1985) outlines a set of generic business strategies, such as a cost leadership strategy, emphasizing low-cost production or distribution of products. Also, differentiation strategy may be used, which distinguishes company products and services on the basis of superior service, quality, unique features, etc. Either strategy may opt to target abroad market or *focus* on a narrow market segment.

Functional strategy flows out of an organization's functional departmental areas, developed in furtherance of the aforementioned corporate and business-level strategies. Functional area strategies include:

- Operations Strategy — Designing production processes that meet customer product/service requirements.
- Financial Strategy — Preparing budgets and securing needed financial resources.
- Marketing Strategy — Identifying customers, customer requirements, pricing strategies, promotional methods, and distribution channels.
- Human Resource Strategy — Recruiting, selecting, training, compensating, and organizing employees.
- Research & Design Strategy — Creating new products or updating existing products and services.

APPLICATIONS

Corporate strategy responds to a number of questions related to how a firm intends to compete on a broad scale. How will the corporation grow? What businesses will the firm compete with? Is growth strategy an appropriate option to choose from? If so, does the firm possess the financial capability to grow? Is the firm's target market attractive enough to allow for growth in their current industry? Must the firm look outside of its current industry for growth opportunities, and if so, which industries? These are but a few of the questions corporate strategy addresses. Depending on the answers to these questions, corporate-level strategy is addressed through growth strategy or a defensive strategy alignment.

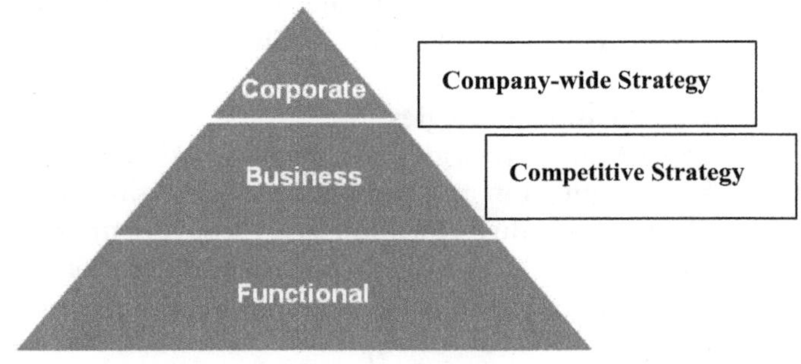

Fig.1

Note that growth strategies may be pursued by internal or external means. For example, when choosing internal growth mechanisms, a firm develops and markets new products, improves upon existing products, or sells existing products to new markets. Alternatively, when a firm implements external growth strategies, the firm acquires growth assets outside of the organization.

Growth Strategy

Growth strategy is that strategy employed to grow a firm's profits and lies within two broad categories: diversification and concentration (Wheelen and Hunger, 2006). Diversification strategy adds products/ services somewhat related or unrelated to the firm's core business. Concentration strategies are those growth strategies whereby a firm maintains a competitive focus within their particular industry. The two types of concentration strategies are vertical integration and horizontal integration.

Concentration Strategies

With vertical integration strategy, a firm takes over the supply function and/or distribution function that was previously handled by outsiders. There are several types of vertical integration strategies: forward vertical integration, backward vertical integration, and full integration.

Forward vertical integration strategy involves a manufacturer assuming the distribution function for their product. A failed attempt at forward vertical integration is personal computer maker Gateway's attempt to distribute PCs through company-owned retail stores. This strategy was a failure due to the high overhead costs associated with their bricks-and-mortar retail stores. Gateway switched to marketing PCs exclusively through their website and over the phone.

More successful examples of companies taking over the distribution function are found in the factory outlet shopping mall phenomenon. In effect, various manufacturers sell their products directly to consumers through company-owned stores — companies such as Nike, Tommy Hilfiger, Sketchers, Pepperidge Farms, Samsonite, etc. However, unlike Gateway, these companies do not rely on forward vertical integration entirely, as they also rely upon third-party retailers for the bulk of their sales. More on the degrees of vertical integration shall be discussed later in the topic.

Backward vertical integration is when a firm assumes the supply function for their respective value chain. With increasing global competition and the rising costs of commodities, (e.g. copper, rubber, aluminum, iron, and oil etc.), a trend shows an increased amount of backward vertical integration activity. In order to ensure reliable supply and to control costs, manufacturers have been acquiring suppliers of critical inputs to their production processes. Examples include: Japan tire manufacturer Bridgestone's purchase of an Indonesian rubber plantation, and Toyota acquiring a controlling interest in its main supplier of batteries for its hybrid vehicles (Gross, 2006).

On the other hand, Bob Evans Farms Inc. has always relied on a backward vertical integration strategy. Best known for offering pork sausage products to the retail grocery market, Bob Evans controls the supply function of their business by raising and slaughtering hogs on company-owned farms, then preparing and packaging their park sausage products for sale.

Full integration occurs when a firm takes over the entire value chain of supplying the inputs of production (i.e., raw materials or component parts), manufacturing the product, and distribution of the product to the ultimate consumer. Examples of complete vertical integration are oil and gas companies such as ExxonMobil, BP, and Royal Dutch Shell PLC, etc. These fully integrated companies engage in oil exploration, extract crude oil with their own drilling operations, refine oil into gasoline at company-owned refineries, and then distribute gasoline products through company-owned gas stations.

Note that vertical integration exists in varying degrees along the value chain. The ranges of vertical integration are: non-integration, quasi-integration, taper integration, and full integration (Harrigan, 1984).

- Full Integration (discussed above) is when a manufacturer retains in-house responsibility for its supplies and is the sole distributor of its products.
- Taper Integration occurs when a firm is forward or backward vertically integrated, yet relies on outside firms for supplying only a portion of production inputs or a portion of distribution needs.
- Quasi-Integration is an arrangement whereby a company does not make any supplies or distribute any of its products, but owns a partial interest in a supplier or distributor to guarantee access to supplies and distribution channels. For example, in a forward quasi-integration arrangement, PepsiCo could purchase a partial equity interest in Kroger supermarket chain in order to ensure access to Kroger's distribution network. Or in a backward quasi-integration arrangement, GM could conceivably acquire a minority equity interest in a supplier of automotive electrical components.
- Non-integration involves the use of contractual arrangements, i.e., long-term agreements between the firm and its suppliers and/or distributors to provide services over a specified time period. With this type of arrangement, no ownership transfer or exchange of assets occurs. The automotive industry commonly makes use of such non-integration arrangements.
- Horizontal Integration is when a firm acquires a competitor in the same industry. Also, horizontal integration tends to be the most preferred growth strategy for many industries. Mergers and acquisitions are the typical method by which horizontal integration is achieved (David, 1996). For example, the personal computer industry has undergone a number of horizontally integrated transactions with Gateway Computer's acquisition of low-cost rival e-Machines, and HP's merger with rival pc-maker Compaq. Likewise, in the telecommunications sector, SBC Communications merged with AT&T. Automotive industry examples of horizontal integration are Ford Motor's acquisition of Volvo, Jaguar, Aston Martin, and Land Rover, as a way of quickly moving into a high-end automotive segment. Other examples include GM's acquisition of Swedish car-maker Saab, and Germany's Daimler-Benz acquisition of US-based Chrysler Corp.

Diversification Strategies

Diversification strategies are of two varieties: concentric diversification and conglomerate diversification.

Concentric diversification is an assortment of *related* products in the firm's portfolio. As one of the world's largest food and beverage companies, PepsiCo Inc. represents an example of concentric diversification (http://pepsico.com/PEP%5fCompany/

BrandsCompanies/index.cfm). The company's related business units include:

- Frito-Lay snacks
- Pepsi-Cola beverages
- Gatorade sports drinks
- Tropicana juices
- Quaker Foods

On the other hand, conglomerate diversification is a collection of *unrelated* lines of business in the corporate portfolio. For example, when many people think of General Electric (GE), they automatically think of light bulbs or appliances; yet the GE of today is a truly diversified conglomerate, made up of six business units:

- GE Infrastructure consists of aircraft engines, energy, oil and gas, rail and water process technologies, and more.
- GE Commercial Finance provides loans, operating leases, financing programs, commercial Insurance, and reinsurance products.
- GE Health offers medical imaging and information technologies, medical diagnostics, patient monitoring systems, performance improvement, drug discovery, and biopharmaceutical manufacturing technologies.
- GE Industrial includes appliances, lighting and inducts, factory automation systems, etc.
- GE Money offers financial products such as credit cards, personal loans, mortgage, and motor solutions.
- NBC Universal is a media and entertainment business consisting of news production, movies, theme parks etc. (http://www.ge.com/en/company/businesses/ge_nbc_universal.htm)

Defensive Strategy

Defensive strategies are those strategies used when experiencing financial trouble, indicated by declining sales and profits. The need for retrenchment strategy may be due to an industry-wide problem (e.g., an unattractive industry such as a typewriter company) or a firm-specific problem (e.g., poor management, lack of financial resources, etc.). With this in mind, there are four types of defensive strategies that firms employ: retrenchment, divestiture, joint venture, and liquidation (David, 1996).

Retrenchment strategy (also known as turnaround strategy) involves the imposition of cost reductions, with an emphasis on improving the operational efficiency of the firm. An example of a successful turnaround effort is Nissan Motors Ltd.

In 1999, after seven straight years of record unprofitability, Nissan named as its new CEO, Carlos Ghosn, an executive vice president from Renault. As part of his retrenchment strategy, Ghosn closed manufacturing plants in Japan, reduced employee headcount by 21,000, cut in half the number of suppliers to around 600, and reduced parts costs by 20 percent. Under Ghosn's leadership, Nissan went from a $5.5 billion loss in fiscal 2000 to a $2.7 billion profit in 2001—far exceeding expectations (http://www.gsb.stanford.edu/news/headlines/vftt%5fghosn.shtml).

Divestiture involves the spin-off of a firm's business units that are unprofitable or do not represent a good strategic fit with the firm's core business. IBM's former desktop personal computer business is a prime example. In 2004, IBM sold its personal computer business to Chinese computer maker Lenovo Group for $1.75 billion. IBM's rationale for the deal was a continuation of IBM's strategy shift from selling low-margin hardware products to selling higher-margin consulting services, software, and high-end computers. Likewise, IBM viewed the deal as an inroad to the vast, fast growing Chinese market for servers and technical services (Spooner and Kanellos, 2004).

Joint ventures are temporary partnerships between two firms, typically utilized when both firms wish to capitalize on a mutually beneficial opportunity. Technically speaking, the IBM/Lenovo deal is a divesture transaction, yet it also contains elements of a joint venture between the two companies, with IBM maintaining an 18% equity investment in Lenovo. For example, Lenovo has been the preferred supplier of PCs to IBM and was allowed to use the IBM brand for five years. Also, IBM has provided marketing support to Lenovo via the IBM corporate sales force. From a benefits perspective, the deal rid IBM of its personal computer business, while gaining an entry point into China for other IBM products and services. On the other hand, Lenovo gained access to IBM's extensive corporate customer base, the IBM name, and IBM's marketing expertise (Spooner and Kanellos, 2004).

Liquidation — Liquidation involves selling off a company's assets for their tangible net worth and signals the end of the firm's existence. This strategy is employed when a firm is losing significant amounts of money with no prospect of recovery; all other retrenchment strategies have been tried, yet were either inappropriate, or ended in failure. Generally, liquidation occurs as part of a court-ordered bankruptcy sale under Chapter 7 bankruptcy. However, a firm may undertake a voluntary path to liquidation outside of bankruptcy, yet this route is less common. Examples of firms forced to liquidate are passenger airline carriers Trans World Airlines (TWA) and Pan American Airways. Note that Chapter 7 liquidation is not to be confused with a Chapter 11 bankruptcy in which a firm is allowed to reorganize its financial affairs in the hopes of remaining an ongoing firm. (For more information on the types of corporate bankruptcies, visit the U.S. Security and Exchange Commission website at: http://www.sec.gov/investor/pubs/bankrupt.htm.)

Factors Influencing Corporate Strategy Choice

There are a number of factors influencing the choice of corporate strategy (David, 1996):

Forward Integration

- Used when a firm's present distributors are too expensive, or incapable of meeting distribution needs;
- The availability of quality distributors is limited in number;
- Competing in an industry experiencing high market growth; or
- Used if the organization has the capital and capability to manage the distribution function.

Backward Integration

- Present suppliers are too expensive, unreliable or incapable of meeting the firm's needs;
- Number of suppliers is limited, with many existing competitors;
- Industry is experiencing rapid growth;
- Resources are needed quickly; or
- Used if the organization has the capital and capability to manage the business of supplying its own parts.

Horizontal Integration

- The industry is a growth industry;
- Increased economies of scale provide competitive advantage;
- Used if the organization has the capital and capability to manage an expanded business; or
- Competitors are failing due to a lack of managerial expertise — expertise your firm possesses.

Concentric Diversification

- Poor growth prospects exist in the current industry;
- New related products or services would enhance the sale of existing products;
- Related products can be offered for sale at competitive prices;
- New products offer a seasonal counterbalance against the seasonality of existing products; or
- Current products are in a decline stage of their life cycle.

Conglomerate Diversification

- Industry is declining in sales and profits;
- Does the organization have the capital and capability to manage a diversified business line?;
- Existing markets are saturated;
- An attractive investment exists in an unrelated business; or
- Antitrust concerns prevent pursuing companies in the same industry.

Also, Porter (1987) identifies three tests for making diversification choices that are most likely to create shareholder value.

1. Attractiveness test — Is the industry attractive or capable of being made attractive?
2. Cost-of-entry test — Is the cost of entry reasonable enough so as not to jeopardize future profits?
3. Better-off test — Does the parent corporation offer competitive advantage to the new unit or will the new unit bring a competitive advantage? In other words, are meaningful synergies likely to result between the new unit and the corporation?

Joint Venture

- The distinctive competencies of the two firms complement one another;
- A reduction in risks results from an alliance;
- Appropriate for smaller firms having trouble competing against larger firms; or
- There is a need to get a new technology to market quickly.

Retrenchment

- The firm has a weak competitive position;
- The firm is plagued by inefficiency, low profits, or stock holder pressure to improve performance;
- The organization has grown so large that an internal reorganization needs to take place; or
- A distinctive competency exists, yet the firm has failed to capitalize on it.

Divestiture

- The retrenchment strategy was a failure;
- A product line or division needs more resources in order to compete and survive;
- A division is performing poorly;
- A division is a poor strategic fit with the firm's overall corporate vision; or
- An infusion of cash is needed but can't be obtained elsewhere.

Liquidation

- Pursued when divestiture and retrenchment have failed;
- When bankruptcy is the only alternative—liquidation allows for the orderly sale of assets; or
- Liquidation allows the firm's stockholders to minimize their losses.

Corporate Portfolio Approaches

As noted previously, "Corporate strategy concerns two different questions: what businesses should the company be in and how the corporate office should manage the array of business units" (Porter, 1987). As for managing the array of business units, there are several corporate portfolio approaches. One of the first portfolio approaches developed is the BCG (Boston Consulting Group) matrix. The BCG matrix is a two-dimensional analysis of a business unit's strength, determined by relative market growth rate and relative market share. Market growth rate is the annual growth rate in which the firm competes, with market share being the firm's market shares relative to all other direct competitors.

1. Cash cows are profitable business units with a low market share and high growth rate. They should be milked for cash, with the cash flow being deployed elsewhere.
2. Dogs possess a low market share and low growth rate and should be liquidated or divested.
3. Question marks are typically found within new product areas and have a low market share with a high growth rate. Given their high growth rates, question marks should be infused with cash to develop them into stars.
4. Successful question marks become stars; stars have a high growth rate and high market shares, hence a growth strategy of integration would be employed here (Thompson and Martin, 2005).

The BCG matrix's simplicity — a recognized strength — is also one of its weaknesses. The market growth rate dimension (one indication of industry attractiveness) and relative market share (one determinant of competitive advantage) overlook other important determinants of profitability. In response to this limitation, consulting firm McKinsey and Co. derived a more comprehensive model from the BCG Matrix, i.e., the GE Business Screen Matrix. The GE matrix, developed for GE by Mckinsey, considers a three-dimensional analysis of high, medium, and low industry attractiveness and competitive position. Industry attractiveness is substituted for BCG's market growth rate, and is comprised of external factors such as entry barriers, market growth, industry profitability, market size, pricing trends, etc. Competitive position replaces BCG's market share measure, and includes internal strengths and weakness factors including market share, relative brand strength, management strength, profitability, size, etc.(Thompson and Martin, 2005).

CONCLUSION

Corporate strategy does not exist in a vacuum — it is a smaller, yet integral part of a larger and distinct process known as the strategic management process, interrelating with the formulation of a firm's business strategy, as well as its functional strategy. Is there one best corporate strategy? The answer is an unequivocal no — there is no single best corporate strategy. Likewise, the process of developing corporate strategy has become a more daunting task in light of the global competitive forces firms must confront. Corporate strategy is dependent on numerous factors as outlined with respect to industry attractiveness and the relative competitive strengths of the respective company. Once again, the fact that corporations operate in a global environment greatly complicates the formulation and coordination of corporate strategy. Hence, the formulation of corporate strategy is a dynamic, interactive, iterative process, sometimes requiring midstream adjustments as a result of unexpected changes in the firm's competitive environment. Therefore, the wrong corporate strategy choices, in addition to improper implementation, can mean the difference between success and failure.

Bibliography

Bharadwaj, A., El Sawy, O. A., Pavlou, P. A., & Venkatraman, N. N. (2013). Digital business strategy: toward a next generation of insights. MIS Quarterly, 37(2), 471–482. Retrieved November 20, 2013 from EBSCO Online Database Business Source Complete. http://search.ebscohost.com/login.aspx?direct=true&db=bth&AN=87371552&site=ehost-live

Caescu, S., & Ploesteanu, M. (2011). Corporate strategies of integrated marketing. *Romanian Journal of Marketing, 6* (3), 22–29. Retrieved November 20, 2013 from EBSCO Online Database Business Source Complete. http://search.ebscohost.com/login.aspx?direct=true&db=bth&AN=69920156&site=ehost-live

David, F. R. (1996). *Strategic management* (6th ed.). Upper Saddle River, NJ: Prentice Hall.

Gobble, M. M., Petrick, I., & Wright, H. (2012). Innovation and strategy. *Research Technology Management, 55* (3), 63–67. Retrieved November 20, 2013 from EBSCO Online Database Business Source Complete. http://search.ebscohost.com/login.aspx?direct=true&db=bth&AN=74700144&site=ehost-live

Gross, D. (2006, August 17). *Dis-integration?* Retrieved April 30, 2007, from http://www.slate.com/id/2147952

Harrigan, K. (1984). Formulating vertical integration strategies. *Academy of Management Review, 9*(4), 638. Retrieved May 02, 2007, from EBSCO Online Database Business Source Complete. http://search.ebscohost.com/login.aspx?direct=true&db=bth&AN=4277387&site=ehost-live

Porter, M.E. (1980). *Competitive strategy.* New York: Free Press.

Porter, M.E. (1985). *Competitive advantage: Creating and sustaining superior performance.* New York: Free Press.

Porter, M.E. (1987). From competitive advantage to corporate strategy. *Harvard Business Review,65*(3), 43–59. Retrieved May 01, 2007, from EBSCO Online Database Business Source Complete. http://search.ebscohost.com/login.aspx?direct=true&db=bth&AN=4126877&site=ehost-live

Spooner J.G. & Kanellos M. (2004, Dec. 8). *IBM sells PC group to Lenovo.* Retrieved March 30, 2007, from http://news.com.com/IBM??????????1042%5f3-5482284.html

Stanford Graduate School of Business (2002, Nov. 11). *Nissan motor CEO Carlos Ghosn is turnaround hero.* Retrieved March 30 2007, from http://www.gsb.stanford.edu/news/headlines/vftt%5fghosn.shtml

Thompson, J. L. & Martin, F. (2005). *Strategic Management — Awareness and Change.* (5th ed.) London: Thomson Learning.

Suggested Reading

Ansoff, H.I. (1957). Strategies for diversification. *Harvard Business Review, 35*(5), 113–124. Retrieved May 07, 2007, from EBSCO Online Database Business Source Complete. http://search.ebscohost.com/login.aspx?direct=true&db=bth&AN=6769323&site=ehost-live

Campbell, A., Goold, M., & Alexander, M. (1995). Corporate strategy: The quest for parenting advantage. *Harvard Business Review, 73*(2), 120–132. Retrieved May 01, 2007, from EBSCO Online Database Business Source Complete. http://search.ebscohost.com/login.aspx?direct=true&db=bth&AN=9503282004&site=ehost-live

Farid, M., & Flynn, D. (1992). The strategic choice of Chapter 11: An examination of the critical factors. *Review of Business, 13*(4), 32. Retrieved May 02, 2007, from EBSCO Online Database Business Source Complete. http://search.ebscohost.com/login.aspx?direct=true&db=bth&AN=9607035565&site=ehost-live

Harrigan, K., & Porter, M. (1983). End-game strategies for declining industries. *Harvard Business Review, 61*(4), 111. Retrieved May 02, 2007, from EBSCO Online Database Business Source Complete. http://search.ebscohost.com/login.aspx?direct=true&db=bth&AN=3868184&site=ehost-live

Henderson, V., & Hobson, D. (2011). Optimal liquidation of derivative portfolios. *Mathematical Finance, 21* (3), 365–382. Retrieved November 20, 2013 from EBSCO Online Database Business Source Complete. http://search.ebscohost.com/login.aspx?direct=true&db=bth&AN=60573352&site=ehost-live

Edwin D. Davison, M.B.A., J.D.

CRISIS MANAGEMENT

ABSTRACT

This article examines the factors that influence a manager's determination of an event or situation as a crisis. Various strategies of responding to a crisis are explained along with factors that may influence the strategy chosen to ameliorate a crisis situation. The methods that companies use to prepare for future crises are also reviewed. Several past business crises and the scope of those crises are reviewed. The selection and execution of crisis response strategies to a recall prompted by Salmonella Typhimurium are examined along with specific actions that several companies in the food industry took in response to the situation. The role of United States Government agencies in the recall process is also explained.

OVERVIEW

The term "crisis" is used to describe a wide variety of events and circumstances. However, what comprises a crisis, or when a company decides that they are experiencing a crisis, is dependent on a number of variables.

- First, to what extent are there internal capabilities in place to deal with an event or situation that is disrupting business?
- Second, what is the magnitude of the event and what are the consequences of not successfully handling the crisis?
- Third, to what extent does the event affect other businesses, the surrounding community, or even the country where the company is located?

In an ideal world a company would be able to predict and be prepared for every possible event and thus minimize the perception that the event had turned into a crisis (Klein, 2007). The larger the company and the more experience that corporate staff have in handling a specific type of event, the less likely it is that the event will be considered a crisis. In a situation involving a product recall, for example, some companies have considerable experience and probably have staff in place to deal with the recall. This is the case in the automobile industry, where products are recalled frequently. On the other hand, in a small company with limited staff, or in one that has never faced a recall of its products, the event may become a crisis.

Identifying & Predicting Crisis Situations

If the magnitude of the event is small and limited to one location or one product, or if that event has little if any impact on day-to-day operations, it is likely the event will not be viewed as a crisis. If the event is wide in scope and devastates operational capability, the event may be viewed as a crisis. In addition, if the negative consequences of not successfully handling the crisis are minimal, then the event will not turn into a crisis. But if the consequences of failing to properly handle an event are extensive, it will likely be treated as a crisis ("Top managers lack confidence," 2009).

The geographical scope of an event or the economic scope of an event may also influence whether or not managers in a particular company will consider the event a crisis. A natural disaster that affects several counties or states, for example, may be seen as a disruption but not particularly as a crisis. In such events, federal, state, or local response deals with many of the consequences of the event. There is also most likely some sort of insurance coverage in place to aid in the recovery.

If the event affects only one company, or the supply chain in which the company operates, managers may consider the event a crisis. In other words, the more the consequences of the event fall singularly on a specific company or industry, the more likely it is that the event will be viewed as a crisis (Freda, Arn & Gatlin-Watts, 1999).

In case of the 2008 economic downturn, the collapse of the mortgage industry was viewed as a crisis, which in turn affected the banking industry in general and many corporations that were dependent on the availability of affected monies (Verma, 2009). However, it could be argued that the media and politicians who continuously emphasized that the events as a crisis contributed to the effects of the downturn (Levinson, 2009). In this vein, the identification of the downturn as a crisis could be seen as strategic, as it allowed Congress to be persuaded into action and also presented certain opportunities to savvy businesses (Garmhausen, 2009) (Maddock & Vitn, 2009).

Strategy Creation & Execution

Once a company has decided that an event is a crisis, a strategy must be executed to minimize the affect of the crisis. One of the first desires that corporate managers have is to control the damage to company operations, reputation, business relationships, and, in some cases, stock prices. This requires the ability to rapidly organize efforts and mobilize the right people for the job (Miller, 2006). Above all, speed is of the essence and the chief executive officer (CEO) should play a key role (Kimes, 2009).

If operations are disrupted it is important to restore normal functioning as quickly as possible and remedy any defects that may be related to the current crisis. But the work is not finished there. During this time, a focus on reputation management, also known as image repair, may have more overall importance and value than an organization's functions. The CEO, with support from the crisis management team, is a key player in this part of the crisis drama. Much of the world outside the walls of the company views the CEO as the chief communicator for a company. In addition, the CEO's reputation is also on the line (Gaines-Ross, 2009).

Corporate Crisis Examples

There have been long lists of companies that have each faced rather severe crises. In 1984, in Bhopal, India, a Union Carbide chemical plant spewed pollution into the local community and caused a disaster for which the company has suffered consequences ever since (Haseley, 2004). In 1980, Proctor and Gamble introduced the Rely Super-Absorbent Tampon, which was later linked to hundreds of cases of toxic shock syndrome and numerous lawsuits (Weinberger & Romeo, 1989).

The Ford Motor Company suffered embarrassment as well as a class action lawsuit over the Ford Pinto, a small compact car introduced in the 1970s that had a tendency to burst into flames if hit from the rear (Weinberger & Romeo, 1989). In the late 1970s, the Firestone 500 series tires were blowing out and coming apart as people drove in their cars, which resulted in deaths and lawsuits (Gatewood & Carroll, 1981).

One of the most dramatic crises to ever befall an organization was the Space Shuttle Challenger explosion, which happened on January 28, 1986, just after lift-off. It was also televised around the world and especially in the classrooms of public schools in the United States. Among its crew was a schoolteacher, to be the first teacher in space. As Challenger exploded, millions of children were traumatized, the education community was outraged, parents were horrified, and politicians held their banners of anger high. NASA managers were tried and then convicted (Watson, 2006).

Another major crisis for a corporation, and the environment, was the 2010 Gulf of Mexico oil spill involving British Petroleum (Valvi & Fragkos, 2013). In response to the spill, BP set up a $20 billion trust to settle claims against the company (King, 2010).

APPLICATION

Crisis Management in Product Recall Situations

During the industrial revolution, innovation and business soared at a rapid rate, and there was little government intervention as to the quality and safety of the products that manufacturers were sending to market. After World War II this started to change. Federal authority to ensure the safety of consumer products, food and drugs, and transportation products was expanded. New laws were passed, federal agencies were created, and the age of product recalls began.

The expansion of regulations and the growth of government oversight have certainly benefited the consumer. From a business perspective, this oversight and resulting recalls have caused a long list of dramatic organizational crises.

Government Agencies Executing Recalls

The United States Consumer Product Safety Commission

The United States Consumer Product Safety Commission (CPSC) is the federal agency responsible for ensuring the safety of consumer products, including toys, baby accessories, electrical tools and appliances, household chemicals, and over 15,000 other products (CPSC, 2009). The CPSC was created in 1972 when the Consumer Product Safety Act became law. The CPSC issues hundreds of recalls every year and has prevented and removed hundreds of millions of items from the market in the United States (CPSC, 2003).

The United States Food and Drug Administration

The United States Food and Drug Administration (FDA) has jurisdiction over most food products, human and animal drugs, therapeutic agents of biological origin, medical devices, radiation-emitting products, cosmetics, and animal feed. The scope of the FDA's monitoring activities is huge; covering over $1 trillion worth of products annually and involving not only manufacturing but also import, transport, and storage. The agency traces its roots back to 1862 as a division of the United States Department of Agriculture. In 1980, the FDA was moved to the newly formed United States Department of Health and Human Services where it took on its current role and structure (FDA, 1998).

The FDA has executed over 3,200 food product recalls since 1980, of which about twenty five percent were Class I recalls (recalls on products that pose a reasonable probability of causing serious adverse health consequences or death if eaten). There have also been hundreds of drug recalls resulting in some drugs being removed from the market permanently (United StatesGovernment Accountability Office, 2000). In some cases, when the FDA does not feel that companies with recalled products are responding appropriately or with due urgency, it will send United States Marshals to confiscation products (Weise, 2008).

The National Highway Traffic Safety Administration

The National Highway Traffic Safety Administration (NHTSA) manages safety recalls involving motor vehicles and motor vehicle equipment. Manufacturers can execute a voluntary recall or a recall can be ordered by the NHTSA. There have been thousands of recalls in the last several decades; while some recalls were very serious, the majority involved relatively non-life-threatening defects. The manufacturer is required to file a public report describing the safety-related defect or noncompliance with a federal motor vehicle safety standard. NHTSA monitors every safety recall, and the law requires that manufacturers provide safe, free, and effective remedies. Manufacturers are also required to attempt to notify owners of recalled products (NHTSA, 2009).

Product Recalls & Business Crisis Management

A product recall can be a serious crisis for many businesses, especially smaller to mid-sized companies without in-house legal counsel or other staff that have experience in dealing with recalls. Many advisers suggest immediate and straightforward action and note that an off-the-shelf response plan may not be the answer to the crisis (Dezenhall, 2009).

There are numerous strategies that a company can take. They can be defensive or they can have a problem-solving orientation. They can communicate openly or they can communicate very little or not at all to the public and their customers (Falkheimer & Heide, 2006) (Huang & Su, 2009).

The Peanut Corporation of America Salmonella Scare

The recalls of the last several years created rather serious business crises involving food products. In terms of analyzing a business crisis, these recalls are interesting because the products involved were part of a complex and lengthy supply chain. Fortunately, the supply chain management systems were useful in helping to mitigate damage.

Much to the surprise of many, an American staple, peanut butter, was at the center of one of the largest, most widespread food recalls in history. Because of its use in the production of numerous other food products, the complexity and costs of the recall were multiplied across the industry. Over 2,500 products were recalled and the tainted products resulted in hundreds of illnesses and perhaps several deaths. The products all had ingredients manufactured by the Peanut Corporation of America (PCA) and were tainted with Salmonella typhimurium (Cook, 2009) (Schmit &Weise, 2009).

PCA voluntarily ceased operations in February and soon filed for bankruptcy. A criminal investigation by the United States Justice Department had been filed on January 30. Four years later, in February 2013, four former company officials were indicted on 75 counts including obstruction of justice and introducing adulterated food into interstate commerce (Tavernise, 2013). One of the PCA products, peanut paste, is commonly found in cookies, crackers, cereal, candy, ice cream, and pet treats, among hundreds of other types of food products (Cook, 2009). On February 20, 2009, PCA issued a statement indicating it had filed for Chapter 7 bankruptcy and that it was no longer able to communicate with customers regarding recalled products (FDA, 2009).

Not only was the PCA in a business crisis, but other manufacturers that used PCA products were also thrown into the crisis. In addition, restaurants, school districts, nursing homes, and probably even the military had to deal with examining over 2,500 products and dispose of any that had hit the recall list. Thus the PCA crisis spilled out of the corporation and into the supply chain, into the wholesalers and retailers selling any of the 2,500 products, and down to the home and the mouth of the food consumer.

While the occurrence of situations that pose a threat to a business are somewhat inevitable, the way the situation is handled can mean the difference between a career-ending crisis and future success. As the Salmonella outbreak unfolded, there was a congressional hearing about the contamination and the conduct of PCA. The House subcommittee wanted the president of PCA, Stewart Parnell, and the Blakely, Georgia, plant manager to testify. By refusing to do so, the PCA set a tone of noncompliance and portrayed a lack of concern for the situation. This, in addition to internal emails deemed unfavorable to the PCA, placed the association in a bad position (Schmit, 2009, Feb. 12).

The companies that used peanut products in their manufacturing process started weighing in publicly and quickly. Perry's Ice Cream initiated a voluntary recall of select products containing peanut butter that could have been contaminated with Salmonella. Dreyer's Grand Ice Cream announced that neither the company nor its suppliers bought ingredients from PCA ("Processors respond," 2009). Unilever publicly stated that it did not use PCA products to make Skippy Peanut Butter, Slim-Fast shakes or bars, or its ice-cream products: Breyers, Good Humor, Klondike, Popsicle, and Ben & Jerry's (Angrisani, 2009).

Kellogg's made public that it recalled several snack products that ended up costing the company between $65 and $75 million (Schmit, 2009, Feb. 6). Kellogg's was strongly criticized during the House subcommittee hearings but has stated that it will now do its own audits on those suppliers making products most vulnerable to bacterial contamination. Nestle officials contended that they had chosen not to use PCA products (Weise & Schmit, 2009).

Retailers Dorothy Lane Market and Costco made public that they had removed products from their stores and notified their customers using personal phone calls, letters, and automated calls (Gallagher, 2009). Wegmans Food Markets made public that it had contacted each of its suppliers to determine where ingredients came from and examined its private-label products, removing from shelves those products that were potentially contaminated. United Supermarkets published an online list of food products it removed from shelves (Angrisani, 2009). Food Lion and Walmart moved quickly and publicly discussed their quality control programs and the requirements they set for suppliers for food safety and testing (Garry, 2009).

This sole crisis example illustrates the wide range of responses that companies can assume during a product recall crisis. Retailers were quick to execute a plan and hope that the plan would be viewed positively by their customers. Food producers that used PCA products also moved quickly, but not all of them will escape further scrutiny for not have better quality control procedures in place. PCA, on the other hand, chose to be silent and to fold the company.

ISSUE

Can a Company Really be Prepared for a Business Crisis?

There are three obvious paths that companies can take to plan for a potential business crisis. Each has its benefits and each has its drawbacks. Business managers sometimes consciously choose their path while others sort of muddle through. Some companies do nothing and survive, others do nothing and perish.

Plan Making

Some companies plan and plan. They make plans. Then they make more plans. There are strategic plans, growth plans, marketing plans, business continuity plans, disaster recovery plans, general emergency plans, succession plans, and dozens of others. In many instances those plans serve companies very well—especially when these plans have a strong communication aspect built into them (Cagle, 2006).

One clear criticism of the process of making plans is that once plans are designed, documented, and bound, they often are put upon a shelf, where they age and become outdated. Staff come and go, and many new staff members do not even know the plans exist or where they are kept (Greek, 1998). The old plans may have misinformation and may not address updated legal requirements.

Team Making

Instead of making plans, some companies train and develop staff that can respond to a variety of situations with a consistent corporate philosophy and a coordinated course of action. This requires developing individuals as well as teams. It also requires staff knowledge of the company, the industry in which it exists, and the potential threats within the industry environment. In the PCA contamination case, it was clear that some of the proactive businesses had dealt with recalls and health issues in the past and knew how to mobilize their resources (Angrisani, 2009) (Gallagher, 2009) (Garry, 2009).

Risk Analysis

One method of selecting crisis action guidelines is to perform a sound risk analysis. To do so requires good research, thorough analysis, and above all, realistic and clear thinking. As research is best accomplished when bias is minimized and analysis is best accomplished when the researcher has not yet decided the answer they are seeking, realistic and clear thinking are the elements most necessary in conducting a sound risk analysis (McConnell & Drennan, 2006).

Many of the companies in the supply chain in the PCA case were realistic. They came to grips with the fact that Salmonella was indeed a risk in the food business. The staff in the companies may even have had to respond to contamination situations in the past. The evidence was there for viewing; there had been numerous contamination cases since the early 2000s. In 2005 and 2006, for example, there were four large multistate outbreaks of Salmonella infections resulting from the consumption of raw tomatoes, mostly in restaurants (Bidol et al., 2007). Cases span the last decade with some being localized and others being rather widespread ("Salmonella outbreak," 1999)

CONCLUSION

What type of event or circumstance constitutes a crisis will vary from company to company. What may be routine business operations for some companies may be a serious crisis for others. Both the perception of events and experience in dealing with events influence the evolution of a crisis.

If a crisis is in fact recognized, it is important to mobilize resources promptly in order to effectively control the damage. Necessary resources include experienced staff as well as outside assistance, if necessary. The CEO should be the leading spokesperson for the company when dealing with the media and the public. This shows that the company is serious about its efforts to address the crisis and can remedy any problems that may have caused the crisis.

As the government started regulating industries more strictly and setting standards for products and processes, more companies found themselves in the public spotlight because of product recalls for defects or safety issues. Regulations and standards now cover virtually every consumer product on the market in the United States. The government also works to keep unsafe products from entering ports in the United States, and officials confiscate and destroy millions of pounds of items every year.

The process of planning and preparing for future crisis can be complex and expensive. Planning certainly helps some companies, but plans are often shelved and become outdated and ineffective. Having well- trained staff with experience in crisis management and effective communication skills can help minimize the impact of a wide range of crisis situations.

Bibliography

Angrisani, C. (2009). Recall keeps retailers on alert. *SN: Supermarket News, 57*(6), 28-30. Retrieved April 9, 2009, from EBSCO Online Database Business Source Complete. http://search.ebscohost.com/login.aspx?direct=true&db=bth&AN=36641161&site=ehost-live

Bidol, S., Daly, E., Rickert, R., Hill, T., Al Khaldi, S., Taylor Jr., T., et al. (2007). Multistate outbreaks of salmonella infections associated with raw tomatoes eaten in restaurants — United States, 2005-2006. *MMWR: Morbidity & Mortality Weekly Report, 56*(35), 909-911. Retrieved April 8, 2009, from EBSCO Online Database Academic Search Complete. http://search.ebscohost.com/login.aspx?direct=true&db=a9h&AN=26651983&site=ehost-live

Cagle, J. (2006). Internal communication during a crisis pays dividends. *Communication World, 23*(2), 22-23. Retrieved April 10, 2009, from EBSCO Online Database Business Source Complete. http://search.ebscohost.com/login.aspx?direct=true&db=bth&AN=20203909&site=ehost-live

Cook, G. (2009). Peanut recall causes concern for schools. *American School Board Journal, 196*(4), 6-7. Retrieved April 8, 2009, from EBSCO Online Database Academic Search Complete. http://search.ebscohost.com/login.aspx?direct=true&db=a9h&AN=36911655&site=ehost-live

Dezenhall, E. (2009, March 9). What to do in a product safety crisis. *Business Week Online,* 23. Retrieved April 7, 2009, from EBSCO Online Database Academic Search Complete. http://search.ebscohost.com/login.aspx?direct=true&db=a9h&AN=36928486&site=ehost-live

Falkheimer, J., & Heide, M. (2006). Multicultural crisis communication: Towards a social constructionist perspective. *Journal of Contingencies & Crisis Management, 14*(4), 180-189. Retrieved April 7, 2009, from EBSCO Online Database Academic Search Complete. http://search.ebscohost.com/login.aspx?direct=true&db=a9h&AN=22999736&site=ehost-live

Fletcher, M., & Casale, J. (2009). Peanut firm's GL insurer seeks coverage ruling. *Business Insurance, 43*(6), 3-21. Retrieved April 9, 2009, from EBSCO Online Database Business Source Complete. http://search.ebscohost.com/login.aspx?direct=true&db=bth&AN=36936154&site=ehost-live

Freda, G., Arn, J., & Gatlin-Watts, R. (1999). Adapting to the speed of change. *Industrial Management, 41*(6), 31. Retrieved April 8, 2009, from EBSCO Online Database Business Source Complete. http://search.ebscohost.com/login.aspx?direct=true&db=bth&AN=2772106&site=ehost-live

Gaines-Ross, L. (2009). Damage control. *Leadership Excellence, 26*(3), 8-8. Retrieved April 8, 2009, from EBSCO Online Database Business Source Complete. http://search.ebscohost.com/login.aspx?direct=true&db=bth&AN=36836519&site=ehost-live

Gallagher, J. (2009). Retailers limit tainted peanut butter's spread. *SN: Supermarket News, 57*(5),12. Retrieved April 9, 2009, from EBSCO Online Database Business Source Complete. http://search.ebscohost.com/login.aspx?direct=true&db=bth&AN=36527134&site=ehost-live

Garmhausen, S. (2009). In turmoil, bankers see a chance to woo advisers. *American Banker, 174*(31), 8-9. Retrieved April 8, 2009, from EBSCO Online Database Business Source Complete. http://search.ebscohost.com/login.aspx?direct=true&db=bth&AN=36586711&site=ehost-live

Garry, M. (2009). Vetting the food supply. *SN: Supermarket News, 57*(8), 24-27. Retrieved April 9, 2009, from EBSCO Online Database Business Source Complete. http://search.ebscohost.com/login.aspx?direct=true&db=bth&AN=36821858&site=ehost-live

Gatewood, E., & Carroll, A. (1981). The Proctor and Gamble rely case: A social response pattern for the 1980s? *Academy of Management Proceedings, 369-373.* Retrieved April 8, 2009, from EBSCO Online Database Business Source Complete. http://search.ebscohost.com/login.aspx?direct=true&db=bth&AN=4977126&site=ehost-live

Greek, D. (1998). Taking the drama out of a crisis. *Professional Engineering, 11*(14), 17. Retrieved April 10, 2009, from EBSCO Online Database Academic Search Complete. http://search.ebscohost.com/login.aspx?direct=true&db=a9h&AN=950127&site=ehost-live

Haseley, K. (2004). Twenty tears after Bhopal: What you need to know about managing today's crises. *Chemical Market Reporter, 266*(18), 21-22. Retrieved April 8, 2009, from EBSCO Online Database Business Source Complete. http://search.ebscohost.com/login.aspx?direct=true&db=bth&AN=15206138&site=ehost-live

Huang, Y., & Su, S. (2009). Public relations autonomy, legal dominance, and strategic orientation as predictors of crisis communicative strategies. *Journal of Business Ethics, 86*(1), 29-41. Retrieved April 7, 2009, from EBSCO Online Database Business Source Complete. http://search.ebscohost.com/login.aspx?direct=true&db=bth&AN=37254454&site=ehost-live

Kimes, M. (2009). How do I keep my company's reputation intact when our industry has been tainted by bad news? *Fortune, 159*(5), 30-30. Retrieved April 8, 2009, from EBSCO Online Database Academic Search Complete. http://search.ebscohost.com/login.aspx?direct=true&db=a9h&AN=36868685&site=ehost-live

Ki, E., & Brown, K. A. (2013). The effects of crisis response strategies on relationship quality outcomes. *Journal of Business Communication, 50*(4), 403-420. Retrieved November 15, 2013, from EBSCO Online Database Business Source Complete. http://search.ebscohost.com/login.aspx?direct=true&db=bth&AN=90066173&site=ehost-live

King Jr., N. (2010, June 22). Feinberg ramps up $20 billion compensation fund. *Wall Street Journal,* p. A6. Retrieved November 14, 2013, from EBSCO Online Database Business Source Complete. http://search.ebscohost.com/login.aspx?direct=true&db=bth&AN=52177134&site=ehost-live

Klein, K. (2007, October 18). Planning ahead for crisis management. *Business Week Online,* 21. Retrieved April 7, 2009, from EBSCO Online Database Academic Search Complete. http://search.ebscohost.com/login.aspx?direct=true&db=a9h&AN=27145925&site=ehost-live

Levinson, M. (2009). The economic collapse. *Dissent (00123846), 56*(1), 61-66. Retrieved April 8, 2009, from EBSCO Online Database Academic Search Complete. http://search.ebscohost.com/login.aspx?direct=true&db=a9h&AN=36407227&site=ehost-live

Linsley, P., & Slack, R. (2013). Crisis management and an ethic of care: The case of Northern Rock Bank. *Journal of Business Ethics, 113*(2), 285-295. Retrieved November 15, 2013, from EBSCO Online Database Business Source Complete. http://search.ebscohost.com/login.aspx?direct=true&db=bth&AN=86660160&site=ehost-live

Maddock, G., & Vitn, R. (2009). Don't let a good crisis go to waste. *Business Week Online,* 10. Retrieved April 7, 2009, from EBSCO Online Database Academic Search Complete. http://search.ebscohost.com/login.aspx?direct=true&db=a9h&AN=36845448&site=ehost-live

McConnell, A., & Drennan, L. (2006). Mission impossible? Planning and preparing for crisis. *Journal of Contingencies & Crisis Management, 14*(2), 59-70. Retrieved April 10, 2009, from EBSCO Online Database Academic Search Complete. http://search.ebscohost.com/login.aspx?direct=true&db=a9h&AN=20923936&site=ehost-live

Miller, J. (2006). Damage control. *InsideCounsel, 16*(181), 42-44. Retrieved April 7, 2009, from EBSCO Online Database Business Source Complete. http://search.ebscohost.com/login.aspx?direct=true&db=bth&AN=23498648&site=ehost-live

The National Highway Traffic Safety Administration (NHTSA), Office of Defects Investigation (ODI). (2009). *What is a safety recall?* Retrieved April 8, 2009, from The National Highway Traffic Safety Administration. http://www-odi.nhtsa.dot.gov/recalls/recallproblems.cfm

Processors respond to peanut recall. (2009). *Dairy Foods,* 110(2), 10. Retrieved April 9, 2009, from EBSCO Online Database Business Source Complete. http://search.ebscohost.com/login.aspx?direct=true&db=bth&AN=36950344&site=ehost-live

Salmonella outbreak hits more than 120 students at California's Pomona College. (1999). *Nation's Restaurant News, 33*(31), 21. Retrieved April 8, 2009, from EBSCO Online Database Business Source Complete. http://search.ebscohost.com/login.aspx?direct=true&db=bth&AN=2157400&site=ehost-live

Schmit, J. (2009, February 6). Peanut plant's practices not 'rampant'. *USA Today,* 4b.

Schmit, J. (2009, February 12). Peanut president refuses to testify. *USA Today,* 1b.

Schmit, J., & Weise, E. (2009, January 29). Peanut butter recall grows.*USA Today,* 1b. Tavernise, S. (2013, February 22). Charges filed in peanut salmonella case. *New York Times,* p. B5.

Top managers lack confidence in corporate leadership's plans to counter economic crisis. (2009). *Corporate Board,* 30(175), 28-29. Retrieved April 7, 2009, from EBSCO Online Database Business Source Complete. http://search.ebscohost.com/login.aspx?direct=true&db=bth&AN=36785062&site=ehost-live

United States Consumer Product Safety Commission. (2003). 2003 *Annual report.* Retrieved April 8, 2009, from The U.S. Consumer Product Safety Commission. http://www.cpsc.gov/cpscpub/pubs/reports/2003rpt.pdf

United States Consumer Product Safety Commission. (2009). *CPSC overview.* Retrieved April 8, 2009, from The U.S. Consumer Product Safety Commission. http://www.cpsc.gov/about/about.html

United States Food and Drug Administration. (1998). *History of the FDA*. Retrieved April 8, 2009 from The United States Food and Drug Administration. http://www.fda.gov/oc/history/historyoffda/default.htm

United States Food and Drug Administration. (2009). Peanut product recalls: *Salmonella* typhimurium. Retrieved April 9, 2009, from United States Food and Drug Administration. http://www.fda.gov/oc/opacom/hottopics/salmonellatyph.html

United States Government Accountability Office. (2000). *Food safety: Actions needed by USDA and FDA to ensure that companies promptly carry out recalls.* Retrieved April 8, 2009, from United States Government Accountability Office. http://www.gao.gov/archive/2000/rc00195.pdf

Valvi, A. C., & Fragkos, K. C. (2013). Crisis communication strategies: A case of British Petroleum. *Industrial & Commercial Training, 45*(7), 383-391. Retrieved November 14, 2013, from EBSCO Online Database Business Source Complete. http://search.ebscohost.com/login.aspx?direct=true&db=bth&AN=90609233&site=ehost-live

Verma, A. (2009). Navigating the financial crisis. *Communication World, 26*(1), 4-7. Retrieved April 8, 2009, from EBSCO Online Database Business Source Complete. http://search.ebscohost.com/login.aspx?direct=true&db=bth&AN=36111901&site=ehost-live

Watson, T. (2006, November 2006). Teacher's space goal delayed 21 years. *USA Today*, 6a.

Weinberger, M., & Romeo, J. (1989). The impact of negative product news. *Business Horizons, 32*(1), 44. Retrieved April 8, 2009, from EBSCO Online Database Business Source Complete. http://search.ebscohost.com/login.aspx?direct=true&db=bth&AN=4527528&site=ehost-live

Weise, E. (2008, November 7). FDA sends in federal marshals to seize tainted heparin. *USA Today*, 10b.

Weise, E., & Schmit, J. (2009, March 20). Nestle did its own peanut inspection. *USA Today*, 1b.

SUGGESTED READING

Ethelberg, S., Lisby, M., Torpdahl, M., SÃrensen, G., Neimann, J., Rasmussen, P., et al. (2004). Prolonged restaurant-associated outbreak of multidrug-resistant Salmonella Typhimurium among patients from several European countries. *Clinical Microbiology & Infection, 10(10), 904-910. Retrieved April 8, 2009, from EBSCO Online Database Academic Search Complete. http://search.ebscohost.com/login.aspx?direct=true&db=a9h&AN=14418354&site=ehost-live*

Haohua Yuhang: Finding opportunities in the crisis. (2009). *China Chemical Reporter, 20*(9), 22. Retrieved April 10, 2009, from EBSCO Online Database Academic Search Complete. http://search.ebscohost.com/login.aspx?direct=true&db=a9h&AN=37218616&site=ehost-live

Harugeri, A., Parthasarathi, G., Ramesh, M., Sharma, J., & Padmini Devi, D. (2008, July). Story of heparin recall: What India can do? *Journal of Postgraduate Medicine, 54(3), 222-224. Retrieved April 8, 2009, from EBSCO Online Database Academic Search Complete. http://search.ebscohost.com/login.aspx?direct=true&db=a9h&AN=33293360&site=ehost-live*

Kallenberg, K. (2007). The role of risk in corporate value: A case study of the ABB asbestos litigation. *Journal of Risk Research, 10*(8), 1007-1025. Retrieved April 7, 2009, from EBSCO Online Database Business Source Complete. http://search.ebscohost.com/login.aspx?direct=true&db=bth&AN=27625533&site=ehost-live

Larson, G. (2007). Two courses in crisis management. *Business & Commercial Aviation, 101*(5), 54-57. Retrieved April 7, 2009, from EBSCO Online Database Business Source Complete. http://search.ebscohost.com/login.aspx?direct=true&db=bth&AN=27741069&site=ehost-live

Michael Erbschloe, M.A.

Critical Thinking in the Management of Technology

ABSTRACT

Managing technology requires the ability to think critically. Besides managing technology assets and human resources, managers of technology must guide organizations and staff in identifying problems, designing solutions, evaluation of solutions and solution providers, implementing selected solutions and closely monitoring results at each juncture. Technology managers can augment technical skills by implementing critical thinking strategies. Critical thinking supports solving complex and unstructured problems. Critical thinking strategies are characterized by taking an active approach to planning and executing problem solving. Using critical thinking helps technology managers adapt to the changing demands of the technology itself and the environment that must support it. Critical thinking can be developed and is often developed through experience. Meanwhile, there have been changes in the existing standards for technology education to place emphasis on teaching critical thinking skills. Educational institutions have come to the realization that technology management no longer depends primarily on technical skills but requires other skills that extend beyond simple knowledge. The inability to apply knowledge in a critical and timely fashion can lead to undesirable results in the real world. In other disciplines, there is disagreement as to whether or not critical thinking has a common definition or can be effectively taught.

OVERVIEW

Critical thinking is a way of conducting mental processes in order to "decide what to believe or do" (Schafersman, 1991). Technology managers are likely to have many inputs into decision making. Technical staff, business oriented operational staff and peer managers are just a few of the internal sources of input. Technology vendors, competitors, government regulators and customers are other groups influencing and providing input to technology decisions made by managers. Skillful technology managers must balance competing and critical inputs to decision making. At times there will be the luxury of making decisions and having ample time, resources and information to do so. In other cases, technology management decisions are based on unforseen problems, product, service or system failures and other undesirable events.

The focus of critical thinking is on evaluating successful alternatives for action. Thinking critically is also an automatic filter that can prioritize activity in a changing environment. Critical thinking allows professionals to manage daily challenges by methodically yet creatively solving problems. Penn State University (2004) considers critical thinking an essential competency for students. Penn State's curricular guide defines critical thinking as:

"a term used to refer to those kinds of mental activity that are clear, precise, and purposeful. It is typically associated with solving complex real world problems, generating multiple (or creative) solutions to a problem, drawing inferences, synthesizing and integrating information, distinguishing between fact and opinion, or estimating potential outcomes, but it can also refer to the process of evaluating the quality of one's own thinking."

Technology managers must check their own thinking because of the risk of bias or personal preference influencing decisions. Riddell (2001, p. 121) suggests that critical thinking requires getting away from "programmed ways of thinking." Programmed thinking can come from personal beliefs, experiences, stereotypical thoughts and even assumptions made about the way decisions will be received within an organization or by other key decision-makers. The management of technology may require creative and multiple solutions because outcomes may be difficult or impossible to predict yet return on investment must be assured. Some technology implementations are based on unrealistic timelines or costs due to the problems with predicting results. The world of technology is fraught with the constant trend toward obsolescence with the advent of many new technologies every day that threaten the stability of any current technology infrastructure. Decision making regarding technology standards may be challenging to managers because there are no guarantees the standards will infinitely support organizational goals. It is also a possibility that staying with standards too long will not guarantee a migration path to new or required technology. Decisions that are not in the best interest of an organization may not manifest themselves until later when it is discovered that the decision can become more costly over time.

Many managers and professionals may possess a large amount of knowledge and skill but the application of that skill within the context of a specific problem or scenario is not necessarily automatic. If problems are simple, concise and unchanging, a manager may have little trouble handling the issue or even handing it off to other less experienced personnel. However, in the real world, problems are seldom of scope or nature where simple knowledge alone will facilitate coordination of a solution. In technology, it is quite likely that the problems a manager will face may be beyond the experience of the manager or technical staff no matter the level of experience or training. One such problem is that of interoperability. Managing technology calls for managing different products and solutions from various vendors that may or may not easily operate together without some or even significant customization or adjustment. Once customization patching is done, it may have to be done and updated on a continual basis. Managing these updates may make the solution more costly than the organization can afford.

Technology tends to change quite often for many different reasons. Some technology change is the result of new capabilities being available such as higher capacity storage devices or greater functionality in software. Technology changes can also be due to vendors adopting new standards, merging technologies with other vendors or otherwise changing the direction of research and development. The speed of change in technology is not easy to predict nor is the direction of change. It is very possible that managers of technology may have to manage technology change without having access to internal resources to support these efforts. In this case, managers have to consider how to complete projects using external resources such as consultants and systems integrators or outsourced staff, assets, networks or facilities.

The management of technology involves bringing technical leadership to the mission and purpose of an organization. Managing technology also requires what Hargrove (2001, p.222) calls "block and tackle" managers who remove obstacles and barriers to staff achievement. Technical staff can exhibit creativity but can be thwarted by management's need to adhere to a set agenda, program, direction or timeline. The technical aspects of managing technology can include project planning and can require an understanding of the systems development life cycle. Technical managers also have to understand typical information technology tasks, what makes up these tasks and how long tasks take in order to estimate and allocate project resources.

How to Solve Technology Problems

Management of technology can range from managing information to applying technology to solve a problem or to meet a user or customer need. The process of solving the problems that management of technology indicates may not be a straight line because of the complex nature of most problems. Laudon & Laudon (2007, p. 18) suggest a four step problem solving methodology that starts with problem identification and is followed by solution design, solution evaluation and choice and ends with implementation of the solution.

When managers examine how technology should be managed, careful consideration has to be given to the needs of users and various stakeholder groups while balancing the features and functionality of technology. Because of competing needs and a requirement to balance technology needs versus organizational needs, the ability to conceive different paths and alternatives becomes a necessity. Hence, the opportunities for critical thinking abound.

Types of management problems in technology can include dealing with technical staff issues. One important technical staff issue is ensuring that internal skills are up to date and useful in meeting organizational needs. Technology training for technical staff is expensive and time consuming. Many technical professionals may also spend a considerable amount of personal time and money getting up to speed on new technology. The problem of technology training is not just reserved for technical staff. Increasingly, end users have to upgrade technology skills to be productive and contribute to organizational success. Managers of technology have to grapple with the most efficient and effective means of training end users given that most are at varying levels of initial knowledge. Sometimes, vendors offer training at no cost when major solutions are implemented. Vendor training is often standardized and may exceed the effectiveness of internally developed training as it is deployed more often in many different situations.

Leadership for the front lines (1999) recognized that increasingly non-technical managers may be responsible for using, recommending and managing technology and has several recommendations from technology consultant Barbara E. Miller. One recommendation is for managers to assess personal technology competence. Managers can be hampered by what is unknown but overwhelmed when trying to determine how much depth of knowledge is really necessary.

Another recommendation is to ask important questions about the use of technology and what benefits are provided at a personal, team or departmental level. A critical question involves the use of technology and whether or not staff people are using technology to its greatest benefit. Miller believes that managers need to "understand the dynamics of change" noting that a small percentage of people are able to adapt easily to change while half have some difficulties and a third or more will resist change. Managing technology can also mean that managers foster a certain type of environment that fosters the type of responses needed. Managers can encourage users and technology professionals to engage in continuous learning for personal and organizational benefit (Leadership for the front lines, 1999, para. 6.).

Managers of technology may have to deliver news that is not well received by some in an organization. Some unpopular decisions may be that all users have to participate in training, make changes to certain practices, have limits on certain resources or that certain projects will not be funded. Other decisions, such as outsourcing may affect whether or not technology employees will have a job in the future. While a decision like this may be very popular with senior managers if it reduces cost significantly, it may cause a work slowdown or quick defection by affected employees. Miller also states that new technology requires new standards to inform employees on the effective use of new technology. A great deal of planning is necessary to visualize the impact and to communicate standards. While some issues may arise in attempting to buy in on standards from users, other problems may be avoided by establishing standards as early as possible.

Managing technology may deal with the problem of managing and qualifying information for use as business intelligence to manage operations and solve problems. This eWeek (2007) discusses service problems that plagued JetBlue Airlines when passengers were stranded for hours on a runway. JetBlue's CEO blamed the mishap on faulty business intelligence. Technology allows access to large amounts of data but cannot always guarantee that the right data is available at the right time or if the data is accurate. JetBlue feels that the problem could have been avoided by using accurate business intelligence that would have informed the airline about previous patterns and decisions.

Difficulties in Incorporating Critical Thinking

Critical thinking is defined as "An ability to evaluate information and opinions in a systematic, purposeful, efficient manner" (Cunningham, Cunningham and Saigo, 2002, glossary). While it may sound great to include critical thinking in the arsenal of technology managers, facilitating critical thinking is not a sure science. Riddell (2007, p.124) suggests that critical thinking may be nice to have but the ability to teach it is not supported by research. The author cites a 28 year study of nursing education that did not show a correlation between increased education and an increased ability to utilize critical thinking skills.

Riddell (2007, abstract) notes that there is no single agreed upon definition of critical thinking and discussion of the topic in theoretical terms is much easier and more prevalent than application to the practice of a discipline. Riddell (2007, p. 122) does go on to cite the commonalities in definitions given over 25 years by experts in the field of critical thinking to include:

- Reflection
- Identification and appraisal of assumptions
- Inquiry, interpretation and analysis
- Consideration of context.

Reflection provides the manager of technology an opportunity to step away from assumptions about technology that may be long-held. However, although a manager may be able to address personal long-term beliefs, there is another step in convincing others to also release assumptions. Reflection tends to expose limitations and many in the technology profession enjoy being thought of as very knowledgeable about technology. Reflection may also take time and the cycle of technology delivery is already long for most end users given design issues, compatibility issues, vendor delays, rollout phases and decision-making to include a technology project into a budget.

Identification and appraisal of assumptions made is somewhat like reflection in that it takes time, however, traversing assumptions can provide valuable input prior to launching a technology project. Knowing whether or not assumptions are valid can be helpful in reducing the cost and time associated with a technology project. Organizational influences can affect the objective appraisal of assumptions because most organizations still have a hierarchy and groups and factions can form that hold onto appraisal methods that prefer a specific school of thought. Vendors can be helpful in the identification and appraisal of assumptions by providing a view of what others are doing. Managers need to balance the views of vendors since providing information can be quickly transformed into a sales pitch.

Inquiry, interpretation and analysis can include research and pilot testing. These valuable activities can be limited by a lack of willingness by managers to be thorough or to consider technology alternatives that are unfamiliar. Managers are often cognizant of staying with safe solutions offered by large and familiar companies to avoid trouble should an explanation be needed to justify a decision. In this case, time is again a factor in the level of rigor applied to research and testing. The prevalence of information can lead to almost limitless searching and evaluation of products and approaches. The beginning of the inquiry phase must include guidelines so managers can tailor the search for information and guide the testing without limiting the evaluation.

Managers of technology must always consider the context of the situation in which decisions are made. Context may end up dictating whether a decision is made or how. If the purse strings are controlled by an end user group that values speed over functionality, the best solution in the technology manager's mind may not be selected. End user managers, for example, may value cost over technology standards. A solution may be appropriate because it is inexpensive but doesn't fit into existing information technology standards. A solution may be selected because it is the best available for the money and allows an end user group to perform specific functions that are needed today. Selecting a slightly inferior solution now may be a preferred course of action when weighed against the cost of not having functionality and waiting for it to appear in a more stable technology at an unknown later date.

Management of technology can benefit if managers possess critical thinking skills, however, most technology decisions are not made in a vacuum and exist in the context of other organizational decisions, opinions and assumptions. Along with critical thinking, managers may need to polish persuasive skills to influence and convince others when decision-making is shared.

Viewpoint

Who controls technology management decisions?

In previous years, some may have assumed that the management of technology was best left to technical wizards who excelled in understanding how technology works. As a result, the more technical personnel were obvious choices to consult about or to control technology management decisions. As technology implementation has matured, organizations have realized that a myriad of skills are needed to truly manage the proliferation and implementation of technology solutions. Just what skills are needed is often up for debate. The level of skill in terms of depth and breadth is often challenging and expensive to acquire. A high level of technical skill may not be a guarantee that decisions are also based on business strategy and organizational goals. Dubie & Duffy (2005, p. 41) feel both technology details and business acumen must be emphasized to be successful in today's organizations. The authors state "Even those pursuing the executive ranks should become conversant in technology."

In some circles, technology managers are required to have significant technical backgrounds in order for technical managers to gain and maintain the respect of technical staff. In other scenarios, technical managers may experience management difficulties due to a lack of business, operational or managerial skills. Critical thinking skills can help managers who are weak in a particular area, technical or business, by allowing identification of barriers to decision making.

The ability to think critically may come naturally to some but can also be incorporated into the education that students in a variety of disciplines receive. Greifner (2007) notes that in 2007 the International Society for Technology in Education revised its National Educational Technology Standards to include what students "should know about technology." The Society has six categories of educational standards including: "creativity and innovation; communication and collaboration; research and information retrieval; critical thinking, problem-solving, and decisionmaking; digital citizenship; and technology operations and concepts."

The management of technology requires a creative approach to problem solving. Robbins (2001, p. 134) described a three component model of creativity that merges expertise, creativity skills and task motivation. Success as a manager of technology is found in a balance of these three components. Some may argue that technology skills are most difficult to acquire for those without technology backgrounds, however, managers who excel at talent selection can surround themselves with technical individuals with specific attributes. Task motivation can dictate the skills technology professionals must have. Technical professionals are needed who can easily summarize technology issues and alternatives and who understand how technology meets business objectives. Translating business objectives into technology requirements is also a key skill. Organizations will determine whether or not the background of the individual is valued by the manner in which professionals are promoted or allowed to participate in technology decision making. Promoting from within sends a signal that whether an individual has a technology, business or industry background, the perception is that the skills necessary are available from within. Organizations can also bolster skills by providing ongoing training in management and technology skills for key employees.

Another battleground is departmental control of information technology. An information technology department may select and deploy various solutions or technology assets. But, once those assets are owned by a business unit and technology knowledge begins to proliferate, information technology departments may find that users want to exert greater control over how technology dollars are spent. Creative application of critical thinking skills can help managers navigate control conflicts.

Creativity in Managing Technology

For most managers of technology, the management of technology incorporates the ability to manage multiple competing objectives, high tolerance for controlling and explaining ambiguity, and discovering creative solutions to complex problems as needed. Creativity is "the ability to produce novel and useful ideas" (Robbins, 2001, p. 133-135).

Creativity is needed because managers have to operate at a "speed of light pace" (Leadership for the Front Lines, 1999, para. 1). Some of this pressure is due to the fact that users of technology have become used to an instantaneous response from computer systems and expect 100% uptime and immediate recovery from failures. Spangler (2006) reported on a 2005 Deloitte and Touche survey of information technology professionals which indicated that 12.1% of those polled has "zero tolerance" for downtime or computer outages. Only 7.8% stated that their businesses could operate for 72 hours without technology. Creativity may also mean dealing with situations that have not occurred before.

As the ability to collect data and analyze it has expanded with the speed and power of computing, technology has developed to capture opportunities for using and monetizing it. Technology managers need to remain current on program updates and available alternatives and be able to integrate new applications and systems as part of a continual upgrading process. The very structure of an industry can change rapidly with introduced technologies, necessitating organizational changes that will depend on the critical thinking and visionary capabilities of technology managers and their subordinates (Drnevich & Croson, 2013).

One of the most important areas in which creativity is needed is in managing relationships. Both internal and external relationships have an impact on the ability to assess technology need, acquire appropriate solutions and effectively implement and manage technology. Managers of technology must purchase talent and technology and establish relationships with vendors to have resources available to provide assistance and information when needed. Relationships in the industry can help managers become aware of the availability of scarce talent resources and competitive trends. Strong internal relationships can ensure that support is available for decisions and projects. Some organizations are trending towards using cross functional teams for technology project implementations meaning that a technology department employee may not be the normal makeup of a project team member. Creative management of individuals who are not direct reports requires developing solid relationships with peer-level managers as well as subordinates and superiors.

Creativity in managing technology and more importantly technology problems will likely find managers looking for new ways to apply critical thinking skills to save time and money. Zhen (2005) defines five steps to the process of managing problems including:

- Detection
- Identification
- Determination
- Resolution
- Reflection.

Zhen suggests that new technology is needed to help determine the root cause of information technology problems. According to Zhen, existing UNIX-based tools provide volumes of data that is difficult to search quickly and that do not have the capability to recognize time-stamped data. So while time data is available, the tools cannot incorporate that information automatically into the research process causing manual and slower processing of information. In addition, programming of complex UNIX commands may be required to create a search argument that adequately addresses the information needed. Zhen suggests that the concepts learned and devised in online search engines are the next step to making information technology problem solving more creative and effective. Technology management requires applying all available skills including creative and critical thinking to ensure productivity increases and costs are contained and reduced where possible.

Guillemette & Paré (2012) suggest that business objectives must be "constantly renewed and adjusted" and that the function of IT departments must be aligned with these objectives. This requires clarification on the part of top management as to what exactly is expected from the company's technology assets. How IT can support the strategic mission is a primary challenge for technology managers. A company's agility in the marketplace in the twenty-first century is directly tied to strategic investment in and use of technology (Lu & Ramamurthy, 2011).

Bibliography

Cunningham, B., Cunningham, M. A., & Saigo, B. W. (2002). Environmental science: a global concern, 7/e [Glossary]. McGraw Hill Online Learning Center. Retrieved April 6, 2007, from http://highered.mcgraw-hill.com/sites/0070294267/student%5fview0/glossary%5fa-d.html

Drnevich, P.L., & Croson, D.C. (2013). Information technology and business-level strategy: Toward an integrated theoretical perspective. *MIS Quarterly, 37*(2), 483-509. Retrieved October 31, 2013, from EBSCO Online Database Business Source Complete. http://search.ebscohost.com/login.aspx?direct=true&db=bth&AN=87371536&site=ehost-live

Dubie, D. & Duffy, J. (2005). The best advice I ever got. *Network World, 22*(47), 40-42.

Greifner, L. (2007). Technology standards. *Education Week. In the News Report Roundup, 26*(25).

Guillemette, M.G., & Paré, G. (2012). Toward a new theory of the contribution of the it function in organizations. *MIS Quarterly, 36*(2), 529-551. Retrieved October 31, 2013, from EBSCO Online Database Business Source Complete. http://search.ebscohost.com/login.aspx?direct=true&db=bth&AN=74717006&site=ehost-live

Hargrove, R. (2001). *E-leader: reinventing leadership in a connected economy.* New York, Perseus Books Group.

Laudon, K.C. & Laudon, J.P. (2007). *Essentials of business information systems (7th ed.).* Upper Saddle River, NJ: Pearson Education, Inc.

Lu, Y., & Ramamurthy, K. (2011). Understanding the link between information technology capability and organizational agility: An empirical examination. *MIS Quarterly, 35*(4), 931-954. Retrieved October 31, 2013, from EBSCO Online Database Business Source Complete. http://search.ebscohost.com/login.aspx?direct=true&db=bth&AN=67129445&site=ehost-live

Master high tech communication tools. (1999, July 15). *Leadership for the Front Lines,* p7. Retrieved March 25, 2007, from EBSCO Online Database Business Source Premier. http://search.ebscohost.com/login.aspx?direct=true&db=buh&AN=6332572&site=bsi-live

Penn State University. (2004). Guide to Curricular Procedures [Glossary]. Retrieved March 24, 2004, from http://www.senate.psu.edu/curriculum%5fresources/guide/glossary.html.

Riddell MScN, RN, T. (2007). Critical assumptions: thinking critically about critical thinking. *Journal of Nursing Education, 46*(3),121-125.

Robbins, S. A. (2001). *Organizational Behavior (9th ed.).* Upper Saddle River, NJ: Prentice Hall, Inc.

Schafersman, S.D. (1991). An introduction to critical thinking. [Paper]. Retrieved March 24, 2007, from http://www.freeinquiry.com/critical-thinking.html.

Spangler, T. (2006). Out of scope: Tales from the tech front. *Baseline*, (57), 88. Retrieved April 6, 2007, from EBSCO Online Database Business Source Premier. http://search.ebscohost.com/login.aspx?direct=true&db=bth&AN=20432610&site=ehost-live

This eWeek. (2007). *eWeek, 24*(7), 5. Retrieved April 6, 2007 from EBSCO Online Database Business Source Premier. http://search.ebscohost.com/login.aspx?direct=true&db=bth&AN=24447471&site=ehost-live

Zhen, J. (2005). Searching for a root cause. *Computerworld, 39*(45), 36.

SUGGESTED READING

Brookfield, S. (1987). *Developingcritical* thinkers*: Challenging adults to explore alternative ways of thinking and acting.* San Francisco: Jossey-Bass.

Mesirow, J. (1991). *Transformative dimensions of adult learning.* San Francisco: Jossey-Bass.

Paul, R. (2004). *A draft statement of principles.* National Council for Excellence in Critical Thinking Web Site http://www.criticalthinking.org/about/nationalCouncil.shtml#DRAFT.

Marlanda English, Ph. D.

Decision Making

ABSTRACT

This article discusses decision-making in a business environment. While leaders are ultimately responsible for business decisions, problem-solving is a shared responsibility among top managers who make strategic decisions, middle managers who make tactical decisions and lower level managers who make operational decisions. By having accurate information, decisions are more likely to be based on facts, sound reasoning and intelligence. This article will provide an overview of decision making and includes a discussion of factors that lead to good business decisions.

OVERVIEW

Leadership & Decision Making

One of the earmarks of an effective leader is someone who makes decisions while motivating people to implement them. He or she must learn to communicate and deal with high and low-performing workers and bring out the best in both employees and managers while demonstrating authority and creativity. While leaders have different decision-making styles, a leader needs to choose the right people to participate in the decision-making process and there are some basics steps they must follow.

Leaders need to spot and solve problems while seeking opportunities to move the company forward. In order to do so, accurate information needs to be obtained, and a number of alternatives need to be developed and evaluated for strengths and weaknesses. Decisions are made after developing a number of ideas, debating a variety of options and encouraging an exchange of opinions in order to find the best course of action (Garvin, 2001).

While leaders are ultimately responsible for making business decisions, problem-solving is a shared responsibility among people at different levels in a company. Further, there are different types of decision-making responsibilities and these include strategic decisions, tactical decisions and operational decisions.

Strategic Decisions

Top managers are often responsible for making strategic decisions or decisions that concern the long-term goals of the company. For example, a company might decide to develop new products or focus its efforts on increasing the volume of an existing product. Strategic decisions establish company policy and these decisions are often complicated because the future is uncertain and accurate information is often limited. In these cases, managers must rely on their past experiences as well as their instincts (Janczak, 2005).

There are four techniques available to senior managers. They must be able to generate conflict that needs to be resolved; employees should be encouraged to question existing assumptions; the work environment should be one that encourages learning, and finally, managers need to be able to distinguish between available resources and services and customer needs (Young, 2005).

Tactical Decisions

Once a company's goals and policies are established by senior management, tactical decisions aimed at achieving a company's goals and implementing company policy need to be made. Such decisions are usually made by middle managers and require managers to focus on specific actions that will bring about the company's objectives. For example, a mid-level manager might devise a plan to provide employees with incentives in order to increase production. This requires mangers to have accurate information so that their decisions are based on facts (Abukari, 2003).

Operational Decisions

Lastly, decisions regarding the day-to-day functions of a business also need to be made. These decisions are considered operational decisions and they are subordinate to strategic and tactical decisions. While these decisions are the responsibility of low-level managers, good decision making is crucial here since such decisions focus on productivity, quality control and employee performance. Moreover, operational decisions can be broken down into:

- Short term planning needs like ordering supplies, establishing work priorities and enlisting temporary help.
- Medium term planning like hiring and firing personnel, purchasing equipment, training individuals and modifying procedures.
- Long term planning like replacing subcontractors, redesigning production facilities and modifying capacity (Copeland, 1986).

Importance of Debate & Open Exchange of Ideas

Although decision-making and problem solving occurs at different levels of a company, leaders are ultimately responsible for every business decision and this requires a leader to have an understanding of strategic, tactical and operational decisions. Further, decision making rests not only on what decisions are made, but who makes them and how they are made. Business decisions often require an inquiry process, developing and debating a number of ideas in order to find the best course of action. This approach to decision making is a test of strength among competing ideas (Garvin, 2001).

In order to encourage debate and a free exchange of ideas, a leader needs to have a high level of emotional intelligence so that he or she can manage conflict that invariably arises in such an environment. Some leaders have a tendency to make decisions that are not based on sound reasoning while other decision makers can be rigid in their dealings with other people. However, leaders that exercise emotional intelligence can motivate people to be creative and to realize a vision (Batool, 2013). In the end, a decision-making process that relies on debating a number of ideas should strive for a balance and a number of factors.

Successful leaders are flexible and open to the ideas of others, but also adhere to a set of core values — essentially an internal determination regarding what a company's goals and aspirations are and how they plan to achieve them. At the same time, decisions must be made with an awareness of the outside world — leaders and managers must be capable of knowing what the truth is outside of the organization. This means understanding what factors are affecting the market. Understanding these factors will allow for good strategic decisions. Further, decision makers need to understand how that market is changing and to what extent the business can contribute to those changes. Such an understanding will lend itself to good tactical decisions. Finally, everyone involved in the decision-making process must understand what the company needs to do in order to be successful in that market as this will result in effective operational decisions (Unseem, 2005).

In the end, all levels of decision-making — strategic, tactical and operational, require access to accurate information. By having accurate information, leaders and managers will be better equipped to make decisions that are based on facts, sound reasoning and intelligence. This information can also be thought of as business intelligence. Effectively employing business intelligence will enable leaders to provide managers with the right information at the right time. Having the right information will ensure that decisions will be based on facts and allow for decisions to be made more quickly. Moreover, because business intelligence relies on factual information, it encourages a rational approach to management (Abukari, 2003).

APPLICATIONS

Importance of Business Intelligence

Most businesses exist to provide goods and services to their customers and this requires decisions on how to deliver those goods, pricing, the handling of unsatisfied customers, and how to treat repeat or high volume customers (Rhode, 2005). Such decisions require "mission critical business intelligence" and there are technologies that enable businesses to understand "customer buying behaviors and preferences," "product pricing and promotion" and "product assortment." By evaluating this information, a business is better able to make operational decisions (Ross, 2007, p. 25).

Information Gathering

Not only is having access to business intelligence critical for operational decisions, such information also plays a role in strategic and tactical decisions. Supporting such decisions means "gathering actionable information on the competitive environment" (Heath, 1996, p. 52). This type of information has been termed "competitive intelligence" of which there are basically two sources — traditional and nontraditional. Traditional sources of intelligence refer to published material such as newspapers, magazines, government and court documents and company reports, while nontraditional sources include interviews with employees, suppliers, distributors and customers. Having access to this kind of business intelligence will prove valuable as a company makes strategic decisions like whether to enter into a new market. Competitive intelligence will also facilitate tactical decisions regarding how to enter a new market — such as by forming an alliance or merging with a company that already exists in a particular business sector (Heath, 1996).

Manager Instinct

Armed with this information, a successful leader will encourage managers to participate in the decision-making process by debating ideas; however, he or she must also exercise leadership by making the final decision and ensuring that decision is fully understood by employees. Moreover, the final decision must be implemented as soon as possible. Some managers stress intuition and believe they can rely on 'gut instincts' when faced with the necessity for a speedy decision. Some business consultants agree, saying that decision-making is really all about trusting one's intuition (Drury, 2005).

While wisdom may stem from experience, there are many who believe that innovation and invention require a person to be highly intelligent, intellectually and emotionally, and these abilities are not necessarily a matter of experience. Further, decisions are sometimes required in the face of incomplete information. Many managers are able to rely on a minimum amount of information when making decisions in a timely manner. A leader is one who can sense and articulate the aspirations of people and empower them to take action. Even though there are technologies that allow for more timely data analysis, a leader's gut instinct might require a decision that relies on his or her vision more than any technical analysis (Drury, 2005).

Technology Use

In contrast, evaluating more options in less time requires decisions to be based on reason, and relying on gut instincts may lead to unsuccessful outcomes. As situations become more complex, relying on intuition does not lend itself to good decision making since individuals are really basing their decisions on preconceived notions about past events. Technological advances have increased the amount of accessible information and decreased the amount of time available in the decision-making process. At the same time, technology also provides the means to process information more quickly. Today, computer programs are being developed to enhance pre-existing decision-making tools that have been utilized by business people such as system dynamics and decision trees (Bonabeau, 2003).

System dynamics is a way of studying and managing complex feedback systems. This is a method that identifies a problem, explains the cause of the problem, builds a computer model that reproduces those causes, considers alternative ways to solve the problem and finally implements a solution. A decision tree is a tool used when there are choices between several courses of action. Decision trees consider a variety of options and the possible outcomes of choosing those options. They also form a balanced picture of the risks and rewards associated with each possible course of action. In short, these analytical methods assist business people with quickly processing large amounts of information so that the facts about a given situation can be accurately determined. With these facts at their disposal, and after the issues have been thoroughly debated, managers and leaders are in a better position to make good decisions (Bonabeau, 2003).

While there are numerous methods and technologies for analyzing information and a myriad of solutions that can be applied to strategic planning, good decisions ultimately rest on a leader's emotional intelligence and vision. A leader must also be able to make rational decisions and communicate his or her vision and the reason for decisions to all levels of management. In some organizations, however, senior managers often make decisions themselves and then try to persuade people to buy into those decisions. According to Unseem, that approach precludes options and ideas that management may not have even considered. At the same time, all participants need to take responsibility for their involvement in the process. While a leader needs to choose the right people to fulfill managerial roles, it is the leader's job to communicate effectively with the managers. In the end, the role of all employees in a business organization is to represent the company as well as to work together to ensure the business' success. Having the right people engage in an exchange of ideas creates an environment where information flows freely and success is more likely (Unseem, 2005).

VIEWPOINTS

Technological Advancements & Decision Making

The amount of information that people can access has expanded dramatically because of technological advances. In light of these developments, managers and leaders have more choices and data at their disposal, but less time to make decisions.

Communication

As the Internet evolved, many businesses developed their own internal Internets, known as *Intranets*, and these innovations have enabled employees to become more involved in the decision-making process. Moreover, other Internet-based technologies are being deployed on Intranet systems. Currently, the development of social software like web logs (blogs) and podcasting enables people to communicate and exchange information easily. A blog is a web-based journal written by one or more people. For example, CEOs are using blogs to communicate with the rank and file as well as for different groups in the organization to share their accomplishments. A podcast is an audio file that can be used for broadcasting executive speeches throughout the company. Finally, most businesses today have internal e-mail and instant messaging capabilities that allow people to readily share information (Holtz, 2005). Businesses are also starting to utilize popular social media portals such as YouTube, Facebook, and Twitter to enhance workplace communications (Koster, 2012).

Further, having alternative means of communication can lend itself to creating a constructive environment for engaging in critical debate. But the use of e-mail, Intranets, and social media creates a whole other layer of policies as to their proper use. A wrongly-placed or used word in an e-mail can lead to misunderstandings and even legal action and companies must be aware at all times of those implications (Lieber, 2011).

Use of Consultants

Although technological advances can enable people to process and analyze more information quickly, people-not machines or software programs-ultimately make decisions. There are many factors beyond the technical analysis of data that affect these decisions, such as the managerial and decision-making style of a leader, the interpersonal skills of the staff, as well as the corporate culture in general. According to Sargeant, technology does not allow a company to make determinations about the group dynamic and so objective opinions of managerial consultants are needed. To be effective, consultants need to understand the business and be comfortable addressing a variety of issues such as leadership, finance and organization. Further, consultants can be useful if they are called upon to make assessments in a short time period and assist managers and leaders with communicating the goals of the company to those involved in the decision-making process, getting those individuals to cooperate and also enlisting the cooperation of other divisions within the company (Sargeant, 2005).

The fact that leaders are ultimately responsible for making decisions means that they must often make strategic decisions and then delegate tactical and operational decisions to the right managers. Further, leaders must ensure that middle and low level managers have access to sufficient information as well as the technological assets to analyze that information. In the final analysis, a successful business consists of successful people, and so it is reasonable to expect them to work towards implementing a leader's final decision. However, emotions often become a factor in decision making. To be successful, a leader must be able to manage his or her emotions and also recognize the emotions of others. This skill allows a leader to encourage people to work towards implementing strategic decisions. A leader also needs to be an effective communicator and open to new ideas and different views, especially concerning tactical and operational decisions. One way to accomplish this is by asking questions, pushing employees for more in-depth explanations and in the end, explaining the rationale for the final decision (Garvin, 2004).

There are a number of ways a business can improve its decision-making processes. Whether they rely on advanced technology or the advice of independent consultants, successful decisions really require businesses to establish a set of core values. Doing so will allow an organization to attract employees and customers who are aligned with those values.

BIBLIOGRAPHY

Batool, B. (2013). Emotional intelligence and effective leadership. *Journal Of Business Studies Quarterly, 4*(3), 84-94. Retrieved on November 13, 2013, from EBSCO Online Database Business Source Complete. http://search.ebscohost.com/login.aspx?direct=true&db=bth&AN=86874024&site=ehost-live

Bonaneau, E. (2003). Don't trust your gut. *Harvard Business Review, 81*(5), 116-123. Retrieved January 29, 2007, from EBSCO Online Database Business Source Premier. http://search.ebscohost.com/login.aspx?direct=true&db=buh&AN=9721855&site=ehost-live

Copeland, R., & Globerson, S. (1986). Improving operational performance in service industries. *Industrial Management, 28*(4), 23. Retrieved April 10, 2007, from EBSCO Online Database Business Source Complete. http://search.ebscohost.com/login.aspx?direct=true&db=bth&AN=4983608&site=ehost-live

Cryer, B. (2005). Listen to the heart. *Leadership Excellence, 22*(9), 20. Retrieved January 29, 2007, from EBSCO Online Database Business Source Premier. http://search.ebscohost.com/login.aspx?direct=true&db=buh&AN=18419354&site=ehost-live

Drury, M.L. & Kitsopoulos, S.C. (2005). Do you believe in the seven deadly myths? *Consulting to Management, 16*(1), 28-31. Retrieved February 1, 2007, from EBSCO Online Database Business Source Premier. http://search.ebscohost.com/login.aspx?direct=true&db=buh&AN=16308648&site=ehost-live

Garvin, D. & Roberto, M.A. (2001). What you don't know about making decisions. *Harvard Business Review, 79*(8), 108-116. Retrieved January 29, 2007, from EBSCO Online Database Business Source Premier. http://search.ebscohost.com/login.aspx?direct=true&db=buh&AN=5134704&site=ehost-live

Heath, R.P. (1996). Competitive intelligence. *Marketing Tools, 3*(5), 52-59. Retrieved April 10, 2007, from EBSCO Online Database Business Source Complete. http://search.ebscohost.com/login.aspx?direct=true&db=bth&AN=9607180715&site=ehost-live

Holtz, S. (2005). The impact of new technologies on internal communication. *Strategic Communication Management, 10*(1), 22-25. Retrieved January 29, 2007, from EBSCO Online Database Business Source Premier. http://search.ebscohost.com/login.aspx?direct=true&db=buh&AN=19299476&site=ehost-live

Janczak, S. (2005). The strategic decision-making process in organizations. *Problems & Perspectives in Management, 2005*(3), 58-70. Retrieved April 10, 2007, from EBSCO Online Database Business Source Premier. http://search.ebscohost.com/login.aspx?direct=true&db=buh&AN=18427082&site=ehost-live

Koster, K. (2012). Social media tools gain acceptance. *Employee Benefit News, 26*(12), 14. Retrieved on November 13, 2013, from EBSCO Online Database Business Source Complete. http://search.ebscohost.com/login.aspx?direct=true&db=bth&AN=82030092&site=ehost-live

Lieber, L. D. (2011). Social media in the workplace-Proactive protections for employers. *Employment Relations Today (Wiley), 38*(3), 93-101. Retrieved on November 13, 2013, from EBSCO Online Database Business Source Complete. http://search.ebscohost.com/login.aspx?direct=true&db=bth&AN=66694755&site=ehost-live

Rhode, F. (2005). Little decisions add up. *Harvard Business Review, 83*(6) 24-26. Retrieved on February 28, 2007, from EBSCO Online Database Business Source Premier. http://search.ebscohost.com/login.aspx?direct=true&db=buh&AN=17276331&site=ehost-live

Ross, D. (2007). What is BI and what do we do with it? *Retail Merchandiser, 47*(3), 25. Retrieved April 10, 2007, from EBSCO Online Database Business Source Complete. http://search.ebscohost.com/login.aspx?direct=true&db=bth&AN=24415530&site=ehost-live

Seargeant, J.R. (2005). Saving troubled companies. *Consulting to management, 16*(1), 21-24. Retrieved February 1, 2007, from EBSCO Online Database Business Source Premier. http://search.ebscohost.com/login.aspx?direct=true&db=buh&AN=16308642&site=ehost-live

Unseem, J. (2005). Jim Collins on tough calls. *Fortune, 151*(13), 89-94. Retrieved January 29, 2007, from EBSCO Online Database Business Source Premier. http://search.ebscohost.com/login.aspx?direct=true&db=buh&AN=17328693&site=ehost-live

Young, D. (2005). Strategic decision making: It's time for healthcare organizations to get serious. *Healthcare Financial Management, 59*(11), 86-92. Retrieved April 10, 2007, from EBSCO Online Database Business Source Premier. http://search.ebscohost.com/login.aspx?direct=true&db=buh&AN=19773949&site=ehost-live

Suggested Reading

Connelly, S., Helton-Faith, W. & Mumford, M.D. (2004). A managerial in basket study of the impact of trait emotions on ethical choice. *Journal of Business Ethics, 51*(3), 245-267. Retrieved January 29, 2007, from EBSCO Online Database Business Source Premier. http://search.ebscohost.com/login.aspx?direct=true&db=buh&AN=14106986&site=ehost-live

Pech, R. & Durden, G. (2004). Where the decision makers went wrong: From capitalism to cannibalism. *Corporate Governance: The International Journal of Effective Board Performance, 4*(1), 65-75. Retrieved on January 29, 2007, from EBSCO Online Database Business Source Premier. http://search.ebscohost.com/login.aspx?direct=true&db=buh&AN=20037815&site=ehost-live

Sayegha, L., Anthony, W. & Perrewe, P. (2004). Managerial decision making under crisis: The role of emotion in an intuitive decision process. *Human Resource Management Review, 14*(2), 179-2000. Retrieved January 29, 2007, from EBSCO Online Database Business Source Premier. http://search.ebscohost.com/login.aspx?direct=true&db=buh&AN=13941126&site=ehost-live

Richa S. Tiwary, Ph.D., M.L.S.

Decision Making Under Uncertainty

ABSTRACT

Every day, managers make decisions that affect the profitability, effectiveness, and viability of the organization. Sometimes the factors affecting the predictability of events can be determined. However, not all variables affecting outcomes are neatly predictable. Decisions made under uncertainty are decisions for which there is no meaningful probability distribution underlying the various outcomes. In these situations, the decision maker simply does not know what will happen for the various decision alternatives. There are several approaches to decision making under conditions of uncertainty, including application of the Bayes' Decision Rule, Markov processes, and gaming. In the end, however, virtually every decision requires judgment. Knowledge of stochastic processes alone are insufficient to guide decision making.

OVERVIEW

Every day, managers make decisions that affect the profitability, effectiveness, and viability of the organization. Although in some of these cases the parameters are known (e.g., if Harvey gives a raise to the production workers, there will not be enough money left over to buy parts to make widgets), in other cases they are not known (e.g., if Harvey does not give the production workers a raise, he does not know whether or not they will stay and continue to make widgets). Similarly, many of the decisions facing managers are complex (e.g., Harvey can ask the workers to postpone getting a raise and continue to make widgets while the company tries a new marketing strategy; if the workers do not continue to make widgets, the company cannot afford the new marketing campaign. However, there is no way to predict with 100 percent accuracy whether or not the campaign will be successful enough to bring in the added revenue to enable the company to give the workers a raise).

Factors Affecting the Predictability of Events

Trends, Business Cycles & Seasonal Fluctuations

Sometimes the factors affecting the predictability of events can be determined. These deterministic variables are those for which there are specific causes or determiners and include trends, business cycles, and seasonal fluctuations. Trends are persistent, underlying directions in which a factor or characteristic is moving in either the short, intermediate, or long term. In most cases, trends are linear rather than cyclic; growing or shrinking steadily over a period of years. For example, the increasing tendency for business to outsource and offshore technical support and customer service in many high tech companies over the past few years is a trend. However, not all trends are linear. Trends in new industries tend to be curvilinear as the demand for the new product or service grows after its introduction and then declines after the product or service becomes integrated into the economy. Another type of deterministic factor is business cycles. These are continually recurring variations in total economic activity. Business cycles usually occur across most sectors of the economy at the same time. For example, it has been noted that several years of a boom economy with expansion of economic activity (e.g., more jobs, higher sales) are often followed by slower growth or even contraction of economic activity. Business cycles may occur across one industry, a business sector, or even the economy in general. A third type of deterministic factor is seasonal fluctuations. These changes in economic activity occur in a fairly regular annual pattern and are related to seasons of the year, the calendar, or holidays. For example, office supply stores typically experience an upsurge in business in August as children receive their school supply lists for the coming year. Similarly, the demand for heating oil is typically greater during the cool months than it is in the warm months.

Stochastic Variables

However, not all variables affecting outcomes are so neatly predictable. Stochastic variables are caused by randomness or include an element of chance or probability. These include both irregular and random fluctuations in the economy that occur due to unpredictable factors. For example, a natural disaster such as an earthquake or flood, political disturbance such as war or flu epidemic that causes high absenteeism is often unpredictable and can affect a business' profitability. In conditions of uncertainty, there is no meaningful probability distribution for the various outcomes. In these situations, the decision maker does not know what will happen for the various decision alternatives.

Conflicting Interests in Decision Making

Another factor complicating real world decision making processes is the fact that there is often more than one party to the decision and the parties may have conflicting interests. In fact, systems theory posits that the organization comprises multiple subsystems and that the functioning of each affects both the functioning of the others and the organization as a whole. So, for example, in the illustration above concerning giving raises to the workers during a time of flux, there are at least two major parties to the decision. From the workers' point-of-view, getting a raise now is better than maybe getting a raise later. Their raise or lack thereof, in turn, affects other parties not directly in the discussion such as their families (e.g., if there is no raise, the family cannot pay for Johnny's tuition) and their creditors (e.g., if there is no raise, the family cannot meet the increased payment on their adjustable rate mortgage). Management, of course, has a different point-of-view. If they give the workers a raise now, they will not have sufficient funds available for the new marketing campaign that will bring in more revenue. Without the additional revenue, they will have to lay off some of the workers, which means that they will not be able to meet an increased demand for widgets even if they do launch the new marketing campaign. They could take money to pay the production workers from the monies set aside for raises for new product development, but then they would not be able to gain a competitive edge over the companies offering similar items in the marketplace. In addition, management needs to report to its stockholders, and increased wages may mean decreased profits.

Categories of Decisions to be Made

Certainty & Uncertainty

The decisions facing managers in the business world can be classified into several categories: decisions made under certainty or uncertainty, under risk, or under conflict. A decision made under certainty occurs when all the facts of the situation are known and the model provides the decision maker with the exact consequences of choosing each alternative. This knowledge, however, does not mean that the decision is either obvious or trivial. There may be many possible courses of actions that can be taken, each with different consequences, and the decision maker needs to consider the advantages and disadvantages of each and weigh them against each other. Decisions made under uncertainty, on the other hand, are decisions for which there is no meaningful probability distribution underlying the various outcomes. In these situations, the decision maker simply does not know what will happen for the various decision alternatives.

Multiple Criteria Decision Making

Multiple criteria decision making is a discipline that deals with the problem of making decisions in complex situations where there are conflicting objectives. Multiple criteria decision making is founded on two interrelated, key concepts. Satisficing is the attempt to find solutions that satisfy all the constraints rather than optimizing them. For example, the workers may be given a raise, but only in six months after the new marketing campaign goes into effect. This would still give them a raise, but would also give the company an opportunity to get back on its feet. From the workers' point-of-view, the optimal situation would be to get raise now. From management's point-of-view, the optimal situation would be to keep wages low so that there are more profits. Neither one of these situations is optimized in this solution, but the constraints of both are satisfied. The second key concept of multiple criteria decision making is bounded rationality. This process involves setting the constraints of the situation and then attempting to find solutions that satisfy the constraints. This is an iterative process in which the constraints are adjusted as necessary and the search for solutions is continued until a satisfactory solution is found. For example, the workers at Widget Corporation may be willing to postpone getting a raise only if the raise that they get in six months is greater than the one that they would accept today.

Methods for Solving Multiple Criteria Decision Making Problems

As shown in Table 1, there are a number of methods available for solving multiple criteria decision making problems. Deterministic decision analysis is used to find the most preferred alternative in the decision space using value functions. Stochastic decision analysis does the same thing, but uses utility functions and stochastic outcomes. In the stochastic approach, both the utility function and the probability of the various outcomes are estimated by the decision maker. The multi-objective mathematical programming approach includes both multi-objective linear programming and multi-objective integer programming.

Decision Outcomes	Decision Space	
	Explicit	Implicit
Deterministic	Deterministic multiattribute decision analysis	Deterministic multiobjective mathematical programming
Stochastic	Stochastic multiattribute decision analysis	Stochastic multiobjective mathematical programming

Table 1: Taxonomy of Multiple Criteria Decision Making Approaches
(From Ramesh & Zionts, p. 539)

Decision Theory

Decision theory is a body of knowledge and related analytical techniques designed to give decision maker information about a situation or system and the consequences of alternative actions in order to help him/her choose among the set of alternatives. One tool often useful in decision making is modeling building. Models are representations of a situation, system, or subsystem. Conceptual models are mental images that describe the situation or system. This type of model is the first step in creating mathematical or computer models that represent the situation or system using one or a series of mathematical equations. The development of models that accurately represents the real world is typically an iterative process. Models must usually be tested and refined until they represent the real world to the degree desired by the analyst or decision maker. Initially, conceptual models tend to be broad or general representations without much detail but which span the range of variables to be considered. However, the initial model helps the analyst better understand the situation or system under consideration and to refine the representation of the real world. As the model is analyzed and the situation is better understood, the model can be refined to better reflect the underlying reality.

APPLICATIONS

Approaches for Decision Making Under Uncertainty

Bayes' Decision Rule

There are several approaches to decision making under conditions of uncertainty. One of these is the application of Bayes' Decision Rule. This is a decision making strategy in which one chooses the option with the largest expected payoff. This is determined by multiplying the consequences of each act by the probability of the several occurrences and then adding the products together. Decision models in these situations are characterized by several basic elements. First, there is a set of options from which the decision maker may choose as well as a set of consequences that may occur as a result of a given decision. In addition, Bayes' Decision Rule assumes that there is an underlying probability distribution that can be used to quantify the decision maker's beliefs about the relationship between the various choices and resultant consequences. Further, this approach involves a utility function that quantifies the decision maker's preferences among the various consequences.

Markov Processes

Another frequently used approach in this type of situation is the application of Markov processes. These are stochastic processes in which the probabilities of future events are completely determined by the current state of the process. So, for example, if one knows the current state of the process, no additional insight can be gained from previous states of the process. A Markov chain is a random process comprising discrete events in which the future development of each event is either independent of past events or dependent only on the immediately preceding event. Markov chains are often used in marketing, for example, to model subsequent purchases of products (i.e., the probability of the customer making a purchase from a particular business or brand is dependent only on his/her last purchase of that brand or independent of the brand).

Gaming

A third approach to decision making under uncertainty is the application of gaming to real world problems. Gaming is an activity in which two or more independent parties attempt to achieve objectives within a limiting context. In business, gaming involves the use of mathematics in determining optimal strategies and making the best possible decisions in context. Gaming, however, is a controversial approach to decision making, and is typically more art than science. However, it is possible to gain insights into a real world situation by designing, playing, or analyzing a game. Game design is a multi-stage process. First, one sets the objectives for the game and defines the parameters in which the game will be played. Once these constraints are articulated, a conceptual model is developed and decisions are made as to how best to represent it. The game is then constructed and refined. As opposed to other methods for making decisions under conditions of uncertainty, gaming is not a solution method nor does it lead to a forecast, solution, or prediction. However, a game does help the decision maker to better understand the situation about which a decision needs to be made, including its constraints, consequences, and greater ramifications.

Compromises in Decision Making

From a scientific point-of-view, it would be comforting to be able to collect data, build a mathematical model or perform a statistical analysis, and be given a number that could be looked up in a table to tell one whether to choose Option A or Option B. Unfortunately, real world decisions are not so simple. As discussed above, real world decisions often are made in situations where it is impossible to predict or even know all the parameters that affect the decision. Further, real world decisions are more complicated than decisions made in a laboratory setting because even in those few situations where there is only one decision maker in a business setting, a decision can ripple throughout the organization and its stakeholders. A decision that results in an optimal situation for one stakeholder may be disastrous for another stakeholder. Frequently, there is no best answer and the decision must be made as a series of compromises. In addition, it must be remembered that the interpretation of data analysis as, indeed, the very data themselves, are subject to the skill and qualitative assessment of the decision maker or analyst. In addition, it has been argued that the probabilistic and value-related factors of Bayesian methods imply a degree of precision that is impossible to obtain in the real world. As a result, the conclusions drawn on this methodology are too precise to be given much credence. Others have argued against the presumption of normalcy underlying Bayes' rule.

Forecasting for Business Decisions

Opinion about the best way to forecast for business decisions can be sharply divided between those that rely on statistical methodology and those that prefer to use their "gut" to determine where the industry, supply chain, or market is going. Both approaches have advantages and disadvantages, however. Statistical methods can be less prone to bias than are judgments. In addition, statistical methods tend to be more reliable and can more efficiently make use of historical data. On the other hand, statistical techniques can only work with the data they are given. Judgmental decision making can be useful particularly when there are recent events about which the decision maker is aware but which have not yet had sufficient time to result in observable data for analysis. There are, however, risks inherent in decisions that are made purely on subjective criteria. Human error can make the analyst or manager more optimistic (or pessimistic) than actually warranted, trends or factors may be read into the data that are not actually there, or the effects of correlated variables may not be taken into account.

The Importance of Judgment

In the end, virtually every decision requires judgment. First, judgment is key to determining which data are relevant to the model or game or that is considered in the analysis. Potential variables affecting decisions in the real world are virtually limitless. However, no statistical model or analysis can take all variables into account. Even if it could, spurious positive results would be seen due to the effects of probability alone. Therefore, it is essential that expert judgments be used to reduce the inputs into the process. Judgment is also important in decision making because different analytic techniques can yield different results. It is the judgment of the analyst that determines which technique is most appropriate to analyze the data. The worth of the end result of the analysis depends heavily on correctly choosing the most appropriate analytical method. Finally, expert judgments can be essential to help the analyst understand the situation and give insight into the parameters through which the data and subsequent analysis should be interpreted. Statistical processes alone are insufficient to guide decision making.

Bibliography

Armstrong, J. S. (2001). Forecasting. In S. I. Gass, & C. M. Harris (eds.), *Encyclopedia of operations research and management science* (pp. 304-310). New York: Wiley. Retrieved July 18, 2007, from EBSCO Online Database Business Source Complete. http://search.ebscohost.com/login.aspx?direct=true&db=bth&AN=21891406&site=ehost-live

Armstrong, J. S., & Collopy, F. (1998). Integration of statistical methods and judgment for time series forecasting: Principles from empirical research. In Wright, G. & Goodwin, P. (eds.), *Forecasting with judgment.* New York: John Wiley & Sons.

Armstrong, J. S. & Green, K. C. (2006, Sep). Select a forecasting method (selection tree). Retrieved July19, 2007, from http://www.forecastingprinciples.com/selection%5ftree.html

Delage, E., & Mannor, S. (2010). Percentile Optimization for Markov Decision Processes with Parameter Uncertainty. Operations Research, 58(1), 203-213. Retrieved November 15, 2013, from EBSCO Online Database Business Source Complete. http://search.ebscohost.com/login.aspx?direct=true&db=bth&AN=53017824&site=ehost-live

Eggers, J. P. (2012). Falling Flat: Failed Technologies and Investment under Uncertainty. Administrative Science Quarterly, 57(1), 47-80. Retrieved November 15, 2013, from EBSCO Online Database Business Source Complete. http://search.ebscohost.com/login.aspx?direct=true&db=bth&AN=76538844&site=ehost-live

Laskey, K. B. (2001). Bayesian decision theory, subjective probability and utility. In S. I. Gass, & C. M. Harris (eds.), *Encyclopedia of operations research and management science* (pp. 57-59). New York: Wiley. Retrieved August 9, 2007, from EBSCO Online Database Business Source Complete. http://search.ebscohost.com/login.aspx?direct=true&db=bth&AN=21891161&site=ehost-live

Lee, Y., & Baldick, R. (2013). A frequency-constrained stochastic economic dispatch model. *IEEE Transactions On Power Systems, 28*(3), 2301-2312. Retrieved November 15, 2013, from EBSCO Online Database Business Source Complete. http://search.ebscohost.com/login.aspx?direct=true&db=bth&AN=89267611&site=ehost-live

Miller, D. R. (2001). Markov processes. In S. I. Gass, & C. M. Harris (eds.), *Encyclopedia of operations research and management science* (pp. 486-490). New York: Wiley. Retrieved August 10, 2007, from EBSCO Online Database Business Source Complete. http://search.ebscohost.com/login.aspx?direct=true&db=bth&AN=21891583&site=ehost-live

Ramesh, R., & Zionts, S. (2001). Multiple criteria decision making. In S. I. Gass, & C. M. Harris (eds.), *Encyclopedia of operations research and management science* (pp. 538-543). New York: Wiley. Retrieved August 9, 2007, from EBSCO Online Database Business Source Complete. http://search.ebscohost.com/login.aspx?direct=true&db=bth&AN=21891643&site=ehost-live

Schum, D. A. (2001). Decision analysis. In S. I. Gass, & C. M. Harris (eds.), *Encyclopedia of operations research and management science* (pp.194-198). New York: Wiley. Retrieved August 9, 2007, from EBSCO Online Database Business Source Complete. http://search.ebscohost.com/login.aspx?direct=true&db=bth&AN=21891288&site=ehost-live

Schwabe, W. (2001). Gaming. In S. I. Gass, & C. M. Harris (eds.), *Encyclopedia of operations research and management science* (pp.321-323). New York: Wiley. Retrieved August 11, 2007, from EBSCO Online Database Business Source Complete. http://search.ebscohost.com/login.aspx?direct=true&db=bth&AN=21891419&site=ehost-live

Wang, Y. (2012). A fuzzy-normalisation-based group decision-making approach for prioritising engineering design requirements in QFD under uncertainty. International Journal Of Production Research, 50(23), 6963-6977. Retrieved November 15, 2013, from EBSCO Online Database Business Source Complete. http://search.ebscohost.com/login.aspx?direct=true&db=bth&AN=82935625&site=ehost-live

Suggested Reading

Borgonovo, E. (2006). Measuring uncertainty importance: Investigation and comparison of alternative approaches. *Risk Analysis: An International Journal, 26*(5), 1349-1361. Retrieved August 9, 2007, from EBSCO Online Database Business Source Complete. http://search.ebscohost.com/login.aspx?direct=true&db=bth&AN=22674895&site=ehost-live

Courtney, H., Kirkland, J., & Viguerie, P. (1997). Strategy under uncertainty. *Harvard Business Review, 75*(6), 67-79. Retrieved July 31, 2007, from EBSCO Online Database Business Source Complete. http://search.ebscohost.com/login.aspx?direct=true&db=bth&AN=9711071077&site=ehost-live

Eichberger, J., Harper, I. R., Pfeil, C., & Scheid, F. (2002). Decision-making under uncertainty. In J. Eichberger, I. R. Harper, C. Pfeil, & F. Scheid (eds.), *Solutions manual for financial economics* (pp. 1-19). New York: Oxford University Press. Retrieved August 9, 2007, from EBSCO Online Database Business Source Complete. http://search.ebscohost.com/login.aspx?direct=true&db=bth&AN=25608783&site=ehost-live

Foss, N., Mahnke, V., & Sanchez, R. (2000). Demand uncertainty and asset flexibility: Incorporating strategic options in the theory of the firm. In N. Foss, V. Mahnke, & R. Sanchez (eds.), *Competence, governance & entrepreneurship* (pp. 318-332). Retrieved August 9, 2007, from EBSCO Online Database Business Source Complete. http://search.ebscohost.com/login.aspx?direct=true&db=bth&AN=7672238&site=ehost-live

Gottlieb, D. A., Weiss, T., & Chapman, G. B. (2007). The format in which uncertainty information is presented affects decision biases. *Psychological Science, 18*(3), 240-246. Retrieved August 9, 2007, from EBSCO Online Database Business Source Complete. http://search.ebscohost.com/login.aspx?direct=true&db=bth&AN=24719389&site=ehost-live

Goyal, M. & Netessine, S. (2007). Strategic technology choice and capacity investment under demand uncertainty. *Management Science, 53*(2), 192-207. Retrieved August 9, 2007, from EBSCO Online Database Business Source Complete. http://search.ebscohost.com/login.aspx?direct=true&db=bth&AN=24272429&site=ehost-live

Hitsch, G. J. (2006). An empirical model of optimal dynamic product launch and exit under demand uncertainty. *Marketing Science, 25*(1), 25-50. Retrieved July 31, 2007, from EBSCO Online Database Business Source Complete. http://search.ebscohost.com/login.aspx?direct=true&db=bth&AN=19991298&site=ehost-live

Ruth A. Wienclaw, Ph.D.

Decision Processes: A Core Business Activity Supported by Information Systems

Abstract

Decision-making is required in organizations on a daily basis. The decisions that are made can deal with sales, operations, finances, products, competition, employees and a whole host of other topics. Decisions can be short term, long term or emergency in nature. Organizational decisions can model or simulate the future while analyzing past or present performance. Technological advances in information systems provide large amounts of data to support decision-making as well as tools to analyze data in the context of specific problems and 'what-if' scenarios. Every organization has decision processes and protocols. Decisions are impacted by the quality of the decision-making process. The flexibility and inclusiveness of decision processes contribute to the effectiveness and usability of decisions as does the availability of high performance decision support systems. Organizations can use information systems to analyze and predict. Other critical factors include balancing objective and subjective data and collaboration among decision-makers. Decision-makers may use intuition and internal know-how along with performance data to arrive at a decision. There are many ways to use information and decision-making tools. Addressing the need for high quality decisions may cause organizations to make significant investments in information technology that can guide, support and improve internal decision-making processes.

OVERVIEW

It is important that organizations make good decisions. Decisions guide the organization to failure or success. Therefore, the organization needs to have a process in place that increases its chances of making good decisions. Decision activity in organizations can be complex and involved; answers to problems may not be simple or straightforward and may involve many different decision-makers. The organizational decision process is more complex than an individual decision because many types of data must be gathered from different sources and given to multiple decision makers.

Organizations can make good decisions by:

- Recognizing when routine, traditional practices of decision making need to be replaced with creative decision processes
- Encouraging collaboration rather than competitiveness in decision making
- Being adaptable in decision-making to better react to an ever-changing world
- Understanding how certain types of information systems (called decision support systems) can synthesize expertise in the field to assist decision makers. Decision support systems can guide, support and improve decision making. Decision processes are the steps organizations go through to arrive at decisions. These processes vary by size and type of organization. Good decision making means working together with others for creative solutions. Roszkiewicz (2007, p. 13) says collaboration "refers to a rich and interactive relationship similar to the type we experience when brainstorming." An orderly decision process requires that decision makers work together or collaborate on ideas about what information to consider, how solutions to problems look and the decision process itself.

But how do we get rich, interactive relationships? Individual decision-makers may lack strong skills in collaboration and may view decision-making with others as competitive instead of collaborative. One answer may be decision support systems (DSS). Information systems that support decision making are called decision support systems. According to French and Turoff (2007, p.39) decision support systems (DSS) can be used with individuals or groups to assist decision-makers by "organizing and communicating results" so each collaborative team member can come to a "shared understanding." The shared understanding can be of the problem, strategy, solution or in retrospect when viewing a project that is completed.

Organizations need to make numerous decisions to survive. Decisions can be daily shifts directing operational activity, responses to problems or far-reaching and extensive charting of strategic directions. One by-product of having to make so many decisions is that decisions may be made based upon a certain history of success in creating solutions or because of habits and perceptions held by decision-makers. The process of making decisions this way results in a routine or traditional organizational practice which may not lead to a correct result. This means that the decision-making process becomes a traditional organizational practice, instead of a creative one. Once the decision process is set in an organization, it may be used over and over again even if it doesn't fit the current problem type. Frederickson (2006) notes that organizations can be more attached to traditional practices for decision processes and internal data than to industry best practices. He suggests that organizations work to incorporate industry best practices into decision processes for the greatest value and optimal decision-making results.

Organizations need to be adaptable in how they make decisions. Brown, Steyvers, & Hemmer (2007) found that decision-makers need to adjust the methods used to make decisions because the environment in which decisions are made in organizations is constantly changing. Therefore, a decision process that worked for a particular problem at a particular time may not be as effective under other conditions. Similarly, circumstances and conditions may change so rapidly and dramatically that any former decision processes are outdated.

Obviously, an organization's goal is to be profitable and productive. We have already discussed that organizations must sometimes break from the mode of traditional set decision-making for the sake of creativity, but creativity in decision-making must also be managed. The greater the innovation and creativity, the greater value that can be added to products and services that organizations produce. On the other hand, unmanaged creativity and innovation may interfere with decision-making processes and process management because both can interrupt the logical and orderly flow that would occur with traditional, rational decision-making. Elbanna and Child (2007) suggest a connection in research of strategic decision processes between the size of the organization and the likelihood of using traditional, rational processes instead of creative ones. Such research indicates that the larger the organization, the more likely that traditional decision-making will be a set practice.

Organizations also need to closely watch whether their decision makers use logic to make decisions or whether politics plays more of a role. Rajagopalan, Rasheed, & Datta (1993, p. 351) stated that decision processes in organizations can model two types. The first is a rational type where strategic decisions are based on logic. The second is a political or behavioral type that is based on "bargaining and negotiations among individuals and organizational subunits with conflicting perceptions, personal stakes and unequal power." Faulty decisions can occur simply because an individual or group has an unequal percentage yet persuasive amount of power. The organization needs to minimize the role of politics.

The Role of Decision Makers & Decision Support System Impact

Decision-makers assume several roles in the decision making process including analyzing information, making assumptions about the validity of information and setting the parameters in 'what-if' scenarios. Decision-making may put the decision-maker in the role of change agent and require management of expectations from those not involved in decision-making. The decision-maker must be cognizant of the need to include others while balancing external input. In addition, they must also perform the role of expert communicator with other decision-makers and to those outside of the decision-making team. Decision-makers must put results of decisions into context so that the information can be effectively used as input for other decisions and to re-evaluate and modify organizational decision processes.

Today's decision makers must have a global view when it comes to decision making. Stolarczyk (2007) notes the importance of decision-makers having a global view of the world, especially in manufacturing where organizations are likely to deal with suppliers from around the globe. The ability to use information technology related to global supply chains helps companies make "crucial and timely financial decisions" (Stolarczyk, 2007, p. 52).

The decision-maker may be placed in the unenviable role of determining whether a company has a future or not. Crucial decision-making can be supported by effective DSS. Stolarczyk quotes a supply chain and logistics report on Fortune 500 companies as stating that many companies feel the supply chain technology being used doesn't adequately support decision-making in "budgeting and cash flow planning." Some barriers to acquiring adequate systems have been the lack of focus on the global supply chain and the investment cost, according to Stolarczyk.

Kelly, Hutchins, & Morrison, (n.d., abstract) et al conducted an experiment to determine the value of DSS in tactical decision-making. They found that throughout the decision making process, DSS helped guide, support and improve decision making. The experiment used experienced decision-makers engaged in real-life scenarios and found that those using DSS had less communication about simple situational information because of the ability to get the same view of the situation from the DSS. DSS were able to get to the central issues faster and formulate what action was needed. Problems noted by Kelly et al. (p.1) were human issues related to the decision-makers' ability to remember information, difficulty in getting the group centered on the same information at the right time and biases among the decision-makers.

DSS was found to assist decision makers regarding decision bias problems. Decision bias problems include decision-makers continuing to hold to a specific opinion about risk or threat even when presented with new information that contradicted the decision-makers initial opinion (Kelly et al., p. 2). Decision-makers were also found to hold on to information that was not related to the situation in making judgments. The study showed that early in the scenario and through the middle of the scenario, decision-makers supported by DSS outperformed their counterparts without DSS in identifying critical issues of "greatest tactical interest." However, late in the scenario, decision-makers without the benefit of a DSS outperformed their counterparts in identifying critical issues (Kelly et al., p. 3). The authors postulated that these results indicate that the benefits of using a DSS wear off late in a scenario because critical issues are somewhat obvious by that time even without using a DSS. Early identification of the critical factors by the DSS group could also be due to the human tendency to stick to initial information as correct.

The study by Kelly et al. showed that the group using the DSS was less likely to react and suggest tactical action against threats based on ambiguous information. The authors felt that this was due to the ability of the DSS to help the group filter and interpret ambiguous information to a higher degree than the group without the DSS. When analyzing specific performance against tactical threats, the study found that the group using the DSS was better able to defend against these tactical threats than the group not using the DSS. This could be the result of team communication, in that the group using the DSS had a greater shared understanding of the initial threat information.

DSS was also found to be helpful in terms of communication. Kelly et al. (p.4), wanted to determine whether or not using a DSS affected how decisions are made about what action to take and when. The experiment analyzed the amount of verbal communication among the decision-making teams and found that fewer communications were initiated by the DSS team among themselves but slightly more when encountering external information. Kelly et al. examined the content of verbal communications to determine whether or not it was affected by a DSS. The areas of content were coded in the following way:

- Information
- Status
- Clarification
- Assessment
- Orders or commands for action

The Kelly study concluded that with a DSS, the group was able to spend more time on clarifying, assessment and giving orders and less time on exchanging basic information and status because the DSS provided that information. The study concluded that having a DSS caused teams to communicate less frequently but more efficiently, and greater experience with a DSS could affect performance and communication even more. The authors also found that to have the optimum effect, a DSS would have to have specific features to support performance and communication such as being easy to access, having a user friendly interface and the ability to track important tactical data easily.

Using Decision Support Systems

What is a decision support system? One definition from French and Turoff (2007, p. 39) is that decision support systems (DSS) support "operational, tactical or strategic decision-making." The authors suggest that DSS must have the flexibility to make assumptions or allow for decision-maker input. It is important that DSS meet the following important criteria: 1) fit technology to purpose; 2) take a knowledge management perspective and allow collaboration; 3) data quality; 4) audit.

Each of these criteria has a specific meaning, fitting the technology to the purpose means not just the problem at hand but also organizational objectives, management processes and culture. In addition, the organization must be willing to change the technology when another type of technology or technology tool is better suited for the scenario. A knowledge management perspective means considering all the knowledge that is available in the organization that might impact decisions. Collaboration among groups and various organizational units ensures a thorough problem perspective exists. Data quality criteria address the fact that while data exists it may not be 'clean' or verified. In addition, uncertainty can exist because data from various sources may contradict data from other sources. Decision-makers are then put in the position to make judgments even with the uncertainty present in the available information. The audit criteria recognizes that all organizations audit activities in some way and decision support systems should participate by recording and monitoring information and prompting specific activity when required (French & Turoff, p.40). The audit data can also provide management teams with "shared meaning" of events and activities and make sure that actions are thoroughly analyzed after the occurrence so that the information can be input into future decision-making activities.

DSS assists in real-world decision making. In one study, DSS helps to predict change in the future. Kirilenko, Chivoiu, Crick, Ross-Davis, Schaaf, Shao, Singhania, & Swihart (2007) discuss an Internet based DSS for forest landowners whose purpose is to help in the management of family forests. The DSS provides useful information on various species, tree density and size as well as specifics to geographic region and wildlife in the region. A unique modeling capability of the tool is the ability to predict "forest dynamics" "40 years into the future" (Kirilenko et al., abstract). Important details available to users of the tool include the ability to measure and predict changes to the forest in many ways using a "Forest Vegetation Simulator." Since knowledge about forests is highly specialized, a tool of this nature is a requirement to effectively manage a forest and to have social consideration for natural habitats that cannot be easily replaced if destroyed. Unlike the dairy production DSS (Higgins, 2007) where farmers had high levels of sophisticated knowledge and history in the industry, the trend in family forest management is that new owners typically have urban backgrounds and little knowledge of forestry. The forest landowner DSS seeks to connect these new owners with the resources available through the government in the natural resources arena.

DSS can assist in problems that occur when people work in groups. Group Decision Support Systems (GDSS) have the goal of getting past the typical barriers found in group meetings and collaborative situations (Roszkiewicz). Since people are the most important and expensive resource in an organization, investments may be made in systems that corral the capabilities of people which Roszkiewicz (p.13) calls integrating "computer power in our attempt to identify, collect, organize and interpret the thoughts of the most important human resources each company has."

Challenges arising when working in groups include distributing information and hoping that the group understands the significance of the information, and organizing it and applying that information to the problems within the organization. At the same time, the inability to focus on what is important, personality conflicts and personal biases may make it difficult for the group to stick to an agenda and move the agenda forward. GDSS provide discipline and structure to group interactions while helping provide consensus regardless of the social skills of the participants. (Roszkiewicz, 2007). The goal is to capitalize on the value of the intellectual capital of the group without the downside of ineffective interactions. Roszkiewicz (2007) notes that GDSS have the ability to:

- Brainstorm
- Organize
- Prioritize

GDSS pairs web-conferencing capabilities with Internet browser based GDSS to capture free flowing comments while providing "tools for decision-making and reporting." GDSS also allows for the pre-planning of collaboration to ensure that decision processes are mapped to activities.

While decision-making can include everyday and mundane organizational decisions, the process can also include life and death situations. Physicians frequently make life and death decisions and therefore it is critical that there is a decision process in place to help physicians make good decisions. This type of challenging decision-making can be assisted by information systems because such systems can easily synthesize expert opinions for physicians. According to Lamont (2007) decision support systems can be used to ensure correct patient diagnosis. Clinical Decision Support Systems (CDSS) can make physicians aware of the latest information on an illness and also limit the likelihood of misdiagnosis of an illness. Physicians use decision support systems to help them with diagnosing illnesses and correctly interpreting symptoms. The goal of decision support systems in healthcare is to improve the safety of the patient and reduce cost. The better the information available to clinical practitioners, the higher the level of patient care. Developing a CDSS can be quite involved because it requires building a repository of diseases as well as the treatment protocols and drugs used.

The benefit of technology is that a CDSS can electronically store information from the oldest medical texts while including up-to-date information from journals (Lamont, 2007). CDSS allows medical professionals to input patient symptoms and will output possible diagnoses and links to the latest research. Newer CDSS have emphasized decreasing the amount of information that has to be entered about a patient's condition and have simplified the method for getting answers. Now, physicians can combine CDSS with electronic medical records (EMR) to coordinate and integrate information about the patient and the illness in order to improve the quality and speed of care. Integration of these various systems is supported by service oriented architecture (SOA) in which the architecture of systems is oriented towards the processes and uses by end users and is not dependent upon the underlying technology platform. SOA frees users to view information such as patient data through a similar interface no matter where it originated (Lamont, 2007). Without these systems, physicians might rely only on their previous knowledge and education. CDSS allows decision-makers to be flexible in their approach to decision making, so it is possible to include the best ideas.

The practice of using information systems to assist with decision-making has been introduced successfully to the dairy industry. As in the medical industry, synthesizing expert knowledge allows for better decision making. Higgins (2007) notes that effective decision support systems rely heavily on the knowledge of experts in the field and must be based on that knowledge. A decision support system was created for the dairy industry and the design was developed with input from dairy farmers to ensure the value of the farmers' knowledge was included to increase the value of the DSS. Higgins considers the science and technology arguments on who controls design and how system design is heavily skewed towards the designer and not necessarily end users or subject matter experts. The use of decision support systems in the dairy industry has been shown to improve productivity and reduce costs. The value of DSS in dairy production has become increasingly important with increased global competition in farm production (Higgins, 2007).

Viewpoint

Creativity & Decision-Making

The process of decision-making can be tedious or exciting depending on the outlook and tolerance of the individual, the complexity of the problem, the available support tools and the ease of collaborating with others in decision-making. A certain amount of creativity is required as problems and issues may not take the same shape or format and a variety of skills and abilities may be called upon to make successful decisions. This is especially true of decisions that involve performance and prediction. Former levels of performance may not meet current needs and the ability to accurately predict the future may depend on many factors including those over which the decision-maker has no control. Marakas and Elam (2007) call creativity "one of the most vague, ambitious and confusing terms." Matching creativity in a business environment that is accustomed to strict and accurate performance measures is a difficult task. Even if an organization has been successful in creative problem-solving and decision-making, reproducing what is difficult to quantify may seem like an impossible undertaking.

Weber (1986) suggested that decision support systems "should be designed to stimulate learning and creativity." Weber felt that the research supported a responsibility being placed on the designer of a DSS to stimulate the problem-solving and decision-making creativity of the user. Learning and growth can take place in the process of making decisions and solving problems, and a useful DSS supports both. Designers have to be exposed to users and subject matter experts in order to have a full understanding of what design issues are pertinent in making DSS usable and effective. Higgins (2007) describes a two-day workshop for dairy farmers used to examine farmers' "preexisting knowledge" as well as to determine whether or not users (farmers) felt the DSS had benefits and could be used in daily production.

Weber (1986) noted that DSS are by nature supportive of "human cognitive processes and semi-structured situations." He states that the benefit of DSS is the ability to support individual and organizational learning and performance while reducing the "cognitive differences" that people may have. Kelly et al. also found that DSS are useful in reducing the differences between the interpretations of data by decision-makers. Weber saw the shift in DSS evolution in a way that provides decision-makers with learning tools that are more effective in 'ill-structured" problem-solving scenarios. Weber (1986) defined cognitive processes as consisting of "sensation and perception" while learning is comprised of four sub-processes:

- Selection
- Construction
- Integration
- Acquisition

Further, Weber considered problem-solving to be "the active manipulation of perceived, learned, and remembered information." The difficulty in solving a problem is directly related to "the amount of structure," "the power of the chosen solution methods and the knowledge available to the user." "Cognitive strategies" are used to "acquire, store, retrieve and manipulate information" and "affect how creatively we think..." Weber calls creativity "originality in problem solving" and "an outcome of learning."

Weber noted that previous DSS were product oriented instead of process oriented and felt that in order to make DSS "systems to think with (STW)" the DSS must map to the natural cognitive processes decision-makers use in problem-solving. He suggests that designers are most successful when using analytical tools that model situations using analogy and "familiar electronic metaphors."

Marakas and Elam (1997) explored creativity in the context of the process used by the decision-maker, the tool or the DSS used to deliver the process. The findings of this study indicated that the best result to maximize creativity was combining DSS capabilities to guide the decision-making process with a user armed with knowledge and understanding of the decision-making process. This method was found to be superior in enhancing creativity over simply using a DSS or the user using the decision process without a DSS. The need to explore creativity is driven by the fact that more unique solutions are required more quickly and there is a human tendency to continue to use the same processes for finding solutions.

Balancing Intuition (Gut-Feel) & Objective Data

Decision-makers have to balance what they know with what they feel and historical organizational experience. Decision support systems cannot be designed in a vacuum and must take into account the decision processes of the organization, best practices in decision-making, the ability for an organization to learn and the system's ability to capture and ignite the creativity of the decision-maker. Studies have shown that decision-making performance is supported or hampered by:

- The decision-making process employed
- The quality of support tools
- The ability to incorporate creativity into the process and tools, and
- The effectiveness of decision-makers to collaborate with others.

Part of the balance needed in decision-making is between raw data and the decision-makers' ability to interpret meaning from the data and the real-world scenario that requires a solution. Decision-makers today have the benefit of large quantities of information and DSS can offer tools to screen, filter and contextualize data in light of problem-solving scenarios. However, decision-makers must guard against human tendencies and biases that restrict decision-making while allowing intuition to guide the creative process of decision-making. While learning can be a natural outcome of decision-making and even using DSS, decision-makers may be reluctant to shift decision processes or experiment creatively on critical decisions. Decision-makers are likely to feel that there is less risk in deploying pre-existing decision processes than new and creative ones.

Fowler (1979) suggested that information systems fail to reach their goal of "informing managers" because of being based on the assumption that managers can understand and define what information needs to exist before making decisions. Part of the intuitive nature of decision-making rests with systems designers as well as with decision-makers who anticipate the needs for data and customize the organizational decision processes to support and accelerate decision-making. Fowler stated that design strategy is important to avoid creating DSS that only encompass the designer's viewpoint and end up providing the decision-maker with answers that are "irrelevant" or "unasked.

In studying strategic decision processes of organizations, Rajagopalan et al. (1993) found several factors influencing the decision process models used including:

- Organizational context affects decision-making and is influenced by uncertainty and complexity.
- Organizational internal power structure, past performance and strategies exert substantial influence on decision processes and may follow industry patterns.
- Decision processes vary within an organization based on urgency, reason for decision, uncertainty about outcomes and the degree of resource commitment.

These findings underscore the importance of the process as well as the DSS deployed for decision-making. Decision outcomes such as timeliness, speed and quality are easily tied to the quality of a decision support system while outcomes such as organizational commitment and learning are not as easily incorporated into system design. Similarly, decision processes can be connected to organizational commitment and learning without as tangible a connection to timeliness, speed and quality. Organizations that are serious about improving the results of decision-making must work diligently to examine decision processes and incorporate desired processes into the design of decision support systems.

Bibliography

Brown, S., Steyvers, M., Hemmer, P. (2007). Modeling experimentally induced strategy shifts. *Psychological Science, 18*(1), 40-45. Retrieved May 18, 2007, from EBSCO Online Database Business Source Complete. http://search.ebscohost.com/login.aspx?direct=true&db=bth&AN=24281763&site=ehost-live

Dong, C., & Srinivasan, A. (2013). Agent-enabled service-oriented decision support systems. *Decision Support Systems, 55*(1), 364-373. Retrieved November 15, 2013, from EBSCO Online Database Business Source Complete. http://search.ebscohost.com/login.aspx?direct=true&db=bth&AN=87616718&site=ehost-live

Elbanna, S. & Child, J. (2007). The influence of decision, environmental and firm characteristics on the rationality of strategic decision-making. *Journal of Management Studies, 44*(4), 561-591. Retrieved May 19, 2007, from EBSCO Online Database Business Source Complete. http://search.ebscohost.com/login.aspx?direct=true&db=bth&AN=24892407&site=ehost-live

Fowler, F. P., Jr. (1979). The executive intelligence system as a design strategy. *MIS Quarterly, 3*(4), 21-29. Retrieved May 18, 2007, from EBSCO Online Database Business Source Complete. http://search.ebscohost.com/login.aspx?direct=true&db=bth&AN=4679103&site=ehost-live

Frederickson, H.G. (2006). Reconsidering best practices. *PA Times, 29*(12), 11. Retrieved May 18, 2007, from EBSCO Online Database Business Source Complete. http://search.ebscohost.com/login.aspx?direct=true&db=bth&AN=23496700&site=ehost-live

French, S. & Turoff, M. (2007). Decision support systems. *Communications of the ACM, 50 (3),* 39-40. Retrieved May 18, 2007, from EBSCO Online Database Business Source Complete. http://search.ebscohost.com/login.aspx?direct=true&db=bth&AN=24209666&site=ehost-live

Higgins, V. (2007). Performing users: the case of a computer-based dairy decision-support system. *Science, Technology & Human Values, 32*(3), 263-286. Retrieved May 18, 2007, from EBSCO Online Database Business Source Complete. http://search.ebscohost.com/login.aspx?direct=true&db=bth&AN=24768040&site=ehost-live

Hughes, G. D. (2003). Add creativity to your decision processes. *Journal for Quality & Participation, 26*(2), 4-13. Retrieved May 18, 2007, from EBSCO Online Database Business Source Complete. http://search.ebscohost.com/login.aspx?direct=true&db=bth&AN=10295448&site=ehost-live

Kelly, R. T., Hutchins, S.G., & Morrison, J.G. (n.d.). *Decision processes and team communications with a decision support system. [Whitepaper].* Retrieved May 18, 2007, from http://www.pacific-science.com/kmds/c2%5fconf.pdf

Kirilenko, A., Chivoiu, B., Crick, J., Ross-Davis, A., Schaaf, K., Shao, G., Singhania, V., Swihart, R. (2007). An Internet-based decision support tool for non-industrial private forest landowners. *Environmental Modelling & Software, 22*(10), 1498-1508. Retrieved May 18, 2007, from EBSCO Online Database Academic Source Premier. http://search.ebscohost.com/login.aspx?direct=true&db=aph&AN=24711682&site=ehost-live

Lamont, J. (2007). Decision support systems prove vital to healthcare. *KMWorld, 16*(2), 10-12. Retrieved May 18, 2007, from EBSCO Online Database Business Source Complete. http://search.ebscohost.com/login.aspx?direct=true&db=bth&AN=23898467&site=ehost-live

Laudon, K.C. & Laudon, J.P. (2001). Essentials of management information systems: Organization and technology in the networked enterprise. Upper Saddle River, NJ: Prentice-Hall, Inc.

Makris, S.S., & Chryssolouris, G.G. (2013). Web-services-based supply-chain-control logic: an automotive case study. *International Journal of Production Research, 51*(7), 2077-2091. Retrieved November 15, 2013, from EBSCO Online Database Business Source Complete. http://search.ebscohost.com/login.aspx?direct=true&db=bth&AN=85286024&site=ehost-live

Marakas, G. M. (1997). Creativity enhancement in problem solving: Through software or process. *Management Science, 43*(8), 1136-1146. Retrieved May 18, 2007, from EBSCO Online Database Business Source Complete. http://search.ebscohost.com/login.aspx?direct=true&db=bth&AN=9709102751&site=ehost-live

Rajagopalan, N., Rasheed, A.M., and Datta, D. (1993). Strategic decision processes: Critical review and future directions. *Journal of Management, 19*(2), 349-384. Retrieved May 18, 2007, from EBSCO Online Database Business Source Complete. http://search.ebscohost.com/login.aspx?direct=true&db=bth&AN=5711263&site=ehost-live

Riabacke, A., Larsson, A., & Danielson, M. (2011). Business intelligence as decision support in business processes: An empirical investigation. *Proceedings of the European Conference On Information Management & Evaluation*, 384-392. Retrieved November 15, 2013, from EBSCO Online Database Business Source Complete. http://search.ebscohost.com/login.aspx?direct=true&db=bth&AN=60168261&site=ehost-live

Roszkiewicz, R. (2007). GDSS: The future of online meetings and true digital collaboration? *The Seybold Report, 7*(1), 13-17. Retrieved May 18, 2007, from EBSCO Online Database Business Source Complete. http://search.ebscohost.com/login.aspx?direct=true&db=bth&AN=23835707&site=ehost-live

Stolarczyk, M. J. (2007). The IT factor. *The Journal of Commerce, 8*(12), 52. Retrieved May 18, 2007, from EBSCO Online Database Business Source Complete. http://search.ebscohost.com/login.aspx?direct=true&db=bth&AN=24605140&site=ehost-live

Weber, E. S. (1986). Systems to think with: A response to a vision for decision support systems. *Journal of Management Information Systems, 2*(4), 85-97. Retrieved May 18, 2007, from EBSCO Online Database Business Source Complete. http://search.ebscohost.com/login.aspx?direct=true&db=bth&AN=5745637&site=ehost-live

Wikipedia. (2007). *Service Oriented Architecture (SOA). [Definition]*. Retrieved May 18, 2007, from http://en.wikipedia.org/wiki/Service%5foriented%5farchitecture#SOA%5fdefinitions

SUGGESTED READING

IBM white paper: Enhance quality of care and clinical decision making in a security-rich environment. (2005). Retrieved May 18, 2007, from TechRepublic. http://whitepapers.techrepublic.com.com/whitepaper.aspx?docid=292536

Akella, J., Kanakamedala, K. & Roberts, R. (2007, January 4). Efficient IT shops: Two trends foreseen. *CIO Magazine*. Retrieved May 18, 2007, from CIO Magazine Online. http://www.cio.com/article/27979/Efficient%5fIT%5fShops%5fTwo%5fTrends%5fForeseen/2

Davenport, T. H. & Harris, J. G. (2005). Automated decision making comes of age. *MIT Sloan Management Review, 46*(4), 83-89.

Worley, C. G. & Lawler, E. E. III (2006). Designing organizations that are built to change. *MIT Sloan Management Review, 48*(1), 19- 23.

Marlanda English, Ph. D.

DECISION SUPPORT SYSTEMS

ABSTRACT

Every day, managers are faced with decisions about how best to run their organizations in order to gain or maintain a competitive edge. Although some decisions are simple, many are quite complex and require the manager to consider many variables. To help managers in decision making processes, many organizations employ the use of computer-aided decision support systems. These systems can help managers make decisions about semi-structured and even unstructured problems where not all the information is known in advance. Several different types of decision support systems are available. These include model-driven systems, data-driven systems, knowledge-driven systems, and group support systems. These decision support systems can be quite effective in aiding managers in making decisions and improving the effectiveness and performance of organizations.

OVERVIEW

The world around us is constantly changing. Market needs are shaped by numerous factors including political realities, advances in technology, and changing cultural expectations. To be competitive in this environment, businesses cannot be static, but need to grow and change to meet the needs of the marketplace. To do this, businesses need to be able to make good decisions in response to the changing needs of their environment. In some cases, these are simple decisions: Do we produce more widgets in response to increase market demand? Should we order more raw materials so that we can continue to produce gizmos? In other cases, however, the decision is not so simple. The demands of the marketplace may not be easily deciphered. As exemplified by the 8-track tape systems and the Beta video recorder of the latter half of the 20th century, decoding trends and translating them into business strategies is neither a simple nor an obvious process. In addition, management decisions can have far reaching impact within the organization. For example, the decision to increase the production of widgets may mean that more employees are needed for the widget production line. Management is now faced with another decision: Should new production workers be hired or should employees be transferred from the gizmo production line? If the former decision is made, where does the money come from to hire the new workers? If the latter decision is made, what is the impact on the gizmo production line? Considerations of the production rate for new gizmos or even the viability of the gizmo line also need to be taken into account in order to understand the ramifications of the decision in context.

In most complex business situations, it is important to understand the factors of decision making in context. Organizational behavior theorists tend to view the organization as a system, where changes in one subsystem can have far ranging impact throughout the organization as a whole. In this view, an organization is an interactive system in which the actions of one part influence the functioning of another. Rather than merely focusing on the needs of one part or subsystem within the organization in isolation (e.g., the widget production line) when making a decision, it is important to look at the impact of the decision on all subsystems and levels within the organization.

According to systems theory, organizations are systems comprising numerous subsystems. Rather than viewing an organization as a collection of disassociated parts acting independently, systems theory posits that the functioning of each subsystem impacts the functioning of the other subsystems. For example, in the illustration above, the decision to increase production of widgets can affect other parts of the organization. If more production workers are hired for the widget line, there might also be a concomitant need to hire more human resources and accounting personnel to take care of issues and tasks related to a larger work force. Other considerations in the decision might include whether or not suppliers could deliver sufficient raw materials to make the widgets or sufficient boxes to package the widgets so that they could be sold to consumers. In addition to hiring more workers for the widget production line, the organization would also more than likely also have to hire additional supervisors or managers for the new production lines. The increase in workers for the widget line might also cause conflict between the new workers and the workers already working on the widget production line or between the widget workers and the gizmo workers. Such conflict or job dissatisfaction could affect the functioning of the organization as a whole. Personnel issues are not the only factor that needs to be taken into account in this decision. Management would also have to consider where the new production lines would be located. If there was insufficient room in the current production plants, new facilities would need to be bought or leased. Similarly, new lines would probably require additional equipment. If, on the other hand, the organization decides that it is not cost effective to incur the expenses associated with starting new production lines, there would be other impacts on the organization. If workers are transferred from the gizmo line to make widgets, what happens to the gizmo product line? Even if the organization's management decides to convert some of the gizmo lines into widget lines and transfer some of the existing employees to the new line, these employees would have to be trained to become widget line operators; a necessary activity that would also cost the organization money. Each subsystem within the organization (e.g., the various production groups, accounting, human resources, management) affects the ability of the other groups — as well as of the organization as a whole — to do their jobs. Systems theory also recognizes that the organization is not only made up of interlocking subsystems, but is also part of a larger system itself that depends on inputs of raw materials, human resources, and capital and that needs to export goods or services, employee behavior, and capital in order to continue to the viability of other organizations.

To help management make such complex decisions, many organizations use decision support systems. Although there is no universally accepted definition of the term, in general a decision support system is an interactive computer-based system that helps managers and others make decisions. Decision support systems are used both by individuals and groups, and can be stand alone systems, integrated systems, or web-based.

Decision support systems are used when organizations are faced with unique, complex situations where a decision needs to be made. Decision support systems help decision makers better understand the issues underlying the situation and to make decisions in situations where the extent to which certain variables influence the activity or outcome are not initially clear or only part of the information is available in advance. This condition is referred to as an unstructured situation. To answer unstructured questions, decision support systems must be flexible so that the impact of various variables and conditions can be tested and the analysis returned to the user in a form that is useful for the specific situation. The unstructured nature of the problem also means that the use of a decision support system is an iterative process: The answers to the questions are not ends in themselves, but raise other questions for consideration that need to be run through the decision support system.

Decision support systems can help decision makers in such situations by providing the information and structure needed to make a rational decision. The decision support system creates a quantitative model of the situation and then processes data to show the impact of the variables under consideration on the outcomes. Decision support systems can help decision makers answer questions concerning conditions under which an outcome might occur, what might happen if the value of a variable changes, or how many potential customers have certain characteristics. Decision support systems can also help to trim inefficiencies from organizational systems, such as the supply chain, which further can take into account other company priorities such as carbon emissions reduction. Frequently, decision support systems require the processing of data from multiple files and databases.

Decision support systems are not necessarily esoteric software applications. Spreadsheet software is one of the most frequently used decision support tools. These applications help the decision maker design a table of values arranged in rows and columns in which the values have predefined relationships. Spreadsheet application software allows users to create and manipulate spreadsheets electronically. As a decision support system, spreadsheets enable the decision maker to manipulate variables to see the effect of different values on the variables or of changing the assumptions on the outcome. For example, before making an investment in a new manufacturing plant, a manager could make a model on a spread sheet and analyze the effect of changing interest rates on the risk associated with the venture.

APPLICATIONS

Several different general types of decision support systems have been identified in the literature. These include model-driven systems, data-driven systems, knowledge-driven systems, and group support systems.

Model-Driven Decision Support Systems

A wide variety of models can be used to form the basis for decision support systems. Model-driven decision support systems use various financial, optimization, or simulation models as aids to decision making. Model-driven decision support systems use limited data and parameters provided by the decision makers, but do not generally require large databases. For example, in 2000, Pfizer merged with Warner-Lambert to form an integrated company with sales over $30 billion. As part of the process of integrating the two companies, a decision support system was used to combine the distribution systems of the two organizations. Three linked simulation models were developed: a distribution center storage and capacity model, a distribution picking and shipping model, and a distribution center facility sizing model. Using these three models, the distribution center capacity requirements for two to five years in the future were studied. Analysts were able to examine the effects on inventory and distribution of a variety of sales forecasts. Warner-Lambert also developed an optimization model that enabled decision makers to analyze the flow of products through the network during stated planning periods. A fifth model was used to analyze inventory investments for the combined organization. The decision support system and its models were used for a series of long-range studies that helped Warner-Lambert make decisions about expansion of its distribution network, implementation of a new pharmaceutical delivery network, and consolidation of the distribution networks after the merger.

Another example of a model-driven decision support system was employed by General Motors in their decision to incorporate the OnStar two-way vehicle communication system in its new vehicles. In 1996, General Motors tested a prototype of the OnStar system, but found that it was both difficult to install and expensive. When the time came to make a strategic decision about the installation of OnStar in General Motors' vehicles, two models were developed. The conservative model posited that OnStar should only be offered as an option and promoted to improve vehicle safety and security. The more optimistic model assumed that OnStar would appeal to customers enough so that they would subscribe to the service, thereby generating significant monthly income from service fees for General Motors. Although the potential income from this latter model was attractive, it also carried with it concomitant increased risk and the need for a greater initial investment. As opposed to the previous example where data were available about the existing systems, the model developed to analyze the potential profitability of OnStar was for a system that had never been implemented. General Motors developed a six factor simulation model of the system incorporating customer acquisition, customer choice, alliances, customer service, finances, and dealer behavior. The model also incorporated feedback loops to make the simulation more realistic. In the end, the decision support system allowed management to determine that customer service was an important factor in the implementation of OnStar technology: If General Motors did not adequately invest in the project, the system would fail. Using the simulation, the recommendation was made for an aggressive strategy to pursue OnStar technology.

Data-Driven Decision Support Systems

Data-driven decision support systems utilize time series data gathered on the factor or characteristic of interest at regular intervals over a period of time. Basic data-driven decision support systems access simple file systems using query and retrieval tools whereas more advanced data-driven systems allow the manipulation of data or analytical processing. Executive information systems are a type of data-driven decision support system. These data-driven decision support systems are designed to support executive decision making by presenting information about the activities of the company and the industry. Executive support systems offer quick, concise updates of business performance for top executives. These systems have powerful processing capabilities in order to summarize and present data in a format appropriate to executive decision making.

Top executives differ from middle managers because they need to take a more global view of the organization rather than focusing on a particular process or product. Top level managers are also particularly concerned with the systems approach and need to know how decisions made regarding one part of the organization effect other parts of the organization as well. Executive support systems take these needs into account. To support top-level managers in their tasks, executive support systems allow executives to look not only at the organization as a system itself, but at the organization as part of a larger system as well. To do this, executive support systems permit scanning of data and information on both internal activities as well as the external business environment. Since executives tend to look at things from a higher level than do many analysts, executive support systems highlight significant data and present information in summary form rather than giving the user all the details and supporting data, although users are allowed access to these data if desired. This "drill down" feature allows the user to go down several levels to acquire the data necessary to make a well-informed decision.

Executive support systems are generally well accepted by top-level managers. Although these systems have relatively simple user interfaces to support the way that most top-level managers work, they can be used for a wide range of purposes. For example, executive support systems can be used to determine why a company's expenses are higher than expected, gain an overview of a competitor's financial picture, be continually updated on various corporate indicators relating to effectiveness and performance, or check for processes that are not meeting expectations.

Knowledge-Driven Decision Support Systems

Knowledge-driven decision support systems are person/computer systems with specialized problem solving abilities that can make suggestions or recommendations to the user. Knowledge-driven systems are expert systems that may include the application of artificial intelligence to the decision making process. Artificial intelligence is a branch of computer science concerned with development of software that allows computers to perform activities normally considered to require human intelligence. In the realm of decision support systems, artificial intelligence applications can be used in the development of expert systems that allow computers to make complex, real world decisions. Applications of artificial intelligence to decision making include medical diagnosis, manufacturing quality control, and financial planning.

An example of a knowledge-driven decision support system is the expert system for dispatchers used by Con-Way Transportation Services. Con-Way offers premium next-day service for less-than-truckload shipments to meet their customers' just-in-time shipping strategies. In the past, Con-Way dispatchers used the common industry model. This approach, however, was labor intensive and required the dispatchers to handle complex logistics, including assigning deliveries to over 400 locations, ensuring overnight, on-time delivery, assigning loads to optimize utilization of trailer space, developing efficient routes including consideration of bad weather, highway hazards, and other complications. To assist dispatchers in these duties, Con-Way implemented an expert system to aid in the scheduling process. The system was designed to optimize routing, loading, and delivery while minimizing costs. The system is constantly updated throughout the day and flags discrepancies so that the dispatcher can resolve issues before the truck is loaded. Con-Way's expert system for dispatchers takes into account multiple factors including elapsed time, delivery times, and customer priorities that factor into route specifications. The expert system uses artificial intelligence to develop an optimal solution for loading and scheduling. By using the expert system, dispatchers can perform duties in minutes that used to require hours. As a result, they are able to accept customer orders later than was previously possible. The system, which cost over $3 million, paid for itself within two years of implementation.

Group Decision Support Systems

In addition to the types of decision support systems discussed above, there are also group decision support systems. These systems enable workgroups to process and interpret information together even when they are not physically collocated. These systems use network and communications technologies to foster collaboration and communication in support of decision making. Communications-driven systems rely heavily on communications technology, including groupware, video teleconferencing, and electronic bulletin boards.

Like other decision support systems, group support systems support decision making in situations that are not fully structured and assist in analyzing problems. However, group support systems are used by workgroups or teams rather than by individuals. To maximize effectiveness, group support systems emphasize communication and idea generation between and among group members throughout the system using communication networks. Group support systems typically require the involvement of a facilitator to keep the group focused on the problem under consideration and to help expedite the development and sharing of creative solutions. This shared information is input into a database rather than a traditional report, and includes questions, comments, and ideas from the group.

Marriott Hotels use a group support system to help meet the ever-changing needs of business travelers;

one of their biggest customer segments. Periodically, Marriott assembles teams of personnel from various groups involved in providing service to these customers, including managers, housekeeping, front-desk personnel, catering, room-service coordinators, and bellhops. These representatives exchange experiences and ideas via the group support system in an effort to improve service to this market segment. Inputs are made anonymously so that comments can be made frankly.

Bibliography

Koh, S., Genovese, A., Acquaye, A. A., Barratt, P., Rana, N., Kuylenstierna, J., & Gibbs, D. (2013). Decarbonising product supply chains: Design and development of an integrated evidence-based decision support system – the supply chain environmental analysis tool (SCEnAT). *International Journal of Production Research, 51*(7), 2092-2109. Retrieved October 31, 2013, from EBSCO Online Database Business Source Complete. http://search.ebscohost.com/login.aspx?direct=true&db=bth&AN=85286025&site=ehost-live

Liu, S., Leat, M., Moizer, J., Megicks, P., & Kasturiratne, D. (2013). A decision-focused knowledge management framework to support collaborative decision making for lean supply chain management. *International Journal of Production Research, 51*(7), 2123-2137. Retrieved October 31, 2013, from EBSCO Online Database Business Source Complete. http://search.ebscohost.com/login.aspx?direct=true&db=bth&AN=85286027&site=ehost-live

Lucas, H. C. Jr. (2005). *Information technology: Strategic decision making for managers.* New York: John Wiley and Sons.

Renna, P. (2013). Decision model to support the SMEs' decision to participate or leave a collaborative network. *International Journal of Production Research, 51*(7), 1973-1983. Retrieved October 31, 2013, from EBSCO Online Database Business Source Complete. http://search.ebscohost.com/login.aspx?direct=true&db=bth&AN=85286016&site=ehost-live

Senn, J. A. (2004). *Information technology: Principles, practices, opportunities* (3rd ed.). Upper Saddle River, NJ: Pearson/Prentice Hall.

Suggested Reading

French, S. & Turoff, M. (2007). Decision support systems. *Communications of the ACM, 50*(3), 39-40. Retrieved May 14, 2007, from EBSCO Online Database Business Source Complete. http://search.ebscohost.com/login.aspx?direct=true&db=bth&AN=24209666&site=ehost-live

Gadomski, A. M., Bologna, S., DiCostanzo, G., Perini, A., & Schaerf, M. (1999). An approach to the intelligent decision advisor (IDA) for emergency managers. *Proceedings of the Sixth Annual Conference of the International Emergency Management Society,* Delft, Netherlands: IEMS. Retrieved May 14, 2007, from http://erg4146.casaccia.enea.it/wwwerg26701/TIEMS'99.pdf.

Inmon, B. (2006). Real-time decision support systems? *DM Review, 16*(8), 14.

Jones, K. (2006). Knowledge management as a foundation for decision support systems. *Journal of Computer Information Systems, 46*(4), 116-124. Retrieved May 14, 2007, from EBSCO Online Database Business Source Complete. http://search.ebscohost.com/login.aspx?direct=true&db=bth&AN=22536043&site=ehost-live

Lamont, J. (2007). Decision support systems prove vital to healthcare. *KM World, 16*(2), 10-12. Retrieved May 14, 2007, from EBSCO Online Database Business Source Complete. http://search.ebscohost.com/login.aspx?direct=true&db=bth&AN=23898467&site=ehost-live

Weng, S. Chiu, R., Wang, B., Chi, R. & Su, S. (2006/2007). The study and verification of mathematical modeling for customer purchasing behavior. *Journal of Computer Information Systems, 47*(2), 46-57. Retrieved May 14, 2007, from EBSCO Online Database Business Source Complete. http://search.ebscohost.com/login.aspx?direct=true&db=bth&AN=24375428&site=ehost-live

Ruth A. Wienclaw, Ph.D.

Enterprise Resource Planning

ABSTRACT

This essay investigates the topic of Enterprise Resource Planning (ERP) and ways that ERP systems are being used in today's complex business environment. There are two critical requirements in the Enterprise Resource Planning process: Identification of key business processes and functions and implementation of ERP software that will serve as the architecture for those processes. ERP systems can greatly enhance organizational effectiveness by connecting a company's business units internally as well as externally to customers and vendors. Many organizations have benefited greatly from implementing ERP systems and some "best practices" are reviewed. In other cases, organizations have under-utilized their ERP systems or have struggled with successful deployment. The next generation of ERP systems promises to be web-based and highly customizable as ERP is adopted by an even more diverse industry base.

OVERVIEW

The rise of global corporations has meant that organizations need to implement enterprise-wide systems for linking core operations and business units. Organizations have learned that their business units often need access to the same information but at different times during the product/service lifecycle. ERP systems are large, integrated software packages that offer solutions for administrative (back end) and core business processes (Fuβ, Gmeiner, Schiereck, & Strahringer, 2007).

ERP systems allow for integration on the data and functional levels in a way that aims to avoid data redundancy. In today's global economy, companies can also benefit by allowing partners, vendors, and customers access to some internal information; ERP systems lend themselves well to this capability.

"An ERP system is [defined as] an integrated, configurable, and tailorable information system which plans and manages all the resources and their use in the enterprise, and streamlines and incorporates the business processes within and across the functional or technical boundaries in the organization. With ERP, an enterprise can automate its fundamental business applications, reduce the complexity and the cost of the collaboration, force the enterprise itself to take part in the Business Process Reengineering (BPR) to optimize its operations, and finally result in a successful business" (She & Thuraisingham, 2007, p. 152).

ERP systems have their roots in the manufacturing sector of the 1960s, when centralized computer systems for inventory control were being developed. By the 1970s, MRP (materials resource planning) systems were being designed to define manufacturing requirements and production planning; throughout the next decade they were optimizing the manufacturing process.

In the 1990s the ERP concept was introduced and referred to enterprise-wide (cross-functional) systems that included core operations and processes such as

- Accounting and finance
- HR
- Project management
- Inventory management
- Product distribution

Early ERP systems were expensive to implement and maintain, but the cost has come down as service oriented architecture (SOA) and web services have helped to ease implementation. The majority of all Fortune 1000 manufacturing companies have implemented ERP systems. ERP systems have now been adopted in many diverse industries, such as banking, insurance, health care, and higher education. ERP is considered to be "the price of entry for running a business" (Kumar & van Hillegersberg, 2000). Comprehensive reviews of later ERP implementation were conducted by Shaul and Tauber (2013) and by Nazemi, Tarokh, and Djavanshir (2012).

APPLICATIONS

Why Implement an Enterprise Resource Planning System?

Companies do not take lightly the decision to implement major software applications such as ERP. The following list can serve as a sanity check for companies who are thinking of implementing an ERP system. Research indicates that many companies purchase ERP systems and then fail to fully use the application. One of the best things that senior executives can do before authorizing the purchase of an ERP is to realistically determine if the system will meet the following objectives.

Some of the documented benefits of implementing ERP systems (Fuβ, Gmeiner, Schiereck, & Strahringer, 2007):

- increased revenue and market share
- product differentiation
- shortening of post-merger integration by twelve to eighteen months
- substantial cost saving
- data transparency
- interaction with satellite systems

Some challenges to implementing ERP include

- substantial costs (licensing fees and consulting fees)
- danger of eroding competitive advantage processes
- possible lower flexibility (ERP not customizable)
- vendor dependence for maintenance support
- tisk and complexity of replacing legacy systems
- no good industry option for ERP (available options are too generic)

ERP Solutions in Today's Organization

ERP has been a widely accepted business practice since the 1990s. Vendor ERP systems allowed for enterprise integration of many core functions that are a part of many organizations, regardless of industry. Companies in industries as different as manufacturing and insurance share common functional areas, such as human resources, accounting, and project management. Generic administrative (back office) functions are one part of an ERP system that has been successfully implemented by companies. The other part of the ERP system handles the core-business processes and is highly dependent upon the nature of the specific industry.

ERP system vendors (such as SAP and Oracle) are facing challenges in several areas as their products evolve to serve ever more specialized industries with their more generic applications. Some of the challenges that ERP system vendors have faced face include (Katz, 2007) the following:

- Vendors struggled to make their suites web serviceable.
- Service oriented architecture relegated ERP systems to a component of system architecture rather than a core application.
- Vendors faced growing pressure from cheaper offshore vendors who could develop cheaper, more customized options (commodity pieces of ERP)
- Vendors offered split models of ERP systems
- Generic offerings, such as accounting or human resources, became available.
- Specialized services were offered via middleware applications

ERP systems have been most threatened by SOA, which have been introduced in large organizations. Large companies have more money and resources to implement middleware solutions and build sophisticated applications on top of their ERP backbone. Small companies still use vendor ERP systems and rely on vendor upgrades to add functionality at the functional level. As more small and medium enterprises (SMEs) adopt ERP systems, vendors will offer more middleware to allow for customization.

The Future of ERP Systems

The high cost of implementing the ERP processes and systems is well documented. The purchase of the application, maintenance costs, upgrade costs, training, and IT support are just a few of the costs associated with implementing an ERP system. ERP systems serve as the core process infrastructure for many companies; in other companiess, the ERP system will serve as a process backbone for a larger service-oriented architecture system. In either case, the investment in ERP systems is significant for companies, but should provide a high return on investment in improved business results.

Kugel argues that companies would be well advised to "establish steering committees with senior-level authority to ensure that they are examining the IT dimension of their pressing business issues, finding opportunities to improve business processes through technology initiatives and setting priorities for implementing these solutions. This sort of collaborative effort could go along way toward identifying opportunities and implementing innovations that will improve a company's results" (Kugel, 2007, p. 46).

As business needs evolve and core processes are connected through automation, the following have become components of the next-generation of ERP systems (She & Thuraisingham, 2007).

Systems are now

- heterogeneous (components from different vendors will coexist in the system; components and integration are necessary).
- collaborative (the systems include enterprise-centric processes and collaborative [partner/vendor] processes, and interfaces are web accessible).
- intelligent (ERP systems hold more confidential information that is used for analysis, strategy planning, and investigation).
- knowledge-based (analytics from the system support daily business decision-making, including knowledge-based operations, management, and communication).
- wireless (web-based ERPs are accessible from mobile locations).

Next generation ERP systems have been designed with an emphasis on flexibility and scalability. Fast changing business needs, industry consolidation, and rapidly evolving technology all play a role in the design of future enterprise-wide systems. Companies aredeveloping tools to increase productivity, decrease product time to market, and encourage collaborative processes within their supply chains. Companies are anxious to implement systems that will meet their business needs for a decade or more.).

Web Services & ERP

The relentless march of software applications to the web has included the migration of ERP systems to web-based platforms. Today's large organizations are likely to continue to build layers of web-based applications and middleware applications on top of ERP backbones.

"With ERP systems progressively making use of web service technology and their transformation into systems based on service oriented architectures, they turn into open application backbones that can flexibly be extended and integrated" (Fuβ, Gmeiner, Schiereck, & Strahringer, 2007, p. 169).

One of the biggest motivations for moving ERP systems interfaces to the web is that web services help to reduce integration complexity and costs. Clients (vendors, customers, suppliers) can also access some information without having to go through ERP software. ERP vendors are introducing middleware solutions that act as a "broker between Web services and the ERP software" (She & Thuraisingham, 2007). The key point is that these business processes have to be connected across organizations for a business to succeed in supply chain management. These processes are interorganizational.

Web-based access to ERP systems allow a company's vendors and partners to access company data. One example of the value of web-based access is documented by Volkswagon Corporation. Volkswagon provides millions of users (internal and external) across its supply chain with access to its corporate data.

Issues

Fully Utilizing ERP Systems

ERP systems represent a significant capital investment for most organizations, but too often companies are not leveraging the full capability of the applications. Most companies have achieved only simple process efficiencies and have not fully tapped the full power of their ERP systems. "The Hackett Group found that the cost of running the average finance organization shrank by nearly half during the 1990s; this achievement can be attributed largely to the nearly universal adoption of ERP systems over that period" (Kugel, 2007, p. 45).

Accounting modules have long been a core function of ERP systems and are widely used by many different organizations. The capture of specific operational data is not as widely recorded within ERPs, and this represents a missed opportunity for many organizations.

" Many companies are not using nonfinancial metrics to improve performance, either because they ignore data they already collect or they fail to collect the data their ERP system is capable of delivering" (Kugel, 2007, p. 45).

Perceptions by executives as to the value that ERP systems bring to an organization may be one of the biggest obstacles to successful full-scale ERP system optimization. Without complete support and buy-in from C-level executives to drive organizational effectiveness through ERP implementation, the systems will never realize their full potential. "If there is no attempt to make better use of ERP software because executives do not believe it will produce results, then it cannot deliver those enhancements" (Kugel, 2007, p. 45). If the deployment of ERP systems is not made a strategic initiative within an organization, individual business units could see it as "someone else's job to find new and better ways to use the software to improve the effectiveness and productivity of their organization" (Kugel, 2007, p. 45).

There is certainly an opportunity for IT departments to play a more strategic role in showing the value of optimizing software applications such as ERP systems. Business leaders may not even be aware of the value that such a powerful software application can have for solving critical business issues. Leaders in the IT department can use such opportunities to position themselves and their departments as key business partners.

Using IT to Drive Innovation & Implementation for ERP Systems

Mergers and acquisitions within industries can pose challenges to companies who desire to customize their existing ERP systems. In 2006, Mittal Steel merged with one of its competitors, Arcelor, to form the world's largest steel company. Corporate mergers offer opportunities for companies to evaluate organizational practices, and consolidate systems and processes. One of Mittal's core applications was an ERP system by SAP. The company initiated a project to standardize business processes into one world-wide ERP system.

After nearly a year of analysis, Mittal Arcelor decided that trying to organize all business processes into one ERP system would actually be too difficult to implement in a reasonable time frame. Executives at the company realized that resources put into such a huge project might actually pose a threat to the company's ability to deliver on its core business objectives.

"We have dropped the idea of having one process model at group level because it was too complex and there was too high a diversity in business models and intrinsic complexity in the different segments," said Patrick Vandenberghe, group CIO at Arcelor Mittal (Clark, 2007). Mittal Arcelor decided to standardize the company's business processes into ten distinct business units (by market and geography). Instead of integrating the ten distinct business units into one single ERP system, the company maintains seven global SAP competency centers. The smaller ERP systems share experiences, resources, and applications across the company.

Vandenberghe said "Arcelor Mittal's goal was to buy the entire supply chain for steel manufacturing, from raw materials to finished products, but these processes could not always be integrated" (Clark, 2007). The idea of deploying a single ERP system was a worthy one, but had been described as a "mammoth one." AMR research director Jane Barrett stated "Companies such as Arcelor Mittal, which grow through acquisition, change their structure as they go along and are rarely able to put in a single instance of SAP because it takes too long. The managing value chain overtakes the advantage of having a single system."

Security for ERP

Increased user interaction, storage of more confidential information, and a move toward web-based services all add to the complexity of managing security across enterprise applications. Security control will continue to be increasingly difficult and time consuming to maintain and update; system administrators will spend much time trying to keep up. In addition, the more detailed the security information is, the higher the cost and the worse the performance for the system. Detailed user information will be logged in reports. The double-edged sword of security can be summed up in the following statement: "Usually better [security] solutions will bring higher cost and lower performance to a system" (She & Thuraisingham, 2007).

Today's security solutions are primarily based on role-based access control. RBAC components are

- permissions: Allows access to one or more objects within the system.
- roles: Assigned typically by job function within an organization.
- users: The person (employee) who is assigned one or more roles.
- constraints: The role-to-permission assignment.

As the complexity of enterprise systems grows, so will the need to implement more complex security solutions for managing user access to key data.

Extended RBAC (ERBAC) is the next iteration of role-based security permissions. Two additional parameters have been added to the traditional RBAC predicates:

- obligation: The mandatory requirements required by user.
- condition: The environmental or system requirement (for example, time, date, location).

She and Thuraisingham explain that "In this ERBAC model, an extra decision manager is added since obligation and condition predicates will be taken into account. In the decision process, condition requirements will be checked first; if all the environmental conditions are met, the checking procedure for the obligations will be triggered; and, at last, the decision process will check whether the user is intended to access the information" (She & Thuraisingham, 2007, p. 160).

CONCLUSION

This discussion of ERP and systems implementation reveals that ERP systems are being implemented across many organizations as standard enterprise applications. Companies see the necessity of linking internal processes and capturing relevant data and statistics at critical links in order to assess operational efficiencies. ERP systems, once found almost exclusively in the manufacturing sector, are now be implemented across a variety of industry sectors, including insurance, banking, higher education, and health care. As nonmanufacturing sector industries embrace ERP systems, vendors will need to continue offering customized solutions for niche markets.

Web-based delivery of ERP system solutions will continue unabated as companies seek to enable collaborative access to systems and data. Large organizations will customize web-based delivery by purchasing middleware solutions to link ERP and SOA architectures. The next generation of ERP systems is being developed with scalability, flexibility, and security in mind. There are many documented examples of best practices of implementing ERP software solutions, and companies can benefit greatly from enterprise-wide planning and support for such initiatives. Companies that are about to undertake the ERP process or purchase software applications would do well to investigate what has worked well for other companies in their industry. ERP systems have been in existence for decades in one form or another; due diligence in learning from organizational successes and failures will go a long way in helping organizations to successfully implement ERP systems and processes.

Bibliography

Clark, L. (2007, May 22). Mittal scraps global standardisation plan. *Computer Weekly*, 1. Retrieved August 6, 2007, from EBSCO Online Database Business Source Complete. http://search.ebscohost.com/login.aspx?direct=true&db=bth&AN=25348028&site=ehost-live

Fuβ, C., Gmeiner, R., Schiereck, D., & Strahringer, S. (2007). ERP usage in banking: An exploratory survey of the world's largest banks. *Information Systems Management, 24*(2), 155-171. Retrieved August 6, 2007, from EBSCO Online Database Business Source Complete. http://search.ebscohost.com/login.aspx?direct=true&db=bth&AN=24654646&site=ehost-live

Kamath, J. (2007, June 19). Volkswagen gives IT staff bigger say in ERP systems. *Computer Weekly*, 4. Retrieved August 6, 2007, from EBSCO Online Database Business Source Complete. http://search.ebscohost.com/login.aspx?direct=true&db=bth&AN=25615287&site=ehost-live

Katz, J. (2007). SOA: The next disruptive force. *Industry Week/IW, 256*(3), 41-41. Retrieved August 6, 2007, from EBSCO Online Database Business Source Complete. http://search.ebscohost.com/login.aspx?direct=true&db=bth&AN=24309899&site=ehost-live

Kugel, R. (2007). Getting more from ERP. *Business Finance, 13*(5), 45-46. Retrieved August 7, 2007, from EBSCO Online Database Business Source Complete. http://search.ebscohost.com/login.aspx?direct=true&db=bth&AN=25139045&site=ehost-live

Nazemi, E., Tarokh, M., & Djavanshir, G. G. (2012). ERP: A literature survey. *International Journal Of Advanced Manufacturing Technology, 61*(9-12), 999-1018. Retrieved November 27, 2013, from EBSCO Online Database Academic Search Complete. http://search.ebscohost.com/login.aspx?direct=true&db=a9h&AN=78307374&site=ehost-live

Shaul, L., & Tauber, D. (2013). Critical success factors in enterprise resource planning systems: Review of the last decade. *ACM Computing Surveys, 45*(4), 55-55:39. Retrieved October 31, 2013, from EBSCO Online Database Business Source Complete. http://search.ebscohost.com/login.aspx?direct=true&db=bth&AN=90108290&site=ehost-live

She, W., & Thuraisingham, B. (2007). Security for enterprise resource planning systems. *Information Systems Security, 16*(3), 152-163. Retrieved August 6, 2007, from EBSCO Online Database Business Source Complete. http://search.ebscohost.com/login.aspx?direct=true&db=bth&AN=25728921&site=ehost-live

Shukla, R. (2012). Novel approach to compare an established open-source ERP and a next generation cloud computing ERP. *Researchers World: Journal Of Arts, Science & Commerce, 3*(2), 8-15. Retrieved November 27, 2013, from EBSCO Online Database Academic Search Complete. http://search.ebscohost.com/login.aspx?direct=true&db=a9h&AN=90322418&site=ehost-live

Swanton, B. (2007, June 12). Using SOA as a competitive weapon. *Computer Weekly*, 20. Retrieved August 6, 2007, from EBSCO Online Database Business Source Complete. http://search.ebscohost.com/login.aspx?direct=true&db=bth&AN=25636469&site=ehost-live

Suggested Reading

Griffin, J. (2007). BI and ERP integration: Five critical questions. *DM Review, 17*(5), 6-6. Retrieved August 6, 2007, from EBSCO Online Database Business Source Complete. http://search.ebscohost.com/login.aspx?direct=true&db=bth&AN=24911549&site=ehost-live

Kumar, K., & Van Hillegersberg, J. (2000). ERP experiences and evolution. *Communications of the ACM, 43*(4), 22-26. Retrieved August 7, 2007, from EBSCO Online Database Business Source Complete. http://search.ebscohost.com/login.aspx?direct=true&db=bth&AN=12070056&site=ehost-live

Carolyn Sprague, M.L.S.

Enterprise Risk Management

ABSTRACT

This article examines the development of Enterprise Risk Management (ERM) processes and systems. The types of risks addressed by ERM are explained along with how enterprise risk analysis can assist boards of directors, corporate managers, investors, and industry analysts. The Integrated Framework for ERM of the Committee of Sponsoring Organizations of the Treadway Commission (COSO) is also reviewed. The processes and challenges of implementing ERM and information systems to support ERM are examined along with steps that stakeholders can take to address technical and cultural issues. Past experiences in developing and implementing large-scale systems that drive organizational change are also reviewed.

OVERVIEW

Enterprise Risk Management (ERM) is a data intensive process that measures all of a company's risks. This includes providing managers with an understanding of the full array of a company's risks including financial risks, investment oriented risks, operations based risks, and market risks, as well as legal and regulatory risks for all of the locations in which a company operates or invests (Peterson, 2006). Risk can also be a result of political or social conditions in locations where a company has operations, suppliers, or customers (Woodard, 2005). Risk to a company's reputation is also an important aspect and element of ERM (Ruquet, 2007).

In each of the risk areas there are two primary types of risks that companies face:

- External Risk
- Manufactured Risk

External risk is the risk of events that may strike organizations or individuals unexpectedly (from the outside) but that happen regularly enough and often enough to be generally predictable. Manufactured risk is a result of the use of technologies or even business practices that an organization chooses to adopt.

A technological risk is caused or created by technologies that can include trains wrecking, bridges falling, and planes crashing (Giddens, 1999). Business practice risk is caused or created by actions which the company takes which could include investing, purchasing, sales, or financing customer purchases.

ERM analytical models should encompass both external and manufactured risks which can be identified through historical analysis as well as reviews of current operations and exposures ("Expect the Unexpected," 2009). Once identified, risks can be validated through discussions with corporate executives, operations managers, production managers, and business unit executives. In addition to gaining a better understanding of risks these discussions can also provide insight into existing mitigation practices that have been designed to reduce specific risk (Muzzy, 2008).

The data intensity of ERM requires risk managers to obtain data from numerous sources, test the integrity and accuracy of that data, and to assure that the data is being properly applied and interrupted. Assumptions about the models or analytical approaches behind an ERM analysis must also be carefully examined and tested (Cotton, 2009; Vlasenko & Kozlov, 2009). The internal audit department can help validate some of the financial data used in ERM models as well as provide other potentially relevant financial information (Gramling & Myers, 2006).

The 2008 economic downturn caught many corporate executives working with analytical models that assumed that the housing market would not decline so drastically or on such a widespread basis (Korolov, 2009). Clearly the assumptions and the analytical model had not undergone stringent enough testing. However, most risk managers had also not previously seen the convergence of negative economic trends occur so quickly and across so many sectors simultaneously (Morgan, 2009).

Putting ERM to Work

The ERM process is designed to enable corporate executives as well as investors to quantify and compare risks and to gauge the overall health of a company (Coccia, 2006; Panning, 2006). Investment advisors, institutional investors, and credit rating agencies are adding to the pressure for companies to develop ERM systems and disclose their risks (Karlin, 2007). ERM enables top managers of a company to aggregate, prioritize, and effectively manage risks while enabling business-unit managers to improve decision making in operations and product management (Kocourek & Newfrock, 2006). In managing risks there are several options that corporate executives can take including accepting, preventing, mitigating, transferring, sharing, or avoiding the risks (Woodard, 2005).

The ERM process can also support strategic planning activities as well as provide insight into alternative business practices and goals (Millage, 2005). One of the biggest challenges in implementing ERM strategies is to make sure that selected analytical methods are appropriate for the type and size of organization to which they are being applied (Milligan, 2009). ERM strategies and models as well as the utilization of ERM analyses will vary with corporate culture, business goals, and risk management objectives. This means that a one-size-fits-all approach towards ERM is not likely to be successful (Lenckus, 2006).

The Push for ERM

Although many companies have used ERM over the last decade, the economic downturn of 2008 showed that some companies had not done well when it came to managing their risks (Korolov, 2009; McDonald, 2009). In some of these situations it is entirely possible that corporate executives were not taking newly developed models of risk analysis as seriously as they should have (Lenckus, 2009). However, the attention paid to risk analysis and the ERM concept is changing as more and more companies attempt to recover from the downturn and better plan for the future (Hofmann, 2009). There is also a growing advocacy base for using ERM to help manage companies through all phases of business cycles (Van der Stede, 2009)

In addition to pressure from the investment community, corporations also face new legal requirements that have increased the interest in ERM. After Enron, WorldCom, Tyco, and other large business failed, the United States Congress passed the 2002 Sarbanes-Oxley Act. Sarbanes-Oxley addressed risks related to financial reporting issues. Sections 302 and 404 of the act have spurred considerable interest in ERM. Section 302 mandates disclosure controls and procedures so that companies could disclose developments and risks of the business and section 404 requires an assessment of the effectiveness of internal control over financial reporting (Barton, Shenkir & Walker, 2009).

The United States Securities and Exchange Commission (SEC) has also implemented requirements for publicly traded companies to disclose risk factors in section lA of their 10-Ks. The SEC and Public Company Accounting Oversight Board (PCAOB) also developed Section 404 guidance that supports top-down risk assessment that holds boards of directors more accountable for oversight of company operations (Stein, 2005; Barton, Shenkir & Walker, 2009).

In September 2004, the Committee of Sponsoring Organizations of the Treadway Commission (COSO) published its Integrated Framework for ERM. The framework identifies four types of objectives for ERM:

- Strategic,
- Operations,
- Reporting, and
- Compliance.

In addition, organizations are charged with examining eight components for each of the four objectives:

- Internal environment,
- Objective setting,
- Event identification,
- Risk assessment,
- Risk response,
- Control activities,
- Information and communication, and
- Monitoring (Bowling & Rieger, 2005a, p. 31; Wheeler, 2009).

A summary as well as detailed information about the COSO framework is available at www.coso.org.

Thus, the stage is set and the pressure is on for organizations to use ERM to gain greater insight into company-wide risk. But it may not all be that easy. Even after ERM systems are in place the analysis they render must then be applied to the business decision making process. Even at that point, it will require an added dose of knowledge, wisdom, and experience to develop a competitive strategy and support that strategy with rational day-to-day business management skills before ERM becomes an integral part of a company's success formula.

APPLICATIONS

Implementing ERM

As companies begin to implement ERM processes and systems the most important decisions they face is to decide who will be in charge of the ERM processes and systems and where in the organization the structure the ERM function will be placed. Many companies have opted to create a position of chief risk officer (Wheeler, 2009). This trend has created new career paths for those interested in risk management, especially those that are interested in working in the highest levels of organization management (Branham, 2006).

Establishing an effective risk management organizational structure also requires that the risk management department or director be provided an adequate degree of independence similar to that of an internal auditor. This includes the ability and the resources to build an ERM information system that can support data collection, information-gathering, modeling, and risk analysis (Shan, Xin, Xiaoyan & Junwen, 2009).

ERM staff also need to develop a broad knowledge of the company in which they work and cultivate relationships with key players in all parts of the company in order to promote risk management (Loghry & Veach, 2009). Once relationships are established they must be maintained through continuous, meaningful, and understandable communications regarding the company's risks. ERM staff may also need to develop new skills and will always need to keep their skills and knowledge base updated through continuing education and training in the risk analysis and risk management fields (Zaccanti, 2009).

Corporate executives who are responsible for directing risk analysis need to have enough influence in their organization to gain the attention and respect of other executives (Baker, 2008). The quality of risk analysis and the sophistication or risk inventories and projections may help to persuade corporate executives that there is value to the ERM processes, systems, and staff (Johnson & Swanson, 2007).

ERM staff also need tools to help them crunch through the vast amounts of data that can be used to support risk analyses. The marketplace for applications software programs is beginning to emerge and ERM staff are faced with selecting from tools that may have had little actual real world use (Lenckus, 2006; Ramamoorti & Weidenmier, 2006). Tools and people cost money and if ERM programs are not adequately funded results are likely to be anemic at best (Panning, 2006).

Back to Basics in Information Management

The fundamental principle behind ERM is that it is designed to take a broad and comprehensive view of risks and focus on the basic causes and effects that can keep companies from achieving their strategic business goals (Loghry & Veach, 2009). Some analysts view this as a departure from the past when risk management was depicted as a fragmented, silo-ridden function in most organizations (Bowling & Rieger, 2005). However, ERM systems of this scope are largely based in information creation and analysis and thus the basic rules and processes of information management apply to ERM systems just as they do to any other information system.

Database Software

There are four basic steps to business data management:

- Data creation,
- Data storage,
- Data processing, and
- Data analysis.

A considerable amount of data is created through every-day business processes such as production of items, consumption of supplies or resources, sales of goods or services, and customer service activities. The primary tool for processing and managing such large amounts of data is database software. Database software is used in virtually all industries especially those that are transaction focused and need to track large quantities of items or activities. Enterprise storage systems are capable of storing vast amounts of data and modern storage management tools have eased many of the problems associated with this task.

Complex data analysis, beyond what database software provides, has become essential to manage large organizations and may be more essential in ERM. This type of data analysis can be performed with a variety data mining, statistical analysis, and decision support software packages. This software helps managers and analysts compile or create statistics on millions of business transactions. These statistics can support business forecasting and planning efforts as well as ERM analysis.

Data analysis software has evolved over the last 60 years. For decades most such software was rather cumbersome and required custom programming. In the 1970s decision support systems (DSS) were introduced that provided assistance for specific decision-making tasks. While DSSs can be developed for and used by personnel throughout the organization, they are most commonly employed by line staff, middle level managers, and functional area specialists. Among the latest developments are expert systems, which capture the expertise of highly trained, experienced professionals in specific problem domains.

In the 1990s executive information systems (EIS) or executive support systems (ESS) were being developed in large organizations. At first these systems were cumbersome and most were stand alone systems requiring time consuming data entry processes. As expected, the technology for EIS has evolved rapidly, and new systems are more integrated with other applications like the DDS or Enterprise Resource Planning (ERP) systems (Watson, Rainer & Koh, 1991).

Information System Development Life Cycle (ISDLC)

Regardless if the ERM team is going to use off-the-shelf products such as DSSs or an EIS or develop their own in-house applications, they still need to apply the Information System Development Life Cycle (ISDLC) model to implementation. The traditional and well established approach to the ISDLC is that a development project has to undergo a series of phases where the completion of each is a prerequisite to the commencement of the next and where each phase consists of a related group of steps. The general scheme for the ISDLC is similar almost everywhere. It typically contains four major phases consisting of several steps each:

- Definition Phase: consisting of preliminary analysis, feasibility study, information analysis, and system design.
- Construction Phase: consisting of programming, development of procedures, unit testing, quality control, and documentation.
- Implementation Phase: consisting of user training, conversion of old systems to new systems, thorough field testing, and then a move to full operations.
- Maintenance Phase: after the system is full operation updates are made to assure continued operations as new equipment or upgrades to operating systems occur. Enhancements to the system can also be made to meet changing user requirements.

Effective management of information systems requirements analysis, and thus the design of appropriate systems, is critical to the success of an ERM systems project. Systems development methodologies must be selected and applied based on requirements and goals stated by staff who will ultimately use the system (Avison & Taylor, 1997). ERM practitioners can benefit from these basic information systems practices and should look to traditional development procedures and processes instead of going it alone and trying to reinvent the world of information management.

Issue: Overcoming the Hurdles

The last several years have been a rocky road for many ERM programs and many have been viewed as failures in their early stages. When ERM programs are driven by individuals, single divisions or business units, or function as silos they do not have the ability to bridge with other parts of the company and become integrated into the management process. In addition, ERM has often been viewed as a costly program that takes years to implement and years can pass before any real benefits are derived from the expenditure of time and money (Chase-Jenkins & Shimpi, 2006).

When looking at ERM from the inside, such an evolutionary process can be appreciated. However, when looking at ERM from the outside, the evolutionary process may be viewed as a lack of maturity and easily become a reason for skepticism and mistrust by corporate executives (McDonald, 2008; Schanfield, 2008). Adding to the turmoil is that many of the risk analysis software tools that have come to market during the last few years are in their infancy and many risk analysts remain skeptical about the usability and reliability of the tools (Downes, 2006; Leopoulos, Kirytopoulos & Malandrakis, 2006).

There are many nuts and bolts to implementing an ERM information system especially when it comes to obtaining the data required for risk analysis. In many companies silos of data and information have evolved in various business units. Some of these business units may have been acquired and never fully integrated into a company's overall data infrastructure. In other cases distance from headquarters or levels of contribution to the overall revenue of a corperation may have resulted in a lack of attention about the quality and quantity of data a business unit may possess (Hershman, 2007). In many cases it is likely that data policies and the development of centralized data controls have just not matured (Bryce, 2007).

Another common data and information management scenario is that data control, and thus data management, is much more important in some parts of a corporation than it is in other parts. In a diversified business environment, for example, some business activities may be regulated and have external reporting or control requirements (Psica, 2008). Thus those responsible for implementing ERM information systems need to understand how a company's history, culture, and business sector involvement may impact the existence, management, and availability of data that is needed for risk analysis (Wu, 2004).

The problems ERM practitioners may face when it comes to identifying, collecting, cleansing, and analyzing data may be frustrating to them but the problems are not new to the realm of information management. Often adding to this frustration is a lack of guidance on how to create an information infrastructure to accomplish their goals. ERM practitioners also face the challenge of dealing with cultural, organizational, and political obstacles to data transformation efforts that seem to be almost universal in organizations of all types (Fraser, Schoening-Thiessen & Simkins, 2008).

ERM information systems are facing the same hurdles as other systems that have required changes in procedures, processes, or culture, There are many lessons to be learned from the past implementation of other large systems. Above all, patience and persistence are keys to the process of implementation. The people that have worked on prior large implementations and who have led change in their organizations in the past may very well be among those that can help ease the way for the development or acquisition and the launch of new information systems to support ERM.

CONCLUSION

Over the last decade there have been several corporate financial scandals which were followed shortly thereafter by a widespread economic downturn that many believe resulted from inaccurate forecasting and inadequate risk management. As the age of corporate social responsibility dawns elected officials, regulators, and individual citizens all feel a sense of rage, partially because many people that were in trusted positions did not follow their long-standing professional codes of conduct to guide their ethics and their behavior.

Elected officials responded by passing new laws, many regulators remain unspoken about their actions or inaction, and citizens voiced their opinions at the polling place and in the marketplace bringing political change and drastic declines in consumer spending. The professional organizations, which set the codes of ethics for the trusted, also responded by supporting a change, in fact almost a revolution in how risk will be managed in the business arena.

ERM as a discipline is evolving as tools improve, best practices are developed, and staff gain more experience (Zaccanti, 2009). It is now widely accepted that thorough risk management analysis combines the best of quantitative and qualitative methods and models. Among other things, this approach allows analysts to develop and test scenarios that can address specific concerns and test specific assumptions. However, these methods only work when the company culture encourages alternative perspectives to management assumptions and prevailing strategic thinking (Rudolph, 2009). To maintain momentum ERM staff and corporate executives need a common view of the state of ERM as well as a common language to discuss risks. This means ERM terms must be defined and concepts explained and illustrated as the processes and systems evolve ("How Do We Broaden...," 2008).

Winning over corporate executives may require continuous communication of examples of the cost of risk management failures as well as the potential returns from managing business opportunities in manners that reduce risk but still enable success (Baker, 2008). Corporate executives need to be shown that ERM investments are worthwhile and they need to be shown in ways that they understand and which they can relate (Panning, 2006). However, communication is not an end in of itself. To maximize the benefits gained from ERM risk analysis should be embedded into the strategic planning process and hold a firm place along with market share and profitability analysis (Paladino, 2008).

To some extent ERM is a cultural shift (Coccia, 2005). But the near-term goal is to move executives and boards of directors to the point where they are convinced that they need ongoing analyses of current and future risks (Dickhart, 2008). Beyond that, the long-term goal is the development and perpetuation of a risk management culture (Jones, Santori & Ingram, 2006). ERM staff should recognize that resistance to change in business practices has occurred in the past and it is likely that it will occur in the future (Ballou & Heitger, 2005; Hampton, 2006).

The responsibility for risk management, the methods of analyzing and managing risk, and the information systems to support risk management are all undergoing a radical change. ERM is rapidly emerging but in many places it still flounders in need of both leadership and tools. The complexity of ERM has shocked many boards of directors, corporate managers, and industry analysts. The responsibility for ERM is overwhelming for some and the complexity, detail, and expense is overwhelming for others. ERM is not a quick fix. It is a change that will take time and results will only be accomplished over the long term. To achieve the promise of ERM will require patience and persistence.

Bibliography

Avison, D., & Taylor, V. (1997). Information systems development methodologies: a classification according to problem situation. *Journal of Information Technology (Routledge, Ltd.), 12*(1), 73-81. Retrieved August 4, 2009, from EBSCO online database, Academic Search Premier. http://search.ebscohost.com/login.aspx?direct=true&db=aph&AN=6270862&site=ehost-live

Baker, N. (2008). Real-world ERM. (cover story). *Internal Auditor, 65*(6), 32-37. Retrieved July 29, 2009, from EBSCO online database, Business Source Premier. http://search.ebscohost.com/login.aspx?direct=true&db=buh&AN=35654519&site=ehost-live

Ballou, B., & Heitger, D. (2005). A building-block approach for implementing COSO's enterprise risk management — integrated framework. *Management Accounting Quarterly, 6*(2), 1-10. Retrieved August 3, 2009, from EBSCO online database, Business Source Premier. http://search.ebscohost.com/login.aspx?direct=true&db=buh&AN=16939145&site=ehost-live

Barton, T., Shenkir, W., & Walker, P. (2009). ERM: The evolution of a balancing act. *Financial Executive, 25*(5), 30-33. Retrieved July 29, 2009, from EBSCO online database, Business Source Premier.

http://search.ebscohost.com/login.aspx?direct=true&db=buh&AN=41326828&site=ehost-live

Bowling, D., & Rieger, L. (2005a). Making sense of COSO's new framework for enterprise risk management. *Bank Accounting & Finance (08943958), 18*(2), 29-34. Retrieved August 3, 2009, from EBSCO online database, Business Source Premier. http://search.ebscohost.com/login.aspx?direct=true&db=buh&AN=19726851&site=ehost-live

Bowling, D., & Rieger, L. (2005b). Success factors for implementing enterprise risk management. *Bank Accounting & Finance (08943958), 18*(3), 21-26. Retrieved August 3, 2009, from EBSCO online database, Business Source Premier. http://search.ebscohost.com/login.aspx?direct=true&db=buh&AN=19726858&site=ehost-live

Branham, J. (2006). ERM: A fork in the road for risk mgrs. *National Underwriter / Life & Health Financial Services, 110*(16), 31-31. Retrieved July 30, 2009, from EBSCO online database, Business Source Premier. http://search.ebscohost.com/login.aspx?direct=true&db=buh&AN=20843766&site=ehost-live

Bryce, T. (2007). What is information resource management? *AIIM E-DOC, 21*(3), 46-47. Retrieved August 3, 2009, from EBSCO online database, Business Source Premier. http://search.ebscohost.com/login.aspx?direct=true&db=buh&AN=25162378&site=ehost-live

Chase-Jenkins, L., & Shimpi, P. (2006). ERM helps RMs cope with wider risks. *National Underwriter / Property & Casualty Risk & Benefits Management, 110*(7), 28-29. Retrieved July 30, 2009, from EBSCO online database, Business Source Premier. http://search.ebscohost.com/login.aspx?direct=true&db=buh&AN=19986599&site=ehost-live

Coccia, R. (2005). Enterprise risk management must be part of companies' culture: Panel. *Business Insurance, 39*(43), 37-39. Retrieved July 30, 2009, from EBSCO online database, Business Source Premier. http://search.ebscohost.com/login.aspx?direct=true&db=buh&AN=19067106&site=ehost-live

Coccia, R. (2006). ERM plans cut costs, help risk managers bring added value. *Business Insurance, 40*(21), 4-4. Retrieved July 30, 2009, from EBSCO online database, Business Source Premier. http://search.ebscohost.com/login.aspx?direct=true&db=buh&AN=21129654&site=ehost-live

Cotton, B. (2009). Seven sins of risk management. *Chartered Accountants Journal, 88*(6), 68-69. Retrieved July 29, 2009, from EBSCO online database, Business Source Premier. http://search.ebscohost.com/login.aspx?direct=true&db=buh&AN=43091253&site=ehost-live

Dickhart, G. (2008). Risk: Key to governance. *Internal Auditor, 65*(6), 27-30. Retrieved July 29, 2009, from EBSCO online database, Business Source Premier. http://search.ebscohost.com/login.aspx?direct=true&db=buh&AN=35654518&site=ehost-live

Downes, D. (2006). Risk management software solutions it's a fragmented marketplace. *Accountancy Ireland, 38*(4), 22-24. Retrieved July 29, 2009, from EBSCO online database, Business Source Premier. http://search.ebscohost.com/login.aspx?direct=true&db=buh&AN=21901189&site=ehost-live

Expect the unexpected. (2009). *Best's Review,* 110(2), 62-62. Retrieved July 29, 2009, from EBSCO online database, Business Source Premier. http://search.ebscohost.com/login.aspx?direct=true&db=buh&AN=42430727&site=ehost-live

Fraser, J., Schoening-Thiessen, K., & Simkins, B. (2008). Who reads what most often? A survey of enterprise risk management literature read by risk executives. *Journal of Applied Finance, 18*(1), 73-91. Retrieved August 3, 2009, from EBSCO online database, Business Source Premier. http://search.ebscohost.com/login.aspx?direct=true&db=buh&AN=34667282&site=ehost-live

Giddens, A. (1999). Risk and responsibility. *Modern Law Review, 62*(1), 1. Retrieved July 29, 2009, from EBSCO online database, Academic Search Premier. http://search.ebscohost.com/login.aspx?direct=true&db=aph&AN=10453500&site=ehost-live

Gramling, A., & Myers, P. (2006). Internal auditing's role in ERM. (cover story). *Internal Auditor, 63*(2), 52-58. Retrieved July 30, 2009, from EBSCO online database, Business Source Premier. http://search.ebscohost.com/login.aspx?direct=true&db=buh&AN=20500886&site=ehost-live

Hampton, J. (2006). Reducing the complexity of ERM might give system more traction. *Business Insurance, 40*(36), 33-33. Retrieved July 30, 2009, from EBSCO online database, Business Source Premier. http://search.ebscohost.com/login.aspx?direct=true&db=buh&AN=22478014&site=ehost-live

Hershman, R. (2007). Insurers eye road map for ERM highway. *National Underwriter / Property & Casualty Risk & Benefits Management, 111*(40), 26-27. Retrieved July 29, 2009, from EBSCO online database, Business Source Premier. http://search.ebscohost.com/login.aspx?direct=true&db=buh&AN=27392868&site=ehost-live

Hofmann, M. (2009). Interest in enterprise risk management is growing. *Business Insurance, 43*(18), 14-16. Retrieved July 29, 2009, from EBSCO online database, Business Source Premier. http://search.ebscohost.com/login.aspx?direct=true&db=buh&AN=40628117&site=ehost-live

How do we broaden our awareness of incidents and risks? (2008). *Directorship, 34*(6), 12-13. Retrieved July 29, 2009, from EBSCO online database, Business Source Premier. http://search.ebscohost.com/login.aspx?direct=true&db=buh&AN=35905103&site=ehost-live

Johnson, K., & Swanson, Z. (2007). Quantifying legal risk: A method for managing legal risk. *Management Accounting Quarterly, 9*(1), 22-30. Retrieved July 29, 2009, from EBSCO online database, Business Source Premier. http://search.ebscohost.com/login.aspx?direct=true&db=buh&AN=30046154&site=ehost-live

Jones, R., Santori, L., & Ingram, D. (2006). Credit FAQ: Enterprise Risk Management one year on. *Reactions, 26,* 66-68. Retrieved July 30, 2009, from EBSCO online database, Business Source Premier. http://search.ebscohost.com/login.aspx?direct=true&db=buh&AN=22552799&site=ehost-live

Karlin, B. (2007). Sweating out the ERMs. *Treasury & Risk,* (Dec/Jan). Retrieved July 29, 2009, from EBSCO online database, Business Source Premier. http://search.ebscohost.com/login.aspx?direct=true&db=buh&AN=28144191&site=ehost-live

Kocourek, P., & Newfrock, J. (2006). Are boards worrying about the wrong risks? *Corporate Board, 27*(157), 6-11. Retrieved July 30, 2009, from EBSCO online database, Business Source Premier. http://search.ebscohost.com/login.aspx?direct=true&db=buh&AN=19887261&site=ehost-live

Korolov, M. (2009). Enterprise Risk Management: Getting holistic. (cover story). *Securities Industry News, 21*(15), 1-6. Retrieved July 29, 2009, from EBSCO online database, Business Source Premier. http://search.ebscohost.com/login.aspx?direct=true&db=buh&AN=43249547&site=ehost-live

Lenckus, D. (2006). RIMS launches online tool to advance ERM. *Business Insurance, 40*(49), 2-31. Retrieved July 30, 2009, from EBSCO online database, Business Source Premier. http://search.ebscohost.com/login.aspx?direct=true&db=buh&AN=23455515&site=ehost-live

Lenckus, D. (2006). No two approaches to ERM the same. *Business Insurance, 40*(19), 15-18. Retrieved July 30, 2009, from EBSCO online database, Business Source Premier. http://search.ebscohost.com/login.aspx?direct=true&db=buh&AN=20876684&site=ehost-live

Lenckus, D. (2009). Demonstration of ERM's usefulness key to winning over management. *Business Insurance, 43*(20), 16-17. Retrieved July 29, 2009, from EBSCO online database, Business Source Premier. http://search.ebscohost.com/login.aspx?direct=true&db=buh&AN=41880299&site=ehost-live

Leopoulos, V., Kirytopoulos, K., & Malandrakis, C. (2006). Risk management for SMEs: Tools to use and how. *Production Planning & Control, 17*(3), 322-332. Retrieved July 29, 2009, from EBSCO online database, Business Source Premier http://search.ebscohost.com/login.aspx?direct=true&db=buh&AN=20855872&site=ehost-live

Loghry, J., & Veach, C. (2009). Enterprise risk assessments. (cover story). *Professional Safety, 54*(2), 31-35. Retrieved August 3, 2009, from EBSCO online database, Business Source Premier. http://search.ebscohost.com/login.aspx?direct=true&db=buh&AN=36616707&site=ehost-live

McDonald, C. (2008). Insurer ERM falling short, survey finds. *National Underwriter/ Property & Casualty Risk & Benefits Management, 112*(32), 28. Retrieved July 29, 2009, from EBSCO online database, Business Source Premier. http://search.ebscohost.com/login.aspx?direct=true&db=buh&AN=34359846&site=ehost-live

McDonald, C. (2009). Will ERM survive the economic meltdown? *National Underwriter / Property & Casualty Risk & Benefits Management, 113*(15), 27-34. Retrieved July 29, 2009, from EBSCO online database, Business Source Premier. http://search.ebscohost.com/login.aspx?direct=true&db=buh&AN=40085724&site=ehost-live

Millage, A. (2005). ERM still in its infancy. *Internal Auditor, 62*(5), 16-17. Retrieved July 30, 2009, from EBSCO online database, Business Source Premier.

http://search.ebscohost.com/login.aspx?direct=true&db=buh&AN=18520854&site=ehost-live

Milligan, J. (2009). Adopting an approach to ERM. *Community Banker, 18*(6), 34-37. Retrieved July 29, 2009, from EBSCO online database, Business Source Premier. http://search.ebscohost.com/login.aspx?direct=true&db=buh&AN=41037778&site=ehost-live

Morgan, J. (2009, May 7). Firms adjust to new world of risk. *Investment Management Weekly,* Retrieved July 29, 2009, from EBSCO online database, Business Source Premier. http://search.ebscohost.com/login.aspx?direct=true&db=buh&AN=40730215&site=ehost-live

Muzzy, L. (2008). Approaching Enterprise Risk Management. *Financial Executive, 24*(8), 59-61. Retrieved July 29, 2009, from EBSCO online database, Business Source Premier. http://search.ebscohost.com/login.aspx?direct=true&db=buh&AN=34736453&site=ehost-live

Paladino, B. (2008). Strategically managing risk in today's perilous markets. (Cover Story). *Strategic Finance, 90*(5), 27-33. Retrieved July 29, 2009, from EBSCO online database, Business Source Premier. http://search.ebscohost.com/login.aspx?direct=true&db=buh&AN=35127283&site=ehost-live

Panning, W. (2006a). ERM report card. *Best's Review, 107*(6), 112. Retrieved July 30, 2009, from EBSCO online database, Business Source Premier. http://search.ebscohost.com/login.aspx?direct=true&db=buh&AN=22884933&site=ehost-live

Panning, W. (2006b). Making ERM happen. *Best's Review, 106*(9), 88. Retrieved July 30, 2009, from EBSCO online database, Business Source Premier. http://search.ebscohost.com/login.aspx?direct=true&db=buh&AN=19773391&site=ehost-live

Perera, H., & Costa, W. (2008). Analytic hierarchy process for selection of ERP software for manufacturing companies. *Vision (09722629), 12*(4), 1-11. Retrieved August 4, 2009, from EBSCO online database, Business Source Premier. http://search.ebscohost.com/login.aspx?direct=true&db=buh&AN=36659221&site=ehost-live

Peterson, J. (2006). Ready for ERM. (Cover Story). *ABA Banking Journal, 98*(1), 19-23. Retrieved July 30, 2009, from EBSCO online database, Business Source Premier. http://search.ebscohost.com/login.aspx?direct=true&db=buh&AN=19357897&site=ehost-live

Psica, A. (2008). The right fit auditing ERM frameworks. *Internal Auditor, 65*(2), 50-56. Retrieved July 29, 2009, from EBSCO online database, Business Source Premier. http://search.ebscohost.com/login.aspx?direct=true&db=buh&AN=31639592&site=ehost-live

Ramamoorti, S., & Weidenmier, M. (2006). Is IT next for ERM? (cover story). *Internal Auditor, 63*(2), 45-50. Retrieved July 30, 2009, from EBSCO online database, Business Source Premier. http://search.ebscohost.com/login.aspx?direct=true&db=buh&AN=20500885&site=ehost-live

Rudolph, M. (2009). Do firms need a chief skeptical officer? *National Underwriter / Property & Casualty Risk & Benefits Management, 113*(13), 23. Retrieved July 29, 2009, from EBSCO online database, Business Source Premier. http://search.ebscohost.com/login.aspx?direct=true&db=buh&AN=37563028&site=ehost-live

Ruquet, M. (2007). Firms unprepared for reputational risks. *National Underwriter / Property & Casualty Risk & Benefits Management, 111*(46), 25-26. Retrieved July 29, 2009, from EBSCO online database, Business Source Premier. http://search.ebscohost.com/login.aspx?direct=true&db=buh&AN=27889675&site=ehost-live

Schanfield, A. (2008). 12 top ERM implementation challenges. *Internal Auditor, 65*(6), 41-44. Retrieved July 29, 2009, from EBSCO online database, Business Source Premier. http://search.ebscohost.com/login.aspx?direct=true&db=buh&AN=35654520&site=ehost-live

Shan, H., Xin, G., Xiaoyan, L., & Junwen, F. (2009). A study on the integration risk management for the insurance enterprises. *Management Science & Engineering, 3*(1), 41-50. Retrieved July 29, 2009, from EBSCO online database, Academic Search Complete. http://search.ebscohost.com/login.aspx?direct=true&db=a9h&AN=42512669&site=ehost-live

Songini, M. (2004). S50M SAP rollout runs into trouble in Tacoma. *Computerworld, 38*(47), 1-52. Retrieved August 4, 2009, from EBSCO online database, Academic Search Complete. http://search.ebscohost.com/login.aspx?direct=true&db=a9h&AN=15277720&site=ehost-live

Stein, R. (2005). ERM: An indispensable tool. *Best's Review, 106*(6), 76. Retrieved July 30, 2009, from EBSCO online database, Business Source Premier. http://search.ebscohost.com/login.aspx?direct=true&db=buh&AN=18534036&site=ehost-live

Van der Stede, W. (2009). Enterprise governance: Risk and performance management through the business cycle. *CMA Management, 83*(3), 24-27. Retrieved July 29, 2009, from EBSCO online database, Business Source Premier. http://search.ebscohost.com/login.aspx?direct=true&db=buh&AN=40208368&site=ehost-live

Vlasenko, O., & Kozlov, S. (2009). Choosing the risk curve type. *Technological & Economic Development of Economy, 15*(2), 341-351. Retrieved July 29, 2009 from EBSCO online database, Business Source Premier http://search.ebscohost.com/login.aspx?direct=true&db=buh&AN=43181065&site=ehost-live

Watson, H., Rainer Jr., R., & Koh, C. (1991). Executive information systems: A framework for development and a survey of current practices. *MIS Quarterly, 15*(1), 13. Retrieved August 4, 2009, from EBSCO online database, Academic Search Premier. http://search.ebscohost.com/login.aspx?direct=true&db=aph&AN=9604086246&site=ehost-live

Wheeler, J. (2009). The rise of the Chief Risk Officer. *Internal Auditor, 65*(3), 55-57. Retrieved July 29, 2009, from EBSCO online database, Business Source Premier. http://search.ebscohost.com/login.aspx?direct=true&db=buh&AN=41566021&site=ehost-live

Woodard, M. (2005). Measuring the payoffs of strategic risk management. *CMA Management, 79*(7), 30-35. Retrieved July 30, 2009, from EBSCO online database, Business Source Premier. http://search.ebscohost.com/login.aspx?direct=true&db=buh&AN=19666922&site=ehost-live

Wu, J. (2004). The information repository. *DM Review, 14*(9), 74-77. Retrieved August 3, 2009, from EBSCO online database, Business Source Premier. http://search.ebscohost.com/login.aspx?direct=true&db=buh&AN=14532935&site=ehost-live

Zaccanti, B. (2009). ERM bolsters evolution of insurance RM. *National Underwriter / Property & Casualty Risk & Benefits Management, 113*(15), 29-35. Retrieved July 29, 2009, from EBSCO online database, Business Source Premier. http://search.ebscohost.com/login.aspx?direct=true&db=buh&AN=40085726&site=ehost-live

Suggested Reading

Barlas, S., Shillam, P., & Williams, K. (2006). Companies still struggle with enterprise risk. *Strategic Finance, 88*(2), 25. Retrieved July 30, 2009, from EBSCO online database, Business Source Premier. http://search.ebscohost.com/login.aspx?direct=true&db=buh&AN=21722426&site=ehost-live

Beasley, M., Pagach, D., & Warr, R. (2008). Information conveyed in hiring announcements of senior executives overseeing enterprise-wide risk management processes. *Journal of Accounting, Auditing & Finance, 23*(3), 311-332. Retrieved August 3, 2009, from EBSCO online database, Business Source Premier. http://search.ebscohost.com/login.aspx?direct=true&db=buh&AN=33064755&site=ehost-live

Bradford, M. (2009). Managing the full spectrum of corporate risk. *Business Insurance, 43*(20), 11. Retrieved July 29, 2009, from EBSCO online database, Business Source Premier. http://search.ebscohost.com/login.aspx?direct=true&db=buh&AN=41880293&site=ehost-live

Burnes, G. (2008). TOP 10 Enterprise Risk Management MYTHS. *Financial Executive, 24*(4), 56-58. Retrieved July 29, 2009, from EBSCO online database, Business Source Premier. http://search.ebscohost.com/login.aspx?direct=true&db=buh&AN=31896904&site=ehost-live

Cameron, M., & Bergentoft, N. (2009). Industry trends in treasury software. *Financial Executive, 25*(1), 62-63. Retrieved July 29, 2009, from EBSCO online database, Business Source Premier. http://search.ebscohost.com/login.aspx?direct=true&db=buh&AN=36219784&site=ehost-live

Ceniceros, R. (2007). Team weighing environmental impact more often includes risk managers. *Business Insurance, 41*(49), 18-20. Retrieved July 29, 2009, from EBSCO online database, Business Source Premier. http://search.ebscohost.com/login.aspx?direct=true&db=buh&AN=28044502&site=ehost-live

Cox Jr., L. (2008). What's wrong with risk matrices? *Risk Analysis: An International Journal, 28*(2), 497-512. Retrieved August 3, 2009 from EBSCO online database, Business Source Complete http://search.ebscohost.com/login.aspx?direct=true&db=buh&AN=31683028&site=ehost-live

Csiszar, E. (2008). Managing risk and uncertainty. *Business & Economic Review, 55*(1), 3-7. Retrieved July 29, 2009, from EBSCO online database, Business Source Premier. http://search.ebscohost.com/login.aspx?direct=true&db=buh&AN=34773986&site=ehost-live

De La Rosa, S. (2005). ERM-based audit reports. *Internal Auditor, 62*(6), 73-75. Retrieved July 30, 2009, from EBSCO online database, Business Source Premier. http://search.ebscohost.com/login.aspx?direct=true&db=buh&AN=19281456&site=ehost-live

Engle, P. (2009). Enterprise risk management time. *Industrial Engineer: IE, 41*(5), 20. Retrieved July 29, 2009, from EBSCO online database, Academic Search Complete. http://search.ebscohost.com/login.aspx?direct=true&db=a9h&AN=39775623&site=ehost-live

ERM enigma. (2005). *Canadian Underwriter, 72*(8), 10-14. Retrieved July 31, 2009, from EBSCO online database, Business Source Premier. http://search.ebscohost.com/login.aspx?direct=true&db=buh&AN=18443678&site=ehost-live

Field, A. (2006). Now, ERM counts. *Treasury & Risk, 16*(11), 19-20. Retrieved July 30, 2009, from EBSCO online database, Business Source Premier. http://search.ebscohost.com/login.aspx?direct=true&db=buh&AN=25776841&site=ehost-live

Friedman, S. (2009). Out-of-work risk managers must face up to the 'reality of necessity'. *National Underwriter / Property & Casualty Risk & Benefits Management, 113*(15), 14-36. Retrieved July 29, 2009, from EBSCO online database, Business Source Premier. http://search.ebscohost.com/login.aspx?direct=true&db=buh&AN=40085719&site=ehost-live

Friedman, S. (2009). What are risk managers worth? *National Underwriter /Property & Casualty Risk & Benefits Management, 113*(15), 14-38. Retrieved July 29, 2009, from EBSCO online database, Business Source Premier. http://search.ebscohost.com/login.aspx?direct=true&db=buh&AN=40085720&site=ehost-live

Gangl, W. (2008). Implementing an Enterprise Risk Management evaluation. *InsideCounsel, 18*(Supplement), 8. Retrieved July 29, 2009, from EBSCO online database, Business Source Premier. http://search.ebscohost.com/login.aspx?direct=true&db=buh&AN=34100475&site=ehost-live

Gorzen-Mitka, I. (2013). Risk management as challenge to today's enterprises. *Problems of Management in the 21St Century,* 74-5. Retrieved November 15, 2013, from EBSCO Online Database Business Source Complete. http://search.ebscohost.com/login.aspx?direct=true&db=bth&AN=89641544&site=ehost-live

Gurevitz, S. (2009). Manageable risk. (Cover story). *University Business, 12*(5), 39-42. Retrieved July 29, 2009, from EBSCO online database, Academic Search Complete. http://search.ebscohost.com/login.aspx?direct=true&db=a9h&AN=39755484&site=ehost-live

Hoyt, R., Powell, L., & Sommer, D. (2007). Computing value at risk: A simulation assignment to illustrate the value of enterprise risk management. *Risk Management & Insurance Review, 10*(2), 299-307. Retrieved July 29, 2009 from EBSCO online database, Business Source Premier http://search.ebscohost.com/login.aspx?direct=true&db=buh&AN=26846288&site=ehost-live

Jeffery, C. (2005). Enterprise Risk Management: Opportunity for the Treasurer. *Financial Executive, 21*(8), 71-71. Retrieved July 30, 2009, from EBSCO online database, Business Source Premier. http://search.ebscohost.com/login.aspx?direct=true&db=buh&AN=18523322&site=ehost-live

Jie, L. (2012). The Enterprise Risk Management and the risk oriented internal audit. *I-Business, 4*(3), 287-292. Retrieved November 15, 2013, from EBSCO Online Database Business Source Complete. http://search.ebscohost.com/login.aspx?direct=true&db=bth&AN=84536005&site=ehost-live

Lenckus, D. (2006). ERM an opportunity for risk managers. *Business Insurance, 40*(21), 20-20. Retrieved July 30, 2009, from EBSCO online database, Business Source Premier. http://search.ebscohost.com/login.aspx?direct=true&db=buh&AN=21129665&site=ehost-live

Lenckus, D., Gonzalez, G., Parekh, R., & Roberts, S. (2006). Brokers starting to see the value in ERM services. *Business Insurance, 40*(29), 13-22. Retrieved July 30, 2009, from EBSCO online database, Business Source Premier. http://search.ebscohost.com/login.aspx?direct=true&db=buh&AN=21770578&site=ehost-live

Leopoulos, V., Kirytopoulos, K., & Malandrakis, C. (2006). Risk management for SMEs: Tools to use and how. *Production Planning & Control, 17*(3), 322-332. Retrieved July 30, 2009 from EBSCO online database, Business Source Premier http://search.ebscohost.com/login.aspx?direct=true&db=buh&AN=20855872&site=ehost-live

Mariga, V. (2007). ERM, temples and pyramids: Mysteries solved. *Canadian Underwriter, 74*(11), 42-44.

Retrieved July 29, 2009, from EBSCO online database, Business Source Premier. http://search.ebscohost.com/login.aspx?direct=true&db=buh&AN=28005670&site=ehost-live

Marshall, J., & Heffes, E. (2005). Most firms agree: ERM is a challenge. *Financial Executive, 21*(8), 10. Retrieved July 30, 2009, from EBSCO online database, Business Source Premier. http://search.ebscohost.com/login.aspx?direct=true&db=buh&AN=18522370&site=ehost-live

McCourt, M. (2009). Risk assessment: The view from ten miles above your enterprise. *Security: For Buyers of Products, Systems & Services, 46*(6), 12. Retrieved July 29, 2009, from EBSCO online database, Business Source Premier. http://search.ebscohost.com/login.aspx?direct=true&db=buh&AN=41522225&site=ehost-live

McShane, M.K., Nair, A., & Rustambekov, E. (2011). Does Enterprise Risk Management increase firm value?. *Journal of Accounting, Auditing & Finance, 26*(4), 641-658. Retrieved November 15, 2013, from EBSCO Online Database Business Source Complete. http://search.ebscohost.com/login.aspx?direct=true&db=bth&AN=69640261&site=ehost-live

Mills, R. (2006). Developments in risk management. *Henley Manager Update, 18*(2), 19-29. Retrieved July 30, 2009, from EBSCO online database, Business Source Premier. http://search.ebscohost.com/login.aspx?direct=true&db=buh&AN=24276150&site=ehost-live

Panning, W. (2009). The why and how of risk-based planning. *Best's Review, 110*(3), 78. Retrieved July 29, 2009, from EBSCO online database, Business Source Premier. http://search.ebscohost.com/login.aspx?direct=true&db=buh&AN=43154340&site=ehost-live

Quinn, L. (2007). Camera-shy risk managers can benefit from media exposure. *National Underwriter / Property & Casualty Risk & Benefits Management, 111*(15), 23-32. Retrieved August 3, 2009, from EBSCO online database, Business Source Premier. http://search.ebscohost.com/login.aspx?direct=true&db=buh&AN=24819027&site=ehost-live

Roberts, S. (2005). ERM widely accepted but not widely implemented, study says. *Business Insurance, 39*(31), 6. Retrieved July 31, 2009, from EBSCO online database, Business Source Premier. http://search.ebscohost.com/login.aspx?direct=true&db=buh&AN=17979898&site=ehost-live

Sclafane, S. (2006). S&P: A vision of the future. *National Underwriter/Property & Casualty Risk & Benefits Management, 110*(30), 14-31. Retrieved July 30, 2009, from EBSCO online database, Business Source Premier. http://search.ebscohost.com/login.aspx?direct=true&db=buh&AN=22013895&site=ehost-live

Simkins, B. (2008). Enterprise Risk Management: Current initiatives and issues journal of applied finance roundtable. *Journal of Applied Finance, 18*(1), 115-132. Retrieved August 3, 2009, from EBSCO online database, Business Source Premier. http://search.ebscohost.com/login.aspx?direct=true&db=buh&AN=34667285&site=ehost-live

Smiechewicz, W. (2009). ERM 2.0 makes everybody a risk manager. *Financial Executive, 25*(3), 61. Retrieved July 29, 2009, from EBSCO online database, Business Source Premier. http://search.ebscohost.com/login.aspx?direct=true&db=buh&AN=41237596&site=ehost-live

Sutton, S., Khazanchi, D., Hampton, C., & Arnold, V. (2008). Risk analysis in extended enterprise environments: Identification of critical risk factors in B2B E-commerce relationships. *Journal of the Association for Information Systems, 9*(4), 151-174. Retrieved August 3, 2009, from EBSCO online database, Business Source Premier. http://search.ebscohost.com/login.aspx?direct=true&db=buh&AN=31949122&site=ehost-live

White, L. (2004). Management accountants and Enterprise Risk Management. *Strategic Finance, 86*(5), 6-7. Retrieved August 3, 2009, from EBSCO online database, Business Source Premier. http://search.ebscohost.com/login.aspx?direct=true&db=buh&AN=14831289&site=ehost-live

Michael Erbschloe, M.A.

Executive Leadership

ABSTRACT

Leadership is slightly more obvious than it is valuable. One can exemplify leadership in a variety of ways. Maintaining an awareness of the bodies of knowledge on the topic is one among many. With an ability to draw from various sources and perspectives in a timely manner, an effective leader demonstrates preparation and readiness to articulate ideas, to specify recommendations, and to convince others of rationale soundness. This essay covers transactional leadership, transformational leadership, and servant leadership and it conveys some tenets from each. In addition, it summarizes leadership thought from a historical viewpoint. About eighty years ago, most experts believed that leaders were individuals who were born possessing specific characteristics. Those older approaches gave way to some seeking to find the one best way to lead. More recent thinking suggests executive leadership effectiveness depends on the degree to which there is a match between style and organization of situations. A recent shift in thinking holds the potential for emphasizing service over results. It is likely that service to others will gain importance given the expected growth of jobs and leadership opportunities in the nonprofit sector. The main focal points of executive leadership include mission accomplishment, resource acquisition, and external affairs. In brief, this essay aims to help readers recognize some requirements for leadership so prospective leaders may prepare to act on them.

OVERVIEW

Leadership is both valuable and obvious. Most people would probably define leadership according to their observations of people with whom they interact daily. In terms of the workplace, some of us would agree that our managers, supervisors, and executives are leaders in a formal sense though they may fall short of the leadership we expect to see in them. Fortunately, a few of our co-workers and associates with whom we enjoy informal relationships fit the leadership role better than others who occupy authoritative positions. The need for leadership is present at every level within and between organizations; this essay tends to focus on the top level and makes frequent references to the nonprofit sector.

Aside from job growth projections, significant differences exist between nonprofit organizations and governmental or for-profit entities. "To measure its effectiveness, a nonprofit must ask itself, 'Are we really delivering on our mission, not just meeting budget, and are we getting maximum impact from our expenditures?'" (Epstein & McFarlan, 2011). Leaders of nonprofit organizations should hold or acquire skills that allow them to fulfill missions, acquire resources, develop strategies, and navigate external and political environments. In short supply, some publications on the topic of nonprofit executive leadership are available and tend to focus reader attention on interactions between presidents of the organization and its board. It takes time to rise to the top of the organizational ladder, yet prospective leaders begin developing their skills now rather than later, for the benefits of doing so will become more evident with the passage of time and through service in diverse settings.

Regardless of the sector(s) in which today's undergraduates and tomorrow's leaders seek or will find gainful employment, it is likely they may find the contents of this essay insightful and informative. One of the aims here is to provide content that is applicable across the landscape of organization types. Furthermore, at the very least, readers will finish this essay knowing the difference between a manager and a leader, or between management and leadership. The current state of knowledge on the topic asserts that leadership has more to do with influencing others than it does with exercising authority over others through title or position. Moreover, that literature suggests that leaders influence followers and vice versa while formal authority often fades away into the background. In other words, some scholars and practitioners assert that a leader usually gains authority because his or her followers are willing to lend it. In essence, leaders exist only if they have followers and, as we shall discover in the pages ahead, some leaders function by serving their followers. Indeed, some studies have shown that, for example, to improve service quality and maintain customers, organizations must ensure their employees' job satisfaction (Pansoo & Jang-Hyup, 2013).

APPLICATIONS

Through what approaches can one become an exemplary leader? In attempting to answer that question, it is interesting to note that a countless number of today's college students and high school students are satisfying graduation requirements by earning credits for service learning projects, community service tasks, experiential learning arrangements, and the like. This fact alone may serve to demonstrate the immediate and future needs to pursue effective leadership through various means. Another fact of interest is that the literature on this topic contains a lot of material debating whether experience or instruction is the most effective approach for learning about leadership.

Corporate governance is said to be related to corporate performance (Chun-Yao, Zong-Jhe, & Chun-Yi, 2013). Taken here as evidence of real tension between the academic sector and the corporate sector on the subject of leadership program effectiveness, corporations and management consultants argue from a standpoint that leadership is a topic essentially self-taught. In contrast, business school representatives claim those corporate entities offer programs primarily geared toward issues facing a specific firm and industry concluding that they fall short of exposing participants to larger environmental contexts in which leaders truly operate. Casting those arguments aside for the moment, this essay merely scratches the surface addressing subjects such as leadership traits, styles, and skills and noting the interdependencies among them.

In brief, it is important to assert that personal traits are ineffective and leadership styles are irrelevant in the absence of skillful communications. Some combination of them will keep workers and organizations moving toward their futures. In the broadest sense, an organization is by definition a group of individuals who come together to share responsibility for achieving three general goals common across the universe of organizations: Growth, stability, and survival.

One of the challenges an executive faces is how to channel individual energy and group activities toward goal achievement and how to maximize performance levels and improve output and service qualities. In essence, organizational results are a function of leadership skill development and its perpetual application to challenging situations. As the reader will see, there are a variety of approaches and perspectives on how executives and their subordinates can pursue and meet those challenges. A good place to begin is with an overview of various perspectives on leadership. By understanding those perspectives, readers will find themselves prepared and ready to handle a variety of situations they might encounter during the course of their personal or professional livelihoods.

Leadership Foundations & Perspectives

Able to borrow from various perspectives in a timely manner, an executive leader must be ready to articulate ideas, to specify recommendations, and to convince others that the underlying rationale is sound. Those analytical and communication skills also arise, in part, due to the leader's exposure to opportunities for interactions with highly respected leaders. In addition, the number of interactions and those abilities are a result of the passage of time because individuals will accumulate experiences and encounter a variety of settings as they tend to their personal and professional lives. In the process, leadership learning will occur as they sharpen their self awareness and recognize the influences they have on others.

According to Chester Barnard, leadership is the ability of a superior to influence the behavior of a subordinate or group and persuade them to follow a particular course of action. In addressing the topic of executive leadership, it is necessary to introduce readers to the primary responsibilities or functions of executives. In his classic book *Functions of the Executive* (1968), Barnard outlines those responsibilities. Many recognize them in abbreviated form as POS-D-CORB, which is a device by which to remember respectively the following list of functions: Planning; organizing; staffing; directing; coordinating (drops one letter); and, budgeting. It may serve students of executive leadership well to gain some experience in each in addition to memorizing them.

Efficiency & Effectiveness

Barnard also drew attention to the efficacy of organizations at a time when there was a mechanistic-type fixation on efficiency. Long before the organic and systems perspectives on organizations came into existence, some problems arose as subunits attempted to maximize their own efficiencies in isolation from each other. In effect, subunits would look inward, thereby creating some operating distance between them and other subunits and between the organization and those on the outside whom it serves. Obviously, it takes multiple subunits to deliver a good or service to a customer, but the fixation on departmental efficiencies virtually disrupted the focus on deliveries to clients, customers, and the like. In sum, the organization became highly efficient but it did so at the expense of becoming highly ineffective. That is, it began to lose sight of external demands and it was able to do so at minimal cost, a serious problem indeed.

Management scholars and organization theorists during the 1970s were asking questions something like this: Does it matter if organizations do the right thing when there is a prevailing emphasis on doing whatever they do at the lowest average cost? Certainly, making more of an unwanted item will enhance efficiency as will cutting the costs of producing that item. One could go as far as saying very few leaders arise from the ranks of accountants, for instance, who typically form and implement cost-cutting measures. An inward-looking focus on efficiency will only last until another set of problems arises. Consequently, an ongoing challenge for executive leadership is to provide the right bundles of goods and services at an acceptable level of cost.

Drawing a lesson using the example above, cost-cutting while ignoring market situations may lead the organization to produce the wrong bundles at the lowest cost, which is probably a situation most organizations should avoid. Acquisition of additional resources is far more challenging than keeping an eye toward reduction of existing expenses. Organization survival requires providing, offering, and selling bundles that members of society value, want, and demand. This means executives should opt for effectiveness over efficiency whenever given a choice between them, especially when the cost-effectiveness point remains uncharted and unproven. Efficiency and effectiveness are two concepts integral to advancing Barnard's notion of cooperative systems.

A systems perspective takes into account characteristics of the internal operation and highlights the need to pay attention to the external environment in which the organization operates. In brief, a cooperative system of efficiency and effectiveness is required, according to Barnard. In addition, he asserts that purpose is the unifying and coordinating principle. Basic leadership requires individuals who know with precision an organization's purpose whether it is generating financial returns at the pleasure of stockholders, covering social services at the pleasure of stakeholders, or fulfilling other needs and desires.

Values, Mission & Vision

Values, mission, and vision are elements that frequently define an organization's purpose. Warren Bennis, who is a leadership scholar and a former university president, pointed out in the late 1990s that the foremost responsibility of a leader is defining a vision for the organization and then building the capacity of realizing the vision. Around the same timeframe, as a temporary point of departure, the shared leadership view emerged independently of Bennis and from within the context of quality improvement in academe. It suggests a durable vision is one that a relevant community crafts in concert with a formal leader or authority figure. Whatever the method, a vision may unite the masses and its fruition is the result of bringing people together as they go about their work internalizing the vision. In his book *On Becoming a Leader*, Bennis elaborates on the distinction between managers and leaders.

Three Forms of Leadership

That distinction serves as an introduction to two traditional and one emergent form of leadership. On one hand, transactional leadership takes a short-term view in which managers keep an eye on profitability and focus on doing things right. Managers typically use existing systems, maintain controls, and create anguish while striving to answer questions of how and when. In contrast, leaders create trust, facilitate innovation, and use inspiration as they strive to answer questions of what and why. On the other hand, transformative leadership takes a long-term view in which leaders keep an eye toward the future and focus on doing the right things. The next section presents those two basic forms and it resurrects servant leadership theory while covering a few of the conceptual and empirical overlaps and distinctions among them.

Leadership thought has come a long way since the 1920's and 1930's when most experts held the view that some individuals are born with specific traits and innate characteristics that make them natural leaders. That trait approach gave way to a style approach, which represented the continuous attempt to define the best way to lead. More recent thinking is much broader in scope and seems to signify arrival at a consensus. Apparently, leader effectiveness depends on the degree to which a leadership style matches current and future organization situations.

Transactional Leadership

In a context of the political realm, Burns (1978) introduced transactional leadership and transformative leadership as a dichotomy into which leaders receive classification as being one or the other. That seminal work generated a lot of studies and empirical results. Some of those scholars, including Bass (1985) and others, converted Burns's original classification into a continuum with each form at opposite ends. Drawing from those works before them, researchers (Bass, 1985; Bass & Avilio, 1990) constructed four behaviors typically exhibited through transactional leadership. The first is contingent reward, which refers to a focus on resource exchanges. Followers receive various types of support and resources in exchange for their efforts and performance. The second two are variants of management by exception (MBE), which may be active or passive in nature. With a focus on setting standards, active MBE leaders intervene by taking corrective action when it is required whereas passive MBE leaders intervene only when problems become serious. The last is laissez-faire. It refers to leaders who adopt a hands-off approach, allowing followers to find their own way to meet organizational goals, sometimes avoiding leadership responsibilities altogether.

Executive Leadership

The topic of executive leadership represents a brief opportunity for departure from transactional leadership theory before arriving into a discussion of transformational leadership. In contrast to the routine oriented, transactions view of the workplace, executive leadership highlights behaviors that create and communicate clear direction for the organization's future, for implementing changes in structures and processes, and for evaluating critical success factors. It is obvious that leaders of effective organizations focus on doing the right things, which involves strategies that extend leadership beyond an organization's boundaries and into the external environment. As a chapter worthy of further investigation and exploration by readers of this essay, Herman and Heimovics (2005) advance the executive leadership concept by noting that strategies often cross organization boundaries and require political acumen. In short, executive leadership focuses on the relevance of accomplishing missions and acquiring resources and it strikes a close resemblance to transformational leadership theory.

Transformational Leadership

Drawing from the works of Burns and others, Judge and Piccolo (2004) constructed four behaviors that delineate genuine transformational leadership.

- The first is idealized influence, which refers to leaders who form high standards for conducting business in a moral and ethical manner, who gain respect by doing so, and who receive loyalty from followers.
- The second is inspirational motivation, which refers to leaders who articulate a strong vision based on ideals and values, thereby generating enthusiasm, instilling confidence, and producing inspiration among followers. Frequently, they employ symbolic actions and persuasive speeches. Significant in their association, when these first two behaviors congeal, the result is charisma.
- The third is intellectual stimulation, which refers to leaders who challenge the status quo by encouraging divergent perspectives and innovative strategies.
- The last is individual consideration, which refers to leader behaviors that involve developing, coaching, and consulting followers.

Servant Leadership

It is noteworthy that the year before Burns published *Leadership*, Robert K. Greenleaf (1977) introduced the notion that a servant leader places the interests of followers ahead of his or her own. From a historical perspective, servant leadership received attention from a few researchers who proclaim it is a sound theory worthy of further study and application. Unfortunately, academic journal references to Greenleaf's works are scant in comparison to those of Burns. Nonetheless, the research that is available shows that servant-leaders exhibit the following the characteristics: listening; empathy; healing; awareness; persuasion; conceptualization; foresight; stewardship; commitment as mentors; and, community building. It is rather odd that a servant leader's motivation prompts him or her to serve followers as opposed to leading them. Until recently, its popularity appears to be greater as a topic more suitable for professional workshop and seminar settings than for academic settings and college classrooms.

Servant leadership theory is ripe for empirical support and especially more so now and into the distant future. The world of today is emphasizing the importance of servant leadership as evident in the fact that service learning is becoming an integral part of secondary and postsecondary education. Washington (2007) points out that servant leadership theory is a subject of growing interest in the leadership literature. Her research examines relationships of servant leadership theory to transformational and transactional theories of leadership.

Some key findings from that original research indicate that servant leadership compares with transformative leadership, contingent rewards, and active management by exception (MBE). Conversely, it contrasts with passive MBE and laissez faire. These findings hold promise for future leaders as they seek to uncover which leadership styles are most appropriate where, when, and why. Washington (2007) concludes that servant-leaders and transformative leaders share a common orientation to people, but the focal point of the former is organizational service, whereas the focal point of latter is organizational results. These findings are both timely and informative.

As one might guess, service to others will gain importance given the growth of jobs and leadership opportunities in the nonprofit sector. Executive leadership is likely to evolve naturally through those who choose to serve a nonprofit's need for mission fulfillment and resource acquisition and those who want to develop skills enabling them to span boundaries and navigate political environments. Until additional results from studies on servant leadership become available, the extant body of knowledge on transformative leadership seems to be an appropriate source for individuals aspiring to become tomorrow's leaders.

Leadership for the Future

As mentioned throughout this essay, the state of the art in leadership remains divided over whether practice or instruction is the best teacher. Academicians assert that the ideal environment for leadership development is one that teaches students technical business and communication skills and helps them gain a better understanding of ethics, self-awareness, and values. In contrast, practitioners assert that development occurs primarily through on-the-job training. This begs the question: How, then, do the inexperienced become leaders? In actuality, leadership instruction in college classrooms and in corporate workplaces has occurred for the past 50 years, but recent research is beginning to illuminate similarities and differences among the various perspectives.

A wide array of sources on leadership is available. Many of them focus on developing skills in the following areas: intrapersonal, interpersonal, intercultural, organizational, and nonverbal communications; listening; feedback; small group interactions; persuasion; public speaking; interviewing; question formation and articulation. It is obvious that communication skills play a vital role not only in type but also in transmission medium. The three major communication media are oral, written, and electronic. Those media and skills often determine leadership effectiveness.

It takes a lot more than courses, seminars, and books to master leadership skills. A scan of documents or a search over the Internet will produce a significant amount of information in a short period. An initial pass through some of the course offerings found suggest approaches by which someone aspiring to be an executive leader can realize their goal. In general, the nature of executive leadership involves the ability to serve as a change agent and to communicate effectively. More specifically, it involves crafting visions and anticipating their consequences on an organization. Usually, linkages between organization performance and executive leadership appear on a daily or quarterly basis, which illustrates the need for preparation and readiness.

Developing a personal leadership plan may provide benefits to your organization, other leaders, and one's subordinates, for example, is another suggestion one will find during a search. Other points include how to garner trust while attempting to implement change all the while avoiding as many pitfalls as possible during those processes. Still others mention the importance of acquiring, interpreting, and using information whether it originates from inside or outside the organization. Embedded with all those suggestions, recommendations, and anecdotes are strands of theory intertwined with strands of reality. In essence, leaders will likely serve themselves and others well by combining the best that theory and practice have to offer. Obviously, this will take a considerable amount of time to navigate the work, readings, and conversations. However, an acceleration of those processes often begins with some initial guidance that theoretical frameworks afford.

Whether experience or education is the best teacher, a need for outcomes assessment seems to exist. Assessment may take the form of using three basic steps and asking specific questions.

- First, there is a need for direct observation that compares learning outcomes and objectives as stated on paper to the contents of seminars and assignments. Did teaching occur?
- Second, examinations of participant portfolios over time will allow the teacher and the learner to see progress and to enhance self-awareness. Did feedback occur?
- Lastly, follow-up via open-ended questions may reveal individual outcomes providing at the least some anecdotal evidence of learning. Did teaching and learning occur? Some leadership scholars contend that leaders reach their pinnacle by acting in accordance with their values and intuitions.

A large portion of leadership is a function of the specific time in which we live and the opportunities that present themselves. In conclusion, this essay on executive leadership is time-bound as well though it aims to help readers recognize the requirements for leadership. It closes with a list of challenges. Prospective leaders need to:

- Gain an understanding of personal strengths and weaknesses
- Assure their possession of various traits and qualities; build the capacity to become whatever type of leader and to use any type of style that an organization needs at a given time
- Hold an interest in honing communication and other essential skills
- Develop a dual desire to locate a mentor and to become a protégé
- Invoke a constant search for opportunities to practice leadership

In closing, readers who want to improve their leadership abilities will most likely need to enroll in a variety of courses, workshops, and seminars and work toward convening their own as an instructor.

Bibliography

Barnard, Chester I. (1968). *The functions of the executive.* Cambridge, MA: Harvard University Press.

Bass, B. M. (1985). *Leadership and performance beyond expectations.* New York: Free Press

Bass, B. M. & Avolio, B. J. (1990). *The multifactor leadership questionnaire.* Palo Alto, CA: Consulting Pyschologists Press.

Burns, J. M. (1978). *Leadership.* New York: Harper & Row.

Chun-Yao, T., Zong-Jhe, W., & Chun-Yi, L. (2013). Corporate governance and innovation ability. *International Business Research, 6*(7), 70-78. Retrieved November 22, 2013, from EBSCO Online Database Business Source Complete. http://search.ebscohost.com/login.aspx?direct=true&db=bth&AN=89231988&site=ehost-live

Greenleaf, R. K. (1977). *Servant Leadership.* Mahwah: NJ: Paulist Press

Herman, R. D. & Heimovics, D. (2005). Executive leadership. In Herman, R. D. & Associates'

The Jossey-Bass Handbook of Nonprofit Leadership & Management (153-170). San Francisco: John Wiley & Sons, Inc.

Judge, T.A. & Piccolo, R.F. (2004). Transformational and transactional leadership: a meta-analytic test of their relative validity. *Journal of Applied Psychology,* 89, 755-768.

Pansoo, K., & Jang-Hyup, H. (2013). Effects of job satisfaction on service quality, customer satisfaction, and customer loyalty: The case of a local state-owned enterprise. *WSEAS Transactions on Business & Economics, 10*(1), 49-68. Retrieved November 22, 2013, from EBSCO Online Database Business Source Complete. http://search.ebscohost.com/login.aspx?direct=true&db=bth&AN=88117275&site=ehost-live

McClesky, J. A. (2014). Situational, transformational, and transactional leadership and leadership development. *Journal of Business Studies Quarterly, 5*(4), 117–30. Retrieved November 17, 2014, from EBSCO Online Database Business Source Complete. http://search.ebscohost.com/login.aspx?direct=true&db=bth&AN=96783710

Rao, M. S. (2014). Transformational leadership: An academic case study. *Industrial and Commercial Training, 46*(3), 150–4. Retrieved November 17, 2014, from EBSCO Online Database Business Source Complete. http://search.ebscohost.com/login.aspx?direct=true&db=bth&AN=95891807

Washington, R. (2007). Empirical relationships between theories of servant, transformational, and transactional leadership. *Academy of Management Proceedings*, 1-6. Retrieved November 21, 2007, from EBSCO Online Database Business Source Premier. http://search.ebscohost.com/login.aspx?direct=true&db=buh&AN=26509311&site=ehost-live

Suggested Reading

Antonakis, J., & House, R. J. (2014). Instrumental leadership: Measurement and extension of the transformational-transactional leadership theory. *Leadership Quarterly, 25*(4), 746–71. Retrieved November 17, 2014, from EBSCO Online Database Business Source Complete.http://search.ebscohost.com/login.aspx?direct=true&db=bth&AN=96660745

Allio, R. (2007). Band leaders: How they get that way and what to do about it. *Strategy & Leadership*, 35(3), 12-17. Retrieved November 18, 2007, from EBSCO Online Database Business Source Premier. http://search.ebscohost.com/login.aspx?direct=true&db=buh&AN=25609277&site=ehost-live

Burke, R. (2006). Why leaders fail: Exploring the darkside. *International Journal of Manpower, 27*(1), 91-100. Retrieved November 18, 2007, from EBSCO Online Database Business Source Premier. http://search.ebscohost.com/login.aspx?direct=true&db=buh&AN=21556926&site=ehost-live

Chandran, Jay P. (nd) The relevance of Chester Barnard for today's manager. Retrieved November 14, 2007, from http://www.telelavoro.rassegna.it/fad/socorg03/14/barnard.pdf.

Choi, J., & Wang, H. (2007). The promise of a managerial values approach to corporate philanthropy. *Journal of Business Ethics*, 75(4), 345-359. Retrieved November 12, 2007, from EBSCO Online Database Business Source Premier. http://search.ebscohost.com/login.aspx?direct=true&db=buh&AN=26691059&site=ehost-live

Day, D. V. & Lord, R. G. (1988). Executive leadership and organization performance: Suggestions for a new theory and methodology. *Journal of Management*, 14, 453-464.

Epstein, M. J., & McFarlan, F. (2011). Measuring the efficiency and effectiveness of a nonprofit's performance. *Strategic Finance, 93*(4), 27-34. Retrieved November 26, 2013, from EBSCO Online Database Business Source Complete. http://search.ebscohost.com/login.aspx?direct=true&db=bth&AN=66447413&site=ehost-live

Hackman, J., & Wageman, R. (2007). Asking the right questions about leadership. *American Psychologist, 62*(1), 43-47. Retrieved November 18, 2007, from EBSCO Online Database Business Source Premier. http://search.ebscohost.com/login.aspx?direct=true&db=buh&AN=23745897&site=ehost-live

Lakshman, C. (2005). Top executive knowledge leadership: Managing knowledge to lead change at General Electric. *Journal of Change Management*, 5(4), 429-446. Retrieved November 12, 2007, from EBSCO Online Database Business Source Premier. http://search.ebscohost.com/login.aspx?direct=true&db=buh&AN=19302077&site=ehost-live

Maak, T. (2007). Responsible leadership, stakeholder engagement, and the emergence of social capital. *Journal of Business Ethics, 74*(4), 329-343. Retrieved November 18, 2007, from EBSCO Online Database Business Source Premier. http://search.ebscohost.com/login.aspx?direct=true&db=buh&AN=26210817&site=ehost-live

Tonidandel, S., Avery, D., & Phillips, M. (2007). Maximizing returns on mentoring: Factors affecting subsequent protégé performance. *Journal of Organizational Behavior*, 28(1), 89-110. Retrieved November 12, 2007, from EBCSCO Online Database Business Source Premier. http://search.ebscohost.com/login.aspx?direct=true&db=buh&AN=23463959&site=ehost-live

Steven R. Hoagland, Ph.D.

Forecasting Methods for Management

ABSTRACT

Managers frequently need to make decisions about the future of the organization. Forecasting is the science of estimating or predicting future trends to support managers in this process. Forecasting methods can be used to provide information to support decisions about many aspects of the business including buying, selling, production, and hiring. Many statistical techniques are available for use in forecasting. However, each is not equally applicable in every situation. In addition to quantitative methods for forecasting, there are also subjective or qualitative forecasting methods that are used by many managers. Experienced and insightful managers can take advantage of years of experience to extrapolate trends in ways that are still not possible through the use of quantitative techniques alone. As a result, quantitative and qualitative analyses are inseparable for most forecasts.

OVERVIEW

Every day, managers are faced with decisions that need to be made. Some of these are simple such as the routine reordering of supplies or approval of timesheets. Others are more complex, such as determining how to rate someone in an annual review or determining who should be included in the company's layoffs. Another category of complex decision making that managers face is forecasting. This is the science of estimating or predicting future trends. Forecasting is used to support managers in making decisions about many aspects of the business including buying, selling, production, and hiring. For example, managers need to be able to predict the demand for a product or service over a given time period. This will allow them make a number of other decisions. If there will be an increased demand for the organization's product, management can feel confident that they can meet their financial obligations for that time period. However, they may also need to hire additional workers, lease additional facilities, and acquire or store additional raw materials or components to meet the increased demand. Further, a reasonable forecast about demand can also enable the organization to make better strategic decisions about where to take the business line in the future, whether or not to invest in an additional product line, and so forth. On the other hand, if the organization knows that there will be a decreased demand for their products or services for the foreseeable future, they can make other decisions such as whether or not layoffs are called for, if the design of the product needs to be reconsidered, if the business needs to be taken in another direction, and other decisions regarding corporate strategy. The ability to forecast future events with some degree of accuracy is necessary not only for the operation of the organization itself but also for all the members of the supply chain. The same knowledge about the demand for widgets that will affect the widget manufacturer will also affect the organizations providing raw materials or component parts, storing parts or products, delivering products, and selling them to the customer. For these and other reasons, it is important for successful business operations that forecasts be made and that these forecasts be as accurate as possible. With good forecasts, an organization is able to make decisions, develop strategy, and plan for the future.

Deterministic Variables that Affect Operations & Profitability

There are a number of deterministic variables for which there are specific causes or determiners that can affect the operations and profitability of a business. A trend is the persistent, underlying direction in which something is moving in either the short, intermediate, or long term. Identification of a trend allows managers to better plan to meet future needs. For example, a market trend for an increasing reliance on electronic gadgets may mean that a business needs to rethink its strategy of increasing its emphasis on manual tools. Business cycles are continually recurring variations in total economic activity. These expansions or contractions of economic activity tend to occur across most sectors of the economy at the same time. For example, several years of a boom economy with expansion of economic activity (e.g., more jobs, higher sales) are frequently followed by slower growth or even contraction of economic activity. Seasonal fluctuations are changes in economic activity that occur in a fairly regular annual pattern. Seasonal fluctuations may be related to seasons of the year, the calendar, or holidays. In most situations, for example, it would be unwise for a retail store to hire holiday workers on a permanent basis rather than only for the holiday shopping period.

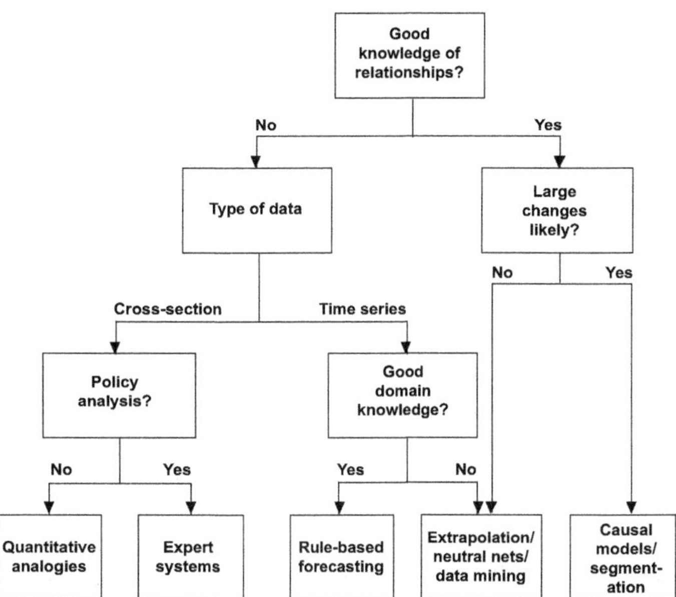

Figure 1: Simplified Forecasting Method Selection Tree for Situations Where Sufficient Objective Data Are Available
(Adapted from http://www.forecastingprinciples.com/selection_tree.html)

Determining the Technique for Forecasting

There are many statistical techniques that can be used in forecasting. However, each is not equally applicable in every situation. The first decision a manager needs to make in choosing a forecasting method is to determine whether or not there are sufficient data available for quantitative analysis. If there are not, qualitative methods must be used. On the other hand, as shown in Figure 1, if there are sufficient data available, there are a number of techniques from which to choose. In order to choose the best technique for the data available, several questions must be asked. First, it must be determined whether or not there is useful knowledge available concerning the relationships and associations between the various factors of interest for the forecast. If there are not, then the type of data available — cross-section or time series — is a determining factor in which analysis techniques are most appropriate. For cross-section data, it must be considered whether or not the forecast needs to assess policy options or otherwise choose between alternative courses of action. If not, quantitative analogies are the most appropriate tool. In this approach, managers or other experts identify analogous situations and these inputs are used to derive the forecast (e.g., to determine how many seats are needed in a movie theatre in a new development, one could look at average data from movie theatres in similar developments). If, on the other hand, the forecast will be used to make decisions between alternatives, a better approach would be to employ an expert system. These are decision support systems that utilize artificial intelligence technology to evaluate a situation and suggest an appropriate course of action. Expert systems develop rules for forecasting following the reasoning processes used by decision making experts.

Forecasting Techniques Using Time Series Data

If time series rather than cross-section data are available, other techniques are more appropriate. If there is a good knowledge about the subject domain of the forecast, rule-based forecasting should be used. These approaches use an expert system that utilizes both expert domain knowledge and statistical techniques. If there is little or no knowledge about the domain, however, other options are available. Extrapolation techniques analyze times series data in an attempt to forecast future events (see below). Neural nets are an approach to artificial intelligence in which computer processors are connected in a way similar to the connections between neurons. These systems are able to learn through trial and error. Data mining can also be used for this type of situation. In data mining, large collections of data are analyzed to establish patterns and determine previously unknown relationships.

If there is a good knowledge of the relationship between variables and the future which is being forecast is unlikely to differ significantly from the past, extrapolation, neural nets, and data mining techniques are available. If, however, it is expected that the future events being predicted will differ significantly from the past, causal models or segmentation are better options for analyzing the data and making forecasts. In causal models, a combination of theory, research, and expert understanding of the domain are used to specify the relationships between variables and make a forecast. Regression analysis is one technique frequently used in this situation. However, although econometrics has been found to improve the accuracy of forecasts in this situation, the use of system dynamics has not.

Subjective & Qualitative Methods for Forecasting
In addition to quantitative methods for forecasting, there are also subjective or qualitative forecasting methods that are used by many managers. These are particularly useful when there are insufficient quantitative data for analysis or if a decision needs to be made quickly. These approaches are used when sufficient quantifiable data are not available for statistical analysis and are based on the manager's experience and intuition about a situation rather than on the application of mathematics or an attempt to reduce the situation to quantifiable terms. There are two major disadvantages of the use of qualitative techniques for forecasting. First, although some managers have good instincts and can make reasonable forecasts using subjective methods, quantitative methods are less dependent on the insights and experiences of one individual and use empirical, verifiable data. Second, because they are subjective, the results of subjective approaches are typically not reproducible because the variables cannot be quantified and applied to future situations.

This is not to say that qualitative techniques are not without merit. Experienced and insightful managers can take advantage of years of experience to extrapolate trends in ways that are still not possible through the use of quantitative techniques alone. In some instances, there are insufficient data to use quantitative techniques, necessitating the use of qualitative forecasting methods. Even when sufficient data are available, it is the human being who must decide which variables to include in the analysis and who must interpret the results of the forecast. Judgment is key to determining which data are relevant to the model. However, a statistical model or analysis cannot take every possible variable into account. Even if this was possible, spurious positive results would be seen due to the effects of probability alone. Expert judgments are essential to determine which inputs need to be considered during the forecasting process. In addition, in many instances, the determination of which analysis methodology is most appropriate to use for forecasting is a matter of judgment. There are a number of statistical techniques available for model building, analysis, and forecasting, many of which are closely related. The validity of the result depends heavily on correctly choosing the most appropriate analytical method. In addition, expert judgments can be helpful in understanding the situation and giving the manager insight regarding the parameters within which the data and subsequent analysis should be interpreted (e.g., "given the current economy and our market plan, we expect widget sales to rise by two percent over the next quarter"). As a result, quantitative and qualitative analyses are inseparable for most forecasts.

APPLICATIONS

One frequently used statistical approach to forecasting is the analysis of time series data. These are data gathered on a specific characteristic over a period of time at intervals of regular length. Unlike *ad hoc* approaches to forecasting where it is impossible to tell whether or not the formula chosen is the most appropriate for the situation; time series analysis allows one to study the structure of the correlation of variables over time to determine the appropriateness of the model. The resultant model can be adjusted as needed to make it more representative of the real world situation.

Goal of Time Series Analysis
The goal of time series analysis is to build a model that will allow managers to forecast future needs. To do this, one must first specify the parameters of the model, including the degree of homogeneity in the time series and the order of the moving average and autoregressive components of the analysis. After the model has been specified, it is next estimated, frequently through nonlinear regression. The autocorrelation function is next examined using a simple

chi-square test to determine whether the residuals are uncorrelated. The model must next be evaluated to determine its validity and whether or not it can be used to make accurate forecasts. Methods to do this include historical simulation starting at different points of time. Model building is an iterative process. The model can be refined as necessary to make it better fit the real world.

Techniques to Smooth out Fluctuation Effects

There are several types of techniques are used to smooth out irregular fluctuation effects in time series data. Naïve forecasting models are simple models that assume that the best predictors of future outcomes are the more recent data in the time series. Because of this assumption, naïve forecasting models do not consider the possibility of trends, business cycles, or seasonal fluctuations. Therefore, the naïve forecasting models work better on data that are reported more frequently (e.g., daily or weekly) or in situations without trends or seasonality. However, care must be taken since naïve model forecasts are often based on the observations of one time period so they can easily become a function of irregular fluctuations in data.

A second approach to smoothing time series data uses averaging models. These models help neutralize the problem of naïve models in which the forecast is overly sensitive to irregular fluctuations. In averaging models, data from several time periods are taken into account. In the simple average model, the forecast is the average of the values for a specified number of previous time periods. Moving averages, on the other hand, use both the average value from previous time periods to forecast future time periods, and update this average in each ensuing time period by including the new values not available in the previous average and dropping out the date from the earliest time periods. Moving averages have the advantage of taking into account the most recent data available. However, it can be difficult to choose the optimal length of time over which to compute the moving average. Further, moving averages do not take into account the effects of trends, business cycles, and seasonal fluctuations. To help neutralize these problems, a weighted moving average can be used which gives more weight to some time periods in the series than to others.

A third approach to smoothing time series data is exponential smoothing techniques. These techniques use weight data from previous time periods with exponentially decreasing importance. Although all these approaches to time series modeling can be helpful for simple data sets, they do not account well for trends. However, there are several approaches available that can help managers forecast the influence of long-term changes in the business climate, including linear regression and regression quadratic models. However, the time series data cannot be influenced by seasonal fluctuations if these methods are to produce accurate forecasts. Otherwise, other techniques must be used. One of these is decomposition, in which the time series data are broken down into the four component factors of trend, business cycle, seasonal fluctuation, and irregular or random fluctuation.

Dealing with Spurious Data

One consideration that must be taken into account in the analysis of time series data is the possibility of spuriousness occurring as the result of error terms of the model being correlated with each other. This autocorrelation (or serial correlation) causes problems in the use of regression analysis because regression analysis assumes that error terms are not correlated because they are either independent or random. When this situation occurs, the estimates of the regression coefficients may be inefficient. Further, both the variance of the error terms and the true standard deviation may be significantly underestimated because of their effect. Autocorrelation also means that the confidence intervals and *t* and *F* tests are no longer strictly applicable. There are, a number of ways to determine whether or not autocorrelation is present in time series data including the Durbin-Watson test. Autocorrelated data can be corrected through techniques such as the addition of independent variables and by transforming variables.

Autoregression Analysis

Another approach to forecasting using time series data is autoregression. This is a multiple regression technique in which future values of the variable are predicted from past values of the variable. Autoregression takes advantage of the relationship of values in different time periods. In autoregression, one tries to forecast a future value of a variable from knowledge of that variable's value in previous time periods. The autoregressive approach can be useful for locating both seasonal and cyclic effects.

Integrated Techniques to Time Series Data Analysis

Another approach to analyzing time series data is to use mixed or integrated techniques that utilize both moving average and autoregressive techniques. For example, the autoregressive integrated moving average (ARIMA) model (also called the Box-Jenkins model) is an integrated tool for understanding and forecasting through the use of time series data. Although ARIMA models can be difficult to compute and interpret, they are powerful and frequently result in a better model than either the use of moving averages or autoregressive techniques alone. They can be used to determine the length of the weights (i.e., how much of the past should be used to predict the next observation) and the values of these weights.

BIBLIOGRAPHY

Armstrong, J. S. (2001). Forecasting. In Saul I. Gass, S. I. & Harris, C. M. (eds.), *Encyclopedia of Operations Research and Management Science* (pp. 304-310). New York: Wiley. Retrieved July 18, 2007, from EBSCO Online Database Business Source Complete. http://search.ebscohost.com/login.aspx?direct=true&db=bth&AN=21891406&site=ehost-live

Arrfelt, M., Wiseman, R. M., & Tomas M. Hult, G. G. (2013). Looking backward instead of forward: aspiration-driven influences on the efficiency of the capital allocation process. *Academy of Management Journal, 56*(4), 1081-1103. Retrieved November 15, 2013, from EBSCO Online Database Business Source Complete. http://search.ebscohost.com/login.aspx?direct=true&db=bth&AN=89878847&site=ehost-live

Armstrong, J. S. & Green, K. C. (2006, Sep). Select a forecasting method (selection tree). Retrieved July 19, 2007, from http://www.forecastingprinciples.com/selection%5ftree.html

Black, K. (2006). *Business statistics for contemporary decision making* (4th ed. update). New York: John Wiley & Sons.

Krupnik, Y. (2013). Deploy business-specific predictive analytics in three easy steps. *Supply & Demand Chain Executive, 14*(3), 32-34. Retrieved November 15, 2013, from EBSCO Online Database Business Source Complete. http://search.ebscohost.com/login.aspx?direct=true&db=bth&AN=88842117&site=ehost-live

Ma, Y., Wang, N., Che, A., Huang, Y., & Xu, J. (2013). The bullwhip effect on product orders and inventory: a perspective of demand forecasting techniques. *International Journal of Production Research, 51*(1), 281-302. Retrieved November 15, 2013, from EBSCO Online Database Business Source Complete. http://search.ebscohost.com/login.aspx?direct=true&db=bth&AN=83404185&site=ehost-live

Nazem, S. M. (1988). *Applied time series analysis for business and economic forecasting.* New York: Marcel Dekker.

SUGGESTED READING

Armstrong, J. S. & Collopy, F. (1998). Integration of statistical methods and judgment for time series forecasting: Principles from empirical research. In Wright, G. & Goodwin, P. (Eds.). *Forecasting with Judgment.* New York: John Wiley & Sons.

Dauten, C. A. & Valentine, L. M. (1978). *Business cycles and forecasting* (5th ed.). Cincinnati: South-Western Publishing Co.

Di Giacinto, V. (2006). A generalized space-time ARMA model with an application to regional unemployment analysis in Italy. *International Regional Science Review, 29*(2), 159-198. Retrieved May 24, 2007, from EBSCO Online Database Business Source Complete. http://search.ebscohost.com/login.aspx?direct=true&db=bth&AN=20711879&site=ehost-live

Makridakis, S. & Wheelwright, S. C. (1982). Introduction to management forecasting: Status and needs. In Makridakis, S. & Wheelwright, S. C. (Eds.). *The Handbook of Forecasting: A Manager's Guide.* New York: John Wiley & Sons.

Morrell, J. (2001). *How to forecast: A guide for business.* Burlington, VT: Gower.

Nelson, C. R. (1973). *Applied time series analysis for managerial forecasting.* San Francisco: Holden-Day.

Wynne, B. E. & Hall, D. A. (1982). Forecasting requirements for operations planning and control. In Makridakis, S. & Wheelwright, S. C. (Eds.). *The Handbook of Forecasting: A Manager's Guide.* New York: John Wiley & Sons.

Ruth A. Wienclaw, Ph.D.

Forecasting Techniques

ABSTRACT

In order to make decisions that will enable an organization to be successful, managers need to be able to predict the needs of the future so that the organization can act appropriately in order to gain or maintain a competitive edge. Forecasting is the science of estimating or predicting future trends. Forecasts are used to support managers in making decisions about many aspects of the organization including buying, selling, production, and hiring. Statistical techniques are available to help managers examine the impact of trends, business cycles, seasonal fluctuations, and irregular or random events on future needs. However, in isolation, these methods are not sufficient for developing good forecasts. Expert judgment needs to be used in combination with statistical techniques in order to optimize the effectiveness of each.

OVERVIEW

Since the beginning of written history, human beings have been interested in learning what the future holds. From our vantage point in the 21st century, we read with bemusement in history books about signs and omens and oracles, and wonder why people ever thought they could read the future in the entrails of a goat. Despite our relative sophistication, however, the desire to know the future persists, and we still long to know what is going to happen. We listen to the television meteorologist to find out whether or not to carry an umbrella. We read the business section of the newspaper to find out the cost of a barrel of oil to determine whether we should wait a few days to buy gas or get it today. We plan our vacations for sunny climes at times when we expect to be knee-deep in snow at home.

Importance of Trends to Business Operations

However, it is not only in our daily lives or in these relatively trivial examples that we need to know what will happen. In the business world, organizations need to know the trends of the marketplace in order to best position themselves to leverage this knowledge into profits. The production manager needs to know if there will be a continuing need for widgets and how much raw material is needed to meet the anticipated demand. The marketing manager needs to know whether changing demographics in the marketplace mean that a new marketing strategy will be needed. The shipping manager needs to know whether or not the price of oil will continue to rise and how this cost affects the outsourcing for the production of gizmos. The human resources manager needs to know whether or not the turnover in the organization will continue and new sources of qualified employees need to be found. To answer these and other questions about the future of the business and how best to respond to the changing needs of the environment and marketplace, businesses rely on forecasting. This is the science of estimating or predicting patterns and variations. Forecasts are used to support managers in making decisions about many aspects of the business including buying, selling, production, and hiring. It is part of the responsibility of management to determine the goals and direction of the organization for both the short and long terms. To do this, it is helpful to be able to predict the variations of economic activity that may affect the business and plan to either leverage these into successes or prepare the organization to survive until the next boom.

Causes of Variation in Economic Activity

There are a number of causes of variation in economic activity: trends, business cycles, and seasonal fluctuations as well as irregular and random fluctuations. Trends are persistent, underlying directions in which something is moving in either the short, intermediate, or long term. Many trends tend to be linear rather than cyclic, steadily growing (or shrinking) over a period of years. For example, in the US there is an increasing trend for outsourcing and offshoring of technical support and customer service in the high tech industry. On the other hand, trends in new industries tend to be curvilinear as the demand for the new product or service grows after its introduction then declines after the product or service becomes integrated into the economy.

Business Cycles

Business cycles are continually recurring variations across the total economy. Such expansions or contractions of economic activity tend to occur across most sectors of the economy at the same time. For example, several years of a boom economy with expansion of economic activity (e.g., more jobs, higher sales) are frequently followed by slower growth or even contraction of economic activity. Business cycles tend not to occur only across one industry or business sector, but often occur across the economy in general.

Seasonal Fluctuations

Many industries also experience seasonal fluctuations — changes in economic activity that occur in a fairly regular annual pattern. Seasonal fluctuations may be related to the seasons of the year, the calendar, or holidays. For example, office supply stores experience an upsurge in business in August as children receive their school supply lists for the coming year. Retail stores make a significant portion of their profits in the weeks between Thanksgiving and Christmas. Travel agencies experience a rise in clients in the winter who want to visit warmer climes and in the summer for families who need to go on vacation when their children are not in school.

Economic Fluctuations

In addition, there are irregular and random fluctuations in the economy that occur due to unpredictable factors. For example, natural disasters, political disturbance, strikes, and other external factors can cause fluctuations in the economy. In addition, there are unpredictable or random factors that can affect a business's profitability such as high absenteeism due to an epidemic. Although this category is by definition difficult if not impossible to predict, there are tools available that can help the manager recognize and predict the other kinds of variations. Identification of a these variations in economic activity allows managers to better plan to meet future needs and keep the business profitable.

Approaches to Forecasting in Business

There are a number of approaches to forecasting that are used in business. Subjective forecasting methods are used by many managers, particularly when a decision needs to be made quickly.

Subjective Approaches

Subjective approaches to forecasting are qualitative rather than quantitative and based on the manager's experience and intuition about a situation rather than on the application of mathematics or an attempt to reduce the situation to quantifiable terms. Depending on the manager and his/her experience, however, subjective approaches to forecasting may or may not be effective. Further, because they are subjective, even when they are effective, subjective approaches are typically not reproducible. There is also no way to quantify the variables used in the forecasting process so that the process can be applied to future situations. The quality of a subjective forecasting approach is completely dependent on the skill and expertise of the manager using it.

Structural & Economic Model Approaches

A second category of approaches to business forecasting are structural and economic models. These approaches use mathematical and statistical techniques to support the development of a forecasting model. Structural models are sets of mathematical functions that are designed to represent the causal relationships within the organization's environment. For example, if an organization was interested in investing in a new venture, it would be helpful to know the future price of its current product in order to forecast its profits and the resultant availability of funds for the new venture. To do this, the manager or analyst might build a specification model of the factors affecting the supply and demand for the current product and the relationship between the factors. There are, however, a number of sources of error associated with this approach to forecasting. First, actual future wages and income will more than likely differ from the estimated values used in the development of the model. Second, the predictive value of the model will be affected by the sampling error in the estimates used in the construction of the model. Third, the model may not take into consideration some important variable which, in turn, could skew the results.

Deterministic Model Approach

A third approach to business forecasting is the use of deterministic models. These models assume that the variable of interest is a deterministic function of time and does not include the effects of any underlying data uncertainty or variability in the time series. Although this type of model means that the observed changes are due solely to changes in the components of the model, there are some drawbacks. Perhaps the biggest objection to deterministic models is that they assume that the time series used as a basis for the model is systematic and highly predictable. This assumption is typically not valid when dealing with real life problems, particularly when they are complex.

Ad Hoc Forecasting Formulas

Another approach to forecasting is the use of ad hoc forecasting formulas based solely on past history. This approach typically uses weighted moving averages. Although this approach simplifies computation, there is no way to determine whether the formula chosen is the most appropriate. This means that there can be no concomitant confidence in the worth of the resultant forecasts.

Time Series Analysis

A final approach to forecasting is the use of time series analysis. Time series data are data gathered on a specific characteristic over a period of time. To be useful, time series data must be collected at intervals of regular length. In time series analysis the sequence of observations is assumed to be a set of jointly distributed random variables. Unlike the ad hoc approach to forecasting where it is impossible to tell whether or not the formula chosen is the most appropriate for the situation, in time series analysis one can study the structure of the correlation of variables over time to determine the appropriateness of the model. The model can be adjusted as needed to make it more representative of the real world situation.

APPLICATIONS

There are a number of statistical techniques that can be used to analyze time series data and forecast industry or marketplace trends or other factors of interest to the business. Some of these techniques are regression models to analyze trends and decomposition techniques to determine seasonality. Statistical methods are not the only important factor in forecasting, however. The analyst and decision maker both must integrate statistical techniques with human judgment in order to maximize the utility of time series forecasting.

Trend Analysis

In business, it is often helpful to be able to forecast trends in the industry, the supply chain, applicant pool, or other factors that affect the ability of the organization to do its job. Using time series data, it is possible to analyze trends to give managers the information that they need to make decisions about the direction the business should take. One of the ways that times series data can be analyzed is through the use of regression analysis. This is a statistical technique used to develop a mathematical model for predicting one variable from the knowledge of another variable.

Lumber Industry & Regression Analysis

An example of the use of regression analysis in determining trends comes from the lumber industry. Black spruce is the most important source of structural lumber in eastern Canada as well as the most important tree for reforestation. There is currently a higher demand for structural lumber than there was in the past, and this trend is expected to continue. To help the lumber industry better choose trees that will meet industry standards for structural lumber, it would be helpful to have a model to predict lumber grade yield for the black spruce. Liu, Zhang, and Jiang used regression analysis to develop a model for forecasting lumber grade and yield. A number of tree characteristics are important to the yield and quality of black spruce lumber including tree size, tree taper, stem form, crown size, and branchiness. To help the industry better identify trees to meet industry standards for structural lumber, they developed a model to identify the variables that significantly influence the yield and quality of black spruce lumber. The purpose of this model was to identify which characteristics are most predictive of lumber grade yield and help improve the prediction of lumber grade yields for the visual grading system.

To develop the model, measurements of various characteristics of interest were taken from 139 randomly selected trees. The trees were then processed and the quality of the resultant lumber graded. The authors used stepwise multiple regression analysis to build a model to predict lumber grade and yield using these data. The first attempt at model building utilized data from all the variables collected. A subsequent model was developed that used only those variables that seemed to be most directly related to yield and lumber grade. The latter model proved almost as effective as the first model. It was determined that either model developed in the study could provide an estimation of black spruce lumber grade and yield either from individual trees or stands of trees using only forest industry data. These models can aid significantly in choosing the trees most likely to have the highest yield of lumber and can also be helpful for forest management and preservation of black spruce supplies.

Seasonal Effects

Another important factor in forecasting is industry seasonality. Seasonal effects are patterns that occur in cycles of less than one year and that are associated with time cycles such as the calendar, seasons, or holidays. However, seasonal effects are not the only source of variability in time series data. As discussed above, time series data can also be affected by trends, business cycles, and irregular or random fluctuations. To determine the effects of these variables, a technique called decomposition is often used. This technique allows the analyst to break down time series data into the component factors of trends, business cycles, seasonal fluctuations, and irregular or random fluctuations.

Seasonality & the Non-OPEC Oil Supply

An example of the importance of determining seasonality and the techniques to do so is given in a recent study of the seasonality of non-OPEC oil supply. For reasons that are obvious at the gas pump each week, short-term changes in oil supply are constantly under scrutiny by analysts. The perceptions of immediate supply have implications not only on energy prices but on crude oil transport prices as well. Therefore, it is important to forecast oil supply fluctuations as accurately as possible. Two-thirds of the oil supply is produced by non-OPEC countries. Whereas OPEC decisions about supply are coordinated between the member countries, this is not true for non-OPEC countries. Decisions in these countries are made by each producer individually. This fact makes analysis of this industry segment particularly important for forecasting supply.

There are a number of reasons for seasonality in oil supply in non-OPEC countries. These include demand for oil, price of oil, stock levels, annual maintenance schedule at production facilities, the psychology and manipulation of the market, timely completion of development projects, as well as irregular and random factors including severe weather, floods, earthquakes, and strikes. There is also a seasonal component to the non-OPEC supply. Cold weather in the winter in the northern hemisphere where the major consumers are located leads to a higher demand for heating oil than in the spring months. During the summer, cooling systems and vacation travel again raise the demand for oil. The resultant seasonal fluctuations in demand for oil yield concomitant variations in non-OPEC oil supply. Because of this cycle, regularly scheduled maintenance — another seasonal factor in oil supply — is frequently scheduled for periods of lower consumption and more temperate weather.

Jazayeri & Yahyai performed an analysis of seasonality of non-OPEC supply in order to help improve the accuracy of short-term supply forecasts. Their study was based on the assumption that observed seasonality cycles are independent of other factors and that they will continue into the future. To analyze the time series data on oil supply in non-OPEC countries, the authors decomposed the data into the four components of trends, business cycles, seasonal fluctuations, and irregular or random variables. Using the decomposition technique of Fourier spectral analysis, it was found that non-OPEC supply follows a seasonal pattern that repeats annually irrespective of other trends. These results can be very useful for analysts forecasting oil supply at various times of the year.

Integrating Statistics & Judgment

Opinion about the best way to forecast for business decisions often seems to be sharply divided between those that rely on statistical methodology and those that prefer to use their "gut" to determine where the industry, supply chain, or market is going. However, both approaches have advantages and disadvantages. Statistical methods are less prone to bias than are judgments. In addition, they tend to be more reliable and can more efficiently make use of historical data. However, statistical techniques can only work with the data they are given. Judgmental decision making, on the other hand, can be useful particularly when there are recent events about which the decision maker is aware but which have not yet had sufficient time to result in observable data in a time series. This type of data includes information about events that have happened in the past but are not expected to recur in the future or events that will affect the future but have not occurred in the past (e.g., the effect of an innovation on the marketplace; governmental or industry policy changes). There are, however, risks with judgmental-only forecasts. Human error may make the analyst or manager more optimistic (or pessimistic) than actually warranted, trends or factors may be read into the data that are not actually there, or the effects of correlated variables may not be taken into account.

Three Ways to Integrate Judgment & Statistical Forecasting

There are three ways in which judgment can be integrated into statistical forecasting using time series data. First, judgment is key to determining which data are relevant to the model. Potential variables are virtually unlimited. However, a statistical model or analysis cannot take all these into account. Even if they could, spurious positive results would be seen due to the effects of probability alone. Therefore, it is important that expert judgments be used to reduce the inputs into the process. Another way in which judgment is important in forecasting is the determination of which statistical technique is most appropriate to analyze the data. There are a number of statistical techniques available for model building, analysis, and forecasting. Many of these are closely related. However, the worth of the end result depends heavily on correctly choosing the most appropriate analytical method. Third, expert judgments can be helpful in aiding the analyst to understand the situation and give insight into the parameters in which the data and subsequent analysis should be interpreted (e.g., "given the current economy and our market plan, we expect widget sales to rise by two percent over the next quarter"). Figure 1 shows some of the considerations for integrating judgment and statistical methods for forecasting.

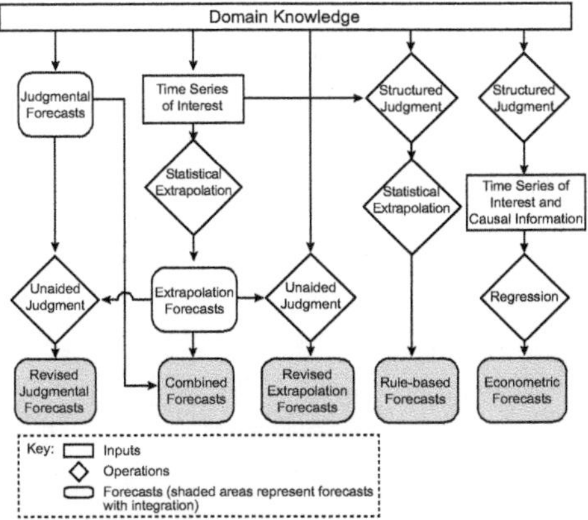

Figure 1: Integration of Judgment & Statistical Methods (From Armstrong & Collopy, p. 275)

Bibliography

Armstrong, J. S. & Collopy, F. (1998). Integration of statistical methods and judgment for time series forecasting: Principles from empirical research. In Wright, G. & Goodwin, P. (Eds.). *Forecasting with Judgment.* New York: John Wiley & Sons.

Black, K. (2006). *Business statistics for contemporary decision making* (4th ed.). New York: John Wiley & Sons.

Dauten, C. A. & Valentine, L. M. (1978). *Business cycles and forecasting* (5th ed.). Cincinnati: South-Western Publishing Co.

Jazayeri, S. M. T. & Yahyai, A. (2004). An analysis of seasonality of non-OPEC supply. *Maritime Policy & Management, 30*(3), 213-224. Retrieved May 23, 2007, from EBSCO Online Database Business Source Complete. http://search.ebscohost.com/login.aspx?direct=true&db=bth&AN=14352172&site=ehost-live

Liu, C., Zhang, S. Y., & Jiang, Z. H. (2007). Models for predicting lumber grade yield using tree characteristics in black spruce. *Forest Products Journal, 57*(1/2), 60-66. Retrieved May 23, 2007, from EBSCO Online Database Business Source Complete. http://search.ebscohost.com/login.aspx?direct=true&db=bth&AN=24255405&site=ehost-live

Ma, Y., Wang, N., Che, A., Huang, Y., & Xu, J. (2013). The bullwhip effect on product orders and inventory: a perspective of demand forecasting techniques. *International Journal of Production Research, 51*(1), 281-302. Retrieved November 15, 2013, from EBSCO Online Database Business Source Complete. http://search.ebscohost.com/login.aspx?direct=true&db=bth&AN=83404185&site=ehost-live

Nelson, C. R. (1973). *Applied time series analysis for managerial forecasting.* San Francisco: Holden-Day.

Sperrazza, C. A., & McManus, D. J. (2013). Net job creation using time series forecasting. *International Journal of Business Management & Economic Research, 4*(3), 714-720. Retrieved November 15, 2013, from EBSCO Online Database Business Source Complete. http://search.ebscohost.com/login.aspx?direct=true&db=bth&AN=89462676&site=ehost-live

Voineagu, V., Pisica, S., & Caragea, N. (2012). Forecasting monthly unemployment by econometric smoothing techniques. *Economic Computation &*

Economic Cybernetics Studies & Research, 46(3), 255-267. Retrieved November 15, 2013, from EBSCO Online Database Business Source Complete. http://search.ebscohost.com/login.aspx?direct=true&db=bth&AN=85469422&site=ehost-live

Suggested Reading

Dishman, P. (2006). A typology of psychological biases in forecasting analysis. In Lawrence, K. D. & Geurts, M. D. (Eds.). *Advances in Business and Management Forecasting.* Boston: JAI Press.

Makridakis, S. & Wheelwright, S. C. (1982). Introduction to management forecasting: Status and needs. In Makridakis, S. & Wheelwright, S. C. (Eds.). *The Handbook of Forecasting: A Manager's Guide.* New York: John Wiley & Sons.

Morrell, J. (2001). *How to forecast: A guide for business.* Burlington, VT: Gower.

Nazem, S. M. (1988). *Applied time series analysis for business and economic forecasting.* New York: Marcel Dekker.

Pindyck, R. S. & Rubinfeld, D. L. (1998). *Econometric models and economic forecasts.* Boston: Irwin/McGraw-Hill.

Wynne, B. E. & Hall, D. A. (1982). Forecasting requirements for operations planning and control. In Makridakis, S. & Wheelwright, S. C. (Eds.). *The Handbook of Forecasting: A Manager's Guide.* New York: John Wiley & Sons.

Ruth A. Wienclaw, Ph.D.

G

Gender & Management

ABSTRACT

This article examines the impact of gender in the workplace. The impact of gender on the composition of the management team is analyzed and current trends of women in management are reviewed. Changes in the workplace over the last three decades as the number of women in the workplace has increased are explained including the emergence of the family-friendly workplace. The types of benefits offered by family-friendly companies are reviewed. Employment statistics on women in the workplace, the occupations in which women work, and the salary differentials between women and men are presented.

OVERVIEW

Gender presents at least two primary challenges to organization managers. One is the impact of gender on management staffing and the composition of the management team. This has most often been discussed in terms of women moving into management positions which has been, and still is in parts of the world, positions traditionally held by men. The second area of impact is in human resource management, which has changed how management deals with a mixed gender non-management workforce who is now often split rather evenly between men and women.

Women in Management

As the society and the economy changes many companies have had to reexamine their workforce composition and their hiring practices. One shift that has been significant is that more companies have become interested in recruiting and promoting women into senior management positions. This provides women the opportunity to work their way to the executive levels of many corporations. Women are succeeding in a wide variety of positions and industries traditionally considered inappropriate for women. They are also beginning to succeed in areas that have historically been male-dominated including manufacturing, engineering, and financial services.

Companies are seeking women for senior management roles for several reasons. One of the most significant reasons is that women represent a very large untapped pool of talent. This is especially true for senior level positions. Companies that desire to strengthen management teams want to remain competitive in a rapidly changing marketplace. They recognize that by including women in the upper echelons of management can add new sources of talent and expand the perspectives of the management force.

The expanded perspective of the management team is achieved because of inherent differences between men and women. Many organizations believe that women bring alternative perspectives to the table. The ultimate goal of course, is to gain and sustain a competitive advantage for the company. As the management team becomes more diverse the customers and clients of the company tend to view the diversity as positive. It should also be noted that women do account for over 80% of all consumer spending in the United States. Women now routinely buy cars and invest in stocks. They also make the majority of the family buying decisions. This being the case, the input of women at the executive level of a company becomes more valuable as well.

When women are on the management team, it signals to current and potential employees that the organization is changing with the times and is embracing gender diversity. Furthermore, the presence of women on the management team can expand the perceptions of the market place and helps to ensure that existing as well as new business opportunities are not overlooked. This is logical in that women constitute a large and rapidly growing consumer base. Organizations with a relatively high percentage of women executives have come to understand and capitalize on gender differences in leadership style and management behavior. These companies are also considered more likely to address actual and perceived inequalities in the workplace and have accomplished that in part by not leaving gender diversity to chance ("Gender and organizational performance," 2002).

Overcoming Obstacles to Female Advancement

Even though the composition of the management work force is changing there still are some issues that impede the progress of women. One major obstacle for women working at senior executive levels is how to overcome the inherent difficulties of balancing career and family. Many things in society have changed, but it is clear that women remain the primary caregivers in most societies and probably will continue that role. It is also likely that women who become senior managers will also be raising a family and may even be caring for their aging parents.

Many companies recognize the dual social role of women and there have been many programs implemented to accommodate their needs such as flextime schedules and generous maternity leave packages. Women know, however, that utilizing many of these opportunities can stifle or even derail a career. To improve their return on investment for making these opportunities available, many companies have limited their generosity only to women who have proven track records of success within the company. There is also a pattern in recruiting executive women from outside which shows recruiters and managers alike do not actively consider female candidates that are likely to make use of these programs.

Many corporate CEOs are white, male, and 60 years of age. Some of these men still find it difficult to picture women like their wives and daughters in senior-level positions. There could be many reasons for this, even including a lack of confidence in their wives and daughters. In some industries, competition is heavy and business is not always neat and clean. The aging CEO may feel that women cannot play aggressively enough to win the market. Thus, many older CEOs let the bias of their personal experiences guide the recruiting process. Many of these CEOs had mothers who stayed at home, and many still have wives who stay at home and attend to family and social matters.

Another not so subtle discrimination in the executive corps is that male executives may exclude women managers from informal activities outside the office. These activities tend to strengthen business relationships. Season tickets to sporting events, for example, may not be offered to female vice presidents. This discrimination results in women losing important opportunities to build relationships outside the structure of the office environment (Landon, 1996).

At lower management levels, women are typically placed in non-strategic sectors, in personnel and administrative positions, rather than in professional and line management jobs leading to the top. Thus, women are cut off from networks (both formal and informal) essential for advancement within enterprises. Unfortunately in some large companies and organizations women in high-level managerial positions such as human resources and administration are often considered less vital to the organization. This may be because managers tend to work long hours in order to gain recognition and even gain promotions ("Women in management," 1998).

Forces that may be underlying explanations of women's inequality in the workplace are the result of structural barriers, stereotypical assumptions, individual choice, and work-family conflict. These issues are broad, power-implicated, ideological forces (Gazso, 2004). The "think manager-think male" attitude still dominates many organizations. Research shows that managerial and executive-level positions are still male sex-typed. Many executives perceive that women do not fit in these positions as well as men. Thus one conclusion that the research supports is that women are considered to be less effective managers than men (Bergeron, Block & Echtenkamp, 2006).

Programs for Advancement

Many governments, enterprises, and organizations, through policy as well as practice, have committed to programs to advance women. Some of these programs have met with limited success while others may have gained a higher profile. Generally, they are having a positive effect, especially in influencing younger generations of men and women.

The development of detailed training, promotion, and career plans in organizations has been shown to be an impetus for promoting equal opportunities in career progression. This may require specific support through networks, coaching, or mentoring. In addition, these must be continued even during downsizing, decentralization, and delayering. ("Women in management," 1998).

Further Insights

Analyzing the Workforce Participation of Women

The workplace faces several challenges in the new millennium, among them that employers face a fairly serious labor shortage. There will not be enough younger people to fill jobs left vacant by retiring baby boomers. Estimates on the labor shortage in the United States range from three million to ten million workers by 2010.

The demographics of the American workforce have also changed in the last forty years. In 2013 it was reported that 74 percent of American women are in the workforce; these women make up approximately 47 percent of the total labor force. In addition, in 2012 mother accounted for over 70 percent of working women and 40 percent of working wives out-earned their husbands.

The modern working woman generally enters into the workforce after completing her education, and moves in and out of the workforce several times until retirement. About three fourths of women work in administrative support or as executives, administrators, and managers. Women are obtaining the majority of bachelor's degrees and are receiving a high percentage of medical, law, and MBA degrees.

There are about 36 million "Generation X" women in the United States and over 15 million are mothers, according to the 2000 Census Bureau. The Gen-X woman has achieved the greatest one-generation leap in social and gender equality in American history. They were the first to enter the legal, medical, and business professions in large numbers and percentages. In 2006 Gen-X women comprised just over 50 percent of all workers in executive, administrative, and managerial occupations, and that number continued to rise through 2013. At the time, this was over 25 percent higher than it was for that age group in 1983. Gen-X women work longer hours than their elders did and are sought graduate degrees, pushing hard for their futures.

In 2006 the breakdown of gender participation in the workforce by race was as follows:

- White women: 59.0%
- White men: 74.3%
- Black women: 61.7%
- Black men: 67.0%
- Hispanic women: 56.1%
- Hispanic men: 80.7%
- Asian women: 58.3%
- Asian men: 75.0% ("Employment & earnings," 2006).

In 2006, for women who worked full-time, wage and salary workers, the ten most prevalent occupations and number of women workers in each occupation were:

- Secretaries and administrative assistants (3,348,000)
- Registered nurses (2,309,000)
- Cashiers (2,291,000)
- Elementary and middle school teachers (2,220,000)
- Retail salespersons (1,740,000)
- Nursing, psychiatric, and home health aides (1,694,000)
- First-line supervisors/managers of retail sales workers (1,436,000)
- Waiters and waitresses (1,401,000)
- Bookkeeping, accounting, and auditing clerks (1,364,000)
- Customer service representatives (1,349,000) ("Employment & earnings," 2006).

Women accounted for 51% of all workers in the high-paying management, professional, and related occupations. They outnumbered men in such occupations as financial managers; human resource managers; education administrators; medical and health services managers; accountants and auditors; budget analysts; property, real estate, and social and community service managers; preschool, kindergarten, elementary, middle, and secondary school teachers; and registered nurses. Ten of the occupations with the highest median weekly earnings in the 2000s are pharmacists, CEOs, attorneys, information systems managers, medical doctors, software engineers, physical therapists, management analysts, health service managers and computer systems analysts. There is a disparity in salaries between women and men; in 2012 women earned approximately 81 percent of what men earned. Women also leave their jobs more frequently than men and in scientific or engineering jobs, women leave their jobs at about twice the rate as men (Jesse, 2006).

Issues

Establishing the Family Friendly Workplace

The management challenge of dealing with a mixed gender non-management workforce, often split evenly between men and women, has attracted considerable attention during the last decade. This challenge is not just to deal with increased numbers of women in the workplace but to also address the needs of men who are married to women who have jobs and families; or, the dual-income household which totals over 33 million families.

Much of the human resource development efforts over the last decade have focused on women. Currently the age of working women spans multiple generations. They may be married. They may be single. They may or may not have children. The array of potential characteristics is important because it means that there is not a one-size fits all recruitment strategy or benefits package that will meet the needs of all working women. Women of baby boomer age face the challenges of eldercare more so than of child care. Some, however, take on the care of their grandchildren if their children are divorced or live in two-income households. When companies or non-profit organizations target women recruits they need to bear in mind that of women's family responsibilities may reach far beyond their own household.

Single mothers can have difficulties in keeping home and work balanced. For instance if there is a problem with a child at school a single mother will need to attend to the problem unless they have support from grandparents or nannies. However, many single mothers would still prefer to be at a child's doctor appointment or a parent-teacher conference. This means that they need a flexible work schedule so they can take time off from work for these important appointments.

Many single mothers do not have the support of parents or family and will need to take time off work as needed to address domestic issues. This may jeopardize their career advancement or even the stability of their jobs. Still, the middle-class single mother is basically far better off than her predecessors of previous generations (Piscione, 2004).

As business conditions changed and competition stiffened one of the easy ways for a company to expand their market share was through a merger or acquisition. The ever changing landscape of leadership that this created, along with post acquisition or merger lay-offs, substantially altered the employee loyalty that many companies spent decades building. Women may have borne the brunt of many of these changes. The need for corporate family-friendly benefits and non-traditional employment approaches has suffered through the corporate consolidations of the last two decades. In attempts to avoid high turnover rates, which in turn cause an increase in hiring and training costs, employers needed to devise new strategies to recruit and retain quality employees.

Benefits of a Family-Friendly Workplace

The term "family-friendly" encompasses a wide range of workplace benefits and practices that help to support the well-being of an employee and his or her family. This includes benefits designed to help reduced life's stress and contribute to a sense of comfort and security. Such benefits often include options that enable employees to have more control of their lives. They could include flexibility in working hours or providing assistance with financial issues. The benefits that an employer gains by establishing a family friendly workplace include:

- Being known for practices that contribute to the support family needs which actually produce real economic results, such as higher profits, higher productivity, and lower attrition.
- Establishing a strong correlation between a company's culture of family support that is recognized among employees, and with customers that are looking to do business with socially responsible companies, and in the communities in which the company has facilities.
- An image of corporate social responsibility that can attract potential investors and new customers.
- An increase in the quality of life and job satisfaction of employees as well as upper management.

Benefits Offered

Since the turn of the century, the most common family-friendly benefits that employers have rolled out are related to dependent care spending accounts, job-sharing, child care, flexible work schedules and compensatory time off. Other benefits include liberal family leave options that go beyond the legal requirements for such leave. There has also been an increase in part-time telecommuting working arrangements and compressed workweeks which allow employees to work forty hours in less than five days.

Many organizations are becoming creative about the types of benefits they include in their family-friendly benefit portfolios. These may include wellness programs, employee assistance programs and home buying assistance. There have also been several education related benefits thrown into the mix, such as scholarship programs for children of employees and tuition reimbursement programs. Community building benefits have included volunteer release time and even concierge services (Clark & Reed, 2004).

Worker's Unions & Women

Another way that a workplace can be transformed or be made more worker-friendly is through unionization of workers. Women are becoming union members at a faster rate than men. This means that unions need to focus on issues that concern women if they choose to capitalize on the trend of more women joining. This could benefit the unions as well as women who join because the women need benefits and representation and the unions need to stem the tide of declining memberships. It may take some unions a while to shift their emphasis because many unions have been traditionally male dominated.

In terms of benefits, unions could win more women members if they would think more like the corporations that have shifted their benefit packages to appeal to and serve women better than they have in the past. Unions may need to have more women as organizers and as leaders in order to convince potential women members that the unions are actually changing and shifting their emphasis. Some unions may be able to make the shift while others may need to wait for a new generation of leadership.

Unions may also need to shift their organization targets and start forming more union cells in places where women traditionally work. If the union offers a good package of benefits to women they may very well succeed in organizing in places that they have failed to organize in the past. It may take decades for this to happen but it is possible to see a resurgence in unions if they can appeal to the growing number of women in the workforce (Yates, 2006).

CONCLUSIONS

Organizations face several challenges in dealing with gender in the workplace. In basic terms, men and women are different in their perceptions of work, success, and life in general. Both men and women want to rise within their organization and to make more money. While they share this similarity there are others issues and goals that are completely different for men and women.

Women have far greater social pressure than men to be both successful in their careers and to be mothers and daughters. The mother role is fairly clear and it is demanding both physically and emotionally. Many women are also daughters and in current times this means that they are often cast into the role of primary care taker for their parents as they age. Although the role of men in the family setting has certainly changed over the last few decades, men still have less of this pressure in their roles of father and son.

Given that women are both increasing their presence in the work place and their power in the consumer market, organizations need to come embrace women on both fronts. First they must provide a workplace and benefits package that is appropriate to meet the needs of working women and their roles as mothers and daughters. Secondly, companies need to address how they position themselves as a producer, seller, or service provider to women as consumers. To do this they need to understand the marketplace and how women view their products and services. It is not likely that men will be able to accomplish that without the help of women in management positions.

Bibliography

Bergeron, D., Block, C., & Echtenkamp, A. (2006). Disabling the able: Stereotype threat and women's work performance. *Human Performance, 19*(2), 133–158. Retrieved December 15, 2007, from EBSCO Online Database Academic Search Premier. http://search.ebscohost.com/login.aspx?direct=true&db=aph&AN=20237021&site=ehost-live

Clark, S., & Reed, P. (2004) Win-win workplace practices: Improved organizational results and improved quality of life. Retrieved December 15, 2007 from United States Department of Labor Women's Bureau. http://www.choose2lead.org/Publications/Study%20on%20Win-Win%20Workplace%20Practices.pdf

Conti, M., & Sette, E. (2013). Type of employer and fertility of working women: Does working in the public sector or in a large private firm matter?. *Cambridge Journal Of Economics, 37*(6), 1303–1333. Retrieved November 22, 2013 from EBSCO Online Database Business Source Premier. http://search.ebscohost.com/login.aspx?direct=true&db=buh&AN=90054040

Devillard, S., Sancier-Sultan, S., & Werner, C. (2014). Why gender diversity at the top remains a challenge. *Mckinsey Quarterly, 2*, 23–25. Retrieved November 17, 2014, from EBSCO Online Database Business Source Complete. http://search.ebscohost.com/login.aspx?direct=true&db=bth&AN=95690599&site=bsi-live

Duberley, J., & Carrigan, M. (2013). The career identities of 'mumpreneurs';: Women's experiences of combining enterprise and motherhood. *International Small Business Journal, 31*(6), 629–651. Retrieved November 22, 2013 from EBSCO Online Database Business Source Premier. http://search.ebscohost.com/login.aspx?direct=true&db=buh&AN=91828462

Eisner, S. (2013). Leadership: Gender and executive style.*SAM Advanced Management Journal, 78*(1), 26–41. Retrieved November 17, 2014, from EBSCO Online Database Business Source Complete. http://search.ebscohost.com/login.aspx?direct=true&db=bth&AN=88038526&site=bsi-live

Employment and earnings. (2006, January). United States Department of Labor, Bureau of Labor Statistics. Retrieved December 15, 2007 from United States Department of Labor, Bureau of Labor Statistics. http://www.bls.gov/cps/cpswom2006.pdf

Gazso, A. (2004). Women's inequality in the workplace as framed in news discourse: Refracting from gender ideology. *Canadian Review of Sociology & Anthropology, 41*(4), 449–473. Retrieved December 11, 2007, from EBSCO Online Database Academic Search Premier. http://search.ebscohost.com/login.aspx?direct=true&db=aph&AN=15621260&site=ehost-live

Gender and organizational performance. (2000). *Worklife Report, 12*(4), 10. Retrieved December 11, 2007, from EBSCO Online Database Academic Search Premier. http://search.ebscohost.com/login.aspx?direct=true&db=aph&AN=3536936&site=ehost-live

Goudreau, J. (2012). A golden age for working women. *Forbes, 190*(11), 56. Retrieved November 22, 2013 from EBSCO Online Database Business Source Premier. http://search.ebscohost.com/login.aspx?direct=true&db=buh&AN=84353430

Jesse, J. (2006). Redesigning science: Recent scholarship on cultural change, gender, and diversity. *Bioscience, 56*(10), 831-838. Retrieved December 15, 2007, from EBSCO Online Database Academic Search Premier. http://search.ebscohost.com/login.aspx?direct=true&db=aph&AN=22726014&site=ehost-live

Landon, S. (1996). Women in the workplace: Making progress in corporate America. *USA Today Magazine, 125*(2618), 66. Retrieved December 11, 2007, from EBSCO Online Database Academic Search Premier. http://search.ebscohost.com/login.aspx?direct=true&db=aph&AN=9611017673&site=ehost-live

Piscione, D. (2004, September) The many faces of 21st century working women. A report to the Women's Bureau of the United States Department of Labor.

Yates, C. (2006). Challenging misconceptions about organizing women into unions. *Gender, Work & Organization, 13*(6), 565-584. Retrieved December 11, 2007, from EBSCO Online Database Academic Search Premier. http://search.ebscohost.com/login.aspx?direct=true&db=aph&AN=22642647&site=ehost-live

Women in management: It's still lonely at the top. (1998). *Women's International Network News, 24*(4), 78. Retrieved December 11, 2007, from EBSCO Online Database Academic Search Premier. http://search.ebscohost.com/login.aspx?direct=true&db=aph&AN=1210148&site=ehost-live

SUGGESTED READING

Bajdo, L., & Dickson, M. (2001). Perceptions of organizational culture and women's advancement in organizations: A cross-cultural examination. *Sex Roles, 45*(5/6), 399–414. Retrieved December 11, 2007, from EBSCO Online Database Academic Search Premier. http://search.ebscohost.com/login.aspx?direct=true&db=aph&AN=6431690&site=ehost-live

Bernstein, A. (2004, June 14). Women's pay: Why the gap remains a chasm. *Business Week*, (3887), 58–59. Retrieved December 15, 2007, from EBSCO Online Database Academic Search Premier. http://search.ebscohost.com/login.aspx?direct=true&db=aph&AN=13374148&site=ehost-live

Browne, B. (1997). Gender and beliefs about work force discrimination in the United States and Australia. *Journal of Social Psychology, 137*(1), 107–116. Retrieved December 11, 2007, from EBSCO Online Database Academic Search Premier. http://search.ebscohost.com/login.aspx?direct=true&db=aph&AN=9704143189&site=ehost-live

Cohen, L. E., & Broschak, J. P. (2013). Whose jobs are these? The impact of the proportion of female managers on the number of new management jobs filled by women versus men. *Administrative Science Quarterly, 58*(4), 509–541. Retrieved November

17, 2014, from EBSCO Online Database Business Source Complete. http://search.ebscohost.com/login.aspx?direct=true&db=bth&AN=92688562&site=bsi-live

Fournier, V., & Kelemen, M. (2001). The crafting of community: Recoupling discourses of management and womanhood. *Gender, Work & Organization, 8*(3), 267. Retrieved December 11, 2007, from EBSCO Online Database Academic Search Premier. http://search.ebscohost.com/login.aspx?direct=true&db=aph&AN=4673616&site=ehost-live

Ganey, J., Battle, A., & Wilson, W. (2007). The black woman's workplace survival guide. *Essence, 37*(12), 160–186. Retrieved December 13, 2007, from EBSCO Online Database Academic Search Premier. http://search.ebscohost.com/login.aspx?direct=true&db=aph&AN=24357096&site=ehost-live

Gatenby, B., & Humphries, M. (1999). Exploring gender, management education and careers: Speaking in the silences. *Gender & Education, 11*(3), 281–294. Retrieved December 11, 2007, from EBSCO Online Database Academic Search Premier. http://search.ebscohost.com/login.aspx?direct=true&db=aph&AN=2291591&site=ehost-live

Hymowitz, K. (2013). Think again: Working women. *Foreign Policy,* (201), 59–64. Retrieved November 22, 2013 from EBSCO Online Database Business Source Premier. http://search.ebscohost.com/login.aspx?direct=true&db=buh&AN=88429406

Moore, C. (2006). Climbing the ladder to success. *Career World, 35*(2), 16-19. Retrieved December 15, 2007, from EBSCO Online Database Academic Search Premier. http://search.ebscohost.com/login.aspx?direct=true&db=aph&AN=22697798&site=ehost-live

Perriton, L. (1999). The provocative and evocative gaze upon women in management development. *Gender & Education, 11*(3), 295–307. Retrieved December 11, 2007, from EBSCO Online Database Academic Search Premier. http://search.ebscohost.com/login.aspx?direct=true&db=aph&AN=2291592&site=ehost-live

Prichard, C., & Deem, R. (1999). Wo-managing further education; gender and the construction of the manager in the corporate colleges of England. *Gender & Education, 11*(3), 323. Retrieved December 11, 2007, from EBSCO Online Database Academic Search Premier. http://search.ebscohost.com/login.aspx?direct=true&db=aph&AN=2291594&site=ehost-live

Ribbens, B. (1999). Women in management: Current research issues. *Journal of Occupational & Organizational Psychology, 72*(1), 121–122. Retrieved December 11, 2007, from EBSCO Online Database Academic Search Premier. http://search.ebscohost.com/login.aspx?direct=true&db=aph&AN=1700171&site=ehost-live

Rotolo, T., & Wilson, J. (2003). Work histories and voluntary association memberships. *Sociological Forum, 18*(4), 603–619. Retrieved December 15, 2007, from EBSCO Online Database Academic Search Premier. http://search.ebscohost.com/login.aspx?direct=true&db=aph&AN=11398082&site=ehost-live

Smith, C. (2000). Notes from the field: Gender issues in the management curriculum: A survey of student experiences. *Gender, Work & Organization, 7*(3), 158–167. Retrieved December 11, 2007, from EBSCO Online Database Academic Search Premier. http://search.ebscohost.com/login.aspx?direct=true&db=aph&AN=4519202&site=ehost-live

Solomon, C. (2000). Cracks in the glass ceiling. *Workforce, 79*(9), 86. Retrieved December 11, 2007, from EBSCO Online Database Academic Search Premier. http://search.ebscohost.com/login.aspx?direct=true&db=aph&AN=3567820&site=ehost-live

Teasdale, N. (2013). Fragmented sisters? The implications of flexible working policies for professional women's workplace relationships. *Gender, Work & Organization, 20*(4), 397–412. Retrieved November 22, 2013 from EBSCO Online Database Business Source Premier. http://search.ebscohost.com/login.aspx?direct=true&db=buh&AN=87564166

Whitehead, S. (2001). Woman as manager: A seductive ontology. *Gender, Work & Organization, 8*(1), 84. Retrieved December 11, 2007, from EBSCO Online Database Academic Search Premier. http://search.ebscohost.com/login.aspx?direct=true&db=aph&AN=4519177&site=ehost-live

Wyn, J., Acker, S., & Richards, E. (2000). Making a difference: Women in management in Australian and Canadian faculties of education. *Gender & Education, 12*(4), 435–447. Retrieved December 11, 2007, from EBSCO Online Database Academic Search Premier. http://search.ebscohost.com/login.aspx?direct=true&db=aph&AN=3978116&site=ehost-live

Michael Erbschloe, M.A.

Human Resource Issues in High Performing Organizations

ABSTRACT

High performing organizations are companies that consistently out-perform their competitors. Although high levels of performance are due to a number of factors, human resource policies and procedures are a significant contributor to on-going success in these organizations. One of the foundations of human resource management success in high performing organizations is the objective understanding and definition of the nature of the jobs within the company, based on empirical evidence, and the establishment of hiring, performance appraisal, and other functions on that basis. In addition, high performing organizations support and empower their workers through continued training to help them acquire even more job-related skills, involvement in organizational decision-making, and financial rewards for contributing to the success of the organization.

OVERVIEW

In recent years, significant attention has been given to high-performing organizations — those companies that consistently outperform their competitors — in an attempt to determine what factors contribute to their success. In organizations that produce goods, it is tempting to point to the efficiency of the production line or automation as a factor in performance. However, the outputs of many companies today are not quite so tangible. Even in traditional production facilities, there are many more factors to performance efficiency than having the newest or best equipment. Organizations are made up of people, and human resources are the most important resource in any organization. Therefore, one of the areas that need to be analyzed in determining the factors that contribute to success in high-performance organizations is human-resource management.

Although the fundamental functions of human-resource management — recruitment and placement, training and development, compensation, and employee relations — are the same in every organization, research has found that there are significant differences between human-resource functionality in low-performing organizations and that in high-performing organizations. In high-performing organizations, human-resource departments tend to operate at a higher level: generating more candidates for job openings and screening them more effectively, offering more and better training opportunities for employees, linking pay and other incentives directly with employee performance, and providing a safer working environment for employees at all levels within the organization. Not only do the processes and outcomes of human-resource activities differ in high-performing organizations, so do their goals. In general, in high-performing organizations, human-resource activities are at the heart of the organization's functioning rather than on the periphery, with the goal of maximizing the potential, utilization, and commitment of all employees at all levels in the organization.

As modern organizations were beginning to take shape after the Industrial Revolution, there was a great distinction between the various types of workers in an organization. Business owners and managers were viewed as the driving force behind the organization, with production workers, clerks, secretaries, and others often viewed as easily replaceable entities. To run an organization under this philosophy, the command-and-control model was adopted from the military. However, in the 21st century, this paradigm has changed. In the Information Age, it is recognized that virtually all employees within organizations are highly skilled and can contribute to the effectiveness and performance of the organization. In current thinking among human-resource managers, employees are not easily replaceable entities but rather human capital. This view regarding an organization's employees takes into account an employee's potential within the scope of his or her current tasks, as well as the employee's overall expertise, including his or her knowledge, skills, abilities, training, and education. Employees are no longer viewed merely as bodies needed to fill positions; they are a type of corporate wealth that can be used to further the objectives of the organization in much the same way as financial capital is used. Therefore, employees need to be nurtured and helped to realize their potential. In addition, their contributions need to be recognized and rewarded and their inputs considered in order to help the organization perform at a consistently high level.

Under this philosophy, human-resource departments need to set up policies and procedures that promote a high-performance work system. This means that just as performance and success in the rest of the organization needs to be objectively measurable and evaluated against objective standards, so too must the performance of the activities within the human-resource department itself. Dessler (2005) describes the results of research published in 2001 that compared the human-resource practices in high-performing versus low-performing organizations. A significant difference found between the two types of organizations was the emphasis placed on various functions that encourage high performance. For example, when hiring new employees, high-performing companies were more likely to promote from within (61.46%) than were their low-performing counterparts (34.90%). This difference is due in part to the fact that high-performing organizations tend to groom their employees for advancement. High-performing companies also tend to be systematic about their approach to hiring new employees. Significantly more high-performing organizations based hiring decisions in part on validated selection tests (29.67%) than did low-performing companies (4.26%). High-performing companies were more likely to attract applicants to the job, whether because of their reputation or their recruiting efforts: 36.55 applicants on average in high-performing companies versus 8.24 applicants on average in low-performing companies. On a practical level, what this means is that high-performing companies have a greater applicant pool from which to fill their open jobs and, as a result, are typically more likely to find the best available person for the job (Dessler, 2005).

The impact of human-resource policies on organizational effectiveness and performance does not stop with hiring practices, however. Even when one has hired from within and the person in the new job is familiar with the general practices and culture of the organization, he or she will still need to learn how to perform the tasks required on the new job. Therefore, one of the functions of the human-resource department is to provide training for employees. According to Dessler (2005), high-performing companies gave new employees an average of 116.87 hours of training their first year, while low-performing organizations gave new employees an average of 35.02 hours of training within their first year. Experienced employees were given an average of 72.0 hours of training in high-performing companies but only 13.4 hours of training in low-performing companies. Although training costs can have a significant impact on an organization's budget, it is very important to train employees. Initial training is necessary to teach new employees how to successfully do their new jobs. However, additional training throughout the employee's tenure is also important. Continued training enables employees to acquire the additional skills that will help them grow and make them better able to contribute to the performance of the organization.

Human-resource practices and procedures are important in other aspects of the organization's functioning. In high-performing companies, for example, 95.17% of the employees received a regular performance evaluation, as opposed to only 41.31 percent in low-performing companies. In addition, in the high-performing companies, 51.67% of the employees received performance feedback from multiple sources, compared to only 3.9% in low-performing companies (Dessler, 2005). Such feedback gives employees a better overall picture of how they are doing on the job. This means that employees in high-performing companies have more information about the quality of their performance so that they know how and when to improve.

Encouraging high performance within organizations is not just a matter of prodding the employees to use their knowledge, skills, and abilities in furtherance of the organization's goals. The high-performing organization also recognizes that employees will be motivated to greater performance if they are rewarded for their efforts with something of value. For example, in the high-performing companies, pay increases and incentive pay were tied to performance for 87.27% of the employees; in contrast, only 23.36%

of such remuneration was tied to performance in low-performing companies. This means that the employees in the high-performing companies not only know how they are doing against organizational standards and how they can improve; they are also given tangible monetary incentives to motivate them to improve their performance and, by extension, the performance of the organization. This is demonstrated by the fact that 83.56% of employees in high-performing organizations were eligible for incentive pay, while only 27.83% of employees in low-performing organizations were eligible (Dessler, 2005). In addition to monetary incentives, high-performing organizations typically try to offer employees other incentives that will meet their individual needs, such as prestige, opportunities to socialize, or job security.

Such differences play themselves out in the performance of the organization. According to Dessler (2005), high-performing organizations had lower turnover (20.87%) than low-performing organizations (34.09%). Reducing turnover helps not only because of the continuity of having high-skilled workers who know the job but also because it reduces the costs associated with hiring and training replacement workers.

The US General Accounting Office (GAO) has been very involved in analyzing high-performing organizations in an attempt to determine what practices differentiate them from other companies. The GAO has found that leadership at the highest levels in high-performing organizations is committed to doing whatever is necessary for success. This includes envisioning what changes are necessary, implementing those changes, and communicating openly with employees. Another discovery was that high-performing organizations tend to work effectively with labor unions to resolve issues quickly. They also make sure that their employees receive the training that they need to better contribute to the organization's goals. In addition, high-performing organizations encourage the use and development of teams as a way to advance the goals of the organization. In high-performing organizations, employees are encouraged to get involved, particularly in planning and sharing performance information and helping design strategic plans.

APPLICATIONS

In the early twentieth century, many organizations were looking for ways to improve organizational performance by taking away work from human beings and automating it. In some ways, we still do this, using computers instead of manual typewriters and PDAs instead of calendars, for example. However, because of the intellectual nature of work in many modern organizations, we also recognize that human capital is an invaluable asset that needs to be nurtured and utilized. To this end, high-performing organizations recognize that the organization's performance is dependent on the employees' performance, and they develop and implement policies and practices that will support high performance. At its most basic, this involves finding employees who have the potential to excel, setting objective performance standards that give them the criteria to know what kind of performance the organization is seeking, and linking performance to rewards in order to encourage high performance.

Defining & Assessing Success

The desire to become a high-performing organization is easy to understand. However, without an objective definition of what this means, it will be difficult, if not impossible, to reach this goal. On the organizational level, achieving high performance means that the organization must perform strategic planning and set clear goals and objectives. The organization also needs to define in objective terms what high performance looks like in order to encourage employees to become high-performing workers in furtherance of these goals.

The definition of what high performance entails is aided by the development of a solid job description based on an objective, thorough job analysis. A well-written job description delineates not only the tasks and responsibilities of a job but also the knowledge, skills, and abilities necessary to do these things. In addition, a good job description sets standards for satisfactory and unsatisfactory behavior on the job. Good job descriptions are competency based, describing the job in terms of measurable, observable, behavioral competencies that the employee must demonstrate in order to perform well. The development of an objective, empirically based job description helps the organization better determine what knowledge, skills, and abilities are needed for employees in each job. Good job descriptions and their concomitant performance standards also help employees know what kind of behavior will be rewarded (or not rewarded) by the organization.

It is not sufficient, however, to merely set standards for job performance. It is also necessary to give the employee feedback on how well he or she is meeting the set standards in order to encourage high performance. The traditional way to do this is through performance appraisal. This is the process of objectively assessing the employee's current performance or performance over the past appraisal period and determining how well it meets predetermined standards. Performance appraisals may describe the performance strengths and weaknesses both of the individual worker and between two or more workers. They may be based on objective data (e.g., average number of widgets produced per day; number of sales made per quarter), personnel data (e.g., number of days late to work), judgmental data (e.g., rating scales), or some combination of the three. Judgmental data in particular can be very subjective and victim to a host of rating errors or bias on the part of the person doing the rating. Therefore, in high-performing organizations, human-resource policies or procedures are developed and implemented to help increase the objectiveness of the appraisal feedback or give the employee feedback from multiple sources.

It is important to give feedback on an employee's performance by measuring it against a predetermined standard or set of specific goals to be achieved for the appraisal period. One way to do this is through a method called management by objectives (MBO). In MBO, the manager, often in concert with the employee, sets objectives for the employee to meet during the coming appraisal period. At the next performance appraisal, the employee is evaluated in terms of how well he or she has met these goals. Although this can be done on an informal level, MBO is frequently instituted across the organization. MBO instituted at this level starts first with the organization setting enterprise-wide goals and objectives based on its strategic plan (e.g., increase company profits from a particular product line by $500,000 over the next year). Using this information, each department then sets its own goals and objectives for how they will support and help reach the organization's goals (e.g., increase sales of the product in the eastern region by 10% over the next year). Departmental goals are then discussed with the employees in each department to help them understand what the organization is trying to achieve and to encourage them to think about how they as individuals can contribute to those goals. Individual employees and their supervisors then discuss the goals and possible contributions that can be made by the individual and set specific, short-term goals (e.g., obtain 10 more customers per quarter; call on 5 more potential customers per week; include two more cities in the region). The performance or progress toward these goals is periodically assessed at predetermined times, and the employee is given feedback on his or her progress.

Although MBO can be a step in the right direction in the attempt to link individual performance with organizational performance goals, it is not without its drawbacks. The most frequently encountered problem with MBO is the setting of unclear or unmeasurable objectives. For example, the objective to "come up with a better widget design in the next quarter" may be valid in principle (if the current design is unsatisfactory), but it is difficult to objectively define (how, exactly, does one define "better"?) and challenging to measure. In addition, it is not a reasonable goal: it is futile to put a time limit on creativity. Further, the process of managing by objectives is time consuming and requires involvement at all levels of the organization to make it work. Although one can define objectives for the individual, if these are not tied in to organizational-level objectives, they probably will not meaningfully or intentionally improve the performance of the organization. Also, it can be difficult to achieve agreement between management and employees on what is a reasonable objective. Supervisors have a tendency to set the bar too high when writing objectives, while many employees tend to set the bar too low so that they can be sure to meet their objectives, particularly if their pay raises are tied to performance. For example, although a manager may want to give a programmer the objective of writing 50 pages of code a week, the programmer may know that this is both unreasonable and impossible. To increase the effectiveness of performance-appraisal goals and feedback, it is important that the employee's goals be reasonable, objective, measurable, and based on the performance goals of the organization.

Even when reasonable, objective, measurable goals are set, receiving feedback from one source is often not sufficient to encourage the type of high performance that many organizations are looking for in their employees. A technique called 360-degree feedback can help improve the feedback the employee receives by increasing the amount of feedback and the sources from which it comes. This technique is called 360-degree feedback because the feedback comes from people who work all around the employee, not just from one person working above him or her. Employees receive feedback on their job performance from representatives of the major groups with whom they interact on the job, both inside and outside the organization. For example, employees may receive feedback not only from their supervisors, as in the traditional performance-appraisal paradigm, but also from their subordinates, coworkers, customers, and other groups with whom they interact. This technique gives the employee more feedback than he or she would receive from one person alone. It also gives the employee better feedback by involving those who work directly with him or her. In addition, this approach to feedback can help neutralize a biased opinion from one person by giving the employee and the supervisor a range of reactions to look at, allowing them to examine the preponderance of evidence rather than one person's reactions. The increased level of feedback received from techniques such as 360-degree feedback gives the employee a better idea of how he or she can improve performance.

Linking Performance to Rewards

Although it is important to specify what kind of behavior is expected in the organization and to encourage employees to meet or exceed these standards by providing feedback, in most cases employees need more from the organization than to know that they are helping it succeed. Even in a non-profit or volunteer organization, workers need to get something out of the situation, whether it is a monetary reward or a feeling of accomplishment or personal growth. To motivate employees to perform at a consistently high level, the organization must give them what they want or need. The process of determining what these things are and giving them to the employee in return for excellent performance is called motivation. One of the things that high-performing organizations do to motivate employees to contribute to the company's high performance is to link the desired performance to rewards.

Many theories have been advanced about motivation. Some theorists have tried to reduce motivation to an equation that connects the probability of increased performance with such things as the employee's perceived expectancy of obtaining a reward for doing so. Other theorists have stated that different people are motivated by different things, from having one's physical needs met (e.g., food on the table and a roof over one's head) to earning the esteem of others or some other internal incentive.

No matter the theory, most motivation theorists recognize that people working in organizations both need and expect remuneration. Sometimes this is required to meet basic physical needs or to have the security of knowing that those needs will continue to be met for the foreseeable future. In other cases, pay incentives in the form of bonuses, raises, or promotions fill a need for recognition from others. No matter what motivators an employee has — and high-performing organizations typically seek to meet those needs within the constraints of the organization — pay is always a consideration.

One of the approaches to motivating desired behavior in high-performing organizations is an approach frequently referred to as pay for performance. In this approach, the employee is rewarded financially for high performance and their contribution to the organization's goals. This is true not only for workers at the bottom of the organizational structure, such as production workers, but for all employees, all the way up to the chief executive officer.

The GAO has researched pay-for-performance systems and has found a number of factors that make them successful. First, such systems must use objective competencies to assess the quality of the employee's performance. As stated earlier, these should be based on empirical research and directly related to the goals of the organization. Second, employee performance ratings should be translated into pay increases or awards so that employees can see a direct, positive consequence of their actions. Third, when making decisions about compensation, both the employee's current salary and his or her contribution to the organization should be considered so that rewards for similar contributions are equitable. Finally, to be successful and to prevent possible abuse, pay-for-performance systems should be clear and well publicized so that employees know the basis on which decisions are made and what kinds of awards are given across the organization.

There are many ways that human-resource functions can aid the organization's goal for high performance. These include recognizing that employees are valuable assets to the organization (i.e., human capital) and increasing the objectiveness of standards, feedback, and the grounds on which rewards are given. By encouraging high performance in individual employees, the organization as a whole can become high performing, too.

Bibliography

Dessler, G. (2005). *Human resource management* (10th ed.). Upper Saddle River, NJ: Pearson/Prentice Hall.

Kim, H., & Sung-Choon, K. (2013). Strategic HR functions and firm performance: The moderating effects of high-involvement work practices. *Asia Pacific Journal of Management, 30*(1), 91–113. Retrieved November 21, 2013, from EBSCO Online Database Business Source Complete. http://search.ebscohost.com/login.aspx?direct=true&db=bth&AN=85399270&site=ehost-live

Kroon, B., Voorde, K., & Timmers, J. (2013). High performance work practices in small firms: A resource-poverty and strategic decision-making perspective. *Small Business Economics, 41*(1), 71–91. Retrieved November 21, 2013, from EBSCO Online Database Business Source Complete. http://search.ebscohost.com/login.aspx?direct=true&db=bth&AN=87910378&site=ehost-live

McShane, S. L. & Von Glinow, M. A. (2003). *Organizational behavior: Emerging realities for the workplace revolution* (2nd ed). Boston: McGraw-Hill/Irwin.

Ming-Chu, Y. (2013). The influence of high-performance human resource practices on entrepreneurial performance: The perspective of entrepreneurial theory. *International Journal of Organizational Innovation, 6*(1), 15–33. Retrieved November 21, 2013, from EBSCO Online Database Business Source Complete. http://search.ebscohost.com/login.aspx?direct=true&db=bth&AN=90515790&site=ehost-live

Sun, L., & Pan, W. (2011). Differentiation strategy, high-performance human resource practices, and firm performance: Moderation by employee commitment. *International Journal of Human Resource Management, 22*(15), 3068–3079. Retrieved November 21, 2013, from EBSCO Online Database Business Source Complete. http://search.ebscohost.com/login.aspx?direct=true&db=bth&AN=65643359&site=ehost-live

US General Accounting Office. (2001). *Human capital: Practices that empowered and involved employees.* (GAO-01-1070). Retrieved 27 March 2007 from EBSCO Online Database Business Source Complete http://web.ebscohost.com/ehost/pdf?vid=6&hid=122&sid=6c11f73f-cb64-441f-8ccf-a2a8b38d1861%40sessionmgr104.

US General Accounting Office. (2004). *Human capital: Implementing pay for performance at selected personnel demonstration projects* (GAO-04-83). Retrieved 27 March 2007 from EBSCO Online Database Business Source Complete http://web.ebscohost.com/ehost/pdf?vid=7&hid=2&sid=cfb3dec4-539c-4fe1-97cd-ac6c01b1a75d%40sessionmgr104.

Suggested Reading

Chang, Y. K., Oh, W., & Messersmith, J. G. (2013). Translating corporate social performance into financial performance: Exploring the moderating role of high-performance work practices. *International Journal of Human Resource Management, 24*(19), 3738–3756. Retrieved November 21, 2013, from EBSCO Online Database Business Source Complete. http://search.ebscohost.com/login.aspx?direct=true&db=bth&AN=90399478&site=ehost-live

Thor, C. G. (1994). *The measures of success: Creating a high performing organization.* New York: John Wiley & Sons.

US General Accounting Office. (2003). *Results-oriented cultures: Creating a clear linkage between individual performance and organizational success* (GAO-03-488). Washington, DC: US Government Printing Office. Retrieved 27 March 2007 from EBSCO Online Database Business Source Complete http://web.ebscohost.com/ehost/pdf?vid=4&hid=102&sid=cfb3dec4-539c-4fe1-97cd-ac6c01b1a75d%40sessionmgr104.

Urwin, P., Michielsens, E., Murphy, R., & Waters, J. (2006, 14 Sep). Think outside the black box: How employee relations links to performance. *People Management, 12* (18), 52. Retrieved 27 March 2007 from EBSCO Online Database Business Source Complete http://search.ebscohost.com/login.aspx?direct=true&db=bth&AN=22536136&site=bsi-live

Walker, D. M. (2004). *Comptroller general's forum: High-performing organizations: Metrics, means, and mechanisms for achieving high performance in the 21st century public management environment* (GAO-04-3434SP). Retrieved 27 March 2007 from EBSCO Online Database Business Source Complete http://web.ebscohost.com/ehost/pdf?vid=5&hid=2&sid=cfb3dec4-539c-4fe1-97cd-ac6c01b1a75d%40sessionmgr104.

Ruth A. Wienclaw, Ph.D.

I

Inclusive Leadership

ABSTRACT

Inclusive leadership is a style of management that has risen to prominence in recent years, and is widely seen as a significant improvement over the relatively uninspiring transactional leadership styles common in previous generations of leaders. While it has several different interpretations, most of these agree that the inclusive leader is one who is available to subordinates, who cares about their ideas and motivations, and who is willing to hear input from all levels of the organization.

OVERVIEW

Inclusive leadership is closely related to transformational leadership, a style that seeks to inspire the members of an organization to work together in order to create a system that is greater than the sum of its parts. In the literature of the fields of business and management, the idea of inclusive leadership generally has two possible interpretations. The first interpretation revolves around an understanding of the value of diversity in organizations (Naudé, Stanley & Ratcliffe, 2015). The traditional approach to management and organizational staffing was to hire people who fit into the corporate mold, the so-called "organization man" discussed in studies of the Japanese business world. The goal was to hire the "right kind" of people who would see the world in the same way that the organization's leadership did, so that there would be a harmonious and productive working environment. The problem that arose with this approach was that it leads to tunnel vision, because people tend to see things only from their own perspective, and if everyone in an organization has more or less the same perspective, then problems that require analysis through a different type of lens may be difficult or impossible for that organization to solve. This is why there is a need for leadership that sees the importance of including many different kinds of people, each with their own background and beliefs (Hafford-Letchfield et al., 2014; Ashikali & Groeneveld, 2015).

The origins of this appreciation for diversity in organizations can be traced back to the 1960s and the beginnings of the Civil Rights movement, which encouraged members of many different racial and ethnic groups to advocate for their communities' needs. This work helped the struggle for women's rights and rights for lesbian, gay, bisexual, and transgendered persons. Companies have realized that building diverse teams is not only the right thing to do morally, ethically, and legally—it also makes good business sense. Companies develop and market products and services to all different kinds of people, so hiring only one type of person (such as white males) and expecting that group to be able to understand the needs and desires of every other group would be a recipe for disaster. Inclusive leadership understands this, and draws upon a rich variety of people and experiences in order to form a better connection with its diverse customer base (Mitchell & Conference Board, 2010).

The second interpretation of inclusive leadership found in management texts refers to a leader's interpersonal style rather than to the leader's attitude toward diversity. Here again, it is useful to consider styles of leadership that have predominated in earlier time periods. In the past, a leader was expected to have all of the answers, because the assumption was that the person who best understands how things should be done is the person who should be in charge, telling everyone else what to do. Sometimes this approach made sense, especially during periods of history prior to the start of public education, because leaders back then might very well be the only ones in the group with the relevant experience and education to see how a problem should be approached.

Further Insights

In the modern period, it has gradually become clear that it is not very common for only the leader to understand the situation an organization faces. More often, leaders are faced with problems that arise from many different areas, and it is not uncommon for leaders to be unfamiliar with these. A factor that has contributed to this trend is the increasing specialization of the modern economy. People do jobs that are more and more detailed, requiring ever greater amounts of specialized training, so that it is beyond the capacity of a single individual to understand every task that is carried out on a day to day basis within the organization (Burrello, Sailor, & Kleinhammer-Tramill, 2013).

One hundred years ago, the leader of a company might very well have experience doing every single job in the firm, such that he—it would almost certainly have been a man—could walk along the factory line, giving the workers advice about their tasks. If one imagines trying to do something similar at one of Silicon Valley's giant technology firms, the need for new leadership styles suddenly becomes clear. Because it is no longer possible for one person to have all of the answers, leaders are realizing that the most useful approach they can adopt is one of inclusion, where they get employees at the organization to commit their time, energy, and expertise to helping the company succeed (Hollander, 2012). Modern leadership theories rely heavily on ideas around social exchange, the idea being that people follow their leaders because the leaders provide them with something in exchange for their cooperation.

Employee work engagement is a measurement of an employee's level of interest in the work he or she has been assigned to complete. Generally, employee work engagement is higher when employees are assigned tasks they know how to do and have the proper authority to perform. Inclusive leadership strives to ensure that employee work engagement remains high by aligning workers with tasks to which they are best suited. Further, inclusive leaders are seen as workers' allies, addressing workplace issues fairly and helping solve problems. Social exchange theory states that if one person performs a task for another, then the person who benefitted will be more likely to reciprocate. Modern leadership theories rely heavily on ideas around social exchange, the idea being that people follow their leaders because the leaders provide them with something in exchange for their cooperation.

VIEWPOINTS

Much of the discussion about inclusive leadership focuses not on whether it is a good idea—few dispute this—but on how it should be practiced. These conversations are of two broad types: things that a leader should do in order to be inclusive, and ways that a leader should behave as part of being inclusive.

Availability

Perhaps the foremost quality that should be in an inclusive leader's toolkit is availability. This means that the leader needs to be willing to sit down with his or her staff whenever they need to discuss an issue related to their work or which might have an effect on their work. Some leaders, especially those with introverted tendencies, find it difficult to cope with this much personal contact, so they devise ways to distance themselves from staff in order to avoid it, such as closing the office door, choosing an office further away from the rest of the department, or requiring everyone to work with a secretary or administrative assistant to schedule a meeting, instead of simply answering their own phone. Those leaders who understand the importance of inclusion, however, make themselves available to their staff, because they feel that part of a leader's role is to listen and interact with everyone on the team. After all, before everyone can be included, everyone has to be able to be heard (Rumsey, 2013).

Accessibility

A quality closely related to availability is accessibility. At first the two might seem almost synonymous, but there is a distinction to be found because it is possible for a leader to be "technically" available yet remain not very accessible. This is best illustrated by an example. In a hypothetical call center, thirty technical support people are supervised by a manager. The manager has an open door policy which is much spoken of, and all employees are reminded on a regular basis that they can go and see the manager any time they have an issue to discuss. This manager can say that she makes every effort to be available for her staff whenever they might need her. However, it turns out that the call center also keeps very strict metrics about how much time staff spend away from their phones. Any time spent away must have a documented explanation, and the paperwork required to document a conference with the manager is considerable.

The effect of this policy would be that very few people would take the time to go and speak to the manager, unless there was a very compelling reason to do so. The manager is available (the door is always open) but not very accessible (because the call center policy acts as an obstacle to meeting with the manager). A more inclusive approach in this scenario might be for the manager to schedule fifteen minutes with each employee, each week, so that they would all feel that they have access to someone who will hear their ideas or can help them, should the need arise (Couto, 2010).

Openness

Along with availability and accessibility, the quality most often seen in inclusive leaders is openness. Openness refers to the leader's ability to be honest and authentic with followers, instead of refusing to share information with them or help them to understand how their work fits into the larger picture of the work being carried on by the organization. Some transactional leaders feel that in order to maintain a position of superiority above those around them, they need to limit others' access to information about the organization's operations. These leaders will typically give orders to others but will refuse to clarify why the orders are being given or what the ultimate use for the work being requested will be.

To continue with the call center example above, the manager of the call center might inform all employees that they must reduce their average call times to under one minute per call. Employees who have a higher level of affective organizational commitment will immediately want to know more about this directive (Wuffli, 2015)—whose idea is it, and what is the reason for it? It could be an attempt to reduce costs by using the phones less, or it could be an effort to make customers happier by resolving their problems more quickly. Knowing the answers to questions like these will help the employees understand how they should act: Should they rush people off the phones at all costs, because the head of the company is adamant that this change happen immediately, or should they just make a mild effort to be more terse, as might be indicated if the project were just a low stakes experiment being conducted by the office leader for a few days.

Whatever the answers to these questions might be, it is how the manager responds to them that shows the extent to which the office embraces an inclusive leadership model. A person following the traditional model of leadership would be very likely to refuse to share any additional information, making clear that the only information the employees needed was that which had been given (Brennan, 2014). This type of response is frustrating for employees and can cause some to feel that there actually is no useful purpose to the orders they have been given, other than to harass people and raise their levels of anxiety.

An inclusive response, on the other hand, would be one in which the leader openly shared why the change in procedure is needed. Possibly, the supervisor does not know either and is just following orders from her superiors, in which case she may empathize with the potential issues that the change might cause. Responding in this way removes barriers between leaders and followers, instead of reinforcing them. Followers who receive an inclusive response feel that they and their leader are working together, both trying to help each other get the work done even if they do not have as complete an understanding of the big picture as they might wish (Esposito & Normore, 2015).

While some advocates of more charismatic leadership argue that using an inclusive style in this way could erode the authority that is traditionally associated with a leadership role, allowing staff to feel that they are on a par with the leader in terms of expertise and knowledge, this is not what usually happens. Instead, those who are exposed to an inclusive style tend to feel more committed to the organization and more willing to use their own creativity and initiative to develop improved products and processes. This is known as affective organizational commitment. Katz & Miller (2014) argue that inclusive leadership is no longer optional in the rapidly evolving business environment in which agility is key to survival. Inclusive leadership's benefits include higher levels of optimism among employees, attributable to the fact that being able to share their views with their leaders gives them the feeling that ideas that they share with the management will actually be heard, considered, and possibly even implemented (Mac, Ottesen, & Precey, 2013).

BIBLIOGRAPHY

Ashikali, T., & Groeneveld, S. (2015). Diversity management in public organizations and its effect on employees' affective commitment: The role of transformational leadership and the inclusiveness of the organizational culture. *Review of Public Personnel Administration, 35*(2), 146–168. Retrieved January 3, 2016 from EBSCO Online Database

Business Source Complete. http://search.ebscohost.com/login.aspx?direct=true&db=bth&AN=102598689&site=ehost-live

Brennan, D. (2014). *As a leader: 15 points to consider for more inclusive leadership.* S.l.: Tate.

Burrello, L. C., Sailor, W., & Kleinhammer-Tramill, J. (2013). *Unifying educational systems: Leadership and policy perspectives.* New York, NY: Routledge.

Couto, R. A. (2010). *Political and civic leadership: A reference handbook.* Los Angeles, CA: SAGE Reference.

Esposito, M. C. K., & Normore, A. H. (2015). *Inclusive practices and social justice leadership for special populations in urban settings: A moral imperative.* Charlotte, NC: Information Age Publishing.

Hafford-Letchfield, T., Lambley, S., Spolander, G., & Cocker, C. (2014). *Inclusive leadership in social work and social care.* Bristol, UK: Policy Press.

Hollander, E. P. (2012). *Inclusive leadership: The essential leader-follower relationship.* New York, NY: Routledge.

Katz, J. H., & Miller, F. A. (2014). Leaders getting different. *OD Practitioner, 46*(3), 40–45. Retrieved January 3, 2016 from EBSCO Online Database Business Source Complete. http://search.ebscohost.com/login.aspx?direct=true&db=bth&AN=97081019&site=ehost-live

Mac, R. G., Ottesen, E., & Precey, R. (2013). *Leadership for inclusive education: Values, vision and voices.* Boston, MA: Sense Publishers.

Mitchell, C., & Conference Board. (2010). *Mind the gap: Overcoming organisational barriers to develop inclusive leaders.* New York, NY: Conference Board.

Naudé, S., Stanley, M., & Ratcliffe, V. (2015). Inclusive leadership matters to performance. *Human Resources Magazine, 20*(4), 16–17. Retrieved January 3, 2016 from EBSCO Online Database Business Source Complete. http://search.ebscohost.com/login.aspx?direct=true&db=bth&AN=110349030&site=ehost-live

Rumsey, M. G. (2013). *The Oxford handbook of leadership.* New York, NY: Oxford University Press.

Wuffli, P. A. (2015). *Inclusive leadership.* New York, NY: Springer.

SUGGESTED READING

Booysen, L. (2014). The development of inclusive leadership practice and processes. In B. M. Ferdman, B. R. Deane, B. M. Ferdman, B. R. Deane (Eds.), *Diversity at work: The practice of inclusion.* San Francisco, CA: Jossey-Bass.

Choi, S. B., Tran, T. H., & Park, B. I. (2015). Inclusive leadership and work engagement: Mediating roles of affective organizational commitment and creativity. *Social Behavior and Personality, 43*(6), 931–944.

Edmunds, A. L., & Macmillan, R. B. (2010). *Leadership for inclusion: A practical guide.* Rotterdam: Sense Publishers.

Fierke, K. K., Lui, K. W., Lepp, G. A., & Baldwin, A. J. (2014). Teaching inclusive leadership through student-centered practices. *Journal of the Academy of Business Education, 15,* 51–65. Retrieved January 3, 2016 from EBSCO Online Database Business Source Complete. http://search.ebscohost.com/login.aspx?direct=true&db=bth&AN=101788621&site=ehost-live

Inclusive leadership still thin on the ground. (2015). *Coaching at Work, 10*(1), 8. Retrieved January 3, 2016, from EBSCO Online Database Business Source Complete. http://search.ebscohost.com/login.aspx?direct=true&db=bth&AN=100214369&site=ehost-live

Prime, J., Otterman, M., & Salib, E. R. (2014). Engaging men through inclusive leadership. In R. J. Burke, D. A. Major, R. J. Burke, D. A. Major (Eds.), *Gender in organizations: Are men allies or adversaries to women's career advancement?.* Northampton, MA: Edward Elgar Publishing.

Scott Zimmer, J.D .

INDUSTRIAL ORGANIZATION & FINANCE

ABSTRACT

This article focuses on industrial organization and finance. Industrial organization and corporate finance have evolved into two distinct fields of study. Both topics place minimum emphasis on the strategic relationship between financial decisions and output market decisions. There is an exploration of market structures. Market structures take into consideration: The number of firms in an industry, the relative size of the firms (industry concentration), demand conditions, ease of entry and exit, and technological and cost conditions. Profit and wealth maximization is discussed. In addition, the value of firm-bank relationships is introduced.

OVERVIEW

In the past, the field of industrial organization has not focused on corporate finance, and vice versa. However, a working knowledge of both fields may assist scholars in understanding "how product markets perform when firms participating in a market are constrained financially, and for understanding how capital structure and corporate governance contribute to product market strategy" (Riordan, 2003, p. 1). Industrial organization and corporate finance have evolved into two distinct fields of study. Brander and Lewis (1986) suggested that the research on financial structures and oligopoly have something in common. Both topics are concerned with the strategic relationship between internal economic decisions and external market decisions. Harris and Raviv (1991) identified the industrial organization effects of capital structure as one of the four major topics when studying the theory of capital structure.

Roe (2001) asserted that "the relative value of shareholder wealth maximization for a nation is partly a function of that nation's industrial organization. When much of a nation's industry is monopolistically organized, maximizing shareholder wealth would maximize the monopolist's profits, induce firms to produce fewer goods than society could potentially produce, and motivate firms to raise price beyond that which is necessary to produce the goods" (p.1).

Profit Maximization

Profits are very crucial to a firm's bottom line. When a firm is able to make a profit, there is an assumption that the company has done a good job of being effective and efficient in controlling the cost while producing a quality product or performing a quality service. However, there are different types of profits. Two types of profits are accounting profits and economic profits.

- Accounting profits are the difference between the total revenue and the cost of producing products or services; they appear on the firm's income statement.
- Economic profits are the difference between overall revenue and the total amount of opportunity costs. The opportunity costs tend to be higher than accounting and bookkeeping costs.

Profit Theories

Profits tend to vary across industries, and there are a number of theories that attempt to provide an explanation as to why this occurs. Five of the most discussed theories in this area are:

- Risk-Bearing Theory. When the owners of a company make investments into the firm, they take on a certain amount of risk. In order to compensate them for their investment, the company will need to have an above average return on economic profits. An example would be a firm that has investors such as venture capitalists or angel investors.
- Dynamic Equilibrium Theory. Every firm should strive to have a normal rate of profit. However, each firm has the opportunity to earn returns above or below the normal level at any time.
- Monopoly Theory. Monopoly Theory. There are times when one firm many have the opportunity to dominate in its industry and earn above average rates of return over a long period of time. These firms tend to take control of the market as a result of economies of scale, dominate the ownership of essential natural resources, control crucial patents and influence government regulations. An example would be utility companies.
- Innovation Theory. A firm may earn above normal profits as a reward for its successful innovations such as patents. An example would be a pharmaceutical organization such as Astra Zeneca.
- Managerial Efficiency Theory. A firm may be able to earn above average profits based on its strong leadership team. This type of organization gains profits as a result of being effective and efficient. An example would be General Electric under Jack Welch's leadership.

Wealth Maximization

Wealth maximization is a long term operational goal. Shareholders continue to exert a claim on a firm's net cash flows even after anticipated contractual claims have been paid. All other stakeholders (i.e. employers, customers) have contractual expected returns. There tends to be a preference for wealth maximization because it takes into consideration (Shim & Siegel, 1998):

- Wealth for the long term.
- Risk or uncertainty.
- The timing of returns.
- The stockholders' return.

Criterion for this goal suggests that a firm should review and assess the expected profits and or cash flows as well as the risks that are associated with them. When conducting this evaluation, there are three points to keep in mind.

- First, economic profits are not equivalent to accounting profits.
- Second, accounting profits are not the same as cash flows.
- Lastly, financial analysis must focus on maximizing the current value of cash flows to firm owners when attempting to maximize shareholder benefit.

Application

Market Structure

Market structures take into consideration:

- The number of firms in an industry.
- The relative size of the firms (industry concentration).
- Demand conditions.
- Ease of entry and exit.
- Technological and cost conditions.

The preferred structure is dependent on the type of industry. Therefore, the financial management team of each firm determines which of the above-mentioned factors will be a part of the decision making process.

The level of competition tends to be dependent on whether there are many (or a few) firms in the industry and the firm's products are similar or different. Given this information, four basic approaches to market structure and the types of competition have been established.

Perfect (Pure) Competition (Many sellers of a standardized product)

Characteristics of perfect competition are:

- Large number of buyers and sellers.
- Homogeneous product.
- Complete knowledge.
- Easy entry and exit from the market.

A firm using this approach tends to be small relative to the total market, and it will offer its product at the going market price. A firm in this format operates at an output level where price (or marginal revenue) is equal to the marginal cost and profit maximized. This format is more theoretical because there is no firm that operates at this level.

Monopolistic Competition (Many sellers of a differentiated product) Characteristics of monopolistic competition are:

- One firm.
- No close substitutes.
- No interdependence among firms.
- Substantial barriers to entry.

In addition, there tends to be many buyers and sellers, there is product differentiation, easy entry and exit and independent decision making by individual firms. An example of a firm fitting this profile would be a small business selling differentiated, yet similar, products. These firms will utilize three basic strategies in order to obtain their principal goal of maximum profits. The strategies are:

- Price changes.
- Variations in the products.
- Promotional activities.

Oligopoly (Only a few sellers of either standardized or differentiated products)

Characteristics of oligopoly are:

- Few firms.
- High degree of interdependence among firms.
- Product may be homogenous or differentiated.
- Difficult entry and exit from market.

The market fits this approach when there are a small number of firms supplying the dominant share of an industry's total output. Oligopolists are interdependent based on all levels of competition — price, output, promotional strategies, customer service policies, acquisitions and mergers, etc. Therefore, decision makers may have a hard time anticipating what rivals will do in reaction to their position, which makes the process complex. Two popular models are Cournot's duopoly model and kinked demand curve. An example would be the NCAA. This organization controls the revenues and costs of its member schools. It has the power to limit the number of games and times that a school can have its games televised. The NCAA retains control over costs through its restrictions on the compensation of student athletes.

Monopoly (A single seller of a product for which there is no close substitute)

A monopoly occurs when one firm produces a highly differentiated product in a market with significant barriers to entry. It may be large or small, and it must be the only supplier. In addition, there are no close substitutes. Since the monopoly is the only producer, it is equivalent to the overall industry and its individual demand curve is the same as the industry demand. An example would be an electric utility company in a specific geographic area.

What is the difference between the monopoly and pure approach? A profit-maximizing monopoly firm will produce less and charge a higher price than firms collectively in a purely competitive industry. However, both demand and cost may be different for a monopoly firm (i.e. a monopoly may be able to take advantage of economies of scales).

VIEWPOINT

Firm-Bank Relationships

There tends to be a variety of information problems in the financial markets and those responsible for overseeing the processes attempt to find different ways to address the issues that arise. One such attempt explores long-term relationships between firms and banks. Some believe that these types of relationships are crucial to the structure of credit markets. As a result, Degryse and Ongena (2002) reviewed the firm-bank relationship and the structure of banking markets on a global level. In addition, Yafeh and Yosha (2001) conducted a study where they reviewed how standard industrial organization tools could be used to analyze the relationship between competition in financial markets and the prevalence of bank-firm relationships.

Benefits

A firm-bank relationship is established when the two entities have a close interaction and the banker is allowed to observe and collect a variety of information about the firm. The banker has the opportunity to evaluate whether or not the firm can meet future financial obligations. Although the banker has a chance to observe how the relationship will benefit the lender in the long term, there are some advantages for the firm as well. For example, the firm can increase its access to credit at a lower cost and with less collateral if it has established a relationship with a bank. Also, the firm may have the opportunity to enter into complex and high risk projects as a result of having an established relationship with a bank. Finally, a firm's reputation and image may be seen as favorable due to an established and credible relationship with a bank (Dass & Massa, 2011).

Negatives

Although this is seen as a positive endeavor, there is a down side. There may be some individuals who will become concerned with the type and amount of information a bank knows about a firm. "The ability for a bank to privately observe proprietary information and maintain a close relationship with its customer can also impose costs on the customer" (Degryse & Ongena, 2002, p. 404). For example, a bank can devise a campaign that will lock customers into maintaining a relationship with it and prevent customers from receiving competitive financing from another bank. This will lead to the original bank having a monopoly over the market as a result of having privileged client information. One solution to this type of problem would be for firms to enter into more than one bank relationship. The banks will offer competitive services, which will minimize the possibility of any one bank getting the upper hand and creating a monopoly situation.

World-Wide Bank-Firm Relationships

Firms can diversify their financial portfolio by entering into relationships with banks across the world. There will be opportunities for banks to form consortiums and market to a variety of firms. The banks could come together and establish rules and regulations for different types of organizational projects around the world. The Second European Banking Directive and the 1994 United States Riege-Neal Act created large international banking markets. Established bank-firm relationships are critical to the present development process for financial systems worldwide (Degryse & Ongena, 2002).

CONCLUSION

Industrial organization and corporate finance have evolved into two distinct fields of study. Brander and Lewis (1986) suggested that the research on financial structures and oligopoly have something in common. Both topics are concerned with the strategic relationship between internal economic decisions and external market decisions. Harris and Raviv (1991) identified the industrial organization effects of capital structure as one of the four major topics when studying the theory of capital structure.

Market structures take into consideration: The number of firms in an industry, the relative size of the firms (industry concentration), demand conditions, ease of entry and exit, and technological and cost conditions. The preferred structure is dependent on the type of industry. Therefore, the financial management team of each firm determines which of the above-mentioned factors will be a part of the decision making process.

A firm-bank relationship is established when the two entities have a close interaction and the banker is allowed to observe and collect a variety of information about the firm. The banker has the opportunity to evaluate whether or not the firm can meet future financial obligations. Although the banker has a chance to observe how the relationship will benefit the lender in the long term, there are some advantages for the firm as well. For example, the firm can increase its access to credit at a lower cost and with less collateral if it has established a relationship with a bank. Also, the firm may have the opportunity to enter into complex and high risk projects as a result of having an established relationship with a bank. Finally, a firm's reputation and image may be seen as favorable due to an established and credible relationship with a bank.

Bibliography

Brander, J., & Lewis, T. (1986). Oligopoly and financial structure: The limited liability effect. *American Economic Review, 76*(5), 956-970. Retrieved October 16, 2007, from EBSCO Online Database Business Source Complete. http://search.ebscohost.com/login.aspx?direct=true&db=bth&AN=4498297&site=ehost-live

Dass, N., & Massa, M. (2011). The impact of a strong bank-firm relationship on the borrowing firm. *Review of Financial Studies, 24*(4), 1204-1260. Retrieved on November 14, 2013, from EBSCO Online Database Business Source Complete. http://search.ebscohost.com/login.aspx?direct=true&db=bth&AN=59962417&site=ehost-live

Degryse, H., & Ongena, S. (2002). Bank-firm relationships and international banking markets. *International Journal of the Economics of Business, 9*(3), 401-417. Retrieved July 5, 2007, from EBSCO Online Database Business Source Complete. http://search.ebscohost.com/login.aspx?direct=true&db=bth&AN=8797206&site=ehost-live

Harris, M., & Raviv, A. (1991). The theory of capital structure. *Journal of Finance, 46*(1), 297-355. Retrieved October 16, 2007, from EBSCO Online Database Business Source Complete. http://search.ebscohost.com/login.aspx?direct=true&db=bth&AN=4653270&site=ehost-live

Riordan, M. (2003, December). How do capital markets influence product market competition?. *Review of Industrial Organization, 23*(3/4), 179-191. Retrieved October 16, 2007, from Business Source Premier database. http://search.ebscohost.com/login.aspx?direct=true&db=bth&AN=14156611&site=ehost-live

Roe, M. (2001). The shareholder wealth maximization and industrial organization. Retrieved October 16, 2007, from http://www.law.harvard.edu/programs/olin%5fcenter/corporate%5fgovernance/papers/No339.01.Roe.pdf

Yafeh, Y., & Yosha, O. (2001, January). Industrial organization of financial systems and strategic use of relationship banking. *European Finance Review, 5*(1-2), 63-78. Retrieved October 16, 2007, from EBSCO Online Database Business Source Complete. http://search.ebscohost.com/login.aspx?direct=true&db=bth&AN=18661426&site=ehost-live

Suggested Reading

Andreani, E., & Neuberger, D. (2006). Corporate control and relationship finance by banks or by non-bank institutional investors? A review within the theory of the firm. *Corporate Ownership & Control, 3*(3), 9-26. Retrieved October 16, 2007, from EBSCO Online Database Business Source Complete. http://search.ebscohost.com/login.aspx?direct=true&db=bth&AN=24766948&site=ehost-live

Birt, J., Bilson, C., Smith, T. & Whaley, R. (2006). Ownership, competition and financial disclosure. *Australian Journal of Management, 31*(2), 235-263. Retrieved October 16, 2007, from EBSCO Online Database Business Source Complete. http://search.ebscohost.com/login.aspx?direct=true&db=bth&AN=24275071&site=ehost-live

Castelli, A., Dwyer, Jr., G., & Hasan, I. (2006). Bank relationships and small firms' financial performance. Working Paper Series (Federal Reserve Bank of Atlanta), (5), 1-26. Retrieved October 16, 2007, from EBSCO Online Database Business Source Complete. http://search.ebscohost.com/login.aspx?direct=true&db=bth&AN=20960850&site=ehost-live

Marie Gould, Ph.D.

L

Labor Relations & Human Resource Management

ABSTRACT

This article examines the different business activities Human Resources participate in. These areas cover employment activities, training and development, and legal compliance. Human Resources should have core competencies which contribute to the overall growth and profitability of the company. Core competencies include ethics, communication, and strategic planning. By combining Human Resources experience and knowledge with the above areas and core competencies, Human Resources can be a valuable asset for a company.

OVERVIEW

This article explains the evolution and growth of Human Resource Management (herein referred to as HR) from simple labor relations functions (or complicated as the case may be) to modern HR functions in all areas of a company's activities. HR, in addition, provides an important resource to address areas where job responsibilities are ill defined or muddied. In today's business world, HR also provides much needed expertise in company newsletter publishing, web site maintenance, morale boosting and wellness programs.

In addition, and most importantly, HR has core competencies which add value to the company's bottom line. These competencies are discussed because they are the heart and soul of any company's success. HR's involvement in business is limited only to HR's imagination, ability, expertise, and competency. Anca-Ioana (2013) demonstrates the key role of HR in finding and exploiting competitive advantages that underpin a company's success against rivals who also seek to recruit the best talent and establish lean and purposeful organizational structures.

The core competencies of HR are: Communication, ethics, training, conflict resolution, motivation, record keeping, recruitment, negotiation, strategic planning, morale building, and legal knowledge.

Of the many core competencies listed above, few are extremely critical to the success of HR. Communication is the most important competency. Communication includes both the spoken and written word. Whether it is writing a company newsletter, a mission statement, or employee handbook, every employee must clearly understand what the company expects and what the company stands for. Well written documents allow for better understanding and a more effective work environment.

Legal competency requires the HR department to thoroughly know the rules and laws for equal treatment of employees. No company can afford to be labeled as discriminatory towards employees; the company's reputation is at stake. Bad press or bad public relations will make recruiting and retention difficult, and is financially damaging.

Strategic planning is a newer area for HR. In the past, most companies left strategic planning to upper management. Today, however, with globalization and complicated work environments, HR is asked to assist management and give input on many aspects of planning for the future in areas such as: future training needs, recruitment requirements, and work environments. HR must have the tools and knowledge to help develop these long range plans. The twenty-first century company is likely multinational in at least some respects. Marler (2012) explores and compares HR strategies from the United States, China, and Germany — three large economies with strongly cultural based business practices. Edwards et al. (2013) suggest that rather than attempting to impose a single monoculture on a multinational company, or even apply a primarily socioeconomic model based on national economic systems, HR practices should strive to harmonize local cultures with overall company strategies.

With employee contact on a day to day basis, ethics is endemic to all areas of the company's operations and this is especially true for HR. Every organization must have a value system to operate under. HR must insure that every employee knows and understands the business ethics of the company. If employees know the company follows and acts within sound and moral business practices, the employees will aspire to these ideals. HR must act in the same manner as the company. Where HR provides leadership, others will follow.

In the last century and before, HR, also known as the personnel department, grew out of the need for businesses to manage and work with labor unions. Labor unions grew in response to capitalism and the industrial revolution.

On a day to day basis, businesses needed a department to manage the ever present issues and difficulties between management and labor. Labor relations demanded mechanisms to deal with labor grievances against management. As labor contracts became more complicated and sophisticated, HR's role increased. HR continues to participate in grievance committees and grievance procedures, but management demands that HR assist with bargaining talks over labor contracts. HR also reviews other company's labor contracts and surveys these companies regarding salaries and wages. Federal and state laws need to be read and contracts brought into compliance.

Today, HR accomplishes the above tasks and responsibilities, but as the modern world has become more complicated, so has the HR role. HR should develop a reasonable and specific procedure to handle employee grievances. The procedure should be simple and clear. Employees must believe HR is unbiased and reasonable in the pursuit of resolving differences. Employees must believe their problems will be handled in a professional and timely manner. Both employees and managers should believe HR will not take sides in favor of one party or the other.

HR also takes on the role of developing training programs so the company has a trained and skilled workforce. HR continues to grow in response to many companies' development and continued growth.

Application

HR still holds grievance hearings, etc. but only 12.5 percent of the US workforce is unionized. Most unions are in the government sector and the traditional heavy industries such as automobile manufacturing.

HR still processes employment applications, but now, instead of advertising in newspaper help wanted ads, HR helps departments to advertise employment on the company's web site or other employment web sites such as monster.com. Resumes now come to HR via e-mail or through on-line applications. Job descriptions should be available to assist HR.

HR is also tasked with developing and updating job descriptions. Job descriptions are necessary for managing the employment process. They inform an employee of responsibilities, duties, reporting hierarchy, and evaluation parameters. Job descriptions are the joint responsibility of HR and the department actually employing the employee. These descriptions should be concise and specific — making sure to avoid generalities. For new candidates, the description provides an accurate idea of what is expected from an employee.

Because job evaluations and success monitoring are based on the job description, the employees can measure their success against the employment standard; the job description. All job descriptions should be reviewed by HR and each department head annually or sooner if the position is being revised and changed.

In many companies, HR is the initial screener of candidates. For example, if a company is planning to add another accountant, the initial HR screening maybe used to "weed out" the non-degreed candidates or candidates without the necessary background. The needs and requirements will vary from department to department.

To assist in the hiring process, HR must ensure the candidate is acceptable and qualified. The information provided on the employment application must be verified. All references should be checked. Work history must be verified. Educational background and degrees should be checked. If the company requires back ground and credit checks, these also must be reviewed and verified. Please note that not all companies require these types of checks. Many companies now require drug testing. HR has the responsibility to order the tests and review them when received. All these requirements assure the company that the candidate is acceptable.

In another important area, the company should have an employee handbook which is given to all employees, particularly new employees. Normally, the handbook is written by HR because HR is the repository of company rules and procedures regarding employment. The handbook should cover and include all areas of employment activities such as holidays (paid or not), grievance procedures, company's mission statement, promotion guidelines, vacations, etc. The handbook should be as detailed and specific or as general as management requires.

HR is routinely tasked with reviewing and updating the handbook. Many companies use ring binders for their handbook so old pages can be removed and new revised pages inserted without having to reprint a new handbook every time a change takes place. It is most important that HR keep the handbook up to date to reflect changes in company policies and the legal changes required by law.

Another area of HR's involvement is the development of the company's organizational chart. Many companies use the organization chart to identify reporting responsibilities, e.g. who reports to whom. The best organizational chart is one based upon functionality. Who, for example, should the accounting function report to? A well-conceived chart should address all company functions. People come and go, but the functions will remain. Organizational charts are a pictorial representation of a company's activities. Employees will find a reporting hierarchy easier to visualize. HR needs to maintain and update the chart as needed, but must, at the very least, perform annual reviews of the chart.

HR is responsible for maintaining current benefits information for all employees. If benefits are to be changed or adjusted, HR will research and then advise management of the best choice(s). Once management has decided, HR will install and administer the new benefit program. The task of administration includes enrollment, answering questions, verification of enrollment, distributing benefit pamphlets or booklets, and maintaining liaison with the benefit provider. HR becomes the information resource for employee benefits.

Part of the benefits monitoring process includes the benefit improvements and employment practices of competing companies. In order to stay competitive and attract the best candidates, HR should closely monitor other companies for competitive wages and benefits.

HR must be knowledgeable and familiar with all types of benefit programs the company offers so that programs can be monitored for effectiveness and usage. Benefits range from medical benefits to dental benefits to death benefits to disability benefits to adoption benefits to vision benefits, etc. Employees normally come to HR for answers and help. HR should be familiar with all insurance forms used by benefit providers so employees can fill out the forms accurately to receive payment with no delay.

HR also maintains and updates legal changes in company rules and policies with regards to employment and benefits. Management will undoubtedly request HR to give its opinion and input about legal changes. Such changes may include the areas of diversity, discrimination and harassment, equal employment opportunity (EEO), affirmative action, privacy, and employee rights.

Federal and state legislation normally applies to most companies and therefore provides a "level" playing field. Beyond the level field, opportunities exist for a company to present itself as an attractive employer and recruit the best candidates. HR should reveal these opportunities.

HR also takes part in the bidding process between benefit providers. HR's job is to solicit bids for services in order to maximize benefits and minimize cost. If HR develops strong working relationships with benefit vendors, every cost saving opportunity can be exploited.

In union/management negotiation, HR has a major role to play regarding benefits. Every wage and benefit addition has a cost and HR must be able to calculate that cost. Management will rely on HR to provide dollar amounts to the labor contract changes so that everyone in the negotiations will have knowledge of the true costs of doing business. HR becomes a valuable tool in the negotiations.

Another area of a company's activities in which HR performs a critical function is training and employee development. Every employee brings to the company some education and skills. It's HR's task to harvest and improve employee skills to help all to become more valuable and contributing employees.

The whole process of training and development begins with the new employee's orientation. First impressions are lasting impressions. Usually, the first people an employee meets are the HR people. These people need to be bright, enthusiastic, helpful, and positive. New employees will have many questions about the company and the employee's coming role in the company. HR should put the employee at ease and provide all necessary information to allay any doubts or questions.

As employees learn their jobs and settle into the work environment, HR will continue to provide information and assistance to insure a smooth transition in company employment. HR will also help to provide any training needed to bring the employee up to the job requirements and skill levels. In order to perpetuate job improvements for the employee, the employee should be encouraged to attend local schools for upgrading skills or obtaining a relevant degree. HR should be available to assist and inform the employee on these matters. There also may be a possibility that the employee needs career advice.

The largest area of training for HR is in management training. Most companies try to promote from within. In order to have a solid and effective management team, employees' skills need to be developed by the company. HR is responsible for providing internal and external management training. Local colleges can provide management or management related courses. HR should have working relationships with these educational vendors that offer courses that are valuable to honing in-house talent.

Some employees have yearly professional development courses they must take to retain their licenses, e.g. accountants, nurses, doctors, etc. HR should be familiar with these professional needs and arrange with the employee to fulfill these requirements. In job descriptions and career development rules, training and educational requirements will be listed. Employees focused on promotion may need course(s) to satisfy job requirements.

Training can also keep employees fresh in their outlook and skills. Employees performing the same job day after day, week after week, month after month . . . can become stagnant and bored. New challenges can revitalize employees' outlook and morale. HR can provide a positive and forward thinking work environment.

If a company has a stated preference for promoting from within, HR should review employment files for possible promotions and promotion requirements. Promoting from within is a powerful and effective morale builder. If employees know opportunity exists, they will strive to perform well in their job, knowing that if the job is well done, there maybe other jobs with better pay available. Promotion is also a great retention tool. If an employee is unable to succeed in one area of employment, perhaps movement to another area will improve the employee's performance.

HR also has responsibilities in the area of motivation. Not every employee will be positive and happy every day. On any given day, some employees will have low morale. Maybe a supervisor is having medical problems affecting their attitude and work. HR should identify these difficulties and problems and try to alleviate the issues surrounding these problems. Not every problem is solvable, but HR must be in the forefront to try and help.

Another way to motivate employees and increase morale and teamwork is company sponsored leisure activities. These can take many forms. Some companies have setup co-ed basketball teams between different departments. These activities allow employees to relax and get to know their fellow employees in an informal atmosphere. Or maybe an employee has a hobby which others are interested in. Seminars and workshops can be presented. The number of leisure activities is only limited to HR's imagination. Traditional motivators are employee of the month awards, suggestion boxes, and production achievement (individual or team) awards.

Ultimately, HR is in the business of working with employees (people). It is a peoples' business. Employees are the company's greatest resource. HR can provide an open positive environment so employees have answers and help. HR can help resolve employee-management issues with a fair and open-minded demeanor in order to deal with important differences. Maybe an employee has a serious drinking problem. Terminating the employee may be the final solution, but if the employee is a good worker, maybe alternate steps can be taken to help the employee overcome his problem or maybe some type of rehabilitation.

Wellness programs are an area where HR can take the lead and encourage employees to live a healthier lifestyle. This can range from quit smoking seminars to exercise programs for all ages. If a company has a web site, the employee section can offer healthy eating tips and cooking recipes for better living.

Beside the more traditional HR activities, there are other areas in which HR can be involved due to a lack of necessary resources within the company. Sometimes, HR manages the receptionist and the business office. Or HR can become the travel agency for the company.

Health and safety is sometimes handled by HR. HR many times is part of software development or part of a purchasing group. Sometimes, company newsletters and internal memorandums are the responsibility of HR. In addition, HR sometimes maintains the company web site and updates the site as needed, particularly in the employment area. On-line applications should be handled by HR.

One of the biggest issues facing businesses today is employee privacy. HR should assist management in developing and establishing a company-wide policy regarding privacy, both corporate and personal. No information should be given out or released to any one outside the company without management's approval. Internally, anyone requesting information regarding an employee must justify the request and have upper management's approval. All employee information must be safeguarded and secure. All files should be reviewed annually by the employee and management and any unnecessary information should be removed and destroyed.

CONCLUSION

In closing, HR people should possess a wide range of knowledge in the management and the operation of a company. To complete their training and education, HR personnel should take a variety of business courses in school so HR can have a firm grip on all areas of management. HR people should be generalists in the company. HR employees need to continually sharpen and learn new skills to be a beneficial contributor to the value of the company. The core competencies mentioned previously are the necessary starting point for HR. As the business grows and changes, HR must continue to expand and develop new expertise.

Bibliography

Anca-Ioana, M. (2013). New approaches of the concepts of human resources, human resource management and strategic human resource management. *Annals of the University Of Oradea, Economic Science Series, 22*(1), 1520-1525. Retrieved October 31, 2013, from EBSCO Online Database Business Source Complete. http://search.ebscohost.com/login.aspx?direct=true&db=bth&AN=90545849&site=ehost-live

Arnold, J.T. (2006). Enrolling online. *HR Magazine,51*(12), 89-92. Retrieved March 2, 2007, from EBSCO Online Database Business Source Premier. http://search.ebscohost.com/login.aspx?direct=true&db=f5h&AN=23337750&site=ehost-live

Bingham, T. & Gelagan, P. (2007). Finding the right talent for critical jobs. *T & D, 61*(2), 30-36. Retrieved March 6, 2007, from EBSCO Online Database Business Source Premier. http://search.ebscohost.com/login.aspx?direct=true&db=f5h&AN=23909596&site=ehost-live

Edwards, P.K., Sánchez-mangas, R., Tregaskis, O., Levesque, C., McDonnell, A., & Quintanilla, J. (2013). Human resource management practices in the multinational company: A test of system, societal, and dominance effects. *Industrial & Labor Relations Review, 66*(3), 588-617. Retrieved October 31, 2013, from EBSCO Online Database Business Source Complete. http://search.ebscohost.com/login.aspx?direct=true&db=bth&AN=88923800&site=ehost-live

Marler, J.H. (2012). Strategic human resource management in context: A historical and global perspective. *Academy of Management Perspectives, 26*(2), 6-11. Retrieved October 31, 2013, from EBSCO Online Database Business Source Complete. http://search.ebscohost.com/login.aspx?direct=true&db=bth&AN=79351873&site=ehost-live

Workers: Onward & upward. (2007). *Computerworld, 41*(4), 39-39. Retrieved March 15, 2007, from EBSCO Online Database Business Source Premier. http://search.ebscohost.com/login.aspx?direct=true&db=f5h&AN=23803419&site=ehost-live

Suggested Reading

Gagne, E.T. (2006). The unfair advantage: The right talent fit-the most significant business challenge over the next 20 years. *Business Credit, 108*(10), 61. Retrieved March 8, 2007, from EBSCO Online Database Business Source Premier. http://search.ebscohost.com/login.aspx?direct=true&db=f5h&AN=23101630&site=ehost-live

Hildreth, S. (2007). HR gets a dose of science. *Computerworld, 41*(6), 24-26. Retrieved March 8, 2007, from EBSCO Online Database Business Source Premier. http://search.ebscohost.com/login.aspx?direct=true&db=f5h&AN=23953420&site=ehost-live

Jack, S., Hyman, J. & Osbourne, F. (2006). Small entrepreneurial ventures culture, change and impact on HRM: A critical review. *Human Resource*

Management Review, 16(4), 456-466. Retrieved March 20, 2007, from EBSCO Online Database Business Source Premier. http://search.ebscohost.com/login.aspx?direct=true&db=f5h&AN=22963874&site=ehost-live

Kramer, R. (2006). The right resources. *BRW, 28*(43), 54-54. Retrieved March 21, 2007, from EBSCO Online Database Business Source Premier. http://search.ebscohost.com/login.aspx?direct=true&db=f5h&AN=23139907&site=ehost-live

Mayson, S. & Barrett, R. (2006). The 'science and practice' of HRM in small firms. *Human Resource Management Review, 16*(4), 447-455. Retrieved March 1, 2007, from EBSCO Online Database Business Source Premier. http://search.ebscohost.com/login.aspx?direct=true&db=f5h&AN=22963873&site=ehost-live

Parker, J. (2007). The spirit of enterprising HR. *HR Magazine, 52*(1), 66-70. Retrieved March 4, 2007, from EBSCO Online Database Business Source Premier. http://search.ebscohost.com/login.aspx?direct=true&db=f5h&AN=23623205&site=ehost-live

Shea, T. F. (2007). Zeroing out 401k. *HR Magazine, 52*(1), 12. Retrieved March 13, 2007, from EBSCO Online Database Business Source Premier. http://search.ebscohost.com/login.aspx?direct=true&db=f5h&AN=23623184&site=ehost-live

Smith, A.E., (2006). Short on skills. *Incentive, 180*(12), 12. Retrieved March 20, 2007, from EBSCO Online Database Business Resource Premier. http://search.ebscohost.com/login.aspx?direct=true&db=f5h&AN=23642009&site=ehost-live

Surowiecki, J. (2005). Networth. *The New Yorker Magazine, 81*(4), 62-63. Retrieved March 10, 2007, from EBSCO Online Database Business Source Premier. http://search.ebscohost.com/login.aspx?direct=true&db=f5h&AN=23257695&site=ehost-live

Fred Westmark, Ph.D.

Leadership & Motivation

ABSTRACT

This article will focus on the relationship between leadership and motivation. A history of leadership theory is presented, followed by the link between leadership and motivation as it pertains to today's mainstream leadership theories. The major theories of motivation are presented in the context of leadership. This article will explore how leadership theories have developed and converged, and how motivation has become an integral part of the leadership construct.

OVERVIEW

Leadership is not a new concept in organizational theory. While many leadership theories have developed and converged in the last century, most business professionals and scholars consider leadership to be a critical individual skill set for employees that are committed to helping their organization succeed and to helping their own careers develop. Part of the leadership construct is the ability to motivate one's constituents, whether they are subordinates, peers, or others in an employee's work group. The best leaders know how to intrinsically motivate and inspire their employees through a variety of techniques. This article will explore how leadership theories have developed and converged, and how motivation has become an integral part of the leadership construct.

Evolution of Leadership Theory

In the last two centuries, many theories of leadership were developed and considered valid during their time. However, in most cases, each new theory was generally short-lived, with a new one quickly following. There is a logical progression of leadership theories through which many of them converged to create Transformational Leadership Theory, today's predominate and current mainstream leadership theory.

The Great Man Theory & Scientific Management

In the 1920's, Frederick Taylor was instrumental in applying a much-needed management model, based on productivity, after the tremendous factory boom caused by the Industrial Revolution. No longer were organizations small, and operating out of the home through small shop owners or agricultural farmers. Instead, the birth and fast expansion of large-scale factories were changing the face of the workplace. Wren (2005) stated, "The Industrial Revolution had provided the impetus; Taylor provided the synthesis" (p. 274). Taylor was the first to expose the importance of worker productivity through studying the motions and habits of production workers. He was the first to functionally separate the "manager" from the "worker," by essentially classifying the worker as the one who does the work, and the manager as the one who makes the decisions.

At the same time, simple yet formal leadership theories began to develop. These theories were simplistic and without scholarly research and empirical data. The predominate leadership theory that existed during the Scientific Management era was the Great Man Theory developed by Thomas Carlyle (1841-1907). Dorfman's study (as cited in Tirmizi, 2002) stated, "According to this theory, a leader was a person gifted by heredity with unique qualities that differentiated him from his followers" (p.270). This was the first theory that laid the foundation for several subsequent trait-based theories that evolved decades later, and were often referred to as the *Trait Period* or *Trait Theories.* In the meantime, beside Carlyle's Man theory, the practice of leadership was being molded by the factories and production lines, and by the work of Frederick Taylor. Taylor's work in these areas was very authoritarian. According to Rost (as cited in Harrison, 1999), "From 1900 to 1930, leadership definitions focused on control and centralization of power." Taylor's work clearly had influences not only management development, but also on leadership methods.

As new leader's emerged, scholars realized that there were some inconsistencies in the Great Man Theory. The reality was that there were many respected leaders that were quite different from each other, which questioned the validity of Carlyle's assertion. In addition, Taylor's work with management theory also demonstrated some inadequacies. There was clearly something missing with viewing the employee as just a 'tool' to get the work done, and the theories' ineffectiveness was likely due to the lack of in-depth scholarly research and empirical data. This led to the next era of leadership theory, which was primarily centered on relationships and behavior.

Behavior Era of Leadership

Mary Parker Follet was one of the first people to introduce elements of psychology theory into the workplace, and viewed leadership from a group and organizational perspective. These views subsequently developed into the fields often referred to as *Organizational Behavior* and *Human Relations,* of which leadership is a critical component. This period in time is often referred to as the Behavior Era in leadership theory development (Van Seters & Field, 1990).

The Behavioral Era in leadership theory was the genesis of the classic argument about whether leaders are born or made: nature versus nurture. Where the trait theories supported the idea that leaders are born (leadership skills are hereditary), the behavioral theories contented that leaders can be trained by modifying their behavior to emulate the behavior of past effective leaders. These two schools of thought diverged after World War II. Stogdill (1975) opined that one theory was based on the *role* of the leader while the other was based on relationship between leaders and their followers, and the effectiveness of group performance. Nearing the tail end of this period, behavioral theories took over as "Carter (1953) and Startle (1956) maintained that the trait approach had reached a dead-end and suggested that the attention be directed toward the behavior of the leader" (Stogdill, 1975).

The early behavioral theories began with studies done at Ohio State University and the University of Michigan. The focus of these theories was on what effective leaders do, and not on what they are. For the first time in history, leadership theories now became multi-dimensional. Johns and Moser (1989) stated, "The University of Michigan leadership studies under the direction of Likert and the Ohio State leadership studies under the direction of Stodgill and Shartle were antithetical to the trait or single-continuum approach" (p. 116). Leadership theories now included both task and relationship elements.

Behavioral theories subsequently converged with the continued development of management principles. One example is Blake and Mouton's managerial grid, which plotted consideration against initiating structure, and another example is McGregor's development of the Theories X and Y (Van Seters et al., 1990). From this point forward, the development of leadership theories had begun to emerge at a progressively rapid rate.

Where supporting research in the past had been thin to none, this era was full of scholarly research and empirical data relating to leadership. As a result, the theories became more applicable than ever, and researchers felt as if they have made tremendous progress toward finally defining leadership. In their studies, Johns and Moser (1989) stated, "Empirical research began to challenge personal trait and one-dimensional views of leadership. Empirical studies suggested that leadership is a dynamic process varying from situation to situation with changes in leaders, followers, and situations" (p. 116). Scholarly research had *finally* taken foot in the development of leadership theories.

Situational, Contingency, & Transformational Era of Leadership

The pace of management development and the evolution of new management theories accelerated significantly from the 1960s to the present, and the knowledge and information available for continued management and leadership studies is abundant. Wren (2005) stated, "It is not possible to examine the full extent of modern management writings, for they are too diverse and too extensive for any in-depth analysis" (p. 395). During this time, the evolution of leadership theories was also at a record pace, and research findings were at an all-time high as more scholars set out to finally define the concept of leadership.

Scholars continued to discover that trait and behavior theories were not enough, and that there was still something missing. They discovered that leaders who went beyond modeling their behavior after previous leaders by adjusting how they act to situations became more effective. This led to two theories that are commonly used in organizations today: the Situation and Contingency theories. Fielder's concept of Situational Favorability was based on influencing others (Maslanka, 2004). The Hersey-Blanchard situational model continued building on previous task-relationship models, and added the element of the readiness of the follower. This was a significant development, because it meant that leadership might be more about the relationship between the manager and subordinate, and less about the leader himself, including his or her traits or behavior. The idea of leadership being a function of the relationship was expanded upon by House and Mitchell's path-goal theory (Maslanka, 2004). Leadership theories had evolved from being based on the individual, to being based on the relationship between the leader and the follower.

Leadership theories began to emerge around the concept that *it takes two to tango.* Theories now went beyond the relationship, and included groups and teams. From Vroom and Yetton's Normative model came the idea that the environment also plays a critical role for the effective leader, by placing significance on the need for acceptance and/or quality within the organization. In addition, scholars began to realize that theories were starting to converge. Leadership theories during the contingency stage included elements from past throes, such as behavior, personality, influence, and situation (Van Seters et al., 1990). For example, Wren (2005) points out that Max Weber's Charisma theory from the scientific Management era returned to leadership theory after remaining dormant for many years. The research and empirical data became as sound and valid as ever, yet scholars still maintained that something was missing. The theories were not well-integrated, and they were difficult to put into practice (Van Seters et al., 1990). In other words, while the research and data was sound, the theories could not be effectively employed.

This led to the development of the two most recent leadership theories, transactional and transformational leadership. Kinicki & Williams (2003) define transactional leadership as "focusing on clarifying employees' roles and task requirements and providing rewards and punishments contingent on performance" (p. 464). While effectively gaining compliance, transactional leadership failed to gain commitment from followers. Transformational leadership solved this dilemma. Kinicki and Williams (2003) defined Transformational leadership as something that "transforms employees to pursue organizational goals over self-interests" (p.465). Tirmizi (2002) opined, "Transformational leadership is defined in terms of the leader's effect on followers. They feel trust, admiration, loyalty, and respect toward the leader and they are motivated to do more than they originally expected to do" (p. 270). Most scholars today agree that the most effective style of leadership is one that combines elements of both transactional and transformational leadership. Antonakis and House (as cited in Kinicki and Williams, 2003. p.465) have researched this subject and came to the conclusion that a combination of these two leadership styles, with an emphasis on the transformational portion, is the best method for leaders to *motivate* their employees. The implication of this suggests that a good leader must adapt to the necessary leadership style for different situations and objectives. These two leadership theories finally closed the loop with research and effectiveness. They are validated through extensive research, and are also effectively employed in the workplace.

Current State of Leadership Theory

The evolution of leadership theories clearly shows a convergence of ideas over more than two centuries into the mainstream theories of today. The first main convergence of ideas came in the 1970s with the contingency theories. The theories combined new ideas with elements of past theories that had been discarded as invalid or inapplicable. These theories contained elements of the Great Man and Trait theories, behavioral theories, influence-based theories and situational theories (Van Seters et al., 1990), but remained stand-alone theories. The second main convergence of theories came with the transactional and transformational leadership theories. Not only did these theories contain elements from past theories but they were well-integrated and could easily be applied to today's organizations. Wren (2005) stated, "Leadership theories cycled from traits through contingency notions and back to leader styles and leader-member relations in transformational, charismatic, transactional, and leader-member exchange theories (p. 454). In addition to these points of convergence, theories have progressed from being based on the individual, to dyad of manager and subordinate, to the group, and finally to the organization.

Today's leadership theories have become complex and specialized. Since the development of transformational leadership, other mainstream theories have emerged. Some examples include Level 5 leadership (Collins, 2001), leadership best practices (Kouzes & Posner, 2003), Servant leadership (Joseph & Winston, 2005), contingent leadership (Manning, 2013), and leadership by creating a learning organization (Senge, 1990). Transformative leadership is described by Caldwell et al. (2012) as an ethical approach that seeks the benefit of all stakeholders with sustained wealth creation as a goal.

A Linkage between Motivation & Leadership

With the historical evolution of leadership in perspective, one can begin to understand the linkage between motivation and leadership. In a well-known Harvard Business Review article, Kotter (2001) set out to describe the differences between leadership and management. In the article, Kotter suggested that leadership is about dealing with change, while management is about dealing with complexity. Kotter explained that leaders set directions while managers plan and budget; leaders align people while managers organize and hire staff, and leaders motivate people while managers control and problem solve. The article was based on the continued discussion on this topic since being introduced by Abraham Zeleznik in 1977 (Kotter, 2001). In the article, Kotter referred to the argument by stating, "the theoreticians of scientific management, with their organizational diagrams and time-and-motion studies, were missing half the picture-the half filled with inspiration, vision, and the full spectrum of human drives and desires. The study of leadership hasn't been the same since. Within this perspective, motivation is clearly a significant part of the leadership construct.

Another example of how motivation and leadership are linked can be seen in how transformational leadership is defined. Bass (1999) discussed the importance of the leader-follower relationship in a transformational leadership setting. Bass stated, "Transformational leadership refers to the leader moving the follower beyond the immediate self-interest through idealized influence (charisma), inspiration, intellectual stimulation, or individualized consideration. It elevates the follower's level of maturity and ideals as well as concerns for achievement, self-actualization, and the well-being of others, the organization, and society" (p.11). Further, Bass (1999) asserts that these four factors will result in the followers wanting to identify with this leadership. In other words, a leader who embraces and practices these elements of leadership would certainly help motivate his or her employees to achieve common organizational goals.

A third linkage between leadership and motivation can be observed in the five best leadership practices as presented by Kouzes and Posner (2003). Kouzes and Posner (2003) stated, "As we looked deeper into the dynamic process of leadership, through case analysis and survey questionnaires, we uncovered five practices common to personal-best leadership experiences" (p.73). These five practices are (1) model the way, (2) inspire a shared vision,

(3) challenge the process, (4) enable others to act, and (5) encourage the heart. The authors asserted that by following these practices, employees could be intrinsically motivated to be committed to the organization's goals and objectives. These five behaviors are directly related to motivating the employee, especially in reference to inspiration, encouragement, and empowerment.

By looking at these examples of current leadership theory, one can see how motivation is linked to leadership and how motivation is a critical aspect within modern leadership theory. With this link now set, a closer look of what motivation is, and how a leader can incorporate motivational techniques in the workplace can be discussed.

Application

Organizational practitioners often concentrate on developing leaders and managers to effectively motivate their employees. Kinicki and Kreitner (2006) defined motivation as "those of psychological processes that caused the arousal, direction, and persistence of voluntary actions that are goal directed" (p.149). The employee's performance is directly related to how motivated they are to achieve their goals. Having the skills alone is often not enough for an employee to achieve high performance at their job. As such, it is the leaders' jobs to motivate their employees to the extent that they can achieve high performance with their current skills and limitations. Motivation can be looked at from three perspectives: needs, process and reinforcement (Lussier, 2005). The needs theories of motivation are critical to the effectiveness of one's leadership. It is in the context of the needs theories that the leadership principles discussed in the first section can be applied. The process and reinforcement theories of motivation are better viewed from a management perspective, rather than a leadership perspective. The following sections give an overview of the most well-known needs theories of motivation.

Maslow's Hierarchy of Needs

The most widely known motivational theory preached by today's organizational practitioners is Maslow's Hierarchy of Needs Theory. Tutt (1989) noted that human behavior continues to be based on instinct, and that humans desire to fulfill their institutional needs. The theory suggests that one's needs are categorized into five categories of a hierarchy- that is, one must satisfy the lowest level of needs before satisfying the higher level needs. These levels, from lowest to highest, are physiological needs, safety needs, social needs, esteem needs, and the need for self-actualization (Lussier, 2005). Many suggest that excellent leaders understand where their employee's needs fall within this hierarchy, and as such can satisfy them accordingly.

McClelland's Needs Theory

A second widely-used needs theory was developed by David McClelland (Kinicki et al., 2006). McClelland suggested that individuals have three needs: a need for achievement, a need for power, and a need for affiliation. He suggested that every individual is different with regards to his or her needs, and in order to adequately motivate someone, a leader should have a clear understanding of their own employees needs with regards to these three areas. For example, someone with a high needs for affiliation might be well-suited for a human resources position, while someone with a high need for achievement might be well-suited for a sales position. Understanding each employee as a unique individual can help a leader or manager determine the best position and the best job tasks for a particular employee.

Herzberg's Hygiene Theory

The third prevalent "needs" theory was developed by Frederick Herzberg, and is often referred to as Hygiene theory of job satisfaction (Kinicki et al., 2006). Herzberg suggested that organizations have things that can be classified as satisfiers and dissatisfiers, and that in order to satisfy and motivate employees; a leader and manager should alleviate the things that dissatisfy employees and improve the things that satisfy employees. Such things as rules and regulations, salary, work environment, and supervisors are examples of things that are classified as dissatisfiers, or hygiene factors. Promotion opportunities, learning opportunities, job recognition, and challenging work are things that are classified as satisfiers. While both are important to motivating an employee, oftentimes organizations only concentrate on removing the dissatisfiers, which does not intrinsically motivate the employee, especially in the long run.

Viewpoint

Leadership and motivation have a direct relationship to employee performance. Leadership theories have evolved since the late 1800s, and today's current leadership theories include motivation as a major part of their construct. Mainstream leadership theories such as Bass's transformational leadership, Collins' Level 5 leadership, and Kouzes and Posner's best practices of leadership are built on the concept that effective leaders need to know how to motivate their employees. Motivation theories can be broken down into needs, process, and behavioral reinforcement. Leadership relies heavily on understanding the needs of theories of motivation, such as Maslow's hierarchy of needs, McClelland's need theory, and Herzberg's hygiene theory of job satisfaction. A leader can be most effective by understanding the needs of his or her employees, which will result in optimizing the overall performance of the leaders' constituents as well as the organization.

BIBLIOGRAPHY

Bass, B. M. (1999). Two decades of research and development in transformational leadership. *European Journal of Work & Organizational Psychology, 8*(1), 9-32. Retrieved on March 14, 2007 from EBSCO Online Database Business Source Premier. http://search.ebscohost.com/login.aspx?direct=true&db=bth&AN=4437836&site=ehost-live

Caldwell, C., Dixon, R., Floyd, L., Chaudoin, J., Post, J., & Cheokas, G. (2012). Transformative leadership: Achieving unparalleled excellence. *Journal of Business Ethics, 109*(2), 175-187. Retrieved October 31, 2013, from EBSCO Online Database Business Source Complete. http://search.ebscohost.com/login.aspx?direct=true&db=bth&AN=78333229&site=ehost-live

Collins, J. (2001). *Good To Great* (1st ed.). New York, N.Y.: HarperCollins Publishing.

Harrison, R. (1999). The nature of leadership: Historical perspectives & the future. *Journal of California Law Enforcement, 33*(1), 24.

Johns, H. E., & Moser, H. R. (1989). From trait to transformation: The evolution of leadership theories. *Education, 110*(1), 115. Retrieved on March 14, 2007 from EBSCO Online Database Business Source Premier. http://search.ebscohost.com/login.aspx?direct=true&db=aph&AN=4717838&site=ehost-live

Joseph, E., E., & Winston, B., E. (2005). A correlation of servant leadership, leader trust, and organizational trust. *Leadership & Organization Development Journal, 26*(1/2), 6.

Kinicki, A., & Kreitner, R. (2006). *Organizational Behavior; key concepts, skills, and best practices* (2nd ed.). New York, N.Y.: McGraw Hill.

Kinicki, A., & Williams, B. (2003). *Management: A practical introduction* (2nd ed.). New York, N.Y.: McGraw-Hill.

Kotter, J., P. (2001). What leaders really do. *Harvard Business Review, 79*(11), 85-96. Retrieved on March 14, 2007 from EBSCO Online Database Business Source Premier. http://search.ebscohost.com/login.aspx?direct=true&db=bth&AN=5634852&site=ehost-live

Kouzes, J., & Posner, B. (2003). *The Leadership Challenge* (3rd ed.). San Francisco, CA.: Jossey-Bass.

Lussier, R., N. (2005). *Human Relations in Organizations* (6th ed.). New York: McGraw-Hill.

Manning, T. (2013). A "contingent" view of leadership: 360 degree assessments of leadership behaviours in different contexts. *Industrial & Commercial Training, 45*(6), 343-351. Retrieved October 31, 2013, from EBSCO Online Database Business Source Complete. http://search.ebscohost.com/login.aspx?direct=true&db=bth&AN=90609232&site=ehost-live

Maslanka, A. M. (2004). *Evolution of leadership theories.* Unpublished M.S., Grand Valley State University, United States – Michigan.

Senge, P. (1990). *The fifth discipline: The art & practice of the learning organization* (1st ed.). New York, N.Y.: Doubleday Dell Publishing.

Stogdill, R. M. (1975). The evolution of leadership theory. *Academy of Management Proceedings,* 4-6. Retrieved on March 14, 2007 from EBSCO Online Database Business Source Premier. http://search.ebscohost.com/login.aspx?direct=true&db=bth&AN=4975786&site=ehost-live

Tirmizi, S. (2002). The 6-L framework: A model for leadership research and development. *Leadership & Organization Development Journal, 23*(5/6), 269.

Tutt, B. (1989). Great instincts: nature vs. nurture Questions fire ongoing debate. *Houston Chronicle (pre-1997 Fulltext),* p. 6.

Van Seters, D. A., & Field, R. H. G. (1990). The evolution of leadership theory. *Journal of Organizational Change Management, 3*(3), 29. Retrieved on March 14, 2007 from EBSCO Online Database Business Source Premier. http://search.ebscohost.com/login.aspx?direct=true&db=bth&AN=6552392&site=ehost-live

Wren, D. (2005). *The History of Management Thought* (5th ed.): John Wiley and Sons.

SUGGESTED READING

Humphreys, J., Einstein, W. (2004). Leadership and temperament congruence: Extending the expectancy model of work motivation. *Journal of Leadership and Organizational Studies. 10(4),* 58. Retrieved on March 14, 2007 from EBSCO Online Database Business Source Premier. http://search.ebscohost.com/login.aspx?direct=true&db=bth&AN=14746484&site=ehost-live

Ilies, R., Judge, T., Wagner, D. (2006). Making sense of motivational leadership: The trail from transformational leaders to motivated followers. *Journal of Leadership and Organizational Studies. 13(1),* 1. Retrieved on March 14, 2007 from EBSCO Online Database Business Source Premier. http://search.ebscohost.com/login.aspx?direct=true&db=bth&AN=21955772&site=ehost-live

Ellemers, N., De Gilder, D., Haslam, S. Motivating individuals and groups at work: A social identity perspective on leadership and group performance. *Academy of Management Review. 29(3)* 459. Retrieved on March 14, 2007 from EBSCO Online Database Business Source Premier. http://search.ebscohost.com/login.aspx?direct=true&db=bth&AN=13670967&site=ehost-live

John D. Benson, M.B.A.

LEGAL ENVIRONMENT OF BUSINESS

ABSTRACT

Article explores the legal environments that directly impact today's businesses and corporations by providing an overview of the major legal realms and legal structures that impact business and business practices. The role law plays in the world of business and its implications to the business professional, as well as, the major sources of law and their intent to either control, regulate, or assist current business practices.

OVERVIEW

The legal environment of business refers to the code of conduct that defines the legal boundaries for business activity. To understand these boundaries, it is essential to first have a basic understanding of the law and how it affects businesses and business practices. The nature of business spans over a number of legal realms, all of which are continuously influenced by the needs and demands of the business community, consumers, and the government. Each has a distinct stake and voice in this vibrant legal environment.

Nature of Law

The study of the legal environment of business encompasses numerous approaches and philosophical theories. The exploration of what law is and how it is defined has been examined by numerous legal philosophers.

Legal Traditionalists

The legal traditionalists view law as a body of principles and rules that courts `utilize when deciding disputes. The traditionalist approach is steeped in the belief that the basic constructs of right and wrong are fixated even though society is continuously changing its beliefs.

Environmental Approach

The environmental approach views law as an arm of societal control that must continuously reflect the current society's moral constructs through the enforcement of rules, regulations, and laws. This approach is much broader in scope, since the law is an institution that reflects the societal need for social order.

Sociological Jurisprudence Theorists

Sociological jurisprudence theorists profess that society ultimately shapes and molds the law and the mechanisms for its enforcement. This school of thought views the legal system and the law as a means of providing an orderly, predictable system of social order, change, and legal reform.

These theories lead to similar conclusions; the primary function of law is to maintain social, political, and economic stability, while simultaneously balancing the need and ability to implement change. To accomplish this successfully, laws have been categorically classified.

Classifications of Law

To make sense out of huge body of information, laws are placed into various categories. Although a number of classifications are possible, the most useful categories utilized are:

- Substantive and Procedural
- Civil and Criminal

Basic to the understanding of these classifications are the terms *right* and *duty*.

A right is the ability of a person with the help of the law, to demand someone else to perform or to cease engaging in a certain activity.

A duty on the other hand, is a commitment placed upon a person to engage in or desist engaging in a certain activity. These two concepts are correlatives, meaning that no right can rest upon one person without a corresponding duty resting upon some other person.

Substantive Law & Procedural Law

Substantive Law

Substantive law includes all those laws that define, regulate, and create legal rights and obligations. A rule stating that promises are enforced only where each party receives something of value from the other party is part substantive law. An example of this would be business contracts and contract obligations.

Procedural Law

Procedural law, on the other hand, establishes the methods for enforcing the rights that are established by substantive law. For example, questions about how a lawsuit should begin, what papers need to be filed, which court the suit should go to, which witnesses can be called, and so on are all questions of procedural law.

Essentially, substantive law relays our rights and entitlements under the law, while procedural law delineates our legal obligations and duties that need to be undertaken to obtain the benefits of those rights.

Civil Law & Criminal Law

Civil Law

Civil law refers to the laws that define the duties existing between individuals or legal entities (meaning corporations). This body of law (better known as *torts*) deals with the infringement of one person or legal entity on the legally recognized rights of another. Civil law violations appear in business in numerous ways. It is the basis of employment violations, breaches of contracts, product liability and copyright infringement.

Criminal Law

Criminal law differs from civil law in that it is an act prohibited by law for the protection of the public at large. Criminal violations in business occur when individuals, in a position of authority, commit criminal actions either against individuals, the company, or the consumer.

"Under the doctrine of respondent superior, a corporation may be held criminally liable for the illegal acts of its directors, officers, employees, and agents. To hold a corporation liable for these actions, the government must establish that the corporate agent's actions were within the scope of his/her duties and were intended, at least in part, to benefit the corporation" (Michel, 2003, p.1).

These types of criminal acts are often referred to as white collar crimes. This catch-all phrase was originally coined by Edwin Sutherland in 1939. Sutherland defined it as "a crime committed by a person of respectability and high social status in the course of his occupation." White-collar crimes usually involve fraud, bankruptcy fraud, bribery, insider trading, embezzlement, computer crime, medical crime, public corruption, identity theft, environmental crime, pension fund crime, RICO crimes, consumer fraud, occupational crime, securities fraud, financial fraud, and forgery.

Sources of Law

With a basic understanding of the classifications of law, the next question that comes to mind is what are the sources of law and where are laws found? Laws derive from federal and state constitutions, federal treaties, interstate compacts, federal and state statutes and executive orders, ordinances of municipal governments, the rules and regulations of federal and state administrative agencies, and federal and state court decisions.

The United States Constitution

The U.S. Constitution (adopted 1787, ratified 1788) is considered the "supreme law." A law in violation of the Constitution, no matter what the source, will not be enforced by the courts. Similarly, the state constitutions are supreme within their respective borders, though keep in mind that all law in the United States is subordinate to the Federal Constitution. No law, Federal or State, is valid if it is in violation of the Federal Constitution.

The U.S. Constitution also creates and limits the power of the government. Examples of the exclusive regulatory federal powers created by the US Constitution include: the power to establish laws regarding bankruptcy, to grant patents, trademarks, and copyrights, and to coin currency. One area of the US Constitution that perhaps has the greatest impact on U.S. businesses is the commerce clause contained in the Tenth Amendment. The commerce clause grants virtually complete power to the Federal Government to regulate the economy and business. This includes transportation of goods across state lines, consumer warranties and credit transactions, electronic funds transfers, residential and commercial real estate transactions, consumer and employee safety, labor relations, civil rights in employment, transactions in securities, environmental protections, and taxation.

The federal government's power to tax is subject to three limitations. First, taxes (excluding income tax) must be apportioned among the states. Second, all custom duties and excise taxes must be uniform throughout the United States. Lastly, no duties may be levied upon exports from any state. Taxes also have regulatory effects. For example, import taxes and custom duties that are meant to protect domestic industry from foreign competition and tax credits which are meant to encourage investments in favorable enterprises and disadvantage unfavorable enterprises.

Statutory Law

Statutes are enacted by Congress and the various state legislative bodies. This constitutes what is better known as statutory law.

An example of a statutory scheme that has had a tremendous impact on corporations has been the Securities Act of 1933 and The Securities Exchange Act of 1934. Both of these were enacted by congress to avoid another stock market crash like the one in 1929. Congress designed both these Acts to prohibit various forms of fraud and to stabilize the securities industry by requiring that all essential information concerning the issue of stock be made available to the investing public.

The 1933 Act is basically a disclosure statute and paper act. This means that the act permits a corporation to sell "junk" (or referred at the time as junk bonds) as long as appropriate disclosures are made through registration statements and prospectus delivery. The major aspects of the act include:

- Issuers of securities must file registration statement
- Prospectuses must be provided to all purchasers of new issues with full and fair disclosures
- Fraudulent activity in connection with underwriting and issuing of all securities is prohibited.

The Securities Exchange Act of 1934 was a further reaction by the legislature to the crash of 1929. It picks up where the Act of 1933 finished, by addressing fraudulent practices in the secondary market.

The Securities Exchange Act of 1934 has often been referred to as the *People Act* since it regulates all persons involved in trading securities on behalf of customers. It encompasses the regulation and registration of brokers and dealers and national security associations.

What is most fascinating about the 1934 Act are the agencies and regulations it was responsible for creating. For example, the creation of the SEC (Security and Exchange Commission), regulations of credit by the Federal Reserve Board, regulations of insider trading, and reporting requirements for issuers are all the direct result of the enactment of the Securities Exchange Act of 1934.

In the early twenty-first century, the most significant statutory scheme regulating corporations was the passage of the Sarbanes-Oxley (SOX) Act in 2002. SOX requires top management to personally certify the accuracy of financial information, boosts the oversight responsibilities of boards of directors, and prohibits the outsourcing of internal audit functions to a company's external auditor. Prawitt, Sharp & Wood (2012) find that accounting risk is more closely associated with the quality of IAF and that oursourcing all or parts of IAF to an external auditor reduced rather than exacerbated risk; however, Singer & You (2011) reported greater invester confidence following SOX and the resulting flurry of financial restatements. After the financial crisis of 2008, in which large companies failed while their executives received substantial compensation packages, the Dodd-Frank Wall Street Reform and Consumer Protection Act (2010) was passed. Dodd-Frank requires a nonbinding shareholder vote on compansation for top executives. Though a number of lawsuits were brought by shareholders after negative votes were overruled by boards, courts were inclined to dismiss cases on procedural grounds. As plaintiff switched tactics, legal expenses for companies mounted and settlements became common. By 2013, the legal environment surrounding executive compensation at public companies remained troubled (Wilkerson, 2013).

Case Law & Judicial Precedent

Courts are responsible for adjudicating alleged violations of and disagreements that arise under legal jurisdiction. The courts are responsible for interpreting the law. A courts interpretation of the law is dependent upon previous court interpretations of the law; this is referred to as the "principle of stare decisis," or simply, precedent. Stare decisis ensures consistency and predictability in the law and in interpretation. In situations where the precedent is unfavorable to a particular case, attempts are made to differentiate the current case from the former case and decision.

It is the responsibility of the higher courts to resolve any inconsistencies in rulings; the ultimate court being The Supreme Court, whose rulings apply to all the lower federal courts. Stare decisis also applies in the various state court systems.

Stare decisis is exemplified in the case that was brought against Enron's accounting firm Arthur Anderson. Charges of obstructing an official proceeding of the Securities and Exchange Commission was filed against the accounting firm in a Texas District Court in 2002. The jury found Arthur Anderson guilty. Anderson Corporation appealed the decision to the United States Court of Appeals for the Fifth Circuit. The fifth circuit affirmed the district court's decision (stare decisis). *Arthur Andersen v. United States,* 73 U.S.L.W. 4393 (2002)]

Common Law

When there is no particular statute or provision, common law is said to exist. Common law is a collection of judicial decisions, customs, and general principles upon which federal and state courts rely. Because many state legislatures refrain from ruling on multiple contigencies, common law holds high importance, especially in contract disputes.

In response to common law, a secondary area of legal authority was developed. Beginning in the 1920's a distinguished group of judges, lawyers, and law school professors established the American Law Institute, known as the ALI. The ALI composed "restatements of the general common law of the United States, including in that term not only the law developed solely by judicial decision, but also the law that has grown from the application by the courts of statutes that were generally enacted and were in force for many years." [Wolkin, (1940) *Restatements of the Law: Origin, Preparation, Availability,* 21 Ohio B.A, Rept. 663] These restatements cover many important areas of common law that include: torts, contracts, agency law, property, and trusts.

Administrative Law

Administrative law is the branch of public law created by administrative agencies. It is important that we look at Administrative law, since Administrative agencies create rules, regulations, orders, and act as the primary interpreters and enforcers of business regulatory schemes like the Security and Exchange Commission, U.S. Federal Trade Commission, Equal Employment Opportunity Commission, Occupational Safety & Health Administration, and Environmental Protection Agency. They possess both judicial authority as well as executive powers. Keep in mind that Administrative agencies are created by federal, state, and local governments. When Congress enacts a statute, it often creates an administrative agency to administer the statute and creates administrative rules and procedures that reflect the agency's needs and ability to effectively operate.

Codification of Law

Codifications of law came about due to demands by the business community lobbying for uniformity in commercial transactions. These tenacious efforts led to the development of uniform business protocols. One of the best known of these codifications has been the Uniform Commercial Code; better known as the UCC. After its completion in 1952, the UCC was systematically adopted by 49 states (except Louisiana).

The NCCUSL (National Conference of Commissioners on Uniform State Laws) besides drafting the UCC also drafted more that 200 uniform laws including the Uniform Partnership Act, the Uniform Limited Partnership Act, and the Unified Probate Code. These codifications expanded and codified existing commercial transaction law; unifying the states' business legal frameworks specific to the business community's needs.

Keep in mind the impact this has had on the expanding national economy. Prior to these codifications, most states had enacted statutes dealing with branches of commercial law, resulting in great diversity among states which ultimately was detrimental to commerce on a national scale. These codifications unified commercial enterprise leading to a more effective and productive national economy.

CONCLUSION

The legal environments of business and the areas of existing legal precedence that touch and affect businesses and the business community on a daily basis are vast. Whether it is criminal, civil, constitutional, statutory, common, or administrative, all have a stake in business and commerce and therefore influence the business horizon as we know it today. Business professionals need to not only think and act globally, but also understand the underling legal fabric that surrounds businesses in our global economy.

Bibliography

Franklin, M.A., Rabin, R.L. (2001). *Tort Law and Alternatives.* New York: University Casebook Series.

Geldart, W., (1984) *Introduction to English Law,* 146 D.C.M. Yardley ed. 9.

Klein, W.A., Ramseyer, M.J., & Bainbridge, S.M. (2001). *Business Associations.* New York: University Casebook Series.

Knapp, C.L., Crystal, N.M., & Prince, H.G., (2003). *Problems in Contract Law.* New York: Aspen.

Michel, S.D. (2003, Nov-Dec). Corporate tax departments and the new focus on corporate criminality. The Tax Executive. Retrieved March 14, 2007, from FindArticles.com. http://findarticles.com/p/articles/mi_m6552/is_6_55/ai_n6049582/pg_1

Prawitt, D.F., Sharp, N.Y., & Wood, D.A. (2012). Internal audit outsourcing and the risk of misleading or fraudulent financial reporting: Did Sarbanes-Oxley get it wrong? *Contemporary Accounting Research, 29*(4), 1109-1136. Retrieved October 31, 2013, from EBSCO Online Database Business Source Complete. http://search.ebscohost.com/login.aspx?direct=true&db=bth&AN=84385459&site=ehost-live

Singer, Z., & You, H. (2011). The Effect of Section 404 of the Sarbanes-Oxley Act on earnings quality. *Journal of Accounting, Auditing & Finance, 26*(3), 556-589. Retrieved October 31, 2013, from EBSCO Online Database Business Source Complete. http://search.ebscohost.com/login.aspx?direct=true&db=bth&AN=66335781&site=ehost-live

Sloan, A. (2013). Are we ready for the next meltdown?. *Fortune, 168*(5), 151. Retrieved October 31, 2013, from EBSCO Online Database Business Source Complete. http://search.ebscohost.com/login.aspx?direct=true&db=bth&AN=90052547&site=ehost-live

Subrin, S.N., Minow, M.L., Brodin, M.S., & Main, T.O. (2000), *Civil Procedure: Doctrine, Practice, and Context.* New York: Aspen.

Wilkerson, A.T. (2013). The continuing evolution of litigation regarding the say-on-pay voting requirements under the Dodd-Frank Wall Street Reform and Consumer Protection Act. *Benefits Law Journal, 26*(1), 75-87. Retrieved October 31, 2013, from EBSCO Online Database Business Source Complete. http://search.ebscohost.com/login.aspx?direct=true&db=bth&AN=85940593&site=ehost-live

Wolkin, (1940). Preparation, Availability, *Restatements of the Law: Origin.* 21, Ohio B.A, Rept. 663

Suggested Reading

Arewa, O. B. (2005). Comment: Corporate governance events: legal rules, business environment and corporate culture. *Case Western Reserve Law Review, 55*(3), 545-550. Retrieved March 14, 2007, from EBSCO Online Database Academic Search Complete. http://search.ebscohost.com/login.aspx?direct=true&db=a9h&AN=18622622&site=ehost-live

Dickerson, C. (2005). Ignorance of the law. *InfoWorld, 27*(11), 20. Retrieved March 14, 2007, from EBSCO Online Database Academic Search Complete. http://search.ebscohost.com/login.aspx?direct=true&db=a9h&AN=16406918&site=ehost-live

Ennico, C. (2005). New year's resolutions for businesses in 2005. *Enterprise/Salt Lake City, 34* (29), 9. Retrieved from EBSCO Online Database Regional Business News. http://search.ebscohost.com/login.aspx?direct=true&db=bwh&AN=15632179&site=ehost-live

Sara Rogers, J. D.

LOGISTICS MANAGEMENT

ABSTRACT

This article examines the subject of Logistics Management. Topics covered include working definitions of the terms logistics management and supply chain management, and an outline of the various activities involved in the logistics management process. Also, we highlight the key supply chain management processes and the relationship each plays in conjunction with logistics management. A practical example of logistics management in action is provided, along with the various logistic management activities and terms of art.

OVERVIEW

Supply Chain Management

Supply chain management is not a new concept—nor is logistics management. The actual practice of logistics management has its first recorded origins in annals of military history from the times of the ancient Romans and Greeks, whereby armies employed basic logistics principles to make sure that their respective armies were adequately equipped with needed supplies for waging warfare. Commercial businesses, driven by the process of transforming raw materials in the manufacturing process, have always engaged in supply chain management on some level. However, the phrase supply chain management was first coined by the consulting firm Booz Allen Hamilton back in 1982.

Oftentimes, logistics management and supply-chain management are used interchangeably by supply chain management professionals. Yet, they are entirely separate concepts. The distinction lies in the fact that logistics management is a subset of activities within the broader supply chain management process. Thus, no meaningful discussion of logistics management can take place without a solid footing in supply chain management. The Council of Supply Chain Management Professionals (CSCMP) recognizes this distinction of logistics management as a component of supply-chain management.

Definitions of Supply Chain Management

The CSCMP defines supply chain management as:

"Supply chain management encompasses the planning and management of all activities involved in sourcing and procurement, conversion, and all logistics management activities. Importantly, it also includes coordination and collaboration with channel partners, which can be suppliers, intermediaries, third party service providers, and customers. In essence, supply chain management integrates supply and demand management within and across companies" (CSMP, n.d.).

Similarly, yet in more plain language, the National Alcohol Beverage Control Association (NABCA) defines supply chain management as:

"Supply chain management is a set of approaches used to efficiently integrate suppliers, manufacturers, warehouses, and customers so that merchandise is produced and distributed at the right quantities, to the right locations, and at the right time in order to minimize system wide costs while satisfying service-level requirements" (NABCA, 2004).

Therefore, a typical supply chain consists of an integrated, coordinated network of suppliers, manufacturers, warehouses, distributors, and retailers, through which parts, raw materials, and subassemblies are acquired, transformed, and delivered to the ultimate customer (see Figure 1). Simply stated, supply chain management (also known as SCM) includes the following supply chain functions of: planning, buying decisions, making products, storing products, moving products, selling products, and handling of returns from customers. By its very nature, supply chain management requires effective collaboration, i.e., real-time, accurate communication and information exchange among the various supply chain partners, as well as the functional areas in a company, such as marketing, finance, and operations.

Note that an AMR Research study of supply chain organizations identified the following goals related to supply chain management (Hillman, 2006):

- Manage and reduce materials costs;
- Optimize overall internal supply chain costs;
- Reduce supply chain risk;
- Improve manufacturing efficiency;
- Enhance customer service;
- Understand customer/end-user demand.

Figure 1: Traditional Manufacturer Supply Chain

Cleary, firms gain a competitive advantage when they are able to achieve these stated goals. The benefits of effective supply chain management can range from higher productivity, lower supply costs, greater customer loyalty, lower inventory carry costs while increasing inventory turnover, decreasing transportation costs, and order fulfillment costs—to name a few. Combined together, these improvements normally translate into increasing company profits and increased market share—certainly a desirable state of affairs for any company.

Core Business Processes

Aside from understanding the goals related to supply chain management, a fundamental grasp of supply chain management requires an essential understanding of the core business processes involved in supply chain management. The Global Supply Chain Forum of the Ohio State University identifies eight key supply chain management processes and the relationship each plays with respect to the logistics management function (Lambert, 2004):

1. Customer relationship management—key customers and customer groups are identified. The logistics function interfaces with customer relationship management in that logistics capabilities are determined in light of the firm's identified customers.
2. Customer service management is the administration and coordination of key suppliers and customers. The role of logistics management is to outline key performance specifications for suppliers in alignment with customer requirements and expectations.
3. Demand management balances customer requirements with supply chain capabilities, matching supply and demand with minimal disruptions. Logistics' role is to produce reliable and accurate forecasts for the demand management process.
4. Order fulfillment entails those activities for defining customer requirements and designing an order fulfillment network, which enable firms to meet customer requests. Network planning is provided by logistics management in designing and operating the information systems necessary for accurate and cost-effective order fulfillment.
5. Manufacturing flow management includes all activities necessary to provide the timely and efficient ability to manage a variety of products in the supply chain and to move products through a company's plants. Prioritization criteria are developed by logistics in moving products through the manufacturing plant.
6. Supplier relationship management identifies key suppliers based on the capabilities of these suppliers and the needs of the firm. In turn, the logistics management function manages the inbound flow of parts, supplies, and raw materials needed in the production process.
7. Product development and commercialization provides the structure for working with customers and suppliers to develop products and market them to potential customers. Working closely with marketing and operations, logistics management establishes movement requirements that enable the delivery of products to the final consumer.
8. Returns management is the process dealing with product returns, namely through returns-management and return-avoidance (i.e., getting it right the first time). In logistics management parlance, this is known as reverse logistics—to be discussed later.

Logistics Management & Supply Chain Management

As our definition states, supply chain management also encompasses logistics management, which is mainly concerned with transportation, inventory management, and distribution, comprised of a flow of goods and information. In particular, logistics management concerns all levels of the supply chain, which includes supplying raw materials, parts, subassemblies, and finished goods—which have inventory that must be managed, transported, and distributed. Vast arrays of firms employ logistics management, such as: government and military organizations, manufacturers, transportation firms, retailers, warehousing companies, merchandising firms, and wholesale distributors. The enormity and importance of logistics management is apparent based on figures obtained from CSCMP's annual "State of Logistics Report." The 2015 report indicates that logistics expenditures in the United States totaled more than $1.45 trillion U.S. dollars in 2014. Comparatively speaking, this expenditure equals 8.3 percent of nominal U.S. GDP (gross domestic product) for year 2014—a massive expense (Schulz, 2015).

Logistics Management

The Council of Supply Chain Management Professionals (CSCMP) defines logistics management as:

"Logistics management is that part of supply chain management that plans, implements, and controls the efficient, effective forward and reverse flow and storage of goods, services and related information between the point of origin and the point of consumption in order to meet customers' requirements. Logistics may have either internal focus (inbound logistics), or external focus (outbound logistics) covering the flow and storage of materials from point of origin to point of consumption" (CSCMP, n.d., 4).

"Logistics management activities typically include inbound and outbound transportation management, fleet management, warehousing, materials handling, order fulfillment, logistics network design, inventory management, supply/demand planning, and management of third-party logistics services providers. To varying degrees, the logistics function also includes sourcing and procurement, production planning and scheduling, packaging and assembly, and customer service. It is involved in all levels of planning and execution—strategic, operational and tactical. Logistics management is an integrating function, which coordinates and optimizes all logistics activities, as well as integrates logistics activities with other functions including marketing, sales manufacturing, finance, and information technology" (Rao, 2009). See figure 2.

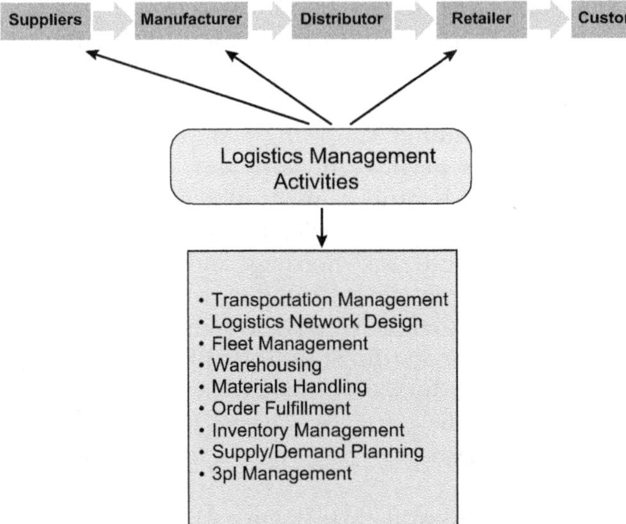

Figure 2: Logistics Management Activities

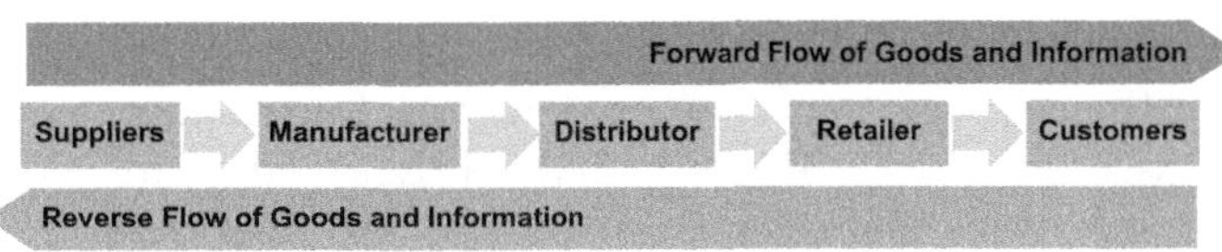

Figure 3: Flow of Goods

Notice that within this definition of logistics management, it refers to the forward and reverse flow of goods and information from the point of origin to the point of consumption. This reverse flow is known as reverse logistics (see Figure 3). "Reverse logistics is the process of moving returned goods from their consumer destination for the purpose of capturing value or proper disposal. It includes processing returned merchandise due to damage, seasonal inventory, restock, salvage, recalls, and excess inventory, as well as packaging and shipping materials from the end user or reseller" (Blanchard, 2007). Reverse logistics costs are sizable—estimated to be approximately a half percent of the total US GDP—accounting for approximately $ 58.34 Billion in expense for year 2004 in the U.S. (Rogers, Lambert, Croxton & Garcia-Dastugue, 2002).

Essentially, logistics management is the management of the movement of goods and information, i.e., all of the shipping and delivering decisions, getting raw materials, parts or supplies, from vendorto the manufacturer and delivering the finished products from the manufacturer to the distributors, who in turn deliver to retailers for ultimate delivery to consumers. In practical terms, logistics management involves the art and science of getting the right materials, to the right place, in the right quantities, at the right price, with the right quality, at the right time. Due to the fact that effective logistics are so vital to the success of a business, managing these decisions is critical. The bottom line is this: logistics management is an important way for companies to minimize costs and to enhance their overall customer service.

Firms Providing Integrated Logistics Management Solutions

Firms such as Schneider Logistics, DHL Logistics, Exel, UPS Supply Chain, and FedEx Supply Chain Services, are examples of firms that offer integrated logistics management solutions to other companies. They are known as third-party logistics providers (3PL providers). Stated another way, 3PL provider refers to the outsourcing of a logistics function(s). On the flip side, you have what are known as fourth-party logistics providers (4PL providers). 4PL providers are organizations that select and manage 3PL providers based on what they determine to be the most optimal logistics management solutions for a given firm. In other words, a 4PL organization creates unique logistics management solutions that cannot be achieved by any single 3PL provider.

As mentioned before, the main objectives of a logistics management system are to maximize customer service and to minimize the total cost of its activities. In other words, the goal is to add value to the customer and reduce the cost of adding that value. Unfortunately, not all firms manage logistics management effectively or efficiently. For example, failures may be rooted in poor data quality upon which logistics decisions rely, improper management of the overall logistics management function, or some unexpected natural calamity. These failures cause disruptions along the entire supply chain, e.g., missing raw material and parts, which cause production delays, causing late orders, in turn generating customer dissatisfaction. Realizing that such disruptions ultimately result in a loss of customers, interruptions along the supply chain are something no business can afford in today's competitive global marketplace.

APPLICATIONS

Let's consider a real-life example of how the logistics management process flows in the overall supply chain. A good illustration is that of Campbell Soup Company—well-known for their variety and quality soups provided to the food industry. When opening a can of soup, few people wonder how a can of soup and its various component parts ended up in their kitchen cabinet. It all starts with the supply chain and the logistics management function (see Figure 4 below).Though our example only shows a single supplier, distributor, and retailer for Campbell Soup Co., a large manufacturer of their size and scope likely has numerous suppliers, distributors, and retailers. Also, in this example, we are viewing the supply chain only from the viewpoint of Campbell Soup. Yet, we can also diagram the supply chain from the perspective of the other companies involved, such as Alcoa, Silgan Holdings, or Kroger, as well, or any other Campbell Soup Co. supplier, distributor, or retailer.

For illustrative purposes, the supply chain process for Campbell Soup Co. begins with Alcoa—a supplier of extracted aluminum necessary in the production of aluminum cans. Alcoa then ships rolls of aluminum to Silgan Holdings, a producer who converts the aluminum into soup cans. Since Alcoa is an indirect supplier to Campbell, Alcoa is known as a tier-2 supplier. Silgan Holdings, a customer of Alcoa and supplier to Campbell Soup, in turn sells their manufactured aluminum cans to Campbell Soup Co., who at this point is a customer of Silgan Holdings. As a supplier to Campbell Soup Co., Silgan Holding is known as a tier-1 supplier in that they directly supply cans to Campbell Soup Co. Campbell Soup then supplies its customer, Bridgetown Foods, (a wholesale food distributor), with cans of soup, who in turn ships and distributes Campbell's Soup to grocery retailers, such as Kroger Company, who then sell Campbell's Soup to the ultimate customer. This is noteworthy in the sense that most of the participants along a supply chain are both suppliers and customers.

Inbound & Outbound Logistics

Through it all, the entire process of moving raw materials, parts, and supplies to the manufacturer, and the process of moving the finished good (i.e., soup) is the designated role carried out by the logistics management function. At this point, a couple of terms need defining: inbound logistics and outbound logistics.

- Inbound logistics involves the materials handling, transportation, receipt, and warehousing of raw materials, parts, and supplies, and their distribution to manufacturing as they are needed in the production process. In the case of Alcoa and Silgan Holdings supplying Campbell Soup Co., this represents inbound logistics.
- Outbound logistics consists of activities involving materials handling, order fulfillment, packaging, transportation, warehousing, and distribution of finished products to the ultimate consumer. When Campbell forwards cans of soup (the finished product) to its distributor (Bridgetown Foods), which then forwards the product to the retailer (Kroger), these transactions are examples of outbound logistics.

As the diagram below (Figure 4) shows, the flow of goods and information travels in a forward and reverse direction along the entire supply chain. For instance, Silgan Holdings places an order with Alcoa for a certain amount of aluminum rolls, resulting in Alcoa shipping the order of aluminum to Silgan—this is a forward flow of goods. Or, Silgan Holdings may return a quantity of aluminum to Alcoa for some reason, such as unacceptable quality, resulting in a reverse flow of goods—i.e., reverse logistics—a concept discussed earlier. Similarly, Campbell Soup Co., after receiving cans from its supplier Silgan Holdings, may likewise return defective aluminum cans to Silgan, again resulting in a reverse flow of goods back through the supply chain.

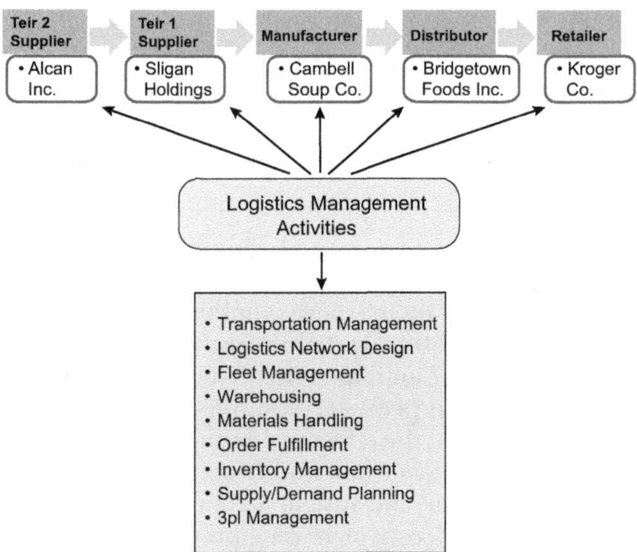

Figure 4: Campbell Soup Company Supply Chain

Logistics Management Activities

The following is a run-down of the various logistic management activities enumerated above in Figure 4. This outline gives a clearer perspective on the various activities inherent in the logistics management function and their interrelationships.

Transportation Management is concerned with determining the most efficient means of executing the movement of product, utilizing various modes of transportation whether it is rail, trucking, shipping, or air transport. The objective is to optimize loads, vehicles, and drivers, with the overall objective of reducing cost and increasing transportation efficiencies.

Logistics Network Design concerns the design of information management systems to aid in the systematic planning, organizing, managing, and control in the areas of order fulfillment, warehouse management, transportation management, materials handling, inventory management, and supply/demand planning. The system integrates with enterprise resource systems in the purchasing of raw materials and parts, manufacturing, marketing and sales functions. Likewise, by necessity, logistics professionals interface with all of an organization's functional areas, i.e., operations, marketing, sales, and finance. Thus, logistics network design facilitates collaboration and integration amongst the various parties in the supply chain relationship.

Logistics Collaboration has been encouraged through an industry-wide initiative known as Collaborative Planning Forecasting and Replenishment (CPFR). CFRR is a Voluntary Inter-Industry Commerce Standards Association (VICS) committee made up of retailers, manufacturers, and solution providers. In this system, partner firms exchange information on product sales and predictions in order to align their operational plans to enable automatic product replenishment and consequently increase the overall efficiency of the supply chain (http://www.vics.org/committees/cpfr/).

Fleet Management involves managing a firm's private and/or contracted fleet for optimal use in transporting goods, involving such issues as fleet availability, condition, fleet location, maintenance, replacements, etc.

Warehouse Management is the management of the movement and storage of materials throughout the warehouse—including receiving, picking, and shipping activities.

Materials Handling concerns the physical handling of goods from the time of procurement to the shipment phase.

Order Fulfillment refers to the activities necessary in responding to customer orders, e.g., receiving and processing orders, delivery, and handling customer inquiries, etc.

Inventory Management involves managing inventory to match supply with demand in the most cost-effective and efficient manner. Decisions include how much inventory to hold, how much to order, and when to order.

Supply/Demand Planning is the planning process of matching sources of supply according to customer demand requirements, as well as supply chain capabilities, over a given time frame.

3PL Management is the process of choosing and managing relationships between the firm and any third-party logistics management providers such as DHL, UPS Logistics, Schneider Logistics, etc.

CONCLUSION

In light of recurring natural disasters, threats of global terrorism, increasing global competition, and rising fuel costs, the effective administration of the supply chain and the logistics management function are even more of an imperative. The logistics management function plays a critical role in this regard. It also follows that the effective administration of the logistics management function is an important way for firms to create and sustain a competitive advantage by reducing costs, increasing productivity, while improving customer service and increasing profits along with market share. At the opposite side of the spectrum, the end results of poor logistics management are higher costs, a possible loss of customers, lower market share, and not surprisingly, lower profit. Indeed, the threat of poor logistics execution represents an enormous incentive for firms to "get it right the first time." Hence, the call for effective logistics management is made abundantly clear.

BIBLIOGRAPHY

An introduction to supply chain and logistics. (2007). *GS1.* Retrieved 27 July 2010 from http://www.acs.org.au/nsw/meetings/IntroductionToSupplyChainAndLogistics.pdf

Blanchard, D. (2007). Supply chains also work in reverse. *Industry Week/IW, 256*(5), 48-48. Retrieved July 11, 2007, from EBSCO Online Database Business Source Complete. http://search.ebscohost.com/login.aspx?direct=true&db=bth&AN=25063653&site=ehost-live

CSCMP, (2006, June). *17th Annual State of Logistics Report.* Retrieved June 25, 2007, from http://www.loginstitute.ca/files/pdfs/17th%5FAnnual%5FState%5Fof%5FLogistics%5FReport.pdf

CSCMP Supply Chain Management Definitions. *CSCMP.* Retrieved 27 July 2010 from http://cscmp.org/aboutcscmp/definitions.asp

Gunasekaran, A., & Choy, K. (2012, May). Industrial logistics systems: Theory and applications. *International Journal of Production Research.* 2377–2379. Retrieved November 20, 2013 from EBSCO Online Database Business Source Complete. http://search.ebscohost.com/login.aspx?direct=true&db=bth&AN=76312392&site=ehost-live

Hillman, Mark, (2006). Risk and reward are found in logistics, transportation, and global trade. *Manufacturing Business Technology, 24*(12), 31–32. Retrieved July 11, 2007, from EBSCO Online Database Business Source Complete. http://search.ebscohost.com/login.aspx?direct=true&db=bth&AN=23507937&site=ehost-live

Jian, L., & Bao, J. (2013). A synthetic cloud model for third-party logistics partner evaluation. *Proceedings for the Northeast Region Decision Sciences Institute (NEDSI),* 1140–1147. Retrieved November 20, 2013 from EBSCO Online Database Business Source Complete. http://search.ebscohost.com/login.aspx?direct=true&db=bth&AN=88837790&site=ehost-live

Lambert, D.M. (2004). The eight essential supply chain management processes. *Supply Chain Management Review, 8*(6), 18–26. Retrieved June 28, 2007, from EBSCO Online Database Business Source Complete. http://search.ebscohost.com/login.aspx?direct=true&db=bth&AN=14354622&site=ehost-live

Mishra, N. N., Kumar, V. V., & Chan, F. S. (2012). A multiagent architecture for reverse logistics in a green supply chain. *International Journal of Production Research, 50*(9), 2396–2406. Retrieved November 20, 2013 from EBSCO Online Database Business Source Complete. http://search.ebscohost.com/login.aspx?direct=true&db=bth&AN=76312394&site=ehost-live

NABCA, (2004, Nov.). National Alcohol Beverage Control Association—Supply Chain Management Industry Presentation. Cincinnati, Ohio. Retrieved June 25, 2007, from http://www.nabca.org/media/28%5F1industrysupplychainmgmt.ppt

Rao, Narayana. (2009). *Supply chain management.* Retrieved 27 July 2010 from http://knol.google.com/k/narayana-raok-v-s-s/supply-chain-management/2utb2lsm2k7a/526#

Rogers, D., Lambert, D., Croxton, K., & García-dastugue, S. (2002). The returns management process. International Journal of Logistics Management, 13(2), 1. Retrieved July 11, 2007, from EBSCO Online Database Business Source Complete. http://search.ebscohost.com/login.aspx?direct=true&db=bth&AN=10036672&site=ehost-live

Schulz, J. D. (2015). 26th Annual State of Logistics: Freight moves the economy. *Logistics Management, 54*(7), 24–28. Retrieved Dec. 3, 2015 from EBSCO Online Database Business Source Complete. http://search.ebscohost.com/login.aspx?direct=true&db=bth&AN=108402736&site=ehost-live&scope=site

Suggested Reading

Bai, C., & Sarkis, J. (2012). Supply-chain performance-measurement system management using neighbourhood rough sets. *International Journal Of Production Research, 50*(9), 2484–2500. Retrieved November 20, 2013 from EBSCO Online Database Business Source Complete. http://search.ebscohost.com/login.aspx?direct=true&db=bth&AN=76312400&site=ehost-live

Fassoula, E. (2005). Reverse logistics as a means of reducing the cost of quality. *Total Quality Management & Business Excellence, 16*(5), 631–643. Retrieved April 19, 2007, from EBSCO Online Database Business Source Complete. http://search.ebscohost.com/login.aspx?direct=true&db=bth&AN=17588624&site=ehost-live

Lynch, D., Keller, S., & Ozment, J. (2000). The effects of logistics capabilities and strategy on firm performance. *Journal of Business Logistics, 21*(2), 47–67. Retrieved April 22, 2007, from EBSCO Online Database Business Source Complete. http://search.ebscohost.com/login.aspx?direct=true&db=bth&AN=4315158&site=ehost-live

McGinnis, M., & Kohn, J. (2002). Logistics strategy revisited. *Journal of Business Logistics, 23*(2), 1–17. Retrieved April 22, 2007 from EBSCO Online Database Business Source Complete. http://search.ebscohost.com/login.aspx?direct=true&db=bth&AN=8566921&site=ehost-live

Myerson, P. (2015). *Supply chain and logistics management made easy: Methods and applications for planning, operations,integration, control and improvement, and network design.* Old Tappan, NJ: Pearson Education.

Stock, G., & Greis, N. (1999). Logistics, strategy and structure. *International Journal of Physical Distribution & Logistics Management, 29*(3/4), 224. Retrieved April 22, 2007, from EBSCO Online Database Business Source Complete. http://search.ebscohost.com/login.aspx?direct=true&db=bth&AN=2019116&site=ehost-live

Edwin D. Davison, M.B.A., J.D.

M

Management Competencies

ABSTRACT

The purpose of this article is to explore the subject of management competencies and provide a framework for contextualizing competency modeling within organizations. First, a background discussion will ensue with an examination of the origins of competency modeling, along with a definition of the term "competencies." From there, we'll highlight the types of competencies typically employed in the construction of competency models. We'll then transition to the various approaches for developing competency dimensions, typical organizational uses for competency models, types of competency models, and management competencies as predictors of performance. The article concludes with an example of an actual competency model and an outline of some perceived drawbacks of competency modeling.

OVERVIEW

Global interest in the utilization of management competencies as a management tool parallels the recognition of human resources as the most valuable asset within any organization. Directly in line with this recognition, management competencies are gaining widespread usage in organizations. Competencies clarify work expectations, generating a common language that catalyzes and reinforces changes in individual behavior. In short, competency models develop a set of expectations within organizations that serve as benchmarks for superior performance. However, as shall be seen, there are several beneficial aspects associated with competency models.

Origins of competency-based methodology are grounded largely in the research of Harvard behavioral psychologist David McClelland in the 1970s, and management theorist Richard Boyatzis's research in the 1980s. McClelland (1973), in his article "Testing for competence rather than for intelligence," made the case for competency modeling as opposed to intelligence testing, proposing that intelligence test scores are not reliable predictors of job success. Essentially, McClelland's competency methodology focused on the identification of key behaviors in high performers versus lesser performers.

Management competency pioneer, Richard Boyatzis (1982), is noted for his work in competency modeling as a predictor of effective manager performance. Boyatzis defines competencies as "an underlying characteristic of an employee (i.e., motive, trait, skill, aspects of one's self image, social role, or a body of knowledge) which results in effective, and/or superior performance in a job" (Boyatzis, 1982, p.20). Likewise, Seal, Boyatzis and Bailey (2006, p. 193) state:

"In the purest sense, a competency is defined as a capability or ability that leads to a successful outcome. It is a set of related but distinct sets of behaviors organized around an underlying purpose or goal, called the "intent." Competencies, therefore, are the result of appropriate behaviors used effectively in the situation or time to further the underlying goal or purpose that emerges from the intent."

Additionally, LeBleu and Sobkowiak (1995), summarize competency modeling by stating: "In its crudest form, it is a yardstick for measuring how someone is performing, comparing current performance to an ideal, and suggesting actions that can be taken to improve that performance."

Types of Competencies

Competencies span three broad categories (Byham & Moyer, 1996).

1. Organizational Competencies—those unique competitive attributes that form the basis upon which organizations compete—sometimes referred to as core competencies. It is an organizational strength that gives an organization a competitive advantage over competitors. For example, Dell Computer's core competence lies in superior supply chain man-

agement—namely their superior efficiency in the procurement of production parts/supplies, manufacturing processes, and their distribution system.

2. Personal Competencies—characteristics representing general standards for acceptable performance (level of achievement or output) in a given role. Consider the job of a sales manager. A sales manager is said to have personal competency if they can adequately perform at a level typically expected of a sales manager. Thus, personal competence is the ability to adequately perform in a given job—as opposed to superior performance.
3. Job/Role Competencies—skills and behaviors necessary to achieve superior performance in a specific job, role, function, task, duty, organizational level, or entire organization. Job/role competencies are the focus of this article. These job/role competencies exist on a number of job levels (Byham & Moyer, 1996):
   - A role (leader of a meeting);
   - A job or position (a manufacturing team leader);
   - A job level (first-line leaders);
   - Several job levels (middle management);
   - A broad band of jobs (professional/ technical jobs);
   - An entire organization.

It is these job/role competencies that provide the footing for our discussion. Job/role competencies measure knowledge, skills, and abilities shown to predict superior performance. As applied to managers in organizations, job/role competencies define effective management performance and are thought of as management competencies. Throughout the remainder of this article, the terms competency and management competencies shall be used interchangeably.

Job/role competencies may be broken down into a number of observable items, i.e. behavior, knowledge, and motivation (Bynam & Moyer,1996).

Behavioral Competency: Behaviors a person exhibits that result in good performance—that which a person says or does that determines performance.

Example: Consider the HR competency dimension of performance management. A manager would be expected to exhibit certain behaviors such as communicating clear performance standards, monitoring employees' performance, providing performance feedback and recommending corrective action when necessary.

The most widely used behavioral competencies are:

1. Team orientation;
2. Communication skills;
3. People management;
4. Customer focus;
5. Results orientation;
6. Problem-solving; and
7. Planning and organizing (Rankin, 2005).

Knowledge Competency: A person's knowledge of facts, technologies, processes, or procedures related to their job. Diplomas, licenses, certificates, as well as a person's ability to apply their knowledge, are signs of such knowledge competency.

Motivational Competency: An individual's feeling about their job, organization, or geographic location which may impact upon performance. Motivational competencies focus on the motivational aspects of proper job fit, organizational fit, or location fit. Generally motivational competencies cannot be developed.

Example: The position of sales manager requires an entrepreneurial orientation as manifested by a predisposition to seeking out opportunities, and a willingness to take calculated risks. If a sales manager is lacking these qualities, a poor job fit results and that individual would most likely lack the motivation and ability to perform at high levels.

Competency Models in Organizations

Research affirms that competency models are widely deployed, with adoption rates likely to increase in the future. A UK-based benchmarking study (Rankin, 2005) of competencies in organizations found that 60% of respondents had a competency framework in place. Of those firms lacking a competency framework, about half (48%) intended to introduce one in the future. Furthermore, among those organizations with competency frameworks, approximately four out of five employees (78%) were included in their competency model. Also, one-half (50%) of the firms reported having a single, common competency framework across the entire organization.

Changes in the business world have made the use of management competency models more prevalent for the following reasons (Byham & Moyer, 1996):

- Rapidly changing, team-oriented, and "virtual" organizations mean that the traditional definitions of jobs are increasingly rare. Thus, management competencies fill the void by clearly defining what is expected of employees.

- Flattened organizations with fewer layers have fewer advancement opportunities that translate to a more horizontal selection process—creating less room for error due to a smaller number of promotional jobs. This phenomenon increases the need for defining and using competencies to aid in selection accuracy.
- With a more dynamic workplace and the path to advancement less clear, well defined competencies provide better self-guidance in career planning. As individuals become increasingly responsible for their career planning, career guidance assistance is needed. Competencies provide this needed assistance.
- With increased overlap between employee and management roles, clearly defined work roles are imperative. Competencies fill the void by clarifying organizational expectations and individual responses.
- Global workforce requirements require an ability to operate effectively in cross-cultural assignments. Competencies are uniquely suited to providing benchmarks for uniform standards that can be applied worldwide (Byham & Moyer, 1996).

APPLICATIONS

Approaches to Defining Competencies

There are two basic approaches to defining and developing competencies in organizations—the behavioral approach and the clinical approach (Byham & Moyer, 1996). The behavioral approach concentrates on behaviors, motivations, and knowledge relevant to a particular job—i.e. job-relevant behavior. On the other hand, the clinical approach identifies underlying personal characteristics of the individual as the basis for defining competencies; independent of any job connection. In essence, the clinical approach targets the personal characteristics of superior performers. Unless otherwise stated, our discussion relies on the behavioral approach—the approach most widely used in developing competencies.

Competency Model Types

The following is an overview of competency models involving US-based firms (Rothwell & Lindholm, 1999). Though the models are based on data specific to the US, these models may be found across cultures to varying degrees, regardless of country origin.

- Borrowed Approach—The easiest and least expensive competency modeling approach, the borrowed approach simply borrows an approach from an existing organization, without taking into consideration the uniqueness of the adopter. An obvious shortcoming lies in the possibility of the borrowed model not being appropriate for the borrowing organization.
- Borrowed and Tailored Approach—A variation of the borrowed approach is the borrowed and tailored approach—which borrows a competency framework from an existing organization, yet tailors the model to the borrower's structure, culture and resources (human, technical, financial, informational, etc.).
- Tailored Approach—As its name suggests, the tailored approach tailors a competency model according to the unique needs of the organization. The process-driven and outputs-driven approaches are classic tailored approaches that have been in use for some time and are more commonly utilized. Several new approaches are the invented approach, the trends-driven approach, and the work responsibilities approach.
- Process-driven Approach—Emphasizes work process (job activities, personal characteristics, behaviors) required for exemplary job performance.
- Outputs-driven Approach—Identifies key outputs of a given job that successful performers produce. Competencies are then developed based on these key outputs.
- Invented Approach—A new competency model is developed without regard to an existing approach. This approach is used when exemplary performers are unavailable or the organization is about to undergo drastic changes.
- Trends-driven Approach—Focuses on what people must know or be able to do in response to managing a changing environment.
- Work responsibilities-driven Approach—"Derives work outputs, competencies, roles, and quality requirements from work responsibilities or activities" (Rothwell & Lindholm, 1999, p.99).

Competency Model Uses

Early usage of competency models focused on two areas: performance management and career development. These early models typically applied primarily to senior managerial personnel (Rankin, 2005). However, management competency frameworks are now being applied across the entire range of the human resource management function. For example, the various uses of competency models are:

- Executive development
- Recruitment and selection
- Compensation
- Performance appraisal
- Career development
- Job design
- Organization design
- Training and development
- Training needs analyses
- Succession Planning (LeBleu & Sobkowiak, 1995) (Bynam & Moyer, 1996)

Also, Rankin (2005) goes further in identifying (in order) the primary applications of competency models in organizations:

- Performance reviews/appraisal
- Improving employee effectiveness
- Achieving greater organizational effectiveness
- Training needs analysis
- Career management

Management Competencies & Performance

In the 1970s, the American Management Association (AMA) and McBer Company (a consulting company founded by David McClelland) studied 1800 managers over a 5 year period, with the aim of identifying the competencies of successful managers. The result of their research yielded five management competencies deemed essential in determining a manager's job success (Rothwell & Lindholm, 1999):

1. Specialized knowledge
2. Intellectual maturity
3. Entrepreneurial maturity
4. Interpersonal maturity
5. On-the-job maturity

Research verifies a number of management competencies serving as accurate predictors of outstanding manager performance (Boyatzis, R., Stubbs & Taylor, 2002). These competencies reside within three broad categories:

Cognitive or intellectual ability, as in the ability to make sense out of complex scenarios with any number of conflicting and sometimes obscure variables which may affect decisions;

Intrapersonal abilities, such as personal adaptability, i.e. the ability and willingness to deal with change;

Interpersonal abilities, (sometimes referred to as emotional intelligence), motivating others to perform, network, communicate, etc.

An important additional ingredient is a person's desire to apply their ability in any one of the aforementioned areas. Without the requisite desire to use these abilities, competencies lose their quality for predicting outstanding performance (Boyatzis, R., Stubbs, & Taylor, 2002).

A Competency Model

The National Institutes of Health (NIH), (the primary federal agency for conducting and supporting medical research) developed an organization-wide competency model for its entire workforce. NIH defines competencies as "the combination of knowledge, skills and abilities that contribute to individual and organizational performance." Suggested uses for the model are decisions pertaining to recruitment and selection, promotion readiness, selection and approval of training, and leadership readiness (http://hr.od.nih.gov/workingatnih/competencies/faqs.htm).

The NIH Competency Model comprises of three components: Core competencies, administrative leadership and management, and occupation-specific areas. Core competencies form the foundation of the NIH model and represent the knowledge, skills and abilities required of all NIH employees—regardless of function. Occupation-specific competencies represent the set of knowledge, skills and abilities expected within a particular functional area (e.g., Accounting, Contracting, Human Resources, Information Technology, etc.). Also, NIH managers and supervisors must display an additional set of competencies in Leadership and Management. Within each competency dimension, individuals are rated on a proficiency scale of 'not applicable' to a high score of 5 which indicates Expert proficiency. (The rating NIH Proficiency Scale is as follows: N/A—Not applicable, 0—Not Demonstrated, 1—Fundamental Awareness, 2—Novice, 3—Intermediate, 4—Advanced, 5—Expert.)

I. Core competencies are split into Business Competencies and Communications/Interpersonal Competencies:

Business Competencies
- Enterprise Knowledge
- Analysis, Decision Making & Problem Solving
- Customer Service
- Driving Results
- Personal Effectiveness

Communications/Interpersonal Competencies
- Written Communication
- Oral Communication
- Interpersonal Effectiveness

II. Leadership & Management Competencies
- Visionary Leadership
- Developing & Managing Talent
- Strategic Decision Making

III. Occupation-Specific Competencies
Occupation-specific competencies vary according to occupation, i.e., an Accountant will have a different set of occupational competencies from that of an Information Technology specialist. The following list illustrates the occupation-specific competencies for NIH Information Technology Management staff (http://hr.od.nih.gov/workingatnih/competencies/occupation-specific/2210/default.htm)

NIH Information Technology Management Competency Model

1. **Information Technology (IT) Adeptness** Possesses the ability to learn new technologies and the aptitude to understand IT concepts.
2. **Information Technology Expertise** Able to use the technologies needed to perform in one's IT-specific area and understands the technologies of importance to NIH Institutes.
3. **Information Technology Awareness** Keeps up to date with trends and changes in the technology market relevant to one's area of professional expertise.
4. **Information Technology Legislative Requirements** Understands and applies comprehensive knowledge of government IT laws, regulations, policies and procedures.
5. **Federal and Departmental Acquisition Policies and Procedures Knowledge** Understands the Federal Government industry and how it functions as a buyer of services and products.
6. **Project Management** Creates and maintains an environment that guides a project to its successful completion.
7. **Technical Information Communication** Communicates technical information in a manner consistent with the level of the target audience.

Note that within each defined competency, a list of key behaviors serve as benchmarks for rating purposes. For example, for IT Adeptness, note the key behaviors:

Information Technology Adeptness In-Depth Possesses the ability to learn new technologies and the aptitude to understand IT concepts.

Key Behaviors:

- Grasps the "how and why" of information technology and its opportunities and limitations.
- Shares information learned at conferences, seminars, and training on new tools and technologies.
- Enhances knowledge and capabilities by engaging in discussions with other IT professionals.

Issues

A number of criticisms have been leveled at the concept of competency modeling over the years (Rankin, 2005). Some of the major criticisms of competency frameworks are:

Competency-based models can be overly elaborate and bureaucratic, affecting their utility to varying degrees. Also, they can be expensive—costing 2 to 3 million dollars for larger organizations, and are likewise very time consuming to implement. Furthermore, in a rapidly changing environment, a given competency model may quickly become outdated, thus consuming additional time and expense in ensuring it remains relevant and up-to-date.

Also, when placing too much emphasis on employees' inputs (competencies) instead of their actual production (outputs), there is a danger of favoring employees who are good performers in theory, but not in actual practice. In a similar vein, because some behavioral competencies are essentially personality traits a person is unable to change, it may be more prudent to judge someone on what they actually achieve.

Competency modeling runs the risk of producing clones that mimic one another, at the risk of minimizing work teams with diverse skill sets who offset and balance the strengths and weaknesses of other team members. Also, because competencies are based on models of good performers' past performance, this potentially overlooks a dynamic environment whereby new ways of addressing work issues may be needed. Also, if an organization is not very proficient in differentiating between successful and unsuccessful performers, competency modeling adds little value to the organization.

CONCLUSION

Used correctly, competency models can be powerful, unifying agents for change—changing and directing individual behavior toward organizational goals. Through the clarification of organizational expectations, competency models can be instrumental drivers of superior performance. Aside from enhancing the performance management process, competency models can be effective tools for recruiting and selecting the right person for the right job. Yet, competencies are also useful tools for designing jobs, career development, compensation planning, determining training and development needs, and making organizational design decisions. Though there are some drawbacks to the use of competency models, the positive contributions tend to outweigh any negative aspects. In light of the wide-ranging benefits of competency models and their ability to elicit superior performance, competency modeling has continued to gain traction.

Bibliography

Boyatzis, R.E. (1982). *The competent manager: a model for effective performance.* London: Wiley.

Boyatzis, R., Stubbs, E., & Taylor, S. (2002). Learning cognitive and emotional intelligence competencies through graduate management education. *Academy of Management Learning & Education, 1*(2), 150–162. Retrieved May 21, 2007, from EBSCO Online Database Business Source Complete. http://search.ebscohost.com/login.aspx?direct=true&db=bth&AN=8509345&site=ehost-live

Byham, W., & Moyer, P. (1996). *Using competencies to build a successful organization.* Development Dimensions International. Pittsburg, PA. http://www.ddiworld.com/pdf/ddi%5Fusingcompetenciesto build%5Fmg.pdf

Hsiu-Chuan, L., Yen-Duen, L., & Chein, T. (2012). A study on the relationship between human resource management strategies and core competencies. *International Journal of Organizational Innovation, 4*(3), 153–173. Retrieved November 15, 2013, from EBSCO Online Database Business Source Complete. http://search.ebscohost.com/login.aspx?direct=true&db=bth&AN=89082709&site=ehost-live

Kronenburg, M. A. (2014). Evaluating Important Healthcare Management Competency Areas and Preparation for Healthcare Reforms. *International Journal of Business & Public Administration, 11*(1), 31–40. Retrieved December 1, 2014, from EBSCO Online Database Business Source Complete. http://search.ebscohost.com/login.aspx?direct=true&db=bth&AN=97887446

Latukha, M. O., & Panibratov, A. Y. Top management teams' competencies for international operations: Do they influence a firm's result? *Journal Of General Management, 40*(4), 45–68. Retrieved December 4, 2015 from EBSCO Online Database Business Source Premier. http://search.ebscohost.com/login.aspx?direct=true&db=buh&AN=108369252&site=bsi-live

LeBleu, R. & Sobkowiak, R. (1995). *New workforce competency models. Information Systems Management, 12*(3), 7. Retrieved May 28, 2007, from EBSCO Online Database Business Source Complete. http://search.ebscohost.com/login.aspx?direct=true&db=bth&AN=9506273274&site=ehost-live

McClelland, D.C. (1973). Testing for competence rather than for intelligence. *American Psychologist, 28*(1), 1–14.

Mendenhall, M. E., Arnardottir, A., Oddou, G. R., & Burke, L. A. (2013). Developing cross-cultural competencies in management education via cognitive-behavior therapy. *Academy of Management Learning & Education, 12*(3), 436–451. Retrieved November 15, 2013, from EBSCO Online Database Business Source Complete. http://search.ebscohost.com/login.aspx?direct=true&db=bth&AN=90436672&site=ehost-live

Montier, R., Alai, D. & Kramer, D. (2006). Competency models develop top performance. *T+D, 60*(7), 47–50. Retrieved May 23, 2007, from EBSCO Online Database Business Source Complete. http://search.ebscohost.com/login.aspx?direct=true&db=bth&AN=21463711&site=ehost-live

Mukhopadhyay, K., Sil, J., & Banerjea, N. R. (2011). A competency based management system for sustainable development by innovative organizations: a proposal of method and tool. *Vision, 15*(2), 153–162. Retrieved November 15, 2013, from EBSCO Online Database Business Source Complete. http://search.ebscohost.com/login.aspx?direct=true&db=bth&AN=89431363&site=ehost-live

Parry, S. (1998). Just what is a competency? *Training, 35*(6), 58.

Rankin, N. (2006). The competency researcher's toolkit. *Competency & Emotional Intelligence, 14*(1), 26–29. Retrieved May 23, 2007, from EBSCO Online Database Business Source Complete. http://search.ebscohost.com/login.aspx?direct=true&db=bth&AN=22713633&site=ehost-live

Rankin, N. (2005). The DNA of performance: the twelfth competency benchmarking survey. *Competency & Emotional Intelligence, 13*(1), 2–24. Retrieved May 09, 2007, from EBSCO Online Database Business Source Complete. http://search.ebscohost.com/login.aspx?direct=true&db=bth&AN=18619211&site=ehost-live

Rejas-Muslera, R., Urquiza, A., & Cepeda, I. (2012). Competency-Based Model Through It: An Action Research Project. *Systemic Practice & Action Research, 25*(2), 117–35. Retrieved December 1, 2014, from EBSCO Online Database Business Source Complete. http://search.ebscohost.com/login.aspx?direct=true&db=bth&AN=73277004

Rothwell, W., & Lindholm, J. (1999). Competency identification, modeling and assessment in the USA. *International Journal of Training & Development, 3*(2), 90. Retrieved May 28, 2007, from EBSCO Online Database Business Source Complete. http://search.ebscohost.com/login.aspx?direct=true&db=bth&AN=4519388&site=ehost-live

Seal, C., Boyatzis, R., & Bailey, J. (2006). Fostering emotional and social intelligence in organizations. *Organization Management Journal, 3*(3), 190–209. Retrieved May 21, 2007, from EBSCO Online Database Business Source Complete. http://search.ebscohost.com/login.aspx?direct=true&db=bth&AN=24012807&site=ehost-live

Suggested Reading

Boyatzis, R. E. (1994). Rendering unto competence the things that are competent. *American Psychologist, 49*(1), 64–66. Retrieved May 31, 2007, from EBSCO Online Database Business Source Complete. http://search.ebscohost.com/login.aspx?direct=true&db=bth&AN=9406080383

Dubois, D. D. (1993). *Competency-based performance improvement: a strategy for organizational change.* Amherst: HRD Press Inc.

Griffiths, B., & Washington, E. (2015). *Competencies at work: Providing a common language for talent management.* New York City, NY: Business Expert Press.

McLagan, P. (1980). Competency models. *Training & Development Journal, 34*(12), 22. Retrieved May 31, 2007, from EBSCO Online Database Business Source Complete. http://search.ebscohost.com/login.aspx?direct=true&db=bth&AN=9072115&site=ehost-live

Spencer, L. M., & Spencer, S. M. (1993). *Competence at work: Models for superior performance.* New York: John Wiley & Sons.

Strobel, K. (2014). Competency Proficiency Predicts Better Job Performance. *HR Magazine, 59*(10), 67. Retrieved December 1, 2014, from EBSCO Online Database Business Source Complete. http://search.ebscohost.com/login.aspx?direct=true&db=bth&AN=98392711

Edwin D. Davison, M.B.A., J.D.

Management Consulting

ABSTRACT

Like the people who comprise them, organizations are constantly changing. Sometimes these changes are for the better and sometimes they are not, and any resulting problems need to be solved. Although many of the day-to-day problems encountered by organizations can be handled internally, some are so deep, complex, or systemic that the objective observations and expert advice of an outside party are necessary. Management consultants fill this role by applying business or behavioral science knowledge to the situation to diagnose and make recommendations for rectifying existing business problems or to help in the development of future plans. The decision to choose a consultant is not necessarily an easy one, but there are several indicators to help in making it. Management consultants can work on a short-term basis supporting such activities as risk assessment or strategic planning, or on a longer-term basis in the process of organization development, helping the organization become more effective and managing the concomitant change.

OVERVIEW

A management consultant is a qualified professional who works with upper level management in an organization to analyze the organization's health and effectiveness, identify problem areas, and make recommendations on how to fix the problems. Depending on the problem, the management consultant may also continue to guide the organization during the implementation of the recommendations. The use of management consultants to do these tasks is often a cost-effective approach to problem solving for two reasons. First, qualified management consultants typically have both more training and more experience in solving complex or systemic organizational problems than do managers working in the organization. In addition, management consultants typically can be more objective than persons working within the organization because they are not entrenched in the organization's culture and do not take its norms, values, and working assumptions for granted. Because management consultants are hired on a contract or retainer basis and not involved in the internal politics or day-to-day operations of the organization, they do not have the same assumptions about organizational norms and culture as do those who work directly for the organization. As a result, they are better able to step back and see the big picture and spot where problems lie.

Management consultants can be either independent contractors or employees of a consulting firm. Although there are large firms that offer management consulting services, most management consultants are individuals or small firms who specialize in these services. Some management consultants specialize in a specific type of organization (e.g., healthcare, nonprofit, service) while others are generalists who work with a wide range of organizations. Typically, management consultants are hired by top level management within the organization. This means that the consultant will be perceived by the organization as having the support of top management. If the role of the consultant is properly introduced to the organization, this also means that employees at all levels of the organization will be more likely to cooperate with the consultant because they will see his/her presence as being of importance to the organization. The fact that the consultant is hired by top management also means that s/he will have access to top management should any problems arise in the course of the consulting project or if cooperation needs to be encouraged. Access to top management also is important if the consultant's recommendations are to be taken seriously and implemented properly within the organization. Without such backing, implementations are more likely to fail.

As outside change agents, management consultants have a clear-cut role and are less likely to be affected by organizational norms and culture than is someone who works within the organization. This means that the consultant is freer to approach the problem objectively without the burden of preconceived notions of how the organization should or should not be working, ideas about what the problem is, or assumptions about who is at fault. In addition, most consultants tend to look at the organizational as a system where changes in one part have impact throughout the organization. This helps the consultant better identify and treat underlying problems rather than merely treating symptoms.

There are, however, people who work as direct employees for the organization who also are also sometimes asked to do the same kinds of activities that an external consultant would do. Such internal consultants, however, are more likely to run into problems in their activities and less likely to be successful for a number of reasons. In general, internal consultants are embedded in the culture of the organization, so they take the values, attitudes, and norms of the organization for granted. This makes it difficult for internal consultants to objectively view the organization or diagnose its problems. In addition, since internal consultants are part of the organization, they tend to think in terms of what the organization has traditionally done rather than what can be done, and is more ready to accept the system as given rather than see the ways that it can be improved. For the same reason, they also have a tendency to not want to rock the boat since they must continue to work in the organization once the change has been implemented. For example, the suggestion to reduce the size of the organization's workforce would be more difficult for an internal consultant to make than for an external consultant because the people who were to be laid off might be friends or because the remaining employees would see the internal consultant as a "hatchet" person who laid off their friends. This would make continuing to be successful as an internal consultant difficult since people would be less likely to cooperate with further consulting efforts. Another negative result of internal consultants being part of the organization is that they have difficulty distinguishing the organizational forest from the trees, and tend to focus on a micro view rather than on a wider systems view that is necessary for success.

Management consultants' activities include diagnosing and making recommendations for existing business problems or supporting organizational management in the development of future plans. One of the major activities of many management consultants is organization development, a long-range effort to improve the organization's problem-solving and renewal processes. Organization development involves the application of behavioral science knowledge to the problems of the workplace. Management consultants also may evaluate existing programs, practices, or procedures within the organization to determine their effectiveness and where and how they need to be improved. Management consultants can also provide expertise to organizational management in the areas of strategic planning and risk assessment and management. The management consultant often acts as a change agent, guiding an organization through a change effort to either improve current functioning and effectiveness or to help plan for a new path in the future. To be effective in these tasks, management consultants need to have knowledge of how to conduct a change effort, an understanding of the organization, and sufficient power to be able to implement the change. This latter qualification means that they need the backing of top level management to support their efforts and implement their recommendations.

Once the organization and the consultant mutually agree to enter into a relationship, there are several phases in the process, as shown in Figure 1. During

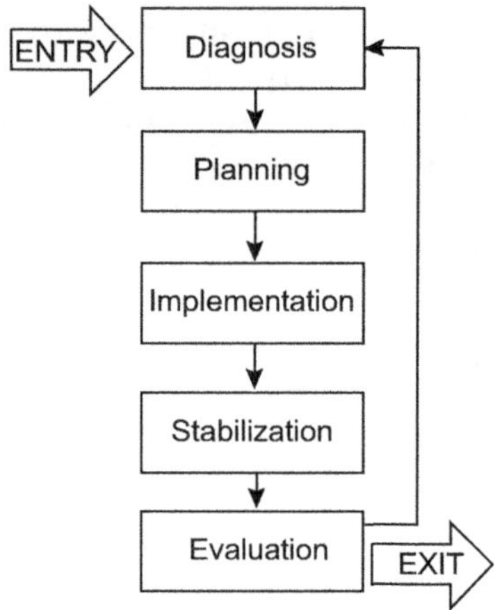

Figure 1: The Organization Development Process

the first phase, the consultant will learn more about the organization, collecting data, and diagnosing the problems facing the organization. During this phase, the consultant may use any number of techniques in an effort to diagnose the problems of the organization and determine the best way to rectify them. Some of these tools and techniques include questionnaires, individual and/or group interviews, personal observations, objective data (e.g., turnover, tardiness, market demographics), outside opinions, confrontation meetings). Once the consultant has diagnosed the problem, s/he will make recommendations to management as to the best way to proceed. These recommendations are then turned into plans and implemented.

After the plans have been implemented, there follows a period of stabilization during which the employees acclimate to the new way of doing things. When this phase is over, the consultant will typically evaluate how well the change fixed the problem. Frequently, the problems being experienced by the organization are deep, complex, and systemic. Therefore, it is unlikely that the single application of any one tool or technique will produce lasting change. Rather, most consulting efforts are iterative. If the organization is still experiencing difficulties, therefore, the consultant will do more data collection and analysis to diagnose the remaining problems. When this is done, the organization and consult sever the consulting relationship.

APPLICATION

Although management consultants can be invaluable to the health and growth of an organization, it can be difficult to know when an organizational problem or opportunity for growth can be handled internally and when a consultant is needed. Once the consultant is hired, it is also important to understand what to expect and how to work with him/her in a way that helps maximize the effectiveness of the client/consultant relationship.

Knowing When a Consultant Is Needed

Many of the day-to-day problems encountered in organizations can be solved by the organization internally. There are, however, some problems that are either outside the capabilities of the organization or so systemic that the help of an outside consultant are not only advisable, but essential. A number of indicators can alert organizational management to the possible need for external, professional help.

Organizational theorists talk about two facets to the organization. The formal organization comprises those aspects of the organization that are obvious to all but the most casual observer. Included in the formal organization are its stated goals, short- and long-term objectives, and other data easily found in its annual report or strategic plan. Another aspect of the formal organization is the structure of the firm: the way it is designed in order to facilitate performance effectiveness, including its division of labor, delegation of authority, and span of control (the number of people who directly work for a person on the next level of the organizational hierarchy). Other aspects of the formal organization include its resources, including its financial capital, equipment, and technology. Resources also include the human capital of the organization and the expertise of the organization's employees, including knowledge, skills, abilities, training and education.

The formal aspects of the organization can often benefit from the services of a management consultant. For example, management consultants can be very helpful to the organization in doing strategic planning; helping the organization better understand the market and its needs, the risks associated with alternate plans, how to implement the plans, and ways to better structure the organization to support the new objectives. Similarly, management consultants can be very helpful for an organization that needs to cope with a merger. Other dysfunctions in the formal organization that can indicate the need for an external consultant include problems in communication systems, difficulties with managerial strategies, or inefficiencies resulting from the structure or roles within the organization. Management consultants can help organizations deconstruct symptoms in these areas to understand the underlying problems and develop and implement appropriate plans that will correct not only the symptom, but the underlying problem.

In addition to the formal organization, there is an informal aspect to each organization comprised of less obvious aspects such as attitudes, values, feelings, interactions, and group norms. Such factors are part of the organizational culture; the set of basic shared assumptions, values, and beliefs that affect the way employees act within an organization. Because these aspects are not written down like the formal aspects of the organization, they can be easily dismissed as not important. However, they have a profound impact on the functioning of the organization and its concomitant health and effectiveness. In fact, like the proverbial iceberg, most theorists believe that the majority of organizational problems stem from aspects of the informal organization. Dysfunction in these aspects of the organization is more likely to be seen by a managerial consultant as an objective outside observer than by someone who is entrenched within those aspects as a member of the organization.

Organizational culture is one of the major factors that can affect the effectiveness of the organization. For example, an organizational culture that is very formal (e.g., with a suit-and-tie dress code and highly structured communication channel requiring multiple layers of approval before an innovation may be implemented) is unlikely to foster the entrepreneurial spirit necessary to be on the leading edge of the industry, surviving on sustainable innovation. Similarly, the norms of the organization – the standards or patterns of behavior that are accepted as normal within the culture—can increase or hamper its effectiveness. Another aspect of the informal organization that can have great impact on effectiveness is its values. For example, a company that builds training devices for the military will have difficulty being successful in its field if it sees itself as an engineering company that happens to build training equipment. To be truly effective in this situation, engineering is a support service that designs the equipment to meet the needs identified by the training function. If this is not understood, the resulting product would be a well-engineered product that does not train well.

Another aspect of the informal organization that is important to the effectiveness of the organization and that often requires the help of an external consultant, is worker motivation. Understanding the values of one's workers, for example, can help the organization understand how to better motivate them. However, such information is often obtained more easily by an external consultant not only because of his/her training, but also because employees are less likely to talk openly about values or offer criticisms to management who has power over them in the organizational setting. Most management consultants are not only neutral third parties who can objectively diagnose the problems of the organization, they also keep the identities of individuals from whom they collected the data confidential—even from management in the organization. This enables them to collect the data needed for this diagnosis and better help the organization.

A parallel in the informal organization to the communication patterns in the formal organization are conflicts or other difficulties in intra- or inter-group cooperation. As discussed above, most employees are typically more willing to give honest feedback to an objective outside party than they would be to their own management. This means that an external consultant will be better able to deconstruct the situation to determine the underlying problem and recommend better, more appropriate potential solutions.

Choosing a Consultant

Choosing a consultant is like choosing any other professional, including a lawyer, accountant, or physician: One must attempt to find the best person for the job based on the need and the consultant's credentials. Although anyone can call themselves a management consultant, it is important to make sure that they have an adequate education to back up their claims. No matter how experienced a person is, if s/he does not have an education in the broader principles, tools, and techniques of management consulting, s/he will only be able to extrapolate what s/he has done on previous jobs. However, every organization is different and the needs of every organization are also different. Some consultants offer solutions looking for problems, however, rather than recognizing the uniqueness of each organization and determining what is needed for each situation and developing a targeted solution based on this information. Similarly, other consultants try to give advice based on a few isolated cases without sufficient knowledge or education to underpin their recommendations. However, mere extrapolation of a few isolated cases is unlikely to be successful. There are a wide range of tools and techniques that can be applied to diagnosing an organization's problems. Successful diagnosis is often based on an iterative process using multiple techniques. If the consultant only offers a single approach based on limited past experience, it is best to be wary.

In addition to the appropriate educational background, a good consultant will also have experience in management consulting. Depending on the needs of the organization, this can be general management consulting experience or consulting experience within a specific industry. As when hiring any professional, it is important to check the consultant's references before making the decision to enter into a formal consulting relationship. In addition, each consultant will have his/own personality just as each organization has its own culture. Most consultants are willing to engage in an initial exploratory consultation to see if there is a good fit between the consultant's expertise and the needs of the organization.

Working with a Management Consultant

Although the management consultant may have more objectivity and be able to bring different insights to bear on the problems facing the organization, s/he cannot solve all the problems of the organization alone. The management consulting process is a collaborative effort requiring the involvement and commitment of both the consultant and the organization. To help ensure that the change process is successful, top management within the organization must support the effort. This includes assurance that change will occur and gives the consultant a power base out of which to operate. If top management is not behind the change effort, no matter how appropriate the consultant's recommendations, they will not be implemented or, worse, not implemented properly. This could potentially leave the organization worse off than it was before.

Top management in the organization is not the only level of employee involvement needed to help ensure the success of the relationship, however. In addition, key management at all levels of the organization need to be involved in the change process.

This will help ensure that plans and decisions are not being made too far from the source of the problem and that the consultant will receive all necessary data and feedback to make the intervention successful. Further, any employees who will be affected by the proposed changes need to be informed and involved as soon as possible. If not, serious repercussions could occur, including job dissatisfaction and lack of motivation (both on the job and in supporting the change effort).

BIBLIOGRAPHY

Cosier, R. A. & Dalton, D. R. (1993, Nov/Dec). Management consulting: Planning, entry, performance. *Journal of Counseling & Development, 72*(2), 191–198. Retrieved April 18, 2007, from EBSCO Online Database Business Source Complete. http://search.ebscohost.com/login.aspx?direct=true&db=bth&AN=9403086503&site=bsi-live

Furusten, S. (2013). Commercialized professionalism on the field of management consulting. *Journal of Organizational Change Management, 26*(2), 265–285. Retrieved October 31, 2013, from EBSCO Online Database Business Source Complete. http://search.ebscohost.com/login.aspx?direct=true&db=bth&AN=88053383&site=ehost-live

Huse, E. F. (1980). *Organization development and change* (2nd ed.). St. Paul, MN: West Publishing Company.

Kipping, M., & Kirkpatrick, I. (2013). Alternative pathways of change in professional services firms: the case of management consulting. *Journal Of Management Studies, 50*(5), 777–807. Retrieved October 31, 2013, from EBSCO Online Database Business Source Complete. http://search.ebscohost.com/login.aspx?direct=true&db=bth&AN=88156397&site=ehost-live

Klarner, P., Sarstedt, M., Hoeck, M., & Ringle, C.M. (2013). Disentangling the effects of team competences, team adaptability, and client communication on the performance of management consulting teams. *Long Range Planning, 46*(3), 258–286. Retrieved October 31, 2013, from EBSCO Online Database Business Source Complete. http://search.ebscohost.com/login.aspx?direct=true&db=bth&AN=89101564&site=ehost-live

McShane, S. L. & Von Glinow, M. A. (2003). *Organizational behavior: Emerging realities for the workplace revolution* (2nd ed). Boston: McGraw-Hill/Irwin.

Pemer, F., & Werr, A. (2013). The uncertain management consulting services client. *International Studies of Management & Organization, 43*(3), 22–40. Retrieved December 4, 2015 from EBSCO Online Database Business Source Premier. http://search.ebscohost.com/login.aspx?direct=true&db=buh&AN=90428767&site=bsi-live

SUGGESTED READING

Gallessich, J. (1982). *The profession and practice of consultation.* San Francisco, CA: Jossey-Bass Publishers.

Kelley, R. E. (1981). *Consulting: The complete guide to a profitable career* (rev.). New York City, NY: Charles Schribner's Sons.

Lippitt, G. L. (1977). Research on the consulting process. *Academy of Management Proceedings*, 153–157. Retrieved April 18, 2007, from EBSCO Online Database Business Source Complete. http://search.ebscohost.com/login.aspx?direct=true&db=bth&AN=4977219&site=bsi-live

Phillips, J. J., Trotter, W. D., & Phillips, P. P. (2015). *Maximizing the value of consulting: a guide for internal and external consultants.* Hoboken, NJ: Wiley.

Ruth A. Wienclaw, Ph.D.

MANAGEMENT INFORMATION SYSTEMS

ABSTRACT

This article will focus on management information systems. The hardware and software components of management information systems are reviewed along with the type of organization functions for which applications software is designed to support. Three business strategies that drive the development and deployment of management information systems - cost-reduction, quality-improvement, and revenue-growth - will be introduced and serve as the foundation for the discussion of the types of management information systems that can be implemented to support the strategies. Opportunities and challenges presented by the use of the Internet as an integral part of management information systems are also examined along with an analysis of staffing challenges for information technology (IT) departments.

OVERVIEW

Management information systems are comprised of computing and communications hardware, operating system software, applications software to support business functions, and specialized staff to analyze and design systems that help to achieve business goals and objectives. Management information systems support a broad array of business operations and enable interaction with an organization's suppliers, customers and service providers.

The selection and deployment of computer systems and communications hardware is driven by the size of an organization, the computing and communications needs of the business sector in which an organization competes and the geographical dispersion of operations. The capacity of computer systems ranges from powerful mainframe systems that support enterprise needs, servers that provide specialized functionality, and desktop units that enable individual employees to access the computing and communications resources of their organization. Each hardware component is controlled and managed by its own specialized operating system software.

Computer systems are comprised of several components including central processors, memory, storage and a communications interface. The central processor is a chip designed to execute commands from the operating system software and applications programs. The memory of the computer provides capacity for the central processor to perform the functions which the operating system and applications software provide computer users. Disk storage provides capacity to store applications programs, databases, text files, and graphic files used in the programs or that are created by users in the performance of their job duties. The communications interface is the device (an interface card for a small computer and a communications processor for a large system) that enables the computer to interact with other computers on a network or across the Internet.

Through the implementation of vendor produced applications software or the deployment of in-house developed customized applications software, management information systems can support a broad array of business operations. Vendor produced applications software such as enterprise resource planning (ERP) software can support large enterprise-wide operational needs. In contrast, vendor produced applications software like Microsoft Office is designed to support the needs of individual users at their workstation. Other applications software packages such as supply chain management systems enable computer users to communicate and conduct business with suppliers and customers. Custom built software is often created to perform functions that vendor produced software cannot adequately support. Business operations that management information systems support include:

- Accounting And Financial Management
- Human Resources Management And Payroll
- Customer Relations Management
- Decision Support
- Business Intelligence
- Knowledge Management
- Inventory Management
- E-Commerce And Internet Sales
- Internet Based Customer Support
- Facilities Management
- Manufacturing Operations

In addition to hardware and software components, specialized information technology (IT) staff is needed to select, implement, manage, and maintain all of the elements of management information systems. The type of IT staff and the number of IT staff required to assure management information systems adequately support business operations varies by the size and type of organization. The specialized skills of IT staff include:

- Systems Analysis
- Systems Design
- Applications Programming
- Data Center Operations
- Network Design And Management
- Information Security
- Help Desk (End User Support)
- Documentation And Quality Control
- Computer System Maintenance

An organization's management information system requires all of the following elements: Computer systems, communications hardware, applications software, and qualified IT personnel to select, design, implement, and maintain all of the components in a manner that supports business strategies.

APPLICATIONS

Aligning Business Strategies & Management Information Systems

The strategic alignment of IT refers to the degree to which the capabilities of the management information systems are aligned with the priorities, goals, and objectives of the firm's business strategy (Wonseok & Pinsonneault, 2007). Alignment is a complex process that requires IT staff to have an in-depth understanding of company operations and a clear understanding of what type of technology is needed to support those activities. It also requires that company management clearly identify and articulate company strategies and related goals and objectives.

There are three types of business strategies that drive the implementation of management information systems. The cost-reduction strategy focuses on reducing the acquisition costs of goods and materials, the costs of producing items, and reducing related operating costs. The quality-improvement strategy focuses on improving quality control, enabling an organization to offer products in higher-priced markets, or to inexpensively provide extended warranties as a product line feature or an add-on sales option. The revenue-growth strategy focuses on areas such as product development, customer service, niche marketing, and competitive pricing. The three strategies and the objectives that management information systems help achieve are listed below (Miller & Toulouse, 1998).

Cost-Reduction

- Strategic Procurement Of Supplies
- Process Innovations
- Just-In-Time Manufacturing
- Efficient Inventory Management
- Honing Operating Efficiency
- Reducing Production/Operating Costs

Quality-Improvement

- Tight Quality Control
- Ensuring Products For High Price Markets
- Marketing Products For High Price Markets
- Warranties And Guarantees
- Production Of Luxury Products

Revenue-Growth

- New Product Development
- Ongoing Development Of Existing Products
- Having A Broad Selection Of Products
- Excellent Customer Service
- Prompt Delivery
- Catering To Market Niches
- Amassing Special Data On Clients
- Customizing Products For Users
- Competitive Pricing
- Advertising
- Promotion/Brand Identification
- Attractive Design Or Packaging

Each of the three business strategies requires different types of activities which in turn require different types of computing abilities and different types of data. Thus, it is important that IT staff understand the organization's information needs in order to better support a wide variety of strategic activities. To complicate matters further, it is realistic to expect that an organization may simultaneously be pursuing more than one business strategy. Management information systems that serve as cost-reduction strategies may not be suitable to support revenue-growth strategies. In such a case, the mix of applications software will need to be expanded in order to support all the activities in the organization.

Communications between business operations managers and IT developers is essential to successfully implement appropriate management information systems. Participation of key business managers in planning management information systems is essential for the identification of appropriate IT applications (Booth & Philip, 2005). Without continued communication it is possible for the alignment between IT development efforts and business strategy to erode, resulting in an organization being without the management information systems it needs to remain competitive.

Applications Software for Cost-Reduction Strategies

Cost-reduction strategies generally attempt to reduce cost associated with procurement activities, inventory management, and production operations. To support cost-reduction strategies, one of the products offered by the information technology industry is Enterprise Resource Planning (ERP) software systems. ERP systems are now several decades old and have matured considerably in their capability, as has the ability of industries to implement and utilize the systems. A study of 247 firms adopting ERP systems shows that firms adopting enterprise systems exhibit higher differential performance only after two years of continued ERP system usage (Nicolaou, 2004).

ERP systems are comprised of a group of integrated modules that help organizations manage procurement, logistics, production planning and manufacturing. In general, the software companies that provide ERP systems also provide additional integrated modules that can support business functions such as the needs of human resource management including basic human resource functions, talent management, scheduling, payroll, and workforce deployment. To maximize the use of data, these modules can be integrated with financial management modules that provide support for accounts payable and receivable. There are very few software companies that offer ERP products and acquisition and implementation can be costly and requires months or years to accomplish.

Applications Software for Quality-Improvement Strategies

The road to quality management is complex with many elements that need to be addressed. Quality-improvement strategies generally attempt to address issues in the quality of materials used in the manufacturing process, the processes utilized during production, and the steps in packaging, storage, and distribution of products that may impact quality. As quality is controlled more tightly, a company may be able to produce products for high priced markets or offer extended warranties for their products.

Studies on quality management show that pursuit of ISO 9000 certification is becoming a must in order for many companies to better compete in the global marketplace. In addition, studies have found that quality is a strategic variable that should be taken into account and managed not only within the single firm, but also throughout the supply chain of which the firm is part (Romano, 2002). As a result of a demand for quality and an evolving procurement environment that requires companies to have ISO 9000 certification, companies around the world have taken steps to gain the certification.

Quality management software enables production managers and engineers to evaluate how well the processes they designed and implemented are achieving quality goals. Software to help manage the quality (through measuring and testing output) is used by many companies. In addition, integrated packages like SAP PLM allow users to begin quality planning during the product design phase. It also creates a foundation for quality inspection processes and in-process control during production. SAP PLM also meets the criteria for ISO 9000 and Good Manufacturing Practice (GMP). Selecting appropriate quality management software for a company requires input from product designers and engineers, production specialists as well as the managers responsible for quality programs.

Applications Software for Revenue-Growth Strategies

Revenue-growth strategies can impact more organization functions than cost-reduction or quality-improvement strategies. Growth strategies can be divided into three sub-categories:

1. Development, which includes new products and improvements to existing products
2. Service, which can include product customization for customers, packaging and delivery processes, or serving niche markets through supply chains
3. Marketing, which addresses analysis of existing and the creation of new data on customers or potential customers, developing and testing pricing strategies, advertising, and image building and branding.

The product development aspects of revenue-growth strategies include the design of new products and the implementation of improvements to existing products. Software packages that support these efforts are usually acquired by the engineering or product development departments and, for the most part, fall out of the realm of the central management information systems departments. The packages include three-dimensional graphics software used in the design process and simulation software to run tests on product functioning and ability under various conditions.

The service aspects of revenue-growth strategies can be driven by several types of software packages, many of which are referred to as customer relations management (CRM) applications. CRM became a popular software application in the middle 1990s and there are dozens of CRM type packages offered by software manufacturers. CRM packages can be rather simple and provide support for retail sales or supply chain relationship management. CRM packages can be complex and have several modules, like ERP systems, and be capable of supporting a wide array of activities. These activities include market analysis, marketing plan development, sales analysis and management, service contract management, workforce management, and partner channel management. Many CRM packages have web interfaces to support remote access and provide a portal for customers to obtain or provide information.

Although competition in the CRM market is driving innovation, the myriad of products makes selecting an appropriate CRM package for a company a lengthy and complex process. Selecting a CRM package includes two very important steps. As Colombo and Francalanci explain, "First, one must calculate the quality-to-cost ratio and support opportunity. Second, one must set a maximum budget for implementation and limit pre-selection to packages satisfying budget constraints. Both objectives share a common attitude towards costs as an organizational control variable that complements, rather than determines, the ranking of packages. Larger companies inevitably involve greater software complexity and consequently incur higher costs. Conversely, smaller companies may not need the most expensive packages and, in this respect, cost limits constitute a legitimate orientation that precedes the ranking of alternatives" (2004, p. 188).

The marketing aspects of a revenue-growth strategy include the analysis of existing data and creation of new data on customers or potential customers, developing and testing pricing strategies, advertising, image building, and branding. Contemporary marketing efforts are most often data driven and there are two types of applications software that currently support analysis for marketing efforts: Business data mining and statistical analysis.

Statistical analysis software packages have been in use for decades, but data mining as a business and market analysis practice and the data mining software products to support those efforts, are relatively new to the field of management information systems. According to Smyth (2005), "By the late 1980s and early 1990s, relational database technology had successfully established itself in the commercial sector, i.e. many businesses and organizations were now using these relational models and tools to manage their data. Worth noting is the fact that these relational database systems were never explicitly designed to support data analysis tasks. Instead they are primarily designed for the purposes of storage, query, and transaction management, i.e. supporting day-to-day operations of organizations that handle large volumes of data (e.g., airlines, banks hospitals, retail organizations, etc.)" (p. 5).

Interest in data warehousing began to grow in the early 1990s, namely maintaining a historical repository of all transactions ever recorded.

"Database researchers quickly realized that companies not only wanted to store, manage, and access their data in a systematic fashion, but they also wished to be able to analyze it. This analysis could not take place in the traditional statistical fashion since these data sets were typically far too large to be handled by conventional statistical software packages. Thus was born the concept of data analysis algorithms which are designed to operate directly on relational databases, and form the main components of modern database-oriented research in data mining" (Smyth, 2000, p.5).

There are dozens of data mining software tools on the market. They are designed to help achieve several types of business goals ranging from customer acquisition, cross- and up-selling, churn prediction, fraud detection, market-basket analysis, and forecasting (Giraud-Carrier & Povel, 2003). As with CRM and ERP software, selecting the appropriate data mining tool for a company can be a lengthy and complex project. The relationship between functionality provided and the cost of data mining tools is also similar to that of CRM and ERP packages; the more you spend the more you get.

APPLICATIONS

The Internet as a Component of Management Information Systems

The Internet has added a new element to management information systems. In about a ten year period from 1995 to 2004, the commercial use of the internet transformed from a researcher's tool to a common business necessity. A large portion of the boom in business investment in information technology was driven by new business applications and infrastructure using Internet related technology (Formanz, Goldfarb, & Greenstein, 2004).

One new application is Internet based Business-to-business (B2B) systems, which can be implemented to support cost-reduction strategies by bringing new efficiencies to operations management. These include supply chain systems, online ordering for business products, just-in-time inventory methods, and collaborative design processes.

A complimentary application is Internet business-to-consumer (B2C) systems, which can be implemented to support revenue-growth strategies by providing new sales, marketing, and customer service opportunities. These include advertising, promotion of brand identification, order processing, dissemination of technical and product information, and email marketing efforts.

Both B2B and B2C applications provide opportunities for companies to expand their markets to new countries and new target populations. With these opportunities also come many challenges including language barriers, varied business customs and social perceptions, as well as different local laws and government regulations. These issues challenged both IT professionals and corporate staff responsible for marketing, sales, product delivery, and customer support. Many companies found it necessary to develop Internet applications in multiple languages as well as hire developers and marketers that were familiar with local customs and laws. They also faced a myriad of state and national privacy laws around the world.

"The Internet has contributed to the awareness of privacy issues in four ways. First, the Internet has resulted in a huge increase in the number of people using computers to seek information and make purchases. Second, several privacy-related incidents have resulted in considerably less than favorable press coverage for enterprises that have suffered from privacy management problems. Third, many organizations had their first experiences in dealing with large-scale privacy issues. Fourth, the global cross-border nature of the Internet presented totally new challenges to governments and enterprises. The combination of these trends set the stage for many potential privacy conflicts" (Erbschloe & Vacca, 2001, p.xv). It also resulted in the creation of a new position in many organizations — the Chief Privacy Officer.

The deployment of Internet applications also presented new security challenges beyond privacy management. An information security program now requires the identification of an organization's electronic informational assets, as well as planning steps that must be carried out to ensure its continued availability, confidentiality and integrity. Any computer that has direct or indirect access to the outside world is potentially at risk, and can further risk all assets connected to the network (Hinojosa, 2005).

Issue

IT Staffing Challenges

Human capital is imperative in the knowledge-intensive IT profession. Chief Information Officers (CIOs) must reward valuable IT skills for important projects while constantly predicting additional requirements over the next three to five years. Even in organizations that are scaling down in size, top executives must possess the skills that will enable them to respond efficiently to future technological challenges (Schwarzkopf, Mejias, Jasperson, Saunders, & Gruenwald, 2004).

Managers face several problems in staffing IT departments. Many organizations have on-call requirements for IT staff and in many cases there is not additional compensation for on-call time. In other cases, work hours for IT employees can be long, especially during critical points during development cycles, the launch of new systems, or the migration from old systems.

IT workers also face a relatively constant need to renew their skill sets. This can occur several times during their career. When systems that an IT worker has supported for several years become obsolete, they must learn new systems and often new programming languages. As new technology emerges in the marketplace, IT workers also face the challenge of rapidly learning about the new technology as it is brought into their organization. New skill development is often done independently and with limited support from employers.

Several steps can be taken to help maintain a stable IT workforce. Striving to develop a professional workplace that meets the needs of the organization and IT employees is an important step in retaining IT employees. It is also important that the hiring process identifies employees that are a right fit for the organization, the IT department, and the teams on which they will be working. The issue of continued skill development and training must also be addressed in personnel policies, management practice, and in the IT budget (Erbschloe, 2003).

CONCLUSION

Management information systems are comprised of a combination of computer systems, communications systems, and applications software that are designed and maintained by professional IT staff. They support organization functions such as financial management, manufacturing and production, human resource management, and office administration. Management information systems also support communications (i.e. email) between employees within the organization as well as workers in supplier or customer organizations. A company's selection of systems and applications software is determined by its business strategy and business needs.

Bibliography

Booth, M., & Philip, G. (2005). Information systems management: Role of planning, alignment and leadership. *Behaviour & Information Technology, 24*(5), 391-404. Retrieved June 27, 2007, from EBSCO Online Database Academic Search Premier. http://search.ebscohost.com/login.aspx?direct=true&db=aph&AN=18406091&site=ehost-live

Colombo, E., & Francalanci, C. (2004). Selecting CRM packages based on architectural, functional, and cost requirements: Empirical validation of a hierarchical ranking model. *Requirements Engineering, 9*(3), 186-203. Retrieved July 2, 2007, from EBSCO Online Database Academic Search Premier. http://search.ebscohost.com/login.aspx?direct=true&db=aph&AN=14259123&site=ehost-live

Davenport, T.H. (2013). Analytics 3.0. *Harvard Business Review, 91*(12), 64-72. Retrieved November 15, 2013, from EBSCO Online Database Business Source Complete. http://search.ebscohost.com/login.aspx?direct=true&db=bth&AN=92545710&site=ehost-live

Deng, X., & Chi, L. (2012). Understanding postadoptive behaviors in information systems use: a longitudinal analysis of system use problems in the business intelligence context. *Journal of Management Information Systems, 29*(3), 291-326. Retrieved November 15, 2013, from EBSCO Online Database Business Source Complete. http://search.ebscohost.com/login.aspx?direct=true&db=bth&AN=85985311&site=ehost-live

Erbschloe, M (2003) *Socially Responsible IT Management*, 16-22. Digital Press.

Erbschloe, M & Vacca, J. (2001) Net Privacy: *A Guide to Developing & Implementing an Ironclad eBusiness Privacy Plan*, XV. McGraw-Hill.

Formanz, C., Goldfarb, A., & Greenstein, S. (2004). City or country: Where do businesses use the Internet? *FRBSF Economic Letter, 2004*(24), 1-3. Retrieved June 27, 2007, from EBSCO Online Database Academic Search Premier. http://search.ebscohost.com/login.aspx?direct=true&db=aph&AN=14269460&site=ehost-live

Giraud-Carrier, C., & Povel, O. (2003). Characterizing data mining software. *Intelligent Data Analysis, 7*(3), 181-192. Retrieved July 2, 2007, from EBSCO Online Database Academic Search Premier. http://search.ebscohost.com/login.aspx?direct=true&db=aph&AN=10388834&site=ehost-live

Hinojosa, P. (2005). Information security: Where we've been and where we need to go. *T H E Journal, 32*(7), 36-36. Retrieved June 27, 2007, from EBSCO Online Database Academic Search Premier. http://search.ebscohost.com/login.aspx?direct=true&db=aph&AN=16277356&site=ehost-live

Miller, D., & Toulouse, J. (1998) Quasi-rational organizational responses: Functional and cognitive sources of strategic simplicity. *Canadian Journal of Administrative Sciences 15*(3), 230-244. Retrieved June 25, 2007 from EBSCO Online Database Academic Source Premier. http://search.ebscohost.com/login.aspx?direct=true&db=bth&AN=1170310&site=ehost-live

Nicolaou, A. (2004). Firm performance effects in relation to the implementation and use of enterprise resource planning systems. *Journal of Information Systems, 18*(2), 79-105. Retrieved June 27, 2007, from EBSCO Online Database Academic Search Premier. http://search.ebscohost.com/login.aspx?direct=true&db=aph&AN=15672357&site=ehost-live

Oh, W. & Pinsonneault, A. (2007). On the assessment of the strategic value of information technologies: Conceptual and analytical approaches. *MIS Quarterly, 31*(2), 239-265.

Romano, P. (2002). Impact of supply chain sensitivity to quality certification on quality management practices and performances. *Total Quality Management, 13*(7), 981-1000. Retrieved July 2, 2007, from EBSCO Online Database Academic Search Premier. http://search.ebscohost.com/login.aspx?direct=true&db=aph&AN=7558650&site=ehost-live

Schwarzkopf, A., Mejias, R., Jasperson, J., Saunders, C., & Gruenwald, H. (2004). Effective practices for

IT skills staffing. *Communications of the ACM, 47*(1), 83-88. Retrieved June 27, 2007, from EBSCO Online Database Academic Search Premier. http://search.ebscohost.com/login.aspx?direct=true&db=aph&AN=12006238&site=ehost-live

Smyth, P. (2000). Data mining: Data analysis on a grand scale? Statistical Methods in Medical Research, 9(4), 309-327. Retrieved July 2, 2007, from EBSCO Online Database Academic Search Premier. http://search.ebscohost.com/login.aspx?direct=true&db=aph&AN=4166086&site=ehost-live

Vieira da Cunha, J. (2013). A dramaturgical model of the production of performance data. *MIS Quarterly, 37*(3), 723-748. Retrieved November 15, 2013, from EBSCO Online Database Business Source Complete. http://search.ebscohost.com/login.aspx?direct=true&db=bth&AN=89477783&site=ehost-live

SUGGESTED READING

Gerard, G.J., Grabski, S. (2002) International Lumberyards, Inc.: An information system consulting case. *Journal of Information Systems, 16*(2), 117-140.

Grant, G.G. (2003). Strategic alignment and enterprise systems implementation: The case of Metalco. *Journal of Information Technology, 18*(3), 159-165.

Cecez-Kecmanovic, D., Janson, M., & Brown, A. (2002). The rationality framework for a critical study of information systems. *Journal of Information Technology, 17*(4), 215-227.

Kettinger, W. J., Grover, V., Guha, S., Segars, A. H. (1994). Strategic information systems revisited: A study in sustainability and performance. *MIS Quarterly, 18*(1), 31-58.

Moynihan, T. (1990). What chief executives and senior managers want from their IT departments. *MIS Quarterly, 14*(1), 15-25.

Michael Erbschloe, M.A.

MANAGEMENT OF AN INSURANCE ENTERPRISE

ABSTRACT

The insurance industry is essential to the world economy and many companies offer coverage for a wide range of risks that people and businesses face everyday. From a consumer's perspective, the transaction may be as simple as paying a premium every month in exchange for the piece of mind of knowing that recovery from a loss is possible. Within a complex framework of government regulation, an insurance company must evaluate risks and assign probabilities to determine a price for the protection sought. They need to invest funds and even seek to insure their own risks with other insurers. The marketplace demands efficiency and insurance companies are turning to technology to address the need. This article discusses the basic components on an insurer's business model and the fundamental forces that affect the management of an insurance enterprise.

OVERVIEW

Risk in some form is present in every act. Whether the risk is remote or closer to assured, disasters both natural and otherwise have the potential to destroy fortunes. The prospect of catastrophic loss can halt progress. Insurance companies address these concerns by spreading the economic impact of a loss over a large group of people. The products they provide are essential to the normal operation of our non-agrarian society. The insurance industry in the United States is composed of some four thousand companies that sell policies to protect against a wide variety of the risks faced by individuals, organizations and entities alike. The industry is also important to the economy as an employer of over two million people. This article discusses some of the major functions, challenges and techniques unique to the management of an insurance company.

Businesses have many basic functions and principles in common. Every business must produce something of value to the market, employ techniques to sell that product, and manage human resources with the appropriate knowledge, skills and abilities to complete the tasks. Each industry has a particular group of core efficiencies necessary for production and distribution to profit from its chosen product line. For example, General Motors, on a fundamental level, must be able to efficiently produce cars at a cost below the price a consumer is willing to pay for those cars. While there are certainly many other factors that determine the success of a company, it would be difficult to imagine a successful company that lacked expertise and efficiency in those areas fundamental to its nature. For an insurance company, the basic model to generate revenue involves two areas; underwriting and investing. The cost of administration and the total amount of claims paid are subtracted from the revenue centers to form the basic insurer business model. To employ this basic model, the insurance industry must operate within a legal framework of state and federal laws and regulation (Encyclopedia of Business & Finance, 2008).

An insurance company can make money in two basic ways.

- First, the insurance company can profit from underwriting. When an insurance company underwrites a risk they assume responsibility for an agreed amount of economic consequences arising from the occurrence of certain events. The premiums earned are applied toward potential profit once they become earned premiums. The amount of premium that is considered earned is a function of the time the insurance company has been exposed to loss under a given policy. For example, if a person purchases a one-year policy and 100 days have elapsed since the policy took effect, the insurance company has earned 100/365 of the total premium paid. Conversely, 265/365 of the premium paid is unearned. An insurance company makes an underwriting profit when the total of earned premiums exceeds the total claims under those policies.
- Second, there insurance company makes money by investing the premiums they receive. Insurance companies invest insurance premium payments as soon as they are received and leave those funds invested until claims are paid. The total amount of cash that an insurance company has on hand and not paid out in claims is called "float," or available reserve. While the company may not be able the keep the investments themselves, they are able to keep the interest that accrued on the funds while in the company's possession. For this reason, insurance companies are important investors in the economy, putting billions of dollars in credit and equity markets. The profits made from investing the "float" are an important source of income for insurance companies and can offset underwriting losses.

The other end of the business equation for an insurance company is largely composed of the underwriting administrative expense and losses incurred. The full equation in total profit earned by an insurance company is the underwriting profit plus the investment income less the losses incurred, or claims paid, and the underwriting expenses. Insurance company mangers have to apply this business model within a highly regulated industry, at both state and federal levels. Each of these areas will be discussed in more detail.

Underwriting

Underwriting is at the heart of the insurance business and it is likely the most difficult part of the business. An insurance policy distributes the economic losses arising from a specific type of risk to a group of people. The term derives from the times when the person assuming the risk actually signed their name on the contract under the risk assumed. In modern usage, it refers to a party who has assumed risk under an insurance policy. The term is also commonly used in investment banking and in that context; the underwriter assumes the risk of the sale of particular securities.

Underwriting is the assumption of a risk; the decision as to assume a particular risk involves a process of quantifying risks and then assigning a price for the assumption. That quantification is a prediction about the claims that will be made under a policy and pricing of the policies accordingly. To perform this prediction, insurers use actuarial science. Actuarial science is a formal mathematical discipline used to calculate the likelihood and frequency of occurrence of covered risks and therefore the funds required to provide the anticipated insurance benefits. For those interested in mathematics and statistics, many universities offer both undergraduate and graduate degree programs in the area.

The discipline uses a number of related fields, including probability, statistics, finance and economics. An actuary analyzes a variety of data to determine the range and probability of the range of risks associated with a covered event and to calculate an insurer's overall exposure under a given policy. For example, mortality rates are important to compute risks and premiums for a life insurance policy. When an insurance company terminates a particular insurance policy the amount of total premiums collected (the earned premium less the administrative expense and total claims paid) equal the underwriting profit for that policy. Insurance companies make money on some policies and lose on others.

After the insurance company assumed risks and paid claims, the measure used to compute and report its profit or loss is called the combined ratio. This ratio is a relationship between income from premiums, claims paid, administrative expenses and dividends distributed. A ratio under 1.00 indicates a profit and a ratio over 1.00 indicates a loss. For example, a combined ratio of .97 means the insurance company made a 3% underwriting profit and a ratio of 1.15 indicates a loss of 15%. The percentages refer to a percentage of each dollar received in premiums; in the above example, a loss of three cents and gain of fifteen cents for each dollar of premium paid. This ratio is reported on company financial statements and to government regulatory agencies.

Underwriting profits vary according to internal company actuarial predictions and actual events. For example, natural disasters, as in the case of a hurricane or earthquake can cause significant claims of which insurance companies are bound to pay. Other times, underwriting may be profitable. Between 1998 and 2003, property and casualty insurers lost over 140 billion; while in the first quarter of 2005, the same sector reported record underwriting profits of over $7 billion on a combined ratio of approximately .92 ("P/C underwriting," 2005).

Investing

The investing income is very important to the overall profitability of an insurance company. In the United States for five years ending in 2003, property and casualty insurance companies had an underwriting loss of approximately $140 billion. However, for that same period, insurance companies reported profits of over $68 billion. These profits were made on investing the float and are dependent upon the condition of the financial markets. Profits derived from the float may be difficult to maintain during times of economic depression; poor economic conditions generally translate to high insurance premiums. The general tendency for insurance profits to fluctuate over time is commonly referred to as the underwriting or insurance cycle. For property and casualty insurers, property losses due to natural disasters cause volatility in the cycle. On the other hand, automobile lines tend to be more profitable due to reliable statistics that are greatly aided by advances in computer technology.

Underwriting Expenses & Claims Handling

From the perspective of the customer, claims handling is the critical function of an insurance company. When a customer suffers a loss, they want to be compensated with all possible speed. From the perspective of the insurance company, mangers must balance the customer's expectations of rapid resolution and satisfaction with administrative expenses, overpayment leakages and fraudulent insurance practices. To satisfy the needs of speed and reliability, insurance companies turn to technology deployed both in the field and over the internet. A range of portable communication technology can be deployed in the field so that adjusters may assess and process claims more rapidly and efficiently than ever before. An adjuster armed with a laptop computer, portable printer, and scanner can evaluate a claim and enter information directly into the insurance company's system without the need for duplicate work, as is the case with paper forms. Once the adjuster has completed the evaluation, they can then print the estimate and issue a check on-site.

The internet also offers the insurance company an opportunity for increased efficiency; both in terms of data entry and accuracy. Once information is entered on a website and added to an insurance company's database, it is unlikely that information need ever be reentered. The internet also allows a greater degree of control over the type and amount of data entered. A website can be programmed to insist on certain information of a particular form and react to information by leading the consumer to additional information that may be required or beneficial; paper lacks these dynamic qualities.

Insurance companies may then pass on the savings from increased efficiency to the consumer in the form of lower premiums and increased customer service, which help business. Management techniques and systems of this kind are employed by individual companies for their own benefit. However, that does not mean that insurance companies are alone; insurance companies share risk through a practice called reinsurance.

Reinsurance

The fundamental purpose and defining feature of insurance is the distribution of risks over a large base. For example, the costs of a car accident suffered by one insured are spread to all insured paying premiums under the policy. The same principle applies to insurance companies who spread risks to other companies with the use of reinsurance. Reinsurance is when one insurance company assumes all or part of a risk already undertaken by another insurance company. The portion of the risk that exceeds the primary insurance company's coverage is said to have been layed-off, or ceded, to the reinsurer. Reinsurers may also reinsure a part of the risk assumed from the primary insurer. This practice is called retroceding.

Reinsurance is an important tool for managers because it allows for increased capacity, stability and financial strength. With reinsurance, an insurance company may assume large risks that it would otherwise not be able. Reinsurance increases stability because it allows a company to make accurate predictions as to potential future liability. Reinsurance is also important to consumers seeking significant coverage because it allows them to deal with one company as opposed to shopping around. Reinsurance unifies the insurance industry around the globe and losses incurred in one can be felt in many other places. For example, Western Europe is an important source of worldwide reinsurance and the Caribbean is an important foreign source for the United States.

Regulation & Control

The insurance industry is governed by a blend of statutes, administrative agency regulations, and court decisions at both the state and federal levels. State laws typically seek to protect insureds by controlling premium rates, preventing unfair insurer practices, and guarding against the financial insolvency of insurers. Federal law permits states to exercise regulatory control over insurance; provided state laws and regulations do not conflict with federal antitrust laws on rate fixing, rate discrimination, and monopolies.

Most states have created agencies to administer state statutes and promulgate rules to address procedural details that are missing from the statutory framework. As an initial matter, to do business within a state, an insurer must register and obtain a license from that state. The registration process is usually managed by the same state administrative agency charged with the responsibility of enforcing the statute and developing rules and regulations. To carry out their enforcement responsibilities, administrative agencies develop a range of rules and regulations. For example, states may require reporting related to company financial stability, define acceptable types of policies, and review the competence and ethical standards of insurance company employees. All the regulations are designed and implemented to fulfill the goals of the consumer protection goals outlined in state statutes.

Legislatures pass laws that are often enforced and developed by agencies in the executive branch. Consistent with the doctrine of separation of powers built into our system of government, the judicial branch has the authority to review and interpret the activities and enactments of both legislatures and agencies. In this way, the courts have an important role in determining what the law means and how it applies to everyday life. Statutes and regulations attempt to control behavior in relatively broad areas and the application of those rules can be ambiguous, disputed or unfair when applied to a specific set of facts. In such a case, the parties often turn to the courts for resolution. When a court decides a dispute between an insurance company, insured, or third party, it must interprets statutes and regulations as applied to each case. Each of those interpretations becomes a precedent that will apply to future cases with similar facts. The sum of all court decisions is called case law. Case law is always changing in response to factual variations and insurance companies must be vigilant to ensure that their practices and policies are in accord with the current law in the states in which they operate.

Case law joins with statues and administrative regulations to form a comprehensive and complex set of controls on the insurance industry. Insurance companies in violation of the law may be fined or may have their license to do business suspended or revoked. Court's may impose significant costs and fees on insurance companies found to have unreasonably denied coverage or failed to defend their insured.

BIBLIOGRAPHY

Coyne, F. (2013). Getting to the efficient frontier. *Best's Review, 113*(12), 72. Retrieved November 15, 2013, from EBSCO Online Database Business Source Complete. http://search.ebscohost.com/login.aspx?direct=true&db=bth&AN=86701357&site=ehost-live

Federal and state legislative update. (2007). *Journal of Insurance Regulation,* 26(1), 123-131. Retrieved January 26, 2008, from EBSCO Online Database Business Source Premier. http://search.ebscohost.com/login.aspx?direct=true&db=buh&AN=28339235&site=ehost-live

Hofmann, M. (2007). Washington heavyweights have shaped insurance industry. *Business Insurance, 41*(41), 35-35. Retrieved January 26, 2008, from EBSCO Online Database Business Source Premier. http://search.ebscohost.com/login.aspx?direct=true&db=buh&AN=27141366&site=ehost-live

Hofmann, M.A. (2013). Winning ways. *Business Insurance, 47*(20), S008. Retrieved November 15, 2013, from EBSCO Online Database Business Source Complete. http://search.ebscohost.com/login.aspx?direct=true&db=bth&AN=91519065&site=ehost-live

Insurance. (n.d.). *Encyclopedia of Business and Finance.* Retrieved January 08, 2008, from Answers.com Web site: http://www.answers.com/topic/insurance

Kawai, Y., & Windsor, P. (2013). The globalisation of insurance: A supervisory response. *Journal of Risk Management in Financial Institutions, 6*(2), 151-159. Retrieved November 15, 2013, from EBSCO Online Database Business Source Complete. http://search.ebscohost.com/login.aspx?direct=true&db=bth&AN=86738327&site=ehost-live

P/C underwriting profits up during first quarter. (2005). *Insurance Advocate, 116*(16), 30. Retrieved January 25, 2008, from EBSCO Online Database Business Source Premier. http://search.ebscohost.com/login.aspx?direct=true&db=buh&AN=17822019&site=ehost-live

Souter, G. (2000). Internet changing face of personal lines sales. *Business Insurance, 34*(34), 12F. Retrieved December 22, 2007, from EBSCO Online Database Business Source Premier. http://search.ebscohost.com/login.aspx?direct=true&db=buh&AN=3571849&site=ehost-live

Underwrite. (n.d.). *West's Encyclopedia of American Law.* Retrieved January 25, 2008, from Answers.com Web site: http://www.answers.com/topic/underwrite

Underwrite. (n.d.). *Dictionary of Finance and Investment Terms.* Retrieved January 25, 2008, from Answers.com Web site: http://www.answers.com/topic/underwrite

SUGGESTED READING

Actually, I'm an actuary. (2007). *Career World,* 36(3), 5. Retrieved January 25, 2008, from EBSCO Online Database Business Source Premier. http://search.ebscohost.com/login.aspx?direct=true&db=aph&AN=27330267&site=ehost-live

Insurance regulation is broken, needs fixing. (2007). *Business Insurance,* 41(25), 8. Retrieved January 26, 2008, from EBSCO Online Database Business Source Premier. http://search.ebscohost.com/login.aspx?direct=true&db=buh&AN=25564470&site=ehost-live

Rappaport, A. (1999). Life insurance assets will grow faster than policies in force. *Best's Review / Life-Health Insurance Edition, 100*(7), 31. Retrieved January 25, 2008, from EBSCO Online Database Business Source Premier. http://search.ebscohost.com/login.aspx?direct=true&db=buh&AN=25002459&site=ehost-live

Seth M. Azria, J.D.

MANAGEMENT OF FINANCIAL INSTITUTIONS

ABSTRACT

This article focuses on the management of financial institutions. It provides an overview of the main management strategies used in financial institutions, including activity-based costing, asset-liability management, profitability analysis, risk management, technology and information management, crisis management, and issues management. The management issues associated with federal and state regulation of financial institutions are addressed.

OVERVIEW

Financial institutions, which move money throughout society in both complex and simple financial transactions, include banks, credit unions, thrifts, savings associations, trust companies, offices of foreign banks, and issuers of travelers checks and money orders. The success and strength of financial institutions depends in large part on their effective management. Management refers to the work or act of directing and controlling a group of people within an organization for the purpose of accomplishing shared goals or objectives. Classic management, as defined by Henri Fayol and Frederick Taylor, consists of five main functions, roles, or actions: Planning, organizing, leading, coordinating, and controlling. Management theory, practice, and scholarship are characterized by a focus on issues of leadership, group dynamics, and employee motivation.

Managers in financial institutions must respond to new technologies, new organizational models, the economic forces of globalization, and increased diversity in the workforce. Modern financial institutions, responding to new technology, increased competition, and changes in trade regulations around the world, are transitioning from hierarchical and centralized forms to group-model and decentralized organizations. In response to the new forms of business organizations, such as large-scale financial institutions, high-tech companies and multinational corporations, management has evolved its skill set to include greater facility for managing change, information, and human differences.

Financial institutions face unique management concerns and challenges due to the degree of government regulation within the financial industry. The management of financial institutions is a complex process involving management sectors of accounting, investment, human resources, and risk assessment. Common management practices used in financial institutions include account-balance costing, asset-liability management, profitability analysis, information management, crisis management, issues management, technology and information management, and risk management. The management of financial institutions has changed significantly since the 1970s. Changes in the following areas have affected management practices in financial institutions: Regulation and deregulation, product diversification, and industry convergence (Kafafian, 2001).

- Regulation and deregulation: The financial industry has undergone significant periods of regulation and deregulation since the 1970s when interest rate limits and geographic quota restrictions were ended. The government regulatory agencies vie for control over regulatory issues such as consumer privacy, merchant banking, community reinvestment, and consumer disclosure.
- Product diversification: The diversification of financial products, particularly traditional banking products, began in the 1970s as a result of regulatory changes. The Gramm-Leach-Bliley Financial Modernization Act, passed in 1999, increased the financial products and services available to consumers in the areas of brokerage, trust, money management, insurance, credit cards, and securitization. The Gramm-Leach-Bliley Financial Modernization Act replaced earlier laws that had prohibited financial institutions from engaging in insurance and investment activities. The Gramm-Leach-Bliley Financial Modernization Act resulted in the creation of numerous commercial and full service banking and financial service institutions. Financial institutions are currently working to adapt the products and services they offer to the needs of their customers. Internet banking has expanded the products and services that financial institutions offer and consumers expect.
- Industry convergence: Financial institutions, such as banks, brokerage firms, money managers, insurance companies, insurance agencies, and data processing vendors, are consolidating their business domains. For example, there are fewer banks in operation than there were in the 1970s. The financial industry is in flux as once discrete businesses attempt to combine operations, product offerings, markets, customers, and internal employee cultures.

In the United States, and developed nations in general, financial institutions facilitate economic growth through lending, savings, and commerce. The early history of formal financial institutions in the United States established the pattern of connection between the health of financial institutions and the economy at large. In the 18th century, banks, life insurance companies, and trading companies were established in the United States. These financial institutions facilitated large-scale economic growth in the United States manufacturing industry, infrastructure, home ownership, business development, international trade, and market formation. Due to the importance of financial institutions for the economic and social health of the nation as a whole, the government actively regulates financial institutions. Clearly, the management practices of financial institutions, as well as the products and services offered by financial services, are scrupulously monitored and regulated by the government. The successful management of financial institutions has a significant impact and influence on the nation.

The following section provides an overview of the main management strategies used in financial institutions including activity-based costing, asset-liability management, profitability analysis, risk management, technology and information management, crisis management, and issues management. This section will serve as the foundation for later discussion of the ways in which management of federal institutions is influenced by state and federal regulations.

APPLICATIONS

Management Strategies in Financial Institutions

Management of financial institutions is a multifaceted endeavor involving the oversight and direction of human resources, accounting, investment, resource-allocation, production, research and design, and finance areas. Common management practices used in financial institutions include activity-based costing, asset-liability management, profitability analysis, risk management, technology and information management, crisis management, and issues management.

Activity-Based Costing

Activity-based costing is an accounting or finance-based management tool used in management accounting. Managers use activity based accounting to identify, describe, assign costs to, and report on operations. Activity-based costing is used in three main ways: a tool to aid strategic decision-making; a lens into the decision-making process; and a resource allocation mechanism. Activity-based costing facilitates strategic decision-making and cost reduction. It allows management to make decisions from an informed and objective basis (Rafiq & Garg, 2002).

Asset-Liability Management

Asset-liability management refers to a risk management practice used to make investment or disinvestment decisions and maintain the credit service ratio. The asset-liability management process generates graphical analysis, data analysis, and interest rate simulation for use in the budget making process. Asset liability management includes the important area of gap analysis. Gap analysis, a tool for comparing actual and potential performance, helps managers answer the following questions: Where are the fundamental mismatches of cash flows and maturities on the balance sheet? Does the institution have a positive or negative gap between actual and potential performance? What is the effect of interest rate changes on the profitability, viability, and safety and soundness of the corporation? Federal regulators require financial institutions to create and distribute a formal asset-liability management report for investors.

Profitability Analysis

Profitability analysis, often part of a larger project of cost-volume profitability analysis, is an analytical tool which compares the inner workings and profitability of a financial institution. Profitability analysis, which has applicability and uses in all areas of a financial institution, examines fund transfer pricing, capital assignment, and costing techniques to predict annual profitability by lines of business, organizational units, products, and customers. Federal regulators, lead by the Financial Accounting Standards Board, require financial institutions to create and distribute a formal profitability analysis report for investors which analyzes profit by categories such as business, geographies, product lines, and customers.

Risk Management

Risk management, which refers to the process of evaluating, classifying, and reducing risks to a level acceptable by stakeholders, is an established practice in financial institutions. Federal regulators require that financial institutions prepare and distribute comprehensive risk management reports to investors. Federal regulators have created risk category checklists which financial institutions can use to create risk management plans. For example, the Office of the Comptroller of the Currency (OCC) includes the following risk categories in their checklist: Credit, liquidity, interest rate, price, reputation, strategic, transaction, foreign exchange, and compliance risk. The Federal Reserve Bank (FRB) includes the following risk categories in their checklist: Credit, market, liquidity, reputation, legal, and operational risk (Kafafian, 2001).

Technology & Information Management

Technology and information management has changed significantly since the 1970s. The main areas of change include: Core technology of accounting and application systems; internal systems such as fax machines, e-mail, Internet access, local networks, remote accessibility, and technology training; external technologies including banking systems, ATMs, telephone banking, call centers, and Internet banking; and management information systems such as budgeting and planning; and data mining and mapping; and product, service and demographic analysis (Kafafian, 2001). Managers in financial institutions are responsible for information and knowledge management. Managers in modern organizations are increasingly applying information technologies (IT) to the problems and challenges of knowledge management (KM). Information technology helps organizations create knowledge management systems (KMS) that structure information storage, use, and distribution within an organization. Organizational knowledge management systems include elements such as data mining, learning tools, intranets, email, telecommunication and video-conferencing technologies, knowledge directories, decision support tools, expert systems, workflow systems, social network analysis tools, and knowledge codification tools. Knowledge management systems create searchable document repositories to support the digital storage, retrieval, and distribution of an organization's explicitly documented knowledge and information (Butler & Murphy, 2007).

Crisis Management

Financial institutions are vulnerable to organizational crisis, such as extortion, hostile takeover, product tampering, copyright infringement, security breach, bribery, information sabotage, sexual harassment, plant explosion, counterfeiting, and boycott. Organizational crisis refer to a low-probability, high-impact event that threatens the viability of the organization and is characterized by ambiguity of cause, effect, and means of resolution, as well as by a belief that decisions must be made swiftly. Organizational crisis management refers to a systematic attempt by organizational members with external stakeholders to avert crises or effectively manage those that do occur. An organization's crisis management framework or model for analyzing often includes the 4C frame of causes, consequences, caution, and coping.

- Causes refer to the immediate failures that triggered the crisis.
- Consequences refer to the immediate and long-term impacts.
- Caution refers to the measures taken to prevent or minimize the impact of a potential crisis.
- Coping refers to the measures taken to respond to a crisis that has already occurred.

Organizational crisis management effectiveness is demonstrated when potential crises are averted or when the major stakeholders of an organization believe that the success outcomes of short-term impacts outweigh the failure outcomes. Crisis management outcomes are often evaluated on a success-failure continuum based on the idea that all organizational crisis results in degrees of success and failure (Pearson & Clair, 1998).

Issues Management

Managers in financial institutions often face ethical issues that arise in the workings of their institution. Issues managers are responsible for integrating business decisions and ethical decisions. Strategies for handling ethical dilemmas in organizations involves the identification of issues, research, analysis, and the creation of responsive organization-wide policies. Issues management provides a framework for analysis of ethical dilemmas and situations that arise in the workplace. One of the main challenges of ethical issues management involves practical implementation of strategies and policies. Issues managers must match the degree of ethics formality to the style of organization. Issues managers may strengthen their ethical issues-management process by adopting a formal code of ethics for the organization and conducting issues-management meetings. Ethics statements articulate the values with which employees should make work-related decisions. In addition to an ethics code, issues managers may work with employees to evaluate work-related decision prior to making definitive and final decisions. This decision-making model is a less formal approach to ethical decision-making than an ethics code (Bowen, 2005).

Issues

Regulation of Financial Institution Management

The regulation of management practices in financial institutions occurs at the state and federal levels. State governments regulate financial institutions, and their management, as a means of ensuring a stable and growing economy. For example, in 2006, the Tennessee Department of Financial Institutions, which is a representative example of the state financial institutions office, was responsible for regulating 160 state-chartered banks, eight trust companies, three business and industrial development corporations, 118 credit unions, 849 industrial loan and thrift offices, 75 insurance premium finance companies, 1,591 mortgage companies, 573 check cashers, 1,484 deferred presentment services companies, 703 title pledge lenders and 57 money transmitters, and thousands of mortgage loan originators. The Tennessee Department of Financial Institutions oversees the state banking system, processes all financial institution related consumer complaints, offers education and outreach programs and generates state-level bank-related legislation.

There are six federal regulatory agencies that oversee the management of financial institutions: the Federal Reserve Board (FRB), the Federal Deposit Insurance Corporation (FDIC), the National Credit Union Administration (NCUA), the Office of the Comptroller of the Currency (OCC), and the Office of Thrift Supervision (OTS). The Consumer Financial Protection Bureau (CFPB) was opened in 2010 in response to the 2008 financial crisis that resulted from reckless practices by lending and investing institutions.

- The Federal Reserve Board: The Federal Reserve Board is the central bank of the United States created, by Congress in 1913, to strengthen the nation's monetary and financial system. The Federal Reserve regulates state member banks, bank holding companies, subsidiaries of bank holding companies, edge and agreement corporations, branches and agencies of foreign banking organizations operating in the United States and their parent banks, and institution-affiliated parties. The Federal Reserve Board has four self-described responsibilities: Conduct the nation's monetary policy by influencing money and credit conditions in the economy in pursuit of full employment and stable prices; supervise and regulate banking institutions to ensure the safety and soundness of the nation's banking and financial system and to protect the credit rights of consumers; maintain the stability of the financial system and containing systemic risk that may arise in financial markets; and provide financial services to the U.S. government, to the public, to financial institutions, and to foreign official institutions.
- The Federal Deposit Insurance Corporation: The Federal Deposit Insurance Corporation, created in 1933 in response to national financial instability of the 1920s and 1930s, regulates state non-member banks and insured branches of foreign banks. The Federal Deposit Insurance Corporation insures deposits in banks and thrift institutions for at least $100,000; identifies, monitors, and addresses risks to the deposit insurance funds; and limits the effect on the economy and the financial system when a bank or thrift institution fails. The Federal Deposit Insurance Corporation, which has an insurance fund of approximately $49 billion, insures more than $3 trillion of deposits in U.S. banks and thrifts. The Federal Deposit Insurance Corporation is the primary federal regulator of banks that are chartered by the states that do not join the Federal Reserve System.
- The National Credit Union Administration: The National Credit Union Administration regulates and supervises credit unions. Credit unions are non-profit financial institutions that are owned and operated entirely by its members and provide financial services for their members including savings and lending. The Federal Credit Union Act, passed in 1934, established the National Credit Union Administration and federally chartered credit unions in all states. The not-for-profit credit unions were originally established to promote savings and limit the potential for profit from profit-motivated lending arrangements.
- The Office of Thrift Supervision: The Office of Thrift Supervision is the federal agency responsible for chartering and supervising the thrift industry. Thrift associations refer to savings and loan associations, credit unions, or savings banks. The Office of Supervisory Operations, and The Office of Thrift Supervision as a whole, analyzes the financial marketplace to see how federal regulation affects the thrift industry. The Office of Thrift Supervision advises Congress on regulatory policies.
- The Office of the Comptroller of the Currency: The Office of the Comptroller of the Currency, established in 1863, charters, regulates, and supervises all national banks including national banks, federally chartered branches, and agencies of foreign banks. The Office of the Comptroller of the

Currency performs the following functions: Examines the banks; approves or denies applications for new charters, and branches; takes supervisory actions against banks that do not comply with laws and regulations; removes officers and directors, negotiates agreements to change banking practices, and issues cease and desist orders as well as civil money penalties; and issue rules and regulations governing bank investments and lending. The Office of the Comptroller of the Currency is directed by the Comptroller, a presidentially-appointed position, for a five-year appointment.
- The Consumer Financial Protection Bureau (CFPB) Created by the Dodd-Frank Wall Street Reform and Consumer Protection Act of 2010, the Consumer Financial Protection Bureau (CFPB) has broad authority. The CFPB issues regulations under a number of consumer protection laws and has supervisory and enforcement authority over financial institutions with assets over $10 billion, including banks, savings associations, credit unions, consumer mortgage companies, payday lenders, and private college loan servicers (Mogilnicki & Malpass, 2013).

In addition to the regulatory efforts and powers of individual agencies, there are interagency commissions that oversee the management of financial institutions. The regulatory agencies come together in formal and informal ways to coordinate their policies and approaches. The Federal Financial Institutions Examination Council (FFIEC) established in 1979, is an example of a formal collaboration. The Federal Financial Institutions Examination Council is a formal interagency body with the power to develop uniform principles, standards, and report forms for the federal examination of financial institutions by the Board of Governors of the Federal Reserve System, the Federal Deposit Insurance Corporation, the National Credit Union Administration, the Office of the Comptroller of the Currency, and the Office of Thrift Supervision. In addition, the Federal Financial Institutions Examination Council is empowered to make recommendations to promote uniformity in the supervision of financial institutions.

CONCLUSION

In the final analysis, management consists of five main functions, roles, or actions: Planning, organizing, leading, coordinating, and controlling.

- Planning refers to management forecasting, strategizing, and deciding what needs to happen in the future.
- Organizing involves making efficient use of human and material resources.
- Leading refers to motivating, commanding and exhibiting skills to inspire and lead employees.
- Coordinating refers to unifying and harmonizing all organizational activity and effort.
- Controlling involves monitoring and checking employee performance for conformity and uniformity.

The management of financial institutions involves these five management functions as well as additional management functions specific to financial institutions. The management of financial institutions differs from the management of other types of institutions in the degree of government oversight and regulation. Financial institutions operate under a high degree of risk due to the effect that their operations have on the health and strength of the economy in general. Managers of financial institutions use a variety of management approaches and practices, including activity-based costing, asset-liability management, profitability analysis, risk management, technology and information management, crisis management, and issues management, to promote stability and growth in their institutions and the economy at large.

Bibliography

About the FFIEC. (2007). The Federal Financial Institutions Examination Council. Retrieved September 6, 2007, from http://www.ffiec.gov/default.htm

Basic tenets of performance management in financial institutions. (2005). *Journal of Performance Management, 18*(2), 17-21. Retrieved September 6, 2007, from EBSCO Online Database Business Source Premier. http://search.ebscohost.com/login.aspx?direct=true&db=buh&AN=18930678&site=ehost-live

Bowen, S. (2005). A practical model for ethical decision making in issues management and public relations. *Journal of Public Relations Research, 17*(3), 191-216. Retrieved September 6, 2007, from EBSCO Online Database Business Source Complete. http://search.ebscohost.com/login.aspx?direct=true&db=bth&AN=17408195&site=ehost-live

Butler, T., & Murphy, C. (2007). Understanding the design of information technologies for knowledge management in organizations: a pragmatic perspective. *Information Systems Journal, 17*(2), 143-163. Retrieved September 6, 2007, from EBSCO Online Database Business Source Complete. http://search.ebscohost.com/login.aspx?direct=true&db=bth&AN=23983454&site=ehost-live

Department resources. (2007). Tennessee Department of Finncial Instituions. Retrieved September 6, 2007, from http://www.tennessee.gov/tdfi/

Garg, A., & Rafiq, A. (2002). Using activity-based costing to improve performance. *Bank Accounting & Finance, 15*(6), 5. Retrieved September 6, 2007, from EBSCO Onlien Database Business Source Premier. http://search.ebscohost.com/login.aspx?direct=true&db=buh&AN=7582239&site=ehost-live

Is US structured finance facing reform overkill? (2004, July). *International Financial Law Review,* 1.

Jednak, D., & Jednak, J. (2013). Operational risk management in financial institutions. *Management (1820-0222), (66),* 71-80. Retrieved November 15, 2013, from EBSCO Online Database Business Source Complete. http://search.ebscohost.com/login.aspx?direct=true&db=bth&AN=87684579&site=ehost-live

Kafafian, R. (2001). Keys to community bank success: Utilizing management information to make informed decisions-fundamental movements. *The Journal of Bank Cost & Management Accounting, 14*(1), 5-11.

McCormally, B. C., Allen, C. L., & Mayer, H. E. (2012). Navigating the evolving risk management landscape: Considerations for financial institutions. *Journal of Taxation & Regulation Of Financial Institutions, 26*(1), 43-51. Retrieved November 15, 2013, from EBSCO Online Database Business Source Complete. http://search.ebscohost.com/login.aspx?direct=true&db=bth&AN=84617102&site=ehost-live

Mogilnicki, E. J., & Malpass, M. S. (2013). The first year of the consumer financial protection bureau: An overview. *Business Lawyer, 68*(2), 557-570. Retrieved November 15, 2013, from EBSCO Online Database Business Source Complete. http://search.ebscohost.com/login.aspx?direct=true&db=bth&AN=87117574&site=ehost-live

Oldfield, G., & Santomero, A. (1997). Risk management in financial institutions. *Sloan Management Review, 39*(1), 33-46. Retrieved September 6, 2007, from EBSCO Online Database Business Source Premier. http://search.ebscohost.com/login.aspx?direct=true&db=buh&AN=9712194811&site=ehost-live

Pearson, C., & Clair, J. (1998). Reframing crisis management. *Academy of Management Review, 23*(1), 59-76. Retrieved Thursday, March 22, 2007, from EBSCO Online Database Business Source Complete. http://search.ebscohost.com/login.aspx?direct=true&db=bth&AN=192960&site=ehost-live

Rafiq, A. & Garg, A. (2002). Activity based costing and financial institutions: Old wine in new bottles or corporate panacea? *The Journal of Bank Cost & Management Accounting, 15*(2), 12-30.

Raihall, D. & Hrechak, A. (1994). Improving financial institution performance through overhead cost management. *The Journal of Bank Cost & Accounting, 7*(1), 44.

Suggested Reading

Preble, J. (1993). Crisis management of financial institutions. *American Business Review, 11*(1), 72. Retrieved September 6, 2007, from EBSCO Online Database Business Source Premier. http://search.ebscohost.com/login.aspx?direct=true&db=buh&AN=5632288&site=ehost-live

Robb, S. (1998). The effect of analysts' forecasts on earnings management in financial institutions. *Journal of Financial Research, 21*(3), 315. Retrieved September 6, 2007, from EBSCO Online Database Business Source Premier. http://search.ebscohost.com/login.aspx?direct=true&db=buh&AN=1178402&site=ehost-live

Wee, L., & Lee, J. (2000). Seven challenges to implementing shareholder value management. *Bank Accounting & Finance (Euromoney Publications PLC), 13*(3), 7. Retrieved September 6, 2007, from EBSCO Online Database Business Source Premier. http://search.ebscohost.com/login.aspx?direct=true&db=buh&AN=3185550&site=ehost-live

Simone I. Flynn, Ph.D.

Management of Human Resources

ABSTRACT

The management of human resources has undergone much transformation over the past decades, due to changes in markets, industry, technology, costs, workforce, and employer-employee relationships. The management of human resources is no longer restricted to a single department: it is now a shared responsibility across organizations. In an era of heightened competition, firms are turning to innovative human resource practices for competitive advantage, and human resource policies and practice are increasingly integrated with business strategy, both domestically and internationally.

OVERVIEW

People are the most important asset of every organization. This is especially true in the twenty-first century's challenging business environment, where human resources are seen as an indispensable input for organizational effectiveness. Since there is a strong relationship between the quality of human resources and the performance and success of an organization, organizations the world over are now striving for effective management of their human resource base.

The management of human resources has evolved in several phases over the twentieth and into the twenty-first century. As an occupation or a department within an organization, this area first came to light between the first and second world wars, under the term "human relations." Subsequently, as trade unions became increasingly powerful in the middle of the century, the term "industrial relations" became popular. The terms "personnel administration" and "personnel management," together with the less popular "employee relations" and "manpower management" emerged in the late 1960s and 1970s, due to the growing complexity of employment law, and ongoing concern about trade unions.

At the time, the management of people in organizations was seen to be the responsibility of the personnel function. As the personnel function grew in scope and importance, monopolizing the management of people, those in managerial and supervisory positions were left with little to do when it came to such activities as the acquisition, development and compensation of human resources; the design of work systems; and labor relations. At the same time, because personnel specialists were increasingly concerned with rules and regulations and were mainly seen as preoccupied with problem-solving, they were often left out of the strategic thinking of their firms.

The 1980s presented new challenges for business organizations. In an era of increasing competition, as the global playing field became far more competitive and volatile than ever before, firms had to strive to gain competitive advantage whenever and wherever possible. Business was also changing at a much faster rate and this was accompanied by high uncertainty.

As a result of rising costs and increasing competitive pressures on profit margins, firms also realized the need to be more cost-effective. Trade union power declined, and the "me" generation emerged, with its emphasis on individualism. There were also changes in organization structure, as firms decentralized responsibility to business units built around products and markets to get closer to their customers. Organizations became flatter, leaner, and more flexible.

The technological revolution also posed great challenges for businesses, with innovations such as the introduction of information technology and computer-integrated manufacturing, which led to issues that had to be managed 'across' the organization and which themselves called for a more integrated view of the organization. The accelerated pace of new product development also meant that people in different functions such as design, marketing, production and finance had to work much more closely together than before. Rapid technological change also led to increased demands for new skills through sourcing, educating, and retraining.

In addition, workforce values were changing: the higher proportion of better-educated "knowledge workers" were increasingly likely to demand self-actualization, causing greater attention to be paid to such issues as communications, participation and motivation. Firms in countries with aging populations faced the extra challenge of limited availability of labor, amid a shrinking workforce. Thus, a premium was placed on the recruitment and retention of high quality employees.

In general, the firms that survived or came on the scene after these changes, have been more complex in terms of products, location(s), technologies, business functions, customers and markets. These changes led to a change in the image and role of the personnel function, leading to another change in name to "Human Resource Management." At the same time, the management of human resources moved from a department function, to a shared responsibility among managers and non-managers, personnel or human resource directors, and line managers. In the highly competitive, internationalized business structure that emerged in the twenty-first century, human resource management became essential to gaining or retaining an edge on rivals (Anca-Ioana, 2013; Brauns, 2013).

APPLICATIONS

With the changes in image, role and name of the human resource management function, came a quest for a new kind of innovation, as firms recognized that the traditional sources and means of competitive advantage, such as capital, technology or location, had become less significant. Innovative human resource practices have now become one of the bases for competitive advantage—no longer as a matter of trend, but rather of survival.

Categories of Human Resource Practice

Agarwala (2003) has identified fourteen categories of human resource practice, highlighting examples of innovative practices for each:

1. Employee Acquisition

Employee acquisition refers to internal and external selection and recruitment of employees to jobs. It includes the hiring of temporary work assistance and the use of external consultants (Grønhaug and Nordhaug, 1992). Pre-acquisition tasks include planning and forecasting, job analysis, job evaluation, job design and work system design. The latter relates to how tasks and responsibilities in the firm are distributed among job incumbents and the degree to which sharp borderlines exist between jobs (Grønhaug and Nordhaug, 1992).

Employee acquisition tasks are best performed in the context of an organization's culture. All things being equal, selection should favor those candidates who appear to "fit in" with the prevailing organizational culture, be it a culture of empowerment, participation, equal opportunity, and/or any one of the many other facets of culture.

Innovative employee acquisition strategies include (Agarwala, 2003):

- greater importance attached to the fit between person and company culture
- emphasis on "career," not "job"
- selling company image to attract potential employees
- referral bonuses
- sign-on bonuses for new employees
- psychological testing
- developing industry-academia interface

2. Employee Retention Strategies

Employee retention refers to the measures put in place to keep employees in an organization, thus reducing the labor turnover rate.

Innovative employee retention strategies include (Agarwala, 2003):

- evolving a pleasant work environment
- deferred compensation
- competitive salaries
- faster promotions
- greater work autonomy

3. Compensation and Incentives

Compensation includes the whole range of rewards and incentives that are applied in relation to employees. Intrinsic rewards are those that are internal to a person, such as job satisfaction and self-esteem; extrinsic rewards are more tangible, and range from wages to employee stock ownership plans (Grønhaug and Nordhaug, 1992). Compensation must be managed, along with employee attitudes towards compensation. Incentives are those offerings that have a tendency to motivate employees to will or to act as the organization desires.

Innovative compensation and incentive strategies include (Agarwala, 2003):

- increasing the component of variable pay
- stock options
- combining individual and team incentives
- performance-linked incentives

- customization of perks to individual needs
- offering a variety of allowances
- conducting compensation surveys

4. Benefits and Services

Similar to compensation and incentives, benefits and services may form part of an employee's remuneration package, and may include medical care, loans, travel, accommodation, catering, and so on. Many employers, for instance, offer Employee Assistance Programs, which are employee benefit programs typically offered in conjunction with a health insurance plan. Such Employee Assistance Programs aim to help employees handle personal problems so that they do not negatively impact their work ability, health, or well-being. These programs usually include assessment, short-term counseling and referral services for employees and their household members.

Innovative benefits and services strategies include (Agarwala, 2003):

- a focus on long-term benefits for employees through alternative insurance and health management schemes
- giving benefits directed at employees' families
- flexible employee benefits or the cafeteria approach, where employees choose from a menu of benefits
- child and elder care programs
- Improvements in retirement benefits

5. Rewards and Recognition

Rewards and recognition are used to encourage and motivate an organization's employees, and effective reward management will promote consistency of practice in this area.

Innovative rewards and recognition strategies include (Agarwala, 2003):

- performance-linked rewards
- flexible rewards
- cash rewards for extraordinary performance
- rewarding team performance
- rewarding team performance
- public recognition of good performance at a company meeting or function
- recognition from co-workers
- a blend of financial and non-financial rewards

6. Technical Training

Human resource development concerns the maintenance, refinement and advancement of competencies possessed by the firm's employees (Grønhaug and Nordhaug, 1992). Technical training refers to training for specific competence on the job, with regard to technology and/or business process change. Training may take place on-the-job or outside the workplace.

Innovative technical training strategies include (Agarwala, 2003):

- systematic training needs assessment
- cross-functional training
- providing job relevant training
- facilitating transfer of training to actual job performance

7. Management Development

The effectiveness of management is recognized as one of the determinants of organizational success, and investment in management development can have a direct economic benefit to organizations, since management development helps to develop leadership, supervision and control.

Innovative management development strategies include (Agarwala, 2003):

- linking management development to individual needs
- linking management development to organizational objectives
- using innovative management development methods, like stress management programs
- adventure training
- leadership and attitudinal training
- study leave

8. Career Planning and Development

Career planning and development refer to the assistance given to employees, to help them plan for, execute and manage their career development within an organization. Some organizations may link the career progress of their members to succession planning.

Innovative career planning and development strategies include (Agarwala, 2003):

- developing career paths
- providing fast-track career plans
- providing mentors to employees

- cross-functional career paths
- providing mentors to employees
- career counseling

9. Performance Appraisals

Performance management is the process linking goal setting and rewards, coaching for performance, aspects of career development and performance evaluation and appraisal into an integrated process (Sparrow et al, 1994). Performance appraisals are a key component of performance management; they may seek to measure and motivate customer service, quality, innovation and risk-taking behavior.

Innovative performance appraisal strategies include (Agarwala, 2003):

- giving weight to individual, team and organizational performance while appraising
- using quantifiable criteria for appraisals
- participative appraisals
- open appraisals to increase transparency
- giving appraisal feedback
- linking rewards to appraisals
- 360-degree appraisals, where feedback comes from all around the employee: from subordinates, peers and managers in the organizational hierarchy, as well as a self-assessment, and in some cases external sources such as customers and suppliers or other interested stakeholders.

10. Potential Development

Potential development is a company-wide management development program that seeks to cultivate performance and leadership at the top of the organization, through the provision of the necessary training, support and opportunities.

Innovative potential development strategies include (Agarwala, 2003):

- job rotations
- use of assessment centers
- coaching
- conducting potential appraisals

11. Succession Planning

This is a management development program aimed at filling specific positions with one of two potential candidates.

Innovative succession planning strategies include (Agarwala, 2003):

- identifying replacements
- provision of fall-back positions in case of failure
- preparing to assume higher responsibility

12. Employee Relations

As firms seek to empower and include employees in the organization, they ought to treat their employees with concern through effective internal communication flows; enhancement of the quality of work life; good labor relations; and health, welfare and safety programs.

Innovative employee relations strategies include (Agarwala, 2003):

- information sharing
- open and transparent communication
- family get-togethers
- humanizing work environment
- respecting employees
- ensuring fairness in management practices
- encouraging risk-taking

13. Employee Exit and Separation Management

Employee exit and separation management refers to the planning, facilitation and management of the departure of employees from an organization. Exit and separation may be initiated by employees themselves; by the state, through retirement; or by firms conducting specific "decruitment" activities such as downsizing and skills reprofiling.

Innovative employee exit and separation management strategies include (Agarwala, 2003):

- extending benefits to retirees for lifetime
- retirement planning workshops for about-to-retire employees
- conducting exit interviews
- outplacement services
- voluntary retirement schemes

14. Corporate Responsibility

As their corporate responsibility, firms seek to recognize and incorporate aspects of the external environment such as the general quality of the labor force, legal regulations or concerns about environmental quality, and social responsibility. They also ensure an effective flow and sharing of information outside of the organization.

Innovative strategies for corporate responsibility include (Agarwala, 2003):

- adult education programs
- community development projects
- concern for greening and protection of the environment
- research promotion

When well planned and implemented, the 'right' combination of the above variables should lead to job satisfaction, motivation, employee commitment and participation for employees, and ultimately, competitive advantage for an organization.

Issues

As the management of human resources is seen increasingly in terms of competitive advantage, the question that arises is, what must be done to gain this advantage? The answer is: strategic business change, with human resource processes at its core.

Before the 1990s, attempts to coordinate human resource management with a firm's business strategy had taken one of three limited appoarches: correlating managerial style or personnel activities with strategies; predicting manpower requirements based on strategic objectives or environmental conditions, and discovering ways to assimilate human resource management into the comprehensive attempt to equalize strategy and structure (Lengnick-hall and Lengnick-hall, 1988).

Since the early 1990s, however, the call has been made to integrate the management of human resources with business strategy all the more. Rather than existing in a vacuum, the human resource activities in a firm are now expected to directly support business strategy and the satisfaction of customer needs.

The integration of the management of human resources with business strategy means that the management of human resources involves a wide variety of policies and procedures which are strategically significant for the organization and are typically used to promote employee commitment, flexibility, good quality of work life as well as to realize overall business goals such as organizational values, structure, productivity, and production techniques (Sparrow et al, 1994).

This has led to a concept in the management of human resources called "human resource strategy." This concept refers to the set of decisions or factors that shape and guide the management of human resources in an organizational context. It is also a set of strategic processes communally shared by human resources and line managers to resolve people-related business issues. It is directly related to the business strategy and focuses on the formulation and alignment of human resource activities to achieve organizational competitive objectives. Through human resource strategy, human resource management aims to increase value through issue identification, assessment, and resolution. The main issues targeted are those critical to the organization's viability and success. It is a more action-oriented strategy than traditional human resource planning.

Strategic human resource management works through many means, including the following:

- coordinating available resources with necessary staffing levels and abilities, through recruitment, selection, assignment, and other strategic staffing processes
- aligning individuals and groups with overall business objectives through the management of performance.
- developing needed capabilities and performance through training, education, and job-related learning
- enhancing the quality of management through an emphasis on management development
- bridging the gap between the strategic and the operational through the relationship between employee and line manager. The personnel or human resource management function advises the manager on how he/she can carry out these objectives, and line managers implement the strategic objectives of the organization through their leadership style and the way in which they manage their people.
- conducting human resource planning (predicting future business and environmental costs and generating the personnel requirements determined by those future conditions) as a key aspect of strategic planning. The resultant plans are strategic if they address significant change of direction—not merely continuity.

In the 2010s, companies such as Google and Netflix have been lauded as models of innovation in terms of human resources management. As of 2014, Google had become known for not only its more luxurious employee perks and benefits, but also for its use of data-based analytics in the hiring process and in maintaining more positive employee attitudes (Rafter, 2015). At the same time, Netflix had become famous for its agile approach to managing its workforce, including a dedication to hiring only the most qualified individuals, promoting open communication about employee performance rather than formal review processes, and maintaining a philosophy of treating employees maturely (McCord, 2014).

In the international arena, there has been a growing interest in international human resource management, as more markets internationalize, more nations become integrated into the international world economy, and more businesses choose to expand their operations across national borders. The increasing attention drawn to this area reflects the prevalence of the realization that efficient and effective human resource management internationally is a key factor in the success of a business. Evidence suggests that human resource constraints are often the limiting factor when attempting to implement international business strategies. Recently it has been argued that the fast pace of internationalization and globalization has led to a more strategic role for human resource management, and it also leads to changes in the content of human resource management (Scullion & Starkey, 2000).

It is important for multinational firms to know which human resource policies and practices they can consider using in their worldwide operations, to assist them in gaining competitive advantage. This leads to the questions whether different parts of the world practice human resource management for competitive advantage differently; and whether there is some uniformity that firms can pursue in their efforts to manage their worldwide workforces successfully.

International businesses are increasingly turning their attention to issues such as expatriate management, where employees are transferred by organizations to work outside their country of origin or permanent residence. Effective management in this area helps to reduce the early return of expatriates; to minimize disruption to international operations; and to prevent the situation where expatriates are not retained by the organization after completing their assignments. As it is believed that quality of management is more critical in the international arena than in domestic operations (Tung, 1984), international firms are also looking at the plethora of issues stemming from cross-cultural management, along with those issues surrounding the management of diversity in multicultural domestic workforces. As the pace of internationalization has accelerated, the need for cross-cultural awareness, cross-cultural sensitivity, and understanding the daily operations of international businesses, has become more salient. Academicians too have advanced understanding in these areas through the development of the distinct sub-field of International Human Resource Management, within the management discipline. Marler (2012), for example compares scholarship in the field from the United States, Germany and China, three countries with widely differing histories, economic and political systems, and business cultures.

Bibliography

Anca-Ioana, M. (2013). New approaches of the concepts of human resources, human resource management and strategic human resource management. *Annals of the University Of Oradea, Economic Science Series, 22,* 1520–1525. Retrieved October 31, 2013, from EBSCO Online Database Business Source Complete. http://search.ebscohost.com/login.aspx?direct=true&db=bth&AN=90545849&site=ehost-live

Agarwala, T. (2003). Innovative human resource practices and organizational commitment: an empirical investigation. *International Journal of Human Resource Management, 14,* 175–197. Retrieved March 08, 2007, from EBSCO Online Database Business Source Complete. http://search.ebscohost.com/login.aspx?direct=true&db=bth&AN=9629951&site=ehost-live

Brauns, M. (2013). Aligning strategic human resource management to human resources, performance and reward. *International Business & Economics Research Journal, 12,* 1405–1410. Retrieved October 31, 2013, from EBSCO Online Database Business Source Complete. http://search.ebscohost.com/login.aspx?direct=true&db=bth&AN=91752236&site=ehost-live

Camp, R. (1987). Managing human resources: productivity, quality of worklife, profits/Strategic human resource management: a guide for effective practice/Human resource management: a practical approach (Book). *Personnel Psychology, 40,* 128–133. Retrieved March 08, 2007, from EBSCO Online Database Business Source Complete. http://search.ebscohost.com/login.aspx?direct=true&db=bth&AN=6266152&site=ehost-live

Craft, J. (2005). Human resource strategy. *Blackwell Encyclopedic Dictionary of Human Resource Management.* Retrieved March 17, 2007, from EBSCO Online Database Business Source Complete. http://search.ebscohost.com/login.aspx?direct=true&db=bth&AN=14720676&site=ehost-live

De Cieri, H., Fenwick, M., & Hutchings, K. (2005). The challenge of international human resource management: balancing the duality of strategy and practice. *International Journal of Human Resource Management, 16,* 584–598. Retrieved March 08, 2007, from EBSCO Online Database Business Source Complete. http://search.ebscohost.com/login.aspx?direct=true&db=bth&AN=17132361&site=ehost-live

Grønhaug, K., & Nordhaug, O. (1992). International human resource management: an environmental perspective. *International Journal of Human Resource Management, 3,* 1–14. Retrieved March 08, 2007, from EBSCO Online Database Business Source Complete. http://search.ebscohost.com/login.aspx?direct=true&db=bth&AN=5824679&site=ehost-live

Handy, L., Barham, K., Panter, S., & Winhard, A. (1989). Beyond the personnel function: the strategic management of human resources. *Journal of European Industrial Training, 13,* 13–18. Retrieved March 08, 2007, from EBSCO Online Database Business Source Complete. http://search.ebscohost.com/login.aspx?direct=true&db=bth&AN=5225094&site=ehost-live

Lengnick-hall, C., & Lengnick-hall, M. (1988). Strategic human resources management: a review of the literature and a proposed typology. *Academy of Management Review, 13,* 454. Retrieved March 08, 2007, from EBSCO Online Database Business Source Complete. http://search.ebscohost.com/login.aspx?direct=true&db=bth&AN=4306978&site=ehost-live

Marler, J.H. (2012). Strategic human resource management in context: A historical and global perspective. *Academy of Management Perspectives, 26,* 6–11. Retrieved October 31, 2013, from EBSCO Online Database Business Source Complete. http://search.ebscohost.com/login.aspx?direct=true&db=bth&AN=79351873&site=ehost-live

McCord, P. (2014). How Netflix reinvented HR. *Harvard Business Review, 92*(1/2), 70–76. Retrieved December 4, 2015 from EBSCO Online Database Business Source Premier. http://search.ebscohost.com/login.aspx?direct=true&db=buh&AN=93302820&site=bsi-live

Rafter, M. V. (2015). Just Google him. *Workforce, 94*(4), 40–49. Retrieved December 4, 2015 from EBSCO Online Database Business Source Premier. http://search.ebscohost.com/login.aspx?direct=true&db=buh&AN=101804541&site=bsi-live

Schuler, R., & Walker, J. (1990). Human resources strategy: Focusing on issues and actions. *Organizational Dynamics, 19,* 4–19. Retrieved March 08, 2007, from EBSCO Online Database Business Source Complete. http://search.ebscohost.com/login.aspx?direct=true&db=bth&AN=9607245395&site=ehost-live

Scullion, H., & Starkey, K. (2000). In search of the changing role of the corporate human resource function in the international firm. *International Journal of Human Resource Management, 11,* 1061–1081. Retrieved March 08, 2007, from EBSCO Online Database Business Source Complete. http://search.ebscohost.com/login.aspx?direct=true&db=bth&AN=4219959&site=ehost-live

Sparrow, P., Schuler, R., & Jackson, S. (1994). Convergence or divergence: human resource practices and policies for competitive advantage worldwide. *International Journal of Human Resource Management, 5,* 267–299. Retrieved March 08, 2007, from EBSCO Online Database Business Source Complete. http://search.ebscohost.com/login.aspx?direct=true&db=bth&AN=5812654&site=ehost-live

Tung, R. (1984). Strategic management of human resources in the multinational enterprise. *Human Resource Management, 23,* 129–143. Retrieved March 08, 2007, from EBSCO Online Database Business Source Complete. http://search.ebscohost.com/login.aspx?direct=true&db=bth&AN=12617244&site=ehost-live

Walker, J. (1994). Integrating the human resource function with the business. *Human Resource Planning, 17,* 59–77. Retrieved March 08, 2007, from EBSCO Online Database Business Source

Complete. http://search.ebscohost.com/login.aspx?direct=true&db=bth&AN=9504251742&site=ehost-live

Walker, J. (2005). Strategic human resource planning. *Blackwell Encyclopedic Dictionary of Human Resource Management.* Retrieved March 08, 2007, from EBSCO Online Database Business Source Complete. http://search.ebscohost.com/login.aspx?direct=true&db=bth&AN=14720949&site=ehost-live

Warner, M. (1997). Review symposium: from human relations to human resources. *International Journal of Human Resource Management, 8,* 124–128. Retrieved March 08, 2007, from EBSCO Online Database Business Source Complete. http://search.ebscohost.com/login.aspx?direct=true&db=bth&AN=5819043&site=ehost-live

SUGGESTED READING

Agarwala, T. (2003). Innovative human resource practices and organizational commitment: an empirical investigation. *International Journal of Human Resource Management, 14,* 175–197. Retrieved March 08, 2007, from EBSCO Online Database Business Source Complete. http://search.ebscohost.com/login.aspx?direct=true&db=bth&AN=9629951&site=ehost-live

Armstrong, M. (2006). *A handbook of human resource management practice* (10th ed.). London: Kogan Page.

Noe, R. A. (2015). *Human resources management: Gaining a competitive advantage* (9th ed.). New York City, NY: McGraw-Hill Education.

Sparrow, P., Schuler, R., & Jackson, S. (1994). Convergence or divergence: human resource practices and policies for competitive advantage worldwide. *International Journal of Human Resource Management, 5,* 267–299. Retrieved March 08, 2007, from EBSCO Online Database Business Source Complete. http://search.ebscohost.com/login.aspx?direct=true&db=bth&AN=5812654&site=ehost-live

Vanessa A. Tetteh, Ph.D.

MANAGEMENT SCIENCE

ABSTRACT

Managers today are inundated by data. Often, the correct interpretation of these data can mean the difference between being on the cutting edge of a market and being left behind by the competition. To solve the complex business problems faced by organizations in the 21st century, managers are increasingly turning to management science - the application of statistical techniques, scientific method, and mathematical modeling - to analyze and solve the problems of the organization. Management science can help managers solve a wide range of problems in the workplace and to make better decisions concerning the operation and strategy of the business. Management science offers managers many tools to help analyze and interpret the data with which they are bombarded every day. Some of these tools include data mining, decision support systems, and forecasting techniques.

OVERVIEW

Management is the process of efficiently and effectively accomplishing work through the coordination and supervision of others. Effective management is much more than the effective application of such soft skills as management style, communication ability, and administrative prowess, however. Management also comprises the decisions that managers make to help gain or maintain a market share or to increase profitability within the marketplace. Although management decisions can be made subjectively based on a given manager's experience, the amounts of data that must be processed in order to do this well continue to increase with the proliferation of information technology and systems. As a result, managers are increasingly turning to management science — the application of statistical methods, scientific method, and mathematical modeling — to analyze and solve the problems of the organization.

21st Century Applications of Management Science

Management science has many practical applications in 21st century businesses. The use of probability theory, statistical techniques, and research methodology can help managers solve a wide range of problems in the workplace including optimizing cost/benefit tradeoffs in product design, improving the quality of services or products, forecasting the needs and trends of the marketplace, and improving the effectiveness of supply chain management. By applying mathematical statistical techniques to the real problems of the business world, managers can make better decisions concerning the operation and strategy of the business.

Management science allows organizations to apply scientific method in order to solve many problems in the business world. For example, descriptive statistics are useful in summarizing and describing data. In addition, management science also includes the application of business statistics to real world problems. This discipline is an applied form of mathematics and is a valuable tool for helping analyze and interpret data. In particular, the use of inferential statistics, a collection of techniques that allow one to make inferences about the data, including the ability drawing conclusions about a population from a sample.

Another tool of management science is building models, or the development of abstract representations of situations, systems, or subsystems. Model development typically occurs in two phases. First, a conceptual model is developed to describe the situation or system. Initial conceptual models tend to be broad or general representations without much detail but which span the range of variables to be considered. Models typically must be tested and refined until they represent the real world to the degree desired by the analyst or decision maker. Models are iteratively refined using observations of the real world so that they better reflect the underlying reality of the situaiton. When the conceptual model adequately reflects the major parameters of the real world, data can be gathered and quantitative techniques used to turn the conceptual model into a mathematical model.

APPLICATIONS

In the 21st century, human beings are constantly bombarded with data that need to be sorted, analyzed, and interpreted. In the business world, the correct interpretation of data can mean the difference between being on the cutting edge of a market or being left behind by the competition. Management science offers managers many tools to help analyze and interpret the data with which they are bombarded every day. Data mining allows managers to examine large amounts of data for previously unseen patterns and relationships in order to help forecast the future of an industry or the needs of a market. Decision support systems help managers make reasoned decisions about the semi-structured and unstructured problems with which they are faced every day. Forecasting uses statistical tools to recognize trends and patterns in the data and provides managers with the empirical data necessary to help shape the growth and focus of the organization.

Data Mining

Data mining is the process of analyzing large collections of data to establish patterns and determine previously unknown relationships between the data. The results of data mining efforts are used to predict future behavior. Data mining can be used to help the business better understand the needs and desires of current and potential customers and to identify and acquire high-value customers. The information produced by data mining efforts can also be used to optimize store layout for increased sales by shelving items that are frequently purchased together in close proximity. In addition, data mining can be used to increase the profitability of the store or chain, increase return on investment, decrease the costs of advertising and promotions, monitor performance of the store or business, and detect fraud, waste, and abuse. By detecting previously unrecognized patterns in data, data mining can help managers to make better decisions regarding business problems, develop novel approaches to meeting current organizational objectives, or create a more profitable strategic plan for the future of the organization.

Data Mining & Customer Relationship Management

Although data mining is used to examine the relationships within a wide variety of data across many disciplines, one of the primary uses of data mining in business is to find unknown relationships within sets of customer data. Among other things, data mining is frequently used in business for customer relationship management. This is the process of identifying prospective customers, acquiring data concerning these prospective and current customers, building relationships with customers, and influencing their perceptions of the organization and its products or services. For example, a data mining effort might examine the types of products purchased on line by owners of home computers. One source of data that is increasingly mined for information comes from retail scanners. The customer cards issued by various retail stores (e.g., supermarkets, pet supply stores, drug stores) that many people carry in their wallets that give them discounts or points toward rewards also can be used to collect information that is used in data mining efforts. For example, a grocery store might use data mining software to analyze the purchases made by consumers over the course of a week to determine what items are purchased together. For example, if the store finds that the purchases of fresh sweet corn fluctuate with the purchase of ribs during the summer, they might place pre-shucked corn next to the ribs in the refrigerated meat case. This knowledge would also help the store determine whether or not to purchase more corn for the weeks when ribs were on sale. Alternatively, data mining could be used by the store or chain to push other products. Grocery stores often issue customers coupons at the checkout counter or send them to customer homes based on what purchases they have made. For example, previous purchases of Brand X paper towels might result in the generation of a discount coupon for a future purchase of Brand X paper towels or for a future purchase of the store's brand of paper towels.

Data mining applications can be based on a number of different techniques. The most commonly used of these is classification, which is used to analyze data in a database and build a model to predict future behavior. Among the tools used in data classification are neural networks and decision trees. Neural networks are mathematical structures that are capable of learning. This technique is most effective when there is a large amount of data to be analyzed and the relationships between the data are either complex or imprecise. Decision trees are used to classify data into a limited number of classes. Decision trees classify data based on if-then statements and although they tend to be faster than neural nets, also are more appropriate to data with less complex relationships. Another approach to data mining is clustering. This technique subdivides the database into groups of records that share common traits. The structure of these clusters is unknown before the analysis begins. This means that the clusters usually need to be interpreted before they can be put into use in the real world. Data mining can also be done based on sequence discovery, or the establishment of relationships or associations between items over time. (For example, consumers who purchase maternity clothing this year are more likely than are those who do not to purchase diapers next year.)

Decision Support Systems

To help managers make the unique, complex decisions that frequently arise in today's businesses, many organizations use decision support systems. These are interactive computer-based systems that support managers in their decision making processes. Decision support systems help managers better understand the issues underlying the situation and to make decisions in situations where the extent to which certain variables influence the activity or outcome are not initially clear or only part of the information is available in advance (i.e., unstructured situations). To be of use in answering unstructured questions, decision support systems must be flexible so that the impact of various variables and conditions can be tested and the analysis be returned to the user in a form that is useful for the specific situation. In addition, unstructured problems typically require an iterative process: The answers to the questions are not ends in themselves, but raise other questions for consideration that need to be run through the decision support system.

Decision support systems can help managers by providing the information and structure needed to make a rational decision. A decision support system creates a quantitative model of the situation and then processes data to show the impact of the variables under consideration on the outcomes. Decision support systems can also help decision makers answer questions concerning conditions under which an outcome might occur, what might happen if the value of a variable changes, or how many potential customers have certain characteristics.

Types of Decision Support Systems

There are several different general types of decision support systems including model-driven systems, data-driven systems, knowledge-driven systems, and group support systems. Model-driven decision support systems use various financial, optimization, or simulation models as aids for managerial decision making. Data-driven decision support systems process time series data and access simple file systems using query and retrieval tools. More advanced data-driven systems allow the manipulation of data or analytical processing. Knowledge-driven systems are expert systems that frequently include the application of artificial intelligence to the decision making process. These decision support systems are person/computer systems with specialized problem solving abilities that can make suggestions or recommendations to the user.

Forecasting

Managerial science can also help managers forecast future requirements of the marketplace or the industry so that they can better position the organization to effectively compete and survive. Businesses frequently need to know the trends of the marketplace in order to best position themselves to leverage this knowledge into profits. For example, a production manager may need to know if there will be a continuing need for widgets and how much raw material is needed to meet the anticipated demand. A marketing manager may need to know whether changing demographics in the marketplace mean that a new marketing strategy will be needed. A shipping manager may need to know whether or not the price of oil will continue to rise and how this cost affects the outsourcing for the production of gizmos. A human resources manager may need to know whether or not the turnover in the organization will continue and if new sources of qualified employees need to be found. Managers can answers questions such as these through forecasting — the science of estimating or predicting patterns and variations about many aspects of the business including buying, selling, production, and hiring.

Causes of Variation in Economic Activity

Managers are interested in a number of causes of variation in economic activity: Trends, business cycles, and seasonal fluctuations as well as irregular and random fluctuations. Trends are persistent, underlying directions in which something is moving in either the short, intermediate, or long term. Many trends in established industries tend to be linear rather than cyclic, and steadily grow or shrink over a period of years. For example, in the US, there is an increasing trend towards the outsourcing and off-shoring of technical support and customer service in the high tech industry. Trends in new industries, on the other hand, tend to be curvilinear as the demand for the new product or service grows after its introduction then declines after the product or service becomes integrated into the economy.

Although managers can make forecasts subjectively based on experience or other factors, management science allows forecasts to be made based on quantitative analysis of data through the development of structural and economic models. Structural models are based on sets of mathematical functions designed to represent the causal relationships within the organization's environment. For example, before investing in a new venture, an organization might need to know the future price of its current product in order to forecast its profits and the resultant availability of funds for the new venture. Managers could be supported in this decision through the development of a specification model that contains the factors affecting the supply and demand for the current product and the relationship between these factors. Another approach to business forecasting is the use of deterministic models. This type of model assumes that the variable of interest is a deterministic function of time and does not include the effects of any underlying data uncertainty or variability in the time series. Forecasting can also be done based on *ad hoc* forecasting formulas developed from past history. This type of model typically uses weighted moving averages. Although this approach simplifies computation, there is no way to determine whether the formula chosen is the most appropriate. This means that there can be no concomitant confidence in the worth of the resultant forecasts. Forecasting can also be done through the use of time series analysis. Time series data are gathered on a specific characteristic over a period of time. To be useful, these data must be collected at intervals of regular length. As opposed to the *ad hoc* approach to forecasting (where it is impossible to tell whether or not the formula chosen is the most appropriate for the situation) in time series analysis, one can study the structure of the correlation of variables over time to determine the appropriateness of the model. The model can be refined as necessary to make it more representative of the real world situation.

BIBLIOGRAPHY

Black, K. (2006). *Business statistics for contemporary decision making* (4th ed.). New York: John Wiley & Sons.

Bruns, H. C. (2013). Working alone together: coordination in collaboration across domains of expertise. *Academy of Management Journal, 56*(1), 62-83. Retrieved November 15, 2013, from EBSCO Online Database Business Source Complete. http://search.ebscohost.com/login.aspx?direct=true&db=bth&AN=86645983&site=ehost-live

Lucas, H. C. Jr. (2005). *Information technology: Strategic decision making for managers.* New York: John Wiley and Sons.

Lund, S., Manyika, J., & Ramaswamy, S. (2012). Preparing for a new era of knowledge work. *Mckinsey Quarterly, (4),* 103-110. Retrieved November 15, 2013, from EBSCO Online Database Business Source Complete. http://search.ebscohost.com/login.aspx?direct=true&db=bth&AN=82911532&site=ehost-live

Menon, S. & Ramesh, S. (2001). Data mining. *Encyclopedia of Operations Research & Management Science,* 191-194. Retrieved July 6, 2007, from EBSCO Online Database Business Source Complete. http://search.ebscohost.com/login.aspx?direct=true&db=bth&AN=21891287&site=ehost-live

Schoemaker, P. H., Krupp, S., & Howland, S. (2013). Strategic leadership: The essential skills. *Harvard Business Review, 91*(1), 131-134. Retrieved November 15, 2013, from EBSCO Online Database Business Source Complete. http://search.ebscohost.com/login.aspx?direct=true&db=bth&AN=84424206&site=ehost-live

Senn, J. A. (2004). *Information technology: Principles, practices, opportunities* (3rd ed.). Upper Saddle River, NJ: Pearson/Prentice Hall.

SUGGESTED READING

Bandinelli, R., Rapaccini, M., Tucci, M., & Visintin, F. (2006). Using simulation for supply chain analysis: Reviewing and proposing distributed simulation frameworks. *Production Planning & Control, 17*(2), 167-175. Retrieved May 29, 2007, from EBSCO Online Database Business Source Complete. http://search.ebscohost.com/login.aspx?direct=true&db=bth&AN=19821457&site=ehost-live

Chong, I.-G., Albin, S. L. & Jun, C.-H. (2007). A data mining approach to process optimization without an explicit quality function. *IIE Transactions, 39*(8), 795-804. Retrieved July 6, 2007, from EBSCO Online Database Business Source Complete. http://search.ebscohost.com/login.aspx?direct=true&db=bth&AN=25228067&site=ehost-live

Jones, K. (2006). Knowledge management as a foundation for decision support systems. *Journal of Computer Information Systems, 46*(4), 116-124. Retrieved May 14, 2007, from EBSCO Online Database Business Source Complete. http://search.ebscohost.com/login.aspx?direct=true&db=bth&AN=22536043&site=ehost-live

Levine, D. M., Krehbiel, T. C., & Berenson, M. L. (2005). *Business statistics: First course* (4th ed.). Upper Saddle River, NJ: Prentice Hall.

Rice, G. H. Jr. & Hamilton, R. E. (1979). Decision theory and the small businessman. *American Journal of Small Business, 4*(1), 1-9. Retrieved May 21, 2007, from EBSCO Online Database Business Source Complete. http://search.ebscohost.com/login.aspx?direct=true&db=bth&AN=5751685&site=ehost-live

Shpilberg, D. & de Neufville, R. (1975). Use of decision analysis for optimizing choice of fire protection and insurance: An airport study. *Journal of Risk & Insurance, 42*(1), 133-149. Retrieved May 21, 2007, from EBSCO Online Database Business Source Complete. http://search.ebscohost.com/login.aspx?direct=true&db=bth&AN=5205276&site=ehost-live

Weng, S. Chiu, R., Wang, B., Chi, R. & Su, S. (2006/2007). The study and verification of mathematical modeling for customer purchasing behavior. *Journal of Computer Information Systems, 47*(2), 46-57. Retrieved May 14, 2007, from EBSCO Online Database Business Source Complete. http://search.ebscohost.com/login.aspx?direct=true&db=bth&AN=24375428&site=ehost-live

Ruth A. Wienclaw, Ph.D.

MANAGERIAL LEADERSHIP

ABSTRACT

This paper will provide an overview of the necessary qualities of effective management and discuss how adhering to core values and maintaining standards of ethical conduct are necessary to achieve managerial leadership. There are certain necessary qualities for effective management. Managers need to have strong organization skills, the ability to communicate, and the capacity to make decisions. These skills are essential for effective management whether one is managing a small business, a division within a company, or has oversight responsibility for a group in any other work environment. However, truly successful managing requires a business owner or a manager to go beyond these basic skill sets in order to set a higher standard of quality. In order to accomplish this, managers need to lead. Moreover, managerial leadership requires that a manager adhere to certain core values and standards of ethical conduct.

OVERVIEW

Managerial Skills

Regardless of the type of business or work situation, a successful enterprise requires effective management. There are certain basic skill sets that managers must have in order to be effective.

- First, a manager must be highly organized. This means that they need to manage their time efficiently, prioritize their responsibilities and assume responsibility for the workflow of the group by delegating expediently.
- In order to delegate, a manager must also be able to communicate effectively. Successful communication requires a manager to speak and write clearly as well as to listen intently. In fact, listening is probably one of the more important abilities a manager must have to communicate effectively. This is because managers need to have a clear understanding of the group and what people can and cannot do. The best managers are those that recognize people's capabilities so that they delegate responsibilities effectively. In short, employees should be put into positions where they are most likely to fulfill their duties successfully. By having strong communication skills, a manager will be able to delegate, and to act decisively (Ramona, Emanoil & Lucia, 2012).
- Being able to make decisions, whether popular or unpopular, also lends itself to a successful leadership situation.

Essentially, having a successful business, agency or other enterprise requires having effective managers. Effective managers need to have strong organizational, communication and decision-making skills. More than this, successful managers must be capable of leading.

Managerial Functions

In order to lead, a manager must first master the basic functions of management. In his article, Justice Walton (2005) states that there are four functions of management:

- Short and Long Term Planning.
- Organizing a line or staff.
- Directing (taking charge of a department or organization and controlling).
- Implementing various techniques for managerial control.

Managers are supposed to delegate duties, not perform those duties. Moreover, a manager usually has the responsibility of choosing the people that will be doing the work. This means that the manager is in charge of hiring, firing, training and disciplining employees. Because of this, managers are also responsible for the work that the group performs. To ensure that the group is meeting consistent standards of quality, a manager must be able to motivate people and provide them with a sense of accomplishment. This means that managers need to communicate the big picture to employees by linking their role to the enterprise's main function.

One factor that determines how a manager will perform these functions is his or her personality. A person's temperament, character and personality are directly related to how he or she will not only manage, but also lead. Another important factor is a manager's emotional intelligence (Boyatzis, Good & Massa, 2012; Davis, 2011). There are certain traits that allow one to be an effective leader. Leaders must be able to work with others and show employees that their role does make a difference. To do this, managers must be positive thinkers and perform their role with energy. In so doing, they will instill energy in the team. Some of the traits that will enable a manager to lead include integrity, pride, sincerity, curiosity, passion and courage (Walton 2005). These traits will be further discussed elsewhere in this article.

APPLICATIONS

Indicators of Successful Management

There are ways to determine if a company or enterprise is being successfully managed. Success usually manifests itself in results and this normally is reflected by financial outcomes, such as profit in a sales organization. This can also be reflected by a number of outcomes in an educational setting—such as the test scores of a particular grade level or the percentage of students graduating in a school district. Such results are also referred to as quantitative results and while these are important, there are also other results that need to be reviewed: qualitative results. These results can be reflected in a business enterprise by employee satisfaction, customer satisfaction, quality control, customer retention, and employee retention. Charles Kerns contends that there are six dimensions of quality results: (i) results need to be values driven, (ii) results should be grounded in ethical behavior, (iii) results must be related to the overall purpose of the entity, (iv) results need to be geared toward learning, (v) results must be able to be measured, and (vi) results need to provide a balanced perspective—both quantitative and qualitative, in determining the success of the enterprise (Kerns 2005).

Importance of Core Values & Ethics

It is becoming more evident that the success of businesses, educational institutions, hospitals, and healthcare providers, as opposed to for profit organizations, government agencies, and any other group dynamic where people are working toward a common goal, is directly related to the entity's values. This is reflected in both quantitative and qualitative results. A sales enterprise that is lacking a core set of values may be able to sustain itself in the short run, but at the end of the day, its long-term success will be the result of actions that are rooted in a set of core values. Adhering to a set of values lends itself to actions that are constructive and ethical.

Since values are directly related to the long-term success of an enterprise, these values must first be identified and then become part of the entity's basic function. There should also be a means to ensure that these values are adhered to over time. In order for a manager to achieve this, he or she must follow those values. In so doing, managers set an example for the group and thereby gain credibility.

Once a set of core values has been established, the attitudes and behaviors that arise should be grounded in ethical behavior. Ethics has become a buzzword in the wake of the financial accounting scandals that arose throughout the first decade of the 2000s (for companies like ENRON in 2001 and Bernard L. Madoff Investment Securities in 2008), but ethical behavior in the long run will enable an organization to sustain qualitative and quantitative results. It is ultimately the responsibility of managerial leaders to adhere to standards of ethical conduct. A manager can lead the way by being truthful, having integrity, extending kindness, treating staffers with fairness, taking responsibility for his or her actions, and for the performance of the group, and finally treating others with respect. In the end, a leader must have integrity and his or her effectiveness and leadership will be affected by whether the staff believes in a manager's integrity.

Creating a Successful Environment

In addition to adhering to a set of values and acting ethically, a leader must be able to link the results of the enterprise and its people to the organization's purpose. According to Kerns (2005), "without a positive connection between work and organizational purpose—what we do each day becomes less meaningful."

Making Employees Matter

This simply means that people need to believe that what they are doing has meaning and that their role makes a difference. In a sales organization, sales people can clearly see this link. But what of the operations personnel—the accountants, customer service reps, and clerical staff? At times, people serving these basic but vital functions tend to lose sight of the big picture; after all, the sales people who are successful and receive the most commissions usually are compensated at a higher level than the operations personnel. In order to ensure that they continue to achieve quality results, an operations manager must be able to remind his or her staff how their functions are connected to the overall success of the business, and this can only happen if the manager has mastered one of the basic skills mentioned earlier: the ability to communicate.

A manager can only be successful at connecting a team's work to the larger purpose of the organization if he or she can communicate and thereby create an environment that people believe is a good place to work. Not only must a leader ensure that the people he or she is responsible for managing believe their role is important, a leader can also ensure the quality of a team's performance by putting team members in situations where they can learn. There are a number of ways to accomplish this. First a leader must ensure that he has hired the right people to do the job. Once the right people are in place, the manager is responsible for ensuring that people learn the functions required to perform that role. But what happens when an employee has mastered that role? If employees stop learning they become stagnant. One way to prevent this is for the manager to cross-train his or her team members so that they perform a variety of roles.

Evaluating & Responding to Results

While it is clear that quantitative results can be measured in numbers such as profits for a sales organization or numbers of students in a graduating class, qualitative results must also be measured. This can be achieved by incorporating the aforementioned values and ethical behaviors into the basic functions of the enterprise and into roles and responsibilities of the employees. If a manager has mastered the organizational skills that allow him or her to establish priorities, has communicated these priorities to staff members, and then ensures that these priorities are being fulfilled by providing people with consistent feedback, he or she can then make necessary decisions such as rewarding, firing or disciplining people. At the end of the day, it is the manager's job to determine annual pay raises, bonuses and promotions, and these can be difficult decisions to make. Even harder than rewards, though, comes the responsibility of doling out punishment.

At times, employees in a particular group or a division of a large corporation may not be meeting the objectives and goals to achieve the organization's purpose. In such times, the manager must make the tough decision to discipline certain individuals or even to close entire divisions. In the case of the former, the values of fairness and respect come directly into play. If an employee is treated fairly in a situation that requires disciplinary action, and if they are also treated with respect, the decision and actions required will be handled more effectively. In a situation where an entire division of a company is closed, a leader must ensure that the decision was based on a valid reason and that the action will ensure the long term profitability of the entity. Not everyone can make these tough calls and they go beyond the basic skill sets required for effective managing; such decisions require managerial leadership.

VIEWPOINTS

Measuring Quantitative & Qualitative Results

Quantitative and qualitative results must be balanced, and they must be monitored in a number of areas. These include financial (profits and other similar results), customer satisfaction (easily measured through a strong orientation to customer service) and internal business purposes (linking the role of each group and the people in each group to the entity's overall purpose and potential for learning and growth) (Kerns 2005).

These measurements are ultimately the responsibility of the manager, and in order to effectively assume that responsibility, the manager must master the basic organizational, communication and decision-making skills required of the position. Beyond this, a manager must have the ability to lead. Leadership requires that a manager have certain core values and to act in a way that is ethical. This will encourage others to act ethically as well. By encouraging others to act ethically and in adherence to the organization's core values, a manager will have greater success linking a group's or individual's performance to the business entity's purpose. This can only happen if a manger has integrity. There are other leadership traits such as courage, pride, sincerity, vision, passion, curiosity and daring. These are not theoretical notions and many successful businesses, education and other leaders have spoken and written extensively about such leadership traits.

Jack Welch of GE on Successful Leadership

One such leader is Jack Welch, the former CEO of General Electric Corporation. In his book,

"Winning," Welch elucidates on the very matters discussed in this paper. His long and successful tenure at GE offers a clear and distinct path toward managerial leadership.

Welch contends that before becoming a leader, an individual's success in an organization is about self-development. Becoming a leader changes the focus from growing oneself to growing others. When one becomes a manager, one becomes responsible for other people, and because of this responsibility, a manager must go beyond basic functions of managing and become a leader. This requires a manager to "resolve problems, assume responsibility, offer valid criticism, and set an example by pursuing high quality and acting with integrity" (Welch 2005).

There are a number of ways for a leader to pursue high quality, and for Welch, a leader must emanate positive energy. In addition to this, a leader must also be optimistic. "An upbeat manager that goes through the day with a positive outlook ends up running a team or organization filled with upbeat people" (Welch 2005).

In order to have successful managerial leadership, people in positions of authority must also have the trait of courage. This trait rises from being able to make decisions. These decisions are all centered on ensuring that the organization is fulfilling its purpose. At times, this requires an organization to take risks, and ultimately someone is responsible for making those decisions. As Welch states, "Winning companies embrace risk taking and learning this requires freely admitting mistakes..." (Welch 2005).

In order to make those decisions and to get people to act in a way that will bring about that vision a leader must also have sincerity. People need to be able to trust managers (i.e., leaders) and in order to trust them; people need to believe that leaders have integrity. The way for a leader to establish his or her integrity is to be trustworthy. In turn, the way for a leader to establish trust is by being open and honest. Being candid means that a leader communicates in a way that people know where they stand in terms of their performance. People also need to know how the business is doing. If things are going well, people need to know that their efforts contributed to the organization's success. Accordingly, another way to establish trust is for a leader to credit people for their efforts.

By giving credit when appropriate, people are filled with a sense of pride, and this is another trait necessary for managerial leadership. Not only must a manager take pride is his role, and the goal of the entity, he or she must also take pride in the success of others. One way to ensure this is by having vision. It is the responsibility of the leader to determine the team's vision and bring it to fruition. "The mission must be specific to the company's vision, and the mission in business is to win" (Welch 2005).

To get people to share the vision, a manager must also have passion. Passion is not only a necessary ingredient for attaining managerial leadership. Passion is essential to being successful in any endeavor. This is seen in people who are excited about their work. One way to get people to be passionate about their work is by linking their efforts to the overall purpose of the organization, and it is the leader's responsibility to bring forth this passion by manifesting positive energy. In the end, though, passion comes from within.

Not only does managerial leadership require passion, a leader must have a great deal of curiosity. A leader's job is not to have all the answers, but rather, it is a leader's responsibility to have all the questions. Not only must a leader have all the questions, the questions must engender open and honest debate. Finally a leader needs to ensure that the questions he or she raises will result in effective action. Questions must lead to results and sometimes those results may not be what were originally intended. Because of this, another trait essential to leadership is daring. A leader must be willing to face confrontations that may arise from his or her passion, curiosity and tough decisions. A leader must also be able to resolve those conflicts. In these instances, a leader will be more inclined to be successful if they adhere to a core set of values and establish trust by conducting themselves ethically.

CONCLUSION

There are certain fundamental skills required for effective management. Included in these skills are organizational, communication and decision-making skills. These skills are necessary in order to fulfill the four basic functions of management and these are short and long-term planning, organizing a line or staff, directing (taking charge of a department or organization and controlling), and implementing various techniques for managerial control. Whether an organization is being managed successfully will be reflected in results. There are two types of results, quantitative and qualitative. Quantitative results are normally evidenced by financial outcomes. Qualitative results, on the other hand, can be measured in a number of other ways. Included in those measurements are that results need to be values driven, and that results should be grounded in ethical behavior. Ultimately, the person responsible for these results is the manager. And so not only must a manager have basic skill sets to ensure that the basic functions of management are being fulfilled, a manager must go further and become a leader.

Managerial leadership requires managers to have certain traits, especially integrity. A leader that has integrity will ensure that the business entity's results are values driven, will conduct himself or herself ethically, and in so doing engender the trust of the people under the manager's direction. In the end, that trust will manifest itself in the purpose or goals of the enterprise.

Bibliography

Boyatzis, R. E., Good, D., & Massa, R. (2012). Emotional, social, and cognitive intelligence and personality as predictors of sales leadership performance. *Journal of Leadership & Organizational Studies (Sage Publications Inc.), 19*(2), 191–201. Retrieved on November 20, 2013, from EBSCO Online Database Business Source Complete. http://search.ebscohost.com/login.aspx?direct=true&db=bth&AN=74306127&site=ehost-live

Curtiss, R. & Sherlock, J. J. (2006). Wearing two hats: counselors working as managerial leaders in agencies and schools. *Journal of Counseling and Development, 84*(1),120–126. Retrieved December 11, 2006, from Business Source Premier (19511337). http://search.ebscohost.com/login.aspx?direct=true&db=buh&AN=19511337&site=ehost-live

Davis, S. A. (2011). Investigating the impact of project managers' emotional intelligence on their interpersonal competence. *Project Management Journal, 42*(4), 37–57. Retrieved on November 20, 2013, from EBSCO Online Database Business Source Complete. http://search.ebscohost.com/login.aspx?direct=true&db=bth&AN=62425079&site=ehost-live

Fast, N. J., Burris, E. R., & Bartel, C. A. (2014). Managing to stay in the dark: managerial self-efficacy, ego defensiveness, and the aversion to employee voice. *Academy of Management Journal, 57*(4), 1013–1034. Retrieved November 18, 2014, from EBSCO Online Database Business Source Complete. http://search.ebscohost.com/login.aspx?direct=true&db=bth&AN=97336641&site=bsi-live

Kerns, C. D. (2005). Are all results created equal? Auditing organizational outcomes for quality. *Total Quality Management, 16* (7), 827–840,. Retrieved December 11, 2006, from Business Source Premier (18363733). http://search.ebscohost.com/login.aspx?direct=true&db=buh&AN=18363733&site=ehost-live

Ramona, T., Emanoil, M., & Lucia, F. (2012). Reflections on managerial communication. *Studies in Business & Economics, 7*(1), 153–159. Retrieved on November 20, 2013, from EBSCO Online Database Business Source Complete. http://search.ebscohost.com/login.aspx?direct=true&db=bth&AN=82591342&site=ehost-live

Sprier, S. W., Fontaine, M. H. & Malloy, R. L. (2006). Leadership run amok. *Harvard Business Review,84*(6), 72–82. Retrieved December 11, 2006, from Business Source Premier (20773198). http://search.ebscohost.com/login.aspx?direct=true&db=buh&AN=20773198&site=ehost-live

Vyas, R. (2013). Managing the dimensions of ethos, pathos and logos of change through transformational leadership. *IUP Journal of Soft Skills, 7*(3), 7–22. Retrieved November 18, 2014, from EBSCO Online Database Business Resource Complete. http://search.ebscohost.com/login.aspx?direct=true&db=bth&AN=92607072&site=bsi-live

Walton, J. (2005). Searching for managerial lesdership skills along the yellow brick road. *Healthcare Purchasing News, 29* (8), 60. Retrieved December 11, 2006, from Business Source Premier (17831943). http://search.ebscohost.com/login.aspx?direct=true&db=buh&AN=17831943&site=ehost-live

Welch, J., Welch S. (2005). *Winning.* New York: Harper Business/An Imprint of HarperCollins.

Suggested Reading

Creech, B. (1994). Leadership not manageship. In *The Five Pillars of TQM. How to Make Total Quality Management Work for You* (pp. 294–348). New York: Truman Talley Books/Dutton.

Covey, S. (1989). *The Seven Habits of Highly Effective People.* New York: Simon & Schuster.

Guliani, R.W. (2002). *Leadership.* New York: Miramax Books/Hyperion.

Hall, J. L. (2013). Managing teams with diverse compositions: implications for managers from research on the faultline model. *SAM Advanced Management Journal, 78*(1), 4–10. Retrieved November 18, 2014, from EBSCO Online Database Business Source Complete. http://search.ebscohost.com/login.aspx?direct=true&db=bth&AN=88038524&site=bsi-live

Mckee, A., Johnston, F. & Massimilian R. (2006). Mindfulness, hope and compassion: a leader's road map to renewal. *Ivey Business Journal, 70* (5), 1–5. Retrieved December 11, 2006, from Business Source Premier (21102970). http://search.ebscohost.com/login.aspx?direct=true&db=bth&AN=19511337&site=ehost-live

Richa S. Tiwary, Ph.D., M.L.S.

MANAGING CONFLICT WITHIN ORGANIZATIONS THROUGH NEGOTIATIONS

ABSTRACT

This article will focus on negotiation. Negotiation, as a tool of conflict management and conflict resolution in modern business organizations, will be described and analyzed in the following sections. The article will provide an overview of organizational conflict and conflict management. The role of conflict manager will be described. The article will include discussion and analysis of the main models, tactics, and strategies for negotiation. Integrative and distributive approaches to negotiation will be addressed.

OVERVIEW

Negotiation, which refers to the process of bargaining preceding an agreement, is part of a larger process of managing conflict within organizations. While this article focuses on business negotiations, negotiation should be understood as a central and fundamental conflict resolution and management tool used by individuals, governments, and businesses alike. Negotiation skills, used to manage interpersonal, intergroup, inter-organizational, and international conflict, are crucial for participation in the modern business world. Organizational conflict and organizational change, and related negotiation mechanisms and tools for managing these processes, are characteristic of current business practices across businesses and industries.

Changes in contemporary business practices are causing the role of negotiation in business to evolve from conflict resolution to conflict management. In the twenty-first century, private sector organizations are increasingly moving from traditional authoritative, hierarchical structures to cooperative, team-based structures. The new team-based model of organizations, dependent upon cooperation and functioning work relationships, requires high-level knowledge of negotiation skills, conflict management skills, and mediation tactics. This structural change is occurring in large part as a result of globalization and its related processes as well as the Internet and related technologies. Businesses and industries are increasingly transnational, decentralized operations. Goods and services may be produced in one region and sold in another. Telecommuting is a common work choice made in businesses with virtual rather than brick-and-mortar headquarters and stores. The increased pace of technological development and innovation requires businesses to become learning organizations to remain competitive in the marketplace. Cooperative management and participatory problem solving, both requiring negotiation skills, are common in team-based, decentralized business organizations. Furthermore, a culture that includes conflict as creative tension but not as a destructive force is an element of successful team-based organizations (Boni & Weingart, 2012).

Negotiation, as a tool of conflict management in modern business organizations, will be described and analyzed in this article. The following sections provide an overview of organizational conflict and conflict management. These sections will serve as the foundation for a discussion and analysis of negotiation, mediation, and the relationship between negotiation and conflict management.

Organizational Conflict

Organizational conflict, which refers to an interactive process manifested in incompatibility, disagreement, or dissonance within or between social entities, creates organizational change. Types of conflict include interpersonal, inter-group, inter-organizational, and international conflict. Conflict is a social process. Contextual antecedents, such as individual, team, project, and organizational characteristics, influence and may exacerbate conflict (Barki & Hartwick, 2001). The conflict process can be positive or negative. Functional conflict creates positive change within the organization. Dysfunctional conflict creates negative change within the organization. Organizational conflict can arise from problems within work activities as well as incompatible preferences and goals.

Singleton, Toombs, Taneja, Larkin, and Pryor (2011) suggest that definitions of *conflict* will differ depending on the level of volatility, or perceived volatility, in the conflict. In the least volatile realm, the word *conflict* implies dissension, disagreement, opposition, and lack of consensus among two or more people. In the most volatile realm, the implication is associated animosity, anger, antagonistic words and/ or behavior, and increasing levels of frustration. In either case, those involved in the conflict should understand the difference between functional and dysfunctional conflict and whether, and the extent to which, conflict management and conflict resolution theories and tools are needed.

Occurrence of Organization Conflict

Organizational conflict often occurs in the following situations and scenarios (Rahim, 2002):

- Parties are required to engage in an activity that is incongruent with their needs or interests.
- Parties hold behavioral preferences that are incompatible with another person's implementation of his or her preferences.
- Parties want some mutually desirable resource that is in short supply.
- Parties possess attitudes, values, skills, and goals that are appropriate for directing their behavior but contradict the attitudes, values, skills, and goals held by others within an organization.
- Two parties have contradictory preferences regarding their joint actions.

Interpersonal Conflict

"Interpersonal conflict" refers to a phenomenon that occurs between interdependent parties as they experience negative emotional reactions to perceived disagreements and interference with the attainment of their goals. Interpersonal conflict within organizations often occurs on project teams involving multiple parties with potentially conflicting agendas, goals, styles, personalities, and objectives. Symptoms of interpersonal conflict include hostility, jealousy, steam rolling, poor communication, political maneuvering, a proliferation of technical rules, norms, and regulations, frustration, and low morale. Interpersonal conflict is characterized by interdependence, disagreement, interference, and negative emotion. Interpersonal conflict within organizations can produce positive or negative results or change. Examples of negative outcomes from interpersonal conflict include distrust of others, hostility, decreased group coordination and cohesiveness, reduced job satisfaction and motivation, higher absenteeism and turnover, grievances, and lower performance and productivity. Examples of positive outcomes from interpersonal conflict include greater self-awareness, creativity, adaptation, and learning (Barki & Hartwick, 2001).

Diagnosis of Organizational Conflict

Most people, groups, and organizations have conflict thresholds that must be exceeded for conflict to occur. Managers are generally responsible for the diagnosis of organizational conflict. The diagnosis of organizational conflict generally specifies the type of conflict, parties involved, and level and type of intervention needed. A diagnosis should indicate whether there is need for an intervention and the type of intervention needed.

Goals & Objectives of Intervention

Interventions in situations of organizational crisis are designed to accomplish the following goals and objectives (Rahim, 2002):

- Interventions in situations of organizational crisis are designed to attain and maintain a moderate amount of substantive conflict in non-routine tasks at various levels.
- Interventions in situations of organizational crisis are designed to reduce affective conflict at all levels.
- Interventions in situations of organizational crisis are designed to enable the organizational members to select and use the appropriate styles of

handling conflict so that various situations can be effectively dealt with.

- Despite the fact that conflict often serves a function within organizations, conflict management most often attempts to reduce, resolve, and minimize conflict (Rahim, 2002).

Conflict Management

Managers, across a wide range of businesses and industries, oversee organizational conflict to ensure successful resolution. Conflict is managed by organizational leaders often referred to as "conflict managers." "Conflict management," which refers to designing effective macro-level strategies to minimize the dysfunctions of conflict and enhance the constructive functions of conflict in order to enhance learning and effectiveness in an organization, is recognized as its own field (Rahim, 2002). Examples of conflict management include negotiation, bargaining, mediation, and arbitration. There are two main categories of conflict management techniques including conflict stimulation and conflict resolution. "Conflict stimulation" refers to the creation of conflict within organizations to promote change. Conflict resolution includes techniques (such as problem solving, expansion of resources, avoidance, compromise, authoritative command, altering human variables, and altering structural variables) to reduce conflict within the organization.

Conflict Management Styles

Different conflict management styles have different outcomes. "Conflict management styles" refer to general strategies or behavioral orientations individuals adopt when dealing with conflicts. There are five different modes or styles of conflict management including asserting, accommodating, compromising, problem-solving, and avoiding (Barki & Hartwick, 2001):

- Asserting: Conflict, within the asserting management approach, is considered a win-lose situation. This approach is also referred to as "competing," "dominating," and "forcing."
- Accommodating: The accommodating approach to conflict management involves individuals obliging or yielding to others' positions or cooperating in an attempt to smooth over conflicts. This approach is also referred to as "cooperating," "obliging," "yielding," and "sacrificing."
- Compromising: The compromising approach to conflict management involves give and take behaviors where each party wins some and loses some. This approach is also referred to as "sharing" and "splitting the difference."
- Problem-solving: The problem-solving approach to conflict management occurs when individuals in conflict try to fully satisfy the concerns of all parties. This approach is also referred to as "integrating," "cooperating," and "collaborating."
- Avoiding: The avoiding approach to conflict management occurs when individuals are indifferent to the concerns of either party and refuse to act or participate in conflict. This approach is also referred to as "withdrawing," "evading," "escaping," and "apathy."

Research has shown that demographic and personality traits affect which mode or style of conflict management individuals choose to employ in the workplace. For instance, gender research suggests women tend to accommodate, compromise, or avoid conflict while men tend to assert or compete more (Sone, 1981; Cardona, 1995, qtd. in Prause & Mujtaba, 2015). Similarly, a person's dominant values influence his or her conflict management style: those who value self-transcendence (humility, cooperation, etc.) are more accommodating; those who prize conservation (self-image, recognition, etc.) are inclined to avoid conflict; those for whom self-enhancement (authority, power, wealth, etc.) is of prime import tend to dominate; and those with an openness to change (independence, curiosity, harmony) are likely to engage in problem solving (Anjum, Karim & Bibi, 2014).

Criteria Necessary for Successful Conflict Resolution

Team-based organizations increasingly work to manage conflict rather than resolve conflict. All conflict management strategies, including asserting, accommodating, compromising, problem-solving, and avoiding, must satisfy certain criteria to be effective. These criteria include organizational learning and effectiveness, needs of stakeholders, and ethics:

- Organizational learning and effectiveness: Conflict management strategies, designed to enhance organizational learning, enhance critical and innovative thinking. Organizational members, including employees and managers, are expected to learn the process of conflict diagnosis and intervention.

- Needs of stakeholders: Conflict management strategies, designed to satisfy the needs and expectations of the strategic stakeholders and to attain a balance among them, involve these parties in a problem-solving process that will lead to collective learning and organizational effectiveness. This conflict management strategy is intended to lead to stakeholder satisfaction and confidence.
- Ethics: Conflict management designed to define organizational problems so that it leads to ethical actions that benefit humankind is referred to as "ethical conflict management."

Conflict management in a contemporary business organization's functions requires a supportive organizational culture. Employees in contemporary business organizations that value conflict management are encouraged by managers and leadership to engage in the process of diagnosis of and intervention in problems. An organizational culture that supports conflict management encourages task-related conflict and discourages emotional conflict; supports organizational learning; risk taking, openness; diverse viewpoints; continuous questioning and inquiry; and sharing of information and knowledge. Conflict management, within a supportive organizational culture, has the potential to enhance organizational learning that involves knowledge acquisition, knowledge distribution, information interpretation, and organizational memorization (Rahim, 2002).

APPLICATIONS

Negotiation

In the business sector, negotiation is used within and between organizations. Negotiation is used in the commercial arena of buying and selling and solving industrial relations problems (Baines, 1994). "Commercial or business negotiation" refers to the process for resolving differences of opinion that arise in contract dealings between a buyer and seller. Commercial negotiations can involve a complex range of financial, business, and contractual issues. Planning, conducting, and analyzing the outcomes of commercial negotiations are key elements of a successful business (Ashcroft, 2004). Negotiations between individuals and organizations can be adversarial, coercive, emotional, cooperative, logical, courteous, or mutually advantageous. Negotiation of all kinds requires preparation, discussion, offers, and bargaining. While these are viewed as distinct stages, they build on one another. Preparation involves clarifying basic assumptions, selecting the negotiating team, choosing the leaders, discovering information, deciding on aims for the process, and arranging the physical environment or meeting place. The negotiating session involves introductions, presentation of cases, listening, offering options, summarizing, taking breaks, not rushing, making a deal when appropriate, and formalizing the negotiated agreement by signing a document (Baines, 1994).

Traditional Models of Negotiation

Traditionally, there have been three main models of negotiation: integrative, distributive, and interdependence (Donohue & Roberto, 1996):

- Integrative model of negotiation: The integrative model of negotiation focuses on multiple issues, engages in problem solving, offers concessions and acceptances, and focuses on mutually beneficial solutions.
- Distributive model of negotiation: The distributive model of negotiation involves parties within a distributive orientation that may conceal information, exaggerate their positions, and use threats, attacks, demands, and repetitive arguments. Distributive negotiation behavior works to create a context that makes integration less acceptable.
- Interdependence model of negotiation: The interdependence model of negotiation combines integrative and distributive models. Negotiators continuously and explicitly define their interdependence by offering information, strategies, and tactics that foster both cooperation and competition. The interdependence model exists along a continuum of integrative-distributive processes.

Contemporary Models of Negotiation

Changes in contemporary business practices, due to globalization, new technology, and emergence of team-based organizations, have expanded the field of negotiation strategies to include additional approaches (and models) of negotiation such as power-based, interests-based, needs-based, dignity model, comprehensive systemic, SWOT, and stage:

- Power-based model of negotiation: The power-based model of negotiation, based on distributive principles, is characterized by selfishness, aggressive behavior, and competition. Power-based disputants will work to maximize their individual self-interest (Chaterjee, 2006).

- Interest-based model of negotiation: The interest-based model of negotiation, also referred to as "interest-based bargaining" or "mutual gains bargaining," refers to bargaining processes that are focused on understanding and building on interests and using problem-solving tools as a way of avoiding positional conflicts and achieving better outcomes for all stakeholders. Interest-based negotiation skills and tactics include active listening, converting positions into underlying needs or interests, joint data collection, brainstorming, joint task forces, facilitation, and effective communication with constituents (Fonstad, 2004). The interest-based model of negotiation, based on integrative negotiation, separates disputants from the problem, focuses on interests and not positions, generates a variety of possibilities before creating an agreement, and insists that the results be based on some objective criteria (Chaterjee, 2006).
- Need-based model of negotiation: The human needs approach to conflict negotiation treats disputants as socio-psychological beings with certain needs that require fulfillment not as rational actors interested in the furtherance of self-interest. The need-based approach assumes that conflict arises from a threat to fundamental needs. The need-based model of negotiation works toward win-win solutions (Chaterjee, 2006).
- Dignity model of negotiation: The dignity model of negotiation assumes that situations of conflict arise from inhuman physical and verbal violence that compromise individual and group dignity. The dignity model of negotiation is based on the following premises: acceptance of humanity, validation of gender, class, race identities, recognition of each party, understanding, fairness, security, inclusion, autonomy, trust, and access to relationship recovery (Chaterjee, 2006).
- Comprehensive systemic model of negotiation: The comprehensive systemic model of negotiation addresses conflict as mediation between structure and agency. "Structure" refers to the broad framework that a social system functions within, and "agency" refers to individual and collective action (Chaterjee, 2006).
- SWOT model of negotiation: The SWOT model of negotiation is used to evaluate the company's strengths, weaknesses, opportunities, and threats. This business management tool is an effective business negotiation strategy. Looking at a firm's production and marketing goals and assessing the firm's operations and management policies and practices in light of those goals, the SWOT model is used to plan negotiating tactics and strategy. Knowledge of company's strengths, weaknesses, opportunities, and threats allows for savvy and informed negotiation (Cellich, 1990).
- The stage model of negotiation: The stage model of negotiation specifies a fixed number of stages that negotiators move through as they interact and move toward closure. Negotiators begin in a distributive mode, concealing information and using aggressive and contentious strategies, and then move toward an integrative mode emphasizing problem solving and supportive strategies (Donohue & Roberto, 1996).

Determining the Negotiation Model to be Used

Conflict managers, and individual parties or disputants, decide which negotiation model or approach to use based on multiple factors including consistency of frame, nature of negotiator training, time allocated to negotiate, goals of disputants, and level of uncertainty (Donohue & Roberto, 1996):

- Consistent frame: Numerous factors emerge during negotiations that push parties into a consistently integrative or distributive frame.
- Nature of negotiator training: Negotiators are usually trained to use a specific sequence of behaviors in the course of their negotiation proceedings.
- Time to negotiate: The amount of time available or allocated to negotiation sessions varies by negotiator, organization, business, and industry.
- Goals of disputants: The goals of disputants involved in negotiation may initially be implicit or explicit as well as reasonable or unreasonable. Negotiators describe the key points of each disputant's case, claim, or position to make goals clear to everyone involved in the negotiation session.
- Level of uncertainty: When disputants enter into a negotiation session uncertain of their knowledge of the issues, their understanding of their oppo-

nent's position, or their ability to predict their opponent's goals and strategies, instability and volatility is likely to result.

Steps to Negotiation

Ultimately, despite the specific negotiation model or approach chosen by the negotiator, similar processes or sub-processes will be present in all negotiations. For example, negotiators are competitors with their counterparts in claiming scarce resources; negotiators are collaborators with their counterparts in creating value; negotiators are relationship-shapers; and negotiators are coalition managers and consensus builders within their own organization (Fonstad, 2004). In addition, all the negotiation models described above include the same basic steps. The standard steps of the negotiation process include preparation, the opening phase, reaching agreement, and closure (Manning & Robertson, 2004):

- Preparation: Preparation establishes the issues, gathers quality information, prepares the case, and prepares for the encounter.
- The opening phase: The opening phase creates a positive climate in which disputants state their individual cases.
- Reach agreement: Reaching agreement involves disputants challenging the opponent's case, responding to challenges, making concessions, and trading, linking, and moving to reach agreement.
- Closure: Closure summarizes and records agreements as well as establishes monitoring and review procedures.

Issues & Variables that Impact Negotiation Processes

Issues and variables that impact all steps of the negotiation process described above include clarity of focus, flexibility of strategy, win-win values, and interactive skills (Manning & Robertson, 2004):

- Clarity of focus: Clarity of focus includes defining the issues, having a clear and simple case, using different types of information from a variety of sources, taking time before making decisions, agreeing to the outcome, monitoring, and reviewing.
- Flexibility of strategy: Flexibility of strategy involves finding out about the other party and what they want, taking a long-term perspective, planning around issues rather than in a strict sequence, and using concessions, adjournments, and doing whatever is necessary to reach an agreement.
- Win-win values: Win-win values involves having respect for the other party and what they want, considering a wide range of options and outcomes, ensuring both parties clearly present their case, and cooperating openly to achieve mutually acceptable outcomes.
- Interactive skills: Interactive skills involve showing personal warmth, seeking information and clarification throughout, summarizing and testing understanding of what is said, and being open and non-defensive.

Negotiation has the potential to manage conflict and promote collaboration, learning, and more effective business operations. If the negotiation process is ineffective and conflict persists within the organization or between parties, then parties or disputants move toward mediation or arbitration. "Mediation" refers to the use of a third party in the negotiation process to facilitate a resolution through persuasion or alternative ideas. "Arbitration" refers to the involvement of a neutral third party in the negotiation process who has the authority to decide on an agreement. Mediation is one of a group of alternative methods to resolve business disputes including arbitration, mini-trials, expanded use of value billing, and alternative fee arrangements with counsel. Mediation of business disputes often allows disputants to avoid the filing of a lawsuit entirely (Berman, 1994). Mediation is a dispute resolution tool used to settle disputes between individuals, companies, workers, and states that fosters agreement and reduces conflict. Mediators or arbitrators are disinterested and are neutral third parties (Greig, 2005).

CONCLUSION

Ultimately, conflict management strategies, which range from negotiating, asserting, accommodating, compromising, problem-solving, and avoiding, serve to minimize conflicts at various levels as well as work to attain and maintain a moderate amount of substantive conflict to promote healthy change and growth within business organizations. Conflict managers have the responsibility to select and use the appropriate conflict management strategy for the conflict and the disputants (Rahim, 2002). General guidelines for negotiating, relevant to all the negotiation models described in this article, include taking time to break the ice, presenting the case, listening, being prepared to suggest many options, summarizing regularly, and being prepared to take a break when negotiation stalls (Baines, 1994). Negotiation outcomes tend to vary based on the perspective and orientation of disputants. Parties with integrative orientation view negotiation as a win-win endeavor. Parties with a distributive orientation view negotiation as a win-lose endeavor. Additionally, there is evidence that the perceived effectiveness and use of different conflict resolution behaviors varies across cultures (Sadri, 2013). Conflict managers must assess the positional bias of each participant to ensure a successful negotiation outcome for all involved.

BIBLIOGRAPHY

Anjum, M. A., Karim, J., & Bibi, Z. (2014). Relationship of values and conflict management styles. *IBA Business Review, 9*(1), 92–103. Retrieved December 10, 2015, from EBSCO online database Business Source Premier. http://search.ebscohost.com/login.aspx?direct=true&db=buh&AN=97342467&site=bsi-live

Ashcroft, S. (2004). Commercial negotiation skills. *Industrial and Commercial Training, 36*(6/7), 229–233. Retrieved May 31, 2007, from EBSCO online database Business Source Complete. http://search.ebscohost.com/login.aspx?direct=true&db=bth&AN=15169435&site=ehost-live

Baines, A. (1994). Negotiate to win. *Work Study, 43,* 25–27.

Barki, H., & Hartwick, J. (2001). Interpersonal conflict and its management in information system development. *MIS Quarterly, 25,* 195–228. Retrieved May 31, 2007, from EBSCO online database Business Source Complete. http://search.ebscohost.com/login.aspx?direct=true&db=bth&AN=4626798&site=ehost-live

Bazerman, M., & Curhan, J. (2000). Negotiation. *Annual Review of Psychology, 51,* 279. Retrieved May 31, 2007, from EBSCO online database Business Source Complete. http://search.ebscohost.com/login.aspx?direct=true&db=bth&AN=3076147&site=ehost-live

Berman, P. (1994). Resolving business disputes through mediation and arbitration. *CPA Journal, 64,* 74. Retrieved May 31, 2007, from EBSCO online database Business Source Complete. http://search.ebscohost.com/login.aspx?direct=true&db=bth&AN=9501114967&site=ehost-live

Boni, A.A., & Weingart, L. (2012). Building teams in entrepreneurial companies. *Journal of Commercial Biotechnology, 18,* 31–37. Retrieved November 5, 2013, from EBSCO online database Business Source Complete. http://search.ebscohost.com/login.aspx?direct=true&db=bth&AN=84497033&site=ehost-live

Cellich, C. (1990). Skills for business negotiations. *International Trade Forum, 26,* 8. Retrieved May 31, 2007, from EBSCO online database Business Source Complete. http://search.ebscohost.com/login.aspx?direct=true&db=bth&AN=9611212959&site=ehost-live

Cheung, S., Yiu, K., & Suen, H. (2004). Construction negotiation online. *Journal of Construction Engineering & Management, 130,* 844–852. Retrieved May 31, 2007, from EBSCO online database Business Source Complete. http://search.ebscohost.com/login.aspx?direct=true&db=bth&AN=16217300&site=ehost-live

Fonstad, N., McKersie, R., & Eaton, S. (2004). Interest-based negotiations in a transformed labor-management setting. *Negotiation Journal, 20,* 5–11. Retrieved May 31, 2007, from EBSCO online database Business Source Complete. http://search.ebscohost.com/login.aspx?direct=true&db=bth&AN=18353380&site=ehost-live

Greig, J. (2005). Stepping into the fray: when do Mediators mediate? *American Journal of Political Science, 49,* 249–266. Retrieved May 31, 2007, from EBSCO online database Business Source Complete. http://search.ebscohost.com/login.aspx?direct=true&db=bth&AN=15074371&site=ehost-live

Manning, T. (2004). Influencing, negotiating skills and conflict-handling: some additional research and reflections. *Industrial and Commercial Training,* 36(2/3), 104.

Prause, D., & Mujtaba, B. G. (2015). Conflict management practices for diverse workplaces. *Journal of Business Studies Quarterly, 6*(3), 13–22. Retrieved December 10, 2015, from EBSCO online database Business Source Premier. http://search.ebscohost.com/login.aspx?direct=true&db=buh&AN=101770173&site=bsi-live

Rahim, M. (2002). Toward a theory of managing organizational conflict. *International Journal of Conflict Management (1997-2002), 13,* 206. Retrieved

May 31, 2007, from EBSCO online database Business Source Complete. http://search.ebscohost.com/login.aspx?direct=true&db=bth&AN=9905175&site=ehost-live

Sadri, G. (2013). Choosing conflict resolution by culture. *Industrial Management, 55,* 10–15. Retrieved November 5, 2013, from EBSCO online database Business Source Complete. http://search.ebscohost.com/login.aspx?direct=true&db=bth&AN=90447258&site=ehost-live

Singleton, R., Toombs, L.A., Taneja, S., Larkin, C., & Pryor, M. (2011). Workplace conflict: a strategic leadership imperative. *International Journal of Business & Public Administration, 8,* 149–163. Retrieved November 5, 2013, from EBSCO online database Business Source Complete. http://search.ebscohost.com/login.aspx?direct=true&db=bth&AN=60073584&site=ehost-live

SUGGESTED READING

Adair, W., & Brett, J. (2005). The negotiation dance: time, culture, and behavioral sequences in negotiation. *Organization Science, 16,* 33–51. Retrieved May 31, 2007, from EBSCO online database Business Source Complete. http://search.ebscohost.com/login.aspx?direct=true&db=bth&AN=16285252&site=ehost-live

Hunt, C., & Kernan, M. (2005). Framing negotiations in affective terms: methodological and preliminary theoretical findings. *International Journal of Conflict Management, 16,* 128–156. Retrieved May 31, 2007, from EBSCO online database Business Source Complete. http://search.ebscohost.com/login.aspx?direct=true&db=bth&AN=21409072&site=ehost-live

McKersie, R., Eaton, S., & Kochan, T. (2004, January). Kaiser Permanente: Using interest-based negotiations to craft a new collective bargaining agreement. *Negotiation Journal, 20,* 13–35. Retrieved May 31, 2007, from EBSCO online database Business Source Complete. http://search.ebscohost.com/login.aspx?direct=true&db=bth&AN=18353379&site=ehost-live

Rosenthal, M. (2015). Mediating conflict. *Training, 52*(4), 72. Retrieved December 10, 2015, from EBSCO online database Business Source Premier. http://search.ebscohost.com/login.aspx?direct=true&db=buh&AN=103722592&site=bsi-live

Simone I. Flynn, Ph.D.

MANAGING IN A TURNAROUND ENVIRONMENT

ABSTRACT

Turnaround is the process of reviving and growing underperforming companies. Turnaround efforts are usually led by experienced turnaround managers, who are consultants brought into a company during its decline phase. The turnaround process has three phases, namely, the crises stage, stabilization stage, and recovery stage. Turnaround managers, already working under difficult conditions, face many challenges from factors both internal and external to their company.

OVERVIEW

A turnaround is a process whereby a company that has been experiencing an extended period of poor performance, is led to experience substantial and sustained positive performance. As a topic in the field of business management, turnaround is attracting increasing attention from researchers, educators, investors, managers and consultants. Developments in this area have led to the establishment of the discipline of turnaround management, the profession of turnaround managers, and the practice of turnaround investing.

Turnaround managers are consultants who are hired during financial crises, to save distressed companies from bankruptcy and turn around their fortunes. Turnaround managers join a company either as CEO or consultant, so that they can direct the turnaround process. This is largely preferable to the situation where a company's owners or senior mangers attempt to turn around their company themselves, since their lack of objectivity and emotional involvement often lead them to create new problems without resolving any of the old ones. Much depends on the turnaround manager: If he or she is not able to save a company from bankruptcy, or if the company's core business is not profitable, the company will be liquidated.

Even though turnarounds can be one of the best means by which a company can attain long-term sustainability, many of those in top positions in ailing companies find it difficult to even accept that they need a turnaround. This is one of the biggest obstacles to turnaround, and it is based on several factors:

- Firstly, many corporate executives believe that to initiate a turnaround is tantamount to admitting failure.
- Secondly, some corporate executives believe that turnarounds lead to mass redundancies, and this leads them to resist the idea of a turnaround. However, this is not the case: It is only those employees who do not add value in the workplace that will typically be laid off during the turnover process.
- Thirdly, there is a misconception that other companies will cease to do business with a company undergoing a turnaround. On the contrary, however, firms tend to be drawn to a company in turnaround, because the very fact that it has initiated a turnaround implies that it is a responsible and serious company.

Even when CEOs accept that their company needs a turnaround, they often take a long time to arrive at such a decision. Due to such hesitation, turnarounds are often initiated by third parties such as lenders (such as banks), bankruptcy attorneys, or investors who have a stake in the company.

Companies that need a turnaround most often experience underperformance in the areas of management, finances, competition, operations, and strategy. Management underperformance can usually be seen in areas such as leadership issues; skills issues; micromanagement instead of delegation; organizational structure issues; ineffective communication; misplaced compensation and incentives; and high employee turnover.

Financial underperformance is usually evident in excessively low sales volume; excessively low prices; excessively high expenses; poor balance sheet management; debt; and insufficient working capital. Competitive under-performance tends to be characterized by factors such as uncompetitive products; service and support issues; obsolescence; and quality issues. These can lead to a loss of established business and/or a failure to get new businesses.

Operational underperformance is characterized by lean manufacturing opportunities; poor capacity planning; poor scheduling; and process inefficiencies. The last area of underperformance, strategic underperformance, is characterized by market channel issues; supply chain tier issues; and scale issues.

Further Insights

A turnaround environment can be defined as the social, technological, economic and political environment in which a turnaround company functions. The internal turnaround environment consists of stakeholders such as customers, suppliers, employees, board of directors, and creditors; the external turnaround environment consists of factors and forces beyond the control of the company, including the economic environment, technical environment, legal environment, political environment and cultural environment. The nature of a company's internal and external turnaround environment has an effect on that company's decisions, turnaround strategies, processes and performance.

Needless to say, managing a turnaround is a challenging experience. For instance, those managing in a turnaround environment must do so under intense time pressure. Today's turnaround managers are being given less time to carry out their tasks, with some being expected to complete a turnaround in six months. Turnaround managers need special skills and competencies to effectively manage the unique planning and control processes that are required in managing and turning around a distressed and loss-making company. As if these challenges were not enough, turnaround managers also have to deal with opposition from within their assigned company, for instance from senior managers who resist replacement, or from employees who fear losing their jobs.

Stages of the Turnaround Process

The turnaround process comprises three stages: Crises, stabilization and recovery. Each stage has a different objective and requires a different type of action by the turnaround manager. The objectives and turnaround actions of each stage are depicted in the table below.

Pre-Turnaround Stage: Decline

Before the beginning of any turnaround, there is a significant phase that the company must have gone through, which is worth discussing here. This stage is called 'decline,' and it is characterized by sustained poor performance. Management perceptions and actions during this phase will determine whether or not a

Table 1: Stages of the Turnaround Process

Turnaround Actions	Crises Stage Objective	Stabilization Stage Objective	Recovery Stage Objective
Financial	Positive cash flow situation		
Operational		Profit	
Strategic			Growth

(Fredenberger, Lipp & Watson, 1997, adapted)

company requires a turnaround, since timely intervention can reverse the decline process. Even if a company does require a turnaround, management perceptions and actions during this phase will determine whether the company actually embarks on the turnaround; and how successful the turnaround is likely to be.

Decline can be caused by internal and external factors. For example, an internal factor such as the processing and analysis of company information, if ineffective, can lead to a decline. Likewise, companies that fail to keep up with changes in the external environment are also likely to decline.

Crisis Stage

The first of the three stages of a turnaround is the crises stage. At this stage, a company is close to bankruptcy or liquidation. By this stage, a company would have sustained heavy losses, and therefore, cash outflows would have exceeded cash inflows. As such, the crises stage calls for financial action to create a positive cash flow situation.

The dire situation may lead to changes in the top management team (this tends to happen often in Western countries, and in companies which have relatively high outsider control of the Board of Directors). A turnaround manager would typically be hired at this stage. The main reason why top managers are asked to leave companies that are embarking on a turnaround, is that the top managers find it difficult to recognize problems, since they are usually responsible — at least in part — for those same problems, and it would be difficult for them to put together the necessary creative solutions while having the same mindset that led to the problems in the first place.

Analysis

To be able to make proper evaluation and diagnoses of the situation at hand, a turnaround manager would need to conduct seven types of analyses with current — not past or future — company information. These seven analyses are: Financial analyses, working capital analyses, cost analyses, expense analyses, personnel analyses, asset analyses, and market analyses. Of the seven, financial and working capital analyses tend to be considered by turnaround managers to be the most important. Financial analyses are used to first of all improve cash flow, and secondly, they are used to reschedule debt, reduce expenses, reduce costs, and scale back operations. All seven analyses are prepared into reports and their contents are typically as follows (Fredenberger, Lipp & Watson, 1997):

- Financial Analyses: Balance statements & income statements.
- Working-Capital Analyses: Cash-flow statements (daily, weekly, monthly and quarterly); accounts receivable sales/collection/aging analyses; notes receivable aging analyses; inventory turnover, on-hand, sales per day, ABC analyses; accounts payable aging analyses; notes payable aging analyses; secured debt analyses; lender availability.
- Cost Analyses: Direct and indirect labor compensation (monetary value and percentage of sales); product material cost (percentage of sales); product material cost per supplier (percentage of sales).
- Expense Analyses: Sales/marketing other expense (percentage of sales); finance/administration other expense (percentage of sales); engineering in-house/contract product-related expense (percentage of sales); warranty expense (percentage of sales).
- Personnel Analyses: Burden people-related variable and fixed expense (percentage of sales); compensation expense per direct and indirect labor employee; overtime premium expense per direct and indirect labor employee; sales/marketing people-related expense (percentage of sales); finance/administration people-related expense (percentage of sales); engineering in-house/contract people-related expense (percentage of sales).
- Asset Analyses: Burden plant-related variable and fixed expense (percentage of sales); sales income per plant square foot; capacity utilization as a percentage of plant, equipment and machinery.
- Market Analyses: Product line gross margin as a percentage of profitability; product, model, catalog number gross margin percentage; cumu-

lative margin funds by product, model, catalog number; customer gross margin funds profitability and as a percentage of profitability; cumulative gross margin funds by customer/region/channel/rep; product line margin/customer/region/channel/representative; sales dollars per employee.

Turnaround managers face the challenge of gathering a lot of information as quickly as possible. As important as it is to have the necessary information at the right time, many turnaround managers find that the information available to them is often not in a usable condition, and even when it is usable, it usually gets to the turnaround manager too late. When it comes to information, turnaround managers specifically have to deal with problems such as neglected information systems, inadequate or missing financial information, 'creative' accounting, improper information formats, reports that are not matched to problems, and so on. Information is such a key part of any turnaround, that in order to resolve these kinds of information problems, some companies go to the extent of hiring experienced turnaround chief information officers (CIOs).

The lack of information faced by turnaround managers can partly be attributed to a deliberate ploy on the part of employees, to either hold back information, or to misinform the turnaround manager. This is often done out of fear, and it is therefore imperative that the turnaround manager quickly gains the trust of employees to prevent fear from arising, and to facilitate access to information. These can be achieved through effective collaboration with the human resources department to ensure that the entire company buys into the turnaround process; that the employees are kept informed about what is happening throughout the turnaround; that the employees are constantly reminded of the strengths of the company; and that the employees are ultimately allocated jobs that make the best use of their skills and talents.

Strategy Formulation

Next during the crises stage, a turnaround manager would need to formulate a strategy to recover from the crises. The turnaround strategy will be based on the factors which led to the corporate decline, and for this reason, it is imperative that the problem which caused the underperformance be accurately identified. For instance, if a company has had a single large financial setback such as a legal settlement, fraud or embezzlement, the solution will be mainly financial. If a company is facing efficiency problems, the solution will be mainly operational. If the problem is to do with the reconfiguration of the firm's portfolio of businesses or the positioning of units within that portfolio, the solution will be mainly strategic. In general, however, the primary cause of company non-performance is some form of managerial incompetence, especially related to improper control of the internal elements of a company.

Once a turnaround manager has discovered the core reason for the underperformance, he or she would need to develop a strategic and operating plan. This is quite a challenging task, because the revival of a declining company often calls for the improvement of operations, but under decline conditions, a company can hardly invest in the necessary plant and equipment. This weakness affords the company the opportunity to fully utilize its creative ability through initiatives like extended targets and suggestion forums. Creative negotiations with financial institutions will also support the financial management undertaken during the crises.

The strategic and operating plan may include details of the following actions:

- Retrenchment, which may involve all or some of the following:
  - The reduction of expenses;
  - The reduction of receivables;
  - The reduction of inventory levels;
  - The reduction of personnel.

- Raising the necessary capital, through means such as:
  - Lenders (for example, banks and finance companies);
  - Equity capital from turnaround investors and strategic acquirers;
  - Asset sales;
  - Bankruptcy reorganization.

- Management of the external stakeholders, including, for example:
  - Joint cost reductions with suppliers;
  - Improved trade credit;
  - New strategic partnerships with suppliers;
  - Change in distribution channels;
  - Outsourcing of inefficient processes.

- Management of the internal climate through such means as:
  - Management of the decision processes;
  - Transformation of organizational structures;
  - Formalization of control structures;
  - Restructuring of lines of communication.

- Process improvement, which may result in quality improvement and improved productivity; as well as a reduction in expenses and inventory investment.
- Continuous improvement based on market needs.
- Strategic pricing for certain customers, where possible.

Stabilization Stage

Once the turnaround manger has decided on the best strategy to implement, he or she must take action to address the crises. At the point when cash inflows are at least equal to or greater than cash outflows, the crises would have passed, and it can be said that the company has reached the stabilization stage (also known as renewal). This second stage of the turnaround process calls for operational action to bring about profits. At this stage, the turnaround manager endeavors to motivate the company and allow it to become profitable and grow.

Depending on the circumstances and the turnaround manager's leadership qualities, a turnaround manager can stabilize and motivate a company by either exercising authoritarian leadership to get employees to follow a highly structured turnaround plan; or by empowering employees. Employee empowerment in a turnaround situation involves inverting the organization, practicing team-based problem-solving with cross-functional teams, putting in place a simple reporting structure, supporting senior management and corporate staff, setting measurable customer-driven goals for the entire organization, and measuring results.

Recovery Stage

The third and final stage of the turnaround process is recovery, also termed the expansion stage. This stage calls for strategic action to bring about a return to normal profits and growth. A turnaround manager can achieve growth through improved performance by selling more units of a company's product; by adding more products to its range; by raising prices; and/or by reducing fixed and variable expenses. The achievement of growth, however, should not be an end in itself — the ultimate aim of a turnaround is to strengthen the company's position so that it will not fall back into a loss situation. At this stage, a turnaround manager will typically leave for the next assignment, possibly helping the owners of the company to hire a professional manager, before departing.

Issues

Turnaround management differs from country to country, and this is so because of variations in culture, institutional factors, commercial practices, and other environmental factors. The actions of individuals and organizations — including managers and employees — toward any given activity are largely determined by institutional factors such as culture. For instance, cultural differences can account for differences in the rate of recognition of company decline; differences in the speed of initiating or starting a turnaround effort; and so on. In some countries, due to the prevailing culture, it is extremely difficult to get a CEO to agree to step down for a turnaround consultant to take over.

In the West, top management typically has sufficient autonomy to make the necessary changes and cutbacks during a turnaround, but in some developing countries there may be significant constraints on managerial action, or there may be conflicting stakeholder priorities posing obstacles to a turnaround.

No matter the cultural setting, for a turnaround effort to have any chance of success, it must be adapted to suit the local setting.

Bibliography

Abebe, M.A., Angriawan, A., & Yanxin, L. (2011). CEO power and organizational turnaround in declining firms: Does environment play a role?. *Journal of Leadership & Organizational Studies (Sage Publications Inc.), 18*(2), 260-273. Retrieved November 15, 2013, from EBSCO Online Database Business Source Complete. http://search.ebscohost.com/login.aspx?direct=true&db=bth&AN=60516781&site=ehost-live

Ahlstrom, D., & Bruton, G. (2004). Guest editors' introduction to special issue. Turnaround in Asia: Laying the foundation for understanding this unique domain. *Asia Pacific Journal of Management,*

21(1/2), 5-24. Retrieved December 6, 2007, from EBSCO Online Database Business Source Complete. http://search.ebscohost.com/login.aspx?direct=true&db=bth&AN=13541052&site=ehost-live

Banaszak-Holl, J. (2000). Advances in applied business strategy, volume 5: Turnaround research: Past accomplishments and future challenges. *Administrative Science Quarterly, 45*(3), 633-635. Retrieved December 6, 2007, from EBSCO Online Database Business Source Complete. http://search.ebscohost.com/login.aspx?direct=true&db=bth&AN=3798344&site=bsi-live

Barker, V. III, Patterson, J., & Mueller, G. (2001). Organizational causes and strategic consequences of the extent of top management team replacement during turnaround attempts. *Journal of Management Studies, 38*(2), 235-269. Retrieved December 6, 2007, from EBSCO Online Database Business Source Complete. http://search.ebscohost.com/login.aspx?direct=true&db=bth&AN=4335802&site=ehost-live

Bruton, G., Ahlstrom, D., & Wan, J. (2001). Turnaround success of large and midsize Chinese owned firms: Evidence from Hong Kong and Thailand. *Journal of World Business, 36*(2), 146. Retrieved December 6, 2007, from EBSCO Online Database Business Source Complete. http://search.ebscohost.com/login.aspx?direct=true&db=bth&AN=4498268&site=ehost-live

Feder, W. (2003, Spring). Keeping the doors open: Financing options for troubled companies. *Investment Guides Series: Turnaround Management II,* 91-95. Retrieved December 6, 2007, from EBSCO Online Database Business Source Complete. http://search.ebscohost.com/login.aspx?direct=true&db=bth&AN=14892653&site=ehost-live

Fredenberger, W., Lipp, A., & Watson, H. (1997). Information requirements of turnaround managers at the beginning of engagements. *Journal of Management Information Systems, 13*(4), 167. Retrieved December 6, 2007, from EBSCO Online Database Business Source Complete. http://search.ebscohost.com/login.aspx?direct=true&db=bth&AN=1813579&site=ehost-live

Harker, M., & Harker, D. (1998). The role of strategic selling in the company turnaround process. *Journal of Personal Selling & Sales Management, 18*(2), 55-67. Retrieved December 6, 2007, from EBSCO Online Database Business Source Complete. http://search.ebscohost.com/login.aspx?direct=true&db=bth&AN=826670&site=ehost-live

Milite, G. (1999). Turnaround management: Charting a new beginning. *HR Focus, 76*(11), 9. Retrieved December 6, 2007, from EBSCO Online Database Business Source Complete. http://search.ebscohost.com/login.aspx?direct=true&db=bth&AN=2491371&site=ehost-live

Mueller, J. (1999). Turnaround investing in one easy lesson. *Secured Lender, 55*(2), 38. Retrieved December 6, 2007, from EBSCO Online Database Business Source Complete. http://search.ebscohost.com/login.aspx?direct=true&db=bth&AN=1707564&site=ehost-live

Murak, G. (2004). Turnaround with help from your staff. *Restaurant Hospitality, 88*(7), 68-72. Retrieved December 6, 2007, from EBSCO Online Database Business Source Complete. http://search.ebscohost.com/login.aspx?direct=true&db=bth&AN=14159755&site=ehost-live

O'Kane, C., & Cunningham, J. (2012). Leadership Changes and Approaches During Company Turnaround. *International Studies Of Management & Organization, 42*(4), 52-85. Retrieved December 3, 2014, from EBSCO Online Database Business Source Complete. http://search.ebscohost.com/login.aspx?direct=true&db=bth&AN=84461668&site=bsi-live

O'Kane, C., & Cunningham, J. (2014). Turnaround leadership core tensions during the company turnaround process. *European Management Journal, 32*(6), 963-980. Retrieved December 3, 2014, from EBSCO Online Database Business Source Complete. http://search.ebscohost.com/login.aspx?direct=true&db=bth&AN=99209175&site=bsi-live

Pant, L. (1991). An investigation of industry and firm structural characteristics in corporate turnarounds. *Journal of Management Studies, 28*(6), 623. Retrieved December 6, 2007, from EBSCO Online Database Business Source Complete. http://search.ebscohost.com/login.aspx?direct=true&db=bth&AN=4555029&site=ehost-live

Raina, B., Chanda, P., Mehta, D., & Maheshwari, S. (2003). Organizational decline and turnaround management. *Vikalpa: The Journal for Decision Makers, 28*(4), 83-92. Retrieved December 6, 2007, from EBSCO Online Database Business Source Complete. http://search.ebscohost.com/login.aspx?direct=true&db=bth&AN=11961133&site=ehost-live

Rose, K.H., & Dalcher, D. (2013). Managing projects in trouble: Achieving turnaround and success. *Project Management Journal, 44*(1), 109. Retrieved November 15, 2013, from EBSCO Online Database Business Source Complete. http://search.ebscohost.com/login.aspx?direct=true&db=bth&AN=85016497&site=ehost-live

Sutton, G. (2003, Spring). Confessions of a turnaround guy. *Investment Guides Series: Turnaround Management II,* 14-22. Retrieved December 6, 2007, from EBSCO Online Database Business Source Complete. http://search.ebscohost.com/login.aspx?direct=true&db=bth&AN=14892468&site=ehost-live

Turnaround. (n.d.). *Dictionary of Business Terms.* Retrieved December 06, 2007, from Answers.com Web site: http://www.answers.com/topic/turnaround

Turnaround. (n.d.). *Investopedia.* Retrieved December 06, 2007, from Answers.com Web site: http://www.answers.com/topic/turnaround

Yandava, B. (2012). A capability-driven turnaround strategy for the current economic environment. *Journal of Business Strategies, 29*(2), 157-185. Retrieved November 15, 2013, from EBSCO Online Database Business Source Complete. http://search.ebscohost.com/login.aspx?direct=true&db=bth&AN=90139427&site=ehost-live

SUGGESTED READING

Arogyaswamy, K., Barker, V. III, & Yasai-Ardekani, M. (1995). Firm turnarounds: An integrative two-stage model. *Journal of Management Studies, 32*(4), 493-525. Retrieved December 6, 2007, from EBSCO Online Database Business Source Complete. http://search.ebscohost.com/login.aspx?direct=true&db=bth&AN=9510114617&site=ehost-live

Bibeault, D. B. (1982). *Corporate turnaround: How managers turn losers into winners.* New York: McGraw-Hill.

Gadiesh, O., Pace, S., & Rogers, P. (2003). Successful turnarounds: Three key dimensions. *Strategy & Leadership, 31*(6), 41-43.

Hofer, C. W. (1980). Turnaround strategies. *Journal of Business Strategy, 1,* 19-31.

Hoffman, R. (1989). Strategies for corporate turnarounds: What do we know about them? *Journal of General Management, 14*(3), 46-66.

O'Callaghan. Shaun (2010). *Turnaround Leadership: Making Decisions, Rebuilding Trust and Delivering Results After a Crisis.* Philadelphia: Kogan Page.

Robbins, D. K., & Pearce, J. A. II (1992). Turnaround: Retrenchment and recovery. *Strategic Management Journal, 13,* 287-309.

Scherer, P.S. (1988). From warning to crises: A turnaround primer. *Management Review, 77*(9), 30-36.

Scherer, P.S. (1989). The turnaround consultant steers corporate renewal. *Journal of Management Consulting, 5*(1), 17-24.

Vanessa A. Tetteh, Ph.D.

MANAGING INTER-FIRM ALLIANCES

ABSTRACT

Companies may engage in inter-firm alliances in order to obtain something of value. The specific value may be financial, expertise or market position. Alliances can be formal or informal and can be short or long term. Some companies are looking for a long term partner and may engage in joint ventures in order to boost their qualifications for certain types of business. Meanwhile, others are looking for an informal partnership for the purpose of joint marketing. Some companies will acquire various entities to create a certain position in the market. The biggest management challenge in setting up an alliance with another firm is upfront planning. Advanced planning can be used to anticipate possible obstacles to effective alliances. Some of these obstacles can be in the sharing of information and staff, which entities will shoulder the financial burden, or how the financial burden will be distributed.

OVERVIEW

Companies may turn to inter-firm alliances for many reasons. These alliances may be formal or informal but in some way provide benefits for the parties involved. Some of the inter-alliances may be in the form of formal and legal partnerships and joint ventures. Companies may also align through merger and acquisition activity. Companies that are dependent on each other such as suppliers in an automobile manufacturer's supply chain may find value in alliances. Pietras and Stormer (2001, p.9) described strategic alliances as "a way for companies with complementary strengths to enter a given market more effectively and efficiently than either alliance partner could manage alone." Alliances can be a way for companies to avoid risk due to unforeseen factors, technology or market risk (Vaidya, 2011).

Dyer, Kale, and Singh (2001) called strategic alliances "a fast and flexible way to access complementary resources and skills that reside in other companies — an important tool for achieving sustainable competitive advantage." These benefits and others could explain why so many companies engage in alliances of all kinds. Dyer et al (2001, p.37) noted that "the top 500 global businesses have an average of 60 major strategic alliances each." However, about half of strategic alliances fail.

Reasons for Alliances

Best Practices

Alliances can take place because one company may have technology that another needs or may have demonstrated best practices in an area that can save a company money. For example, many online companies align themselves with specific shipping companies such as FedEx or UPS because these companies have demonstrated expertise in shipping. Online companies that sell merchandise that must be shipped may be experts in their business but may not be experts in the best and most efficient ways to ship. Similarly, online giant Amazon.com has become proficient in selling online and has built credibility online. The Amazon.com marketplace allows vendors to align themselves with Amazon.com using the online giant's proven system for getting customers, selling products and delivering those products quickly. Amazon.com has also proven that it knows how to protect customer personal information online. Many online shoppers are reluctant to shop with a company they have not done business with before. However, Amazon.com has set up a system for tracking orders and allows customers to access its customer service system if there are problems with an order sold through Amazon.com by a marketplace vendor.

Alliances can help companies get a product to market faster. One company may partner with another company with research and development expertise. Or, companies that are working in the same area of product development may pool their resources to complete a better product faster. Some products cross different fields making it important to find partners in the different industries needed. For example, a computer company might partner with a telecommunications company on a phone product with computer capabilities.

Mutual Benefit

Alliances usually take place because one firm has something that another wants and jointly they can create opportunities for all parties involved (Mitchell & Canel, 2013). For example, a small company may offer a service but may need help in getting the word out about that service. The small company may partner with a well-known company that offers a similar service or even a different one. This type of alliance may only be needed for a short period of time. A company may develop a self-improvement product or service and may need to generate leads. The company may be aware that companies like Stephen Covey's CoveyLink.com or Donald Trump's TrumpUniversity.com attract people interested in self-improvement. The smaller company may align themselves with these giants in self-improvement to be positioned to target a large audience without having to build that list on its own. The larger company may benefit by being able to offer another product that someone else created giving customers another reason to visit the company website.

Problem Solving

Sometimes alliances are formed to solve the joint problems that groups of companies share. For example, small manufacturers in the U.S. may form an alliance to address manufacturing competition from China. The companies in this type of alliance may work together to share ideas or even partner by trying to open up facilities overseas where appropriate. These companies could coalesce to identify joint purchasing opportunities or determine how they might lobby the government as a group to receive assistance. Similarly, technology vendors may form an alliance to ensure that technology is developed around open standards to ensure that products are compatible. If companies make a product that is far ahead of the competition but not compatible with the hardware, software and equipment that customers currently own, the advanced products are not very useful. The technology cemetery is loaded with very advanced but proprietary hardware and software that ended up failing because of the lack of interoperability and compliance with other products in use.

Alliance Organization

A non-profit organization called the Quoted Companies Alliance advocates for small companies listed in the United Kingdom (Binham, 2006). Companies might join an alliance like this to have a unified voice to represent their interests. Alliance groups like this one will only be successful as long as they stay in touch with the real needs of their membership. Pietras and Stormer (2001) give examples of strategic business alliances including "contracts, limited partnerships, general partnerships, or corporate joint ventures, or may take less formal forms, such as a referral network." Alliances are relationships between companies for mutual benefit.

Management of Alliances

The management of alliances starts at the very beginning of the relationship. Before the alliance is formalized, there is a need to do a great deal of planning and due diligence. Parties involved in the alliance will likely also exchange information, financial and otherwise, as part of the vetting process. There may be a need to sign nondisclosure agreements depending on the depth of the relationship and what internal information will be shared. Each party must manage and analyze information and manage the deployment of resources.

Alliances work when each side is able to get a result of value. Managing strategic alliances requires continual monitoring of the relationship to determine whether or not it is still effective. Collecting data on the cost of the alliance is also a factor in understanding if the alliance is useful. Evaluation at regular intervals will help the parties determine if the relationship should continue and if so, in what way. Keeping abreast of business activity in the industry and region can provide clues on which companies are engaging in strategic alliances and which companies may be ripe for that type of relationship.

Cisco Systems

Managing alliances can be tricky if the companies are in similar industries because a partner could also be partners with the competitor of their alliance partner. Careful thought must be given to this possibility up front and swift action will be needed as these situations arise. Cisco Systems is well known for products in the networking sector of the technology industry. Although Cisco has been successful, it still has ideas for expanding to other parts of the industry (Capron, 2013).

Cisco has entered the AON (Application-Oriented Networking) market by introducing products and by targeted merger and acquisition activity of at least ten companies per year in 2006 and 2007 (Manufacturing Business Technology, 2007). Cisco has a partnership with SAP to network enable enterprise applications. The partnership helps Cisco do what they do best (networking) while taking advantage of the reach that SAP has with enterprise customers. Companies like Cisco may also acquire companies to eliminate competition. The benefit to the acquired company is investment in the products and services offered and a means to take those products to market quickly to the automatically built Cisco customer base. It might take much longer for a smaller company to attract top tier clients which tend to be conservative in deploying technology due to cost, implementation, roll-out and compatibility issues. Similarly, advances in research and development can be supported and taken farther by partnering with a company that has the financial and human resources to push development forward.

A similar alliance between Cisco and SAP ended that allowed for co-branding and marketing of risk and compliance products. Cisco and SAP regularly enter into various types of partnerships likely because they have felt a level of trust and reaped benefits from their ongoing alliances. However, Cisco is engaged in a business partnership with IBM which owns a company that competes in the same area of a company that Cisco recently acquired. Within the technology industry, this is called co-opetition or a scenario in which these technology vendors realize that they will always have some overlap or competition with other technology vendors. But, as all try to expand their reach and embrace new technology, these competitors may have to work together as partners to ensure their mutual survival.

Companies seeking alliances should set specific goals and objectives for the alliance and always consider the impact of time. Putting together an alliance could mean a partnership on a short project or it could mean a multi-year agreement. In the case of a merger, the partnership might exist forever. As a result, companies must protect themselves by getting as much information as possible up front and to engage in careful planning. In addition, company employees have to be prepared for the upheaval that might result from certain kinds of alliances. Dyer (2001) suggested companies put a due diligence team in place to assess the suitability of potential alliance partners.

Viewpoint

The Value of Alliances

Time can cost companies money. The time it takes to develop products and services, the time it takes to train employees and the time it takes to acquire and convince customers to buy are all expensive. The value of an alliance can be the cost savings associated with time and catapulting a company into the next phase of development.

Strategic Alliance Processes

Dyer et al (2001) studied 200 businesses and found them engaged in 1572 alliances. A 1% rise in stock price was noted with the announcement of each alliance "which translated into an increase in market value of $54 million per alliance" (Dyer, 2001, p.37). Dyer et al also identified certain companies that were much more efficient at creating value than others such as HP, Oracle and Parke-Davis. These companies were extraordinarily successful because within their organizational structure was a dedicated strategic alliance function. The dedicated function can provide training to company employees to improve the internal capabilities of the firm to judge strategic alliances. Some companies provide intensive training for employees on alliances.

Successful alliance companies with units dedicated to identifying and analyzing strategic alliance opportunities can be more successful because of an institutional strategy. Dyer (2001, p.38) reported that "Enterprises with a dedicated function achieved a 25% higher long-term success rate" than companies engaging in alliances without an institutional approach. A dedicated strategic alliance function also helps companies become more familiar with the process and increases the knowledge available internally to the firm about strategic alliances. Dedicated resources can also spend the time needed to evaluate the progress and results of alliances. The increased knowledge helps companies devise strategies and tactics for every part of the strategic alliance process.

The University of Pittsburgh Medical Center has partnered with Alliance Imaging to deliver advanced technology for the treatment of cancer. The Medical Center reaps several benefits from the alliance. First, the center gets the opportunity to commercialize proven technology and resell the technology to hospitals that don't have advanced cancer technology. Second, the company only made a 20% financial investment but will receive 50% of the control (Becker, 2006). In addition, the medical center has 16 hospitals and 42 cancer centers so if has an opportunity to use and develop cancer treatments regularly. The partnership gives the hospital a distribution network for their technology. The market for radiation therapy is said to be $20 billion and not all hospitals can afford the equipment.

Alliance Evaluation

Alliances have to be reevaluated periodically to determine their relative value based on a company's objectives. Hershey Candy ended a long term relationship with advertising and public relations giant Ogilvy & Mather. Instead, Hershey established a new relationship and chose to expand other relationships as a solution to new advertising problems. The purpose of the change was to take a new direction and make changes that consumers might notice (Beirne, 2005). The distinctions are needed based on the large number of new products Hershey produced. Some retailers have suggested that the constant influx of new products is confusing to customers. Hershey must keep a critical eye on its market given that it spent a projected $580 million in advertising in 2013 alone (Schultz, 2013).

Sometimes alliances help companies penetrate a market quickly. HSBC North America partnered with Debitman Card, Inc. to serve a common customer base (Breitkopf, 2006). HSBC brings merchants to the table like Best Buy and HP while Debitman brings a payment network to process debit payments. The value of this alliance is it allows all of the players including HSBC who provides the credit card system for merchants, the retailers and Debitman to all concentrate on their core business area. Concentrating on a core business area is essential to success and efficiency. Partnering with those who are also experts in their lines of business can give companies access to expertise that would take a long time, money and effort to build. In addition, the largest retailer (Wal-Mart) only issues credit cards, not debit cards meaning that Debitman would have been shut out of Wal-Mart's business (Breitkopf, 2006). Together, HSBC and Debitman are working to convince retailers about the additional revenue opportunities in the debit business. The alliance can also help these strategic partners to work jointly on common problems.

There are times when alliances of particular companies affect entire industries. Examples can be seen in the automotive, telecommunications and retail sector. Becker (2005) reported on an merger between Alliance Medical Corporation and Vanguard Medical Concepts to consolidate two of the top three companies involved in the reprocessing of used medical equipment for reuse. Hospitals used to perform this task themselves and soon outsourced to contract re-manufacturers. This action makes the two medical device re-manufacturers together the largest company performing these tasks. Since both companies had different customers and specialized in servicing different devices, they can now sell to each other's customers and increase the revenues and demand associated with their products.

Alliance Need

Alliances should not be entered into simply because a company wants to be bigger or wants to prevent competition. To find the real value means the companies involved must actually have a need. Geographic interests are an example of a specific need for an alliance. Magnum Semiconductor is a semiconductor manufacturer based in California with a need to expand worldwide (Electronic News, 2006). Strategic alliances in foreign companies might involve finding local people to manage the company or setting up subsidiaries in the foreign country that would do business for the company. Other strategies if a company wants a presence in another country could be to align with distributers that are already set up allowing a company to capitalize on local country knowledge.

One of the greatest benefits of alliances is the ability to get more customers. More customers can come from taking a new view of your business and industry and to focus on the needs of these potential customers. A financial services company chose to partner with a pharmaceutical company to get more customers (Ramachandran, 2006). By partnering with a pharmaceutical company, a financial services firm has access to the names of physicians and others who might have financial service needs.

How to Make Strategic Alliances Work

There are as many ideas about making strategic alliances work as there are ways to construct them. However, any company interested in a strategic alliance will have to process a lot of information. Information can include data about the company, company interests and needs, industry players and dependent industries. Knowledge about other industries affected by a company's industry or that in some way has impact on an industry can offer unique ideas for possible alliances. Customers can also be a source of key information and possible referrals to strategic alliance opportunities.

Harper (2001) suggested that companies should avoid jumping into strategic alliances too quickly in order to solve problems. Avoid strategic alliance failure requires being realistic from the beginning. Painting too rosy a picture could lead to great disappointment. Disappointment can occur even if companies are industry leaders and spend a great deal of time vetting each other. Different styles in management, structure and methods may make it hard for different cultures to work together (Rooks, Snijders & Duysters, 2013). Harper (2001) outlined several important steps to help make strategic alliances work and provide win-win results for the parties involved. Using these steps makes it possible for companies to truly reap the benefits of lower costs, better market penetration, access to expertise or any other benefits they are looking to achieve.

To make strategic alliances work:

- Companies can make a careful assessment of the company goals for strategic alliances. This can mean looking internally at the needs and objectives in order to create a picture of the right kind of strategic partner candidate. A company should also look at alliances from the perspective of all stakeholders such as customers, employees and stockholders. A thorough look from these perspectives will also help companies identify what factors of an alliance are most important and which, if not in place, will sabotage an alliance. Companies should also evaluate whether or not another action other than an alliance might make more sense or provide some value such as cost savings.

- Formulate an alliance strategy with the candidate before signing formal agreements. In this way, both can try out ideas and see how working together feels. A true alliance that is not a merger provides what Harper (2001, p.26) calls "equal power"; allowing each company to be independent. Identification of the benefits for both must be compelling enough to balance out the effort and cost of working together. Both companies will have to share information about the strengths and weaknesses they bring to the table.
- Both sides of an alliance will have to contribute to making it work and have the ability to participate in making the alliance work from business development to process improvement.
- Similarly, both companies have to be honest about the effect and performance of the alliance when evaluating success.

"Frequent milestones" are a tactic suggested to ensure that risk is low and that problems are easily identified and handled early (Harper, 2001, p.27). The continuous feedback and continuous learning approach will make certain that the relationship between the alliance members is constantly improving.

Bibliography

Alliances keeps network management specialist moving up the application stack. (2007). Manufacturing Business Technology, 2(7), 22. Retrieved November 21, 2007, from EBSCO Online Database Business Source Complete. http://search.ebscohost.com/login.aspx?direct=true&db=buh&AN=25887801&site=ehost-live

Becker, C. (2006). Spreading out. *Modern Healthcare, 36*(7), 36. Retrieved November 21, 2007, from EBSCO Online Database Business Source Complete. http://search.ebscohost.com/login.aspx?direct=true&db=buh&AN=19939088&site=ehost-live

Becker, C. (2005). Alliance, Vanguard join forces. *Modern Healthcare, 35*(33), 14. Retrieved November 21, 2007, from EBSCO Online Database Business Source Complete. http://search.ebscohost.com/login.aspx?direct=true&db=buh&AN=18373321&site=ehost-live

Beirne, M. (2005). Hershey candy is dandy, but shelf space is thicker. *Brandweek, 46*(35), 6. Retrieved November 21, 2007, from EBSCO Online Database Business Source Complete. http://search.ebscohost.com/login.aspx?direct=true&db=buh&AN=18590624&site=ehost-live

Binham, C. (2006). QCA wins lobbying battle as Govt drops increased AIM regulation. *Lawyer, 20*(41), 5. Retrieved November 21, 2007, from EBSCO Online Database Business Source Complete. http://search.ebscohost.com/login.aspx?direct=true&db=buh&AN=23291918&site=ehost-live

Breitkopf, D. (2006). HSBC to issue for merchants using Debitman. *American Banker, 171*(98), 12. Retrieved November 21, 2007, from EBSCO Online Database Business Source Complete. http://search.ebscohost.com/login.aspx?direct=true&db=buh&AN=20908302&site=ehost-live

Capron, L. (2013). Cisco's corporate development portfolio: A blend of building, borrowing and buying. *Strategy & Leadership, 41*(2), 27-30. Retrieved on November 20, 2013, from EBSCO Online Database Business Source Complete. http://search.ebscohost.com/login.aspx?direct=true&db=bth&AN=87116218&site=ehost-live

Dyer, J., Kale, P. & Singh, H. (2001). How to make strategic alliances work. *MIT Sloan Management Review, 42*(4), 37-43. Retrieved November 21, 2007, from EBSCO Online Database Business Source Complete. http://search.ebscohost.com/login.aspx?direct=true&db=buh&AN=4834186&site=ehost-live

Harper, P. (2001). Four steps to making strategic alliances work for your firm. *Journal for Quality & Participation, 24*(4), 24-27. Retrieved November 21, 2007, from EBSCO Online Database Business Source Complete. http://search.ebscohost.com/login.aspx?direct=true&db=buh&AN=5982707&site=ehost-live

Magnum opens Japan office. (2006). *Electronic News, 52*(33), 7. Retrieved November 21, 2007, from EBSCO Online Database Business Source Complete. http://search.ebscohost.com/login.aspx?direct=true&db=buh&AN=22161207&site=ehost-live

Mitchell, S., & Canel, C. (2013). Evaluating strategic alliances in small and medium-sized enterprises. *Advances in Management, 6*(4), 2-9. Retrieved on November 20, 2013, from EBSCO Online Database Business Source Complete. http://search.ebscohost.com/login.aspx?direct=true&db=bth&AN=86941105&site=ehost-live

Pietras, T. & Stormer, C. (2001). Making strategic alliances work. *Business & Economic Review, 47*(4), 9. Retrieved November 21, 2007, from EBSCO Online Database Business Source Complete. http://search.ebscohost.com/login.aspx?direct=true&db=buh&AN=5426867&site=ehost-live

Ramachandran, A. (2006). Alliances the formula for adviser business. *Money Management, 20*(34), 1. Retrieved November 21, 2007, from EBSCO Online Database Business Source Complete. http://search.ebscohost.com/login.aspx?direct=true&db=buh&AN=22161207&site=ehost-live

Rooks, G., Snijders, C., & Duysters, G. (2013). Ties that tear apart: The social embeddedness of strategic alliance termination. *Social Science Journal, 50*(3), 359-366. Retrieved on November 20, 2013, from EBSCO Online Database Business Source Complete. http://search.ebscohost.com/login.aspx?direct=true&db=bth&AN=89488685&site=ehost-live

Schultz, E.J. (2013, September 2). Hershey's ad-budget rethink pays off with sweet rewards. *Advertising Age.* Retrieved from http://adage.com/article/special-report-marketer-alist-2013/hershey-s-ad-budget-rethink-pays-sweet-rewards/243761/

Vaidya, S. (2011). Understanding strategic alliances: An integrated framework. *Journal of Management Policy & Practice, 12*(6), 90-100. Retrieved on November 20, 2013, from EBSCO Online Database Business Source Complete. http://search.ebscohost.com/login.aspx?direct=true&db=bth&AN=78858339&site=ehost-live

SUGGESTED READING

Forest Laboratories and Schering-Plough case studies. (2005). *Pharmaceutical Licensing Strategies,* 1-17. Retrieved November 21, 2007, from EBSCO Online Database Business Source Complete. http://search.ebscohost.com/login.aspx?direct=true&db=buh&AN=21120550&site=ehost-live

Hirings. (2005). *Pensions & Investments, 33*(21), 35-37. Retrieved November 21, 2007, from EBSCO Online Database Business Source Complete. http://search.ebscohost.com/login.aspx?direct=true&db=buh&AN=18673053&site=ehost-live

Solheim, S. (2006). Virtualization vendors take aim at desktop. *Network World, 23*(16), 23. Retrieved November 21, 2007, from EBSCO Online Database Business Source Complete. http://search.ebscohost.com/login.aspx?direct=true&db=buh&AN=20634474&site=ehost-live

Theodore, S. (2005). New age 'Infuzion.' *Beverage Industry, 96*(12), 32-34. Retrieved November 21, 2007, from EBSCO Online Database Business Source Complete. http://search.ebscohost.com/login.aspx?direct=true&db=buh&AN=19443540&site=ehost-live

Westera, W., Herik, J. & Vrie. (2004). Strategic alliances in education: The knowledge engineering web. *Innovations in Education & Teaching International, 41*(3), 317-328. Retrieved November 21, 2007, from EBSCO Online Database Business Source Complete. http://search.ebscohost.com/login.aspx?direct=true&db=buh&AN=14910724&site=ehost-live

Marlanda English, Ph.D.

MANAGING PURE RISKS: OPERATION & MARKETS

ABSTRACT

This article focuses on managing pure risk. It provides an overview of the main approaches and challenges to managing the pure risks associated with and resulting from business operations and market activity. Topics of discussion include pure risk management strategies, operational risk, market risk, and formal risk disclosure requirements. This section serves as a foundation for a discussion of the issues associated with pure risk transfer and terrorism catastrophe bonds.

OVERVIEW

Corporate risk can be divided into the two broad categories of pure risk and speculative risk. Pure risk exclusively involves the potential for loss and no potential for profit. The occurrence of pure risk cannot be controlled nor reliably predicted. Examples of pure risk include terrorism, fire, death of key employees, customer injuries on the premises of the business, and natural hazards such as earthquakes and hurricanes. Pure risk can devastate a company. In contrast, speculative risk involves the equal chance of making a profit or taking a loss.

There is debate within the corporate world about how pure and speculative risks should be managed. Risk management refers to the process of evaluating, classifying, and reducing risks to a level acceptable by stakeholders. Risk management tactics include risk avoidance risk transfer, risk reduction and risk assumption. Since the emergence of risk management in the 1960s, corporations have created strategies for managing the pure risks associated with scientific research, market fluctuations, operations, engineering inventions, computer systems, and liability (Barlow, 1993). There is a tendency in many corporations to combine pure risk management and speculative risk management into the same program and initiatives. These corporations base this decision to have a widely-applied risk management approach on the belief that corporate risk represents a single exposure to the corporation. In practice, managing pure and speculative risk requires two very different skill sets.

Pure risk management involves minimizing negative outcomes by avoiding losses and accidents and preparing for natural and man-made disasters and catastrophes. Speculative risk management involves working to achieve the best passive results for events beyond the company's control (Lansdale, 1997). Speculative risk, which can be used to create profit and is also referred to as financial risk, is the domain of corporate managers, company owners, and the board of directors; pure risk, with no potential to bring profit, growth, or increased performance to the firm, is the domain of risk managers (Vann, 1990). Pure risk is assessed and managed almost exclusively by risk mangers. Pure risk managers plan for eventualities never knowing if or when the pure risk scenario will occur.

Corporations choosing to handle risk through a unified management strategy rather than separate pure risk and speculative risk strategies are continuing the industry's practice of the last forty years. While corporate insurance dates back to the nineteenth century, the practice of risk management, characterized as a singular approach to business risk, did not emerge until the 1960s and was not widely adopted until the 1980s. The 1980s were characterized by increasing government regulations, a growing economy, and insurance crisis. The federal government passed laws, such as the Occupational Safety and Health Act, the Environmental Protection Act, and Superfund legislation, which required corporate compliance. Corporations created new positions, such as risk manager, to address liability, safety, and environmental compliance issues. In addition, the business-boom of the mid 1980s, characterized by an increase in production plants, business locations, operations and workers, required new types and larger amounts of insurance. Companies demanded more insurance options and coverage from their insurers and insurance companies balked at the demands. Companies struggled both with financing their increasing insurance needs and finding insurance policies that met the needs of their expanding businesses. Corporations increasingly hired risk managers to assess their risks and select the best insurance options for their expanding businesses (Englehart, 1994).

Over the last ten years, insurance companies, in response to the of events such as the September 11, 2001 attacks on the World Trade Center, the collapse of the Enron Corporation and the unstable global geopolitical risk, are increasingly unwilling or unable to insure pure risk. Insurance companies are increasingly requiring shared risk scenarios with corporations and governments. Clearly, the current business and political environment is creating a greater divide between pure risk and speculative risk than ever existed before. While firms face the potential for numerous types of pure risk, within the areas of operational risks, market risks, cultural risks, economic risks, political risks and credit risks, pure risk managers are possibly most challenged by the need to manage operational risk and market risk. The pure risks associated with operations and market behavior, along with pure risks in general, are characterized by their unpredictability and potential to create devastating losses.

The following section provides an overview of the main approaches used to manage the pure risks associated with and resulting from business operations and market activity. Topics of discussion include formal management approaches, operational risk, market risk, and risk disclosure requirements. This section will serve as a foundation for a discussion of the issues associated with pure risk transfer and terrorism catastrophe bonds.

APPLICATIONS

Managing Operational & Market Risk

Pure risk managers are responsible for assessing, anticipating, minimizing, and mitigating the pure risks associated with operations and market activity. Like all pure risks, the pure risks associated with operations and market activities are always unexpected, negative, and destructive. Pure risk managers develop response scenarios and prepare their organizations for surviving pure risk situations such as fire, terrorism, death of key employees, customer injuries on the premises of the business, and natural hazards such as earthquakes and hurricanes.

Operational Risk

Operational risk refers to the financial losses that could potentially result from either internal procedural failures or external affairs. Examples of operational risk include the following: Procedural errors; internal control failures; failure of information processing equipment; malicious or fraudulent actions by individuals; workplace safety issues; succession failures; unintentional failures to protect clients; damage to physical assets; failures to follow regulations; business disruptions including terrorism and vandalism; computer and network crashes; service or product quality lapses; fraud; failure to comply with regulations or company policies; shifting political landscapes; and other unpredictable events (Beans, 2003, p.22). Operational risk is created by multiple factors including overly complex production processes; over-engineered products; too many vendors; complex or unclear organizational structures; and fragmented financial or control systems (Lynn, 2006). The results of operational risks can be potentially far-reaching and devastating for firms of all sizes and in all industries. Regulators and corporations have struggled since the 1990s to come to a consensus on the definition and meaning of operational risk. Firms of all sizes and in all industries struggle to decide the best means to allocate capital for managing operational risk and determine what role the board of directors has in assessing and managing operational risk. While a working definition of operation exists across industries, operational risks vary significantly between different industries and sectors (Garver, 2006).

The Basel Committee on Banking Supervision has led the way in the effort to define operational risk and develop tactics for management of operational risk. The Basel Committee on Banking Supervision has issued two international accords or international agreements, Basel I in 1988 and Basel II in 2004, which have standardized corporate perception of and management of operational risk. The Basel Accords have been widely adopted by regulatory commissions around the world. In the United States, the main federal banking agencies, including the Office of the Comptroller of the Currency, the Federal Reserve System, the Office of Thrift Supervision, and the Federal Deposit Insurance Corporation, have revised and implemented the Basal II Accord. The Basel Committee on Banking Supervision reported that the most serious operational risks arise from breakdowns in internal controls and corporate governance. Operational risk, according to the Basel Committee, can also be caused by failures of information technology systems or events such as major fires or other disasters (Aerts, 2001).

The Basel II Accord, officially titled the International Convergence of Capital Measurement and Capital Standards, promotes three approaches to quantifying operational risk:

1. The first is a basic indicator approach based on the annual revenue of the institution
2. The second is a standardized approach based on the annual revenue of each broad business lines institution
3. The third is advanced analytical approached based on an internal risk measurement framework.

U.S. firms, under pressure from the Basel II Accord requirements and the federal Sarbanes-Oxley Act, are increasingly revamping their organizations to handle operational risks. The operational risk management framework generally includes identification, measurement, monitoring, reporting, control and mitigation frameworks (Garver, 2006). Creating a framework for operational risk requires defining operational risk. More and more companies and countries are adopting the Basel Committee's definition of operational risk. That said, operational risk frameworks are not wholly general to all firms and industries. For example, the banking industry has unique needs, investment tools, and objectives and cannot adopt the operational risk frameworks of large corporations in other industries such as manufacturing or real estate. In the banking industry, operational risk often overlaps with credit risk and interest-rate risk.

Operational Risk Manager's & Management

Operational risk managers are responsible for anticipating, minimizing, mitigating, and preparing for operational risk. Operational risk managers work to minimize operational risk through engaging in the following risk management strategies: Foster a culture of risk awareness throughout the organization; back up all data, information, and procedures; practice contingency plans; take time to get to know customers; understand the firm's products; visit all branches and offices of the firm; and streamline and optimize all processes (Beans, 2003). Operational risk managers mitigate operational risk through the use of multiple strategies including: Looking and planning for the unexpected; instituting quality control programs; evaluating financial processes and transactions as if they were manufacturing processes, adopting internal performance metrics such as customer-oriented metrics, product oriented metrics, and financial oriented metrics; aligning insurance closely with the desired unit of value; and training for the unexpected. Operational risk managers prepare for operational risk through the use of multiple strategies including adopting the mindset of production managers with a concern for reducing defects in the products they produce for their customers; evaluating low frequency but high value risk/return tradeoffs; and increasing resources devoted to training, communication, and teamwork. Increased training, especially cross training, increases the likelihood that individuals throughout the organization remain alert for sources of defects or risk.

Ultimately, operational risk management is important for numerous reasons. For example, companies that experience fraud, errors, and systems failures are generally granted less capital by their financial lenders and become less competitive in the marketplace over time. In addition, companies that experience fraud, errors, and systems failures generally do not garner customer, employee, and vendor trust and develop a negative reputation in their industry or business sector (Lynn, 2006).

Market Risk

Market risk refers to exposure to the uncertain market value of a portfolio. Investors experience market risk as a result of the fluctuations in securities prices. Market risk extends to entire classes of assets or liabilities. Pure risk managers assess market risk through value-at-risk analysis. Value-at-risk analysis refers to a measure of how the market value of an asset or of a portfolio of assets is likely to decrease over a certain time period under usual conditions. Market risk anticipates the value or amount that an investment will decrease due to changes in market factors. The main factors, source, or variables effecting market risk include the following: Equity risk, equity index risk, interest rate risk, currency risk, commodity risk, unanticipated inflation and exchange rate change, decline in customer buying habits, and a shrinking market.

The United States government has strict corporate market risk reporting requirements. The Securities and Exchange Commission (SEC) requires that all corporations include a 10-K form in their annual reports describing the ways in which their own results may depend directly on financial markets. The SEC requires this reporting practice as a means of consumer protection for current or potential investors. In 2005, the Securities and Exchange Commission issued new corporate risk reporting and disclosure requirements. The SEC requires reporting on risk factors in three main categories of market behavior including industry risks, company risks, and investment risks. The SEC's new corporate risk reporting requirements, as represented by changes to annual report requirements on Form 10-K and quarterly reports on Form 10-Q, further the SEC's commitment to integrating corporate disclosure and processes first described in the Securities Act of 1933 and the Securities Exchange Act of 1934. Corporations must now disclose risk factors in their annual reports and describe changes in previously disclosed risk factors in their quarterly reports. Risk factors are believed to present a summary of the risks facing the company and identify factors that investors should consider when making an investment.

The SEC's new corporate risk disclosure requirement, as described in Item 503(c) of Regulation S-K, instructs that, when appropriate, a company has to engage in a discussion regarding the most important factors that may negatively affect the issuer's business, operations, industry, financial position or its future financial performance. The SEC argues that the new reporting requirements should not be burdensome as the SEC noted that companies should already be in a position to recognize new or changing material risks affecting their businesses. The SEC argues that disclosure of risk factors will alert investors to risks specific to the company or its industry that make an offering speculative or high risk.

The SEC requires, as stated in Rule 421 (d) of Regulation C, that the risk factors section of annual and quarterly reports be written using plain English principles. The SEC specifies six basic plain English principles that must be followed when drafting and explaining corporate risk factors: Short sentences; definite, concrete, everyday words; active voice; tables or bullet point lists, whenever possible; no legal jargon and highly technical business terms; and no multiple negatives. The SEC's plain English requirements are intended to make the risk factors easier for investors to understand. Ultimately, the SEC reports that the new risk disclosure requirements should help rather than hinder corporations. The disclosure of market risks limits the future liability of the company should such a market loss occur (Robbins & Rothenberg, 2005). In addition to the SEC market risk disclosure requirement, the Sarbanes-Oxley Act, passed in 2002 in response to corporate auditing scandal, requires that corporations engage in risk assessment and risk auditing to monitor its financial reporting and auditing processes. Section 404 of the Sarbanes-Oxley Act, which focuses on management's assessment of internal control over financial reporting, instructs corporations to conduct a top-down market risk assessment to evaluate the corporation's internal controls systems (Banham, 2004).

Issues

Pure Risk Shifting & Terrorism Catastrophe Bonds

Risk philosophy refers to a predetermined goal concerning the allocation of risk. Two of the most common risk philosophies are risk sharing and risk shifting. In the case of pure risk, risk shifting or risk transfer involves causing the other contracting party to sustain the full consequences of unanticipated events. In contrast, pure risk sharing occurs when an owner is willing to assume the risk of increased costs in the future caused by unanticipated events in exchange for a contract price today. Corporations and risk managers choose their risk philosophy based on their appetite for and ability to finance risk (Kozek & Hebberd, 1989). Catastrophe bonds, also referred to as cat bonds, are an example and increasingly common form of pure risk shifting. Traditionally, catastrophe bonds have been used to transfer the pure risk of natural disasters like hurricanes, storms, and earthquakes. Following the September 11, 2001 attacks on the World Trade Center, catastrophe bonds that transfer the pure risk of a manmade disaster have become common. Recent economic and political events, such as September 11, 2001 terrorist attacks and the collapse of the Enron Corporation, have brought a new awareness of pure risk and exposure to corporations around the world. More businesses are employing pure risk management strategies and tools to address this new awareness of corporate risk and vulnerability.

The Fédération Internationale de Football Association (FIFA), soccer's international governing body, issued the first terrorism catastrophe bond in 2003. The Fédération Internationale de Football Association issued a catastrophe bond worth an equivalent $260 million to cover the risk of a terrorism related cancellation of the World Cup 2006 in Germany. The bond covered the marketing revenue that the Fédération Internationale de Football Association would have to refund if the matches were cancelled due to natural or terrorist related catastrophe. The Fédération Internationale de Football Association earns most of its revenue from World Cup Soccer. The Fédération Internationale de Football Association based its decision to create the bond on a risk analysis in the form of an extensive model of potential terrorism-related pathways to FIFA World Cup disruption and cancellation. The bond's scheduled maturity was September 2006. The 2006 World Cup did in fact happen as planned and was unmarked by terrorist acts. Since the FIFA terrorism catastrophe bond was issued in 2003, terrorism catastrophe insurance, as a form of pure risk insurance, has grown extremely popular. The demand for terrorism catastrophe bonds is so great that they are often oversubscribed. The current geopolitical environment is currently so unstable that few insurers or companies can or will finance the pure terrorism risk alone. Insurers and companies use terrorism catastrophe bonds as one form of pure risk shifting (Trot & Jenkins, 2003).

CONCLUSION

In the final analysis, managing pure risk requires a thorough knowledge of the relevant workings of business and industry as well as an awareness of dangers to the business posed from real-world political and environmental events. Pure risk managers must oversee loss and risk associated with people, property, liabilities, and finance. Examples of pure risks include bomb explosions, fire, windstorm damage, theft, fraud, environmental pollution, an employee accident, an employee illness, loss of a key management figure, exposure to liabilities, or loss of market share for product. Pure risk managers create a framework within which firms can absorb the results of pure risk scenarios. A pure risk management framework will include the coordination and monitoring of risk preparedness and response scenarios and activities as well as an overall statement of the firm's risk management philosophy (Cooper, 1993).

BIBLIOGRAPHY

Aerts, L. (2001). A framework for managing operational risk. *The Internal Auditor, 58*(4), 53-59.

Banham, R. (2004). Enterprising views of risk management. *Journal of Accountancy, 197*(6), 65-71. Retrieved July 3, 2007, from EBSCO Online Database Business Source Complete. http://search.ebscohost.com/login.aspx?direct=true&db=bth&AN=13318843&site=ehost-live

Barlow, D. (1993). The evolution of risk management. *Risk Management, 40*(4), 38-44.

Beans, K. (2003). How to create a framework for managing operational risk. *Community Banker, 12*(4), 22. Retrieved July 9, 2007, from EBSCO Online Database Business Source Complete. http://search.ebscohost.com/login.aspx?direct=true&db=bth&AN=10444077&site=ehost-live

Bloom, L., & Galloway, D. (1999). Operational risk management pays off. *American Banker, 164*(199), 6. Retrieved July 9, 2007, from EBSCO Online Database Business Source Complete. http://search.ebscohost.com/login.aspx?direct=true&db=bth&AN=2381334&site=ehost-live

Cooper-Mitchell, M. (1993, August). A thorough approach to business security. *Director,* 11-17.

Englehart, J. A historical look at risk management. *Risk Management, 41*(3), 65-72.

Ferrer, R., & Mallari, N.C. (2011). Speculative and pure risks: their impact on firms' earnings per share. *Journal of International Business Research,* 10115-136. Retrieved November 15, 2013, from EBSCO Online Database Business Source Complete. http://search.ebscohost.com/login.aspx?direct=true&db=bth&AN=64876714&site=ehost-live

Garver, R. (2006). Operational risk: Who's making progress. *American Banker, 171*(86), 9-16. Retrieved July 10, 2007, from EBSCO Online Database Business Source Complete. http://search.ebscohost.com/login.aspx?direct=true&db=bth&AN=20749794&site=ehost-live

Halek, M., & Eisenhauer, J. (2001). Demography of risk aversion. *Journal of Risk & Insurance, 68*(1), 1-24. Retrieved July 10, 2007, from EBSCO Online Database Business Source Complete. http://search.ebscohost.com/login.aspx?direct=true&db=bth&AN=4862654&site=ehost-live

Kozek, J. & Hebbard, C. (1989). Contracts: Share the risk. *Water Engineering & Management, 136*(6), 20-24.

Kurland, O. (1992). The rise of financial risk management. *Risk Management, 39*(9), 12-15.

Langsdale, G. (1997). Five risk trends to watch. *Financial Executive, 13*(4), 21-23.

Lynn, B. (2006). Operational risk: Are you prepared? *AFP Exchange, 26*(6), 40-46.

McNamara, M. (1991). Managing the risk of employee benefits exposures. *Society of Chartered Property and Casualty Underwriters, 44*(1), 24-35.

Mainelli, M. (2002). Industrial strengths: Operational risk and banks. *Balance Sheet, 10*(3), 25-35.

Marcela-Cornelia, D. (2010). Causal relations between natural risk and business risk. *Annals of the University of Oradea, Economic Science Series, 19*(2), 242-248. Retrieved November 15, 2013, from EBSCO Online Database Business Source Complete. http://search.ebscohost.com/login.aspx?direct=true&db=bth&AN=65287268&site=ehost-live

Powers, M. (2006). Pure vs speculative risk; false choice; sham marriage. *The Journal of Risk Finance, 7*(4), 345.

Robbins, R., & Rothenberg, P. (2005). Writing effective risk factor disclosure in offering documents and exchange Act Reports. *Insights: The Corporate & Securities Law Advisor, 19*(5), 9-15. Retrieved July 11, 2007, from EBSCO Online Database Business Source Complete. http://search.ebscohost.com/login.aspx?direct=true&db=bth&AN=17256492&site=ehost-live

Trott, D., & Jenkins, G. (2003). How FIFA sold terrorist risk to the capital markets. *International Financial Law Review, 22*(12), 49-52. Retrieved July 11, 2007, from EBSCO Online Database Business Source Complete. http://search.ebscohost.com/login.aspx?direct=true&db=bth&AN=11759497&site=ehost-live

Vann, J. (1990). Risk management is relevant. *Management Accounting, 68*(3), 54-55.

SUGGESTED READING

Davis, R. (1989). Different treatment of marketing and design defects in pure risk-utility balancing: Who's the... *American Business Law Journal, 27*(1), 41. Retrieved July 10, 2007, from EBSCO Online Database Business Source Complete. http://search.ebscohost.com/login.aspx?direct=true&db=bth&AN=9701240348&site=ehost-live

Gahin, F. (1967, March). A theory of pure risk management in the business firm. *Journal of Risk & Insurance, 34*(1), 121-129. Retrieved July 10, 2007, from EBSCO Online Database Business Source Complete. http://search.ebscohost.com/login.aspx?direct=true&db=bth&AN=17482328&site=ehost-live

Sundararaj, G., Aravindan, P., Devadasan, S., & Muthu, S. (2000). Risk prevention and management in blast furnace operation through mock drill exercise. *Production Planning & Control, 11*(2), 197-206. Retrieved July 10, 2007, from EBSCO Online Database Business Source Complete. http://search.ebscohost.com/login.aspx?direct=true&db=bth&AN=3977368&site=ehost-live

Simone I. Flynn, Ph.D.

MANAGING THE PROCESS OF INNOVATION

ABSTRACT

This article will focus on managing the process of innovation. The article will provide an overview of the main types of innovation found in organizations, including incremental and breakthrough innovation, the trajectory of innovation, barriers to innovation, and the history of private and public sector innovation. This overview will serve as a foundation for discussion of managing the innovation process. The issues associated with managing breakthrough innovation will be addressed. A case study of Boeing's formalized innovation program will be in included. The case study will provide an example of how a company can effectively manage the innovation process on an extremely large scale and the ways in which successful innovation creates competitive advantage in the marketplace.

OVERVIEW

There is an established relationship between business strategy, innovation, and organizational performance. Innovation, which refers to the use of a new product, service, or method in business practice immediately subsequent to its discovery, influences economic success and market share in increasingly competitive global markets. In response to new technology-driven global markets, companies have increased their use of advanced technologies as well as their innovation efforts (Zahra, 1993). Innovation is associated with competitive advantage in both growing and mature markets. Innovation, unlike most other business practices, can change the competitive balance in mature markets (Brown, 1992). The concept and practice of innovation became closely associated with economic gain and competitive advantage in the 1930s. In the 1930s, economist Joseph Schumpeter (1883-1950) created a theory of economic development based on five types of economic innovations: set up or discovery of a new product, a new manufacturing process, a new market, source or new organization (Leteneyei, 2001). Contemporary business theory argues that companies must compete to keep or gain market share. Innovation is considered to be the key to creating competitive advantage (Stalk, 2006).

The following sections will provide an overview of the main types of innovation found in organizations, the trajectory of innovation, barriers to innovation, and the history of private and public sector innovation. This overview will serve as a foundation for discussion of managing the innovation process. The issues associated with managing breakthrough innovation will be addressed. A case study of Boeing's formalized innovation program will be in included. The case study will provide an example of how a company can effectively manage the innovation process on an extremely large scale.

Types of Innovation

Numerous types of innovation occur in organizations. Examples include marketing innovation, technological innovation, organizational innovation, product innovation, service innovation, and process innovation.

- Marketing Innovation: Marketing innovation refers to a process in which people gradually become familiar and accepting of a new idea. Marketing innovation is a social learning process that results in consumers slowly changing their attitudes and values. Market innovations are often technologically driven. When a technology is developed, the new technology is often in need of a new type of market application. Market innovation is based on the following assumptions: Innovation is driven by a learning process within social groups; some individuals have a higher propensity to try innovative products than others; and the speed of adoption may vary from one business to another (Brown, 1992).
- Technological Innovation: Technological innovation is the process by which industry generates new and improved products and production processes. Technological innovation includes activities ranging from the generation of an idea, research, development and commercialization to the diffusion throughout the economy of new and improved products, processes and services. Effective technological innovation includes either the diffusion process or the spread of the innovation commercially (Zairi, 1992). Technological innovation requires and is followed by new technology exploitation. New technology exploitation (NTE) refers to the utilization of new technology or scientific developments to improve the performance of products or manufacturing processes. The failure of management to recognize and manage breakthrough technology innovation often results in organizational inefficiencies and frustration (Bigwood, 2004).
- Organizational Innovation: Organizational innovation can be defined as the process of changing the organization by introducing different methods of production or administration. Organizational innovation includes the adoption of ideas from outside the organization and the generation of ideas within. Organizational innovation involves planning initiation, execution, selection, and implementation (Spender & Kessler, 1995).
- Product Innovation: Product innovation involves the introduction of a good that is new or substantially improved.
- Service Innovation: Service innovation involves the introduction of a service that is new or substantially improved.
- Process Innovation: Process innovation involves the implementation of a new or significantly improved production or delivery method.

All of the innovation types described above has elements and trajectories in common. There are two main approaches to innovation that span and characterize all innovation processes: incremental and disruptive innovation. Incremental innovation refers to improvement of technology performance or product feature enhancement. Breakthrough innovation, also referred to as disruptive, radical, or discontinuous innovation, refers to innovation based on technologies previously new to the world. These two different types of innovation have separate development trajectories and associated management strategies (Hacklin, 2005).

The Trajectory of Innovation

The trajectory of innovation is most often conceived of as an s-shape pattern with three distinct levels of diffusion and adoption of the innovation. For example, the s-curve for technology innovation includes three main phases (Hacklin, 2005):

- Pacemaker Technology Phase: Emerging technology is called a pacemaker technology as it is new to the world and the future potential and applications are identified. The diffusion of the innovative technology has not yet started in this phase.

- Disruptive Technology Phase: Established technology evolves into disruptive technology when it has managed to outperform competing technologies in respective mainstream markets. The diffusion of the innovative technology is occurring at a rapid pace in this phase.
- Key Technology Phase: The performance of the technology becomes more efficient and the technology become widely-adopted by the customer base. The diffusion of the innovative technology is complete in this phase. The innovative technology, if successful, has saturated its market and become ubiquitous technology among its users.

Organizational Barriers to Innovation

Innovation, which requires active learning, risk-taking, insight and vision, does not occur in every firm. Common organizational barriers to innovation include (Brown, 1992):

- A heavy reliance on market research to minimize risk when drawing up and approving plans for new products.
- The use of financial techniques, such as risk minimization, to assess innovation projects that are inherently risky.
- A tendency to invest in and rely on what has served the company well in the past rather than what may serve it better in the future.
- Systems of rewards and promotion that encourage a low-risk, custodial approach to management rather than a high-risk management approach.

History of Private & Public Sector Innovation

Innovation in the twentieth century was characterized by public and private sector partnerships and relationships. The private and public sectors significantly influence one another's innovation processes. The relationship between public and private sector innovation became very close during the Cold War from the 1940s until the early 1990s. After World War II, and during the Cold War era, publicly-funded science and technology research, development, and innovation grew for three main reasons: First, science and technology research was fueled by the belief in the need for strong national defense technologies. Second, science and technology research was fueled by the belief that scientific research, which had delivered nuclear weapons, antibiotics, and jet aircraft, would produce other innovations of national interest. Third, science and technology research was fueled by the belief that a large national science system was perceived by other countries as representative of national prestige and cultural achievement.

Cold War era, science and technology research and innovation, motivated by concerns for national defense more than economic growth, produced many of the university research and laboratory programs, government laboratories, and other technical institutes such as the National Science Foundation (NSF) and the National Aeronautics and Space Administration (NASA). The United States, along with other countries such as Canada, Australia, Great Britain, France and Switzerland, invested in significant national scientific infrastructures during the Cold War years (de la mothe & Dufour, 1995). Cold War-era defense-related spending resulted in the development of such high-technology industries as semiconductors, computers, and commercial aircraft.

During the 1980s and 1990s, private sector science and technology development and innovation grew and defense-related, military research and innovation slowed. In contrast to the pattern of the previous five decades, technological development began to flow from civilian to military applications. In 2000, the Clinton administration reduced the role of defense-related research and design funding in U.S. technology policy. Instead, the Clinton administration focused resources and policies on commercial technology research, development, innovation, procurement, and adoption (Ham, 1995). The largest high-tech private sector innovators will remain tied to the public sector for two main reasons: First, the public sector, including the military, remains one of the main customers of high-tech innovators. Second, the public sector has the funds available for public-private partnered and cooperative research and development programs.

APPLICATIONS

Managing the Innovation Process

The success of an innovation is connected to a market forecast of customer needs and wants as well as effective management of the innovation process. Firms have numerous economic tools and approaches for successfully developing a market and customer forecasts but are only recently, in the last two decades, developing and articulating management practices for the innovation process. While firms may or may not institute a formalized innovation policy and procedure to guide employees and mangers, there are a set of principles that guide the innovation process across businesses and industries:

- Innovations should meet customer needs, please shareholders, and motivate staff.
- Innovation requires vision to drive the change process.
- Innovation requires a risk-tolerant environment.
- Innovation requires a lifelong learning orientation that involves all members of the organization.
- Innovation requires creative thinking in a diverse and information-rich organizational environment.
- Innovation requires a cross-functional systems perspective for analyzing the impact of change and overseeing implementation.

Managers of the innovation process address numerous issues within the organization to ensure successful development and implementation of an innovation. The main innovation management responsibilities include reducing the sense of risk; managing the customer interface; training customers; managing staff performance; engaging front-line staff; and using information technology (Riddle, 2000).

Managers of the innovation process need feedback about their management performance. While market share will eventually reflect the success of management efforts, there exists another method for management review. Innovation management can be judged and evaluated through an innovation management measurement framework. The framework of the innovation management process consists of seven categories: inputs management, knowledge management, innovation strategy, organizational culture and structure, portfolio management, project management and commercialization. Innovation management measurement is used within firms by managers and executives. The innovation management measurement framework allows managers to evaluate their own innovation activity, explore the extent to which their organization is innovative, and identify areas for improvement (Adama & Bessant, 2006).

ISSUES

Managing Breakthrough Innovation

The process of managing breakthrough innovation, also referred to as disruptive or discontinuous innovation, varies greatly from managing incremental changes in products and technologies. The objectives of incremental innovation, such as speed, cycle time, profit impact, and quick cash recovery, generally do not apply to the breakthrough innovation process. Innovation managers recognize that the evaluation process for new products, processes, or services differs significantly from that used for extension projects. The potential market for incremental innovations is evaluated through conventional market research methods such as written surveys, focus groups, or concept tests. Breakthrough innovation projects are generally evaluated on their long-term value, impact on the market, and magnitude. The potential market for breakthrough innovations is evaluated through three main venues:

- Professional conferences and meetings.
- The demonstration of the product via early prototypes for reaction within the firm.
- Potential customers' evaluations of early working versions.

Determining the value of the innovation within the market is a speculative process. The project life-cycle for breakthrough innovations includes unpredictability, long time horizons, starts and stops, and periods of stagnancy. Management practices that facilitate the breakthrough innovation process include:

- Mechanisms for directing the technology-market arenas in which breakthrough innovations occur;
- Mechanisms for proactively stimulating discontinuous breakthrough innovation;
- Mechanisms for protecting projects that operate with high risk, uncertainty, and potential for failure.

Innovation managers are responsible for encouraging and facilitating the development of new businesses, product lines, and production processes based on breakthrough innovations. In addition, managers are responsible for developing and implementing management practices that reduce the high uncertainty associated with developing and commercializing breakthrough innovations. Managers, responsible for managing the breakthrough innovation process, use five types of managerial strategies to influence the process:

- Innovation Mangers Set Boundaries To Direct And Constrain Discontinuous Innovation Activities;
- Innovation Mangers Take Proactive Approaches To Stimulating Discontinuous Innovation;
- Innovation Mangers Stabilize A Systematic Approach To Evaluation And Screening Breakthrough Innovation;
- Innovation Mangers Create Incubating Organizational Arrangements;
- Innovation Mangers Recognize The Key Role Of Individual Initiative And Capabilities In The Innovation Process.

Ultimately, the breakthrough innovation process is not deliberately managed so much as encouraged and facilitated. Traditional management techniques are unsuitable for breakthrough innovation projects up until the point that uncertainty is reduced. The managers' main job is to reduce uncertainty and fear of failure up until the point where traditional management practices once again are appropriate. Managers of a breakthrough innovation project must be cognizant and accepting of the realities of the life cycle of a discontinuous innovation project. Breakthrough innovation projects are long-term lasting ten years or longer; have highly uncertain and unpredictable outcomes; are sporadic, with many stops and starts, deaths and revivals; have changing leaders and personnel; and require extensive exploring and experimenting rather than targeting and developing. Ultimately, breakthrough innovation projects, though potentially profitable to the business, are most successful when they are separated from traditional business expectations and ongoing business activities (Rice, 1998).

Case Study: Boeing's Global Enterprise Technology System (GETS)

In 2003, Boeing, a $54-billion-a-year aerospace company, developed and applied a new process for managing its enterprise-level research and development called the Global Enterprise Technology System (GETS). The Global Enterprise Technology System (GETS), which combines strategies from systems engineering, software process improvement, organizational psychology, and anthropology, provides a strategically-driven and systems-engineering-based approach to managing innovation. GETS is an example of applying the concepts of systems engineering to research and design.

The Global Enterprise Technology System is a collaboration between Boeing's business units including Boeing Commercial Airplanes, Integrated Defense Systems, and Phantom Works. The scale of Boeing's business operations includes customers in 145 countries with products and services such as commercial airplanes, defense products such as military airplanes, rotor-craft, missiles, communications systems, and space products such as satellites and launch vehicles. Technological innovation within Boeing's huge system and markets occurs primarily at the research organization called Boeing Phantom Works. Boeing Phantom Works is often referred to as Boeing's catalyst of innovation.

The scale of Boeing's enterprise necessitated an approach to managing innovation across many areas in a manner that is focused and connected without squashing vision and creativity. Boeing developed the GETS program to satisfy the following goals and objectives: highly collaborative, systematic, efficient, continuous, traceable, effective, and simple. The Global Enterprise Technology System is organized into four distinct phases including Discover, Decide, Develop, and Deploy. These four phases occur continuously at various levels.

- Discover: The discovering process is rooted in the constant dialog between what is desirable in the marketplace and what is possible to accomplish with technology.
- Decide: The deciding process draws on the outcomes of the discovering phase. Managers ask the following questions: What have we learned about the future? What new opportunities have surfaced? What assumptions have changed? What areas of emphasis are changing?
- Develop: The developing process, characterized by focus and efficiency, is about carrying out the work ideas. Technologists develop plans for the chosen research and design efforts and execute them within existing resource constraints.
- Deploy: The deployment process involves the placement and marketing of the innovative technology.

Boeing's GETS program has produced a generic model of technology and product development management that is used as a guide to establish research and development management processes for different parts of the enterprise. The GETS program facilitates process development workshops, conducts a broad-based formal inspection of the process, and promotes continuous improvement philosophy. Boeing considers the GETS program to be successful in guiding and managing the innovation efforts of their 2,500 researchers and their managers. Boeing reports the followings benefits and gains from the GETS program (Lind, 2006):

- Stronger Working Relationships Across Technology, Product, And Market Arenas;
- More Strategically Focused Portfolio That Delivers Greater Value To Boeing Business Units;
- More Effective Long-Term Focus, Strategic Planning, And Synergy;
- Reduced Meetings And Travel Associated With The Portfolio Planning;
- More Flexible Technology Portfolio To Meet The Changing Needs Of The Business;
- Reduced Complexity And A Stronger Innovation Process That Is Easier To Apply To New Areas.

The GETS program is a model of large scale innovation management. Boeing created GETS as an institutionally approved, supported, and overseen space for creativity and breakthrough innovation.

CONCLUSION

In the final analysis, the management of the innovation processes across businesses and industries shares numerous characteristics. Patterns of disciplined innovation management include understanding the product development process, making support functions time-invisible, grouping critical resources together, and maintaining management continuity (Stalk, 2006). Managers of the innovation process can improve their firm's chances at successful innovation by lowering sales expectations, assessing risks and rewards, sharing the rewards, encouraging innovation, allowing for learning and failure, and promoting experimentation and the need for change (Brown, 1992).

Questions that managers of the innovation process should ask themselves as they develop and implement their management strategies include the following: Is innovation stated as part of your corporate objectives and business plan? Do you provide support to staff that try out new ideas, even if the ideas fail? Do you have experiments or pilots of new service concepts being conducted within your business? Does your financial reporting system reflect innovation as an investment or a cost? (Riddle, 2000). Ultimately, innovation, when properly managed, gives companies competitive advantage in the marketplace.

Bibliography

Adams, R., Bessant, J., & Phelps, R. (2006). Innovation management measurement: A review. *International Journal of Management Reviews, 8*(1), 21-47. Retrieved June 6, 2007, from EBSCO Online Database Business Source Complete. http://search.ebscohost.com/login.aspx?direct=true&db=bth&AN=20387011&site=ehost-live

Bigwood, M. (2004). Managing the new technology exploitation process. *Research Technology Management, 47*(6), 38-42. Retrieved June 6, 2007, from EBSCO Online Database Business Source Complete. http://search.ebscohost.com/login.aspx?direct=true&db=bth&AN=14935409&site=ehost-live

Brown, R. (1992). Managing the 'S' curves of innovation. *Journal of Consumer Marketing, 9*(1), 61. Retrieved June 6, 2007, from EBSCO Online Database Business Source Complete. http://search.ebscohost.com/login.aspx?direct=true&db=bth&AN=5517061&site=ehost-live

Costa Souza, J., & Bruno-Faria, M. (2013). The innovation process in the organizational context: an analysis of helping and hindering factors. *Brazilian Business Review (English Edition), 10*(3), 108-129. Retrieved November 15, 2013, from EBSCO Online Database Business Source Complete. http://search.ebscohost.com/login.aspx?direct=true&db=bth&AN=91678530&site=ehost-live

de la Mothe, J. & Dufour, P. (1995). Techno-globalism and the challenges to science and technology policy. *Daedalus, 124*(3), 219-237.

Eschenbaecher, J., & Graser, F. (2011). Managing and optimizing innovation processes in collaborative and value creating networks. *International Journal of Innovation & Technology Management, 8*(3), 373-391. Retrieved November 15, 2013, from EBSCO Online Database Business Source Complete.

http://search.ebscohost.com/login.aspx?direct=true&db=bth&AN=66183155&site=ehost-live

Ham, R., & Mowery, D. (1995). Enduring dilemmas in U.S. technology policy. *California Management Review, 37*(4), 4-107. Retrieved April 27, 2007, from EBSCO Online Database Business Source Complete. http://search.ebscohost.com/login.aspx?direct=true&db=bth&AN=9510031720&site=ehost-live

Letenyei, L. (2001). Rural innovation chains. *Review of Sociology, 7*(1), 85-100.

Lind, J. (2006). Boeing's global enterprise technology process. *Research Technology Management, 49*(5), 36-43.

Hacklin, F., Raurich, V., & Marxt, C. (2005). Implication of technological convergence on innovation trajectories. *International Journal of Innovation & Technology Management, 2*(3), 313-330. Retrieved June 6, 2007, from EBSCO Online Database Business Source Complete. http://search.ebscohost.com/login.aspx?direct=true&db=bth&AN=18526428&site=ehost-live

Morris, L. (2013). Three dimensions of innovation. *International Management Review, 9*(2), 5-10. Retrieved November 15, 2013, from EBSCO Online Database Business Source Complete. http://search.ebscohost.com/login.aspx?direct=true&db=bth&AN=91879701&site=ehost-live

Rice, M., O'Connor, G., Peters, L., & Morone, J. (1998, May). Managing discontinuous innovation. *Research Technology Management, 41*(3), 52-58. Retrieved June 6, 2007, from EBSCO Online Database Business Source Complete. http://search.ebscohost.com/login.aspx?direct=true&db=bth&AN=575443&site=ehost-live

Riddle, D. (2000). Managing change in your organization. *International Trade Forum,* (2), 26-27. Retrieved June 6, 2007, from EBSCO Online Database Business Source Complete. http://search.ebscohost.com/login.aspx?direct=true&db=bth&AN=4845035&site=ehost-live

Spender, J., & Kessler, E. (1995). Managing the uncertainties of innovation: Extending Thompson (1967). *Human Relations, 48*(1), 35-57. Retrieved June 6, 2007, from EBSCO Online Database Business Source Complete. http://search.ebscohost.com/login.aspx?direct=true&db=bth&AN=12243776&site=ehost-live

Stalk Jr., G. (2006). Hardball innovation. *Research Technology Management, 49*(1), 20-28. Retrieved June 6, 2007, from EBSCO Online Database Business Source Complete. http://search.ebscohost.com/login.aspx?direct=true&db=bth&AN=19962271&site=ehost-live

Mohamend, Z. (1992). Managing user-supplier interactions: management of R & D activity. *Managerial Decision, 30*(8), 49-58.

Zahrah, S., & Covin, J. (1993). Business strategy, technology policy and firm performance. *Strategic Management Journal, 14*(6), 451-478. Retrieved April 27, 2007, from EBSCO Online Database Business Source Complete. http://search.ebscohost.com/login.aspx?direct=true&db=bth&AN=5207188&site=ehost-live

Suggested Reading

Schroeder, R., Van de Ven, A., Scudder, G., & Polley, D. (1986). Managing innovation and change processes: Findings from the Minnesota Innovation Research Program. *Agribusiness, 2*(4), 501-523. Retrieved June 6, 2007, from EBSCO Online Database Business Source Complete. http://search.ebscohost.com/login.aspx?direct=true&db=bth&AN=5138889&site=ehost-live

Tvaronaviciene, M., & Korsakiene, R. (2007). The role of government in implementation of innovation. *Business: Theory & Practice, 8*(1), 9-13. Retrieved June 6, 2007, from EBSCO Online Database Business Source Complete. http://search.ebscohost.com/login.aspx?direct=true&db=bth&AN=24656092&site=ehost-live

Voelpel, S., Leibold, M., & Streb, C. (2005). The innovation meme: Managing innovation replicators for organizational fitness. *Journal of Change Management, 5*(1), 57-69. Retrieved June 6, 2007, from EBSCO Online Database Business Source Complete. http://search.ebscohost.com/login.aspx?direct=true&db=bth&AN=16968319&site=ehost-live

Simone I. Flynn, Ph.D.

MOTIVATION, PRODUCTIVITY AND CHANGE MANAGEMENT

ABSTRACT

This article will focus on the importance for a manager to understand how to motivate employees and manage change within an organization, and how productivity is affected by the nature of the information-based organization. A summary of motivation theories is presented, including the needs-based, process-based, and reinforcement motivation theories. This is followed by an overview of the most mainstream change management models for creating organizational transformation. Finally, the paper presents a discussion on how productivity is affected by employee motivation, and how contemporary fast-paced information-based organizations can take advantage of motivational and change management theory.

OVERVIEW

In the year 2000, the well-known management guru Peter Drucker predicted a changing organizational landscape; one that is centered around information rather than productivity, focusing on worker knowledge, information sharing, and task specialists. Looking at the state of contemporary organizations, one can conclude that Drucker was right. Contemporary organizations face the challenges resulting from exponential growth in global competition, short product life cycles and quickly changing consumer demand (Muthusamy, Wheeler, & Simmons, 2005). These factors, combined with information availability and accessibility described by Drucker, have led organizations to find success through innovative and creative thinking, employee empowerment, and the sharing and management of knowledge. This has created a significant paradigm shift in how organizations motivate employees, how much value they place on worker productivity and where it fits, and how organizations deal with change (the foundational basis of 'innovation' and 'transformation'—popular buzzwords for contemporary organizational practitioners). This paper provides an overview of each of these topics, and how they are interrelated with each other.

Motivation

Never before has motivation played such a critical role in the workplace. Employees, in general, have more freedom than ever in getting their jobs done. The idea of self-managed employees and a democratic workplace is no longer the organization of the future. Rather, companies are beginning to embrace these concepts in order to have a changing organization that can adapt to an unstable and increasingly changing work environment. Some suggest that a completely democratic workplace is inevitable (Collins, 1997). This is creating a shift in emphasis from managing to leading, of which motivation plays a big role. The best leaders understand how to motivate their employees, using a transformational leadership style that is inspiring, intellectually stimulating, and provides individual consideration for each employee (Bass, 1999). Leaders of modern-day organizations must know how to motivate each of their employees in order for them to thrive in dynamic work environments. Understanding the various motivation theories is the first step to putting them into practice.

Motivation Theories can be categorized into three areas; needs-based, process, and reinforcement (Kinicki & Williams, 2003). All three categories should be considered by managers and leaders in the right situational context.

Needs Theories

Maslow's Hierarchy of Needs: Maslow's Hierarchy of Needs theory is probably the most widely recognized motivational theory. Maslow asserted that our needs are fulfilled in a progressively complex way—a hierarchy consisting of five levels. An individual's needs are prioritized by the position in the hierarchy, whereby certain needs cannot be achieved until the needs in the lower level of the hierarchy are fulfilled. The five levels (from bottom to top) are physiological needs, safety needs, social needs, self-esteem needs, and self-actualization. The physiological needs that one has are elements such as food shelter, clothing, and other most basic necessities. The safety needs include protection from physical and emotional harm, and the elimination of conflict. Clearly, in an industry such as construction, safety is a larger concern than it might be for computer programmers (Halepota, 2005). The social needs include the need for love, friendship, affiliation, and belonging. The self-esteem needs include job status, respect, promotion, and recognition. Finally, self-actualization is a level where all of the needs are met, and one is completely satisfied with one's surrounding environment. Organizational leaders should concentrate on where their employee's needs fit within the hierarchy. For example, it would not make sense to promote an employee without first offering an adequate salary.

A second widely-used needs theory was developed by David McClelland (Kinicki & Kreitner, 2006). McClelland suggested that individuals have three needs: a need for achievement, a need for power, and a need for affiliation. He suggested that every individual is different with regards to his or her needs, and in order to adequately motivate someone, a leader should have a clear understanding of their own employees' needs with regards to these three areas. For example, someone with a high need for affiliation might be well-suited for a human resources position, while someone with a high need for achievement might be well-suited for a sales position. A leader can make a critical mistake by exclusively using motivational techniques that concentrate in the wrong area, such trying to fulfill affiliation needs for a group of engineers that enjoy working in solitude.

The third needs theory that is often embraced was developed by Frederick Herzberg, and is often referred to as Hygiene Theory of Job Satisfaction (Kinicki et al., 2006). Herzberg suggested that organizations have elements that can be classified as satisfiers and dissatisfiers, and that in order to satisfy and motivate employees, a leader/manager should remove the elements that dissatisfy employees and improve the elements that satisfy employees. Such elements as rules and regulations, salary, work environment, and supervisors are classified as dissatisfiers, or hygiene factors. Promotion opportunities, learning opportunities, job recognition, and challenging work are classified as satisfiers. While both are important to motivating an employee, oftentimes organizations only concentrate on removing the dissatisfiers, which does not intrinsically motivate the employee, especially in the long run. Take the employee who is not happy with his or her career progression and attempts to resign, only to be tempted to stay with an increase in salary—a short-term solution that does not create the desired satisfaction.

Process Theories

There are three predominant process theories of motivation: Victor Vrooms Expectancy theory, Equity theory, and Goal setting theories.

The expectancy theory of motivation has three components (Kinicki et al., 2003). First, the employee has an expectation that his or her efforts will lead to high job performance. Second, the employee understands that if he or she performs at a high level, there will be a positive outcome. Finally, the employee understands the value of the possible outcome. These components—expectancy, instrumentality, and valence—are three elements of Vroom's theory. An example to demonstrate this needs process might be a commissioned salesman who is preparing for a sales call to a potential new customer. The salesman knows that in order to get the sale, an effort must be made, rather than having the purchase order just "drop in his lap." He spends half the night preparing his presentation, knowing that he will not present well without adequate presentation (effort leading to expectancy). He knows that if the presentation goes well, he will likely get the sales order (performance leading to instrumentality). Finally, he knows that an order will lead to a sales commission, and he'll be closer to his monthly sales goal (outcome leading to value or valence). He is motivated to prepare and get the sale.

Another process needs theory is Adam's Equity Theory. Adam asserted that the employee/employer relationship was a two way street where the employee has a number of inputs into the organization, and expects a number of resultant outputs that are fair and equitable. For example, an employee might bring past job experience, educational accomplishments, and might work 10 hours per week more than the average. To make these inputs feel equitable, the employee is motivated by good pay, promotional opportunities, and a good working environment. When there is an imbalance between input and outputs resulting in a feeling of inequity, the employee will have a feeling of dissonance—something is not right in the relationship. As a result, he or she won't be motivated towards achieving high performance. To remedy this, an employer might consider the individual's inputs separately, and compensate them accordingly to satisfy the inequity. Ramlall (2004) suggested that the Equity theory also considered the comparison to others. In other words, employees are motivated by positioning themselves against their fellow employees through their work inputs, and expect to be rewarded accordingly.

A third process theory is the Goal Setting theory. Drucker (as cited in Hoopes, 2003) asserted that the manager/employee relationship was immoral due to the power imbalance between the manager and the subordinate. His solution was the process of Management-By-Objective (MBO), where the employee has control over his or her work goals and tasks, which result in varying compensation levels and gives the employee a perception of being in control of their performance. Locke and Latham (Kinicki et al., 2003) formalized the Goal-Setting theory as a motivational construct, and this led to the birth of the SMART goals acronym (Smart, Measurable, Achievable, Relevant, and Time bound) that is commonly embraced by organizations, organizational practitioners, and management scholars.

Reinforcement Theory

Reinforcement theory is based on the reasoning that actions lead to consequences, which then lead to future behaviors. In this realm, there are four ways to reinforce behavior: positive reinforcement, negative reinforcement, extinction, and punishment (Kinicki et al., 2003). Positive reinforcement uses rewards to encourage continued behavior, such as a bonus for performing well. Negative reinforcement is the removal of consequences after a positive change in behavior has occurred, such as a sales manager who no longer calls three times a day to check up on a new salesperson. Extinction is the reinforcement process by which rewards are withheld or eliminated due to poor performance, such as the engineering manager who does not offer public recognition of an employee who does not have good performance, while publicly complimenting everyone else in the department. The last way to reinforce is through punishment, such as the manager that docks an employee's pay for coming in late to work on several occasions.

Productivity

Productivity is closely related to motivation. For employees to be effective and efficient in their job tasks, having the technical knowledge and ability is not necessarily enough. The employees also need the resources required to do the job. They need supportive management and leadership with a vision that is aligned with their own goals and objectives. Most importantly, an employee needs to be driven (or motivated) by some means to achieve high performance.

Employees are significantly influenced by the leadership and management styles employed by their managers and supervisors. In a time where innovation and change is expected, the transformational leadership style can be closely tied to employee performance. Much research has indicated that behavior and performance are positively influenced by transformational leadership (Caillier, 2014). Inspiring employees is a major element of that leadership style.

Kouzes and Posner (2003) also discussed how motivation and inspiration could affect employee performance. They claimed that leaders who routinely engaged in their five recommended practices—model the way, inspire a shared vision, challenge the process, enable others to act, and encourage the heart—are not only more productive in their jobs, but they are viewed as better leaders and have higher job satisfaction. They clearly established a link between a motivational style of leadership and employee performance.

Another model of performance was presented by T.R. Mitchell and D. Daniels (as cited in Kinicki et al., 2006). The creators of this model asserted that an employee's motivated behavior results from three things. First, the employee brings certain skills, such as job knowledge, traits, emotions, and beliefs to the workplace and the job setting. Second, the workplace employer provides the job context, such as the environment, support, rewards, task types, and work culture. Third, the manager of the employee uses processes that motivate the employee, such as giving them attention and direction, creating arousal, or being intense or persistent. These three things (employee inputs, job context, and motivating processes) result in the motivating behavior or drive that employees have towards completing tasks or achieving goals. The resulting motivating behavior includes employee focus, effort, strategy, and persistence in accomplishing the desired objectives or tasks. The model is based on the assertion that performance and productivity is directly related to motivated behavior, and that managers and leaders need to understand how to motivate their employees, in addition to providing the technical skills and an accommodating work environment.

In all three instances, performance is directly related to how motivated employees are.

Change Management

With an emphasis on creativity, innovation, and transformation due to the new information-based organizational (Drucker, 2000) and transformational leadership environment (Bass, 1999), understanding how to manage change is critical to the organizational strategy and process. Goodstein and Burke (as cited in French, Bell, & Zawacki, 2005) put it this way, "American corporations are accepting the 'New Age' view of organizations as a 'nested subset of open, living systems, dependent upon the larger environment for survival'" (p. 388). The fast-changing business environments of the twenty-first century, especially due to globalization and increased competition, have resulted in a significant need to not only be open to organizational change, but also to understand how to manage the change process. There are several theories of change that exist, and they all have much in common. Some of the more popular change theories are Kurt Lewin's three-step change theory, Appreciative Inquiry, and John Kotter's 8-step model of change.

Kurt Lewin's 3-step Change Theory

Kurt Lewin is considered the father of understanding organizational change by most. His model suggests that there are three steps one should take when undergoing organizational change: unfreezing, moving, and then refreezing. Through this process, the group undergoing change can first be destabilized—that is, allowing behaviors to move away from the status quo. The second step, moving, allows the change agents to implement the different processes or desired behaviors to the point that seems most desirable. Once this is achieved, the third stage is to refreeze, which stabilizes the change, making it the norm in terms of actions and behaviors (French et al., 2005). This model is one of the more popular change models, but also one that many consider outdated. However, Lewin's work should not be discounted as his theory continues to influence emerging thought, such as complexity theory (Burnes, 2004).

Appreciative Inquiry is a change model that is gaining in popularity and acceptance. Using this model of change, organizational change agents focus on the successes rather than the failures in order to pinpoint areas in which to change. The positive essence of the methodology makes it attractive to those who are generally concerned with employees' natural resistance to change. Johnson (Johnson & Leavitt, 2001) stated, "Appreciative inquiry is an approach that is uniquely suited to organizations that seek to be collaborative, inclusive, and genuinely caring for both the people within the organization and those they serve" (p. 129). In the field of organizational development, where major transformations take place, appreciative inquiry is the most common and most preferred method used by contemporary organizational practitioners (Rita Williams, as cited in French et al., 2005). The appreciative inquiry method not only serves as a catalyst for change, but is also the most easily accepted transformation process for those that resist change. The appreciative inquiry process, by means of looking at possibilities rather than problems, provides a different perspective for those involved in an organizational transformation.

John Kotter, a Harvard University professor, is well known as a leader in change management theory. His most famous work was his eight-step model for creating change (Kotter, 1998). The eight steps in his model were:

1. Establish a sense of urgency
2. Form a powerful guiding coalition
3. Create a vision
4. Communicate a vision
5. Empower others to act on a vision
6. Plan and create short-term wins
7. Consolidate improvements and produce even more change
8. Institutionalize new approaches

This model provided organizational change agents with a logical, action-oriented formula for implementing change, and as such has become popular on most bookshelves of modern managers and leaders. The first four steps are intended to change the status quo—perhaps building on Lewin's model. Steps three through seven allow the organization to introduce and begin implementing the change. The last step is intended to make the change permanently imbedded into the fabric of the organization.

Application

Motivating employees in a changing environment is no easy task. A leader in the twenty-first-century information-based organization is faced with a multitude of challenges (such as keeping productivity high) as information and knowledge-sharing is encroaching into the space that productivity once exclusively held at the top of the organizational priority list. The leader must engage in the leadership style that is most affective for an unstable and constantly changing environment.

Antonakis and House (as cited in Kinicki and Williams, 2003, p. 465) concluded that a combination of transformational leadership and transactional leadership styles, with an emphasis on the transformational portion, is the best method for leaders to motivate their employees. Leaders need to be aware of the individual needs of their employees, including the best way to motivate them. Every employee is different, and as such, leaders would benefit by considering the different types of motivating theories, some based on need, some based on process, and some based on behavior and reinforcement. However, understanding how to motivate each employee should not overshadow the need for the developmental and technical skills needed to perform job tasks, as well as making the appropriate and required resources available to the employees. Michaelson (2005) warns that where motivational theories are applied for the sole purpose of driving productivity, productivity will almost inevitably decline. Management that views workers paternalistically or as units to be manipulated, ultimately dehumanizes its workforce, however fair and beneficial the methods. In fact, respect, justice, and fair compensation may align with a worker's own idea of proper management, but if such reasonable treatment is transparently applied as "motivational" rather than humane, the worker may not respond in a positive way.

In addition to motivating employees, being a transformational leader also means that the leader is constantly striving for change through innovation and creative thinking. As leaders push for change, in order to keep up or stay ahead of the competition, they should expect to see significant resistance, unless an effective change management strategy is employed.

The bottom line is that the concepts of motivation, change management and productivity are intertwined and linked. All three should be a major consideration for a contemporary transformational leader.

Bibliography

Bass, B. M. (1999). Two decades of research and development in transformational leadership. *European Journal of Work & Organizational Psychology, 8*, 9–32. Retrieved on March 14, 2007, from EBSCO Online Database Business Source Premier. http://search.ebscohost.com/login.aspx?direct=true&db=buh&AN=4437836&site=bsi-live

Burnes, B. (2004). Kurt Lewin and complexity theories: Back to the future? *Journal of Change Management, 4*, 309–325. Retrieved on March 31st, 2007, from EBSCO Online Database Business Source Premier. http://search.ebscohost.com/login.aspx?direct=true&db=buh&AN=15980546&site=bsi-live

Caillier, J. G. (2014). Toward a better understanding of the relationship between transformational leadership, public service motivation, mission valence, and employee performance: A preliminary study. *Public Personnel Management, 43*, 218–239. Retrieved on November 5, 2014, from EBSCO online database Business Source Premier. http://search.ebscohost.com/login.aspx?direct=true&db=buh&AN=96205010&site=bsi-live

Collins, D. (1997). The ethical superiority and inevitability of participatory management as an organizational system. *Organization Science, 8*, 489. Retrieved on March 14, 2007 from EBSCO Online Database Business Source Premier. http://search.ebscohost.com/login.aspx?direct=true&db=buh&AN=5170367&site=bsi-live

Cranston, S., & Keller, S. (2013). Increasing the "meaning quotient" of work. *Mckinsey Quarterly*, (1), 48–59. Retrieved December 7, 2015 from EBSCO Online Database Business Source Premier. http://search.ebscohost.com/login.aspx?direct=true&db=buh&AN=85277092&site=bsi-live

Drucker, P. (2000). Coming of the new organization [Electronic Version]. Retrieved March 14, 2006 from http://homepage.mac.com/bobembry/studio/biz/conceptual%5fresources/authors/peter%5fdrucker/neworg.pdf.

French, W. L., Bell, C. H., & Zawacki, R. A. (2005). *Organization development and transformation: Managing effective change* (6th ed.). New York, NY: McGraw-Hill Irwin.

Halepota, H. (2005). Motivational theories and their application in construction. *Cost Engineering, 47*, 14–18. Retrieved October 31, 2013, from EBSCO Online Database Business Source Complete. http://search.ebscohost.com/login.aspx?direct=true&db=bth&AN=16614691&site=ehost-live

Hoopes, J. (2003). *False prophets* (1st ed.). Cambridge, MA: Perseus Publishing.

Johnson, G., & Leavitt, W. (2001). Building on success: Transforming organizations through an appreciative inquiry. *Public Personnel Management, 30*, 129. Retrieved on March 31, 2007, from EBSCO Online Database Business Source Premier. http://search.ebscohost.com/login.aspx?direct=true&db=buh&AN=4387302&site=bsi-live

Kinicki, A., & Kreitner, R. (2006). *Organizational Behavior; key concepts, skills, and best practices* (2nd ed.). New York. NY: McGraw Hill.

Kinicki, A., & Williams, B. (2003). *Management: A practical introduction* (2nd ed.). New York, NY: McGraw-Hill.

Kotter, J. P. (1998). Winning at change. *Leader to Leader,* 27–33.

Kouzes, J., & Posner, B. (2003). *The leadership challenge* (3rd ed.). San Francisco, CA.: Jossey-Bass.

Merrell, P. (2012). Effective change management: The simple truth. *Management Services, 56,* 20–23. Retrieved October 31, 2013, from EBSCO Online Database Business Source Complete. http://search.ebscohost.com/login.aspx?direct=true&db=bth&AN=77508042&site=ehost-live

Michaelson, C. (2005). Meaningful motivation for work motivation theory. *Academy of Management Review, 30,* 235–238. Retrieved October 31, 2013, from EBSCO Online Database Business Source Complete. http://search.ebscohost.com/login.aspx?direct=true&db=bth&AN=16387881&site=ehost-live

Muthusamy, S., K., Wheeler, J. V., & Simmons, B. L. (2005). Self-managing work teams: Enhancing organizational innovativeness. *Organization Development Journal, 23,* 53. Retrieved on March 31, 2007, from EBSCO Online Database Business Source Premier. http://search.ebscohost.com/login.aspx?direct=true&db=buh&AN=19282864&site=bsi-live

Performance measures and rewards: The alignment of management goals and employee motivation. (2014). *Canadian Manager, 39,* 26–27. Retrieved on November 5, 2014, from EBSCO online database Business Source Premier. http://search.ebscohost.com/login.aspx?direct=true&db=buh&AN=95462784&site=bsi-live

Ramlall, S. (2004). A review of employee motivation theories and their implications for employee retention within organizations. *Journal of American Academy of Business, Cambridge, 5*(1/2), 52. Retrieved on March 31, 2007, from EBSCO Online Database Business Source Premier. http://search.ebscohost.com/login.aspx?direct=true&db=buh&AN=13200742&site=bsi-live

Sabine, B., Silke Astrid, E., & Daniel, G. (2007). Follower behavior and organizational performance: The impact of transformational leaders. *Journal of Leadership & Organizational Studies, 13,* 15.

Silvera, I. (2013). Motivation schemes can build long-term engagement. *Employee Benefits,* 7. Retrieved December 7, 2015 from EBSCO Online Database Business Source Premier. http://search.ebscohost.com/login.aspx?direct=true&db=buh&AN=88135273&site=bsi-live

SUGGESTED READING

Berry, J. (2014). Revolutionising motivation. *Training Journal,* 10–13. Retrieved on November 5, 2014, from EBSCO online database Business Source Premier. http://search.ebscohost.com/login.aspx?direct=true&db=buh&AN=98788793&site=bsi-live

Change management needs to change: Interaction. (2013). *Harvard Business Review, 91,* 18–19. Retrieved October 31, 2013, from EBSCO Online Database Business Source Complete.

Clegg, C., & Walsh, S. (2004). Change management: Time for a change! *European Journal of Work and Organizational Psychology, June 2004,* 2. Retrieved on April 5, 2007, from EBSCO Online Database Business Source Complete. http://search.ebscohost.com/login.aspx?direct=true&db=bth&AN=13310790&site=ehost-live

Houkes, I., Janssen, P., de Jonge, J., & Bakker, A. (2003). Specific determinants of intrinsic work motivation, emotional exhaustion, and turnover intention: A multisample longtitudinal study. *Journal of Occupational & Organizational Psychology, 76,* 427. Retrieved April 5, 2007, from EBSCO Online Database Business Source Complete. http://search.ebscohost.com/login.aspx?direct=true&db=bth&AN=11717817&site=ehost-live

Mautz, S. (2015). *Make it matter: How managers can motivate by creating meaning.* New York City, NY: AMACOM.

Schwinn, C., & Schwinn, D. (1996). Lessons for organizational transformation. *Journal for Quality & Participation, 19,* 6. Retrieved on April 5, 2007, from EBSCO Online Database Business Source Complete. http://search.ebscohost.com/login.aspx?direct=true&db=bth&AN=9609301000&site=ehost-live

Strickler, J. (2006). What really motivates people? *Journal for Quality & Participation, 29,* 26. Retreived on April 5, 2007, from EBSCO Online Database Business Source Complete. http://search.ebscohost.com/login.aspx?direct=true&db=bth&AN=20795025&site=ehost-live

John D. Benson, M.B.A.

MULTI-GENERATIONAL MANAGEMENT

ABSTRACT

The study of multi-generational management has recently come into vogue, because an unusual circumstance has developed. Significant numbers of five distinct generations are now present in the workforce of the United States, a phenomenon human resources professionals and social scientists have dubbed "5G." This presents unique challenges for managers because each generation has in place certain stereotypes about itself and about the other four generations. These stereotypes affect the ways the generations interact with one another at work, and have frequently been the source of conflict.

OVERVIEW

The modern workplace has long been struggling to address issues of diversity, as members of more and more groups find themselves needing to understand one another well enough to get along or at least get their work done with a minimal amount of friction. During this process, diversity has usually taken the form of differences in gender, ethnicity, cultural background, sexual orientation, or religious affiliation. Within the past few years, a new category has been added to this list: generational diversity. This is because, for a variety of personal and economic reasons, more generations are simultaneously participating in the workforce than has been seen at almost any other period in history. At present there are five distinct generations working side by side: the traditionalists (born before 1946), the baby boomers (born after 1946 but before 1964), generation X (born after 1965 and before 1980), generation Y (born after 1980 and before 1995, also known as millennials), and generation Z (born after 1996). Each of these generations has distinctive qualities that it is known for; some of these are positive, while others are negative. These stereotypical representations affect the kinds of expectations held by members of one generation when they interact with another generation. As is often the case when people act based on their expectations of others, there are times when the interaction takes on the semblance of a self-fulfilling prophecy.

For example, if a group of millennials expect that their baby boomer supervisor will behave in a self-centered manner, thinking primarily about his or her own needs, then it is likely that most of the supervisor's actions will be interpreted this way, regardless of their true intent. When the supervisor eventually learns that he or she is being perceived in this way, it is likely to create resentment toward the millennials for thinking the worst (Zemke, Raines, & Filipczak, 2013).

APPLICATIONS

In an effort to avoid generational conflicts in the workplace, many managers have begun to study the ways that different generations tend to interact with one another at work. Obviously, there are a great many permutations and combinations that can arise from the five different generations, as well as the many different types of relationships that are possible in the contemporary work environment. Employees can be above or below one another in the hierarchy, or at the same level (Burke, Cooper, & Antoniou, 2015). They can also be members of completely separate hierarchies and power structures, who nevertheless are required by the circumstances of the workplace to interact with one another from time to time.

A good deal has been written about the stereotypical behaviors that each generation supposedly exhibits: Traditionalists are old fashioned and methodical, and tend to resist the use of technology whenever possible, preferring face to face communication. Baby boomers are seen as disliking authority but having a preference for clear organizational structures with well established reporting lines; they are sometimes described as materialistic and even self-absorbed. Generation Xers are thought to be cynical and independent, because they grew up exposed to numerous political and religious scandals, and often had to look after themselves because their parents were divorced, working, or both—the term "latch key kid" dates from Generation X's era, when kids would go home after school to an house because both parents were at work. Millennials share the baby boomers' distrust of authority, but possess great aptitude with technology, since they grew up using the Internet and various gadgets. Generation Z is only just entering the workforce, so it is difficult to tell what all of its distinguishing characteristics will be, though it is clear that its members are even more comfortable with technology than are members of generation Y (Sauser & Sims, 2012).

Perhaps the most interesting piece of research on these issues, from a managerial perspective, at least, is a study that investigated these generational stereotypes in an effort to determine how accurate they really are. The study found, among other things, that virtually all generational stereotypes relevant to workplace performance are experienced as exaggerations by the generation to whom they are attributed. For each generational grouping, questions were asked of that group's members and of members of all of the other groups, about how accurate the stereotypes attributed to that group are. Every group reported feeling that others' understanding of it was exaggerated.

For example, if all groups were asked what percentage of millennials behave awkwardly in social situations, most groups might estimate the answer to be about 80 percent, whereas millennials themselves would estimate about 50 percent. In other words, the stereotypes that each generation has about the other generations tend to be grounded in truth, but are less true than people outside a given group believe they are (Elliott, 2011).

Managing multiple generations of workers requires balancing competing interests, some of which appear to be at odds with one another (Al-Asfour, 2014). This can make management a thankless job, as almost any type of initiative can be relied upon to upset one generation even as it appeases another. For example, if a company sought to introduce an employee benefit that would be paid out in the form of shares in the company that could be redeemed after ten years, younger employees such as millennials and those from generation Z might be quite pleased, but older employees like traditionalists and even some baby boomers might be less thrilled (Abrams & Von, 2013). This would be because the older employees might not want to wait years into their retirement to receive the benefit, while the younger employees, with more working years ahead of them, would find the delay less onerous. Software technologies have been developed specifically to help human resource personnel to deal with a multi-generational workforce (König, 2015).

In order to avoid conflict-generating situations, managers of multiple generations will often try to craft benefit programs in such a way as to make them appealing to each age group of employees at the firm (Bussin & van Rooy, 2014). In the example above, the benefit of company shares might be altered so that it could be redeemed at any time during the ten year period, but the reward would be greater if one waited longer. This way, all generations would have the option of receiving the same benefit, but they would also have the flexibility of cashing it in sooner if that worked better for them.

VIEWPOINTS

One piece of advice that multi-generational managers agree on is that they should be aware of differences among employees of different generations, but try to build on the similarities that exist between them. For example, baby boomers are unusual in the fact that they frequently care for their parents and their children at the same time; they are sometimes called the "sandwich generation," since they are sandwiched between the needs of their parents and their kids. Sometimes this causes baby boomers to resent members of other generations, envying the fact that they do not have as many duties to juggle. A skillful manager could help avoid conflict around this by enlisting both Baby Boomers and members of other groups to help the company design support services for employees in need of child care. This would be a project that focuses on what employees of different generations have in common—the need for high quality child care—rather than what distinguishes them.

Interestingly, most of the generations think other generations have the same negative qualities, the majority of which seem to result from poor communication between members of different generations. This can be seen when one asks members of various generations what they think about other generations' attitudes toward change. Members of younger generations will usually report that members of older generations are resistant to change: Baby boomers say this about traditionalists, generation X says it about baby boomers, and generation Y says it about generation X, and so on. The pattern holds for other stereotypes as well. Millennials think baby boomers are arrogant, baby boomers think millennials are arrogant, and so on—suggesting that the underlying issue is that the generations are not communicating well with one another (Szollose, 2011). Facilitating communication between generations, and in effect "translating" for one generation so that its words and behavior are understood by other generations the way they were meant to be, becomes the role of the multi-generational manager. Ideally this sort of work is done ahead of time, so that misunderstandings and conflicts can be avoided before they begin, but in large organizations where things are constantly on the move, this is not always possible. The manager must then clean up the mess caused by mistaken assumptions, clarifying communications, and repairing bruised egos on all sides (Lindsell-Roberts, 2011).

Recruitment

It is tempting to think of the multi-generational workforce only in terms of the problems it can cause, but there are potential benefits worth considering as well. Having employees from different age groups all working together toward the same organizational goals brings to the work a much wider range of skills and experience than would be present if only one or two generations were represented. Some employers, cognizant of this benefit, design their recruitment efforts to appeal to members of different generations. This can be a tricky affair because it is easy for recruiters to fall back on simplistic stereotypes about the generations, assuming that all millennial and generation Z workers are vegan carpoolers, for example (Reitman & American Society for Training and Development, 2013).

The best multi-generational recruitment efforts are based on detailed research and discussions with members of the groups being targeted, so that a realistic picture of the target generations and their needs can be developed. Sometimes, this involves refining the lens through which the generations are being studied. This can mean not only looking at the year of an employee's birth to determine their generation, but also examining criteria such as career stage. Career stage is an approximation of how long an employee has been in a career, and tends to be classified as early, middle, or late.

Early career is usually five years or less in a role, middle career is five to fifteen years, and late career stage is fifteen or more years in a role (Warnell, 2015). Thus, an employee born in 1975 who has been working as a salesperson for eight years might be described as a member of generation X at the middle stage of his or her career. This gives a clearer picture of the employee's experience and potential attitudes, which can be useful when helping the employee interact effectively with others. For example, more than one generation complains that other generations do not respect its authority or acknowledge the contribution of their experience. Assessing the accuracy of this kind of complaint could be difficult for a manager who does not know more about the employees involved—an early stage baby boomer who does not feel her experience is being respected by a late stage millennial is a very different situation than a late stage traditional who feels that her experience is not being acknowledged by an early stage generation Z employee. When a thorny conflict arises, the wise manager will pause to consider issues such as stage and generation (Finkelstein, 2015).

BIBLIOGRAPHY

Abrams, J., & Von, F. V. (2013). *The multigenerational workplace: communicate, collaborate, and create community*. Thousand Oaks, CA: Corwin.

Al-Asfour, A., & Lettau, L. (2014). Strategies for Leadership Styles for Multi-Generational Workforce. *Journal of Leadership, Accountability & Ethics, 11*(2), 58-69. Retrieved January 3, 2016, from EBSCO Online Database Business Source Complete. http://search.ebscohost.com/login.aspx?direct=true&db=bth&AN=100414801&site=ehost-live

Burke, R. J., Cooper, C. L., & Antoniou, A.-S. G. (2015). *The multi-generational and aging workforce: Challenges and opportunities*. Northampton, MA: Edward Elgar.

Bussin, M., & van Rooy, D. J. (2014). Total rewards strategy for a multi-generational workforce in a financial institution. *South African Journal of Human Resource Management, 12*(1), 1–11. Retrieved January 3, 2016 from EBSCO Online Database Business Source Complete. http://search.ebscohost.com/login.aspx?direct=true&db=bth&AN=103281234&site=ehost-live

Elliott, S. (2011). *Ties to tattoos: Turning generational differences into a competitive advantage*. Dallas, TX: Brown Books.

Finkelstein, L. M. (2015). *Facing the challenges of a multi-age workforce: A use-inspired approach*. New York, NY: Routledge.

König, C. (2015). HR technologies for the multi-generational workforce. *Workforce Solutions Review,*

6(3), 20–23. Retrieved January 3, 2016 from EBSCO Online Database Business Source Complete. http://search.ebscohost.com/login.aspx?direct=true&db=bth&AN=111478863&site=ehost-live

Lindsell-Roberts, S. (2011). *New rules for today's workplace.* Boston, MA: Houghton Mifflin Harcourt.

Reitman, A., & American Society for Training and Development. (2013). *Talent engagement across the generations.* Alexandria, VA: ASTD Press.

Sauser, W. I., & Sims, R. R. (2012). *Managing human resources for the Millennial generation.* Charlotte, NC: Information Age.

Szollose, B. (2011). *Liquid leadership: From Woodstock to Wikipedia: Multigenerational management ideas that are changing the way we run things.* Austin, TX: Greenleaf.

Warnell, J. M. M. (2015). *Engaging millennials for ethical leadership: What works for young professionals and their managers.* New York, NY: Business Expert Press.

Zemke, R., Raines, C., & Filipczak, B. (2013). *Generations at work: Managing the clash of boomers, Gen Xers, and Gen Yers in the workplace.* New York, NY: American Management Association.

Suggested Reading

Barry, M. (2014). Creating a practice environment that supports multigenerational workforce collaboration. *American Nurse, 46*(1), 13.

Carpenter, M. J., & de Charon, L. C. (2014). Mitigating multigenerational conflict and attracting, motivating, and retaining millennial employees by changing the organizational culture: A theoretical model. *Journal of Psychological Issues in Organizational Culture, 5*(3), 68–84.

Cekada, T. L. (2012). Training a multigenerational workforce. *Professional Safety, 57*(3), 40–44. Retrieved January 3, 2016, from EBSCO Online Database Business Source Complete. http://search.ebscohost.com/login.aspx?direct=true&db=bth&AN=72324002&site=ehost-live

Gelbtuch, J. B., Morlan, C., Project Management Institute & PMI Global Congress—North America. (2015). *Successful project management leadership in a multigenerational workplace.* PMI Global Congress 2015—North America.

Wiedmer, T. (2015). Generations do differ: Best practices in leading traditionalists, boomers, and generations X, Y, and Z. *Delta Kappa Gamma Bulletin, 82*(1), 51–58.

Scott Zimmer, J.D.

N

Negotiations

ABSTRACT

Wherever people work together, there is a potential for conflict. This is particularly true in organizations where the needs and focus of the different stakeholders often are often in opposition. Conflict can negatively impact an organization's performance and effectiveness. Negotiation is a process used to help conflicting parties reach a mutually acceptable agreement. There are two primary factors that can affect the effectiveness of negotiations: The skill of the negotiator in conflict management skills and various situational variables. To be successful in negotiations, good preparation is essential. There are a number of tactics that a negotiator can use to help become better prepared for the negotiating table including information gathering about the strengths, weaknesses, and assumptions of the opponent. In addition, it is important for the negotiator to be mentally prepared for the negotiating table through an understanding of his/her own strengths, weaknesses, and assumptions as well.

OVERVIEW

In many ways, globalization has revolutionized the way that many organizations do business. The practice of off-shoring enables organizations to relocate part of their operations to another country with lower costs or to outsource functions or activities to other companies with lower rates both around the country and around the world. Typically, this work was previously performed by domestic employees. However, these practices are often necessary to combat another result of globalization: the increased competition from other organizations at home that are able to charge less because of outsourced work or around the world and are able to compete in the global marketplace. Although organizations potentially have a greater, global marketplace in which to market their products or services, this marketplace is also populated by more competitors than ever before.

Stakeholder Interest & Conflict

Most organizations have multiple stakeholders — persons or groups that can affect or be affected by a decision or action. These may include the organization's employees, suppliers, distributors, and stockholders. Often the interests of the different stakeholders are in conflict. For example, most stockholders will be primarily concerned with earning a high return on their investment. In the abstract, keeping labor prices down or raising the sales price of widgets in the marketplace are equally able to do this. Workers, of course, have a different view of the situation. They want an income that not only represents a living wage but a fair one as well. Therefore, keeping down the organization's costs by keeping down employee wages (particularly *vis à vis* comparable wages within the industry) is likely to harm rather than help the organization's bottom line in the long run as workers leave for organizations with better compensation packages. Another group with a stake in organizational operations is management. This group is often more likely to take the long view of organizational effectiveness, realizing that holding down wages will lead to worker unrest and dissatisfaction and have a negative impact on the viability of the organization. However, they typically also realize the need to stay competitive in the global marketplace with its increased competition and potentially cheaper labor rates.

The needs and focus of the different constituencies within the organization often lead to conflict — the situation where one or more parties believes that its interests are negatively affected by another party. For example, conflict can arise between labor and management over a wage increase. One of the goals of management is to keep costs down, and wages are one of the costs of doing business. Employees, on the other hand, are more concerned about their own costs and taking care of their families, so they seek higher wages in order to do this effectively. There are two ways that such a situation can be viewed. In the win-lose orientation, one or more of the parties in the conflict look at the situation as a fixed pool of resources that can be divided among the parties. In this view of conflict, the more one side receives, the less the other side receives. So, for example, labor might balk at the implementation of a new research and development department because they view it as increasing the number of employees that needs to be paid from a limited source of funds for wages. Management, similarly, might view this as a win-lose situation because the more that they have to pay the current workers, the less money they will have available to support the proposed research function that theoretically can develop new products that will gain more income for the company with which they may be able to give workers higher compensation in the long term.

However, in many conflict situations, it is not necessary for there to be a winner and a loser. In the win-win orientation, one or more of the parties to the conflict believe that it is possible to arrive at a mutually beneficial solution for all parties involved. Continuing with the example of a conflict over wages, a win-win orientation might mean that both sides are cognizant of the fact that having a nominal cost of living raise in the short term so that more monies can be devoted to research and development efforts may mean an overall higher wage in the long term after the success of the research and development efforts.

Resolving Organizational Conflict

One of the ways that conflict between groups within an organization is often resolved is through negotiation. This is an interactive process between two or more conflicting parties in which the parties attempt reach a mutually acceptable agreement about an issue or issues of mutual interest. In negotiation, the conflict is redefined in terms of interdependence of the parties. For example, in the illustration above, although the employees could push for the highest raise possible, if that action would cause the organization to go out of business, neither side would win. Similarly, if the organization refused to listen to the employees' arguments for a raise and only paid minimum wage, they might soon lose not only the current employees but the possibility of hiring new employees at that rate. The employees, similarly, would lose the security of their current job and have to look for new work. Again, both sides would lose because both sides are dependent on each other. Because of this fact, negotiation between the two parties in the wage dispute discussed above would have as one of its goals to move both parties from a win-lose orientation to a win-win orientation. So, the employees might settle for a cost-of-living increase for the next year with a promise of a greater increase after the new research and development effort increases the organization's cash flow or some other agreement in which both sides win.

Approaches to Effective Negotiation

It is generally agreed that competition, accommodation, or other win-lose strategies are not typically effective in negotiations. Although some theorists posit that collaboration is the best negotiating approach, others believe that other win-win orientations can also be effective. One must be careful of adopting a collaborative approach until mutual trust can be established between the parties. In addition, collaboration requires the sharing of information between the parties in the conflict. However, complete transparency in negotiations can be ill advised. Information is power, and if one side in the negotiation has too much power, the situation can quickly become win-lose rather than win-win. Most skilled negotiations tend to share information slowly, particularly at the beginning of the negotiation. This allows trust to be built. In addition, although a win-win approach is typically preferable, if it becomes apparent that such an approach will not work, it may be necessary to switch to a win-lose approach.

As shown in Figure 1, negotiation is a process in which the goal is to move the position of the parties involved to a point where a mutually acceptable agreement can be reached. This area of potential agreement is called the "bargaining zone." In negotiation, each party begins by describing its initial offer for each point on the agenda. This may be what each believes to be the best that it can achieve out of the negotiation, or it may be a best-of-all-possible-worlds scenario. For example, representatives of the employees may start with asking for a cost-of-living increase (i.e., a best achievable approach) or a 25-percent increase (i.e., an ideal-world approach), and representatives of management may start with refusing

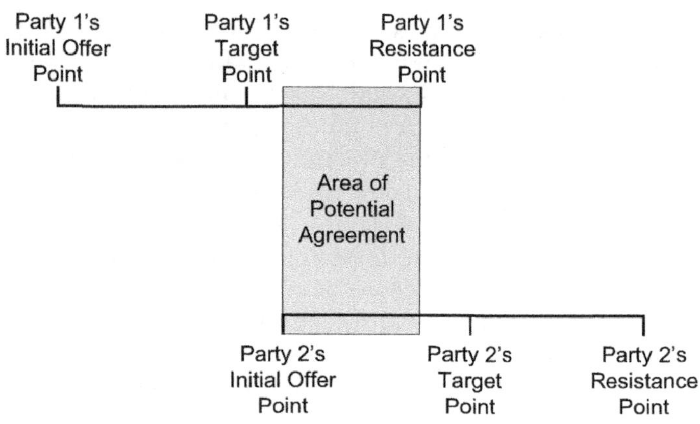

Figure 1: Bargaining Zone Model of Negotiations
(Adapted from McShane & Von Glinow, 403)

to give any raise (i.e., an ideal-world approach). However, this initial offer is typically recognized by all involved to be only a starting point for discussions and that both sides will make concessions (i.e., move closer to the bargaining zone). The target point for each party is what it believes to be a realistic expectation for the outcome of the negotiation. The resistance point is the point beyond which each party is willing to continue negotiations because it will be giving away too much to the other party (i.e., the situation becomes too win-lose).

For example, the employees in the illustration above may start with what they believe to be a good outcome of a cost-of-living increase plus an additional 8 percent as their initial offer. Given the circumstance of the company, however, they may reasonably expect to get a cost-of-living increase plus 2 percent as a target point. Further, they may also have determined that they cannot afford to receive less than a cost-of-living increase with a promise of renegotiations in a year once the research and development effort is finished.

If the negotiation is being conducted with a win-lose orientation, the parties do not reveal their target or resistance points so as not to give an advantage to the other side. In a win-win negotiation situation, however, sharing information often can help to reach a mutually acceptable solution. If, for example, a supplier needs to postpone delivery dates and the buyer does not care as long as the dates are before a certain date, an agreement can be reached. In this scenario, the supplier would probably concede something to the buyer, such as a lower price, financing, or a willingness to deliver more items.

Factors Affecting the Success of Negotiations

The primary factors that can affect the effectiveness of negotiations are the skill of the negotiator in conflict management skills and various situational variables. Research shows that negotiators who plan and set goals are more likely to facilitate a satisfactory agreement for all parties involved. A negotiator needs to carefully consider all known information in order to develop the best possible initial offer, target point, and resistance point. This includes articulating and checking the assumptions that are being made in the situation, what the values of his or her party are, and what the goals are for the situation. In addition, a good negotiator will go through the same thought processes for the other party's position in order to better understand how to reach a mutually acceptable agreement. To aid in this process, the negotiator needs to be skillful at gathering information. Part of this means to engaging in active listening — an approach to improved communication in which the receiver of the message attempts to better understand the message being transmitted, formulates a response based on this understanding, and responds in a way that clarifies the message. Information gathering also involves asking the other party for details about its position in order to better understand what they desire. This process can often be helped by using a team of negotiators rather than a single individual. In this way, more information can be gathered and additional insights applied to help achieve an optimal solution for all parties involved.

Necessary Negotiator Skills

A good negotiator needs not only to be a good listener, but a good communicator as well. Part of this means working to make sure that the emotional or interpersonal conflict is kept to a minimum and that the situation is viewed as objectively as possible. Good negotiators are also persuasive, excelling in the art of convincing the other party to take a particular course of action or hold a particular point of view by using argument, reasoning, or entreaty. In other words, a good negotiator is not only able to clearly articulate the position of his or her side so that the other party can understand it, he or she is also able to get the other party to accept the goals of his or her side.

Particularly in win-win situations, however, negotiation is not just about getting one's way, but also about making concessions in order to reach the optimal solution for all parties involved. When both sides are willing to make concessions, they are able to move closer to the bargaining zone, where they can potentially reach an agreement. Concessions also signal to the other party that one is negotiating in good faith and is truly trying to reach a mutually agreeable solution to the conflict. However, concessions also show the other party what one considers to be of importance in the negotiating situation. As stated before, it is often unwise to give away too much information at least until mutual trust has been established. Therefore, most negotiators offer just enough concessions to keep the lines of communication open without giving away too much. Otherwise, concessions might be perceived as a sign of weakness by the other party and encourage them to employ power and resistance in the negotiation rather than to work toward a mutually acceptable solution.

Situational Factors Affecting the Success of Negotiations

In addition to the skills of the negotiator, the success of negotiations can be affected by various situational factors. One of these is the location of the negotiation. People often try to keep the negotiations in their own environment so that they can keep to their normal routines, not have to cope with travel-related stress, or depend on others for the various resources they might need during the negotiation. For this reason, many negotiations are held in a neutral environment. Although twenty-first-century telecommunications technologies mean that negotiations can potentially be held at a distance so that both parties can be on home ground, most negotiators find that in-person negotiations are preferable. This in true in part because it is easier to read body language and other nonverbal communication in a face-to-face situation and also allows for additional sidebar discussions outside the negotiating room. In addition, the physical layout of the negotiating room can influence the outcome of the process. For example, people who sit on opposite sides of the table in negotiations are more likely to take a win-lose orientation than those who are interspersed around the table or all facing a whiteboard that symbolizes their common problem.

Another factor that can affect the negotiation process is time, including the length of the process and what the associated deadlines are. The longer the process, the more invested the parties will be in resolving the situation. However, this can also mean that the parties are more likely to make unwarranted concessions just to ensure that the negotiation will not fail. Similarly, deadlines may help negotiations stay on track so that a timely agreement is reached. On the other hand, deadlines may also make the parties more willing to make unwarranted concessions, not allow sufficient time for a collaborative approach to succeed, or not give the parties sufficient time to gather the information they need for successful negotiations.

Finally, negotiations do not occur in a vacuum: They are closely watched by various stakeholders and even the general public. When negotiations are closely watched, the negotiators tend to be more competitive and less willing to make concisions. In addition, when they are being watched, negotiators are often more concerned about saving face than they are about reaching an optimal solution.

APPLICATIONS

As discussed above, preparation is one of the keys to successful negotiations. This, however, means not only information gathering, but mental preparation as well. It is frequently observed in the literature that one of the pitfalls in negotiations is overconfidence that one's perceptions of the situation are truly reality. Research has found that negotiator's predictions of their behavior at the negotiating table are frequently incorrect. This is partially due to a tendency to take an optimistic view of the future and to hope for the best. In addition, people often do not fully understand the impact of their motivations and emotions on their behavior, including the desire to reach an agreement even at the cost of giving away more than they should. These factors lead to a situation of overconfidence that is not warranted by the actual negotiating situation.

To better predict one's behavior in a negotiation, it is important to recognize that the assumptions and predictions about what will happen will not necessarily be shown to be true in the actual situation and to develop ways to cope with the unexpected. Negotiations can be very emotionally charged situations. Although one might assume that one will remain calm under pressure, this will not necessarily happen in actuality. To help one cope with the possibility of reacting in an emotional way during a negotiating situation, it is important — in advance

— to determine coping mechanisms that can be employed. For example, when negotiating on what is an emotionally charged issue, it could be helpful to visualize how one would react in such a situation and what tactics could be taken to defuse the situation or keep it from escalating. In addition, one should have a best alternative to a negotiated agreement (BATNA) in mind before negotiations. This is an alternative action that will be taken if a mutually satisfactory negotiated agreement cannot be reached (e.g., if the employees in the earlier example cannot reach a satisfactory agreement, they are willing to strike). Having a BATNA enables the negotiator to have a back-up position to keep from making too many concessions in order to reach an agreement.

To help keep from being overconfident in a negotiation situation, there are several things that one can do. First, it is important to collect as much information about the other party, including their strengths, weaknesses, and motivations. Information is power, and the more one knows about one's opponent, their strengths and weaknesses, their motivations, and the parameters within which they must work, the better one will be able to negotiate. Second, it is important to consider that one's own assumptions may not be accurate and that the opposite might occur. In such a situation, it is helpful to have previously thought through the ramifications of potentially unexpected actions on the part of one's opponent and how one will handle them. Third, it can be helpful to work with a colleague or other trusted person who can play devil's advocate. This person can help the negotiator think through his or her own assumptions and motivations and be better prepared for the actual negotiation.

BIBLIOGRAPHY

Crump, L. (2011). Negotiation process and negotiation context. *International Negotiation, 16*(2), 197–227. Retrieved November 19, 2013 from EBSCO online database Business Source Premier. http://search.ebscohost.com/login.aspx?direct=true&db=buh&AN=60621764

Diekman, K. A., & Galinsky, A. D. (2006, Oct). Overconfident, under-prepared: Why you may not be ready to negotiate. *Negotiation,* 6–9. Retrieved June 19, 2007, from EBSCO Online Database Business Source Complete. http://search.ebscohost.com/login.aspx?direct=true&db=bth&AN=24198881&site=ehost-live

Kuang, X., & Moser, D. V. (2011). Wage negotiation, employee effort, and firm profit under output-based versus fixed-wage incentive contracts. *Contemporary Accounting Research, 28*(2), 616–642. Retrieved November 19, 2013 from EBSCO online database Business Source Premier. http://search.ebscohost.com/login.aspx?direct=true&db=buh&AN=61378248

McShane, S. L., & Von Glinow, M. A. (2003). *Organizational behavior: Emerging realities for the workplace revolution* (2nd ed.). Boston, MA: McGraw-Hill/Irwin.

Miles, E. W. (2013). Developing strategies for asking questions in negotiation. *Negotiation Journal, 29*(4), 383–412. Retrieved November 19, 2013 from EBSCO online database Business Source Premier. http://search.ebscohost.com/login.aspx?direct=true&db=buh&AN=90673532

Moore, D. (2007, June). Are you an overconfident negotiator? *Negotiation,* 7–9. Retrieved June 19, 2007, from EBSCO Online Database Business Source Complete. http://search.ebscohost.com/login.aspx?direct=true&db=bth&AN=25138861&site=ehost-live

Sokolova, M., & Lapalme, G. (2012). How much do we say? Using informativeness of negotiation text records for early prediction of negotiation outcomes. *Group Decision & Negotiation, 21*(3), 363–379. Retrieved November 19, 2013 from EBSCO online database Business Source Premier. http://search.ebscohost.com/login.aspx?direct=true&db=buh&AN=73982401

SUGGESTED READING

Bacon, N., & Blyton, P. (2007). Conflict for mutual gains? *Journal of Management Studies, 44*(5), 814–834. Retrieved June 19, 2007, from EBSCO Online Database Business Source Complete. http://search.ebscohost.com/login.aspx?direct=true&db=bth&AN=25395158&site=ehost-live

Bordone, R. C. (2006, November). Divide the pie — Without antagonizing the other side. *Negotiation,* 4–6. Retrieved June 19, 2007, from EBSCO Online Database Business Source Complete http://search.ebscohost.com/login.aspx?direct=true&db=bth&AN=24198886&site=ehost-live

Hackley, S. (2006, September). Focus your negotiations on what really matters. *Negotiation*, 9–11. Retrieved June 19, 2007, from EBSCO Online Database Business Source Complete. http://search.ebscohost.com/login.aspx?direct=true&db=bth&AN=24198876&site=ehost-live

Kolb, D. M., & Carnevale, P. J. (2007, January). When dividing the pie, smart negotiators get creative. *Negotiation*, 9–11. Retrieved June 19, 2007, from EBSCO Online Database Business Source Complete. http://search.ebscohost.com/login.aspx?direct=true&db=bth&AN=24198900&site=ehost-live

Liljenquist, K. A., & Galinsky, A. D. (2006, September). How to defuse threats at the bargaining table. *Negotiation*, 1–4. Retrieved June 19, 2007, from EBSCO Online Database Business Source Complete. http://search.ebscohost.com/login.aspx?direct=true&db=bth&AN=24198873&site=ehost-live

Malhotra, D. (2006, November). Dealing with distrust? Negotiate the process. *Negotiation*, 7–9. Retrieved June 19, 2007, from EBSCO Online Database Business Source Complete. http://search.ebscohost.com/login.aspx?direct=true&db=bth&AN=24198887&site=ehost-live

Menkel-Meadow, C. (2007, June). Know when to show your hand. *Negotiation*, 1–4. Retrieved June 19, 2007, from EBSCO Online Database Business Source Complete. http://search.ebscohost.com/login.aspx?direct=true&db=bth&AN=25138859&site=ehost-live

Movius, H. (2007, March). When individual bargaining skills aren't enough. *Negotiation*, 4–6. Retrieved June 19, 2007 from EBSCO Online Database Business Source Complete http://web.ebscohost.com/ehost/pdf?vid=10&hid=119&sid=9fb98e2b-b78d-439a-8ac9-452af0533cc3%40sessionmgr3.

Nadler, J. (2007, March). Build rapport — and a better deal. *Negotiation*, 9–11. Retrieved June 19, 2007, from EBSCO Online Database Business Source Complete. http://search.ebscohost.com/login.aspx?direct=true&db=bth&AN=24198912&site=ehost-live

Overbeck, J. R., Neale, M., & Mannix, E. A. (2011). *Negotiation and groups*. Bingley, England: Emerald. Retrieved November 19, 2013 from EBSCO online database eBook Academic Collection (EBSCOhost). http://search.ebscohost.com/login.aspx?direct=true&db=e000xna&AN=375905&site=ehost-live

Schweitzer, M. E. (2006, August). Aim high, improve negotiation results. *Negotiation*, 4–6. Retrieved June 19, 2007, from EBSCO Online Database Business Source Complete. http://search.ebscohost.com/login.aspx?direct=true&db=bth&AN=24198868&site=ehost-live

Susskind, L. (2007, May). Find the sweet spot in your next deal. *Negotiation*, 7–9. Retrieved June 19, 2007, from EBSCO Online Database Business Source Complete. http://search.ebscohost.com/login.aspx?direct=true&db=bth&AN=24687506&site=ehost-live

Swaab, R. I., & Galinsky, A. D. (2007, February). How to negotiate when you're (literally) far apart. *Negotiation*, 7–9. Retrieved June 19, 2007, from EBSCO Online Database Business Source Complete. http://search.ebscohost.com/login.aspx?direct=true&db=bth&AN=24198905&site=ehost-live

Woolcock, S., & Bayne, N. (2011). *The new economic diplomacy: Decision-making and negotiation in international economic relations.* Farnham, England: Ashgate Pub. Retrieved November 19, 2013 from EBSCO online database eBook Academic Collection (EBSCOhost). http://search.ebscohost.com/login.aspx?direct=true&db=e000xna&AN=390189&site=ehost-live

Ruth A. Wienclaw, Ph.D.

Networking

ABSTRACT

Networks have become an integral part of most lives in the modern world of the twenty-first century. There are several types of networks used for communications and information sharing including local area, metropolitan area, and wide area networks. Every network is linked through communications channels that may be physical channels (e.g., copper or fiber optic cables) or wireless channels (i.e., radio waves). In addition, networks can be structured in a number of different ways through various architectures that determine how the various components interact and cooperate. Networks have many applications for twenty-first-century businesses. General applications of networking include transmitting and receiving messages or documents electronically, data communications, providing an infrastructure for holding virtual meetings with participants who are geographically dispersed, and electronic commerce.

OVERVIEW

Networks have become an integral part of most lives in the modern world of the twenty-first century. For example, e-mail has become the standard mode of communication in many situations, and businesses send not only messages but documents, pictures, and audio/visual clips across the office and around the world with ease. In addition, the majority of consumers now count on the Internet to compare and purchase goods and services rather than go to a physical storefront. Social media sites, such as Facebook, Twitter, and LinkedIn, have become important parts of expanding contacts and reaching out to a wider range of individuals all over the world. People not only use networking capabilities at home and at work but also take their laptops and smartphones with them on vacation, feeling adrift at the thought of not being able to keep in touch almost instantaneously. However, networks have other applications as well. In the workplace, networks enable employees to coordinate their activities and to share data, information, and documents in an effort to increase the efficiency and effectiveness of the organization. This ability to share data and information quickly and accurately is increasingly essential to the success of businesses. Particularly as increasing numbers of businesses become active in the global marketplace, networks are becoming integral to work.

Types of Networks

Networks are sets of computers that are electronically linked together. Communications networks are sets of locations (or nodes) with concomitant hardware, software, and information that are linked together to form a system that transmits and receives information. There are several types of networks used for communications and information sharing. Local area networks link multiple local computers to each other and various peripheral devices. Metropolitan area networks link computers over citywide distances at higher speeds than local area networks. Wide area networks link multiple computers that are widely dispersed and use high-speed, long-distance communications networks or satellites to transmit and receive data.

- Local Area Networks A local area network consists of multiple desktop computers located near each other that link into a network. These networks are used to connect computers in an office or series of offices and span distances from a few hundred feet to a few miles. A local area network allows users to share files and peripheral devices such as printers, fax machines, or storage devices. The computers linked into the network are also referred to as workstations, clients, or nodes. They are connected to a server—a host computer for the network that provides services to the clients. The server typically has more storage capacity and can process at higher speeds than the client computers. Cloud computing allows companies to use space on an external server, maintained by a provider, for both file storage and to deliver applications (Yang & Jia, 2013).
- Metropolitan Area Networks Metropolitan area networks transmit data and information citywide (up to 30 miles) and at greater speeds than a local area network. These networks are optimized for both voice and data transmissions and can, therefore, carry more forms of data than can be carried over local area networks, including voice, data, image, and video data. Metropolitan area networks typically operate over a city-wide network of fiber optic cables. These networks enable the metropolitan area network to provide high quality multimedia transmissions at higher speeds than is possible over local area networks.
- Wide Area Networks Wide area networks comprise multiple computers that are widely dispersed and that are linked into a network. These networks typically use high-speed, long-distance communications networks or satellites to connect the computers within the network. Wide area networks can be used for a variety of applications, particularly when the client computers that need to be networked are at a distance from each other. For example, a retail chain may use a wide area network

to connect its stores across the country or across the world, allowing them to share inventory and sales data and to send e-mail messages to each other. These networks can also be used to connect computerized cash registers that can be used to collect and transmit sales data at each location and transmit them to the company's corporate headquarters as part of the closing procedure each day.

Wide area networks use services provided by a common carrier—a company that provides public communications transmission services. The speed at which the data are transmitted over the network is determined by the bandwidth. The higher the bandwidth of a transmission, the more quickly data can be transferred within the network. Bandwidth is expressed in thousands of bits of information per second (kbps), millions of bits per second (mbps), or billions of bits per second (gbps). On a more practical level, a typical page of typed correspondence contains approximately 275 words, which translates to 2,000 bytes or 16,000 bits of information. Transferring this amount of data over a 56 kbps modem takes approximately 0.28 seconds; transferring the same page over a high speed network transmitting at 1.544 mbps, however, only takes approximately 0.01 seconds. Although this may seem to be a small difference, business documents are frequently significantly longer than one page. So, for example, transmission of a 600-page document at 2400 Bps would take nearly two hours, at 56,000 Bps would take only five minutes, and at 1.544 mbps would take only 10.8 seconds. Similarly, higher bandwidths are necessary to transmit video transmissions. Wide area networks sometimes transmit over a T-carrier, a very high-speed channel that connects lower-speed networks or computers at different sites or over fiber optic cables that allow even faster data transmission.

Network Channels

No matter the type, networks are linked through communications channels (also referred to as network media). These channels may be physical channels (e.g., copper or fiber optic cables) or wireless channels (i.e., radio waves). There are a number of different types of media used to transmit data. The transmission speeds of some of these channels are given in Table 1.

Table 1: Transmission Speeds of Communications Channels

Channels	Transmission Speeds
Twisted pair	Over 100 mbps
Coaxial cable	140 mbps
Fiber optic cable	Over 2 gbps
Wireless (Cableless) Channels	**Transmission Speeds**
Microwave	275 mbps
Satellite	2 mbps
Infrared	75 mbps
Radio waves (RF transmissions)	275 mbps

(from Senn, p. 344)

Physical Communications Channels

There are three basic types of physical communications channels: twisted pair, coaxial, and fiber optic cable. Although these have different characteristics, it is the hardware and software attached to the network that determines the actual speed of transmission. No matter how fast data can be transmitted over the network cables, if the information system on the end of the cable is slow, the actual receipt of the data will be concomitantly slow.

- Twisted pair cables are used in telephone wires and are so called because they are made of pairs of copper wire twisted together to form a cable. Twisted pair cable was designed for the transmission of voice and text messages and is considered by information technology specialists to be a voice-grade medium. These channels transmit at a variety of rates ranging from 100 Bps to 100 mbps depending on what the carrier determines is a feasible speed of transmission for the cable.
- Coaxial cable is another commonly used cable for networks. This type of cable is made up of one or more central wire conductors surrounded by an insulator and sheathed in wire mesh or metal.
- Fiber optic cable uses light from a laser to transmit data, providing the fastest data transmission of the physical network media.

Wireless Communications Channels

In addition to physical network media, various wireless channels are available. Wireless networks use radio waves sent over the open air or through space. Most wireless networks utilize microwaves—high-frequency radio signals—for data transmission. Some wireless networks employ terrestrial stations that use relay towers about 30 miles apart. These stations must be unobstructed and have a clear line between them since microwaves travel in a straight line. Increasingly, wireless transmission is done using satellites. The microwaves are beamed from a terrestrial station to a communications satellite, which in turn relays the signal to another terrestrial station or stations.

Network Architectures

Networks can be structured in a number of different ways through various architectures that determine how the various components interact and cooperate. Network architectures comprise the structure of a communications network, including how the various components are linked, interact, and cooperate. Network architectures may be centralized, distributed, or a combination of the two.

- Centralized Architecture In a centralized architecture, the server hosts all of the network's hardware and software, performs all the network's processing, and manages the network from a central site. In this type of architecture, the hardware and software frequently are found in a centralized computer center.
- Distributed Architecture In a distributed architecture, on the other hand, the various computers are at different locations and connected by a network. In this type of architecture, an application may run on one or more locations on the network simultaneously. For example, in a retail store with a distributed network, data on individual sales transactions may be automatically transmitted to a distribution center. In addition, the chain's suppliers may also connect using their own networks to monitor inventory in the distribution centers and replenish them as necessary.

Both of these approaches to network architecture have advantages and disadvantages. Centralized systems are easier to manage, but distributed systems keep information where it is most needed. To leverage the advantages of both types of architectures, some enterprises use hybrid systems that combine the strengths of both approaches.

By 2014, a type of networking architecture that had been in various stages of development for several years began coming to the forefront: software-defined networking (SDN). This architecture gives programmers more immediate control over the way data and resources are operated within a network through the separation of the network's control and forwarding functions (Kirkpatrick, 2013).

APPLICATIONS

Networks have many applications for twenty-first-century businesses. In general, networks have four roles: transmitting and receiving messages or documents electronically, data communications, providing an infrastructure for holding virtual meetings with participants who are geographically dispersed, and electronic commerce.

Electronic Message Transmission

Perhaps the best-known aspect of networking both in business and personal applications is electronic mail (e-mail). This network service transmits text messages from a sender to one or more recipients. The message is sent over the network and stored on a reserved area of space on a drive in the server or host computer that has been set aside for the recipient. This space is referred to as the recipient's electronic mailbox. The message remains there until it is retrieved by the recipient. When the recipient logs onto his/her e-mail account, the system sends a notification that a new message has been received. The recipient can then retrieve and view the message, store it for later reference, forward it to other recipients, reply to the message, or delete it. E-mail messages can also be broadcast, that is, sent to a number of recipients simultaneously. This capability cuts down on the amount of work that the sender needs to do to get information into the hands of multiple people and also helps provide work groups, teams, and others who need to communicate with current information so that communications and projects can proceed more efficiently. In addition, e-mail enables people to send text and other documents electronically across the network.

Another frequently used application of networking capabilities is voicemail. Whereas e-mail involves the transmission of text messages between a sender and recipients, voicemail involves the transmission of spoken messages. The sender speaks into an ordinary telephone connected to the computer network. The message is then digitized and stored in the recipient's voice mailbox. The recipient can retrieve the message using his/her phone. The message is then reconverted to an analog voice message and relayed to the recipient. Voice messages can be stored, replayed, or broadcast to multiple recipients.

Data Communications

Electronic Data Interchange

Networks can also facilitate the flow of money and other data between businesses or between customers and businesses. Electronic data interchange is a standard format that is used to exchange business data such as price or product identification number. Electronic data interchange technology is particularly important for facilitating international commerce where paperwork required for international trade creates costs of up to 7 percent of the value of the items being traded. With electronic data interchange technology, shippers, carriers, customs agents, and customers all can send and receive documents through electronic funds transfer, thereby saving both time and money for international transactions.

Electronic Funds Transfer

A similar network service is electronic funds transfer—the electronic movement of money over a communications network is called electronic funds transfer. This service increasingly affects financial transactions. Credit card transactions are settled by electronic funds transfer between the user and the issuer of the credit card and payroll checks, government support checks, and other deposits can be deposited by electronic funds transfer. Because of such technologies, the Internet is also used for e-commerce to buy and sell goods or services—including products and information retrieval services—electronically rather than through conventional means.

Virtual Meeting Capabilities

Another service that can be provided by networks is videoconferencing. This service provides live two-way audio and video transmissions over the network. Through videoconferencing, people who are geographically dispersed can meet together and participate in a meeting without the inconvenience or expense of travel. Video conferencing is much more than a simple audio/visual hookup, however. Through the use of the network, meeting participants can share documents, images, and even product demonstrations. Information can be retrieved from a central database (a collection of data items used for multiple purposes and which is stored on a computer) and simultaneously shared with all conference participants. Decentralized meetings can also be facilitated through the use of networks even without the audio hookup. In teleconferencing, meeting participants at different sites communicate with each other through the telephone. They use the network to share documents and other information through an electronic bulletin board in near real time. Networks can also allow participants to use presentation software just as in a face-to-face meeting.

Electronic Commerce

The use of networks to support business is not only concerned with internal or business-to-business applications, however. E-commerce (i.e., electronic commerce) is the process of conducting of business online through such transactions as sales and information exchange. One common application of e-commerce is online retailing and electronic storefronts as supported by networks. Customers visit a business's website on the Internet and examine product pictures and information, compare different products, fill an electronic shopping cart, and checkout and pay for their purchases in much the same way that they would in a brick-and-mortar store. Another network application of e-commerce is the electronic market. This is a collection of individual shops that can be accessed through a single location on the Internet that are the virtual equivalent of shopping malls. The use of networks to support e-commerce offers many benefits to businesses. First, businesses are able to extend their geographic reach and literally reach potential customers around the globe without setting up operations in other locations. E-commerce can facilitate selling to a larger market as well as increasing the speed at which transactions can take place. The networking capabilities of e-commerce also enable customers to make better informed decisions in a more timely manner, thereby helping the business's cash flow and saving the customer time.

Bibliography

Casado, M., Foster, N., & Guha, A. (2014). Abstractions for software-defined networks. *Communications of the ACM, 57*(10), 86–95. Retrieved from EBSCO Online Database Business Source Complete. http://search.ebscohost.com/login.aspx?direct=true&db=bth&AN=98606318&site=bsi-live

Cavage, M. (2013). There is no getting around it: you are building a distributed system. *Communications of the ACM, 56*(6), 63–70. Retrieved from EBSCO Online Database Business Source Complete. http://search.ebscohost.com/login.aspx?direct=true&db=bth&AN=87803979&site=bsi-live

Gomes, J. V., Inácio, P. M., Pereira, M., Freire, M. M., & Monteiro, P. P. (2013). Detection and classification of peer-to-peer traffic: A survey. *ACM Computing Surveys, 45*(3), 30:1–30:40.Retrieved from EBSCO Online Database Business Source Complete. http://search.ebscohost.com/login.aspx?direct=true&db=bth&AN=89005465&site=bsi-live

Kantor, E., Lotker, Z., Parter, M., & Peleg, D. (2015). The topology of wireless communication. *Journal of the ACM, 62*(5), 37:1–37:32. Retrieved from EBSCO Online Database Business Source Premier. http://search.ebscohost.com/login.aspx?direct=true&db=buh&AN=110871297&site=ehost-live&scope=site

Kirkpatrick, K. (2013). Software-defined networking.*Communications of the ACM, 56*(9), 16–19. Retrieved from EBSCO Online Database Business Source Complete. http://search.ebscohost.com/login.aspx?direct=true&db=bth&AN=90070287&site=bsi-live

Lucas, H. C., Jr. (2005). *Information technology: Strategic decision making for managers.* New York: John Wiley and Sons.

Senn, J. A. (2004). *Information technology: Principles, practices, opportunities* (3rd ed.). Upper Saddle River, NJ: Pearson/Prentice Hall.

Yang, K., & Jia, X. (2013). An efficient and secure dynamic auditing protocol for data storage in cloud computing. *IEEE Transactions on Parallel & Distributed Systems, 24*(9), 1717–1726. Retrieved from EBSCO Online Database Business Source Complete. http://search.ebscohost.com/login.aspx?direct=true&db=bth&AN=89454656&site=bsi-live

Suggested Reading

Ali, M. G. & Zahir, S. (2006). Performance evaluation for web applications with web caching in a distributed wireless system using OPNET. *Journal of Computer Information Systems, 46*(3), 57–66. Retrieved from EBSCO Online Database Business Source Complete. http://search.ebscohost.com/login.aspx?direct=true&db=bth&AN=20862405&site=bsi-live

Bennet, D., & Bennet, A. (2004). The rise of the knowledge organization. In C. W. Holsapple (Ed.), *Handbook on Knowledge Management 1: Knowledge Matters* (pp. 5–20). New York: Springer-Verlag. Retrieved from EBSCO Online Database Business Source Complete. http://search.ebscohost.com/login.aspx?direct=true&db=bth&AN=20352978&site=bsi-live

Casado, M., Foster, N., & Guha, A. (2014). Abstractions for software-defined networks. *Communications of the ACM, 57*(10), 86–95. Retrieved from EBSCO Online Database Business Source Premier. http://search.ebscohost.com/login.aspx?direct=true&db=buh&AN=98606318&site=ehost-live&scope–site

Juels, A., & Oprea, A. (2013). New approaches to security and availability for cloud data. *Communications of the ACM, 56*(2), 64–73. Retrieved from EBSCO Online Database Business Source Complete. http://search.ebscohost.com/login.aspx?direct=true&db=bth&AN=88141518&site=bsi-live

Varshney, U. (2005). Vehicular mobile commerce: Applications, challenges, and research problems. *Communications of AIS, 2005*(16), 329–339. Retrieved from EBSCO Online Database Business Source Complete. http://search.ebscohost.com/login.aspx?direct=true&db=bth&AN=19323571&site=bsi-live

Ruth A. Wienclaw, Ph.D.

Networks in Business

ABSTRACT

Networks are widely used in business today. Although many businesses use the Internet to market goods and services, an increasing number of businesses use an intranet, a smaller version of the Internet that is used by company employees to communicate with each other and to share data. Intranets are typically protected by firewalls that prevent unauthorized access and keep company propriety or sensitive data or information confidential. Businesses can also share information with partners, customers, or other parties through an extranet, a part of an intranet that is available to authorized parties. By using networks, businesses can communicate more quickly, update information more accurately, and coordinate all members of a supply chain in order to work more efficiently and bring products or services to the customer more expeditiously than is possible using traditional communications media.

OVERVIEW

In many ways, the use of networks has changed our lives. For example, in many situations, e-mail has obviated the need for surface mail, fax transmissions, or even phone calls, and provides us with almost instant access to friends, family, and colleagues. Similarly, data—including documents, photos, and videos—can be easily shared as attachments to e-mails. Social networking allows us to keep track of friends and family. The World Wide Web allows us to easily find or share information, purchase or sell items, or perform a host of other tasks more quickly and easily than was possible before. Just as the Internet has transformed our lives, so, too, network technology has transformed the way that many organizations—large and small—do business.

Communications Networks

Most organizations today have become "netcentric," relying heavily on the use of computers, databases, and telecommunications to conduct their day-to-day business activities (Lucas, 2005). At its most basic, a network is a set of computers that are electronically linked together through communications lines (e.g., telephone lines, fiber optic cables) or wireless technology (i.e., radio signals over the air or through space). Businesses use networks to share data, documents, and programs or to allow employees to communicate with one another or with providers or customers.

One common use of network technology is e-mail communication. Employees are able to send e-mails with or without attachments, just as they would have picked up the phone or used inter-office mail a few decades ago. Network technology allows organizations to take this a step further and actually set up virtual teams in which team members do not always meet face to face but conduct their activities over a distance. In virtual teams, the members are geographically or organizationally dispersed and interact primarily through communication technology. For example, large engineering programs can use experts from around the country—or around the world—who communicate via e-mail or secure networks, sharing documents, giving briefings, discussing problems, and making decisions all using network technology.

Similarly, individuals in different parts of the supply chain can communicate over networks without having to deal with the other members directly. For example, a retail clerk in a point of sale location can use a network to check supply quantity at a warehouse without ever talking directly to warehouse personnel. If the item he needs is available, he can place an order directly from his terminal. The warehouse manager, in turn, can order more stock over a network from her supplier who, in turn, arranges for transportation for the stock through a network.

The use of networks has changed the business model used by many organizations. Because network technology can speed or ease communications between individuals, departments, or business partners, it can be possible for management to eliminate functions from the organization and outsource them to other organizations that can do the task more cost-effectively. For example, a retailer may sell products directly to customers at a brick-and-mortar store, but may also sell to customers over the Internet. The retailer may also outsource the manufacturing of the products that it sells to other firms, and communicate with them over the Internet or other network.

The retailer may outsource billing to yet another company and communicate with its bank through another network.

Types of Networks

LAN, MAN & WAN

In general, a network is a set of locations (or nodes) with concomitant hardware, software, and information that are linked together to form a system that transmits and receives information and data. There are three types of communications networks. Local area networks (LANs) connect multiple computers that are located near one another and linked into a network that allows the users to share files and peripheral devices such as printers, fax machines, and storage devices. LAN technology was developed after the utility of personal computers for business became recognized and organizations wanted to be able to share information and access data for the organization. For example, a LAN may be used to link multiple workstations within a department as well as control a common printer.

Another type of network used by businesses is the metropolitan area network (MAN). These networks are larger than LANs and transmit data and information citywide (typically around 30 miles) and at greater speeds than a LAN. In addition, MANs are capable of transmitting voice, data, image, and video data, although they are typically optimized for voice-data transmission. Rather than using telephone lines, MANs typically use fiber optic cables. Another type of network used by businesses is the wide area network (WAN). These comprise multiple computers that are widely dispersed and that are linked into a network. WANs typically use high speed, long distance communications networks or satellites to connect the computers within the network.

Intranets & Extranets

Certainly, the Internet is one valuable network tool now widely used by businesses. Increasingly, a business needs to have a presence on the web (e.g., a homepage) in order to be competitive. However, the Internet is only one type of network that is used by businesses. In addition, some organizations set up private networks to serve their needs. An intranet is a private network similar to the Internet, and is set up for a given enterprise. Intranets are used to share information and provide computing resources within an organization. Intranets may also be used to facilitate document sharing for workgroups and virtual teams. An intranet requires the installation of servers and clients using Internet protocols (e.g., TCP/IP, http), and a web browser. As with the Internet, an intranet may comprise several networked LANs or use the leased line of a WAN.

Typically, an intranet contains proprietary information. To prevent those outside the organization from gaining unauthorized access to information that the organization does not wish to disclose to the public, information on an intranet is blocked by a firewall so that the information is only available to employees, other stakeholders, or other parties whom the organization authorizes. A firewall is a special-purpose software program or piece of computer hardware that is designed to prevent authorized access to or from a private network. Next-Generation Firewalls (NGFWs) deliver more granular control than traditional firewalls but have their own set of challenges (Erdheim, 2013). However, not all parts of an intranet need to be kept private. Intranets also provide platforms that can be used to develop and distribute applications for use by anyone with a web browser.

When part of an intranet is made accessible to outside parties (e.g., customers, suppliers, partners), it is referred to as an extranet. Extranets can be used to exchange large volumes of data, share catalogs with a select list of users (e.g., wholesalers, other members of an industry), collaborate with other companies on joint projects or ventures, provide limited access to other select companies, or share information with partner organizations.

Many organizations use intranet and extranet technology. For example, rather than merely listing names and phone numbers, intranet phone directories can also include a photograph and job description for each employee.

APPLICATIONS

Business Uses for Networks

Businesses can use networks for a wide variety of purposes, including the transmission of messages, the communication of data, hosting virtual meetings, and conducting electronic commerce. The most common application of networks is electronic mail (e-mail) capabilities that allow employees to communicate with one another, customers, suppliers, or partners electronically rather than using older methods such as faxes, phone calls, interoffice mail, or surface mail. E-mail also allows messages to be broadcast to a number of recipients simultaneously. This capability is advantageous from a business standpoint because it cuts down on the time that the sender needs to transmit the message multiple times, gets information into the hands of a large number of recipients quickly and simultaneously, and facilitates the work of groups. In addition to sending text messages, e-mail also allows senders to transmit documents, video clips, photographs, drawings, and other information as attachments. Some email providers, such as Google, even have their own drives (Google Drive), on which a network of people can edit documents in real time. This reduces the need to make and distribute hard copies and also allows groups to work or comment on common documents together, reducing the need for coordination. Messages can also be transmitted via voice mail, in much the same way as one would leave a message on a telephone answering machine. Voice mail messages can be stored, replayed, or broadcast to multiple recipients.

Virtual Workgroups

Such electronic capabilities make the job of the individual employee easier and facilitate communications across the enterprise. Networks can be used to facilitate virtual meetings and virtual teams and workgroups in which the members are geographically or organizationally dispersed and members interact primarily through communication technology rather than meeting face-to-face. This use of network technology can save the enterprise money associated with travel costs as well as with costs associated with moving expenses or hiring. Virtual teams can incorporate members of the enterprise and also its partners through extranet technology. Through videoconferencing (vcon) and online collaborative tools like Skype and WebEx (Davis, 2012), employees or colleagues who are geographically dispersed can participate in a meeting without the inconvenience or expense of travel. In addition, meeting participants can share documents, images, and even product demonstrations without the need for a face-to-face meeting. Even if some of the meeting or workgroup participants do not have vcon technology, they can communicate with each other through the web or telephone and use the network to share documents and other information through an electronic bulletin board or use presentation software just as in a face-to-face meeting.

Data Communications for E-Commerce

Another common business use of networks is for data communications. The standard format for transmitting business data (e.g., price, part number) is electronic data interchange (EDI). This technology can facilitate commerce not only across the country but across the globe. EDI helps facilitate the data exchange necessary for international commerce, and reduce the cost of global commerce by reducing the cost of the associated paperwork, which can add up to 7 percent to the value of the items being traded. Similarly, electronic funds transfer can be used to move money over a communications network. Electronic funds transfer facilitates international business transactions, and also affects consumers on a local level. For example, the worldwide PLUS ATM network can be accessed by over one billion credit and debit cards. These transactions are settled electronically by the transfer of funds between the user and the issuer of the card. Electronic funds transfer can also be used to deposit payroll checks, government support checks, and other deposits without the need to physically handle the currency.

Electronic funds transfer has enabled another use of networks for businesses: electronic commerce (e-commerce), the conducting of business (e.g., sales, information exchange) over the Internet. For example, many businesses today have electronic storefronts supported by network technologies. These electronic storefronts may be in addition to or in place of brick-and-mortar point-of-sale locations. In electronic commerce, customers visit a business's web site on the Internet and examine the online catalog, compare products, fill an electronic shopping cart, and check out and pay for their purchases in much the same way as if they were in a physical store. Network technology also facilitates electronic markets, or a collection of individual shops that can be accessed through a single location on the Internet that are the virtual equivalent of shopping malls. Through the use of e-commerce, businesses are able reach potential customers around the globe without setting up satellite operations in other locations. In addition, e-commerce can increase the speed at which business transactions take place, thereby helping not only the business's cash flow but also saving the customer time and (potentially) money because the business does not need to have a brick-and-mortar storefront.

Example: Cisco Systems

One example of an organization that has successfully incorporated networking technology into its business model is Cisco Systems (Senn, 2004). Cisco emerged as a world leader in networking technology, designing and selling networking hardware (e.g., routers, switches) and network management software to other enterprises for use in creating intranets and connecting to Internet. In part, Cisco's success has been attributed to its catching the Internet wave in the mid-1990s. Cisco created a new form of supply chain to link customers, manufacturers, and other partners using Internet technology. This use of networking technology allowed Cisco to cultivate and leverage close relationships with other organizations in order to provide its customers with the products that they need without having to hire the full range of experts or facilities that would be required for them to provide the same range of services themselves. The members of this supply chain, in a sense, were partners, including manufacturers, assemblers, distributors, resellers, and transporters. Working in cooperation with these other enterprises, Cisco was able to integrate various supply chains by interconnecting its business systems and key information technology applications. This resulted in an automated order acceptance and fulfillment process which helped Cisco achieve its reputation in the field.

Cisco's suppliers/partners made all of the components for Cisco, performed nearly all of the subassembly work, and performed more than half of the final assembly. Rather than using e-mail, or phone calls to coordinate their activities, Cisco and its partner-suppliers communicate electronically over the network for all phases of the operation. For example, once a product is finished and ready for shipping, the partner-supplier notifies a transportation company within the system and ships the product directly to the customer. Because communications are handled electronically, there are fewer opportunities for error along the supply chain. Cisco is able to work more efficiently because the same information is shared with all partners in the supply chain, requiring less coordination and updating. Further, information can be shared over the network in real time. As a result, changes that occur in one part of the supply chain are immediately disseminated to all parts of the supply chain. This allows the entire network of organizations to respond more expediently to changes. Cisco has moved into promising new businesses: cloud computing, unified enterprise IT systems, mobile device management, and TelePresence (Preimesberger, 2013). It has also initiated the Internet of Everything project, which seeks to connect people, data, and processes like never before, increasing the networking capabilities of devices and the diverse peoples who use them.

CONCLUSION

Networks are widely used in business today. They can be as simple as the posting of a home page on the World Wide Web to advertise the company's products and services or the use of the Internet to provide e-mail capabilities. Many organizations take this a step further, however, and link together their employees with an intranet, a smaller version of the Internet that is used by company employees to communicate with each other and to share data. Intranets are typically protected by firewalls that prevent unauthorized access and keep company propriety or sensitive data or information confidential. In some cases, however, the enterprise may want to share some information with other parties such as partners, customers, or industry members. In this case, they may develop an extranet, or part of the intranet that is available to these parties.

Network technology is much more than a high tech replacement for older communication methods. By using networks, businesses can communicate more quickly, update information more accurately, and coordinate all members of a supply chain in order to work more efficiently and bring products or services to the customer more expeditiously than was previously possible.

Bibliography

Chelariu, C., & Osmonbekov, T. (2014). Communication Technology in International Business-To-Business Relationships. *Journal of Business & Industrial Marketing, 29*(1), 24-33. Retrieved December 3, 2014, from EBSCO Online Database Business Source Complete. http://search.ebscohost.com/login.aspx?direct=true&db=bth&AN=94622162

Davis, B. (2012). Bright picture for vcon. *AV Magazine, 43*. Retrieved November 20, 2013, from EBSCO Online Database Business Source Complete. http://search.ebscohost.com/login.aspx?direct=true&db=bth&AN=70475670&site=ehost-live

Erdheim, S. (2013). Deployment and management with next-generation firewalls. *Network Security, 2013*(10), 8-12. Retrieved November 20, 2013, from EBSCO Online Database Business Source Complete. http://search.ebscohost.com/login.aspx?direct=true&db=bth&AN=91848947&site=ehost-live

Kumar, R. L. (2004). A framework for assessing the business value of information technology infrastructures. *Journal of Management Information Systems, 21* (2), 11-32. Retrieved 20 October 2009 from EBSCO Online Database Business Source Premier http://search.ebscohost.com/login.aspx?direct=true&db=buh&AN=14776227&site=ehost-live

Lucas, H. C. Jr. (2005). *Information technology: Strategic decision making for managers.* New York: John Wiley & Sons.

Preimesberger, C. (2013). Why highly profitable Cisco Systems is cutting 4,000 jobs. Eweek, 2. Retrieved November 20, 2013, from EBSCO Online Database Business Source Complete. http://search.ebscohost.com/login.aspx?direct=true&db=bth&AN=89992382&site=ehost-live

Senn, J. A. (2004). *Information technology: Principles, practices, opportunities* (3rd ed.). Upper Saddle River, NJ: Pearson/Prentice Hall.

Suggested Reading

Ahuja, M. K., Galletta, D. F., & Carley, K. M. (2003). Individual centrality and performance in virtual R&D groups: An empirical study. *Management Science, 49* (1), 21-38. Retrieved 20 October 2009 from EBSCO Online Database Business Source Premier http://search.ebscohost.com/login.aspx?direct=true&db=buh&AN=9092481&site=ehost-live

Chen, K., Tarn, J. M. & Han, B. T. (2004). Internet dependency: Its impact on online behavioral patterns in e-commerce. *Human Systems Management, 23* (1), 49-58. Retrieved 20 October 2009 from EBSCO Online Database Business Source Premier http://search.ebscohost.com/login.aspx?direct=true&db=buh&AN=12255143&site=ehost-live

Dekleva, S., Shim, J. P., Varshney, U., & Knoerzer, G. (2007). Evolution and emerging issues in mobile wireless networks. *Communications of the ACM, 50* (6), 38-43. Retrieved 20 October 2009 from EBSCO Online Database Academic Search Complete http://search.ebscohost.com/login.aspx?direct=true&db=a9h&AN=25301819&site=ehost-live

Flynn, S. I. (2014). Technology in Modern Organizations. *Research Starters Sociology,* 1-7. Retrieved December 3, 2014, from EBSCO Online Database Business Source Complete.

Ruth A. Wienclaw, Ph.D.

O

Operations Management

ABSTRACT

Operations management comprises those areas of management that are concerned with the productivity, quality, and cost in the operations function as well as strategic planning for the organization. This discipline covers not only manufacturing processes, but support processes that add value to the product or service as well as the management of the entire supply chain. There are a number of ways that organizations can streamline their operations to meet the demands of today's marketplace. However, for these to have any significant or lasting effect, they must be done within a coordinated strategy for both short and long-term organizational effectiveness. There are a number of tools and techniques that can be used by managers to improve the effectiveness and efficiency of business operations. These include lean manufacturing, total quality management, and business process reengineering strives to improve the effectiveness and efficiency of the various processes within an organization.

OVERVIEW

Business organizations exist to provide something of value to their stakeholders. For stockholders, this may mean profitability and return on investment. For employees, this may mean job security and a wage that is at or above industry standards. For distributors and suppliers, this may mean sufficient commerce to keep their own operations going. To meet these disparate objectives, organizations need to be able to offer a product or service of value to the customer, whether it is light-weight running shoes, steel rivets, or consulting services. Operations management comprises those areas of management that are concerned with productivity, quality, and cost in the operations function (i.e., activities necessary to transform inputs such as business transactions and information into outputs such as completed transactions) as well as strategic planning for the organization. Business operations include any processes that transform any inputs such as labor, capital, materials, and energy into products and services that are of value in the marketplace. Operations management draws from multiple disciplines in order to optimize the effectiveness of operations within the organization.

Operations management is more than an emphasis on manufacturing processes. There are many activities within an organization that add value to the end product or service but that do not directly provide goods or services to the customer. For example, the accounting department adds value to the organization's activities by making sure that the employees, distributors, and suppliers are all paid promptly and accurately. Human resources also supports business operations by developing and implementing policies and procedures that ensure that employees are treated fairly and are motivated to use their skills and talents in helping the business become a high performing organization. In addition, operations management is not only concerned with the operations within the single organizational entity, but also of the smooth and efficient operations of the entire supply chain. This is the network of organizations involved in the production, delivery, and sale of a product. The supply chain may include suppliers, manufacturers, storage facilities, transporters, and retailers. The supply chain includes the flow of tangible goods and materials, funds, and information between the organizations in the network, all of which adds value to the product or service being offered to the customer.

Historically, operations management focused on providing the highest possible quality for the lowest possible price. Increasingly, however, customers are also demanding greater product variety, short life cycles, and other qualities that require organizations to more closely examine their operations for ways to better meet the needs of the marketplace. In addition, globalization has brought with it increased competition from overseas operations that are able to provide products or services at lower cost. This results not only in greater competition but also in the need to put even more emphasis on optimizing the effectiveness and efficiency of operations in order to stay viable in the marketplace.

There are a number of ways that organizations can streamline their operations to meet the demands of today's marketplace. However, for these methods to have any significant or lasting effect, they must be done as part of a coordinated strategy designed to improve both short and long-term organizational effectiveness. A strategy is a plan of action to help the organization reach its goals and objectives, including organizational effectiveness and marketplace viability. A good business strategy should be based on the rigorous analysis of empirical data, including market needs and trends, competitor capabilities and offerings, and the organization's resources and abilities. The strategic planning process helps the organization determine what goals to set and how to reach them. This process also allows the organization to determine and articulate its long-term goals and to develop a plan to use the company's resources — including materials, equipment and technology, and personnel — in reaching these goals.

Because of its concern with organizational performance and effectiveness, one of the tasks of operations management is to set the strategy — including goals and objectives — of the organization. Strategic planning is the process of determining the best way to accomplish the goals of the organization. Goals and objectives define in practical terms what the organization would like to be within a specific period of time. Determining the organization's business goals requires an examination of all the organization's operations and processes to determine which add value to the organization's products or services and which do not.

APPLICATIONS

There are a number of tools and techniques that can be used by managers to improve the effectiveness and efficiency of business operations. These include lean manufacturing, total quality management, and business process reengineering. Lean manufacturing strives to eliminate waste and continually improve productivity. Total quality management strives to improve customer satisfaction by improving quality. Business process reengineering strives to improve the effectiveness and efficiency of the various processes within an organization.

Lean Manufacturing

Lean manufacturing is manufacturing philosophy that attempts to eliminate all waste from production processes. The objectives of lean manufacturing are to lower production costs, increase output, and shorten lead times. To do this, lean manufacturing efforts attempt to do several things. First, lean manufacturing efforts attempt to reduce defects and unnecessary physical waste during the production process. This includes reducing the excess or unnecessary use of raw materials or other inputs, reducing the number of defects and their associated costs, and reducing or eliminating product features that are not of value to the customer. Lean manufacturing efforts also attempt to reduce manufacturing lead times and production cycle times in the manufacturing process. This can result in less cost associated with storage of materials and products and the ability to get products to the customer in a more timely manner. Similarly, lean manufacturing attempts to minimize inventory throughout the production process. This practice helps reduce the amount of working capital needed to sustain operations. Just-in-time manufacturing is a manufacturing philosophy that strives to eliminate waste and continually improve productivity. The primary characteristics of just-in-time manufacturing include having the required inventory only when it is needed for manufacturing and reducing lead times and set up times. In addition, lean manufacturing attempts to optimize the use of equipment and space to reduce or eliminate bottlenecks in manufacturing processes and optimize the rate of production. Lean manufacturing also examines business processes (see below) and their effect on the productivity of employees. Under the lean manufacturing philosophy, idle time is reduced and workers efforts are streamlined so that they contribute directly to the value of the product or service.

One lean manufacturing approach is the Six Sigma process. This term is a statistical reference to how far (i.e, the number of standard deviations, symbolized by the Greek letter sigma, "s") a data point is from the middle of the normal curve. Six sigma distance signifies the degree to which a product reaches its quality goal. Specifically, at six sigma above "normal," a product is reaching its quality goal 99.9999997 percent of the time, or has only 3.4 defects per million. Six Sigma projects set this as the goal toward which manufacturing and quality control efforts in the organization are focused.

Six Sigma programs are targeted at reducing costs by making changes before defects or problems occur. As part the Six Sigma program, employees and managers are trained in statistical analysis, project management, and problem solving methodology. These skills are used to help them reduce defects in their products. Most organizations that have implemented Six Sigma programs report increased profitability resulting from lower production costs from doing the thing correctly the first time in combination with reduced costs for not having to redo the work previously done.

Total Quality Management

Another strategy for increasing the quality of goods and services and concomitant customer satisfaction is Total Quality Management (TQM). TQM attempts to improve the quality of products or services by raising awareness of quality concerns across the organization. This management strategy emphasizes developing an organizational environment that supports innovation and creativity as well as taking risks to meet customer demands using such techniques as participative problem solving that includes not only managers, but employees and customers as well.

There are five cornerstones to TQM: The product, the process that allows the product to be produced, the organization that provides the proper environment needed for the process to work, the leadership that guides the organization, and commitment to excellence throughout the organization. To be successful, TQM programs need to consider all five of these primary emphases. To help ensure the success of the TQM strategy, it is necessary that an environment of quality be fostered within the organization. This requires not only an emphasis on the efficiency of processes, but also an emphasis on consistency, integrity, and other positive interpersonal relationship skills. To foster the teamwork necessary to bring about high quality, TQM encourages organizations to implement a decentralized authority structure where decisions are made close to those affected and all have a chance to participate in the process. This practice helps employees feel part of the system and that they are a vital part of the organization, not just hirelings. Ownership of team members working on the product can also be fostered by increasing the flow of communication across all levels of the organization and providing each employee the training that s/he needs to successfully add value to the product.

TQM looks not only at the bottom line in terms of profits or other relevant numbers, but also helps link the concepts of value to the customer with the cost of the product. This practice can help with market positioning and increasing market share. This can be enabled by continually assessing the marketplace of the organization's product vis a vis the organization's skills and resources to better position the organization to excel in the marketplace.

Business Process Reengineering

Business process reengineering is a management approach that strives to improve the effectiveness and efficiency of the various processes within an organization. Business process reengineering is a radical rethinking and redesign of business processes so that they achieve dramatic improvements in critical organizational performance criteria such as cost, quality, service, and speed. To be successful, business process reengineering requires organizations to reexamine the assumptions underlying their business operations and to question why they do things the way that they do. The purpose of this analysis is to get at the root of any business process problems that the organization is experiencing. This will allow managers to reinvent the way that things are being done as opposed to modifying current practices to be somewhat more effective. This analysis often reveals obsolete, erroneous, or inappropriate practices or procedures that do not add value to the product or service being offered by the business.

While business process reengineering is not appropriate for every organization, it is most appropriate where more traditional methods fail or where there is a major discrepancy between where the organization is and where the organization needs to be. Businesses that are in serious trouble can often benefit from business process reengineering. Symptoms of this serious trouble can include having costs that are significantly higher the competition's, customer service that is causing the organization to lose a significant number of customers, or failure rates that are significantly above those for the industry. Organizations that find themselves in such situations have little choice than to perform a major overhaul of their business processes if they want to be viable. In addition, organizations that are not yet in such dire straits but that are headed on a trajectory to that condition can also often benefit from reengineering efforts. Symptoms of these situations include increased competition or competitors that have significantly improved their offerings or new customer needs that cannot be adequately met by the current business processes. Business process reengineering may often enable organizations to avoid falling into the first category where reengineering is mandatory if the organization is to survive. Not only failing or inefficient organizations can benefit from reengineering efforts, however: Top performing organizations with aggressive management that wants to take them further may also benefit from this analysis and redesign. Business process reengineering in highly successful organizations can help them further consolidate their position in the marketplace and create further barriers to their competitors.

The goal of business process reengineering efforts is to improve the effectiveness of the organization. This is commonly demonstrated in a number of ways. For example, reengineering frequently results in several jobs being consolidated into one. Business process reengineering efforts also often change processes so that workers who better understand the situation can make decisions rather than submitting these up the line for a supervisor to consider. Similarly, business process reengineering often results in work being performed where it makes the most sense. This situation results in less delays, lower overhead costs, and higher job satisfaction for the employees. As a result, reengineered processes can help improve customer satisfaction by providing quick resolution to their problems.

One of the basic tenets of the business process reengineering process is that steps in any business process must be performed in a natural order and all the steps must add value to the product or service rather than activity for the sake of activity. So, for example, a manufacturing company process might analyze the customer requirements and then translate these into internal product codes, transmit this information to various plants and warehouses, receive the various components, assemble the components into a finished product, and deliver and install the equipment, requiring the involvement of a different organization for each step in the process. Although these steps might traditionally be performed sequentially, if some of the data collected are not needed until delivery, time could be saved by not waiting until all of these steps were completed before starting the rest of the process.

Reengineered processes frequently have different versions that take into account various situations so that value is added to the product or service and the customer is better served. Although standardization of business process works fine in an assembly line, many jobs today do not need this degree of structure. For example, clerks in a retail store could be given the authority to take care of customer problems at the point of sale rather than making the customer go to the customer service department or waiting for a manager to come and authorize a simple activity. Similarly, a technician on a technical help line might be given the authority to treat customers according to their individual needs rather than going through a pre-ordained script. In this way, reengineering processes reduce the amount of time for the transaction. This results in lower costs for the organization as well as increased customer satisfaction and loyalty.

Bibliography

Birshan, M., Engel, M., & Sibony, O. (2013). Avoiding the quicksand: Ten techniques for more agile corporate resource allocation. *Mckinsey Quarterly*, , 60-63. Retrieved November 15, 2013, from EBSCO Online Database Business Source Complete. http://search.ebscohost.com/login.aspx?direct=true&db=bth&AN=91665810&site=ehost-live

Creech, B. (1994). *The five pillars of TQM: How to make total quality management work for you. New* York: Truman Talley Books/Dutton.

Hammer, M. & Champy, J. (1993). *Reengineering the corporation: A manifesto for business revolution.* New York: Harper Business.

Heger, D. A. (2006). An introduction to operations research — benefits, methods & application. Retrieved July 6, 2007, from Fortuitous Online Database http://www.fortuitous.com/docs/primers/OR-intro.pdf

Knoppen, D., Ateş, M. A., Brandon-Jones, A., Luzzini, D., van Raaij, E., & Wynstra, F. (2015). A comprehensive assessment of measurement equivalence in operations management. *International Journal Of Production Research, 53*(1), 166–182. Retrieved

Dec. 3, 2015, from EBSCO Online Database Business Soure Complete. http://search.ebscohost.com/login.aspx?direct=true&db=bth&AN=99545986&site=ehost-live&scope=site

Lowson, R. H. (2002). *Strategic operations management: The new competitive advantage.* New York: Routledge.

Lucas, H. C. Jr. (2005). *Information technology: Strategic decision making for managers.* New York: John Wiley and Sons.

Matthews, R. L., & Marzec, P. E. (2012). Social capital, a theory for operations management: a systematic review of the evidence. *International Journal of Production Research, 50,* 7081-7099. Retrieved November 15, 2013, from EBSCO Online Database Business Source Complete. http://search.ebscohost.com/login.aspx?direct=true&db=bth&AN=83140421&site=ehost-live

Senn, J. A. (2004). *Information technology: Principles, practices, opportunities* (3rd ed.). Upper Saddle River, NJ: Pearson/Prentice Hall.

Thorat, N., Raghavendran, A., & Groves, N. (2013). Offline management in virtualized environments. *Communications of the ACM, 56,* 75-81. Retrieved November 15, 2013, from EBSCO Online Database Business Source Complete. http://search.ebscohost.com/login.aspx?direct=true&db=bth&AN=87497840&site=ehost-live

Vonderembse, M. A. & Marchal, W. G. (2001). Operations management. In Saul I. Gass, S. I. & Harris, C. M. (eds.). *Encyclopedia of Operations Research and Management Science.* New York: Wiley, 585-588. Retrieved June 27, 2007, from EBSCO Online Database Business Source Complete. http://search.ebscohost.com/login.aspx?direct=true&db=bth&AN=21891684&site=ehost-live

Suggested Reading

Nerur, S. & Balijepally, V. (2007). Theoretical reflections on agile development methodologies. *Communications of the ACM, 50,* 79-83. Retrieved June 27, 2007, from EBSCO Online Database Business Source Complete. http://search.ebscohost.com/login.aspx?direct=true&db=bth&AN=24209676&site=ehost-live

Parker, K. (2006). Emerging trends in plant operations management. *Manufacturing Business Technology, 24,* 2. Retrieved June 27, 2007, from EBSCO Online Database Business Source Complete. http://search.ebscohost.com/login.aspx?direct=true&db=bth&AN=23507918&site=ehost-live

Stevenson, W. J. (2015). *Operations management.* New York, NY: McGraw-Hill Education.

Szwejczewski, M. & Cousens, A. (2007). Increasing flexibility: What are your options? *Management Services, 51,* 17-20. Retrieved June 27, 2007, from EBSCO Online Database Business Source Complete. http://search.ebscohost.com/login.aspx?direct=true&db=bth&AN=25188167&site=ehost-live

Ruth A. Wienclaw, Ph.D.

Organization Design

ABSTRACT

Organization design is the process of structuring the organization in a way that facilitates employee productivity and supports the organization in reaching its goals. The basic building blocks of organizational structure are division of labor, centralization of authority, and formalization. The organization can also be departmentalized functionally or divisionally. However, the requirements of today's electronically-enabled organizations have resulted in changes in the way that some organizations are structured. Matrix, network, and even virtual approaches are becoming more common. Organization design is an iterative process, however. As the organization grows and changes, the design may need to be reconsidered in order to keep the organization competitive.

OVERVIEW

Not every organization is created equally. Universities have formal organizational structures at the top of the hierarchy, but individual professors are given the authority to evaluate students and assign grades. Banks are run by strict rules and the individual tellers must follow strict procedures for fund disbursement, record keeping, and other tasks. Engineering firms are often run as teams that direct their own activities, with each person reporting both to a functional or departmental manager (e.g., programming department) and to a project manager (e.g., widget development project).

Depending on what they are trying to accomplish — e.g., encourage creativity, mass produce products, provide services — different types of organizations need to be structured differently. These structures include how labor is divided among employees, how communication flows both down and up the organizational hierarchy, and how formal power is consolidated or distributed. The design of the organization is the structure through which it is organized to conduct its business. Organization design sets limits on how work can be accomplished. An appropriate organization design can support employees in meeting organizational goals by giving them the freedom or the structure necessary to perform their tasks. For example, a team-based structure often works well for creative tasks where employees working together can experience the synergy that results in an outcome that is greater than they could have developed as individuals. An inappropriate organization design, on the other hand, can hinder the employees in their tasks and keep the organization from reaching its goals. For example, giving employees too much freedom in a bank could lead to bad or inconsistent decisions about lending, poor record keeping, and a resultant lack of profits for shareholders.

The design of an organization involves consideration of several things, including the division of labor and concomitant patterns of coordination of work activities, centralization and the structure of power relationships, and the degree of formalization of the organization. Division of labor is the way that work in the organization is divided into separate jobs. The more that work is subdivided, the greater the degree of specialization the individual employee needs to be able to do the job well. The development of a simulator to teach aircraft mechanics how to maintain and repair a fighter jet, for example, would require the inputs of numerous types of employees, including the subject matter experts who know what tasks are involved in these tasks, the training specialists who determine the best way to teach these tasks to students, the engineers who know how to turn the trainers' requirements into a piece of equipment that can be used to teach these tasks, the computer programmers who write the programs that run the simulator and present the information to students, and the production workers who actually put together the equipment for delivery to the customer. In addition to the workers performing the tasks, there are usually supervisors for each type of job. These individuals understand the nature of the work to be done, can support the employees in their tasks and make sure that the needs of the organization are met.

When jobs are divided in this way, they also need to be coordinated so that the work done by the individual employees or groups will fit together to create the work product needed by the organization. There are several general ways to coordinate work. Every organization uses informal communication when employees share information about tasks they are working on or when they form mutual ways to coordinate their work activities. Although informal communication can be quick and easy, it tends to work best when the organization is small and there are few barriers to communication. The mom-and-pop grocery store on the corner, for example, is more likely to use informal communication to coordinate the activities of workers than they are to have a formal set of procedures that cover every possible task. No matter the size of the organization, however, informal communication can occur directly (e.g., Harvey tells Chuck that he needs him to close out the cash register for the day) or through liaison or integrator roles (e.g., the project leader of the simulator development team encourages the various work groups to communicate with each other and coordinate their activities). Coordination can also be done through a formal hierarchy, where formal organizational power is given to an individual who directs work and allocates resources. This often is done through direct supervision (e.g., George's boss tells him to finish the report by the end of the day) or through the corporate structure (e.g., the head of the Zenda operation of the organization coordinates the work for the organization in that country). Coordination can also be accomplished through standardization of skills, processes, or outputs. In this approach to coordination, the organization sets policies and procedures for dealing with various common activities. This is helpful in routine situations (e.g., the receiver in each of the organization's stores enters information into the computer in the same format), but is not so helpful when unusual circumstances arise.

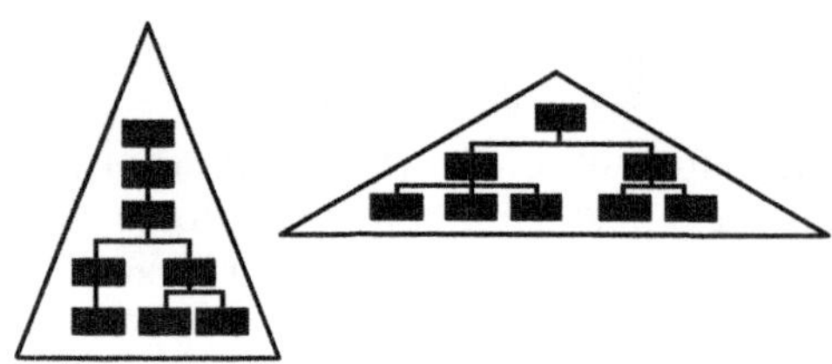

Figure 1: Tall (narrow span of control) vs. flat (wide span of control) organizational structures

The power structure within the organization is determined by its span of control and degree of centralization. Span of control is the number of employees that report directly to a supervisor in the next level up in the organization. At one time it was thought that a narrow span of control of 20 employees or less was the best approach to structuring an organization. Research has found, however, that in today's environment, the average span of control in effective organizations is 31. The most appropriate span of control will depend on what the organization is trying to accomplish and what types of people it employs. Larger spans of control are harder to supervise. However, when the employees self-manage (either as professionals or as self-managing work teams), this task becomes easier.

Another characteristic of an organization's structure is the degree to which formal decision-making power is centralized or carried out by a small group of people. In a centralized organization, a very limited number of individuals — usually at the top of the organizational hierarchy — have the power to make decisions. This is particularly true in smaller or emerging organizations where the founder or CEO tends to make most, if not all, of the decisions. However, as an organization grows, one person (or even a small group of people) is no longer able to make all the decisions, so the authority is distributed throughout the organization. For example, in a multinational firm it is logical to have some of the decisions made at a local level. Similarly, decisions about various activities can be made at a departmental or operational level.

Finally, organizations differ on the degree to which they formalize behavior through the imposition of rules, policies, practices, procedures, or formal training. Formalization can help employees know how to do their jobs. It can also help customers know that they are getting the same product no matter which of the organization's stores they patronize. A franchise coffee shop, for example, may specify the temperature to which the coffee is kept heated, how frequently the coffee is brewed, how much milk is added to a latte, and so forth. Formalization is more effective in organizations where employees' tasks are routine. So, for example, it is easier to formalize an organization such as a fast food franchise than it is to formalize a think tank. Although formalization can make an organization's processes more efficient, it can have the opposite effect when an unusual situation arises and a variance from the normal procedure is needed.

Although very small or emerging companies can function effectively with a simple structure, as the organization expands and grows it is useful to group employees together to perform common tasks. This facilitates supervision of employees and coordination of their work, helps in resource allocation, and provides common goals and measures of performance. There are several traditional ways to organize employees. The functional structure organizes employees around their knowledge or skills (e.g., the engineering department, the production department). This approach to structuring an organization makes supervision easier and can help foster professional identity. However, the functional approach to organizational structure can also result in a situation where the goals of the unit are given priority over the goals of the organization. The very intra-unit cohesiveness fostered by functional structuring can also lead to increased conflict and communication difficulties with other departments. Another way to structure an organization is through the creation of divisions. Divisions can be created based on geographic location (e.g., the US division vs. the Zenda division), clients (e.g., the hospital division vs. the consumer division), or products (e.g., the widget division vs. the gizmo division). Like functional structures, divisional structures can encourage a feeling of camaraderie and belongingness within the group. In addition, such divisional structures support growth and increased complexity better than do functional structures. However, this approach to organizational structure also creates the requirement for duplicate knowledge (e.g., each division needs a human resources function). As with functional structures, the divisional structure also results in more communication problems across groups.

Another type of organization that is used in many complex organizations — particularly those that work on time-limited contracts — is the matrix structure. This approach to organizational structure combines the features of the functional organization and the divisional organization. In a matrix structure, employees typically are hired for a functional department (e.g., programming, engineering, production). They are brought together on a temporary basis, however, as functional teams (e.g., the widget contract) or as part of a division. This means that each employee actually reports to two bosses: the functional boss (e.g., the programming department head) and the divisional boss (e.g., the widget project manager). Matrix structures have the advantage of efficient deployment of talent throughout the organization. This approach to organization design also can help the organization to be more flexible and efficient. However, this approach requires more coordination than the simpler approaches of functional or divisional structures. The dual-reporting relationship can be difficult to manage and the very fluidity of the design that is attractive to the organization can be stressful to the employee.

APPLICATIONS

Organization design for the 21st Century

Globalization, e-commerce, the ability to telecommute, and the high tech nature of many jobs have changed the way that many organizations do business. This fact, in turn, impacts the way that the organizations need to be structured in order to best support the high performance of the employees and the success of the organization. The strict military model of command and control that was often used in the past does not work as well for today's organizations comprised of highly creative or highly educated employees. As a result, new paradigms for organizational structure are emerging.

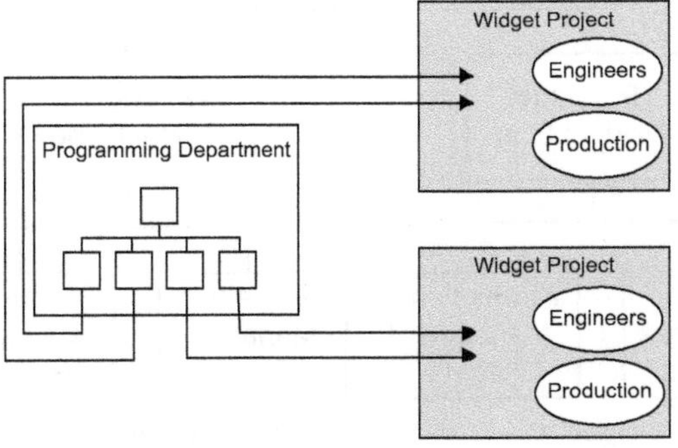

Figure 2: Simplified Matrix Design

Team-based structures (also called lateral, cluster, or circle structures) are departmentalized with a flat span of control and little formalization. The work in these organizations is performed by self-directed work teams — cross-functional groups that work without typical management supervision. When teams work well, they can achieve synergy, producing products or ideas that are greater than those that could have been accomplished by the individuals alone. An increasing number of organizations are finding the team-based structure to be a flexible way to respond to the needs of the organization and to reduce the levels in the managerial hierarchy and their concomitant costs. Since self-directed work teams have more independence and self-determination than other types of groups in an organization, they can respond more quickly to the needs of the organization or process and make better informed decisions. However, team-based structures also require increased interpersonal communication skills and training. In addition, teams cannot merely be created by fiat: It takes time to develop a team that works well together. Further, the very flexible nature of team-based structures can also lead to role ambiguity, increased conflict, and more stress for the team members.

Organizations can also be structured around a network of affiliates that together create a product or serve a client base. For example, a network structure (also called a modular or lattice structure) may comprise an accounting firm, marketing firm, product development firm, and manufacturing firm that all work together. In the network structure, the emphasis is on creating value for the organization, focusing on customer-centered activities that enhance the value of processes and products rather than on management-induced activities that do not. The various units in the network organization form alliances or partnerships to meet organizational needs. Communication in the network organization flows not only vertically along the lines of command, but horizontally between the work units. This approach to organizational structure is particularly appropriate in multinational companies that do a significant amount of communication electronically.

Another contemporary approach to organization design in the 21st Century is the virtual organization. The virtual organization is actually an association of multiple organizations that are allied for the purpose of product development or serving a client. For example, large government contracts such as ship design and development are often bid by such alliances, since it is difficult for any one organization to have all the skills necessary to develop a complex weapons system from cradle to grave. By joining together to form a product team, however, normally separate engineering, ship building, and training companies (among others) can create a temporary organization that will meet all the customer's needs. Virtual organizations usually consist of a prime contractor that performs most of the work and leads the team, and a number of subcontractors that may change as the needs of the project demand.

Redesigning the Organization

A running joke in many organizations is that when management does not know how to solve its problems, they reorganize. Sometimes reorganization is merely the business equivalent of rearranging the deckchairs on the *Titanic*: a way to look like one is doing something while ignoring the bigger, harder problem. However, reorganization also can be a legitimate effort. The goals and operations of organizations change as does the marketplace in which they operate. In order to stay competitive, there are occasions when the organization needs to reinvent itself and reorganize itself in order to be more competitive in the marketplace. For example, when adding operations in a different country, a very hierarchical, centralized structure more than likely will need to be changed. In such situations, managers on the ground need the empowerment to make decisions appropriate to the new location without first asking permission from a corporate headquarters located in a country with a different culture and legal and economic systems.

However, reorganization is not something to be taken lightly. It is a costly undertaking not only in terms of the time it takes to design and implement the new structure, but in terms of the impact on employees and their ability to perform and contribute to the success of the organization. In most re-organizations, there are losers: those whose jobs were downsized, from whom power was taken, or who are now forced to form a new work team. This can result not only in a situation where the employees must learn a new way of doing something or where they need to bond into a new work team, but also can result in employee dissatisfaction or a non-supportive work environment. The pros and cons of any contemplated reorganization must be carefully considered and weighed to determine whether or not a re-organization is appropriate.

Before embarking on the process of reorganization, the management team should consider several things. First, reorganization should be done as part of the organization's on-going strategic planning process. Reorganization should not be attempted unless it would significantly improve the organization's competitive edge. However, different market segments such as separate product lines or operations in different countries frequently benefit from being structured so that they receive sufficient management attention and do not compete with each other. For example, a company manufacturing two products might want to organize itself around the two product lines rather than having each in the same reporting structure. Similarly, it may be strategically advantageous to have different reporting structures for operations that are located in different countries. Organizational redesign should be structured so that the corporate headquarters supports the various operations of the organization rather than makes their tasks more difficult by imposing unreasonable reporting structures or not giving them sufficient management attention to support their success in the marketplace.

The design of an organization should exploit the strengths of its human capital. For example, an organization that employs a significant number of

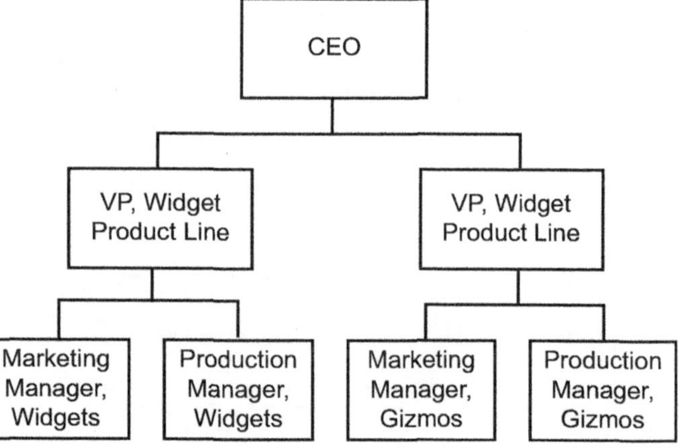

Figure 3: Simplified Organizational Chart Showing Different Reporting Structures

professional workers involved in a creative process (e.g., engineers) should take care not to impose too many strictures on their ability to do their jobs. Such employees need to be able to make decisions on the local level rather than going through a complex chain of command. On the other hand, it is also important that each function within the organization is manageable. If one cannot find competent managers for a given function in a proposed reorganization scheme, the system probably needs to be redesigned. Other constraints that may affect the feasibility of an organizational redesign include the interests of the organization's stakeholders, the ability of the information systems to support the structure, government regulations (including international regulations that may affect a multinational organization), and the organizational culture. Such variables should all be considered carefully before a redesign is attempted.

Once the problems facing the organization have been sufficiently analyzed and it has been determined that redesigning the organization will solve them, there are several considerations for the actual redesign process. One consideration is whether or not there are any groups within the organization with special cultures that need to be separated from the other groups. For example, although marketing functions can fall within product lines, they often are a separate function because of their different tasks and attitudes. Similarly, a new product development laboratory might need to be put in as a separate function so that it is not influenced by the way current products are designed. A related consideration concerns the ease of coordination between groups within the organization. For example, if coordinating the functions of a given product line that has operations in two separate countries is too difficult, it might make more sense to separate them organizationally and not just geographically.

Another consideration that needs to be taken into account, particularly in decentralized organizations, is whether there is sufficient accountability built into the organization design. In particular, it is important to look at the proposed organizational structure to determine if multiple groups have shared responsibilities. In such instances, it is easy for problems to arise when one group assumes that the other will accomplish the task or blames the other group for its own failure. In addition, it is important to determine how groups whose performance is difficult to measure will be held accountable. For example, it is not necessarily reasonable to expect a new product development group to create 20 viable new product ideas a quarter. On the other hand, it is important to ensure that the group is doing its best to produce new ideas.

Finally, the organization design should be flexible enough to accommodate the organization's needs in the future. An organizational structure that cannot do so is not going to be useful for supporting organizational effectiveness and success in the long run. However, molding the structure of an organization can be a continuing process as the needs of the organization and the marketplace change. For the organization to continue to meet the challenges of the future, it is important that the structure be adapted to support those needs as necessary.

BIBLIOGRAPHY

Csaszar, F. A. (2013). An efficient frontier in organization design: Organizational structure as a determinant of exploration and exploitation. *Organization Science, 24*(4), 1083-1101. Retrieved October 31, 2013, from EBSCO Online Database Business Source Complete. http://search.ebscohost.com/login.aspx?direct=true&db=bth&AN=89424518&site=ehost-live

Friesen, G. B. (2005). Organization design for the 21st century. *Consulting to Management, 16*(3), 32-51. Retrieved April 3, 2007, from EBSCO Online Database Business Source Complete. http://search.ebscohost.com/login.aspx?direct=true&db=bth&AN=17951111&site=bsi-live

Goold, M. & Campbell, A. (2002). Do you have a well-designed organization? *Harvard Business Review, 80*(3), 117-124. Retrieved April 3, 2007 from EBSCO Online Database Business Source Complete. http://search.ebscohost.com/login.aspx?direct=true&db=bth&AN=6327095&site=bsi-live

Hearn, S., & Choi, I. (2013). Creating a process and organization fit index: An approach toward optimal process and organization design. *Knowledge & Process Management, 20*(1), 21-29. Retrieved October 31, 2013, from EBSCO Online Database Business Source Complete. http://search.ebscohost.com/login.aspx?direct=true&db=bth&AN=85652503&site=ehost-live

McShane, Steven L. & Von Glinow, Mary Ann. (2003). *Organizational behavior: Emerging realities for the workplace revolution* (2nd ed). Boston: McGraw-Hill/Irwin.

Miozzo, M., Lehrer, M., DeFillippi, R., Grimshaw, D., & Ordanini, A. (2012). Economies of scope through multi-unit skill systems: The organization of large design firms. *British Journal of Management, 23*(2), 145-164. Retrieved October 31, 2013, from EBSCO Online Database Business Source Complete. http://search.ebscohost.com/login.aspx?direct=true&db=bth&AN=75061676&site=ehost-live

Worren, N. (2011). Hitting the sweet spot between separation and integration in organization design. *People & Strategy, 34*(4), 24-30. Retrieved October 31, 2013, from EBSCO Online Database Business Source Complete. http://search.ebscohost.com/login.aspx?direct=true&db=bth&AN=70939319&site=ehost-live

SUGGESTED READING

Brusoni, S. & Prencipe, A. (2006). Making design rules: A multidomain perspective. *Organization Science, 17*(2), 179-189. Retrieved April 3, 2007, from EBSCO Online Database Business Source Complete. http://search.ebscohost.com/login.aspx?direct=true&db=bth&AN=20451811&site=bsi-live

Child, J. & McGrath, R. G. (2001). Organizations unfettered: organizational form in an information- intensive economy. *Academy of Management Journal, 44*(6), 1135-1148. Retrieved April 3, 2007, from EBSCO Online Database Business Source Complete. http://search.ebscohost.com/login.aspx?direct=true&db=bth&AN=5887960&site=bsi-live

Dunbar, R. L. M. & Starbuck, W. H. (2006). Learning to design organizations and learning from designing them. *Organization Science, 17*(2), 171-178. Retrieved April 3, 2007, from EBSCO Online Database Business Source Complete. http://search.ebscohost.com/login.aspx?direct=true&db=bth&AN=20451812&site=bsi-live

Harris, M. & Raviv, A. (2002). Organization design. *Management Science, 48*(7), 852-865. Retrieved April 3, 2007, from EBSCO Online Database Business Source Complete. http://search.ebscohost.com/login.aspx?direct=true&db=bth&AN=7209662&site=bsi-live

Muchinsky, P. M. (2003). *Psychology applied to work: An introduction to industrial and organizational psychology* (7th Ed). Belmont, CA: Thomson/Wadsworth.

Ruth A. Wienclaw, Ph.D.

ORGANIZATION DEVELOPMENT

ABSTRACT

Organization development (OD) is a long-range effort to improve an organization's problem-solving and renewal processes. OD involves the application of behavior science knowledge to the problems of the workplace. OD consultants tend to look at the organization as a symptom and diagnose not only obvious symptoms, but deeper, more systemic problems. The OD process comprises multiple steps, tends to be long-term, and often includes multiple iterations of the diagnosis, planning, action, and stabilization/evaluation steps. OD interventions are typically more successful if carried out by an external consultant as change agent.

OVERVIEW

Each generation brings with it new technologies and new challenges. From a business perspective, this means that the organization needs to adapt and change to meet the changing needs and demands of the marketplace, or fail. Organization development (OD) is a long-range effort to improve the organization's problem-solving and renewal processes. OD involves the application of behavior science knowledge to the problems of the workplace.

Sometimes the changes that need to be made in an organization are relatively simple, even obvious. For example, most modern businesses need to have a presence on the web in order to be taken seriously by potential customers. Other changes are less simple to implement. For example, although it may be obvious to most observers that an organization needs to computerize its inventory, the ramifications of this change may be widespread and complex. The organization will have to hire someone to install the system and input the inventory data into the new system. The human resources department will need to develop or contract training for the people using the new inventory system. Old procedures will need to be updated to take into account the new procedures and their requirements. This illustrates the nature of the organization as a system: changes in one part of the system result in changes in the other parts of the system as well.

Organizational Culture: The Informal Organization

Although the installation of a new inventory database system can be a complex task involving most (if not all) of the organization, other changes can be even more complex, such as those that attempt to change the organization's culture or norms. French and Bell (1973) use the metaphor of an iceberg to describe the nature of an organization (see Figure 1). According to this theory, an organization comprises both a formal organization and an informal organization. When a symptom arises in an organization, it may be due to problems in the formal organization, the informal organization, or both. Like an iceberg, the formal organization — that part of the organization that is easily observable (and more easily fixable) — represents only a small portion of the organization as a whole. The formal organization comprises the goals of the organization, the structure of the organization (i.e., the design of an organization including its division of labor, delegation of authority, and span of control), the skills of its employees, the technology it employs, and the resources it has to accomplish its tasks. The example of the need to install a computerized inventory system is an example of an intervention within the formal organization.

However, as illustrated in Figure 1, like an iceberg, the majority of the organization is harder to see and diagnose. The informal organization comprises such things as attitudes, values, feelings, interactions, and group norms. These are much more difficult to deal with than the aspects of the formal organization. Often, problems that appear to be part of the formal organization may in fact be related to the informal organization or may be a combination of problems in both the formal and the informal organization. Therefore, it is important for the organization's OD practitioner to separate the symptoms the organization is experiencing from the underlying problems. Although some organizational problems (such as the example of the need to implement a new inventory database) are obvious and relatively straightforward to fix, others are more systemic and thus more difficult to diagnose.

There are many symptoms for which an organization requires an OD intervention. For example, communication or intra- or inter-team conflict is frequently cited as a problem in many organizations. Similarly, managerial strategies are often found to be ineffective or onerous by those who must live under them. Other obvious symptoms of organizational problems include:

- Lack of motivation on the part of the worker,
- Lack of clear or functional structure or roles within the organization,
- Problems with the organizational climate, or
- Problems stemming from cultural norms.

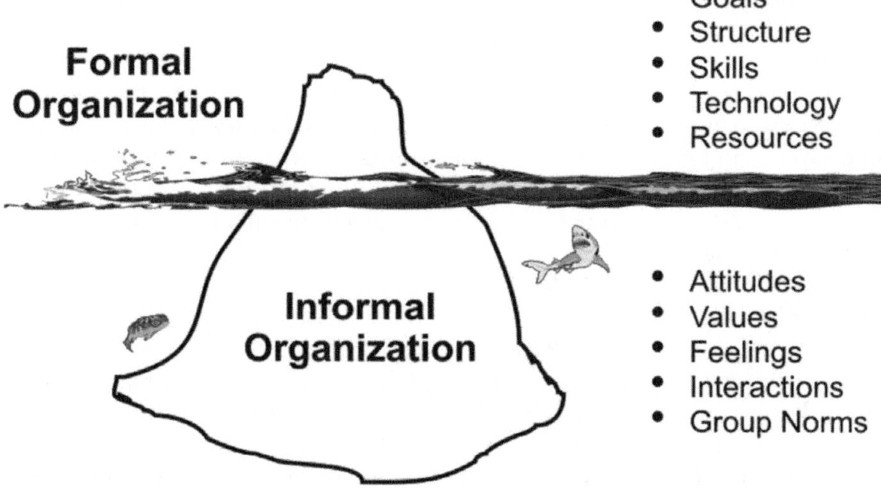

Figure 1: The Formal and Informal Organization (adapted from French & Bell, 1973)

There are some situations where OD interventions should be considered, such as the need to perform strategic planning or cope with a merger. However, for the most part, these are only symptoms. The problems underlying these symptoms are often not the same. Communication problems, for example, might occur because the organization has set two or more groups in competition with each other, and they need to compete for scarce resources. Apparent lack of motivation may be the result of inadequate control, lack of training, or unfair or inadequate rewards. Part of the job of the OD consultant is to determine what underlying problems are responsible for the symptoms being experienced by the organization.

Further Insights

The OD Consultant/Change Agent

Although for the most part, organizations employ their own OD staff, for OD to be effective it requires an outside change agent. This is a person external to the organization who guides an organization through a change effort. To be effective, change agents need to have knowledge of how to conduct a change effort, an understanding of the organization, and sufficient power to be able to implement the change.

There are a number of reasons why an external change agent is more likely to successfully accomplish change within an organization than an internal change agent with the same credentials. External consultants typically have a more clear-cut role than do internal consultants. When an external consultant is hired to do OD for an organization, it is typically with the understanding that his or her purview comprises the activities associated with OD and not with other organizational tasks or objectives. If the external change agent is properly introduced into the organization, everyone will know what purpose this individual serves. An internal consultant, on the other hand, typically has more difficulty articulating his or her role within the organization. Although OD may be part of the internal consultant's role, she or he will often be called upon to perform other human resources activities as well. This makes it more difficult for the organization to see an internal consultant as an expert. It also makes it less likely that the affected employees will be as open with an internal consultant as with an external one, because they will tend to see him or her as part of the organizational hierarchy with loyalties to management rather than to the employees.

External consultants are more likely to be effective as OD change agents because they are less affected by organizational norms than internal consultants. Whereas internal consultants are more ready to accept the organizational system as given, external consultants are more likely to be able to look at the organization objectively and see problems in areas that an internal consultant might take for granted.

An external consultant is also freer to look at the organization from a larger, systems view while an internal consultant is more likely to focus on a micro view of the organization. As discussed above, it is essential that an OD consultant consider the problems in both the formal and the informal organization and to recognize that changing the organization in one area is likely to have a direct or indirect effect on other areas. An internal consultant, however, often is either (a) unable to have that degree of objectivity because she or he is part of the system or (b) is only tasked with very circumscribed activities because she or he is a direct employee of the organization. For example, if the organization is experiencing difficulties in communication, an internal consultant might be tasked with developing and conducting a training course in communication skills. An external consultant, given the same set of symptoms, would more than likely look at the system as a whole and might find out that the communication problem was only a symptom of a deeper underlying problem such as conflict over scarce resources or differing norms between groups. The internal consultant is unlikely to be able to successfully address this problem because she or he has only been tasked with giving a training course.

Finally, external consultants typically have easier access to upper-level management in the organization. Since the support of upper-level management is essential for the success of OD interventions, this makes external consultants more likely to be successful. Internal consultants, on the other hand, are part of the system that they are trying to change. Since they are unlikely to have the same access to upper-level management as an external consultant, they are less likely to have the support necessary to ensure the success of their interventions. As a result, internal consultants typically spend little effort toward organizational renewal, whereas external consultants are free to do so.

OD Processes

Scouting

Organization development is a multistage process (see Figure 2). The first step for both the consultant and the organization is scouting. This is a mutual exploration between the two parties to determine whether or not they can work together. Sometimes,

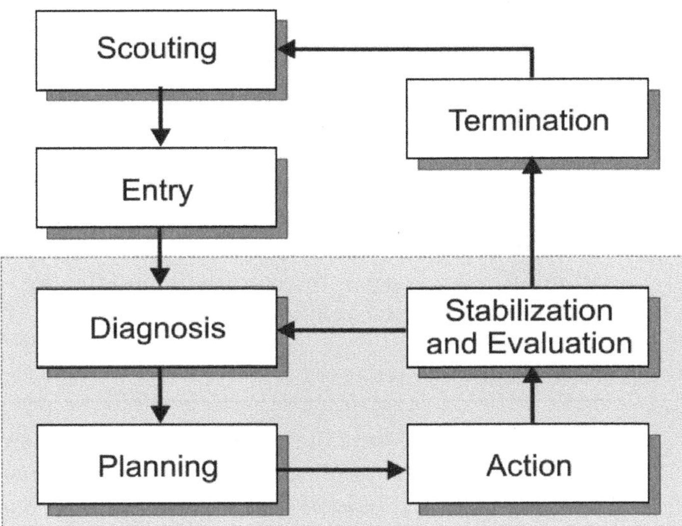

Figure 2: Stages in an Organization Development Intervention

for example, the OD consultant may not have experience or interest in the type of intervention needed by the organization. In other cases, the organization may be unable or unwilling to guarantee the support and resources necessary to ensure that change will occur. In order for the OD intervention to be successful, the organization must be willing to implement the changes suggested by the OD consultant based on the research. Key management within the organization (especially at top organizational levels) must be involved in the change process. Further, those persons who will be affected by the change must be brought on board as soon as possible, and any persons involved must be informed about the change and the reasons for it and motivated to implement it. If the organization cannot make these assurances, it is unlikely that the intervention will be successful.

Entry

If the organization and the consultant mutually decide that working together would be beneficial, they move into the entry stage. During this time, the two parties set roles for the desired change, share expectations for the results of the OD intervention, establish a commitment (typically through contractual arrangement), and establish an effective power base to help ensure that the intervention will be effective.

Diagnosis

The next stage is diagnosis. During this stage, the OD consultant looks at the problems as perceived by the client. Although these are typically symptoms rather than underlying problems, this is usually the most reasonable place to start an intervention. In addition, the change agent at this point will look at the goals of the client and determine how best to meet them. This determination will take into consideration both the resources and commitment of the client to the OD intervention and change process as well as the resources of the consultant.

There are a number of methods that are applied by OD consultants to aid in the diagnostic process. One of the most frequently used is the questionnaire, used in the context of the survey research feedback methodology (see Figure 3). This is a type of research in which data about the opinions, attitudes, or reactions of the members of a sample are gathered using a survey instrument. The phases of survey research are goal setting, planning, implementation, evaluation, and feedback. As opposed to experimental research, survey research does not allow for the manipulation of an independent variable. The questionnaire or survey used in this technique comprises a data collection instrument designed to acquire information on the opinions, attitudes, or reactions of people. The consultant may choose to survey all employees using this instrument or may select a sample of workers who are asked questions concerning their opinions, attitudes, or reactions, which are gathered using a survey instrument or questionnaire for purposes of scientific analysis.

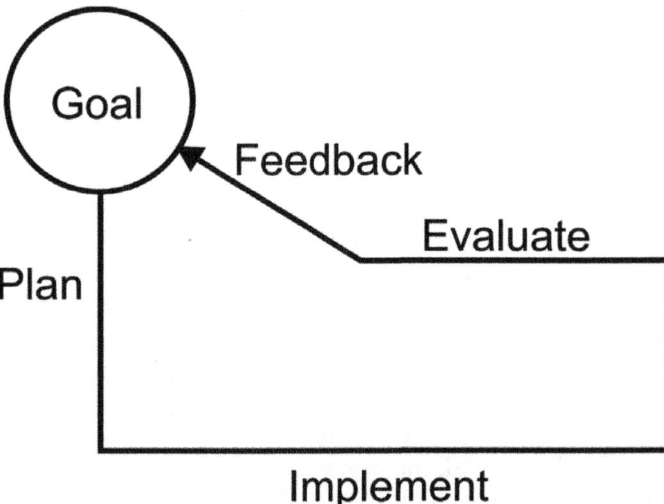

Figure 3: Survey Research Feedback Methodology

In addition to surveys, the OD consultant may conduct interviews with key individuals across the organization. For example, there are typically individuals who better understand the causes of various symptoms and problems, who can better articulate these, or who are informal leaders within the organization. The OD consultant often includes his or her personal observations of the organization. Fruitful sources of such observations come from staff meetings, interdepartmental memos, and other records of communication. Another source of data that is useful in making a diagnosis of problems is objective data. This can include such the statistics as absenteeism, turnover, antiorganizational behavior, production rates, reject rates, or union activity. Similarly, outside opinions of the organization from customers, clients, and competitors can also be useful in determining underlying problems.

Another useful tool for diagnosing problems within the organization is the confrontation meeting. The purpose of confrontation meetings is to tap management resources within the organization and to apply these to solving the organization's problems. To conduct a confrontation meeting, the change agent starts by establishing the proper climate for the meeting by articulating the goals, philosophy, and other ground rules for conduct of the meeting. She or he then describes the task that the group is to undertake. At this point, the consultant emphasizes the need for problem-solving and brainstorming skills. The meeting then breaks into working subgroups that are usually composed of members from different levels and sections within the organization. These subgroups then identify the major problems facing the organization and come back together to discuss and categorize the problems that were identified. These problems may then be assigned to various subgroups for further study and analysis.

Planning, Action & Stabilization

Once the problem has been diagnosed, the next step in the OD process is to plan the intervention. At this point, the decision needs to be made as to whether the intervention should be system-wide or only implemented at certain levels. Once the nature and scope of the intervention has been determined, the next step in the OD process is to implement it. The consultant next works with the organization to stabilize the change so that it becomes internalized. Once this has happened and the change state becomes the status quo, the consultant then evaluates the effectiveness of the change in solving the problem of the organization. At this point, if it is determined that further action it is necessary, the OD process then continues with further diagnosis, planning, action, and stabilization. Eventually, when it is determined that the underlying problem has been adequately addressed and that the change process has been internalized within the organization, the consultant and the organization dissolve their relationship.

CONCLUSION

Organization development is more than management consulting. It is the application of behavior science knowledge to the problems of the workplace. OD is a long-range effort to improve the organization's problem-solving and renewal processes and often takes more than one iteration before the underlying problem is properly diagnosed and adequately addressed. Although some organizations have internal OD consultants on staff, in general, an external change agent is more likely to accomplish the long-term change desired by the organization. Properly applied, the OD process can be very effective in diagnosing and fixing deep or systemic problems in the organization.

BIBLIOGRAPHY

Anderson, D. L. (2012). Organization development interventions and four targets of post-acquisition integration. *OD Practitioner, 44*(3), 19–24. Retrieved November 27, 2013 from EBSCO online database Business Source Premier. http://search.ebscohost.com/login.aspx?direct=true&db=buh&AN=77415368

French, W. (1969). Organization development, objectives, assumptions and strategies. *California Management Review, 12* (2), 23–34. Retrieved April 27, 2010 from EBSCO Online Database Business Source Complete http://search.ebscohost.com/login.aspx?direct=true&db=bth&AN=5049468&site=ehost-live

French, W. L., & Bell, C. H., Jr. (1973). *Organization development: Behavioral science interventions for organization improvement.* Englewood Cliffs, NJ: Prentice-Hall.

Nicholas, J. M. (1982). The comparative impact of organization development interventions on hard criteria measures. *Academy of Management Review,*

7 (4), 531–542. Retrieved April 27, 2010 from EBSCO Online Database Business Source Complete http://search.ebscohost.com/login.aspx?direct=true&db=bth&AN=4285229&site=ehost-live

Rao, T. V., & Ramnarayan, S. S. (2011). *Organization development: Accelerating learning and transformation.* New Delhi, India: SAGE/Response Business Books. Retrieved November 27, 2013 from EBSCO online database eBook Academic Collection (EBSCOhost). http://search.ebscohost.com/login.aspx?direct=true&db=nlebk&AN=421044&site=ehost-live

Yaeger, T. F., Sorensen, P. F., & Johnson, H. H. (2013). *Critical issues in organization development: Case studies for analysis and discussion.* Charlotte, NC: Information Age Pub., Inc. Retrieved November 27, 2013 from EBSCO online database eBook Collection (EBSCOhost). http://search.ebscohost.com/login.aspx?direct=true&db=nlebk&AN=591027&site=ehost-live

Suggested Reading

Akdere, M., & Altman, B. A. (2009). An organization development framework in decision making: Implications for practice. *Organization Development Journal, 27* (4), 47–56. Retrieved April 27, 2010 from EBSCO Online Database Business Source Complete http://search.ebscohost.com/login.aspx?direct=true&db=bth&AN=48656205&site=ehost-live

Bate, P., Khan, R., & Pyle, A. J. (2000). Culturally sensitive structuring: An action research-based approach to organization development and design. *Public Administration Quarterly, 23* (4), 445–470. Retrieved April 27, 2010 from EBSCO Online Database Business Source Complete http://search.ebscohost.com/login.aspx?direct=true&db=bth&AN=3709682&site=ehost-live

Burke, W. W., & Church, A. H. (1992). Managing change, leadership style, and intolerance to ambiguity: A survey of organization development practitioners. *Human Resource Management, 31* (4), 301–318. Retrieved April 27, 2010 from EBSCO Online Database Business Source Complete http://search.ebscohost.com/login.aspx?direct=true&db=bth&AN=7239411&site=ehost-live

Chattopadhyay, S., & Pareek, U. (1984). Organization development in a voluntary organization. *International Studies of Management and Organization, 14* (2/3), 46–85. Retrieved April 27, 2010 from EBSCO Online Database Business Source Complete http://search.ebscohost.com/login.aspx?direct=true&db=bth&AN=5815556&site=ehost-live

Cobb, A. T., & Margulies, N. (1981). Organization development: A political perspective. *Academy of Management Review, 6* (1), 49–59. Retrieved April 27, 2010 from EBSCO Online Database Business Source Complete http://search.ebscohost.com/login.aspx?direct=true&db=bth&AN=4287998&site=ehost-live

Dahl, J. G., & Glassman, A. M. (1991). Public sector contracting: The next "growth industry" for organization development? *Public Administration Quarterly, 14* (4), 483–497. Retrieved 27 April 2010 from EBSCO Online Database Business Source Complete http://search.ebscohost.com/login.aspx?direct=true&db=bth&AN=7162859&site=ehost-live

Deaner, C. M. D., & Miller, K. J. (1999). Our practice of organization development: A work in progress. *Public Administration Quarterly, 23* (2), 139–151. Retrieved April 27, 2010 from EBSCO Online Database Business Source Complete http://search.ebscohost.com/login.aspx?direct=true&db=bth&AN=2794421&site=ehost-live

Gabris, G. T., & King, J. (1989). Making management training more effective and credible through organization development: Results in one city. *Public Administration Quarterly, 13* (2), 215–231. Retrieved April 27, 2010 from EBSCO Online Database Business Source Complete http://search.ebscohost.com/login.aspx?direct=true&db=bth&AN=7284954&site=ehost-live

Huse, E. H. (1978). Organization development. *Personnel and Guidance Journal, 56* (7), 403–406. Retrieved April 27, 2010 from EBSCO Online Database Business Source Complete http://search.ebscohost.com/login.aspx?direct=true&db=a9h&AN=6475520&site=ehost-live

Jaeger, A. M. (1986, Jan). Organization development and national culture: Where's the fit? *Academy of Management Review, 11* (1), 178–190. Retrieved April 27, 2010 from EBSCO Online Database Business Source Complete http://search.ebscohost.com/login.aspx?direct=true&db=bth&AN=4282662&site=ehost-live

Lau, C.-M., & Ngo, H.-Y. (2001). Organization development and firm performance: A comparison of multinational and local firms. *Journal of International Business Studies, 32* (1), 95–114. Retrieved

April 27, 2010 from EBSCO Online Database Business Source Complete http://search.ebscohost.com/login.aspx?direct=true&db=bth&AN=4564768&site=ehost-live

Marshak, R. J., & Grant, D. (2008). Organizational discourse and new organization development practices. *British Journal of Management, 1* (19), S7–S19. Retrieved April 27, 2010 from EBSCO Online Database Business Source Complete http://search.ebscohost.com/login.aspx?direct=true&db=bth&AN=29993787&site=ehost-live

McDonagh, J., & Coghlan, D. (2006). Information technology and the lure of integrated change: A neglected role for organization development? *Public Administration Quarterly, 30* (1/2), 22–55. Retrieved April 27, 2010 from EBSCO Online Database Business Source Complete http://search.ebscohost.com/login.aspx?direct=true&db=bth&AN=24117533&site=ehost-live

Miranda, S. M., & Saunders, C. (1995). Group support systems: An organization development intervention to combat groupthink. *Public Administration Quarterly, 19* (2), 193–216. Retrieved April 27, 2010 from EBSCO Online Database Business Source Complete http://search.ebscohost.com/login.aspx?direct=true&db=bth&AN=7151588&site=ehost-live

Porras, J. I., & Berg, P. O. (1978). The impact of organization development. *Academy of Management Review, 3* (2), 249–266. Retrieved April 27, 2010 from EBSCO Online Database Business Source Complete http://search.ebscohost.com/login.aspx?direct=true&db=bth&AN=4294860&site=ehost-live

Sanchez, M. (2013). Maturing toward enterprise organization development capability. *OD Practitioner, 45*(4), 49–54. Retrieved November 27, 2013 from EBSCO online database Business Source Premier. http://search.ebscohost.com/login.aspx?direct=true&db=buh&AN=90602261

Sinzgiri, J., & Gottlieb, J. Z. (1992). Philosophic and pragmatic influences on the practice of organization development, 1950-2000. *Organizational Dynamics, 21* (2), 57–69. Retrieved April 27, 2010 from EBSCO Online Database Business Source Complete http://search.ebscohost.com/login.aspx?direct=true&db=bth&AN=9609134589&site=ehost-live

Terpstra, D. E. (1981). The organization development evaluation process: Some problems and proposals. *Human Resource Management, 20* (1), 24–29. Retrieved April 27, 2010 from EBSCO Online Database Business Source Complete http://search.ebscohost.com/login.aspx?direct=true&db=bth&AN=12493291&site=ehost-live

Umstot, D. D. (1980). Organization development technology and the military: A surprising merger? *Academy of Management Review, 5* (2), 189–202. Retrieved April 27, 2010 from EBSCO Online Database Business Source Complete http://search.ebscohost.com/login.aspx?direct=true&db=bth&AN=4288717&site=ehost-live

White, B. J., & Ramsey, V. J. (1978). Some unintended consequence of "top down" organization development. *Human Resource Management, 17* (2), 7–14. Retrieved April 27, 2010 from EBSCO Online Database Business Source Complete http://search.ebscohost.com/login.aspx?direct=true&db=bth&AN=12493334&site=ehost-live

White, J. D. (1990). Phenomenology and organization development. *Public Administration Quarterly, 14* (1), 76–85. Retrieved April 27, 2010 from EBSCO Online Database Business Source Complete http://search.ebscohost.com/login.aspx?direct=true&db=bth&AN=7163655&site=ehost-live

Ruth A. Wienclaw, Ph.D.

Organizational Behavior

ABSTRACT

Organization behavior is the study of the functioning and performance of individuals, groups, and teams within organizations as well as of organizations as a whole. Based on scientific research and empirical data, organizational behavioral theorists attempt to understand, predict, and influence behavior at all levels within the organization. There are many practical applications of organizational behavior theory for managers. For example, at the individual level, organizational behavior theory can help managers learn to be better leaders and communicate with and motivate their workers. At a team level, organizational behavior theory helps managers understand how teams are formed and function, and how to best support them so that synergy occurs. At the organizational level, organizational behavior theory can help managers better understand how the organization works and how each subsystem within it works together to make up the organization as a whole.

OVERVIEW

Organizational behavior is the systematic study and application of how individuals and groups think and act within organizations and how these activities affect the effectiveness of the organization as a whole. Organizational behavior theorists take a systems approach, looking not only at individuals or groups as isolated entities, but also as part of an interactive social system in which the actions of one part influence the functioning of another. Rather than merely focusing on the profitability of the organization in isolation, the discipline of organizational behavior attempts to improve organizational effectiveness at all levels within the organization. To do this, organizational behavior theorists attempt to understand, predict, and influence events on the individual, group, and organizational levels.

The field of organizational behavior is based on several principles. First, organizational behavior theory and practice does not operate in isolation, but is multidisciplinary, drawing on the insights arising not only from its own research but also the research and insights of other disciplines. For example, psychology has contributed to organizational behavior theory by helping explain issues relating to individual and interpersonal behavior, as well as the dynamics of groups and teams. Sociology has contributed to the knowledge of organizational behavior by increasing the understanding of how groups and teams act and interact, working together to contribute to the functioning of the organization as a social system. Anthropology contributes understanding of culture and rituals, while political science helps us understand conflict between groups as well as organizational environments, power, and decision making. Newer disciplines, such as information systems theory, help organizational behavior theorists understand the dynamics of teams, how organizations manage knowledge, and how decisions are made.

Just as the disciplines from which it gathers insights are based on empirical evidence, organizational behavior applies the scientific method in an attempt to systematically study the actions and interactions of individuals and teams within an organization. The scientific method involves observing behavior within organizations, formulating a theory based on the observations to explain why the behavior occurs, experimenting and collecting data to determine the truth of the hypothesis, and validating or modifying the hypothesis as appropriate.

This process differs from some early management theorists who often took lessons learned in isolated situations (such as the success of one large manufacturing company) and turned them into a list of simple steps to follow for success in all businesses. Rather, organizational behavior theory takes a contingency approach. This approach assumes that an action does not necessarily always have the same consequences, and may result in a different reaction in different situations. What this means practically is that one solution is not universally the best and behavior cannot be distilled into simple lists of steps that ensure success. In general, it has been found that proposed absolute or universal rules need to be tempered by too many exceptions. For example, in the study of leadership, researchers and practitioners alike have found that there is not one best way to lead, but that the "ideal" management style is contingent on the needs, abilities, and personalities of both the employees performing the tasks and of their leader or manager. Because of real world experiences, organizational behavior theorists tend to temper their theories by trying to better understand when and why a principle works and by not stating absolutes.

One of the reasons that it is necessary to take a contingency approach when trying to understand behavior in organizations is that organizations are systems comprising numerous subsystems. The functioning of each subsystem impacts the functioning of the other subsystems. Therefore, in addition to the contingency approach, organizational behavior theory is also founded on the premise of systems theory. In this approach, the organization is viewed as a system made up of interdependent subsystems, each of which affects the effectiveness of the other as well as the effectiveness of the organization as a whole. For example, a strike by one segment of workers in an organization negatively impacts the ability of the organization as a whole to meet its objectives whether those be to efficiently collect garbage, transport passengers, or produce auto parts. However, systems theory affects organizations in less obvious ways, too. For example, when writing a proposal for a new contract, if one work group fails to meet its deadline for writing the technical response, a budget cannot be developed to submit to the prospective client and the production of a professional-looking proposal cannot be done in a timely manner. If enough of these small actions with negative impacts occur, the organization will not win the contract. This, in turn, could affect the profitability and even the viability of the organization and, along with it, the jobs and lives of the individuals and teams of which it is comprised. Each subsystem (technical work group, accounting or costing group, and proposal production group) affects the ability of the other groups — as well as of the organization in general — to do their jobs.

Although such insights are interesting in the abstract, organizational behavior is a practical discipline that not only attempts to understand and predict behavior, but to influence it. To this end, organizational behavior theorists have made significant contributions to management theory and practice.

APPLICATIONS

The field of organizational behavior is concerned with all three levels of functioning within the organization: individual, groups and teams, and the organization as a whole. At the individual level, organizational theorists study the characteristics, thought processes, and behaviors of employees. This subset of organizational behavior includes analyzing employees' personality, motivation, roles, and cultural differences and how such elements affect their behavior and interactions within the organization. Understanding these processes prepares the manager to better motivate individuals and help them reach their full potential within the organization. At the team level, organizational behavior theorists look at such concepts as what distinguishes a team from a group, what processes are involved in the formation of a team, how leadership arises within a team, and the best way to manage teams. At the organizational level, theorists examine how the actions of individuals and teams affect the organization and its effectiveness, as well as how the organization interacts with the greater culture and society.

Individual Behavior

When setting up a new organization, there are many considerations that impact how it will be structured. For example, a computer software development firm will need programmers through necessity. The number and type of employees needed will depend on what product the firm is trying to deliver and what level of work is sustainable. If these employees could work completely on their own, they would each be able to do their jobs however they wished. For example, Harvey may like to start at noon and work through the evening or keep his work area in a constant state of controlled chaos while Chuck may be a morning person who keeps everything in its place. If they could work alone, this would not be a problem. In reality, however, people typically do not work in isolation and individual differences in work style, ability to communicate, and desire to be in charge can bring about clashes. Harvey and Chuck may need to share an office and reach an accommodation about how best to work together. Or, the programmer must depend on input from the designer and must also coordinate with other programmers working on other parts of the project. S/he may also be called on to demonstrate the new software to potential customers or work with marketing personnel to support efforts to maintain and increase the company's market share. One of the roles of the manager in an organization is to help minimize such differences, utilizing the abilities of the workers to meet the needs of the organization and supporting the needs of the workers with the resources of the organization.

Organizational behavior theorists examine many aspects of human behavior in order to help understand, predict, and control how people act and interact in the workplace. One practical application of the knowledge of individual differences is situational leadership theory. In this approach to leadership, theorists state that effective leaders change the style of their leadership depending on the ability and even the personality of the people they are trying to lead. For example, in cases where the workers do not have sufficient knowledge of how to do the job, the leader typically must be more directive than in situations where the workers are highly skilled and experienced. Similarly, the contingency leadership model suggests that effective leadership depends on whether the leader's style is appropriate to the situation. For example, a leader who prefers to wade into a situation and tell people what to do will not be successful in a situation where a team works best through synergy; piggybacking ideas off each other and developing a product or idea may be greater than what they could have done alone.

Another area in which organizational behavioral theorists are interested in, regarding the effects of individual differences and their impact on management effectiveness, is employee motivation. Motivation is the study of the needs and thought processes that determine a person's behavior. Understanding what motivates a person can help a manager better reward that person for behavior that contributes to achieving the objectives of the organization. For example, if a worker is motivated by money, a manager can use the possibility of raises or bonuses to motivate the desired behavior. On the other hand, if the worker is motivated by status or power, a promotion or corner office may offer a greater incentive for desired behavior. There are two general approaches to motivation considered by organizational theorists. Content theories of motivation examine the dynamics of people's needs, and use these to explain why the same person may be motivated differently at different times. Process theories of motivation, on the other hand, examine the processes by which needs are translated into behavior. These theories help both organizational theorists and managers better understand, predict, and influence the performance of employees.

In addition to idiosyncratic differences between people based on individual personality types and preferences, organizational behavior theorists and managers alike are concerned with individual differences between people based on their cultures. Certainly, it is important not to offend others in the course of getting a task done, but this issue goes deeper. Different cultures have different ways of doing things, and unless these differences are understood and accommodated, motivating the worker and meeting organizational objectives will be more difficult than necessary. For example, when communicating, most women prefer to make eye contact with the person to whom they are speaking and tend to devote their full attention to the conversation. Many men, on the other hand, do not expect these things in a conversation and often multitask while talking. This can lead to miscommunication and conflict when such differences in communication styles result in situations where people believe that they are not being listened to or not being taken seriously. In another example, in the Japanese culture one must be able to not only understand what the other person is saying, but to also correctly understand the nonverbal cues that accompany the verbal part of the communication. For example, in order to be polite, Japanese businesspersons may say what they think the other person wants to hear — such as saying that they will give serious consideration to a proposal — while giving nonverbal cues that say that they have already rejected the other person's idea. Each culture has its own subtleties of communication. Such differences must be understood in order to facilitate effective communication so that organizational goals can be met.

Team Behavior & Processes

An increasing amount of work today is performed by teams rather than by groups or individuals. Although some tasks are better performed by the single individual working alone, organizations are finding that many tasks are better accomplished through teamwork. There are several differences between a team and a group of individuals working together. Whereas the group may have a common goal (e.g., complete 100 new widgets before the close of business), work teams tend to develop their own mission and their members are vested in accomplishing it. Therefore, although both groups and teams may be accountable to a manager, team members are also accountable to each other for getting their part of the work done. Therefore, in work groups, leadership is typically held by a single person, whereas in a team, all members tend to share leadership. Another major difference between groups and teams is that groups do not have a stable culture; as a result, conflict frequently arises. True teams, on the other hand, have a collaborative culture in which the team members trust each other. As a result, work groups may or may not accomplish their goals whereas true teams tend to achieve synergy, producing products or ideas that are greater than those that could have been accomplished by the individuals alone.

Not all teams are created equally, however. Organizational behavior theorists have observed four different types of teams. In the manager-led work team, the manger is responsible for the design of the organizational context of the team's activities as well as the design of the team performing the work. Although the team itself is responsible for performing the work, the manager is responsible for monitoring and managing the performance of the team. In the self-managing work team, although the manager designs the organizational context of the team and the structure of the group, the team itself not only performs the task to be done but monitors and manages its performance. In the self-designing work team, the manager sets the organizational context within which the work must be performed, but the team organizes itself and specifies how it will perform this work. Finally, the self-governing work team performs all these tasks as well as designs the organizational context in which they occur. When the manager understands such underlying dynamics of team behavior, s/he can be better able to support the team and promote the synergy that is possible through team efforts.

Whether work is being performed in a work group or in a team setting, eventually conflicts will arise. Organizational behavior theorists study these aspects of the organization also, and help managers understand how best to minimize the negative impact of such situations. The key to conflict resolution often lies in understanding when it is best to be assertive and when it is best to be cooperative. The scientific observation of organizational behavior has led to several theories about what situations are best suited for various conflict resolution styles. For example, when each side knows that it has to work with the other and that the interests of both parties are important, collaboration (when both parties try to find a mutually beneficial solution to a shared problem) or compromise (when both parties give a little and get a little in return) are frequently the best approaches to conflict resolution. However, when one of the parties views the conflict as a win/lose situation, it is often necessary to compete. In other situations it may be best to accommodate the other person's desires in the short-term in order to win a more important battle later on. Even avoidance — walking away from the problem — can be an effective way to manage conflict in the short-term if it allows tempers to cool down and the parties to come back later and resolve the conflict.

Organizational Processes

In addition to the assumptions, values, and beliefs of the individual workers and the shared assumptions, values, and beliefs of work teams, it is important to understand the assumptions, values, and beliefs of the organization as an entity. Although one can learn about an organization from observing formal aspects like its goals, structure, and other resources, such data only gives part of the picture. To truly understand the organization, one also needs to understand the informal aspects of the organization — those things understood by the employees but that are not written down or formalized. These include such things as its attitudes, values, feelings, interactions, and norms. The differentiation between the aspects of the formal organization and the informal organization is often described as an iceberg, with the formal structures being equivalent to the ten percent of the iceberg that is observable above the water line, but the real nature of the organization being hidden beneath—not readily observable to the casual observer but requiring careful study and analysis.

Organizational behavioral theorists and practitioners need to understand not only the easily observable aspects of the organization, but the organizational culture in order to truly understand the behaviors and processes that make the organization run. Although organizations can experience problems stemming from their formal structures and aspects, more often it is the aspects of its informal culture that can create problems.

To be truly effective, a manager must understand not only the requirements set out in the formal organization, but also those implied as part of the informal organization. Understanding the values of one's workers, for example, will help the manager know better how to motivate them. Understanding their values and feelings will help the manager avoid destructive conflict or defuse conflict situations when they occur. Understanding how employees interact with each other and the informal norms of work teams will help the manager be better able to support their efforts and facilitate their synergy and contributions to organizational effectiveness.

BIBLIOGRAPHY

Daniela, P. (2013). The interdependence between management, communication, organizational behavior and performance. *Annals of The University of Oradea, Economic Science Series, 22* (1), 1554–1562. Retrieved November 20, 2013 from EBSCO Online Database Business Source Complete. http://search.ebscohost.com/login.aspx?direct=true&db=bth&AN=90545853&site=ehost-live

De Ven, A., & Lifschitz, A. (2013). Rational and reasonable microfoundations of markets and institutions. *Academy of Management Perspectives, 27* (2), 156–172. Retrieved November 20, 2013 from EBSCO Online Database Business Source Complete. http://search.ebscohost.com/login.aspx?direct=true&db=bth&AN=88419319&site=ehost-live

McShane, S. L. & Von Glinow, M. A. (2003). *Organizational behavior: Emerging realities for the workplace revolution* (2nd ed). Boston: McGraw-Hill/Irwin.

Nahavandi, A. (2000). What is a team? In Nahavandi, Afsaneh. *The Art and Science of Leadership* (2nd ed). Upper Saddle River, NJ: Prentice Hall.

Thompson, Leigh L. (2000). What kinds of teams are there? In Thompson, Leigh L. *Making the Team: A Guide for Managers.* Upper Saddle River, NJ: Prentice Hall.

Yukl, G. (2012). Effective leadership behavior: What we know and what questions need more attention. *Academy of Management Perspectives, 26* (4), 66–85. Retrieved November 20, 2013 from EBSCO Online Database Business Source Complete. http://search.ebscohost.com/login.aspx?direct=true&db=bth&AN=84930149&site=ehost-live

Suggested Reading

Eubanks, J. L.; Johnson, C. M.; Redmon, W. K.& Mawhinney, T. C. (2001). Chapter 14: Organizational behavior management and organization development: Potential paths to reciprocation. In *Handbook of Organizational Performance: Behavior Analysis and Management,* 367–390. Retrieved March 23, 2007, from EBSCO Online Database Business Source Complete. http://search.ebscohost.com/login.aspx?direct=true&db=bth&AN=21700928&site=ehost-live

Johnson, C. M.; Mawhinney, T. C.; & Redmon, W. K. (2001). Chapter 1: Introduction to organizational performance: Behavior analysis and management. In *Handbook of Organizational Performance: Behavior Analysis and Management,* 2001, 3–22. Retrieved March 23, 2007, from EBSCO Online Database Business Source Complete. http://search.ebscohost.com/login.aspx?direct=true&db=bth&AN=21700915&site=ehost-live

Johnson, C. M.; Mawhinney, T. C.; Redmon, W. K. (2001). Epilogue. *Handbook of Organizational Performance: Behavior Analysis & Management,* 2001, 457–459. Retrieved March 23, 2007, from EBSCO Online Database Business Source Complete. http://search.ebscohost.com/login.aspx?direct=true&db=bth&AN=21700932&site=ehost-live

O'Hara, K.; Johnson, C. M.; & Beehr, T. A. (1985). Organizational behavior management in the private sector: A review of empirical research and recommendations for further investigation. *Academy of Management Review, 10*(4), 848–864. Retrieved March 23, 2007, from EBSCO Online Database Business Source Complete. http://search.ebscohost.com/login.aspx?direct=true&db=bth&AN=4279107&site=ehost-live

Raver, J. L., Ehrhart, M. G., & Chadwick, I. C. (2012). The emergence of team helping norms: Foundations within members' attributes and behavior. *Journal of Organizational Behavior, 33* (5), 616–637. Retrieved November 20, 2013 from EBSCO Online Database Business Source Complete. http://search.ebscohost.com/login.aspx?direct=true&db=bth&AN=76169259&site=ehost-live

Wageman, Ruth. (1997, Summer). Critical success factors for creating superb self-managing teams. *Organizational Dynamics, 26*(1), 49–61. Retrieved March 23, 2007, from EBSCO Online Database Business Source Complete. http://search.ebscohost.com/login.aspx?direct=true&db=bth&AN=9708296252&site=ehost-live

Ruth A. Wienclaw, Ph.D.

Organizational Consulting

Abstract

This article will focus on how organizational consultants may use the concept of human performance technology to improve performance in an organization. In order to effectively make changes to the processes and structures, a change agent would need to have the ability to interpret various situations occurring within the organization. One field of study that evaluates how to effectively make change in people and systems is human performance technology. The goal of the human performance technology field is to use systems approaches to ensure that individuals have the knowledge, skills, motivation, and environmental support to do their jobs effectively and efficiently. Human Performance Technology is important to the world's economic future because practitioners, such as organizational consultants, strive to provide organizations with solutions to their performance problems. An effective human performance technologist will use a systematic approach to improve the productivity and competence of the workforce so that organizations are able to compete in a global economy.

OVERVIEW

Organizations can be very complex. There will be times when the management team may decide the organization needs assistance with making changes throughout the different units in the company. As a result, individuals may be assigned to facilitate the change process. In order to effectively make changes to the processes and structures, a change agent would need to have the ability to interpret various situations occurring within the organization. "Reading" an organization requires one to be able to understand situations as they occur and know how to handle any problems that may occur. "Skilled leaders and managers develop the knack of reading situations with various scenarios in mind and of forging actions that seem appropriate to the understandings thus obtained" (Morgan, 1995).

One field of study that evaluates how to effectively make change in people and systems is human performance technology. According to the International Society of Performance and Instruction (ISPI), human performance technology (HPT) can be described as "the systematic and systemic identification and removal of barriers to individual and organizational performance." The meaning of the concept can be broken down by each word in the phrase. "Human" refers to the individuals that make up the organization, and "Performance" implies that the activities of the employees can be assessed by measurable outcomes. "Technology" assumes that a systematic and systemic approach can be developed to resolve problems within the organization.

Human Performance Technology (HPT) draws from many academic disciplines such as psychology, instructional systems design, organizational development and human resources. The focus of the interdisciplinary field requires the practitioner to be able to (1) assess and analyze the performance gap between where the organization is and where it wants to go, (2) identify the causes for the performance gap, (3) make recommendations on how to close the gap and improve performance, (4) facilitate the change management process, and (5) evaluate the results to make sure that the desired change has occurred.

The human performance technology field aims to ensure that the knowledge, skills, motivation and environmental support necessary for employees to complete their work successfully is available through a systems approach. According to Jacobs (1987), the conceptual domain of HPT can be defined by three key aspects:

- Management functions — guides, controls and facilitates the development of human performance systems.
- Development functions — examines all aspects of a problem; relates results from a set of decisions to other decisions; and uses resources to develop performance systems.
- Systems functions — provides the conceptual means for viewing people, materials, events and resources required to achieve goals.

Performance tends to be measured in terms of quality, productivity, and cost. As a result, human performance is tied to the bottom line — organizational success. Both individual and organizational goals must be considered when implementing processes and policies that will improve performance. "Use of systems approaches to develop human performance systems is one of the most significant aspects of the field. The end result of using a systems approach is a combination of materials, events, peoples and strategies called a performance system. A performance system is the structure, within the work setting, in which people use resources and tools to perform their work. Human performance systems have five main components: (1) a job or context; (2) individual abilities, motivations, actions, decisions, and behavior; (3) responses required for performance; (4) consequences of the response; and (5) feedback on the consequences" (Jacobs, 1987).

In summary, organizations may require the services of human performance technologists to facilitate changes, such as process improvement, within the company. These individuals will act as consultants to the organization as it charts a new course and direction. Armed with the concept of HPT and performance systems, organizational consultants will be tasked with improving the bottom line of the company's initiatives so that it remains competitive.

APPLICATIONS

Human Performance Technologists as Organizational Consultants

Human Performance Technology is important to the world's economic future because practitioners such as organizational consultants strive to provide organizations with solutions to their performance problems. HPT uses instructional technologies to improve individual performance so that organizational goals can be achieved. Being a good organizational consultant requires an individual to navigate the company through innovations, changes, and processes. An effective human performance technologist will use a systematic approach to improve the productivity and competence of the workforce so that organizations are able to compete in a global economy. According to Morgan (1995), these individuals must (1) have the capacity to remain open and flexible, (2) reserve judgment until all facts are known, and (3) gain new insight by viewing situations from different angles. These skills are required of both the internal and external organizational consultants.

Guiding Principles

In order to differentiate the concept from other disciplines, ISPI has developed a set of principles for human performance technologists to follow when assisting organizations in managing change. The principles are:

1. HPT focuses on outcomes. If an organization focuses on outcomes, the consultant may use tools that support obtaining data to determine whether or not a process is effective and whether the employees share the same vision and goals. In addition, outcomes can measure whether or not the performance gap has been closed.
2. HPT takes a systems view. There is a need to implement an approach that analyzes the performance of the employees in order to determine if the organization is on track with fulfilling its vision, goals and objectives. A system implies that the divisions and people of an organization are interconnected. The people must support the process. It is important to take a systems approach because the complexity within an organization has the power to affect the performance of its employees. The success of a single unit itself and the success of the entire organization at large are deeply dependent on one another. A systems approach considers the entire organizational environment including inputs as well as pressures, expectations, constraints, and consequences.
3. HPT adds value. At the end of the process intervention, clients should leave with a set of tools which will assist them with making choices, establishing measurable goals, identifying barriers and tradeoffs, and taking control of the destiny of the organization. Although the actual HPT techniques address issues such as improving quality, customer retention and cost reduction, there should be a link to how the efforts impact business goals and outcomes such as sales, profits, and market share.
4. HPT establishes partnerships. HPT is built on collaboration among all of the stakeholders in an effort to improve the overall performance of the organization. Everyone should be involved in the decision making process, and the advice and experience of subject matter experts (SMEs) should be taken into consideration. Working collaboratively includes sharing decisions about goals, determining the next steps to take in the process, and viewing implementation strategies as shared responsibilities. Partnerships are created from listening closely, trusting and respecting each other's knowledge and expertise.
5. Be systematic in the assessment of the need or opportunity. The needs assessment occurs in the beginning of the project. The consultant should analyze and evaluate the effectiveness of different aspects of the organization in order to identify the external and internal pressures affecting it. This process will determine the deficiencies or performance gaps that need to be corrected.

6. Be systematic in the analysis of the work and workplace to identify the cause or factors that limit performance. Cause analysis is about determining why a gap in performance or expectations exists. This step in the systematic process will determine what should be addressed to improve performance.
7. Be systematic in the design of the solution or specification of the requirements of the solution. Design is about identifying the key attributes of a solution. The output is a communication that describes the features, attributes, and elements of a solution and the resources required to implement the solution.
8. Be systematic in the development of all or some of the solution and its elements. Development is about the creation of some or all of the elements of the solution. It can be done by an individual or a team. The output is a product, process, system, or technology. Examples include training, performance support tools, a new or re-engineered process, the redesign of a workspace, or a change in compensation or benefits.
9. Be systematic in the implementation of the solution. Implementation is about deploying the solution and managing the change required to sustain it. This standard is about helping clients adopt new behaviors or use new or different tools.
10. Be systematic in the evaluation of the process and the results. Evaluation is about measuring the efficiency and effectiveness of what was done, how it was done, and the degree to which the solution produced the desired results so that the cost incurred and the benefits gained can be compared. This standard is about identifying and acting on opportunities throughout the systematic process to identify measures and record the data that will help identify needs, adoption, and results.

Issues

Choosing the Best Organizational Consultant External versus Internal Consulting

Many organizations will assign someone to complete the task of assessing the organization. When selecting this individual, the organization must evaluate the environment to determine whether or not it is best to use someone within the organization or outside of the organization. Facilitators, or consultants, are requested as a result of their expertise in a given area as well as their ability to collaborate with others in order to accomplish a given task. Human Performance Technologists can facilitate the process if an organization is attempting to make a change with the workforce and systems that are currently in place. Human Performance Technologists are in various industries such as academia, financial services, manufacturing, government, and pharmaceuticals. In addition, their expertise covers many functions such as human resources, training and development, and line management. Given the vast number of sources for finding these individuals, organizations will have to decide what works best.

Although most references on organizational consulting discuss the role of the external consultant, the role of internal consulting is becoming popular. External consultants are viewed as neutral because they do not have a history with the organization, and they tend to work on a project for a specific period of time. In other words, there is a beginning and an end. They are from outside the company, work for the duration of the contract, and may leave (Kleinberg, 1992). In some cases, part of the external consulting contract is to transition the outcomes into a "Train the Trainer" workshop for a select group of employees. Once they have completed their mission, they may train employees to maintain the changes once they are gone. These employees can become the internal organizational consultants. However, depending on the organization's culture, the management team may elect to use external consultants on a continual basis in order to maintain a sense of trust and objectivity.

Internal consultants are organizational development professionals who work exclusively for one organization and are direct reports to a designated level of management (Lacey, 1995). These individuals may work alone or as part of a team. In addition, there may be others such as specialists in organizational development, human resources, training or communications who report to the internal consultant in an effort to complete the assigned tasks.

Both external and internal organizational consultants are challenged with developing a systematic approach to managing change in an organization. As they go through each phase of the consulting process, they will be faced with obstacles that they must overcome. There are advantages and disadvantages for using internal and external consultants to evaluate an organization.

Cummings and Worley (1993) created a process consisting of five phases in the consulting process. These phases are entering, contracting, diagnosing, intervening, and evaluating.

1. Entering

a. External Consultant — This stage tends to be the most difficult stage for the external consultant because the individual needs to market himself and build a client base. Once clients have been identified, the external consultant must build relationships and become familiar with the organization.
   i. Advantage: Select projects based on their criteria
   ii. Disadvantage: Need to learn company
b. Internal Consultant — Little time is spent on entry for the internal consultant since he is considered an insider of the organization.
   i. Advantages: Ready access to clients
   ii. Disadvantages: Obligated to work with everyone

2. Contracting

a. External Consultant — The consultant must work with the client to develop a mutual understanding of what the expected outcomes and deliverables will be. At this stage, the consultant and client communicate expectations and create a legal contract that both will be bound by. The purpose of the contract is to clarify goals, roles, use of resources, and ground rules (Block, 1981).
   i. Advantages: Can terminate project at anytime; maintain "outsider" role
   ii. Disadvantages: May incur "out of pocket" expenses, especially if unexpected events occur.
b. Internal Consultant — The internal consultant works under a contract as well. However, most are verbal versus written. The internal consultant has internal clients that require services. However, one of the disadvantages is that the internal consultant must be sensitive to the "personalities" and politics of the organization. An external consultant can be more vocal with their opinions because they will eventually leave. However, the internal consultant has to remain within the organization and be sensitive to backlash and retaliation.
   i. Advantages: Information can be open or confidential
   ii. Disadvantages: Must complete projects assigned; may experience client retaliation and loss of job

3. Diagnosing

a. External Consultant — During this stage the external consultant will start collecting data such as employee surveys, meeting with focus groups to get follow-up information and feedback, and conducting individual meetings in order to develop an analysis and make recommendations for change. The consultant may also evaluate leadership styles of key players (Darling & Heller, 2012). Once the plan has been developed, the consultant will schedule a meeting to provide the client, and special guests, with feedback on what needs to occur in order to implement the plan.
   i. Advantages: Prestige from being external
   ii. Disadvantages: Confidential data can increase political sensitivities
b. Internal Consultant — This phase is the same for both the internal and external consultant.
   i. Advantages: Has relationships with many organization members
   ii. Disadvantages: Openly sharing data can reduce political intrigue

4. Intervening

a. External Consultant — The design of what issues need to be addressed are the focus of this stage. It's important that the external consultant can get the participants to buy-in to the process because authentic information is required at this point. There has to be commitment on the part of the participants, and the external consultant may include this request at the beginning when the contract is being written. The external consultant needs to be assured that there will be individuals taking ownership of the outcomes and the process will be implemented and maintained once he has left.
   i. Advantages: Can insist on receiving authentic data and internal commitment
   ii. Disadvantages: Must confine activities within boundaries of client organization

b. Internal Consultant — Although this phase is the same for both the external and internal consultant, there is one exception for the internal consultant. Buy-in is key for the external consultant. However, the internal consultant considers it a luxury. Many employees do not have the opportunity to be authentic and recognize the political ramifications if they are completely honest. The internal consultant recognizes this dilemma. "Although most change projects begin with testing the waters of opportunity, hoping to build critical mass that will sweep in all members and result in commitment to change, all projects are not successful in generating enthusiasm for change" (Lacy, 1995).
   i. Advantages: May run interference for client across organizational lines to align support
   ii. Disadvantages: Cannot require information and internal commitment is a luxury.

5. Evaluating

a. External Consultant — During this phase, the external consultant is constantly assessing the process and results while making revisions to the plan. The external consultant may make some assumptions and solicit feedback from the client to see what level of customer satisfaction is present.
   i. Advantages: Can use project success as a means of gaining repeat business and customer referrals
   ii. Disadvantages: Seldom see long term results
b. Internal Consultant — This phase is similar for both types of consultants. The client will require more measurable results as the amount of money spent on the project intervention increases. In addition, there are potential personal rewards for the internal consultant. If the project is successful, there are opportunities for an increase in salary as well as promotions. However, there is a down side. Being an internal consultant can be lonely because many people within the organization may not understand the job. There will be questions regarding what the consultant actually does and whether or not the work adds value to the bottom line.
   i. Advantages: Can see change become institutionalized
   ii. Disadvantages: Little recognition for a job well done

Both external and internal consultants perform many of the same functions throughout the consulting process as each attempt to create a plan of improvement for the organization However, each will face unique sets of challenges and obstacles as he attempts to obtain his goals.

CONCLUSION

If one has a desire to lead change in an organization, he/she must have the ability to see the organization from the "big picture" perspective. Understanding the mission and vision will assist consultants in determining the best course of action for the organization at any given time. "Effective managers and professionals in all walks of life have to become skilled in the art of reading the situations they are attempting to organize or manage" (Morgan, 1995).

Human Performance Technology is a technique that both external and internal organizational consultants may use in order to assist companies with achieving the bottom-line, implementing process improvement, and navigating change throughout the organization. Jacobs (1987) provided 11 propositions that emerged as a result of his research on HPT.

1. Human performance and human behavior are different, and knowledge of the difference is important for achieving the goals of the field.
2. Any statement about human performance must also include organizational performance.
3. Costs of improving performance should be regarded as investments in human capital, yielding returns in terms of increased performance potential.
4. Both organizational and individual goals must be considered in order to determine the desired performance.
5. Human performance technology consists of management functions, development functions, and systems functions.
6. Knowing how to engineer human performance and the conditions that affect it is as important as explaining why the behavior occurred.
7. In order to diagnose problems in an organization, the consultant must analyze the present system first, then examine the differences between the present and ideal system.
8. Exemplary performance provides the most logical referent for determining job performance standards.

9. Human performance problems can have different root causes, and these causes are generally classified as either originating from the person, from the person's environment, or from both.
10. Performance of one subsystem affects the performance of other subsystems in predictable ways, which will require problem causes to be analyzed at more than one level of an organization.
11. Many different solutions may be used to improve human performance. Selection of any one solution is dependent upon the cause and nature of the performance problem, and the criteria used to evaluate a solution must include its potential to make a measurable difference in the performance system.

BIBLIOGRAPHY

Battenfield, A. E., & Schehl, J. (2013). Practice analysis for human performance technologists. *Performance Improvement, 52*(8), 15-20. Retrieved October 31, 2013, from EBSCO Online Database Business Source Complete. http://search.ebscohost.com/login.aspx?direct=true&db=bth&AN=90470471&site=ehost-live

Block, P. (1981). *Flawless consulting.* Austin, Texas: Learning Concepts.

Cummings, T., & Worley, C. (1993). *Organization development and change* (8th ed). New York: South Western College Publishing.

Darling, J., & Heller, V. (2012). Effective organizational consulting across cultural boundaries: A case focusing on leadership styles and team-building. *Organization Development Journal, 30*(4), 54-72. Retrieved October 31, 2013, from EBSCO Online Database Business Source Complete. http://search.ebscohost.com/login.aspx?direct=true&db=bth&AN=84822096&site=ehost-live

Free Management Library, Human Performance Technology. Retrieved April 20, 2007, from http://www.managementhelp.org/trng%5fdev/hpt.htm.

Handbook of Human Performance Technology (2006). *HRMagazine, 51*(8), 134. Retrieved April 20, 2007, from EBSCO Online Database Business Source Premier. http://search.ebscohost.com/login.aspx?direct=true&db=bth&AN=21865156&site=ehost-live

International Society of Performance and Instruction. (n.d.). What Is Human Performance Technology? Retrieved April 20, 2007, from http://www.ispi.org.

Jacobs, R. L. (1987). *Human performance technology: A systems-based field for the training and development profession.* (SERIES NO. 326). Columbus: ERIC Clearinghouse on Adult, Career, and Vocational Education, The National Center for Research in Vocational Education, The Ohio State University, 1987. (ERIC Document Reproduction Service No. ED 290 936).

Kleiner, A. (1992). The gurus of corporate change. *Business and Society Review,* (81), 39-42. Retrieved April 20, 2007, from EBSCO Online Database Business Source Premier. http://search.ebscohost.com/login.aspx?direct=true&db=bth&AN=4649069&site=ehost-live

Lacey, M. Y. (1995). Internal consulting: Perspectives on the process of planned change. *Journal of Organizational Change Management, 8*(3), 75-84. Retrieved April 20, 2007, from EBSCO Online Database Business Source Premier. http://search.ebscohost.com/login.aspx?direct=true&db=bth&AN=3925451&site=ehost-live

Morgan, G. (1995). *Images of organization.* Thousand Oaks: California: Sage.

Rush, A.J. (2012). Client partnership throughout the performance improvement/human performance technology model. *Performance Improvement, 51*(9), 29-37. Retrieved October 31, 2013, from EBSCO Online Database Business Source Complete. http://search.ebscohost.com/login.aspx?direct=true&db=bth&AN=82764242&site=ehost-live

SUGGESTED READING

Dervitisiotis, K. (2006). Building trust for excellence in performance and adaptation to change. *Total Quality Management & Business Excellence, 17*(7), 795-810. Retrieved April 20, 2007, from EBSCO Online Database Business Source Premier. http://search.ebscohost.com/login.aspx?direct=true&db=bth&AN=22295476&site=ehost-live

Hsu, I., Yeh-Yun Lin, C., Lawler, J., & Wiu, S. (2007). Toward a model of organizational human capital development : Preliminary evidence from Taiwan. *Asia Pacific Business Review, 13*(2), 251-275. Retrieved April 20, 2007, from EBSCO Online Database Business Source Premier. http://search.ebscohost.com/login.aspx?direct=true&db=bth&AN=24404428&site=ehost-live

Old, D. (1995). Consulting for real transformation, sustainability, and organic form. *Journal of Organizational Change Management, 8*(3), 6. Retrieved April 20, 2007, from EBSCO Online Database Business Source Premier. http://search.ebscohost.com/login.aspx?direct=true&db=bth&AN=3925446&site=ehost-live

Prajogo, D., & Ahmed, P. (2006). Relationships between innovation stimulus, innovation capacity, and innovation performance. *R&D Management, 36*(5), 499-515. Retrieved April 20, 2007, from EBSCO Online Database Business Source Premier. http://search.ebscohost.com/login.aspx?direct=true&db=bth&AN=22931166&site=ehost-live

Talaq, J., & Ahmed, P. (2004). Why HPT, not TQM? An examination of the HPT concept. *Journal of Management Development, 23*(3), 202-218. Retrieved April 20, 2007, from EBSCO Online Database Business Source Premier. http://search.ebscohost.com/login.aspx?direct=true&db=bth&AN=13208199&site=ehost-live

Marie Gould, Ph.D.

Organizational Learning

ABSTRACT

Organizational knowledge is a concept that represents the sum total of all of the knowledge and experience that members of the organization both possess and bring to the table as they engage in the work of the organization. Organizational learning is the process developed by an organization with the goal of increasing the overall amount of organizational knowledge available, and of making sure that this organizational knowledge is applied in the most timely and effective ways possible.

OVERVIEW

Organizational learning can be thought of as an aggregation of the process of individual learning by members of a larger group—the organization. As individuals acquire experience at various tasks, the accumulation of this experience eventually produces knowledge. When many individuals are working together in an organization, their acquisition of individual experience and the subsequent production of knowledge at the level of the individual also benefits the organization, because the organization acquires experience and knowledge at the same time as the individuals who compose it do. Seen in this way, organizational learning can seem as an almost natural process that occurs without the need for intentional drive to motivate it, almost like sediment accumulating on the ocean floor. Yet there is also a deliberate aspect to organizational learning, because organizations can choose to focus their knowledge management efforts in ways designed specifically to improve their own learning capacity.

An organization might recognize that one of its weaknesses is in being able to retrieve and analyze sales data for transactions using foreign currency. The organization could either continue to operate "as is," in this area, or it could implement changes in its practices to make such information easier to get a hold of and to analyze (Wellman, 2013). This type of thinking about the ways in which one thinks, whether at the level of an individual or of an organization, is known as metacognition, or "thinking about thinking."

APPLICATIONS

Organizations operate within an environment characterized by constant change, whether due to the weather, the economy, social and political developments, or some combination of these factors. Because the environment is perpetually in flux, organizations cannot afford to approach that environment with the same ideas and thought processes used years or even decades ago. Instead, organizations must continue to build their knowledge by using information acquired through experience operating in the ever changing world. An organization that continues to learn by acquiring experience and analyzing it to produce knowledge will be better equipped to deal with changing circumstances (Gino & Staats, 2015).

Another major motivation for organizations to optimize their learning is to help them stay ahead of their competitors. Many types of organizational knowledge pertain to ways in which the organization can operate more efficiently and more effectively (Argyris, 2012). For example, a company that operates a chain of coffee stores might focus entirely on constant expansion into new markets, while its competitor, who possesses many more years of experience in the coffee business, may have learned to take a slower approach and conduct thorough market analysis of every region it considers moving into, before committing to the move. This methodically analytical, go slow approach could help the more established company avoid rushing into economically unstable regions just for the sake of short-term expansion. In this way, the older company's ability to put its own knowledge to more effective use helps the company to outperform its competition in the long run, by avoiding the unnecessary expense of opening stores in areas where there will not be enough business to sustain them at a profitable level (Cameron & Spreitzer, 2012).

Knowledge management is an umbrella term used to describe all of the different ways that an organization manipulates knowledge, from acquiring it and organizing it to distributing and storing it. Generally speaking, the more adept an organization is at knowledge management, the greater will be that organization's aptitude for organizational learning.

The experience curve describes a theoretical model that explains the tendency for overall production costs to decrease as the volume of production increases. In other words, the experience curve shows how an organization learns how to operate more efficiently and more effectively, the more it engages in a particular type of production. Often, it may not be immediately clear how the savings are being achieved, but the reality of the savings is beyond question.

VIEWPOINTS

The fundamental mechanism of organizational learning is change. This does not refer to any kind of gradual evolution that occurs randomly and without direction. The change at the heart of organizational learning is caused by the process of the individuals who make up the organization acquiring experience through the course of their regular work on the organization's behalf, and sharing that experience with others in the organization (Anderson, 2010). As this experience accumulates it is also analyzed by various sectors within the organization (e.g., the finance department, the marketing department, the research and development department) and the product of this analysis is knowledge.

An example of such knowledge in the scenario discussed above might be the realization that coffee stores do not do well when they are located in zip codes that have experienced more than seven percent unemployment within the last three years. This piece of information is no doubt interesting, but it does not really mean much unless it is put to use by the organization to make a change in its behavior. This is the type of change that is central to organizational learning. Perhaps the more experienced coffee chain, after realizing the importance of the seven percent unemployment metric for predicting the success of its location, would decide to change its business practices to exclude from consideration and potential location that has experienced greater than seven percent unemployment in the last three years. This change would be the result of organizational learning—that is, observing information in the real world, analyzing that information and making predictions about it, and then adjusting company behavior based on those predictions (Boonstra, 2013).

Single and Double Loop Organizations

Because organizational learning is a field that lends itself to multiple layers of abstraction, there have been several theories developed to try to explain the different mechanisms used by organizations to acquire, store, process, and transfer knowledge. Some of these are the single and double loop theories, which analyze the ways in which organizations respond to failure. Single loop organizations that experience a failure in their efforts respond by adjusting the methods used in those efforts and trying again to see if the change produces a success. An example of this might be a company that tries to increase sales of its products by advertising on the radio, only to find this method ineffective. The company might decide to try again, but using television advertising instead of radio.

Conversely, a double loop organization in this situation would be unlikely to try a different advertising medium, and more likely to reconsider whether the product being marketed was actually viable in the marketplace. This is because double loop organizations, upon experiencing failure, tend to reconsider the overall goal of their efforts rather than question the methods used.

While these two different types of organizational learning may seem very different, they actually exist at different times and at different levels of most organizations, and can even be employed side by side under some circumstances (Godwyn & Gittell, 2012).

Learning Curves

A learning curve in the context of organizational knowledge management is a graph that represents how an organization's performance of a task improves over time, as the organization gains experience at performing the task. Often this improvement is due to the organization discovering ways that it can perform the task more efficiently, though other factors may also play a role. The factors that play the most significant role in an organization improving its performance typically fall into one of three categories: individual, structural, and technological. Technological changes are enabled by advanced in technology (Iyengar, Sweeney & Montealegre, 2015). The classic example is of a sales force, in the days before the Internet, receiving personal digital assistants that enable them to collect and share their sales data much more quickly and easily. Individual changes are also fairly straightforward, as these include the experience acquired by individual members of the organization while they perform their duties.

The more complex concept is that of structural change (Eddy, 2014). This refers to adaptations the organization makes in response to information it receives, because these changes affect the structure of the organization's operations and processes. Each of these factors is at play in every organization as it interacts with its environment, but the particular nature of an organization influences the degree to which it responds to information. This explains why different organizations exhibit faster or slower responses to the information they receive, and why some organizational responses are more effective than others.

Different theorists have tried to explain variations in organizational performance using a variety of models.

The models that have garnered the most attention are those developed by John F. Muth, Bernardo A. Huberman, and Christina Fang. Muth's main area of focus was on adaptations that increase an organization's cost effectiveness. Huberman continued this general approach, but sought to simplify the number of steps used in the analysis conducted by the organization. Fang's model explores the propagation of credit throughout the organization as part of the analytical process, making it possible for the organization to more accurately identify information that will help improve institutional processes (Lewis, 2015).

Explicit and Tacit Knowledge

Not all types of information and knowledge that are used in organizational learning are equally accessible. Many researchers acknowledge the distinction between knowledge that is explicit within the organization, and that which is tacit. Explicit knowledge consists of information that the organization "knows that it knows." This is information that the organization is aware of and deliberately tries to put to good use, whether it is sales data, transcripts of focus groups discussing the relative merits of potential products in development, or responses to an annual employee satisfaction survey. The foremost quality that makes explicit information easier to deal with is that the organization knows it exists and has a place to keep it so that it can be put to good use.

This is not the case with tacit knowledge. Tacit knowledge is the organization's set of unwritten rules; those who need to know a particular rule are aware of it, but these rules are not written down anywhere, and might even be at odds with the company's official position statements. An example of tacit knowledge might be the fact that every scientist working for company X's research and development department knows that the only way to get a research proposal approved is to have someone from marketing included as a co-author of the proposal (Burke, 2014). This is not the company's official policy, and the company might prefer not to have this information about its internal workings made public knowledge, but it remains a "fact of life" known to all of the company's employees that are affected by it.

Companies that wish to take fullest advantage of their learning opportunities must make every effort to pay as much attention to tacit organizational knowledge as they do to knowledge that is explicit. Tacit knowledge is often possessed by those members of the organization with the longest tenure or the deepest insight into the hidden machinations of the institution. As such, it tends to be some of the most precious information that the organization possesses, and this means that it is vital to try to capture it before it disappears, either through the departure from the organization of those in possession of it or through its tendency to fade away as more pressing matters confront the organization and demand its collective attention (Argote, 2013).

BIBLIOGRAPHY

Anderson, D. L. (2010). *Organization development: The process of leading organizational change.* Los Angeles, CA: Sage.

Argote, L. (2013). *Organizational learning: Creating, retaining, and transferring knowledge.* New York, NY: Springer.

Argyris, C. (2012). *Organizational traps: Leadership, culture, organizational design.* Oxford, UK: Oxford University Press.

Boonstra, J. J. (2013). *Cultural change and leadership in organizations: A practical guide to successful organizational change.* Chichester, UK: John Wiley & Sons.

Burke, W. W. (2014). *Organization change: Theory and practice.* Los Angeles, CA : Sage.

Cameron, K. S., & Spreitzer, G. M. (2012). *The Oxford handbook of positive organizational scholarship.* New York, UK: Oxford University Press.

Desai, V. (2015). Learning through the distribution of failures within an organization: Evidence from heart bypass surgery performance. *Academy of Management Journal, 58*(4), 1032–1050. Retrieved January 3, 2016 from EBSCO Online Database Business Source Complete. http://search.ebscohost.com/login.aspx?direct=true&db=bth&AN=108801068&site=ehost-live

Eddy, P. L. (2014). *Connecting learning across the institution.* San Francisco, CA: Jossey-Bass.

Gino, F., & Staats, B. (2015). Why organizations don't learn. *Harvard Business Review, 93*(11), 110–118. Retrieved January 3, 2016 from EBSCO Online Database Business Source Complete. http://search.ebscohost.com/login.aspx?direct=true&db=bth&AN=110320478&site=ehost-live

Godwyn, M., & Gittell, J. H. (2012). *Sociology of organizations: Structures and relationships.* Thousand Oaks, CA: Pine Forge Press.

Iyengar, K., Sweeney, J. R., & Montealegre, R. (2015). Information technology use as a learning mechanism: The impact of it use on knowledge transfer effectiveness, absorptive capacity, and franchisee performance. *MIS Quarterly, 39*(3), 615–A5. Retrieved January 3, 2016 from EBSCO Online Database Business Source Complete. http://search.ebscohost.com/login.aspx?direct=true&db=bth&AN=108873991&site=ehost-live

Lewis, H. (2015). *Organizational learning: Individual differences, technologies and impact of teaching.* Hauppauge, NNY: Nova Science.

Wellman, J. L. (2013). *Organizational learning: How companies and institutions manage and apply knowledge.* Houndmils, UK: Palgrave Macmillan.

SUGGESTED READING

Döös, M., Johansson, P., & Wilhelmson, L. (2015). Organizational learning as an analogy to individual learning? A case of augmented interaction intensity. *Vocations and Learning, 8*(1), 55–73.

Evans, S. D., & Kivell, N. (2015). The transformation Team: An enabling structure for organizational learning in action. *Journal of Community Psychology, 43*(6), 760–777.

Jain, A. K., & Moreno, A. (2015). Organizational learning, knowledge management practices and firm's performance: An empirical study of a heavy engineering firm in India. *Learning Organization, 22*(1), 14–39.

Mena, J. A., & Chabowski, B. R. (2015). The role of organizational learning in stakeholder marketing. *Journal of the Academy of Marketing Science, 43*(4), 429–452.

Schilling, M. A., & Fang, C. (2014). When hubs forget, lie, and play favorites: Interpersonal network structure, information distortion, and organizational learning. *Strategic Management Journal, 35*(7), 974–994. Retrieved January 3, 2016 from EBSCO Online Database Business Source Complete. http://search.ebscohost.com/login.aspx?direct=true&db=bth&AN=96312592&site=ehost-live

Scott Zimmer, J.D.

Performance Appraisal

ABSTRACT

Performance appraisal is the process of evaluating an employee's performance and providing feedback. Appraisals are necessary not only for employees to understand and improve their performance on the job and for employers to adequately evaluate and select their employees for rewards (e.g., money, prestige, promotion), but it is also important so that the organization can determine the degree to which its employees are contributing toward meeting strategic goals and objectives. There are many ways to judge an employee's performance on the job ranging from objective performance data to global rating scales to more detailed rating scales that represent each of the important aspects of the job. No matter the method used, however, it is vital that the rating scales be anchored to objective, well-defined criteria of job success. This will help ensure that the performance appraisal system is not only accurate but also fair.

OVERVIEW

There is an old saying that advises, "if you do not know where you are going, you will never get there." Certainly, nowhere is this truer than in a business or organizational setting. From an employee's perspective, knowing where one wants to go may mean wanting to do the things on the job that will help ensure a pay raise or promotion. From the organization's perspective, knowing where one is going may mean wanting to do the things that will improve its effectiveness and efficiency and, in general, help it become a high-performing organization. However, neither the employee nor the organization can meet these goals unless they know how they are currently performing and can determine what changes must be made in order to improve overall performance. For the individual, this information usually comes in the form of feedback from a performance appraisal or review. Performance appraisal is the process of evaluating an employee's work performance and providing feedback on how well he or she is doing, typically against some standard of performance for that job. Performance appraisal can also provide the organization with some of the information that it needs in order to make strategic decisions to help it succeed in the marketplace.

Uses for Performance Appraisal Information

Performance appraisal is one of the key functions of an organization's human resources department. Organizations use the data collected in performance appraisal systems for several purposes. Perhaps the most well known of these is to establish standards and an evaluation system that can be used to form the basis of judgments as to whether to reward employees for good performance or punish them for poor performance. For example, management might set an individual productivity target of manufacturing two hundred widgets per day. Those who meet this standard might be given a pay raise or bonus and those who do not might not receive a monetary reward or may be put on probation. Performance appraisal data are also used to provide the criterion information that is used to select new candidates for the job. For example, the results of a job analysis might tell management what tasks a production worker needs to perform on the job. This information is used in conjunction with performance appraisal data that provide information regarding the standards to which employees must be able to perform these tasks in order to develop criteria to be used in hiring new employees for the job.

Another use for performance appraisal data is to provide objectives for organizational training programs. For example, if a department-wide performance appraisal finds that widget makers do not have the necessary skills to meet the organization's goal of two hundred widgets per employee per day, the human resources department might design or contract for a training program that would teach line workers the skills necessary to be better able to meet this goal. Finally, performance appraisal data can provide management with the data needed to provide feedback to employees and to better control their behavior on the job. In most cases, both the employees and management would like to see improved performance on the job. From the employees' perspective, improved performance can be the key to raises, bonuses, perks, and promotions. Such things can help them better meet their needs on the job or in other areas of their lives. Similarly, management would like to see improved performance because it helps to improve the effectiveness and efficiency of the organization, improves the return on investment for hiring and training, and helps the organization reach its strategic goals and become a high-performing organization.

Job Analyses

Before an objective performance appraisal system can be developed, one must first perform a job analysis to determine what tasks are actually performed on the job, the standards to which these tasks need to be performed, and the knowledge, skills, abilities, and other characteristics necessary in order to adequately perform these tasks. Job analysis is the systematic, empirical process of determining the exact nature of a job, including the tasks and duties to be done; the knowledge, skills, and abilities necessary to adequately perform these tasks and duties; and the criteria that distinguish between acceptable and unacceptable performance. The results of a job analysis are typically used in writing job descriptions, selecting new employees for hire, and setting standards for use in performance appraisals.

Performance appraisals need to be based on the tasks that are actually required to be performed on the job rather than on some general impression of the performance of the employee. These tasks and the standards to which they must be performed are usually based on a solid job description based on an objective, thorough job analysis. Good job descriptions and the performance appraisals that are based on them are competency based, describing the job in terms of measurable, observable, behavioral competencies that the employee must demonstrate in order to perform the job well. For example, rather than saying that a salesperson needs to have good customer rapport, the employee would be required to do such things as greet the customer within thirty seconds of entering the store, immediately drop any tasks not directly related to helping customers in the store if a customer needs help, or any other requirement found to be important to good work performance as determined by the job analysis. The performance standards developed as a product of a thorough job analysis are then used not only to frame the performance appraisal criteria but also to communicate to employees what kind of behavior will be rewarded (or not rewarded) by the organization. Performance appraisal data are then used to give employees feedback on how well they are meeting the standards in order to encourage high performance.

Further Insights

Methods of Data Collection

There are many sources of data that can be used in developing a performance appraisal system. For some jobs, empirical, quantitative data are available to objectively judge the quality of an employee's work. For example, for production workers, one might use a combination of quantitative data such as the average number of widgets produced per hour, the amount of waste material produced as a byproduct of manufacturing that number of widgets, and the number of widgets produced that are within specification.

In addition to objective production data, in some situations there are personnel data that are available that need to be taken into account when judging an employee's performance. For example, one might want to consider the number of days the employee was late to work, excessive days taken off, or other hard data that might be found in the employee's personnel file that address the employee's level of performance on the job. Although sometimes personnel data can be useful adjuncts when judging performance, they are typically not a substitute for more directly related data concerning performance.

Of course, not every job can be neatly reduced to quantifiable data. Although one can judge the performance of manufacturing workers, for example, based on the number of widgets they produce per hour, such objective data are not available for every position. In the twenty-first century, an increasing number of employees are knowledge workers and deal in the realm of information and expertise rather than in the realm of tangible products. For example, although it is possible to collect data on the number of calls a technical support employee takes on a help line, this datum does not provide information on how difficult the problem was, how well it was solved, how polite the employee was to the customer, or how satisfied the customer was with the service. As most of us who use technical support lines know, these are important pieces of information and are not captured in the easily collectible "number of calls per hour" statistic. To help management make better-informed decisions regarding an employee's performance, it is often necessary to collect subjective, judgmental data regarding performance. An example of this kind of data collection instrument is the "short survey" that often pops up after an online interaction with a sales or support employee.

Rating Scales

There are many approaches to designing a rating scale to be used in performance appraisal. The simplest of these is the global rating scale in which each employee is given a single score that rates his or her overall performance. However, global ratings do not give the employee sufficient data for how to improve his or her performance. In addition, such scales are prone to various kinds of rating error (see below). Therefore, many organizations develop rating scales based on job-related data and standards. One can use a job description, for example, to break out the major aspects of the job and then rate employees on each of these aspects. However, without well-defined standards for poor, acceptable, and outstanding performance, such rating scales can also be highly subjective in nature and prone to rating errors. Behaviorally anchored rating scales and mixed standards rating scales are two techniques that can be used to increase the objectivity of rating scales and link them to tangible, job-related criteria. Both these methods are based on the collection of critical incidents to discern between good and poor performance on the job. These critical incidents are used to anchor the rating scales and judge current employees against these criteria of success or failure on the job.

As mentioned above, rating scales and other instruments that are used to collect subjective data can be easily affected by various rating errors. The most common of these are halo error, leniency error, and central tendency error.

The halo error (sometimes referred to as the halo/horn error depending on which direction the error is made) occurs when a manager or other rater judges a person in all aspects of job performance based on a single aspect of the job or, on whether he or she likes the individual. For example, if someone is seen as an excellent worker (or nice person) in general, the rater may overlook performance problems in the individual's work and rate him or her highly on all aspects of the job.

The leniency error (sometimes referred to as the leniency/severity error) occurs when a rater tends to rate employees in general higher (or lower) than they would be if the rater had been objective. For example, some supervisors tend to be lenient in the ratings because they want to be kind to their employees and, as a result, rate them higher than they deserve. Similarly, some supervisors believe that everyone can always improve and, therefore, tend to rate their employees more severely than they objectively deserve.

The central tendency error occurs when a supervisor tends to give ratings toward the middle of the scale, believing that although the employees have room for improvement, they also do not deserve to be punished for their performance.

Management by Objectives (MBO)

It is important to evaluate an employee's performance by measuring it against a predetermined standard or set of specific goals to be achieved during the appraisal period. Rating scales are one way to do this; another popular way is through a method called Management by Objectives (MBO). In MBO, managers or the manager and employee together set objectives for the employee to meet during the upcoming appraisal period. Employees are evaluated in terms of how well they have met these goals in the intervening period. MBO can be used not only to evaluate the performance of an individual employee, but also that of a workgroup, department, or the organization as a whole. Under this approach, organization-wide goals and objectives based on its strategic plan (e.g., increase company profits from the widget product line by $500,000 over the next year) are first set. Using this information, each department or workgroup then sets its own goals and objectives to support the organization's goals (e.g., increase sales of widgets in the Eastern Region by 10 percent over the next year). Managers and individual employees then discuss these goals and possible contributions that can be made by each individual and set specific, short-term goals (e.g., obtain ten more customers per quarter; call on five more potential customers per week; include two more cities in the region), and individual objectives are set.

Like rating scales, however, MBO is not without its drawbacks. One of the most frequent is the development of objectives that are either unclear or unmeasurable. For example, in the example of "good customer rapport," if there is no operational definition of the concept, then the objective is as open to rating error as a poorly written rating scale. Similarly, some objectives are unreasonable, such as the objective for a research scientist to develop a cure for cancer within the next year. Another difficulty with setting MBO objectives is that supervisors tend to set objectives that are too difficult to meet while employees tend to set objectives that are too easy to meet.

360-Degree Feedback

To help ensure fair evaluations under a performance appraisal system, human resource policies or procedures are developed and implemented to help increase the objectiveness of the appraisal feedback or give the employee feedback from multiple sources. A technique called 360-degree feedback (because the feedback comes from people who work all around the employee, not just from one person working above him or her) gives employees feedback on their job performance from representatives of the major groups with whom they interact on the job both inside and outside the organization. Under 360-degree feedback, for example, employees may receive feedback not only from their supervisors but also from their subordinates, coworkers, customers, and other groups with whom they work. By doing this, an employee receives more feedback than he or she would receive under the traditional supervisor-only appraisal system. This approach to feedback can also help neutralize biased opinions of one person by giving the employee and the supervisor and range of reactions to look at so that they can look at the preponderance of evidence rather than reactions from just one person and, in general, give the employee a better idea of how s/he can improve performance.

Issues

Pay-for-Performance

Performance appraisal tools and systems are not ends in and of themselves. Among the major purposes of performance appraisal are the ability to provide employees with measurable criteria of success on the job and to provide feedback on how they can improve their performance in order to better meet their performance goals and objectives. One of the ways in which performance appraisal data are frequently being used is to link pay to performance. Under this paradigm, an employee is rewarded financially for high performance and contributing to the organization's goals. Pay-for-performance systems can be used at all levels of the organization, including "C-level" personnel (e.g., chief executive officer, chief operating officer).

The US Government Accountability Office (GAO) has investigated the viability of pay-for-performance systems and has found a number of factors that make them successful. First, it is important to use objective competencies to assess the quality of the employee's performance. As discussed above, this means that performance objectives need to be based on the empirical data developed through a thorough job analysis and be written in such a way that employees can achieve them. Second, employee performance ratings need to be directly tied to pay increases or awards so that employees can see a direct, positive consequence of their actions. In this way, employees are more likely to continue to perform at a level that will bring rewards. Third, fair pay-for-performance systems need to consider both the employee's current salary and his or her contribution to the organization so that rewards for similar contributions are equitable. Finally, pay-for-performance systems needs to be clear and well published so that employees know the basis on which decisions are made and what kind of awards are made across the organization.

CONCLUSION

Performance appraisal is one of the key elements of the human resources function within an organization. This process of evaluating an employee's performance and providing feedback is necessary not only for the individual to improve his or her performance on the job so that he or she can earn the rewards for which he or she is working, such as a promotion or raise, but it is also important so that the organization can determine the degree to which its employees are contributing to meeting its strategic goals and objectives. Performance appraisal data can also be used for other purposes as well, including as inputs into training programs or to develop criteria on which to hire new employees.

There are many ways to judge an employee's performance on the job ranging from objective performance data to global rating scales to more detailed rating scales that represent each of the important aspects of the job. However, whenever a subjective rating method is used, it is vital that the rating scales be anchored to objective, well-defined criteria of job success. This will help ensure that the performance appraisal system is not only accurate but fair.

Bibliography

Ayers, R. S. (2015). Aligning individual and organizational performance: Goal alignment in federal government agency performance appraisal programs. *Public Personnel Management, 44*(2), 161–191. Retrieved from EBSCO Online Database Business Source Premier. http://search.ebscohost.com/login.aspx?direct=true&db=buh&AN=102387358&site=ehost-live&scope=site

Boachie-Mensah, F. O., & Seidu, P. (2012). Employees' perception of performance appraisal system: A case study. *International Journal of Business & Management, 7*, 73–88. Retrieved from EBSCO Online Database Business Source Complete. http://search.ebscohost.com/login.aspx?direct=true&db=bth&AN=72324348&site=ehost-live

Cascio, W. F. (1998). *Applied psychology in human resource management* (5th ed.). Upper Saddle River, NJ: Prentice Hall.

Dessler, G. (2005). *Human resource management* (10th ed.). Upper Saddle River, NJ: Pearson Education/Prentice Hall.

Farndale, E., & Kelliher, C. (2013). Implementing performance appraisal: Exploring the employee experience. *Human Resource Management, 52*, 879–897. Retrieved from EBSCO Online Database Business Source Complete. http://search.ebscohost.com/login.aspx?direct=true&db=bth&AN=92038573&site=ehost-live

Harrington, J. R., & Lee, J. H. (2015). What drives perceived fairness of performance appraisal? Exploring the effects of psychological contract fulfillment on employees' perceived fairness of performance appraisal in U.S. federal agencies. *Public Personnel Management, 44*(2), 214–238. Retrieved from EBSCO Online Database Business Source Premier. http://search.ebscohost.com/login.aspx?direct=true&db=buh&AN=102387355&site=ehost-live&scope=site

Landy, F. J. & Conte, J. M. (2004). *Work in the 21st century: An introduction to industrial and organizational psychology*. Boston: McGraw Hill.

Muchinsky, P. M. (2003). *Psychology applied to work* (7th ed.). Belmont, CA: Wadsworth/Thomson Learning.

Pichler, S. (2012). The social context of performance appraisal and appraisal reactions: A meta-analysis. *Human Resource Management, 51*, 709–732. Retrieved from EBSCO Online Database Business Source Complete. http://search.ebscohost.com/login.aspx?direct=true&db=bth&AN=80235927&site=ehost-live

U.S. General Accounting Office. (2004). Human capital: Implementing pay for performance at selected personnel demonstration projects. *GAO Reports (GAO-04-83)*. Retrieved from EBSCO Online Database Business Source Complete http://search.ebscohost.com/login.aspx?direct=true&db=bth&AN=18173828&site=ehost-live%5fhl%5f

Suggested Reading

Ahn, T. S., Hwang, I., & Kim, M.-I. (2010). The impact of performance measure discriminability of rate incentives. *Accounting Review, 85*, 389–417. Retrieved from EBSCO Online Database Business Source Complete http://search.ebscohost.com/login.aspx?direct=true&db=bth&AN=48750130&site=ehost-live%5fhl%5f

Chan, H. S. & Gao, J. (2009). Putting the cart before the horse: Accountability or performance? *Australian Journal of Public Administration, 68*, S51–S61. Retrieved from EBSCO Online Database Business Source Complete http://search.ebscohost.com/login.aspx?direct=true&db=bth&AN=36840029&site=ehost-live%5fhl%5f

Cichello, M. S., Fee, C. E., Hadlock, C. J., & Sonti, R. (2009). Promotions, turnover, and performance evaluation: Evidence from the careers of division managers. *Accounting Review, 84*, 1119–1143. Retrieved from EBSCO Online Database Business Source Complete http://search.ebscohost.com/

login.aspx?direct=true&db=bth&AN=43251584&site=ehost-live%5fhl%5f

Ellis, S., Mendel, R., & Aloni-Zohar, M. (2009). The effect of accuracy of performance evaluation on learning from experience: The moderating role of after-event reviews. *Journal of Applied Social Psychology, 39,* 541–563. Retrieved from EBSCO Online Database Academic Search Complete http://search.ebscohost.com/login.aspx?direct=true&db=a9h&AN=36622676&site=ehost-live%5fhl%5f

Goffin, R. D., Jelley, R. B., Powell, D. M., & Johnston, N. G. (2009). Taking advantage of social comparisons in performance appraisal: The relative percentile method. *Human Resource Management, 48,* 251–268. Retrieved from EBSCO Online Database Business Source Complete http://search.ebscohost.com/login.aspx?direct=true&db=bth&AN=37267995&site=ehost-live%5fhl%5f

Iqbal, M. Z., Akbar, S., & Budhwar, P. (2015). Effectiveness of performance appraisal: An integrated framework. *International Journal of Management Reviews, 17*(4), 510–533. Retrieved from EBSCO Online Database Business Source Premier. http://search.ebscohost.com/login.aspx?direct=true&db=buh&AN=110338975&site=ehost-live&scope=site

Kaplan, S. E. & Wisner, P. S. (2009). The judgmental effects of management communications in a fifth balanced scorecard category on performance evaluation. *Behavioral Research in Accounting, 21,* 37–56. Retrieved from EBSCO Online Database Business Source Complete http://search.ebscohost.com/login.aspx?direct=true&db=bth&AN=43248470&site=ehost-live%5fhl%5f

Kumar, M. J. (2009). Evaluating scientists: Citations, impact factor, h-index, online page hits and what else? *IETE Technical Review, 26,* 165–168. Retrieved from EBSCO Online Database Academic Search Complete http://search.ebscohost.com/login.aspx?direct=true&db=a9h&AN=40395847&site=ehost-live%5fhl%5f

Lau, C. M., Wong, K. M., & Eggleton, I. R. C. (2008). Fairness of performance evaluation procedures and job satisfaction: The role of outcome-based and non-outcome-based effects. *Accounting and Business Research, 38,* 121–135. Retrieved from EBSCO Online Database Business Source Complete http://search.ebscohost.com/login.aspx?direct=true&db=bth&AN=33751340&site=ehost-live%5fhl%5f

Narcisse, S. & Harcourt, M. (2008). Employee fairness perceptions of performance appraisal: A Saint Lucian case study. *International Journal of Human Resource Management, 19,* 1152–1169. Retrieved from EBSCO Online Database Business Source Complete http://search.ebscohost.com/login.aspx?direct=true&db=bth&AN=32744010&site=ehost-live%5fhl%5f

Sholinhin, M. & Pike, R. (2009). Fairness in performance evaluation and its behavioural consequences. *Accounting and Business Research, 39,* 397–413. Retrieved from EBSCO Online Database Business Source Complete http://search.ebscohost.com/login.aspx?direct=true&db=bth&AN=44723761&site=ehost-live%5fhl%5f

Tan, H.-T. & Shankar, P. G. (2010). Audit reviewers' evaluation of subordinates' work quality. *Auditing, 29,* 251–266. Retrieved from EBSCO Online Database Business Source Complete http://search.ebscohost.com/login.aspx?direct=true&db=bth&AN=49128040&site=ehost-live%5fhl%5f

Varma, A. & Pichler, S. (2007). Interpersonal affect: Does it really bias performance appraisals? *Journal of Labor Research, 28,* 387–412. Retrieved from EBSCO Online Database Business Source Complete http://search.ebscohost.com/login.aspx?direct=true&db=bth&AN=25149624&site=ehost-live%5fhl%5f

Williams, S. L. & Hummert, M. L. (1990). Evaluating performance appraisal instrument dimensions using construct analysis. *Journal of Business Communication, 27,* 117–135. Retrieved from EBSCO Online Database Business Source Complete http://search.ebscohost.com/login.aspx?direct=true&db=bth&AN=5765771&site=ehost-live%5fhl%5f

Wren, B. M. (2006). Examining gender differences in performance evaluations, rewards and punishments. *Journal of Management Research, 6,* 114–124. Retrieved from EBSCO Online Database Business Source Complete http://search.ebscohost.com/login.aspx?direct=true&db=bth&AN=25175510&site=ehost-live%5fhl%5f

Ruth A. Wienclaw, Ph.D.

PERSONAL LINES INSURANCE & RISK MANAGEMENT

ABSTRACT

People face risks in everyday life that carry the potential of economic ruin. Automobile accidents can cause severe injury, loss of property and liability for injury to another. Sickness and personal injuries can cause significant expenses and prevent a person from working, thereby hastening an economic demise. Houses and possessions can be wiped out without warning and can leave a person homeless or an injury on a person's premises can result in life altering legal liability debt. In the face of all these potential sources of disaster, a person can and should manage the risk they face in their personal lives. Judicious use of the personal lines insurance form a powerful set of tools for the individual to manage risk by exchanging a potentially huge and uncertain future expense for the piece of mind and certainty that the fixed premium payment can bring. This article discusses the nature of insurance, the most common types of personal lines insurances and how individuals may use them to effectively manage risk.

OVERVIEW

The normal activities of daily life can carry the risk of enormous financial loss for individuals and their loved ones. While most of these events are relatively rare and uncertain for a particular individual, they are real and often occur without warning. Therefore, most people are willing to pay a small and predictable fixed amount for protection against the occurrence of an unpredictable event that carries catastrophic economic consequences. This is the basic nature of insurance. Personal lines insurance refers to a subset of insurance products that are purchased by individuals for their personal protection. Popular types of personal lines insurance are home, automobile and health insurance. This article will overview the nature and history of insurance as well as the features and benefits of some popular personal lines mentioned.

Insurance is a contract, commonly called a policy, in which an individual or entity makes regular payments, called a premium. In return for premiums, an insurer promises to reimburse or compensate against losses incurred by the insured. Parties involved in an insurance policy are the insured (individual or entity paying premiums), the insurer (usually an insurance company), and the beneficiary (party designated to receive payment under the policy). The insured and beneficiary may be the same person or a different person, as in the case of life insurance where benefits are paid to one person upon the death of another. The range of occurrences that can result in payment by the insurance company under the policy are sometimes called covered events. The terms of the policy determine the amount of the payment and define the range of covered events; therefore, recovery under the policy may be in either whole or in part upon the happening of a covered event.

This insurance arrangement, in a broad economic sense, transfers the risk of loss from an individual to a larger group that is better able to pay for the losses. In fact, the sharing of risk between members of group is the defining feature of an insurance policy. In other words, a contract that distributes risk is an insurance policy. Insurance companies create insurance policies by grouping certain risks together. This grouping provides the uniformity that covered risks which allows insurers to predict their potential losses and set premiums accordingly. For example, drivers that have been in accidents and who have been ticketed for violations of the traffic law may form a high-risk group that are more likely to collect benefits from the insurance company. Therefore, an insurance policy to protect such drivers would be more expensive. The insurance company profits by investing the premiums it receives. A well-developed area of law governs insurance. Insurance policies are subject to the requirements of statues, administrative agency regulations, and the court decisions interpreting both of them.

To satisfy the insurance needs of the American public, the insurance industry is composed of roughly 1600 life and Health Insurance companies and possibly 3000 property and casualty reinsurance companies. The United States is the world's largest insurance market, accounting for approximately 34% of all the 2.3 trillion dollars of premiums paid in world at the end of the twentieth century. Life and Health Insurance in the United States represents approximately 20% of the worldwide market, second to Japan's roughly 29% and far ahead of the

United Kingdom's 10% ranked third (Encyclopedia of Business & Finance, 2008).

Life Insurance

The life insurance industry reports date back to the colonial times. Early colonists were initially skeptical of life insurance as many considered it a gambling and against their religion. However, the expansion of the United States economy from 1830 to 1837 increased the American need to protect their financial prosperity. Four large mutual companies were founded during that period. The first was the Mutual Life Insurance Company of New York (founded in 1843) and it is currently the oldest practicing insurance company. As the insurance industry became an increasingly important component of the economy, governments began to legislate in the area. Massachusetts was the first state to establish an insurance department in 1855, by 1890 most states had established insurance departments and by 1940 all states regulated insurance (Encyclopedia of American History, 2008).

Life insurance provides financial benefits to a specified person, the beneficiary, upon the death of the insured party. There are several types of life insurance. A major distinction between the types of life insurance policies is whether they are term or whole life. Term life insurance provides benefits for a beneficiary if the insured dies within a specific period of time, or "Term," such as twenty years. Because a person may outlive the defined term of the policy, payment on the policy is not assured. Premium payments are required throughout and those premiums, once paid, are not refunded even if the insurance company does not pay out on the policy. For this reason, term life insurance is typically far less expensive than whole life.

Term life insurance policies have several important uses related to ensuring adequate financing during a specific period of time. For example, a young person that just starting in the working may be takeout a 20 year term policy to protect young children against the economic losses that would arise if the insured died while the children were still minors. Lenders may also require that debtor buy an insurance policy as a term o f a loan to ensure repayment in the event of the debtors death, In that situation the lender would likely require to named beneficiary of the insurance policy.

Whole Life

Whole life insurance is the other major category of life insurance and has several variants. The defining features of whole life insurance are the guaranteed eventual pay out of the agreed upon benefit and the policy accumulation of cash value on the policy. The cash value of policy can generally be recovered by the insured by surrendering the policy for the cash. The cash value can also act as collateral that the insured may borrow against. For this reason, a whole life policy is considered an investment vehicle in addition to an insurance product. The whole life policy has several varieties including "universal life" and "variable life." Universal life allows the insured to vary the amount and timing of premium payments that are otherwise fixed under a traditional whole life model.

Health Insurance

Health Insurance began in the mid 19th century with accident insurance and protection from a small number of diseases. The Travelers Insurance Company, founded in 1863, receives credit for writing the first insurance policy in the United States. This first policy contained a schedule of benefits payable to the insured for each particular illness or injury. In the beginning of the twentieth century, states began to enact workers' compensation laws to protect employees from the economic effects of injury on the job. These laws raised interest in group health insurance contracts for illnesses and non-work related injuries. Towards the middle of the twentieth century, employer provided health insurance plans for employees became an important fringe benefit in collective bargaining agreements. With the costs of medical care rising, Major Medical Insurance developed in response to the increased demand for policies that would protect families against prolonged and serious illnesses.

The insurance industry faced and overcame a number of challenges in the end of the twentieth century. After the 1992 presidential election, health insurance companies came under attack from the Clinton Administration which argued that the insurance industry's methods harmed the medical community. President Clinton advocated a competitive model known as managed competition. The insurance industry, however, launched a successful television campaign against the proposed reform.

Larger insurers responded by developing health maintenance organizations (HMO) to regulate care and costs.

The extreme rises in medical costs, nevertheless, remained a problem and Americans increasingly lost or dropped their unaffordable insurance policies. Barack Obama campaigned on a pledge to deliver universal healthcare to Americans in 2008, and in 2010 the Patient Protection and Affordable Care Act was passed over the vehement protests of many Republicans in Congress and leaders of the rising Tea Party movement. The act required private coverage in order to spread the cost over a large and healthier pool of insureds, but forbid restrictions based on pre-existing conditions. Government exchanges were created at the federal and state levels for the convenience of shoppers, high-deductible plans were eliminated, and subsidies were made available for low-income Americans. Critics on the Left asserted that the act was a gift to private insurance companies while those on the Right pronounced it socialism. Many of the provisions of the act were well received, but with a rocky rollout of the federal exchange, healthcare.gov, wariness of the new system was widespread (Custer2013).

Property & Casualty Insurance

For most people, their homes are their most valuable assets, biggest investment and potential source of liability. Prudent financial planning and savings can be wiped out overnight by natural disaster, fire or legal liability for injury that occurred on a person's property. Property and casualty insurance is intended to protect people from these types of risks. While mortgage lenders typically require borrowers to insure their homes as a condition of the loan, many homeowners may be underinsured against these types of risks, particularly for catastrophic risks to their homes. Homeowners in certain areas of the country must be certain that policies cover the risks specific to their geographic area. For example, Californians may be exposed to risk from brush fires, mudslides, and earthquakes. Floridians must ensure protection from hurricanes and floods. In certain situations when a house may be particularly valuable or unique, securing an appraisal by an appraiser approved by the insurance company may be an important step to avoid a gap in insurance coverage (Stolz, 2007).

To avoid or minimize risk, especially with respect to catastrophic losses, homeowners would be wise to analyze and understand the extent of their coverage in the event of a disaster. For example, a homeowner may be responsible for a "windstorm deductible" in the event of a hurricane. Insurance companies began including these deductibles after the massive losses caused by Hurricane Andrew. As opposed to other deductibles that are stated in dollar amounts, this deductible may appear as a percentage of the policy value. A 1% deductible would mean that on a $400,000 policy, a homeowner would have to pay $20,000 before the insurer would incur any liability.

Automobile Insurance

The first automobile insurance policy was issued by the Travelers Insurance Company in 1898. As the number of drivers in the United States increased, the value of automobile insurance became apparent. Indeed, automobile insurance became so broadly accepted that most states required vehicle owners to carry insurance on their vehicles. The state required insurance is generally considered a bare minimum and well below the recommended amount of coverage for a vehicle. Following consumer dissatisfaction with automobile insurance rates in the late 1980s and 1990s, some states implemented no-fault automobile insurance to reduce litigation. A no-fault system requires all drivers to carry insurance for their own protection, requires the insurance carrier to pay, up to policy limits, for the insured injuries, medical bills and property damages, regardless of who caused the accident. The typical no-fault system limits the ability of drivers to sue one another perhaps except in cases of severe injury. Typical no-fault state insurance laws allow accident victims to receive reimbursement for financial losses such as medical and hospital expenses as well as lost income from their own insurance companies and often place restrictions on the right to sue.

APPLICATIONS

The internet has transformed business and society in general; the insurance industry has likewise been affected by the internet, to the benefit of the consumer. In the past, purchasing insurance meant a visit to a local agent who may or may not have the best rates or coverage for a particular consumer. Shopping around for the ideal coverage and rate meant actually meeting with a number of agents. The internet has enabled consumers to shop and compare offerings of many different insurance companies almost instantly with the use of aggregator cites that rapidly compare quotes from different companies either live on the screen or by email.

However, consumers should understand that this rapid flow of information may not always cause prices to fall into line among competitors as one might expect. Using the internet for an insurance purchase removes the potentially valuable advice and resources of an insurance agent and an inattentive consumer may pay too much for an insurance product that inadequately addresses their needs. For example, auto insurance quotes can vary widely between insurers for the same vehicle, with the difference between the lowest and highest price being as much as 85%. Different insurers also vary widely on the degree of control a consumer may have over the specific content of their policies. To minimize the chances of making an error with an online purchase, consumers may consider visiting many different websites, calculating precisely what rates, plans or special offers actually cost, understanding what a plan actually covers despite its name, remaining weary of ubiquitous promises to save the consumer money, and finally a consumer should consider asking an insurance agent for explanation of foreign concepts and to help in negotiations for the bet rates possible (Trembly, 2007).

In addition to rapid comparison shopping to discover the lowest prices, consumers also benefit from a more rapid and simplified purchasing experience that is powered by interactive forms. The information flow enabled by the internet allows insurance companies to increase efficiency and accuracy with online data collection. Insurance companies are deploying powerful technology to increase overall efficiency in other areas of their business as well. Consumers may now pay premiums, file and track claims and change deductibles online. Insurers use modern information technologies to streamline loss reporting. Insurance company online activity indirectly benefits the consumer both in terms of convenience and by allowing the insurance companies to reflect the efficiency in lower prices The insurance companies are then able to pass on the advantage of those efficiencies to consumers in the form of lower rates.

CONCLUSION

When considered together, there appears to be an overwhelming number of risks in everyday life that carry the potential for personal economic ruin. Automobile accidents can cause severe injury, loss of property and liability for injury to another. Sickness and personal injuries can cause significant expenses and prevent a person from working, thereby hastening an economic demise. Houses and possessions can be wiped out without warning and can leave a person homeless, or an injury on a person's premises can result in life altering legal liability debt. In the face of all these potential sources of disaster, a person can and should manage the risks they face in their personal lives. Judicious use of personal lines insurance forms a powerful set of tools for the individual to manage risk by exchanging a potentially huge and uncertain future expense for the piece of mind and certainty that the fixed premium payment can bring.

While some types of insurance, e.g. house and automobile, may be required by the government or a lender, the consumer should be attentive to personal needs and must not rely on required coverage without understanding their personal needs and the insurance products offered. Effective risk management must include an analysis of the understanding of the risk and attendant losses that a person may face. Fortunately, the internet provides a powerful tool to learn about our insurance needs and make purchases to fulfill those needs.

Bibliography

Custer, W.S. (2013). Risk adjustment and the Affordable Care Act. *Journal of Financial Service Professionals, 67*(6), 25-26. Retrieved November 15, 2013, from EBSCO Online Database Business Source Complete. http://search.ebscohost.com/login.aspx?direct=true&db=bth&AN=91762071&site=ehost-live

Insurance. (n.d.). *Encyclopedia of American History*. Retrieved January 25, 2008, from Answers.com Web site: http://www.answers.com/topic/insurance

Insurance. (n.d.). *Encyclopedia of Business and Finance*. Retrieved January 08, 2008, from Answers.com Web site: http://www.answers.com/topic/insurance

Kerr, D.A., & Avila, S.M. (2013). Personal lines risk management and insurance simulation game.

Risk Management & Insurance Review, 16(1), 123-146. Retrieved November 15, 2013, from EBSCO Online Database Business Source Complete. http://search.ebscohost.com/login.aspx?direct=true&db=bth&AN=86693636&site=ehost-live

Lenckus, D. (2003). Personal lines program proves a multifaceted tool. *Business Insurance, 37*(14), 22. Retrieved December 22, 2007, from EBSCO Online Database Business Source Premier. http://search.ebscohost.com/login.aspx?direct=true&db=buh&AN=9596971&site=ehost-live

Levin, A. (1999). MetLife Buys St. Paul personal lines unit. *National Underwriter / Property & Casualty Risk & Benefits Management, 103*(29), 1. Retrieved December 22, 2007, from EBSCO Online Database Business Source Premier. http://search.ebscohost.com/login.aspx?direct=true&db=buh&AN=2081387&site=ehost-live

Lonkevich, D. (1999). Industry keeps pushing for personal lines deregulation. *National Underwriter / Property & Casualty Risk & Benefits Management, 103*(10), 1. Retrieved December 22, 2007, from EBSCO Online Database Business Source Premier. http://search. ebscohost.com/login.aspx?direct=true&db=buh&AN=1659492&site=ehost-live

Ruquet, M.E. (2013). Personal lines moderating; no signs of hardening. *Property & Casualty 360, 117*(9), 12. Retrieved November 15, 2013, from EBSCO Online Database Business Source Complete. http://search.ebscohost.com/login.aspx?direct=true&db=bth&AN=89964601&site=ehost-live

Souter, G. (2000). Internet changing face of personal lines sales. *Business Insurance, 34*(34), 12F. Retrieved December 22, 2007, from EBSCO Online Database Business Source Premier. http://search.ebscohost.com/login.aspx?direct=true&db=buh&AN=3571849&site=ehost-live

Trembly, A. (2007). When buying auto insurance online, do your homework... or pay the price! *National Underwriter / Property & Casualty Risk & Benefits Management, 111*(31), 12-14. Retrieved January 2, 2008, from EBSCO Online Database Business Source Premier. http://search.ebscohost.com/login.aspx?direct=true&db=buh&AN=26370923&site=ehost-live

Vala, K. (2007). Home insurance: Get the facts. *Smart Money, 16*(10), 132-132. Retrieved January 23, 2008, from EBSCO Online Database Business Source Complete. http://search.ebscohost.com/login.aspx?direct=true&db=bth&AN=26660011&site=ehost-live

Suggested Reading

Geary, L. (2001). What about my home? *Money, 30*(12), 147. Retrieved December 5, 2007, from EBSCO Online Database Business Source Premier. http://search.ebscohost.com/login.aspx?direct=true&db=buh&AN=5363498&site=ehost-live

Higham, T., & Wands, T. (1996). Selling personal lines insurance on the Internet. *CPCU Journal, 49*(3), 13. Retrieved December 5, 2007, from EBSCO Online Database Business Source Premier. http://search.ebscohost.com/login.aspx?direct=true&db=buh&AN=9611040161&site=ehost-live

Stolz, R. (2007). Bridging the property and casualty gap. *Journal of Financial Planning, 20*(11), 32-40. Retrieved January 23, 2008, from EBSCO Online Database Business Source Premier. http://search.ebscohost.com/login.aspx?direct=true&db=buh&AN=27518309&site=ehost-live

Seth M. Azria, J.D.

Principles of Management

ABSTRACT

This article examines how managers execute the primary functions of management including strategy development, business planning, organization, control, and leadership. The impact of contemporary factors such as globalization and information technologies is reviewed and the new methods that managers use to execute primary functions are explained. The use of metrics as a tool to develop strategies and plan and organize business activities is examined. The use of analytics as a tool to control business processes and optimize business resources and opportunities is also examined. The importance of developing human resources is examined along with popular contemporary methods for staff development.

OVERVIEW

The functions and activities of managers have remained relatively unchanged over time. Managers have always had to develop strategy, plan business activities, organize business functions, control processes, and lead and develop people, all in a manner that successfully drives businesses. However, what has changed over time is how managers have viewed and executed these functions (Hill & McShane, 2008). In addition, the challenges faced by managers have also changed as technologies and business conditions have evolved.

Technological innovation can play a significant role in determining how well a company performs. To what extent a company decides to pursue innovative methods may depend on available resources as well as competition in the business arena. From a strategic perspective, companies can commit to a high level of innovation in order to discourage new competitors from enter a business as well as to signal existing competitors that the cost of maintaining a product or service could become more costly for them (Corts, 2000).

Effects of Global Markets

Corporate Governance Systems

Corporate governance is related to corporate performance (Chun-Yao, Zong-Jhe, & Chun-Yi, 2013). Globalization certainly increases competition but it also expands the marketplace. However, increased competition and expanding markets can also strain corporate governance systems that have become accustomed to a smaller sale of operation as well as not having to contend with additional and perhaps previously unknown competitors. Corporate governance systems are also structured differently in some countries, especially those settings where the national governments control competition or are heavily invested in large corporations in those countries. Since companies in countries where the economy is largely market-oriented may be able to achieve greater degrees of efficiency and thus be more competitive over companies in settings where national government ownership or control of companies hinders economic performance, competition with these foreign firms will significantly impact firms.

Organizational Structure

Globalization of competition and of markets may also spur companies to create more decentralized management and control structures. This could result in network-like structures where central management functions may not be able to meet the needs of local operations. This could create some redundancy in functional departments in order to meet local needs, while still maintaining a central headquarters or a primary location for company operations. To a certain extent, the company's divisions or business units located in other countries can become highly independent for centralized control and the oversight of the corporate governance structure (Börsch, 2005).

Historically, corporate structures have fluctuated from highly centralized control structures to strong autonomy at the division level and sometimes back again. Globalization has contributed to shifts in these structures, but it is important to recognize that fluctuations in the level of control that corporate headquarters has over business units are likely to continue to occur.

Global Standards

A global economy has also led to the emergence of global standards. In December 2000, the International Organization for Standardization (ISO) issued revisions to the ISO 9000 Standard series. These revisions had a substantial change in focus, which actually makes the standard more useful for organizations seeking to improve performance and profitability (Vragel, 2001). The year 2000 revisions changed both the structure and focus of the standard. The auditable portion of the standard has changed from 20 sections to five, specifically:

- Quality management system.
- Management responsibility.
- Resource management.
- Product realization.
- Measurement, analysis and improvement (Vragel, 2001).

Competitiveness

While it is important to observe and embrace the global quality improvement movement, the "search for competitiveness and competitive advantage appears to be endless. The pressures of the complex, unpredictable, and dynamic business environment, global market competitions, and organizational change have promoted and sustained the search for competitiveness. The factors influencing and determining competitiveness are numerous and diverse" (Mathews, 2006, p. 158).

Competitiveness is achieved by blending a wide range of processes into a winning combination. The goal is certainly to increase productivity and to operate more efficiently. A firm's economic performance is connected to the performance of a certain sector, region or nation (Hategan, 2012). However, companies need to identify areas in which they can actually become competitive and maintain profitability. As corporate executives examine various business strategies they need to simultaneously assess productivity, efficiency and profits.

A true competitive advantage is achieved when a company develops a value-creating strategy that other competitors are not pursuing. Once the strategy is worked out it can be difficult for competitors to mimic the strategy and achieve the same level of benefits from it (Mathews, 2006).

Decision Making

Managers must continuously make decisions. At almost every moment during every day, most executives are involved in some phase of decision making. They collect and exchange information, review and analyze data, develop scenarios, evaluate alternative business tactics and strategies, and review results of activities that were undertaken based on previous decisions.

At lower levels, decisions focus on day-to-day operations. At higher levels, decisions are focused on long-term goals of the company (Brousseau, Driver, Hourihan & Larsson, 2006). As information technology has evolved, so has the ability of managers to use technology to help in the process of developing strategy, planning business activities, organizing business functions, controlling processes, and leading and developing people. Two new powerful technology-based tools can assist managers in the decision making process — metrics and analytics. Metrics enable managers to develop strategies and plan and organize business activities. Analytics enable managers to control business processes and optimize business resources and opportunities.

APPLICATIONS

Performance Measurement

For decades corporate executives in every industry have worked to fine tune how they affect the performance of their businesses. Managers fully understand that to improve the efficiency of their operations and the effectiveness of their business strategy that they need measurement systems. One major shift in performance measurement perspectives was to go beyond just looking at financial figures and relying on a wide array of measurements to judge how well a company is performing. Customer satisfaction, cash flow, manufacturing effectiveness, and innovation are all part of the new perspective of performance measurement and management. The dissatisfaction with using solely financial measures to evaluate business performance started to develop over 50 years ago. General Electric, among others, developed high-level task forces to identify and analyze alternative corporate performance measures (Eccles, 1991).

Lack of Preventative Action

Many managers worry that income-based financial figures are better at measuring the consequences of yesterday's decisions than they are at indicating tomorrow's performance. Events of the past decade substantiate this concern. In the 1980s, some executives saw the strong financial corporate records fall behind due to declines in quality or customer satisfaction which weren't considered important, or because global competitors gained market share. Even managers who have not been hurt feel the need for preventive action. A senior executive at one of the large money-center banks, for example, grew increasingly uneasy about the European part of his business, its strong financials notwithstanding. To address that concern, he nominated several new measures (including customer satisfaction, customers' perceptions of the bank's stature and professionalism, and market share) to serve as leading indicators of the business's performance.

Solutions

Quality Management

Discontent turns into rebellion when people see an alternative worth fighting for. During the 1980s, many managers found such an alternative in the quality movement. Manufacturers and service providers have come to see quality as a strategic weapon in their competitive battles. Thus, they have delegated significant resources to develop measures such as defect rates, response time, and delivery commitments to evaluate the performance of their products, services, and operations. Quality management has been one of the most popular research areas in the twenty-first century (Ebrahimi & Sadeghi, 2013).

In addition to pressure from global competitors, a major impetus for these efforts has been the growth of the Total Quality Movement and related programs such as the Malcolm Baldrige National Quality Award. (Before a company can even apply for a Baldrige Award, it must devise criteria to measure the performance of its entire operation — not just its products — in minute detail.) Another impetus, getting stronger by the day, comes from large manufacturers that are more and more likely to impose rigid quality requirements on their suppliers. Whatever the stimulus, the result is the same: quality measures represent the most positive step taken to date in broadening the basis of business performance measurement.

Customer Satisfaction

Another step in the same direction comes from embryonic efforts to generate measures of customer satisfaction. What quality was for the 1980s, customer satisfaction was for the 1990s. Work on this class of measures is the highest priority at the two manufacturing companies discussed earlier. It is equally critical at another high-tech company that recently created a customer satisfaction department reporting directly to the CEO. In each case, management's interest in developing new performance measures was triggered by strategies emphasizing customer service. Some studies have shown that, to improve service quality and maintain customers, organizations must ensure their employees' job satisfaction (Pansoo & Jang-Hyup, 2013).

As competition continues to stiffen, strategies that focus on quality will evolve naturally into strategies based on customer service. Indeed, this is already happening at many leading companies. Attention to customer satisfaction, which measures the quality of customer service, is a logical next step in the development of quality measures. Companies will continue to measure quality on the basis of internally generated indexes (such as defect rates) that are presumed to relate to customer satisfaction. But they will also begin to evaluate their performance by collecting data directly from customers for more direct measures like customer retention rates, market share, and perceived value of goods and services.

Competitive Benchmarking

According to Eccles, "just as quality-related metrics have made the performance measurement revolution more real, so has the development of competitive benchmarking" (1991, p. 133). First, "benchmarking gives managers a methodology that can be applied to any measure," financial or nonfinancial, but that emphasizes nonfinancial metrics. Second (and less obvious), it has a transforming effect on managerial mind-sets and perspectives.

Benchmarking involves identifying competitors and/or companies in other industries that "exemplify best practice in some activity, function, or process and then comparing one's own performance to theirs. This externally oriented approach makes people aware of improvements that are orders of magnitude beyond what they would have thought possible." In contrast, internal yardsticks that measure current performance in relation to prior period results, current budget, or the results of other units within the company rarely have such an eye-opening effect. Moreover, these internally focused comparisons have the disadvantage of breeding complacency through a false sense of security and of stirring up more energy for intramural rivalry than for competition in the marketplace.

Information Technology

Finally, information technology has played a critical role in making a performance measurement revolution possible. Thanks to dramatically improved price-performance ratios in hardware and to breakthroughs in software and database technology, organizations can generate, disseminate, analyze, and store more information from more sources, for more people, more quickly and cheaply than was conceivable even a few years back. Newer technologies include handheld computers for employees in the field and executive information systems for senior managers. Overall, the range of measurement options that are economically feasible has radically increased.

Implementation

Placing these new measures on an equal footing with financial data takes significant resources. One approach is to assign a senior executive to each of the measures and hold him or her responsible for developing required methodologies. Typically, these executives come from the function that is most experienced in dealing with the particular measure. But they work with a

"multifunctional task force to ensure that managers throughout the company will understand the resulting measures and find them useful. Another, less common, approach is to create a new function focused on one measure and then to expand its mandate over time. A unit responsible for customer satisfaction might subsequently take on market share, for example, or the company's performance in human resources" (Eccles, p. 1991, 134).

In companies that practice pay-for-performance, compensation and other rewards are often tied fairly mechanically to a few key financial measures such as profitability and return on investment. Convincing managers that a newly implemented system is really going to be followed can be a hard sell. The president of one service company let each of his division general managers design the performance measures that were most appropriate for his or her particular business. Even so, the managers still felt the bottom line was all that would matter when it came to promotions and pay.

Aligning incentives to performance is difficult because the formulas for tying the two together are "rarely effective." Formulas have the advantage of "looking objective, and they spare managers the unpleasantness" of having to conduct truly frank performance appraisals. But if "the formula is simple and focuses on a few key variables, it inevitably leaves some important measures out. Conversely, if the formula is complex and factors in all the variables that require attention, people are likely to find it confusing and may start to play games with the numbers. Moreover, the relative importance of the variables is certain to change more often — and faster — than the whole incentive system can change" (Eccles, 1991, p. 135).

Analytics as a Competitive Tool

Many organizations around the world have been implementing a system of analytics to better measure performance. There are several companies that have achieved a high level of performance measurement in industries such as consumer products, finance, retail, and travel and entertainment. Notable companies have included Marriott International, United Parcel Service, and Progressive Insurance.

Marriott International

Marriott International has worked to fine tune its performance measurement and analytics systems for over two decades. One of the primary focuses of the Marriott system is to establish an optimal price for guest rooms and drive revenue. Marriott has taken the system further and worked to develop a "Total Hotel Optimization program." This system has helped Marriott maximize revenue in conference facilities and catering. Analytics has helped the company develop offerings for frequent customers as well as assessing the potential of its frequent and valued customers defecting to competitors.

Progressive

Progressive Insurance created value and revenue for analyzing insurance industry data in new ways and using those results to improve performance. The company has identified small niches of potential customers. One example is motorcycle riders over age 30, college educated, high credit scores, and no traffic accidents to date. For each niche group of potential customers, Progressive performs a regression analysis to identify factors that can help to predict the likelihood of insured losses that each group will experience. These data are used to set policy prices for the niche groups that will likely enable the insurance company to realize profits from the combined groups of customers.

United Parcel Service

United Parcel Service (UPS) realized decades ago that to manage its parcel delivery business in an efficient and effective way and maintain profitability will require an ongoing analysis of performance data and the application of analytics to help identify new business opportunities. UPS also applies its analytics systems to maximize the use of its parcel moving capacity as well as to understand what influences how customers will respond to services and the likelihood of customers defecting to other carriers. UPS has established a Customer Intelligence Group which is able to predict customer defections through reviewing their service use patterns and complaints. This analysis is continuously generated and if a customer is flagged for potential defection a customer representative contacts that customer and consults on problems and devise solutions to improve customer satisfaction. This approach can reduce the number of accounts the company may see defect.

The Leverage of Commonality

A traditional view of business intelligence is often limited to small narrowly focused analytical activities conducted by functional departments or business units that are looking for guidance in tactical situations. However, the unbridled growth of user-developed analytical tools generally leads to many variations of internal performance indicators that are so disparate that they cannot be integrated into a big picture view of organization performance. In addition, research has repeatedly shown that large percentages of use-developed analytical tools such as spreadsheets contain errors, some of which are very serious. So the more user-developed tools there are, the more errors in analysis and thus decisions made on faculty data.

The key to leveraging analytics is to have a common set of data and analytical resources that are used across the organization. This enables different departments and business units to easily share data. In many organizations this may represent a cultural change as departments are pushed to give up their solitude and independence of data and analytical control.

Issue

The Challenge of Developing People

Achieving competitive differentiation through innovation, not Imitation, is difficult to accomplish without a close relationship between people management and business strategies (Appleby & Mavin, 2000). Each employee has talents, strengths, and weaknesses. These talents and strengths need to be integrated into a well designed skills set that best serves the organization. It is also necessary to continuously assess an individual's weaknesses and, using training tools and mentoring, transform the employee into a stronger executive. The changes that occurred in the marketplace over the past 70 plus years are exceptional and represent significant shifts in the way executives run global hyper competitive enterprises (Heames & Harvey, 2006).

Most highly competitive organizations take into consideration numerous factors that impact their overall competitiveness. Competitiveness is clearly influenced by numerous factors, and human resources is one of the key building blocks for a competitive organization. Employees all have unique abilities, attitudes, behaviors, and experiences and the human resource management process should be designed to improve skills and leverage those skills into a competitive advantage.

A traditional and effective approach of transferring knowledge and skills in an organization is the process and practice of mentoring. This technique is recognized as a valuable approach to staff development as well as socializing new employees into the corporate culture. A well structured mentoring program is a very structured way to communicate the expectations of management strategy, goals, and objectives. Although it is only one of many methods to facilitate learning for new employees, the mentoring process provides a guided learning experience that, if done properly, can expose employees to new skills and knowledge as well as reinforcing good management habits. Mentoring can contribute to develop a high performance work force and establishing and maintaining a competitive advantage (Mathews, 2006).

CONCLUSION

The functions and activities of managers have remained relatively unchanged over time. Managers have always had to develop strategy, plan business activities, organize business functions, control processes, and lead and develop people all in a manner that successfully drives businesses. However, what has changed overtime is how managers have viewed and executed these functions. In many industries, technological innovation is an important determinant of firm performance, and the level of innovative activity is therefore a significant choice for the firm. Global competition means greater access to markets on an international scale and can exert pressures on countries and corporate governance systems that rely on non-market coordination to a significant degree.

This shift from treating financial figures as the foundation for performance measurement to treating them as one among a broader set of measures is rather widespread. The "ranks of companies enlisting in this revolution are rising daily. Senior managers at one large, high-tech manufacturer recently took direct responsibility for adding customer satisfaction, quality, market share, and human resources to their formal measurement system" (Eccles, 1991, p. 131). As quality-related metrics have enhanced the performance measurement revolution, so has the development of competitive benchmarking. Benchmarking gives managers a methodology that can be applied to any measure, financial or nonfinancial, yet emphasizes nonfinancial metrics. It also has a transforming effect on managerial mind-sets and perspectives (Eccles, 1991).

History clearly shows that highly competitive organizations take into consideration numerous factors that impact their overall competitiveness, and human resources is one of the key building blocks for a competitive organization. Employees should be considered assets and managers should recognize that each employee has unique abilities, attitudes, behaviors, and experiences and the human resource management process should be designed to improve skills and leverage those skills into a competitive advantage.

Bibliography

Appleby, A., & Mavin, S. (2000). Innovation not imitation: Human resource strategy and the impact on world-class status. *Total Quality Management, 11(4/5/6), S554. Retrieved November 12, 2007, from EBSCO Online Database Academic Search Premier. http://search.ebscohost.com/login.aspx?direct=true&db=aph&AN=3198791&site=ehost-live*

Börsch, A. (2005). How international competition reinforces corporate governance and product market strategies: The case of Bosch. *German Politics, 14*(1), 33-50. Retrieved November 16, 2007, from EBSCO Online Database Academic Search Premier. http://search.ebscohost.com/login.aspx?direct=true&db=aph&AN=17277512&site=ehost-live

Brousseau, K., Driver, M., Hourihan, G. & Larsson, R. (2006). The seasoned executive's decision-making style. *Harvard Business Review, 84*(2), 110-121. Retrieved November 12, 2007, from EBSCO Online Database Business Source Premier. http://search.ebscohost.com/login.aspx?direct=true&db=buh&AN=19406196&site=ehost-live

Chandler Jr., A. (1998). Corporate strategy and structure: Some current considerations. *Society, 35*(2), 347-350. Retrieved November 16, 2007, from EBSCO Online Database Academic Search Premier. http://search.ebscohost.com/login.aspx?direct=true&db=aph&AN=34434&site=ehost-live

Chun-Yao, T., Zong-Jhe, W., & Chun-Yi, L. (2013). Corporate governance and innovation ability. *International Business Research, 6*(7), 70-78. Retrieved November 22, 2013, from EBSCO Online Database Business Source Complete. http://search.ebscohost.com/login.aspx?direct=true&db=bth&AN=89231988&site=ehost-live

Corts, K. (2000). Focused firms and the incentive to innovate. *Journal of Economics & Management Strategy, 9*(3), 339-362. Retrieved November 12, 2007, from EBSCO Online Database Business Source Premier. http://search.ebscohost.com/login.aspx?direct=true&db=buh&AN=3590240&site=ehost-live

Davenport, T. (2006). Competing on analytics. *Harvard Business Review, 84*(1), 98-107. Retrieved November 12, 2007, from EBSCO Online Database Business Source Premier. http://search.ebscohost.com/login.aspx?direct=true&db=buh&AN=19117901&site=ehost-live

Ebrahimi, M., & Sadeghi, M. (2013). Quality management and performance: An annotated review. *International Journal of Production Research, 51*(18), 5625-5643. Retrieved November 22, 2013, from EBSCO Online Database Business Source Complete. http://search.ebscohost.com/login.aspx?direct=true&db=bth&AN=90169832&site=ehost-live

Eccles, R. (1991). The performance measurement manifesto. *Harvard Business Review, 69*(1), 131-137. Retrieved November 12, 2007, from EBSCO Online Database Business Source Premier. http://search.ebscohost.com/login.aspx?direct=true&db=buh&AN=9102251664&site=ehost-live

Heames, J., & Harvey, M. (2006). The evolution of the concept of the 'executive' from the 20th century manager to the 21st century global leader. *Journal of Leadership & Organizational Studies (Baker College), 13*(2), 29-41. Retrieved November 12, 2007, from EBSCO Online Database Business Source Complete. http://search.ebscohost.com/login.aspx?direct=true&db=bth&AN=23316432&site=ehost-live

Hill, C. & McShane, S. (2008). Principles of management. McGraw-Hill/Irwin.

Mathews, P. (2006). The role of mentoring in promoting organizational competitiveness. *Competitiveness Review,* 16(2), 158-169. Retrieved November 16, 2007, from EBSCO Online Database Academic Search Premier. http://search.ebscohost.com/login.aspx?direct=true&db=aph&AN=21760463&site=ehost-live

Pansoo, K., & Jang-Hyup, H. (2013). Effects of job satisfaction on service quality, customer satisfaction, and customer loyalty: The case of a local state-owned enterprise. *WSEAS Transactions on Business & Economics, 10*(1), 49-68. Retrieved November 22, 2013, from EBSCO Online Database Business Source Complete. http://search.ebscohost.com/login.aspx?direct=true&db=bth&AN=88117275&site=ehost-live

Vragel, P. (2001). Using the new ISO 9001 standard to protect and improve profits. *Forging, 12*(2), 28. Retrieved November 12, 2007, from EBSCO Online Database Business Source Premier. http://search.ebscohost.com/login.aspx?direct=true&db=buh&AN=4459911&site=ehost-live

Suggested Reading

Atwater, L., & Brett, J. (2006). 360-degree feedback to leaders: Does it relate to changes in employee attitudes? *Group & Organization Management, 31*(5), 578-600. Retrieved November 12, 2007, from EBSCO Online Database Business Source Premier. http://search.ebscohost.com/login.aspx?direct=true&db=buh&AN=22361740&site=ehost-live

Darnall, N. (2006). Why firms mandate ISO 14001 certification. *Business & Society, 45*(3), 354-381. Retrieved November 12, 2007, from EBSCO Online Database Business Source Premier. http://search.ebscohost.com/login.aspx?direct=true&db=buh&AN=22174834&site=ehost-live

Harvey, M., Novicevic, M., Leonard, N., & Payne, D. (2007). The role of curiosity in global managers' decision-making. *Journal of Leadership & Organizational Studies (Baker College), 13*(3), 43-58. Retrieved November 12, 2007, from EBSCO Online Database Business Source Complete. http://search.ebscohost.com/login.aspx?direct=true&db=bth&AN=24402027&site=ehost-live

Ha?egan, D. (2012). Literature review of the evolution of competitiveness concept. *Annals of the University Of Oradea, Economic Science Series, 21*(1), 41-46. Retrieved November 22, 2013, from EBSCO Online Database Business Source Complete. http://search.ebscohost.com/login.aspx?direct=true&db=bth&AN=86068715&site=ehost-live

Rivette, K., & Kline, D. (2000). Discovering new value in intellectual property. *Harvard Business Review, 78*(1), 54-66. Retrieved November 12, 2007, from EBSCO Online Database Business Source Premier. http://search.ebscohost.com/login.aspx?direct=true&db=buh&AN=2628907&site=ehost-live

Rucci, A., Kirn, S., & Quinn, R. (1998). The employee-customer-profit chain at Sears. *Harvard Business Review, 76*(1), 82-97. Retrieved November 12, 2007, from EBSCO Online Database Business Source Premier. http://search.ebscohost.com/login.aspx?direct=true&db=buh&AN=16951&site=ehost-live

Wilkinson, G., & Dale, B. (1999). Models of management system standards: A review of the integration issues. *International Journal of Management Reviews, 1*(3), 279. Retrieved November 12, 2007, from EBSCO Online Database Business Source Premier. http://search.ebscohost.com/login.aspx?direct=true&db=buh&AN=3253635&site=ehost-live

Michael Erbschloe, M.A.

Principles of Risk Management

Abstract

This article focuses on the principles of risk management and the current day application of them. The first step is to identify risks; potential and realistic ones. The next step is to prevent or manage the risks. Three common risks are information technology, weather and business ethics. Information technology risks relate specifically to online data theft issues, identity theft and computer viruses. Weather concerns involve all forms of precipitation that can affect businesses like, too much rain, too little rain and not enough snow. This is very impactful to the agricultural, vacation/resort and restaurant business market. All businesses would be adversely impacted due to catastrophic weather that could destroy large geographical areas like Hurricane Katrina did (Louisiana, Mississippi and Alabama). Company leadership entails business ethics and the problems that arise due to the lack of them in the workplace. The banking industry is an example of an industry that is greatly impacted by the risks mentioned in this article because of the great financial impact brought on by the use of technology and the unpredictability of weather. Due to these reasons, it is quite obvious of the need to assess risk in all business industries.

OVERVIEW

Principles of risk management are needed even more today than ever before. In the past, many organizations either ignored the risks altogether or simply lived through the unfortunate consequences caused by them. In many cases, these organizations didn't have anyone dedicated to look at or out for potential risks that could adversely impact the company. It was, for lack of a better word, an afterthought. This apathetic way of conducting business, in turn, has caused many companies to go bankrupt and some to permanently close their business doors. Therefore, a closer look at the topic of risk management is essential.

Two Types of Risk

The process of identifying risk entails examining the likelihood of two types of risk: Potential risk and realistic risk. Regardless of the industry impacted, such an assessment is needed to not only identify risks, but to address them.

- Potential Risks — these types of risks may or may not occur, but a plan must be put in place to stop or reduce the impact. Examples are: Stock market crashes, unusually high-levels of precipitation in a typically dry area, employees leaving the department or company and poor executive level decisions. These risks can come from internal and external forces as shown by the above mentioned examples.
- Realistic Risks — these risks are based on known threats. Typically these threats are common for a specific industry or all industries. Examples are: loss of profits, legislative decisions, overseas regulations, information theft and computer viruses. Many times these risks come from external forces and can, as a result, cause quite a challenge to manage.

Prevention & Management of Risk

Now that the risk has been identified, steps must be taken to prevent or manage the risk. There are four main categories to consider. They are elimination, limitation, acceptance and transfer.

- Elimination — This technique involves avoiding any and all activity that could create a risk. Therefore, a company may choose not to sell products and services in a certain geographical location due to historically inclimate weather. Another example would be a company choosing not to use the Internet as a means of selling their products and services due to concerns of information theft. The decision to eliminate an activity is one that comes with a great deal of consideration. Loss of profits and market capitalization could result from such a decision.
- Limitation — This method entails the reduction of an actual exposure to a risk. A company or entity decides to limit the likelihood of suffering severe losses by taking precautionary steps to reduce risks. One example would be a company that chooses to sell a limited amount of products online to limit its exposure. Those products would most likely be high selling items and ones most commonly sold online. Another example is remote office locations put in place to reduce the impact of catastrophic losses of offices in areas where the weather could become volatile. Office daycares instituted to offset employee absenteeism due to childcare issues could impact work productivity and could prove helpful. Also, work safety programs implemented to educate employees on how to properly operate equipment to reduce employee injuries and/or deaths would be beneficial.
- Acceptance — This method involves accepting certain losses incurred. In particular, risks that can't be insured against and are not worth it in the long run because the expense to insure it will not cover the overall exposure. Common examples are damages caused by War. In most cases, these damages are not covered by insurance and as a result must be accepted as a loss by businesses. Another example is a national catastrophe like a

tsunami. Events like these could potentially bring about a total loss.

- Transfer — This is the process of transferring a risk to another party. One common way of doing this is by obtaining insurance coverage. When contractors are utilized, a contract is established to assign the contractor the appropriate risk responsibility. Consultants are also utilized by some organizations to better manage risk due to the expertise they bring for their respective industry. Attorneys help companies to stay compliant and in proper legal standing. Over the past decade, many industries have incorporated the use of derivatives to hedge potential losses, protect themselves and manage the risk.

Common Risks Companies Face

Some areas that commonly create risk are:

- The weather is a risk in itself due to the potential damage it can cause. The main problem that comes from this risk is a company's inability to do anything about the potential damage. Even if they see something coming, time may not be on their side to properly address it.
- Legislation can be introduced at any time, which could adversely impact a business' practices, productivity and profitability. What was once a normal practice or way of doing business may have to be completely revamped, which could be extremely costly.
- The economy is always a tumultuous factor for businesses. If consumers are unemployed or are dealing with other financial constraints, this will greatly impact their buying power. It can also make the market share even more competitive for businesses.
- People resources are always unpredictable and that in itself is a huge risk for companies. Hiring, training and retaining quality employees is a challenge for companies and causes the biggest expense. An employee's lack of productivity or unexpectant departure can greatly impact project work and plans for implementing new products and services.
- Technology is both exciting and risky. The use of new technology can be very expensive and if it doesn't work properly it can take an organization down. This could cause loss of profitability and consumer retention. Yet, if an organization doesn't keep up with new technology it could be left behind and become uncompetitive.

APPLICATIONS

There are several types of risks an organization faces today. This article will discuss a few of them. These risks involve information technology, weather and business ethics.

Information Technology

Technological advances have improved and made life more enriching for everyone who has taken advantage of them. In particular, the information highway, also known as the Internet, has been a huge contributor to such improvements. The conveniences that a click and a few keystrokes make are priceless to many consumers each day. The Internet is used to conduct research, make purchases, communicate with friends and family across the world, find directions, store data and countless other processes.

Information Theft

Along with access to endless quantities of information comes the risk of such information falling into the wrong hands. This information includes addresses, phone numbers, bank accounts, credit card account numbers and business data. Computer hackers have repeatedly been able to infiltrate confidential data from consumers and businesses. As a result, there have been frequent reports of computer viruses that have crippled companies and in some cases put them out of business. Business transactions conducted on the Internet can be quite profitable and convenient, but at times also very dangerous. That's why information theft has come to the forefront of what concerns corporate executives and consumers as a whole today. It can take months, if not years to clear up this type of information theft problem. Credit reporting information may take even longer to restore.

Cyber-risk Insurance Policies

Though there are issues, businesses have found a saving grace because now they have an option to purchase cyber-risk insurance policies. These policies provide coverage for companies that have experienced breaches in information security on the Internet. This type of insurance provides some relief for businesses, which they haven't had before. Some things cyber-risk insurance protects against are theft of trade secrets, destruction of hardware, software, data and extortion of hackers. Some third-party risks that are covered are computer viruses inadvertently forwarded internally, failure to provide products because a hacker or virus stopped the insured's delivery system, unauthorized contents placed on the company Website and the theft of credit card records. A business seeking this type of insurance coverage can obtain multi-million dollar coverage, which offers a great deal of relief to an ongoing problem (Gordon, Loeb & Sohail, 2003).

Weather

It is estimated that four-fifths of all economic activity worldwide is directly or indirectly affected by weather. Also, the US Department of Commerce says that at least $1 trn of the US economy is weather-dependent. With this type of monumental impact, it is no wonder why businesses should factor in this topic when discussing risk management. Virtually every industry is impacted by the weather. If a major storm (hurricane, tornado or thunderstorm) were to occur the destruction of crops would adversely impact food service, restaurant and grocery store industries, to name a few. This could bankrupt a business, especially the smaller mom and pop businesses. Severe damage could occur if a major earthquake occurred in California destroying homes, roadways, and businesses. Cities in this state could be virtually shutdown. It is very apparent, directly or indirectly, that most industries have the potential to be impacted and must do something to protect themselves (Triana, 2006).

Weather Derivatives

Due to the impending dangers that weather related risks could cause, many companies have adopted the use of weather derivatives. These financial instruments can be customized to determine the amount of risk a company may be exposed to when it comes to weather. Electricity and power firms were the pioneers of using these derivatives to hedge their risks and they are still the leaders of using these tools. With this type of protection, a business dependent on snow (like a ski resort) would be protected if there were a very limited supply during the ski season. This would also be the case for various food service industries if crops did not get enough rain. Companies utilizing these tools would receive compensation due to covered losses. The two most commonly used weather derivatives are temperature risks and rain hedges. The examples stated above would use these two types of weather derivatives (Fischer-Rief & Ward, 2003).

Business Ethics

The onslaught of lawsuits against company leaders has been alarming. Something that used to be unheard of has become fairly common. Companies like WorldCom, Enron and Arthur Andersen gained popularity in recent years not due to profitability, but because of falsified accounting reports. One by one, companies were the topic of discussion by the media for this very reason. In particular, what came to light and became the focus were company leaders and their unethical and illegal practices. They abused their authority and stockholders and employees paid the price. This issue has fueled the discussion on ethics and the risks involved when they are not in operation. It has been proven with the above companies that extremely harmful and sometimes irreparable damages may result.

Developing a Code of Ethics

It is critical for a company to develop and enforce a code of ethics. The following should be done as a way to create such a code of ethics:

- Educational materials should be created to provide structured ethical training in all levels in the business
- Documentation and evaluation of risk management using an ethical performance framework
- Inclusion of ethical codes of practice in organizational handbooks
- Inclusion of self-assessment on ethics in appraisals
- Appointment of ethics officers.

These efforts would show from the top down that good ethical behavior is required and taken seriously. The next course of action would be to address improper behavior immediately. This may mean additional training, job demotion or termination for the employee. If immediate action isn't taken, other employees will not take the ethics code seriously. It is because of disparities in the above practices that company leaders had the impression they could do anything without repercussions. Such an attitude creates great risk (Robertson, 2005).

Since company leaders have been under fire in the scandals mentioned above, it would benefit businesses to consider getting directors and officers (D&O) liability insurance. This insurance and variations of it provide protection for the directors and officers' individual assets, defense costs and payouts. Relief and closure are two main benefits that would derive from this coverage. With the influx of record-breaking settlements, this insurance is critical. It could be the difference of staying in or going out of business. Although it provides definite benefits, company leaders should not allow this insurance coverage to cloud their view of doing what is ethically right. The best defense of risk management is to not put the company leader and company at risk (Ferrillo, 2005).

Issues

Information Technology

As stated above, Internet use poses a serious risk to companies. Since the availability of the Internet is so vast, it can be very difficult to catch culprits in wrongful acts. The Internet can be used at home, on the job (usually), in the public library, at school and at a friend's house. Therefore, it would be difficult to determine who performed the illegal activity. Add to the mix the variety of wireless technology available today, and it is clear why the issue is so complex. Some individuals have multiple aliases and are quite capable of getting around firewalls to cause damage to individuals' and companies' data. The more safeguards that are created and put in place to protect potential victims, the more innovative criminals become to counter them. This will continue to be a problem for years to come since the Internet is so heavily used today. Some businesses are strictly run on the Internet and some businesses have achieved greater profit levels because of the availability of the Internet. The need for this tool would make one think that the world has never been without it.

Weather

As discussed above, weather derivatives have benefited businesses. They have allowed those businesses to continue to function and operate inspite of losses due to weather. Without these tools, it would be virtually impossible for some businesses to succeed. However, the unpredictability of the weather will challenge the validity of the weather derivative results. The weather derivatives cannot supersede Mother Nature's will. Meteorologists have access to some of the most up to date technology to make weather predictions for the world. Making predictions a week or two in advance has become the standard. Meteorologists also report on weather trends and provide historical data regarding record-breaking temperatures and symbolic weather events of the past. With all of this information at their fingertips, it would appear that they have everything they need to get it right, but this is not the case. Unfortunately, earthquakes, hurricanes, tsunamis, snow and ice storms suddenly appear, change directions and escalate without warning or notice. It's a part of life that no one can truly prepare for no matter how much information is available. Due to this reason, the weather will always be a factor for both the consumers and the businesses alike.

Business Ethics

Companies and company leaders have options to offset the risk associated with their business. Developing and implementing a code of ethics program is great, but if the board of directors and senior leadership don't buy-in from the beginning, the code of ethics will not work as intended. Accountability is key regardless of a person's position in the company. D&O liability insurance is a great asset to company leaders and companies, but since there have been so many companies charged with securities lawsuits the courts have been awarding hundreds of millions of dollars to the financial detriment of businesses. Can insurance companies afford to pay untraditionally high payouts? How much premium will need to be paid to ensure proper coverage? Can businesses afford it? Tough questions for tough times as companies consider their risks.

VIEWPOINTS

Banking Industry

The banking industry as a whole has been greatly impacted by various risks. Some of those risks come from the economy, environment and technology. Arguably, this industry is one of the riskiest ones to be in due to the great potential for turbulent results. Taking a deeper look at two of the risks mentioned in this article will explain why this is the case.

Information Technology & the Banking Industry

Online banking is very popular today. People enjoy the convenience of taking care of their financial affairs online. Benefits include the elimination of postage costs, reduced gas consumption and time savings. Other benefits include online bank statements that can be reviewed or printed at any time as well as an online bank ledger that takes away the need for keeping paper records. These banks also allow the account holder to review scanned images of handwritten checks to verify account transactions. All of these perks seem like a win win situation for consumers until such convenience is violated by information theft. Personal financial exposure is an obvious impact, but the potential loss of business due to this problem could prove even more damaging. This risk comes from taking advantage of growth opportunities through the Internet which could prove to be very profitable or expensive. The banking industry or individual banks considering the growth opportunities provided by the Internet must determine if the benefits outweigh the risks.

Weather & the Banking Industry

The banking industry can be severely effected by natural disasters. Hurricane Katrina is a prime example. Banks financed many of the homes that were destroyed due to the hurricane. As a result, those banks had to deal with loan defaults from those impacted states (Louisiana, Mississippi and Alabama) as many home sites were abandoned and the owners relocated. The average homes in those states were valued between $85,000 and $125,000. Had a disaster on the same scale happened in a more expensive area of the nation, such as California where the median home value was $500,000, losses could have been devastating for the banking industry (Esola, 2007).

Unlike the insurance industry, banks haven't had a plan in place to address these risks in the past. As stated above, some businesses don't have a plan and don't appear to be developing one any time soon to deal with or alleviate risks. Banks should consider following the lead of insurance companies. The insurance industry has exclusions and limitations to protect themselves. Instead, banks have made inaccurate assumptions by relying on emergency state and federal programs that have limits on how much they will pay. There will be even greater limitations when catastrophic damages occur like Hurricane Katrina due to the large number of payouts. The business industries can't take this lightly. The potential impact is too great too bear alone. The banking industry must begin to follow the principles of risk management to reduce their exposure (Esola, 2007).

CONCLUSION

The process of evaluating the principles of risk management is essential to a company's success. As shown throughout the article, success in risk management could be the difference of simply going through the motions and being proactive. The need is there and due to the risks that companies are facing today, risk management must be taken seriously. There are a variety of risks that affect the various business industries. Three main risks are information technology, weather and company leaders. Each poses its own serious threat. Fortunately, there are methods to overcome or counter them. The first step is to identify risks, both the known and the potential. Once this has been done, prevention or management should be implemented. The key to effective risk management is doing something about it. It's very important to seek solutions and adjust accordingly. It is equally important to evaluate the effectiveness of those solutions and make changes when needed. The solutions available today are vast. As more data is collected, trended and evaluated, the continued effort of developing innovative risk management solutions will create the most effective means of diminishing risk and eliminating it altogether when feasible. Ultimately, this is the goal for every organization.

Bibliography

Courbage, C., & Mahul, O. (2013). Promoting better understanding on sustainable disaster risk management strategies. *Geneva Papers on Risk & Insurance - Issues & Practice, 38*(3), 401-405.Retrieved November 15, 2013, from EBSCO Online Database Business Source Complete. http://search.ebscohost.com/login.aspx?direct=true&db=bth&AN=88899037&site=ehost-live

Esola, L. (2007). Banking industry faces huge risk in major disasters, insurers tell ABA. *Business Insurance, 41*(6), 4-20. Retrieved May 18, 2007, from EBSCO Online Database Business Source Complete. http://search.ebscohost.com/login.aspx?direct=true&db=bth&AN=24101617&site=ehost-live

Esola, L. (2007). Data protection, pandemic planning among top backer concerns at ABA conference. *Business Insurance, 41*(6), 20. Retrieved May 18, 2007, from EBSCO Online Database Business Source Complete. http://search.ebscohost.com/login.aspx?direct=true&db=bth&AN=24101634&site=ehost-live

Ferrillo, P. A. (2005). D&O liability insurance trends 2005. *Corporate Board, 26*(152), Retrieved June 17, 2007, from EBSCO Online Database Business Source Complete. http://search.ebscohost.com/login.aspx?direct=true&db=bth&AN=16916025&site=ehost-live

Finstam, R. M. (2005). Risk management affects us all. *British Journal of Administrative Management, 45*, 4-6. Retrieved May 18, 2007, from EBSCO Online Database Business Source Complete. http://search.ebscohost.com/login.aspx?direct=true&db=bth&AN=15821156&site=ehost-live

Fischer-Rief, V. (2003). Weatherproof. *Euromoney, 34*, 10. Retrieved May 18, 2007, from EBSCO Online Database Business Source Complete. http://search.ebscohost.com/login.aspx?direct=true&db=bth&AN=11255273&site=ehost-live

Gordon, L. A, Loeb, M. P. & Sohail, T. (2003). A framework for using insurance for cyber-risk management. *Communications of the ACM, 46*(3), 81-85. Retrieved May 18, 2007, from EBSCO Online Database Business Source Complete. http://search.ebscohost.com/login.aspx?direct=true&db=bth&AN=12493505&site=ehost-live

Halperin, A. (2007, January 29). Shielding business from wild weather. *Business Week Online*, 19. Retrieved May 18, 2007, from EBSCO Online Database Business Source Complete. http://search.ebscohost.com/login.aspx?direct=true&db=bth&AN=23854471&site=ehost-live

Heffernan, R. (2012). Managing Mother Nature. *Banking New York*, 218-26. Retrieved November 15, 2013, from EBSCO Online Database Business Source Complete. http://search.ebscohost.com/login.aspx?direct=true&db=bth&AN=73027688&site=ehost-live

Heineman, B. W. (2007). Avoiding integrity land mines. *Harvard Business Review, 85*(4), 100-108. Retrieved June 17, 2007, from EBSCO Online Database Business Source Complete. http://search.ebscohost.com/login.aspx?direct=true&db=bth&AN=24267439&site=ehost-live

Krivkovich, A., & Levy, C. (2013). Managing the people side of risk. *Mckinsey Quarterly, (4)*, 123-128. Retrieved November 15, 2013, from EBSCO Online Database Business Source Complete. http://search.ebscohost.com/login.aspx?direct=true&db=bth&AN=91665820&site=ehost-live

Lustgarten, A. (2004). Banking on the weather. *Fortune, 149*(9), 88. Retrieved May 18, 2007, from EBSCO Online Database Business Source Complete. http://search.ebscohost.com/login.aspx?direct=true&db=bth&AN=13185369&site=ehost-live

Musshoff, O., Odening, M., & Wei, X. (2011). Management of climate risks in agriculture-will weather derivatives permeate?. *Applied Economics, 43*(9), 1067-1077. Retrieved November 15, 2013, from EBSCO Online Database Business Source Complete. http://search.ebscohost.com/login.aspx?direct=true&db=bth&AN=60040835&site=ehost-live

Robertson, I. (2005, August). In my opinion. *Management Today*, 6. Retrieved June 18, 2007, from EBSCO Online Database Business Source Complete. http://search.ebscohost.com/login.aspx?direct=true&db=bth&AN=18298054&site=ehost-live

Triana, P. (2006). Are you covered? *European Business Forum, 26*, 50-55. Retrieved May 18, 2007, from EBSCO Online Database Business Source Complete. http://search.ebscohost.com/login.aspx?direct=true&db=bth&AN=23532583&site=ehost-live

York, J. (2005). Prepare for the worst. *Fleet Owner, 100*(10), 32. Retrieved May18, 2007, from EBSCO Online Database Business Source Complete. http://search.ebscohost.com/login.aspx?direct=true&db=bth&AN=18603709&site=ehost-live

Suggested Reading

Childers, D. & Marks, N. (2005). Ethics as a strategy. *Internal Auditor, 62*(5), 34-38. Retrieved June 18, 2007, from EBSCO Online Database Business Source Complete. http://search.ebscohost.com/login.aspx?direct=true&db=bth&AN=18520883&site=ehost-live

Kuver, P. P. (1999). Managing risk in information systems. *Year 2000 Practitioner, 2*(9), 1. Retrieved May 18, 2007, from EBSCO Online Database Business Source Complete. http://search.ebscohost.com/login.aspx?direct=true&db=bth&AN=2215651&site=ehost-live

Nelson, R (1999). Risk management and insurance. In *Shopping center management* (pp. 193-204). New York, NY: International Council of Shopping Centers. Retrieved May 18, 2007, from EBSCO Online Database Business Source Complete. http://search.ebscohost.com/login.aspx?direct=true&db=bth&AN=24017020&site=ehost-live

Risk management & insurance. (2004). *Meeting News,* 82-86. Retrieved May 23, 2007, from EBSCO Online Database Business Source Complete. http://search.ebscohost.com/login.aspx?direct=true&db=bth&AN=14113697&site=ehost-live

Active hurricane season brings danger. (2005). *Safety Compliance Letter, 2457,* 11-12. Retrieved May 18, 2007, from EBSCO Online Database Business Source Complete. http://search.ebscohost.com/login.aspx?direct=true&db=bth&AN=18379632&site=ehost-live

Sheryl D. McClinton

PROCESS MANAGEMENT FOR QUALITY

ABSTRACT

Successfully producing products and delivering services requires adherence to some standard or level of quality. Quality is an attribute that can be measured and is equivalent to meeting or exceeding customer expectations. It can be built into the act of managing processes to design, produce, deliver, maintain and service products of all kinds. However, process complexity may impact the ability to continuously redesign processes for efficiency and quality. Quality tools are useful in determining current quality status and quality philosophies are valuable in order to approach business process management from a holistic view. A concern for quality determines how processes will be managed and controlled. Interaction with customers to collect feedback is essential in monitoring quality. Technology can help master the modification of processes and reduce complexity. But, technology is only one factor that affects process management success. People who use the processes must be included in the management and modification activity and can benefit from quality training. Senior management must set the tone for organizational emphasis on quality and the integration of quality into managing processes.

OVERVIEW

Businesses of all types have processes that run operations, produce products and services and that communicate with customers. Processes can range from simple to complex. The more efficient the processes the more value a company can create and the faster a product can go to market. Efficient processes are clear and communication flows easily about them. An effective system of managing processes allows these processes to be modified and to easily adapt to the constantly changing environment. Effective process management can provide a benefit in the marketplace to a business because the business will be easily able to integrate information about the market into its operations (Cleaveland, 2006; Sly, 2004).

Businesses can attract customers by exceptional positioning of products, attractive advertising, and skillful promotion and pricing. However, the opportunity for a product to experience longevity depends on the true quality of the product and the ability of the company to keep quality high or improve quality over time. Introducing high levels of quality and maintaining those levels can be costly and time consuming, especially if the quality levels required mean product redesign and process redesign.

The hidden cost of redesign in production is the retraining workers and productivity loss when things have been done a certain way for a period of time and then are changed. The manner in which companies manage processes with quality in mind can help in meeting the challenges companies face today. Some of these challenges are demands from the marketplace for new products even faster and customers demanding new features and functionality (Huang & Stohr, 2007). In addition to market and customer demands, industry and government regulations require "proactive compliance" by companies and cause processes to become more complex. Proactive activities can help companies anticipate changes, become leaders in their market space and avoid the cost of reactionary activity. According to Huang &

Stohr, once processes become complex, it becomes more difficult to manage them because the reasons processes are designed a certain way or even exist is lost. In addition, every layer of complexity requires new business rules that influence or even constrain the processes (Huang & Stohr, 2007). For example, a new government regulation may require tracking of information about the age of an applicant for insurance. To meet this requirement, a process may have to add a new business rule that says if age equals some value then move to another action.

Complexity also influences how companies can allocate resources. If a task of monitoring or managing a process is very complex, the level of knowledge of the worker assigned the task must be high; a factor that limits who can work on what task. In addition, there is natural turnover in companies and documentation of business processes and rules is needed since new workers may not understand the required flow of a particular process.

Business Process Management & Total Quality Management

Yu-Yuan Hung (2006) likened Business Process Management (BPM) to Total Quality Management (TQM). Both require a broad strategic view as well as a connection between internal processes and the external environment. An article about process management programs called TQM a "strategy" where the whole organization is consumed with continuous improvement. This strategy was an outgrowth of U.S. manufacturers trying to thwart Japanese competition by mimicking the Japanese emphasis on quality. Keck (2006) noted that the Total Quality Movement of late 1970s and 1980s inspired quality tools.

Tools for Total Quality Management

According to Keck, quality is meeting or exceeding customer expectations. The quality tools developed during the quality movement were used to help companies understand processes, what variability existed in these processes, and to help in measuring defects and deciding what to do about these situations. The initial quality tools were more concerned with the operational status of processes and the ability to identify and correct process issues. When quality tools are applied to business process management, there is an operational and strategic element to process design. Keck (2006) identified Six Sigma, a management philosophy that measures defects and improves quality as a key quality tool. Since the invention of Six Sigma in 1986 by Motorola, it has become much more comprehensive as a business improvement tool. Keck (2006) noted that Six Sigma involves:

- Understanding and managing customer requirements.
- Aligning key business processes to achieve those requirements.
- Utilizing rigorous data analysis to minimize variation in those processes.
- Driving rapid and sustainable improvement to business processes.

Six Sigma

Applying Six Sigma to business process management starts with a comprehensive evaluation of current processes in order to identify what is not adding value or causing errors, etc. (Keck, 2006). Technology is also effective in the analysis required by Six Sigma. Hydrocarbon Processing compared and contrasted Six Sigma to TQM by noting the use of statistical methods and problem solving techniques for process improvement. However, TQM has a company wide focus with involvement by all employees while Six Sigma is the domain of experts called black belts.

ISO 9000

Another popular quality program called ISO 9000 requires documented standard processes for everything a company does. The ISO 9000 approach requires organizations to ask questions about what is done, how accurate it is and why it is done. Activity like ISO 9000 preparation may result in process redesign as formerly unknown details are captured and scrutinized. With ISO 9000, everything you do must be documented. If you are doing something and it is not documented, this omission is picked up. ISO 9000 certification also has the cache` of having documented processes certified by a third party.

Importance of Consistency

Even measuring the quality of current processes is not enough to completely introduce quality into business process management. Consistency of delivery (Keck, 2006) is a critical factor to measure quality in business processes. Keck suggested the outsourcing of certain functions to ensure quality in business processes, especially those that aren't part of the organization's core skills. Quality product and service delivery is dependent on the following key principles (Keck, 2006):

- Management commitment.
- Understanding expertise in process management.
- Unwavering discipline in the organization to apply quality principles.
- Use of quality tools and methodology.
- Creating a quality culture.

Role of Top Management

Top management is the key to achieving these principles in a real world environment. Top management must understand the concepts of quality and business process management, value expertise in these areas of their organization, recognize the value of tools (technology and quality) and must value and support people. There appears to be limitations on the widespread use of process management improvement techniques ("Can process management," 2006). After some period of time, the gains in efficiency, cost and competitive advantage appear to dwindle. Strategic managers may need to take another view and look for new methods of achieving competitive advantage instead of using the same one over and over again.

What is Quality & is it Important?

Quality is an important concept in business and there are many measures of quality in various industries. Quality is dependent upon what the customer believes constitutes quality. Landryovà & Irgens (2006) defined product quality as "a product's fitness for purpose." Keck (2006) saw a direct relationship between quality and customer satisfaction and noted that even cheap prices do not cover up for poor quality. This is traditionally referred to in quality terminology as the total cost of quality.

The Cost of Quality

The total cost of quality is made up of two types of costs. The first is the cost of conformance (COC) and the second is the cost of nonconformance (CONC) (Keck, 2006). The cost of conformance is the price a company pays to adhere to quality standards. The cost of nonconformance is the price a company pays when a product is found to be not fit while in the hands of the customer. Nonconformance is costly because for any product or service, the farther into the process, the costlier the product or service. If a quality error is caught early and prevented from reaching the customer, the company saves money in processing and packaging a product and the multiple labor cycles in the case of a service.

Taguchi Principles of Quality

Landryovà & Irgens (2006) outlined four quality concepts devised by Taguchi called the Taguchi principles of quality and are often referred to as the most effective quality principles in the world. These principles are:

- Quality should be designed into products not inspected in.
- Quality is realized by minimizing deviations from specification and reducing uncontrolled factors as a cause for deviation.
- Quality measurements are not a result of the features or functional performance of a product.
- The cost of quality is measured by deviations in performance and life-cycle costs.

Reasons for Process & Quality Management

Like other quality guidelines, Taguchi's principles emphasize preventing loss where it occurs and not allowing deviation, variation and lack of control of tolerance to continue through the production process.

So why should companies manage processes and why should they manage them for quality? Hammer (2007) noted that focus on processes yields benefits and improvements in cost, quality, speed and profitability among other key areas where businesses need positive activity. Keck (2006) quoted quality guru Philip Crosby's view that investing in quality is less costly than the ramifications of poor quality. Companies need a balance between short term process management and investment in new opportunities for the future ("Can process management," 2006). Balance is difficult because of the tendency to focus on one process or the other and it is difficult to know when to make appropriate shifts. It is very difficult for an organization to keep the entire organization's focus on anything for a long period of time and once it is set in one direction, it is difficult to change it.

Quality is important because it emphasizes what the customer wants. If customer wants are not addressed, opportunities for competitors open up and the value of products and services is reduced. However, an organization's approach to addressing quality issues and integrating quality into business process management may not succeed in meeting customer expectations.

Sustainable Competitive Advantage

Yu-Yuan Hung (2006) describes business process management as a principle that helps companies "sustain competitive advantage." A sustainable competitive advantage is one that occurs when a company finds ways to continuously adapt to new demands. The key to this competitiveness is to make business processes strategic in importance and recognize the role that people play in business process management (Yu-Yuan Hung, 2006).

Dangers of Business Process Management & Quality Management Technology

There are dangers when engaging in business process management and using quality tools to manage the process. Professors from Wharton School of Business and Harvard have performed research which suggests that adhering to process management causes organizations to become stagnant and "dampens innovation" ("Can process management," 2006). The reasons for these problems are that an organization's focus is exclusively on efficiency at the expense of creative thinking. In addition, the method and pattern of process improvement can become entrenched and stale meaning that the previous ways gains were made no longer work. Companies can even apply the techniques they've learned and used to the wrong situation. This is especially true when discovering new products and when designs are impacted by new technology. Anything brand new can skew the equation in ways organizations may not be able to imagine.

Viewpoint

How Processes are Managed for Quality

Although it seems obvious that quality is important and managing processes is essential, transforming business processes with an eye on quality is not easy to do. Hammer (2007) found that executives responsible for these areas failed regardless of time, manpower and money spent. The reason is due to the difficulty in determining what should be changed, when and by how much. Process transformation is not an exact science.

Process & Enterprise Maturity Model

Hammer worked for five years on a model of how executives could measure progress on transforming processes. This model, called the Process and Enterprise Maturity Model (PEMM) has been used successfully in process management at companies including Michelin, CSAA, Tetra Pak, Shell, Clorox, and Schneider National (Hammer, 2007). PEMM identifies two groups of characteristics that help processes perform well over the long term. The first group of characteristics is called process enablers which affect how well individual processes function. Process enablers depend on each other and if any don't function well or are missing, it can affect the ability of the others to function well. The second group of characteristics is organizational capabilities that support high performance processes. Even if process enablers are in place, an organization can work against itself for effective process management, monitoring and improvement.

Process Enablers

Hammer (2007) identified five process enablers and four enterprise enablers. Process enablers are:

- Design — how comprehensive the process in making a product.
- Performers — who executes the processes as well as their skills and knowledge.
- Owner — the senior leader responsible for the process and results.
- Infrastructure — information and systems to support the process.
- Metrics — the measures a company uses to track the process's performance.

The companies that can identify these enablers are more likely to put actions in place to support the process management activities going on within a firm. However, management cannot be the only ones who possess the knowledge and ability to categorize the attributes that enable processes. The operational employees must understand the connection between these enablers and their daily work to be effective contributors to process management.

Enterprise Capabilities

The Enterprise Capabilities are:

- Leadership — senior executives who support process creation.
- Culture — organizational values: Customer focus, teamwork, personal accountability, and willingness to change.
- Expertise — process redesign capabilities.
- Governance — how complex projects and change initiatives are managed.

These enterprise capabilities are less tangible and harder to influence than the process enablers. Strategic leaders have to develop multiple ways to communicate these capabilities and to obtain information and feedback on them. Hammer (2007) tested these enablers and capabilities with several leading companies and found the PEMM model a successful way to guide, plan and evaluate process transformation. The biggest problem Hammer (2007) saw with the enablers and capabilities was that the intensity with which each was active in an organization varied and affected the outcomes. So, if a company was strong in the capability of leadership but weak in governance, problems would occur.

Importance of Process Design

Hammer (2007) felt that the way a process is designed impacts the performance of the process. The design of processes includes who is performing what task, when the task is done, where and how. Hammer recommended using quality tools to make sure processes are being executed the way they should, but promoted process redesign as the real way to transform processes and improve their performance. One company Hammer (2007) tested with the PEMM model was Schneider National, a large trucking company. Schneider's interest in process improvement was due to a decline in growth. Schneider identified the five core business processes important to the company. One process captured all activity related to sales from the identification of a lead to the ultimate purchase of a product. Schneider identified a key performance indicator that could reverse the decline in growth. This indicator was the time needed to respond to a request for a proposal from a customer. The redesign process reduced the time for a bid or response to the customer's proposal by 90% and increased the bid opportunities that resulted in sales by 70%. This is significant and could influence companies like Schneider to go further in business process transformation.

Tarí (2006) observed public sector integration of quality in operations and documented process management and business process reengineering used to improve public sector service quality in police services. Tarí pointed to TQM as being especially applicable to the public sector because it emphasizes the human component and service delivery is concerned with managing and deploying the appropriate human resources as needed. TQM has been used by police departments in Europe to improve police services. TQM emphasizes openness towards the community in service delivery.

Importance of Employee Support/Education

The literature has shown many examples of companies using quality tools to improve processes but doesn't show efforts by companies to help people adapt to the improved processes (Tarí, 2006). Hammer (2007) agreed noting that management is typically ready to pay for teaching people a new process but not ready to pay for helping people understand how the new process works or fits into the larger organizational processes. Another key mistake is changing processes without changing the associated management responsibility that is also likely to change. Other methods of improving police services for quality include process mapping and using the balanced scorecard. Niven (2003) described the balanced scorecard as a measurement system that comes from the organization's strategy and can also be used as a communication tool. The goal is to create balance between financial indicators of success, internal and external stakeholders, and performance indicators. Process mapping gives a clear, universal view of existing processes and how they relate to each other. Tarí's (2006) research ultimately showed that process management helps the service quality improvement process but is dependent upon the right kind of input from people. Improving the service quality of policing depended heavily on a positive relationship with citizens. In some cases, this means establishing a relationship in the first place before it is possible to move to a positive one.

Hammer (2007) argued that process management also means changing the way an organization looks at goals and rewards. These must also change with processes. People must be held accountable for a broader set of the objectives and held to a higher standard of understanding.

Tools to Manage Processes while Ensuring Quality

Part of the success of business process management (BPM) is becoming knowledgeable about BPM, BPM tools, strategies and processes. Yu-Yuan Hung (2006) defined twelve principles for successful business process management. Some of these principles include:

- Looking at BPM in a holistic way rather than piecemeal.
- Making BPM strategic.
- Using information technology to manage BPM.
- Recognizing that BPM has corporate-wide impact on every part of the organization.
- Cross functional managing of processes needed instead of specialization in managing processes.
- Aligning processes.
- Aligning structure.
- Executive commitment.
- Involving people.

The difficulty with building these success principles is that someone at the strategic level must understand the breadth and depth of them and must be willing to train and allocate the appropriate financial and people resources. Many companies are unwilling to take on a task this complex and end up only scratching the surface in BPM. Others may try to do too much too quickly.

Application of Technology to Business Process Management

Ross (1995) defined business process management (BPM) as "an integrated management philosophy and set of practices that includes incremental change and radical change in business process, and emphasizes continuous improvement, customer satisfaction, and employee involvement." Part of quality management is the selection of technology tools to manage the business process management activity. The demand for this technology is strong and expected to grow two and one half times in the next 5 — 7 years.

Oil Refineries & Business Process Management

Landryovà, & Irgens emphasized the support of product quality by the new generation of knowledge about processes (2006). The authors discussed how rule based expert systems combined with SCADA systems (supervisory control and data acquisition) were used in the oil refinery industry to generate information about processes and equipment and then used in process management activities. The reason process knowledge generation and data collection is important and difficult in the oil refinery industry is that the process industry, unlike discrete manufacturing, does not have clear and distinct processes or an easily identifiable design phase. Variations in manufacturing are costly and must be controlled. The ability to develop knowledge about manufacturing and variability assists in predicting and controlling quality issues. In this case, the tools that help manage processes are collaborative tools that work in concert to provide usable information on demand.

The Health Care Industry & Business Process Management Technology

Another application of technology to business process management is that of clinical decision intelligence (CDI). It has a goal of improving healthcare quality and reducing costs by discovering, managing and applying the multitude of data increasingly available from many sources (Wang, Nayda, & Dettinger, 2007). These sources can include the latest research, clinical observations, laboratory tests and so on. CDI changes healthcare processes by integrating important process components including:

- Business intelligence
- Business rule management and
- Business process management.

CONCLUSION

The concern with quality in healthcare was highlighted by several trade and non-profit organizations in the 1990s whose findings showed unnecessary medical errors that even ended in death. Errors, inconsistent and poor quality coupled with high costs indicated a need to take dramatic action. One of the ways to address the healthcare crisis was an attempt to utilize technology more effectively. CDI systems are unique because they combine knowledge discovery and acquisition, knowledge management, and decision support. No technology before CDI had this capability (Wang, Nayda, & Dettinger, 2007). These three subprocesses are challenging to integrate because the people who do them vary in skill, expertise, and what they are trying to achieve, but the ability to connect these processes can yield better care for the patient. The patient gets better care because instead of the traditional approach of dependence on the knowledge a physician has or has among colleagues, the latest research and techniques are also available. The ability to share the information with other clinicians and providers is also seamless. CDI systems also improve the quality of provider knowledge and allows for faster integration of new knowledge, improving overall healthcare provider skill. Hammer noted that improving processes is a dramatic way to improve performance because of the elimination of anything that is the source of cost or errors. In the case of healthcare quality, cost and errors can lead to serious consequences and even death. Every industry has reasons to improve processes and inject quality in the process transformation.

Freeing an organization from unnecessary steps can also lead to creativity and innovation which can lead to what the customer actually wants — new and better products and high quality service.

Bibliography

Asif, M., de Vries, H. J., & Ahmad, N. (2013). Knowledge creation through quality management. *Total Quality Management & Business Excellence, 24*(5/6), 664-677. Retrieved October 31, 2013, from EBSCO Online Database Business Source Complete. http://search.ebscohost.com/login.aspx?direct=true&db=bth&AN=87821057&site=ehost-live

Can process management programs actually discourage innovation? (2006). *Hydrocarbon Processing, 85(1),* 23-25. Retrieved May 18, 2007, from EBSCO Online Database Business Source Complete. http://search.ebscohost.com/login.aspx?direct=true&db=bth&AN=19644355&site=ehost-live

Cleaveland, P. (2006). Building a better manufacturing future. *Product Design & Development, 61(8),* 8-9. Retrieved May 18, 2007, from EBSCO Online Database Business Source Complete. http://search.ebscohost.com/login.aspx?direct=true&db=bth&AN=21984500&site=ehost-live

Enterprise Service Bus switches into drive as markets reach $190M-plus. (2007). *Manufacturing Business Technology, 25(4),* 53-53. Retrieved May 18, 2007, from EBSCO Online Database Business Source Complete. http://search.ebscohost.com/login.aspx?direct=true&db=bth&AN=24855300&site=ehost-live

Hammer, M. (2007) The process audit. *Harvard Business Review, 85(4),* 111-123. Retrieved May 18, 2007, from EBSCO Online Database Business Source Complete. http://search.ebscohost.com/login.aspx?direct=true&db=bth&AN=24267684&site=ehost-live

Huang, W. & Stohr, E. A. (2007). Design and implementation of a business process rules engine. [Working Paper] Stevens Institute of Technology New Jersey. Retrieved August 2, 2007, from http://howe.stevens.edu/fileadmin/Files/publications/Huang%5fStohr%5fBPRE-DESRIST-Final%5f2%5f.doc

Jeang, A. (2011). Economic production order quantity and quality. *International Journal of Production Research, 49*(6), 1753-1783. Retrieved October 31, 2013, from EBSCO Online Database Business Source Complete. http://search.ebscohost.com/login.aspx?direct=true&db=bth&AN=56448517&site=ehost-live

Keck, C. (2006). Quality a cornerstone for success. Datrose Business Process Outsourcing. Retrieved May 18, 2007, from http://www.datrose.com/images/Quality%5fArticle.pdf

Landryovà, L. & Irgens, C. (2006). Process knowledge generation and knowledge management to support product quality in the process industry by supervisory control and data acquisition (SCADA) open systems. *Production Planning & Control, 17(2),* 94-98. Retrieved May 18, 2007, from EBSCO Online Database Business Source Complete. http://search.ebscohost.com/login.aspx?direct=true&db=bth&AN=19821456&site=ehost-live

Niven, P. R. (2003). *Balanced scorecard: step-by-step for government and nonprofit agencies.* Hoboken, New Jersey: John Wiley & Sons.

Ross, J.E. (1995) *Total Quality Management: Text, Cases and Readings.* Delray Beach: St. Lucie Press.

Sly Ph.D., D. (2004). Manufacturing Process Management. *Technology Trends in PLM by Collaborative Product Development Associates.* Retrieved July 20, 2007, from http://www.proplanner.net/Product/Whitepapers/mpm.slycpd%5ftt040601.pdf

Tarí, J. (2006). Improving service quality in a Spanish police service. *Total Quality Management & Business Excellence, 17(3),* 409-424. Retrieved May 18, 2007, from EBSCO Online Database Business Source Complete. http://search.ebscohost.com/login.aspx?direct=true&db=bth&AN=20219057&site=ehost-live

Yu-Yuan Hung, R. (2006). Business process management as competitive advantage: A review and empirical study. *Total Quality Management & Business Excellence, 17(1),* 21-40. Retrieved May 18, 2007, from EBSCO Online Database Business Source Complete. http://search.ebscohost.com/login.aspx?direct=true&db=bth&AN=19216085&site=ehost-live

Wang, X. S., Nayda, L & Dettinger, R. (2007). Infrastructure for a clinical-decision-intelligence system. *IBM Systems Journal, 46(1),* 151-169. Retrieved May 18, 2007, from EBSCO Online Database Business Source Complete. http://search.ebscohost.com/login.aspx?direct=true&db=bth&AN=24478489&site=ehost-live

Zeng, J., Anh, P., & Matsui, Y. (2013). Shop-floor communication and process management for quality performance: An empirical analysis of quality management. *Management Research Review, 36*(5), 454-477. Retrieved October 31, 2013, from EBSCO Online Database Business Source Complete. http://search.ebscohost.com/login.aspx?direct=true&db=bth&AN=88133586&site=ehost-live

Suggested Reading

Cleaveland, P. (2006). Building a better manufacturing future. *Product Design & Development, 61(8),* 8-9. Retrieved May 18, 2007, from EBSCO Online Database Business Source Complete. http://search.ebscohost.com/login.aspx?direct=true&db=bth&AN=21984500&site=ehost-live

Slater, R. (1991). *Integrated process management: A quality model.* New York: McGraw-Hill.

Yu-Yuan Hung, R. (2006). Business process management as competitive advantage: A review and empirical study. *Total Quality Management & Business Excellence, 17(1),* 21-40. Retrieved May 18, 2007, from EBSCO Online Database Business Source Complete. http://search.ebscohost.com/login.aspx?direct=true&db=bth&AN=19216085&site=ehost-live

Marlanda English, Ph. D.

Productivity

ABSTRACT

This article focuses on productivity. The relationship between inputs, outputs, and productivity levels is analyzed. This article provides an analysis of the main types of productivity measures, including average labor productivity and total factor productivity, and a discussion of how productivity is managed and promoted in organizations. The relationship between productivity and growth is explored. The main productivity measures, including productivity growth indexes, productivity level indexes, and subjective productivity measures, are described and the issues associated with productivity measurement are discussed.

OVERVIEW

Productivity is a measurement of economic efficiency that analyzes whether economic inputs are being turned into outputs in an effective manner. Output refers to products or services and input comprises materials, labor, capital, and energy. Economic analysts study productivity as a means of understanding the current economy. In addition, economic analysts engage in productivity projections as a means of predicting the future health and strength of the economy in aggregate and by sectors. Productivity is the foundation of the economy. Productivity slows inflation and contributes to the financing of health, education, and social welfare programs (Schreyer, 2005). The future growth of productivity is linked to the evolution of technology and business investment patterns. Productivity drives economic growth. For example, the U.S. experienced technology-driven productivity growth in the 1990s (Jorgenson, 2006).

Organizational performance is linked to "effectiveness, efficiency, quality, productivity, quality of work life, innovations, and profitability" (Kemppila & Lonnqvist, 2003, p.1). Productivity is linked to inputs and outputs while profitability is linked to inputs, outputs, and price. Organizations measure productivity as a means of assessing organizational strength and planning for increased productivity. Organizations prefer to measure total productivity whenever possible. The total measure of productivity is the overall output divided by the totality of inputs. Challenges to effectively measuring total productivity arise when inputs and outputs overlap or evolve quickly (Kemppila & Lonnqvist, 2003). Industries with difficult productivity levels and outputs include banking, insurance, computer production, and communication services. These industries are characterized by quickly evolving technologies (Schreyer, 2005).

The following sections provide an overview of the main types of productivity measures, including average labor productivity and total factor productivity, and a discussion of how productivity is managed and promoted in organizations. These sections serve as the foundation for later discussion of the relationship between productivity and growth. The main productivity measures, including productivity growth indexes, productivity level indexes, and subjective productivity measures, are described and the issues associated with productivity measurement are discussed.

Types of Productivity

There are numerous categories of productivity including labor productivity, firm or organizational productivity, and individual or employee productivity. Knowing that human capital is formed by investments to build individual or organizational skills that drive productivity growth (Hazan, Marston, & Rajah, 2013), economists tend to focus on measures and projections of labor productivity. Labor productivity refers to the ratio of output to inputs. Labor productivity reflects the efficiency with which labor is used in production rather than the effort per worker. Economists study the average labor productivity (ALP), which refers to the ratio of output to hours worked. The growth of average labor productivity has three sources: capital deepening, labor quality, and total factor productivity (TFP) growth.

- Capital deepening refers to the increase in capital services per hour worked.
- Labor quality refers to labor input per hour worked.
- Total factor productivity growth reflects the labor productivity growth not attributable to capital deepening or labor quality gains (Jorgenson, 2006).

Economists focus on labor productivity rather than more complex measures of complexity in large part due to the relative ease of gathering and computing labor productivity data (Diewert & Nakamora, 2005). Labor productivity is an important economic indicator because the health and demographics of a nation's labor force affect the nation's productivity and potential for economic growth. National economies rely on steady, and in most instances, growing labor supply and demand. Economic growth is often created by increased productivity from a larger labor supply. Individual and aggregate labor supply is determined by individual and aggregate appetite for leisure and consumption as well as wage rates. The public sector can manipulate wage rates and institute labor policies, controlling work related issues such as child labor and work visas, to raise or lower the labor supply. Labor supply policies are often developed to address the public problem of intractable poverty. Labor supply policies, such as welfare reform, job training, and the Earned Income Tax Credit (EITC), are developed to increase the labor supply, job skills, or wages of the poor (Bartik, 2001).

Productivity & Management

Productivity is one of the main factors influencing the success of organizations. Productivity influences economic growth and living standards. Increases in productivity levels and outputs strengthen profits and the economy in general. As a result of the importance of productivity levels to the public and private sectors, organizations actively manage their productivity. Productivity is managed in large part through ongoing quantitative productivity measurement. Organizational productivity is influenced by the following factors and variables: work habits, work climate, personnel feelings and attitudes, new skills, advancement, initiative, and physical work environment.

- Work habit considerations include absenteeism, tardiness, and safety rule violations.
- Work climate includes the number of grievances, employee turnover, and job satisfaction.
- Personnel feelings or attitudes include attitude changes, favorable reactions, and perceived changes in performance.
- New skills include decisions made, conflicts avoided, listening skills, reading speed, frequency of use of new skills.
- Advancement includes increases in job effectiveness, number or promotions and pay increases, and request for transfer.

- Initiative includes number of suggestion submitted implemented, and successful completion of projects.
- Physical work environment includes order and tidiness, ergonomics, walkways, noise, and lighting (Kemppila & Lonnqvist, 2003).

Productivity is managed and promoted in numerous ways in different firms, sectors, and industries. For example, in the private employee benefit plans sector, benefit plan administrators and managers promote productivity by educating their personnel about the cost of employee benefits. The International Foundation of Employee Benefit Plans, which encourages employers to engage in employee benefit plan education, believes that employee appreciation of and knowledge about benefits contributes to workplace productivity. To fully appreciate the employee benefits that they receive, employees must become familiar with their value. Similarly, an employer can provide the optimal level of pay mix and benefits to improve employee engagement (Davidson, 2013). Employers spend significant financial and human capital resources on benefit plan coverage and administration. For example, in 2003, private sector employee benefit costs averaged 42.3% of payroll. The employee benefit costs for small companies averaged 31.9% of payroll. The employee benefit costs averaged 44.9% for large companies. Few employees realize that, in 2003, employees received approximately $18,000 of employee benefits over and above their earned wages. Health care benefits generally make up approximately 35% of total employee benefit costs. Employers, in 2003, spent an average of $6,277 per employee on health care related benefits. Ultimately, employees who understand the true costs and expenses associated with employer-sponsored benefits plan may appreciate the financial commitment made by their employers and be more productive employees (Feldstein, 2005). In 2014, out of a total of 571 organizations both large and small from approximately twenty different industries surveyed by the International Foundation of Employee Benefits, employee benefit costs averaged 32 percent of payroll costs ("Benefit survey highlights," 2015).

Promoting Productivity

Economists, businesses, and governments recognize that productivity can be promoted and facilitated through technical change and increased trade. Technical change increases economic growth and productivity. As a result, businesses and governments actively promote technical change at the corporate and industry levels. Governments actively diffuse new technologies into society and industry in an effort to increase productivity in their nations and increase their level of international competition. Economists encourage the public and private sectors to cooperate and work together to promote technical change. Governments and firms work together to promote the transfer and diffusion of new technologies in an effort to counteract and address market failures that inhibit the invention, innovation, and diffusion of new technologies (Curlee & Goel, 1989).

In addition to technical change as a means of promoting productivity, nations increase trade as a means of increasing productivity. In the years following World War II, nations have been engaging in trade agreements as a means of increasing economic efficiency, productivity, and growth. Regional trade zones facilitate commercial expansion. Today, trade relationships between nations are also political relationships. Trade relationships, as expressed in customs unions, have become political-economic unions for the world's major trading powers including the United States, the European Union, Japan, China, and South Korea as well as developing nations.

APPLICATIONS

Productivity & Growth

Measuring Economic Growth

Policymakers and private sector investors recognize that productivity is a key indicator of economic growth. As a result, these stakeholders require significant information about productivity levels and projections (Schreyer, 2005). Nations around the world are working to increase their competitiveness in the global economy and marketplace. Economic competitiveness of nations is measured and tracked with tools such as the Growth Competitiveness Index and the Business Competitiveness Index. As global competition increases and influences economic growth, these indexes are being eclipsed by the Global Competitiveness Index, which tracks and measures both macroeconomic and microeconomic factors of a country's performance in the global marketplace. Competitiveness refers to the set of institutions, policies, and conditions that decide productivity levels.

There are also alternate measures such as that made possible by images of "the earth at night." Looking at such images, one sees that the brightness of visible lights is strongly related to both population density and income per capita. The observation that income per capita is one of the determinants of visible light suggests that visible light may have a use in helping to *measure* income. Some have suggested that lights data can augment or entirely replace data on gross domestic product (Henderson, Storeygard and Weil, 2011).

Increased productivity creates growth (Snowdon, 2006). Productivity is the key to the competitiveness of nations. Productivity growth can be input driven or total factor productivity driven. Growth in output per worker is related to advances in physical and human capital per worker, technology, and institutional change.

Extensive vs. Intensive Economic Growth

Economic growth, according to the World Bank, refers to a quantitative change or increase in development in a country's economy. The economic growth of a nation is determined by measuring the percent increase in its gross domestic product over the course of one year. Economic growth occurs in two distinct ways. Economic growth of a nation occurs when a nation grows extensively by using more physical, natural, or human resources or intensively by using resources more efficiently or productively. Economic growth is generally considered to be either extensive or intensive in nature.

- Extensive economic growth refers to growth scenarios in which an increase in the gross domestic product is absorbed by population increase without any increase in per capita income.
- Intensive economic growth refers to growth scenarios in which gross domestic product growth exceeds population growth, creating a sustained rise in living standards as measured by real income per capita (Snowdon, 2006). According to the World Bank's approach to promoting and facilitating the economic growth of nations, intensive economic growth of nations requires economic development.

Labor Productivity & Economic Growth

Economic growth is a focus of study and concern for economists, governments, and private sector development organizations. Economists are concerned with forecasting and measuring economic growth. Governments and private sector development organizations focus on forecasting and promoting economic growth of regions and nations. Economic growth is generally promoted through efforts to increase labor productivity. Labor productivity growth is crucial to the strength and growth of economies.

Labor productivity is promoted in four main ways (Vanhoudt & Onorante, 2001):

- Organizations expand the physical capital of workers through the purchase of better machines, tools, and infrastructure.
- Organizations improve the knowledge capital of the workforce through education and training.
- Organizations foster a new economy by introducing new technologies to improve the productivity of all workers.
- Organizations strengthen relations between public and private sectors to facilitate the working of the labor market and limit economic distortions caused by taxes and passive labor market policies.

Tracking Economic Growth

Economic growth is generally tracked and measured by national governments and non-governmental economic research organizations. For example, in the United States, the National Bureau of Economic Research (NBER), the United State's leading nonprofit economic research organization, determines and records dates for economic growth cycles and business cycles in the United States. The National Bureau of Economic Research published its first business cycle dates in 1929. The National Bureau of Economic Research, established in 1920, is a private, nonprofit, nonpartisan research entity committed to fostering a better understanding of how the economy operates. National Bureau of Economic Research associates, including 600 professors of economics and business, develop new statistical measures, estimate quantitative economic behavior models, assess the impacts of public policies on the U.S. economy, and project the impacts of alternate policy proposals. The National Bureau of Economic Research established itself as the predominant research organization on the topic of U.S. business cycles and economic growth tracking through the bureau's early research on the aggregate economy, business cycles, and long-term economic growth in the United States.

Theories of Economic Growth

The two main theories of the economic growth of nations, neoclassical growth theory and new growth theory, connect growth and productivity levels.

- Neoclassical growth theory, also referred to as the exogenous growth model, focuses on productivity growth. The neoclassical growth theory was the predominant economic growth theory from the nineteenth to mid-twentieth centuries. Exogenous growth refers to a change or variable that comes from outside the system. Technological progress and enhancement of a nation's human capital are the main factors influencing economic growth. Technology, increased human capital, savings, and capital accumulation are believed to promote technological development, more effective means of production, and economic growth (Brinkman, 2001).
- New growth theory, also referred to as the endogenous growth theory, began in the 1980s as a response to criticism of the neoclassical growth theory. Endogenous growth refers to a change or variable that comes from inside and is based on the idea that economic growth is created and sustained from within a country rather than through trade or other contact from outside the system. The new growth theory identifies the main endogenous factors leading to sustained growth of output per capita including research and design, education, and human capital (Park, 2006).

Issues

Measures of Productivity

Economists engage in growth accounting and productivity accounting to assess the strength of the economy and make economic projections. The main productivity measures include productivity growth indexes, productivity level indexes, and subjective productivity measures. Productivity measures include both objective and subjective efforts. Objective productivity measures are based on quantitative data gathered from operations. Subjective productivity measures are based on personnel beliefs, perceptions, or attitudes as described on questionnaires (Kemppila & Lonnqvist, 2003).

Productivity Indexes

There are four different types of productivity level indexes: Single factor productivity (SFP), labor productivity (LP), multifactor productivity (MFP), and total factor productivity (TFP).

- Single factor productivity refers to the measurement of output quantity in relation to a single input.
- Labor productivity refers to the measurement of output quantity in comparison to a specified quantity of labor, such as total amount of hours worked.
- Multifactor productivity refers to the measurement of input quantity which can be used to estimate total inputs.
- Total factor productivity refers to the measurement of total output quantity in relation to a measurement of the total input quantity.

Examples of productivity indexes include the Laspeyres productivity index and Paasche productivity index. These productivity indexes both control for price change. Productivity level index values are a useful tool as the values can be manipulated and compared as needed.

Productivity growth indexes measure changes in productivity over time. Standards of comparison, such as comparison over time, are pre-determined and explicit. As a result, productivity growth indexes invite and facilitate data comparison (Diewert & Nakamora, 2005). Labor productivity measures include the total number of hours worked divided by labor type and category. International development organizations, such as the Organization for Economic Co-operation and Development (OECD), gather and publish productivity data. The Organization for Economic Co-operation and Development keeps an online productivity database, referred to as a statistics portal, that includes the following information on economies worldwide: The growth of gross domestic product (GDP), labor productivity growth, and labor productivity levels (Schreyer, 2005)

When total productivity cannot be measured, partial productivity measures, physical productivity measures, or indirect productivity measurement are undertaken.

- Partial productivity ratios are figured by dividing total output by a given input factor.
- Physical productivity measures are figured by dividing a typical output by an essential input.

- Indirect productivity, also referred to as surrogate productivity, measures are used in situation where it is impossible to get the data needed for partial and physical productivity measures. Indirect productivity measures should be taken in situations that include high defect rates, machine defects, unused capacity, high material scrap, unnecessary transports, poor atmosphere, and long waiting times (Kemppila & Lonnqvist, 2003).

Published Reports

The U.S. Bureau of Labor Statistics (BLS) publishes productivity estimates for the business, non-farm business, and manufacturing sectors of the U.S. economy. The Bureau of Labor Statistics gathers its data from a monthly Current Population Survey (CPS). The U.S. Census Bureau conducts the Current Population Survey, which gathers information on the labor force, employment, and unemployment, for the Bureau of Labor Statistics. The CPS data sample includes 60,000 households from all U.S. states. The productivity index reports business sector productivity on a quarterly and annual basis. The Bureau of Labor Statistics productivity index does not measure the specific production factors such as the contribution of labor or capital and reflects the performance of the economy as a whole. This index only includes half of the industries in the business sector. The main industries reported are manufacturing, mining, wholesale and retail trade, and transportation. Industries with less reliable data sources, such as health care, legal, financial, insurance and real estate services, are not represented in the Bureau of Labor Statistics productivity index (Kedrova, 2004).

Subjective Productivity Measurement

Traditional productivity measurement is a quantitative endeavor in which inputs and outputs are reduced to quantifiable data. In addition to the quantitative measures, described above, subjective productivity measurement is emerging in the field of productivity measurement and assessment. Subjective productivity measurement refers to a process of obtaining productivity data by researching and examining the reports of pertinent stakeholders in relation to direct or indirect productivity. Subjective productivity measurement is based on the subjective assessments of organizational personnel. Assessment data is gathered through questionnaire and interview methods. At this point in the development of the subjective productivity measure, the method has been most often applied to work environment and productivity studies.

Critics of subjective productivity measurement argue that the method lacks validity, reliability and practical applications. Validity refers to the ability of an approach to successfully measure what it intends to measure. Reliability refers to the consistency of measurement data. Subjective productivity measures are influences by respondents' attitudes, values, and social phenomena. Supporters of subjective productivity measurement argue that the method operates as a managerial tool with which organizational management can gather unique insight about the connections between personnel and productivity. Subjective productivity measures may be best suited to the following situations characterized by a lack of output-related information. Examples of ideal subjective productivity measurements include the following: Output is generated after a long time delay; large variations in the quality of input or output; large variations in the quantity of input or output; no tradition of productivity measuring operations; no indirect factors that could relatively easily be measured (Kemppila & Lonnqvist, 2003).

CONCLUSION

In the final analysis, productivity is considered by economists to be one of the main factors in maintaining and promoting economic growth. Economists focus on labor productivity measures as the chief productivity indicator in large part because of the availability of data. In the United States, the Bureau of Labor Statistics and the U.S. Census gather monthly wage and labor data. The importance of productivity as an engine for growth is illustrated by the efforts of international development organizations, such as the Organization for Economic Co-operation and Development and the World Bank, to increase productivity levels in nations worldwide.

Bibliography

Bartik, T. (2001). Fighting poverty with labor demand policies. *W.E. Upjohn Institute for Employment Research.* Retrieved August 13, 2007, from http://www.upjohninst.org/publications/newsletter/tjb%5f701.pdf

Benefit survey highlights. (2015). *Benefits Magazine, 52*(1), 15. Retrieved December 3, 2015 from

EBSCO Online Database Business Source Premier. http://search.ebscohost.com/login.aspx?direct=true&db=buh&AN=99997754&site=bsi-live

Brinkman, R. (2001). The new growth theories: A cultural and social addendum. *The International Journal of Social Economics, 28,* 506–526.

Curlee, T. & Goel, R. (1989). The transfer and diffusion of new technologies: A review of the economics literature. A U.S. Department of Energy Technical Report. Retrieved October 25, 2007, from http://www.osti.gov/bridge/product.biblio.jsp?osti%5fid=814262

Davidson, Jenny. (2013). Jenny Davidson: Proving ROI on reward and benefits spend. *Employee Benefits, 11.* Retrieved November 21, 2013, from EBSCO Online Database Business Source Complete. http://search.ebscohost.com/login.aspx?direct=true&db=bth&AN=90170271&site=ehost-live

Diewert, E. & Nakamora, A. (2005). Concepts and measures of productivity: An introduction. In Lipsey and Nakamura (Eds.), *Services industries and the knowledge based economy.* Calgary: University of Calgary Press.

Feldstein, M. (2005). Rethinking social insurance. *American Economic Review, 95,* 1–24. Retrieved October 25, 2007, from EBSCO Online Database Business Source Complete. http://search.ebscohost.com/login.aspx?direct=true&db=bth&AN=17018326&site=ehost-live

Hazan, E., Marston, N., & Rajah, T. (2013). Innovation, capital, and productivity growth. *McKinsey Quarterly,* 98–99. Retrieved November 21, 2013, from EBSCO Online Database Business Source Complete. http://search.ebscohost.com/login.aspx?direct=true&db=bth&AN=91665816&site=ehost-live

Henderson, V., Storeygard, A., & Weil, D. (2011). A bright idea for measuring economic growth. *American Economic Review, 101,* 194–199. Retrieved November 19, 2013, from EBSCO Online Database Business Source Complete.http://search.ebscohost.com/login.aspx?direct=true&db=bth&AN=60940200&site=ehost-live

Jorgenson, D., Ho, M. Stiroh, K. (2006). Potential growth of the U.S. economy: Will the productivity resurgence continue? *Business Economics, 41,* 7–17.

Kedrova, J. (2004). Measuring productivity. Federal Reserve Bank of Dallas. Retrieved October 25, 2007, from http://www.dallasfed.org/eyi/free/0406product.html

Kemppila, S. & Lonnqvist, A. (2003). Subjective productivity measurement. *Journal of American Academy of Business, 2,* 531–538.

Measuring state and local government productivity. (1988). *U.S. Department of Labor.* Retrieved October 25, 2007, from http://www.bls.gov/lpc/iprprody.pdf

Park, C. (2006). The theory of economic growth: A "classical" perspective. *Science and Society, 70,* 558–562.

Schreyer, P. (2005). Measuring productivity. *Conference on Next Steps for the Japanese SNA.* Retrieved October 25, 2007, from http://www.esri.go.jp/jp/workshop/050325/050325paper06.pdf

Snowdon, B. (2006). The enduring elixir of economic growth. *World Economics, 7,* 73–130. Retrieved October 25, 2007, from EBSCO Online Database Business Source Complete. http://search.ebscohost.com/login.aspx?direct=true&db=bth&AN=20697032&site=ehost-live

Vanhoudt, P. & Onorante, L. (2001). Measuring economic growth and the new economy. *EIB Papers.* Retrieved October 25, 2007, from http://eib.eu.int/Attachments/efs/eibpapers/y01n1v6/y01n1a03.pdf

SUGGESTED READING

Ahmed, E. (2006). Is Malaysia's manufacturing productivity growth input driven? *Journal of American Academy of Business, Cambridge, 9,* 223–229. Retrieved October 25, 2007, from EBSCO Online Database Business Source Premier. http://search.ebscohost.com/login.aspx?direct=true&db=buh&AN=22995054&site=ehost-live

Ataay, A. (2006). Information technology business value: Effects of IT usage on labor productivity. *Journal of American Academy of Business, Cambridge, 9,* 230–237. Retrieved October 25, 2007, from EBSCO Online Database Business Source Premier. http://search.ebscohost.com/login.aspx?direct=true&db=buh&AN=21708027&site=ehost-live

Buchanan, L. (2015). The psychology of productivity. *Inc, 37*(2), 50–103. Retrieved December 3, 2015 from EBSCO Online Database Business Source Premier. http://search.ebscohost.com/login.aspx?direct=true&db=buh&AN=101581402&site=bsi-live

Dearden, L., Reed, H., & Van Reenen, J. (2006). The impact of training on productivity and wages: Evidence from British panel data. *Oxford Bulletin of Economics & Statistics, 68*, 397–421. Retrieved October 25, 2007, from EBSCO Online Database Business Source Premier. http://search.ebscohost.com/login.aspx?direct=true&db=buh&AN=22995055&site=ehost-live

Simone I. Flynn, Ph.D.

PROJECT MANAGEMENT

ABSTRACT

Project management is the process of planning, monitoring, and controlling a unique set of tasks that have a discrete beginning, end, and outcome. The project management process is performed within the three constraints of time, costs, and scope. The goal of project management is to produce a technically acceptable product that is both on-time and within budget. To do this, project management attempts to reduce the risks associated with the project and maximize the benefits, including profit and marketability. A number of tools and techniques are available to help the project manager monitor and control projects.

OVERVIEW

A project is a unique, discrete set of tasks with a defined beginning, end, and outcome. This may be as simple as completing a paper for class or as complex as designing, developing, and testing a new destroyer for the Navy. No project is accomplished in a vacuum, however. Each task must be accomplished under the three constraints of time (e.g., the paper is due on Friday; the first destroyer must be operational and in the fleet ten years from the start of the contract), cost (e.g., research for the paper must be done in the local library rather than paying to download articles from professional sites; the destroyer must be built within the budget set by Congress), and scope (e.g., the paper can only be 5,000 words long, so needs to be limited to a narrow topic even though the background information is very interesting; the destroyer needs to be built to the specifications set at the beginning of the project even though the customer or the project team think that additional features would make it better). Project management is a process that helps the project team accomplish its goals within the three constraints of time, cost, and scope. Using the principles and tools of project management, one can plan, organize, and manage the tasks to be done within the given constraints in order to accomplish the goal of the project.

Unfortunately, not every project is run using sound project management principles. Instead, many companies manage projects by doing the organizational equivalent of putting out brush fires, paying attention to whichever problem is most pressing at the time, while letting other problems grow only to be dealt with later at the expense of other project tasks. In a well-run project, on the other hand, the project manager — the project authority for planning, coordinating, and managing the project — needs to be proactive rather than reactive, keeping a constant eye on all aspects of the project so that no one area is allowed to develop problems that could sabotage the overall project, and accomplishing the project goals.

Project management is essentially the art of project control, with the continuing goal of keeping the project on time and within budget. This is often the interactive process of keeping the project within technical scope (i.e., not adding work to the project outside that which was originally planned), within the budget negotiated for accomplishment of the project tasks, moving along according to the predetermined schedule, and balancing the risks associated with changes in any of these areas and how they affect the accomplishment of the overall goal of the project. To do these things, project management activities focus on three things: the project and its goals, the process of how these goals are met, and the performance of individuals and organizations to accomplish these goals. If a project is managed well, its goals can be accomplished on-time and within budget, not only giving the organization a profit in the short-term, but enhancing its reputation for good work at a reasonable cost; thereby enhancing its ability to continue to make a profit in the future.

APPLICATION

There are a number of tools available to help project managers manage their projects efficiently and effectively. Several project management software packages are available that help project managers crunch the required numbers associated with risk management and other project management activities. However, project management is not a task that can be completely automated; human experience and judgments are necessary.

To successfully manage a project, one must first understand the scope of the project (what needs to be done, what the end result should be and the limits placed on these elements by the schedule and budget). In many cases, technical specifications will have been provided by the customer. For the example of the research paper, this may be simple: The paper needs to be 4,900–5,100 words long, follow a specific broad outline, be on a given topic, and use at least three professional references cited in APA format. For the example of the destroyer, however, the task is more complicated. Although the customer undoubtedly will provide technical specifications for what they want the new ship to be able to do, such specifications are long and complex, and need to be distilled and synthesized so that they can be tracked for project management purposes. One way to do this is through the use of a work breakdown structure (WBS). A good WBS provides a solid foundation for performing the tasks of project management on a complex project. By developing a thorough WBS, project management can be better prepared to control the project proactively, rather constantly react in emergency mode to unforeseen problems.

At its most basic, a WBS is a list of all the tasks that need to be done to complete the project. This is written as a hierarchy, starting with general tasks and then breaking these general tasks into more specific steps that need to be taken. For the project of writing a paper, the general outline of the project might be to define the topic, collect data, write the paper, do quality control on the paper, and submit the paper. The initial step of defining the topic could further be broken down into substeps such as scanning the textbook and materials provided by the professor to narrow the topic into areas of interest, bounding the problem by doing preliminary research in the library or on the Internet to see what the components of the topic are, and developing an outline defining the sections of the paper that will be used both for data collection and for writing the paper itself. An example of a portion of a WBS for writing a paper is shown in Figure 1.

In addition to developing a WBS, for more complex projects it is often helpful to determine the critical path that defines which activities are critical to accomplishing the project in a timely manner. Critical path management (CPM) is a tool that helps project managers analyze the activities that need to be performed to accomplish the project and when each needs to be accomplished so that the rest of the project can proceed in a timely manner. This includes determining the order in which the tasks need to be accomplished, what tasks feed into them, and how long each task will take to accomplish. In the example of writing a paper, the critical path might include a target date for finishing the library research that allows sufficient time to synthesize the material before actually writing the paper. For example, a target date for finishing the first draft of the paper should be in place to leave sufficient time to do quality control on the paper, checking it for coherence and flow, grammar and spelling errors, and inclusion of all needed data. In the more complicated example of ship design and development, the development of the critical path would allow the project manager to determine that the training component could not be started until it was determined what tasks needed to be performed both in normal operations and in battle. An example of a portion of a critical path diagram for writing a paper is given in Figure 2. Note that there are two tasks that cannot be performed until the previous task is accomplished.

WBS Number	Task Description
1.0	Project initiation
1.1	Define topic
1.1.1	Scan textbook and other materials
1.1.2	Preliminary library research
1.1.3	Develop preliminary outline
1.2	Perform research
1.2.1	Gather library books on topic
1.2.2	Search professional database for articles

Figure 1: Work Breakdown Structure (WBS)

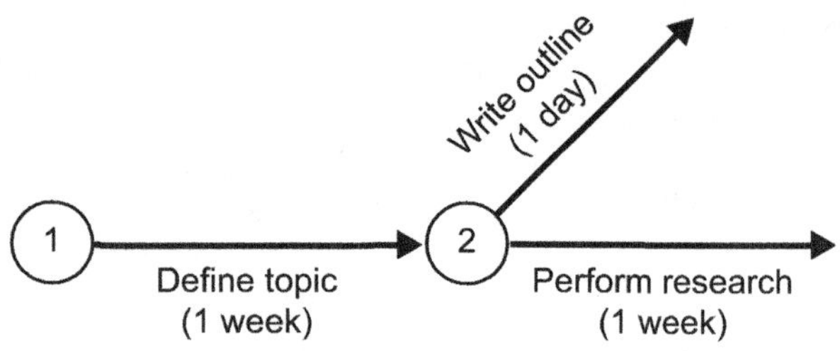

Figure 2: Critical Path Diagram

Another technique that may be of help in project management is resource loading, the process of examining the project to determine which resources are most critical to the success of the project, and proportioning them among the various activities. In the example of the paper, most students find that their most critical resource is time. Resource allocation for writing the paper might include determining how much time can be devoted to the paper from start to finish while still getting other necessary activities accomplished (e.g., eating, sleeping, doing homework for other classes), then allocating that limited time appropriately within the project to each of the activities. For the development of the ship, of course, resources are not limited to time, but also to personnel available to work on the project, materials necessary to perform the activities associated with the project (e.g., computer workstations, software licenses; steel, fiberglass, and other building materials), and the money to acquire both. So, for example, if the budget only allows for the hiring of ten programmers, it must be determined which programming tasks are the most critical and how much of the programmers' time should be allocated to each to best keep the project on time and within budget.

Another widely used project management tool is the program evaluation review technique (PERT). PERT is a variation on the critical path method, and estimates not only the expected length of time to complete each activity in the project, but also the shortest and longest times that each activity could take. This gives project managers a window for each activity and helps them better predict future impact on the project if schedule estimates are not met. This system also helps project managers determine the exact status of the project and predict any potential trouble areas that might negatively impact either the schedule or budget of the project. To do this, PERT divides the project into separate, detailed tasks on a schedule. These tasks are then put together as part of an integrated network that shows how each task impacts the others as well as the overall critical path for the system. Each task is also associated with the appropriate resources — including time, manpower, and capital — that it has been allocated. After the system has been put into place, PERT implements a reporting system so that project managers can compare actual performance and planned progress, and can continually check the status of the project.

Another popular scheduling tool for projects is the Gantt chart. On the vertical axis, the Gantt chart lists all the tasks to be accomplished for the project. On the horizontal axis, the chart lists the time for the accomplishment of these tasks, usually broken down into some pre-defined unit such as days, weeks, or months. Within the body of the chart, the various tasks to be performed are placed on the time line with an indication of the projected start and end dates for each activity. An example of a simplified Gantt chart for part of the paper writing task is shown in Figure 3.

When managing a project, cost and schedule often interact, affecting project performance. For example, budget constraints that prevent the organization from hiring additional programmers mean that there is less programming work that can be done on the project. Alternative solutions could include asking programmers to work overtime, hiring temporary or part-time workers for the short-term, or using only the current programmers and letting them finish their tasks as they can. Each alternative, however, has risks associated with it. The overtime option might require additional money or reduce the effectiveness of overworked human beings, impacting both budget and schedule. The temporary employee option would also require additional funds for personnel, but would minimize these by using the additional personnel on an as-needed status. The option of working only with the current employees without overtime could run the risk of missed deadlines while

Tasks	S	M	T	W	Th	F	S
	Week 1						
1.0 Define the topic	△	—	—	—	—	—	▽
1.1 Scan available material	△	▽					
1.2 Perform library research		△	—	▽			
1.3 Outline paper		△	—	—	—	—	▽

Figure 3: Simplified Gantt Chart

still requiring additional funds as the programmers work not longer hours in the day, but more hours in the project. Risk management is a generic term applied to considering such alternatives and balancing the impacts on the cost, schedule, and design in order to determine which alternative has the least impact on the overall performance of the contract.

The risks associated with not meeting the schedule or budget of a project can affect not only the organization in the short term, but also its long-term viability as well as the career of the project manager. Business risks are the risks that could damage the organization in either the short term or long term if the project fails. Short-term risks might include such things as incurring unexpected expenses on a fixed price contract or not earning an expected incentive if a delivery schedule is not met. In addition, not meeting deadlines or technical requirements could have long-term impact on the organization's reputation and ability to obtain future business. For the project manager, there are also the personal and career risks incurred if the project fails. For all involved, therefore, it is important that risks be honestly recognized before hand and plans put into place so that their negative impact can be minimized if a task or activity runs into trouble.

Some of the risks associated with a contract depend in part on the type of contract that is in place for the project. The two basic types of contracts are the fixed price contract and the cost-reimbursable contract. In the fixed price contract, all project costs are built into the contract and the contractor must pay for any costs incurred over and above the contract amount. This type of contract is generally used where the contract requirements are well-defined in advance and the associated costs can be predetermined. The cost-reimbursable contract, on the other hand, is typically used in situations where the costs associated with the project cannot be adequately and accurately estimated beforehand. In this type of contract, the contractor is reimbursed for costs allowable under the terms of the contract and, therefore, incurs less risk. Contract type is actually a continuum from contracts where the risk is incurred by the contractor (e.g., firm fixed price contracts, fixed price with redetermination contracts, and fixed price incentive contracts in decreasing order of risk) or on the customer (e.g., cost plus fixed fee, cost plus incentive fee, and time and material, in order of increased risk for the customer). Contracts with high risk for the contractor require better risk management.

There are two aspects to risk management. Risk analysis is a planning activity to determine the possibility of risk and ways to reduce its impact. As part of this process, the project manager and key personnel determine three things: (1) what factors could cause the project to fail, (2) what the consequences of such failure might be, and (2) how likely failure is to occur. Various formulas are available to then determine the comparative severity and importance of each risk. For example, an activity that is likely to go wrong but that has little impact on the overall completion of the project is probably less important than an activity that has a smaller chance of failing but that would prevent successful completion of the project. After such determinations are made, a plan can be developed and implemented to handle the possibility of failure at any one of these points.

It is not enough to know what to do if a task or activity on a project fails. Good risk management also requires risk control. This project management responsibility includes such activities as monitoring the project risks so that they can be caught earlier rather than later in the process so that the contingency plan can be put into effect as soon as possible. To maximize the effectiveness of the risk monitoring process, particularly on larger projects, also requires having a risk reporting structure in place so that those working closely on the at-risk activities can report problems to management in a timely manner.

There are a number of tools and techniques available for project risk management including software programs and risk calculation formulas. Computer simulations alone, however, are not adequate to predicting the impact of risk or for preventing it. Large projects typically build in periodic formal reviews held between both the contractor and the customer to jointly determine the status of the project and whether or not mid-course corrections are needed. Two major reviews that are often built into the schedule are the preliminary design review (PDR) and the critical design review (CDR). The PDR is conducted after the preliminary design is complete but before the detail design is begun. During the PDR, the contract describes any changes made to the original design along with the rationale for these changes. At PDR, the contractor may also provide a hands-on demonstration or proof-of-concept for the product.

The CDR is conducted before the design is released for manufacturing. Progressive or incremental CDRs may occur for subsystems of the project, followed by a system-level CDR to determine the completeness and feasibility of the design as a whole.

Bibliography

Hajek, V. G. (1984). *Management of engineering projects* (3rd ed). New York: McGraw-Hill Book Company.

Human, W. J., & Steyn, H. H. (2013). Establishing project management guidelines for successfully managing resettlement projects. *South African Journal of Business Management, 44*(3), 1-14. Retrieved November 25, 2013 from EBSCO Online Database Business Source Premier. http://search.ebscohost.com/login.aspx?direct=true&db=buh&AN=89665393

Kumar, P. P. (2005, Jul). Effective use of Gantt chart for managing large scale projects. *Cost Engineering, 47* (7), 14-21. Retrieved March 19, 2007, from EBSCO Online Database Business Source Complete. http://search.ebscohost.com/login.aspx?direct=true&db=bth&AN=17721066&site=ehost-live

LaBrosse, M. (2004). Project management in the real world. *Plant Engineering, 58* (11), 29-32. Retrieved March 19, 2007, from EBSCO Online Database Business Source Complete. http://search.ebscohost.com/login.aspx?direct=true&db=bth&AN=15089841&site=ehost-live

Lehman, Bill. (2007). Project risk management. *Mortgage Banking, 67* (5), 99-100. Retrieved March 19, 2007, from EBSCO Online Database Business Source Complete. http://search.ebscohost.com/login.aspx?direct=true&db=bth&AN=24083165&site=ehost-live

Linton, Jonathan. (2006). Managing the project. *Circuits Assembly,* 17 (6), 12-14. Retrieved March 19, 2007, from EBSCO Online Database Business Source Complete. http://search.ebscohost.com/login.aspx?direct=true&db=bth&AN=21059488&site=ehost-live

Parker, D., Charlton, J., Ribeiro, A., & Pathak, R. D. (2013). Integration of project-based management and change management intervention methodology. *International Journal of Productivity & Performance Management, 62*(5), 534-544. Retrieved November 25, 2013 from EBSCO Online Database Business Source Premier. http://search.ebscohost.com/login.aspx?direct=true&db=buh&AN=88053523

Ward, J., & Daniel, E. M. (2013). The role of project management offices (PMOs) in IS project success and management satisfaction. *Journal of Enterprise Information Management, 26*(3), 316-336. Retrieved November 25, 2013 from EBSCO Online Database Business Source Premier. http://search.ebscohost.com/login.aspx?direct=true&db=buh&AN=88176684

Suggested Reading

Besner, C., & Hobbs, B. (2012). An empirical identification of project management toolsets and a comparison among project types. *Project Management Journal, 43*(5), 24-46. Retrieved November 25, 2013 from EBSCO Online Database Business Source Premier. http://search.ebscohost.com/login.aspx?direct=true&db=buh&AN=80202137

Grant, K. P., Cashman, W. M. & Christensen, D. S. (2006). Delivering projects on time. *Research Technology Management, 49* (6), 52-58. Retrieved March 19, 2007, from EBSCO Online Database Business Source Complete. http://search.ebscohost.com/login.aspx?direct=true&db=bth&AN=23119319&site=ehost-live

Griffith, A. F. (2006). Scheduling practices and project success. *Cost Engineering, 48* (9), 24-30. Retrieved March 19, 2007, from EBSCO Online Database Business Source Complete. http://search.ebscohost.com/login.aspx?direct=true&db=bth&AN=22743467&site=ehost-live

Krane, H., Olsson, N. E., & Rolstadås, A. (2012). How project manager-project owner interaction can work within and influence project risk management. *Project Management Journal, 43*(2), 54-67. Retrieved November 25, 2013 from EBSCO Online Database Business Source Premier. http://search.ebscohost.com/login.aspx?direct=true&db=buh&AN=73320897

Madlin, N. (1986). Streamlining the PERT chart. *Management Review, 75* (9), 67-68. Retrieved March 19, 2007, from EBSCO Online Database Business Source Complete. http://search.ebscohost.com/login.aspx?direct=true&db=bth&AN=6026402&site=ehost-live

Spencer, G. R. & Lewis, R. M. (2006). Schedule analysis indices. *AACE International Transactions,* 4.1-4.5.

Retrieved March 19, 2007, from EBSCO Online Database Business Source Complete. http://search.ebscohost.com/login.aspx?direct=true&db=bth&AN=22646750&site=ehost-live

Uppal, K. B. (2004). Project management process and action plans. *AACE International Transactions*, 3.1-3.10. Retrieved March 19, 2007, from EBSCO Online Database Business Source Complete. http://search.ebscohost.com/login.aspx?direct=true&db=bth&AN=1.4705182&site=ehost-live

Ruth A. Wienclaw, Ph.D

Resource Planning

ABSTRACT

This article examines resource-planning practices that are used to assure the proper timing and availability of resources. The concepts of optimal and maximum operational velocity are explained and the role of resource planning in the maintenance of operational velocity is examined. The importance of capacity planning and inventory management is reviewed along with methods that many organizations use to manage safety stock in order to smooth production flow. How resource planning practices and methods can be applied to service organizations is also examined.

OVERVIEW

Business Strategy

The business goals of a company as well as the business goals of the channels in which it is a member, dictate overall corporate strategy. The grand strategy, or master strategy, is a result of an analysis of the environment in which the company operates. The grand strategy is the mechanism by which the separate entities within the firm develop their strategies and operational plans and determine their resource requirements. When a company implements its grand strategy it then has a path to follow and has set out long-term goals and a means to measure to what extent those goals have been achieved.

After the grand strategy has been developed and goals and measurement process of goal achievement have been established, then functional strategies can be developed. Each department in the company develops its functional strategy that guides activities in the department that are all designed to help the company achieve its overall strategy. Functional strategies must be consistent with the grand strategy as well as consistent with one another. The resource planning process assures that the acquisition of resources is planned in a manner that facilities efficient work flow across functions.

Goals

Many departments share goals such as making a product available when needed, at the location it is needed and in the quantity it is needed. When the functional strategies of the manufacturing, logistics, sales, and marketing departments are aligned to meet the overall goals of the company then the company is better able to meet customer service demands. These departments and their functional strategies also need to be integrated into the company's supply chain, which includes firms that provide it goods and services as well as its customers to which it supplies goods and services. Thus resource planning goes beyond the activities inside the company and resource needs are highly dependent on sources outside the company (Novack, Dunn & Young, 1993).

Business Processes

Strategies are accomplished through the execution of business processes. Each business process is a collection of activities that combine different inputs to create an output that is of value to the customer. Meeting customer expectations in a timely manner can be challenging if business processes are widely dispersed and inconsistent. Consistent core business processes and data representation are essential to allowing decision makers to respond quickly to the changing market (Singh, 2012).

Businesses generally engage in three main processes: Acquiring and paying for resources, converting resources into goods/services, and acquiring customers, delivering goods and services, and collecting revenues (Klamm & Weidenmier, 2004). Successful implementation of strategies requires that business processes be properly timed and appropriate resources be available when and where they are needed. Both the timing and availability of resources are accomplished through well-managed resource planning.

Resource Planning

One of the major objectives of resource planning is for a business to reach and maintain optimal operational velocity. At this point, the business has sufficient speed in delivering products or services to market, while simultaneously meeting all customer expectations in a timely manner, and obtaining a positive revenue stream from each activity. If addressed appropriately, maximization of operational velocity will drive the enterprise to achieve greater market share and revenue as operational efficiencies are instituted (Stephenson & Sage, 2007). Achieving optimal operations velocity requires that the appropriate resources be in the right place at the right time. This requires advanced planning for the procurement of production materials, production capacity including facilities and equipment, and the workforce necessary for production, operations, distribution and sales.

Birshan, Engel, and Sibony (2013) provide some novel strategies for effective resource planning, including creating a corporate-resources map, benchmarking "resource inertia," and reframing budget meetings as resource reallocation sessions, to name three.

APPLICATIONS

Managing Capacity & Resources in a Changing World

In high-tech industries that are highly competitive, a company's ability to manage and adjust capacity as needed is critical for the long-term success of the company. Demand for products can change rapidly and there are many factors that can impact demand. Some companies and products have demand shifts based on seasons while others may be more tied to long-term economic conditions and still others may be influenced by short term economic shifts.

In addition, product life cycles can be very short for some products which means that companies that produce these products are planning for resources at least one if not several models ahead in the future. In such cases where life cycles are short it is critical that a manufacturer not hold excessive inventory of parts or supplies that may not be usable in the next iteration of the product. On the other hand, if parts or supplies can be used in several iterations in the future, it may be prudent to buy parts when demand for them is low and prices are not rapidly rising.

It is also important to carefully plan the introduction of product innovations. If a company introduces an innovation too soon then they may find that customers are not ready for the innovation, which could impact sales. However, if an innovation is introduced too late and the product line lags behind competitors in functionality, then market share could be lost and sales decline.

So-called *reverse innovation*, in which an innovative product is introduced and adopted first in the developing world before migrating into mature markets, is gaining attention. Pioneered by such companies as GE, Procter & Gamble, and Levi's, the strategy and its successes are described by Natalie Zmuda of *Advertising Age* (2011).

The Semiconductor Industry

The semiconductor industry faces many capacity and resources management issues that other industries do not. Although profit margins on semiconductor products can be attractive the initial costs of introducing a new product can be very high. The majority of this cost is manufacturing equipment and plants which in the semiconductor can be in the billions of dollars. This means that a semiconductor manufacturer needs to have high enough sales levels to justify investing in new plants. Added to the cost are also recent trends of relatively short life cycles for semiconductor products which mean frequent retooling of plants and equipment.

The Biotech Industry

The biotech industry faces similar challenges to that of the semiconductor industry. Although profit margins are favorable, developing manufacturing capacity is expensive with new facilities costing in the hundreds of millions of dollars. Any company in the biotech field must also have sufficient market share and a healthy customer base in order to sustain sales in volume and over time that allows for a return on investment for new manufacturing technology. Many biotech manufacturers and the companies that use their products have developed long-term supplier and purchaser agreements which helps the manufacturer lock in the long term customer and have a steady cash stream. Such agreements can also help the customer of the biotech manufacturer by assuring supply and locking in a favorable price (Wu, Erkoc & Karabuk, 2005).

Resource Planning Optimization Techniques

Supply chain and resource planning optimization techniques are generally used to improve resource planning and maintain a desired level of profitability (Sourirajan, Ozsen & Uzsoy, 2007). As supply chain modeling methods have improved over time a more accurate forecast the need for raw materials, parts, and supplies. Modern supply chain simulation models can account for substitution of parts, time lags in the delivery of supplies or other delays in manufacturing as well as a wide range other resource planning issues (Gresh, Connors, Fasano & Wittrock, 2007).

Safety Stocks

When handling the problem of safety stocks sizing and positioning, safety stocks kept to face demand uncertainty are often positioned on pull managed resources, or the resources that are used to produce items. Positioning for safety stocks on push managed items (those items that are produced and sold by a company) can be expensive for a number of reasons. If parts are customized with company logos or brand names cost will certainly be higher. If parts are perishable or fragile in some way breakage or other damage to the parts can easily occur. If demand for a part suddenly goes up and forecast for an additional supply of the same part is not modified upward safety stock could be depleted and production jobs may be delayed.

When order due dates equal the length of time of the manufacturing pipeline, there is no impact on the lower levels of BOMs, since the time allotted for the replenishment orders makes it possible to manufacture the items unavailable because of resource shortages. As a consequence, safety stock sizing and management are two issues that need to be solved together during the resource planning process. In particular, the best compromise between two alternative scenarios is to be found. On the one hand, replenishment of order due dates can be set equal to the end item lead times. This makes it possible to keep a reduced amount of safety stocks at the lower levels of BOMs. On the other hand, replenishment order due dates can be set equal to the overall length of the pipeline (Caridi & Cigolini, 2002).

The Supply Chain Approach

The supply chain approach to inventory and parts management is designed to reduce the amount of parts inventory and thus to rely on parts suppliers to have a predictable delivery time. In 1995 in the planning and procurement organizations of the Hewlett-Packard Colorado Springs Division, a supply chain project was launched. The objectives of this resource planning effort were to provide planning and procurement organizations with a methodology for setting the best possible resource planning. This was all based on a cost benefit analysis tied to being able to accurately predict the amount of material to have on hand to meet production needs. The success of the system also relied on the ability of suppliers to meet previously agreed upon delivery schedules for parts and materials.

The fundamental challenge was to be able to determine a relatively accurate amount of various products to meet forecasted customer demand. Demand can certainly fluctuate so the supply chain system needed to have a highly predictable turnaround time on parts orders to meet production schedules that could change very quickly. So any company that is going to attempt to keep inventories of parts as low as a possible will always be at some degree of risk that sales forecast will be predicable and that suppliers can meet expected delivery schedules and if necessary accelerate those schedules to meet fluctuations in demand.

Front-end Overdrive

Manufacturing planners have often attempted to hedge their risk of fluctuating demand and the need for parts to meet production schedules by adding a near-term overdrive effort to their production planning. This was usually done by increasing material requirements above the normally expected level of orders. Thus planners create what they feel is an adequate buffer of materials on hand at a production facility. This was a way to beat the existing systems without making permanent modifications to the normal safety stock system.

Although artificially increasing demand may serve short-term purposes the benefits of the supply chain and the previously calculated and determined deliver time on various parts is not utilized and parts inventories may become excessive and impact the cash flow of the company. Production planners work diligently to meet schedules and often without serious regard to the impact of excessive parts on the long-term profitability of a company. In addition, there is a strong possibility that the parts mix on hand may not take into to account those parts that have longer lead times and when the safety stock system is circumvented the imbalance of parts may cause production delays in the future.

The statistical methods utilized by purchasing departments to develop safety stock calculations are designed to make sure that parts are available for completed products. In many situations there are different limits on order sizes for different suppliers. These limits may be set by suppliers of by the purchasing department in the buying organization. IN some cases there are minimum order quantities of the same part and in other cases there are minimum dollars amounts per order. When the production department is inflating projections for demand and parts orders become disorganized it can cause problems in procurement as well as driving parts costs up (Kruger, 1997).

Issues

Resource Planning in Service Industries

IBM and other service organization planners use a Resource Capacity Planning (RCP) Optimizer to provide managers with a adaptable framework to help model what has become known as the human resource supply chain. This type of system can help forecast and schedule human resources in a service environment as well as do double duty as a part of the invoicing process by creating bills of material (BOMs) for customers to whom which services are provided.

This is similar to the process of invoicing customers for whom which a hard product such as a computer or special manufacturing machine was built. In the manufacturing case the invoice would include design, parts, materials, custom programming, testing, and perhaps installation. In a services environment were specialized human skills are provided on a production, as needed, or other special contracting situation the BOM covers the quantity of skilled personnel and their hours and other expenses required to meet the terms of the contract.

In general, a RCP is deployed in a service organization to address several types of problems including dealing with where there are resource or talent gaps. The RCP can also help to reassign staff when there is an excess of specific types of talents o a project or perhaps even a particular city or region. The primary goal is to make sure that human resources are deployed in a manner that adequately covers contractual obligations across clients or across projects based on expected demand.

Human Resource Considerations

Human resource capacity planners in service organizations rely on the RCP to make decisions on how to address talent shortages, deal with the shortages and decide what to do with personnel that have talent and are abundant in the organization (or at least not in short supply). When there is excess supply of physical goods and materials the added cost, until they are eventually used, is for facility space. However, when there is an excess of human resources that cannot be immediately utilized and placed on a project for which there is billable time, the service organization still faces the cost of salary and benefits, and in some cases, if personnel are not at a customer's site, the company may need to also provide office space and computer resources. This is often much higher than the overhead of storing physical materials. Thus an excess in a service organization is far more costly than an excess of materials in a manufacturing company.

Another major difference between managing material resources and human talent is that in the case of material resources there is a very limited range of what most materials can be used for especially if they are fabricated-to-order parts. In the case of human talent it is entirely possible and very likely that employees of a service organization can have more than none talent. When dealing with information technology, for example, many professionals have built a career by moving through the ranks and the various levels of their profession gaining skills and experience as they go through their career. Thus depending on the parameters and complexity of a contract some personnel may be able to fill more than one talent requirement. This means that the RCP needs to be able to take into account the various talents that all staff have as well as their proficiency level in their different areas of expertise.

The Resource Action Problem

In addition to understanding the need for specific talents and who in a service company can perform those talents well, it is also necessary to be able to assign talent to the highest priority project. The challenge at this phase is to have a matrix that can accurately depict what the highest priority project is.

Due dates on projects is certainly one way to determine which projects get which talent first. However, it is not just due dates that count. The importance of performing a certain function during any particular phase of a project may set the stage for the rest of the project plan to be smoothly executed. If a task or module of work takes only two days but four hundred additional days of human time is required to finish the project, and those days cannot proceed until a module or task is done, then the importance of a talent to that project may outweigh considerations on other projects (Gresh, Connors, Fasano & Wittrock, 2007).

CONCLUSION

The business goals of a company as well as the business goals of the channels in which it is a member, dictate overall corporate strategy. The grand strategy, or master strategy, is a result of an analysis of the environment in which the company operates. The grand strategy is the mechanism by which the separate entities within the firm develop their strategies and operational plans and determine their resources requirements.

Each of the functional entities within the firm, and in many manufacturing industries within the supply, must develop and then integrate their strategies in a coordinated manner in order to combine their efforts to accomplish the grand strategy. Each of the departments' strategy must be consistent with the overall grand strategy and complement each other to achieve timely task completion and ultimately higher levels of customer service and satisfaction.

One of the major objectives of resource planning is for a business to reach and maintain optimal operational velocity. At this point, the business has sufficient speed in delivering products or services to market, while simultaneously meeting all customer expectations in a timely manner, and obtaining a positive revenue stream from each activity. If addressed appropriately, maximization of operational velocity will drive the enterprise to achieve greater market share and revenue as operational efficiencies are instituted.

Supply chain and resource planning optimization techniques have long been used to model the behavior of manufacturing supply chains in order to allow better resource planning and improve profitability and efficiency (Sourirajan, Ozsen & Uzsoy, 2007). If a model does not actually depict the reality in which the organization works then the flow of resources will not be managed well enough to optimize a company's performance.

Service industries also face complex resource planning challenges and issues. However, these challenges and issues require a different mindset than required for manufacturing physical objects regardless of how complex that object may be. The matrix of human talent is sometimes difficult to inventory and talents, although they can be identified, may not be equal from employee to the next. Thus service organizations not only need to know what their employees can do they need to have an understanding of well they can actually perform a job.

Bibliography

Birshan, M., Engel, M., & Sibony, O. (2013). Avoiding the quicksand: Ten techniques for more agile corporate resource allocation. *McKinsey Quarterly*, (4), 60-63. Retrieved November 13, 2013, from EBSCO Online Database Academic Search Complete. http://search.ebscohost.com/login.aspx?direct=true&db=bth&AN=91665810&site=ehost-live

Caridi, M., & Cigolini, R. (2002). Managing safety and strategic stocks to improve materials requirements planning performance. *Proceedings of the Institution of Mechanical Engineers — Part B — Engineering Manufacture, 216*(7), 1061-1065. Retrieved November 27, 2007, from EBSCO Online Database Academic Search Premier. http://search.ebscohost.com/login.aspx?direct=true&db=aph&AN=7122849&site=ehost-live

Gresh, D., Connors, D., Fasano, J., & Wittrock, R. (2007). Applying supply chain optimization techniques to workforce planning problems. *IBM Journal of Research & Development, 51*(3/4), 251-261. Retrieved November 27, 2007, from EBSCO Online Database Academic Search Premier. http://search.ebscohost.com/login.aspx?direct=true&db=aph&AN=25732942&site=ehost-live

Klamm, B., & Weidenmier, M. (2004). Linking business processes and transaction cycles. *Journal of Information Systems, 18*(2), 113-125. Retrieved November 21, 2007, from EBSCO Online Database Academic Search Premier. http://search.ebscohost.com/login.aspx?direct=true&db=aph&AN=15672372&site=ehost-live

Kruger, G. (1997). The supply chain approach to planning and procurement management. *Hewlett-Packard Journal, 48*(1), 28. Retrieved November 27, 2007, from EBSCO Online Database Academic Search Premier. http://search.ebscohost.com/login.aspx?direct=true&db=aph&AN=9703095908&site=ehost-live

Novack, R., Dunn, S., & Young, R. (1993). Logistics optimizing and operational plans and systems and their role in the achievement of corporate goals. *Transportation Journal, 32*(4), 29-40. Retrieved November 21, 2007, from EBSCO Online Database Academic Search Premier. http://search.ebscohost.com/login.aspx?direct=true&db=aph&AN=9401101066&site=ehost-live

Singh, P. (2012). Management of business processes can help an organization achieve competitive advantage. *International Management Review, 8* (2), 19-26. Retrieved November 13, 2013, from EBSCO Online Database Academic Search Complete. http://search.ebscohost.com/login.aspx?direct=true&db=bth&AN=82157928&site=ehost-live

Sourirajan, K., Ozsen, L., & Uzsoy, R. (2007). A single-product network design model with lead time and safety stock considerations. *IIE Transactions, 39*(5), 411-424. Retrieved November 22, 2007, from EBSCO Online Database Academic Search Premier. http://search.ebscohost.com/login.aspx?direct=true&db=aph&AN=24196057&site=ehost-live

Stephenson, S., & Sage, A. (2007). Architecting for enterprise resource planning. *Information Knowledge Systems Management, 6*(1/2), 81-121. Retrieved November 21, 2007, from EBSCO Online Database Academic Search Premier. http://search.ebscohost.com/login.aspx?direct=true&db=aph&AN=25215504&site=ehost-live

Wu, S., Erkoc, M., & Karabuk, S. (2005). Managing capacity in the high-tech industry: A review of literature. *Engineering Economist, 50*(2), 125-158. Retrieved November 27, 2007, from EBSCO Online Database Academic Search Premier. http://search.ebscohost.com/login.aspx?direct=true&db=aph&AN=17552396&site=ehost-live

Zmuda, N. (2011). P&G, Levi's, GE innovate by thinking in reverse. *Advertising Age, 82* (24), 2-3. Retrieved November 13, 2013, from EBSCO Online Database Academic Search Complete. http://search.ebscohost.com/login.aspx?direct=true&db=bth&AN=62009231&site=ehost-live

Suggested Reading

Cecil, J., Davidson, S., & Muthaiyan, A. (2006). A distributed internet-based framework for manufacturing planning. *International Journal of Advanced Manufacturing Technology, 27*(5/6), 619-624. Retrieved November 26, 2007, from EBSCO Online Database Academic Search Premier. http://search.ebscohost.com/login.aspx?direct=true&db=aph&AN=18995348&site=ehost-live

Chandler Jr., A. (1998). Corporate strategy and structure: Some current considerations. *Society, 35*(2), 347-350. Retrieved November 16, 2007, from EBSCO Online Database Academic Search Premier. http://search.ebscohost.com/login.aspx?direct=true&db=aph&AN=34434&site=ehost-live

Chiu, S., Shih, C., & Chiu, Y. (2007). A revised cost-benefit algorithm for solving the expediting completion time of end product problem with defective materials in the product structure diagram. *Proceedings of the Institution of Mechanical Engineers — Part B — Engineering Manufacture, 221*(3), 489-497. Retrieved November 22, 2007, from EBSCO Online Database Academic Search Premier. http://search.ebscohost.com/login.aspx?direct=true&db=aph&AN=25208932&site=ehost-live

Heinzelbecker, K., & Taylor, A. (2005). Collective forethought: A new paradigm in strategy. *Futures Research Quarterly, 21*(3), 81-96. Retrieved November 23, 2007, from EBSCO Online Database Academic Search Premier. http://search.ebscohost.com/login.aspx?direct=true&db=aph&AN=19865453&site=ehost-live

Hultqvist, D., & Olsson, L. (2006). Optimization of raw material procurement at pulp or paper mills — the influence of weather-related risks. *International Journal of Systems Science, 37(4), 253-269. Retrieved November 22, 2007, from EBSCO Online Database Academic Search Premier. http://search.ebscohost.com/login.aspx?direct=true&db=aph&AN=20213357&site=ehost-live*

Klemperer, J., Sundararajan, S., & Zimmers Jr., E. (2003). Careful with that warehouse. *Industrial Engineer: IE, 35*(9), 40. Retrieved November 27, 2007, from EBSCO Online Database Academic Search Premier. http://search.ebscohost.com/login.aspx?direct=true&db=aph&AN=10769813&site=ehost-live

Lee, K., & Ball, R. (2003). Achieving sustainable corporate competitiveness. *Greener Management International,* (44), 89-104. Retrieved November 21, 2007, from EBSCO Online Database Academic Search Premier. http://search.ebscohost.com/login.aspx?direct=true&db=aph&AN=15408930&site=ehost-live

Pai, P., Chang, P., Wang, S., & Lin, K. (2004). A fuzzy logic-based approach in capacity-planning problems. *International Journal of Advanced Manufacturing Technology, 23*(11/12), 806-811. Retrieved November 27, 2007, from EBSCO Online Database Academic Search Premier. http://search.ebscohost.com/login.aspx?direct=true&db=aph&AN=16717856&site=ehost-live

Tserng, H., Yin, S., & Li, S. (2006). Developing a resource supply chain planning system for construction projects. *Journal of Construction Engineering & Management, 132*(4), 393-407. Retrieved November 26, 2007, from EBSCO Online Database Academic Search Premier. http://search.ebscohost.com/login.aspx?direct=true&db=aph&AN=20080919&site=ehost-live

Yi, G., Kim, Y., & Lee, E. (2007). Optimal design of multisite batch-storage network under scenario-based demand uncertainty. *Chemical Engineering Communications, 194*(10), 1297-1327. Retrieved November 22, 2007, from EBSCO Online Database Academic Search Premier. http://search.ebscohost.com/login.aspx?direct=true&db=aph&AN=25508406&site=ehost-live

Michael Erbschloe, M. A.

S

Scenario Planning

ABSTRACT

Scenario planning is a way to help organizations think through their assumptions and become better prepared to flexibly respond to possible future conditions. A scenario is a description of a possible future that identifies possible significant events that may happen in the future, major parties involved in that future, and the assumed motivations of those parties. The intuitive approach to scenario planning is based on the assumption that scenarios are not forecasts about the future, but possible alternative pictures of how organizational environments may develop. The formal style is more closely aligned with forecasting and uses computer modeling in an attempt to attach probabilities to the alternative scenarios. Although some organizations find scenario planning to be a useful tool, it is not without its detractors. However, if one is careful to avoid the various potential process and content pitfalls that can affect the quality of the scenario, this approach to strategic planning can be very useful in helping an organization transcend its blind spots and give it the tools to be flexible in responding to future events.

OVERVIEW

The need for an alternative plan has become almost axiomatic in our constantly changing society. Alternative plans may be as simple as planning on staying close to home for vacation if the price of a barrel of oil continues to rise or as complex as planning how to operate in the global market if oil prices continue to rise. The need for planning against various contingencies has even infiltrated our entertainment media as exemplified by the thought bubble above the cartoon character falling over the cliff saying: "Time for Plan B."

One approach to future planning for business is called scenario planning. In this context, a scenario is a description of a possible future that identifies some significant events, the major parties involved in that future, and the assumed motivations of those parties for their actions in that future. Scenario planning is an approach to strategic planning in which a limited number of possible scenarios are drawn to describe possible alternative futures that may affect the functioning of the organization. Scenario planning helps the organization to better understand the nature and impact of forces driving its future. This process emphasizes the open exchange of knowledge from all involved parties and a mutual understanding of issues that are central to the healthy functioning of the organization. Scenario planning has been an important tool for military planning for centuries and more recently has been used in making strategic business decisions. The use of scenario planning can help organizations make decisions based on likely futures such as whether to invest in more brick-and-mortar retail locations or to move more of their retail selling online instead.

Schools of Scenario Planning Thought

There are two general schools of thought on how best to approach scenario planning.

Intuitive Approach

The intuitive approach, taken by such companies as Shell Oil, is based on the assumption that scenarios are not forecasts about the future. Rather, this approach is based on the assumption that the future is uncertain and unknowable. Scenarios developed using the intuitive approach are possible alternative pictures of how the organization's environment may develop. For example, Shell Oil's approach to scenario development is an iterative process comprising five activities. The first phase in this approach to scenario planning is preparation. During this stage of the process, the organization articulates its goals and resources. This phase includes planning the project, allocating responsibilities, securing time for the process, setting research priorities, and conducting interviews with key stakeholders. Phase 2 of the scenario development process is pioneering. During this phase, the organization gathers information across disciplines in order to challenge the conventional wisdom and address its blind spots. During this phase, themes are identified and scenarios outlined and built. Phase 3 of the process is mapmaking. During this phase, dynamics of the situations are clarified, illustrating information is gathered, and endorsements are gained. Phase 4 is navigation. During this phase, the organization navigates its way to the actual events as they unfold. During this phase, scenarios provide a common language that can be used to discuss complex issues and shape strategic conversations. The next phase of the scenario planning process is reconnaissance. During this phase, data are gathered concerning the viability of the scenario and the implications of the scenarios are tested. These steps are repeated in a continuing process over time to improve the scenarios in response to changes in the organization's environment.

Formal Approach

An alternative approach to scenario planning is offered by the formal style used by Rand Corporation and other organizations. Although similar in many ways to the intuitive approach, the formal approach is more closely aligned with forecasting than is the intuitive approach. The formal approach also uses computer modeling in an attempt to attach probabilities to the alternative scenarios.

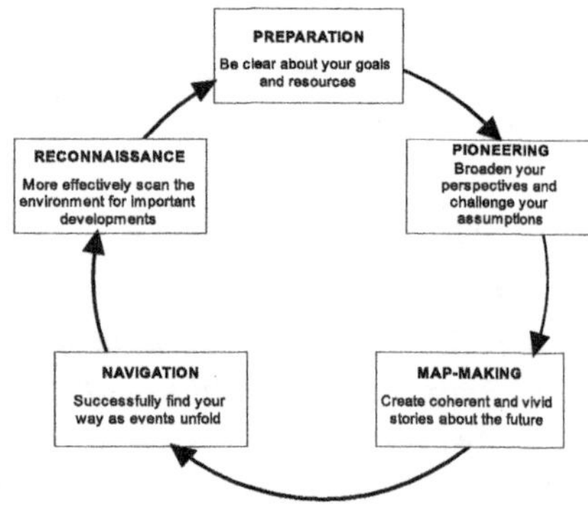

Figure 1: The Shell Oil Approach to Scenario Planning
(Adapted from Shell International, 2003)

Shortfalls of Scenario Planning

Scenario planning is not without its detractors. This approach to strategic planning requires decision makers to be willing to set aside their assumptions and preconceptions and to look objectively at possible futures that may run counter to their existing plans and philosophies. In addition, scenario planning requires research and the insights of external experts. As a result, the development of good scenarios requires more work than some organizations are able or willing to devote to the task. Further, scenarios are only possible futures, not infallible predictions. Peter Schwartz — one of the leading proponents of scenario planning — once famously made a prediction that "our view of the future is positive — but no more so than the times warrant. We live in extraordinary times. The opportunities that are opening up in the next 20 years are enormous" (Stauffer, 2002). This statement, made in 1999, was followed by the first recession in a decade, the terrorist attacks of September 11, and the Enron scandal.

Strengths of Scenario Planning

Despite the fact that some events are simply not reasonably predictable, scenario planning remains a useful tool if one understands its goals. Scenario planning is used to improve the organization's ability to be flexible in responding to rapidly changing environments, not to predict single-point changes in the organization's environment. There are several reasons why scenario planning remains relevant for organizations.

- First, scenarios can help organizations ensure that they are focusing on opportunities that may be provided by a changing environment. Scenario planning is not a substitute for crisis planning. Rather, scenario planning is a long-range planning technique that allows decision makers to investigate the opportunities presented by likely futures. This allows organizations to better plan for both negative and positive future situations.
- Second, scenario planning enables organizations to more prudently allocate their resources. Scenario planning allows the organization to examine a range of potential futures, so that it can be better prepared to respond to any of the envisioned plausible scenarios.
- Third, scenario planning allows the organization to preserve its options. If one understands that the

future is not certain, as well as how to prepare for some of this uncertainty, one can react to future events in a more timely and proactive manner.
- Fourth, scenario planning helps organizations to look ahead rather than to merely assume that the future will be a simple extrapolation of the past. The scenario planning also helps organizations to articulate and question their assumptions as well as to take into account the insights from other stakeholders so that a more realistic picture of the future can be painted.
- Finally, scenario planning offers organizations the opportunity to rehearse for the unexpected. Although the future scenario envisioned will most likely never be exactly the same as the actual future, by envisioning and planning for likely scenarios, the organization can be better prepared to respond to what the future actually brings.

APPLICATIONS

Potential Pitfalls of Scenario Planning

Scenarios are based on the insights of experienced stakeholders as they attempt to consolidate and express their observations of past experience and future trends. As opposed to forecasting — which is an attempt to scientifically quantify and synthesize the data affecting a particular situation — scenario planning is more qualitative. This can be both a benefit and a hindrance for strategic planning.

Integration Problems

Shoemaker (1990) lists a number of potential pitfalls that can be experienced when attempting to do scenario planning for business. These pitfalls stem from two primary sources: process problems in the activities related to scenario development that unfold and build over time and problems with the quality of the content of the scenarios themselves. Process problems include issues related to the failure to integrate the scenario-planning process into the other activities of the organization. For example, as with any organizational change activity, the failure to gain the support and involvement of top management early in the scenario-planning process can derail the process before it even begins. If top management is not a stakeholder in the process and its outcomes, it is unlikely that the process will receive either the resources or support necessary from other stakeholders. Similarly, even if the scenario-planning process leads to valid and important predictions that require changes in the way that the organization does business, if top management is not vested in the process and its outcomes, it is unlikely that these will be acted upon. In addition, when doing scenario planning, it is important to remember that these activities are only one part of the overall planning and decision-making processes within the organization. Activities such as risk assessment and simulation can help integrate the scenario-planning process into the overall organizational decision analysis process.

Incomplete Inputs

A second category of process pitfalls in scenario planning is an outgrowth of the failure to include all the necessary inputs into the mix when developing scenarios. Scenarios are typically centered on external changes, so it is important to get the inputs of representatives of the communities that may affect change in the future (e.g., customers, suppliers, government regulators, academics, and other analysts) to provide their insights to the process. Similarly, it is important to secure the support of both line and staff members in the scenario-planning process. These two groups of people view the organizational universe through different lenses, and the inputs of both are needed. There is often an unfortunate tendency to emphasize the inputs of staff members. However, although staff personnel may understand the "big picture" better, it is the line personnel who understand the minutia of organizational operations that can make an organizational plan a success or failure. It is important to have both line and staff personnel equally involved in the scenario-planning process.

Misunderstandings

Another cluster of potential pitfalls related to process issues in scenario development arises from a lack of understanding of the scenario-planning process and its outcomes. Some organizations, for example, enter into scenario planning without a clear understanding of the process and roles of the various participants in the process. Scenario planning is typically a time-consuming process that requires research and the abilities to abandon one's assumptions and to see situations from alternative perspectives. Scenario planning is not a process that translates into a quick fix for the ills of the organization. The primary purpose of the process is to help stakeholders and decision makers to better understand the ramifications of various possible scenarios on their strategic plans. In addition, scenario planning is only one potential step in strategic planning. To assist in this process, it is helpful to articulate a clear roadmap for the participants so that they know what to expect. Failure to do this can result in participants who are unwilling or unable to put in the work necessary to make the process a success.

Failure to Take All Necessary Steps

Another group of process-based pitfalls that can be encountered in scenario planning stems from not doing all the required steps necessary for the development of realistic scenarios. Scenario planning is — at its core — a learning process that cannot be rushed. Sufficient time needs to be allowed for learning about trends and factors that can affect the organization's future plans. Unlike a math problem, the goal of scenario planning is not to get the "right" answer the first time. Adequate time needs to be allowed to explore various likely alternative scenarios and play them off each other to help participants better understand the underlying factors and assumptions. Because of this, it is also important not to develop too many scenarios. Scenarios should be distinctly different from each other in order to maximize the usefulness of the technique (usually between three and five). Finally, scenario planning can be a continuing process as more data are acquired and processed. Scenarios and resultant strategies alike need to be refined to better fit the continuing stream of data and changes in trends over time.

Failure to Address Underlying Issues/Problems

In addition to process-based pitfalls, the scenario-planning process can also suffer from problems with the quality of the input to the process. For example, it can be difficult for many organizations to objectively think about long-term scenarios when they already are successfully thriving in the marketplace. Too many organizations tend to deal with the symptoms (i.e., "put out fires") rather than the underlying problems. Although this may be a successful strategy in the short term, it tends to be counterproductive in the long term. Particularly in this age of rapidly emerging technology, emphasis on information, and increasing globalization, it is essential that organizations carefully consider the impacts of such changes in the marketplace on their strategies. To do this, the organization must take into account the historical perspective without being bound by it. It can be helpful, for example, for the organization to compare itself with other industries that have experienced unexpected discontinuities or progressed further in terms of various issues of concern (e.g., regulation, technological advances). However, focusing too intently on trends can lead to scenarios that simply project the past into the future without truly applying the type of out-of-the-box thinking required for the development of good scenarios.

Lack of Diverse Viewpoints

Another problem that can be experienced during scenario development is that all the scenarios are merely variations on a single theme. A set of scenarios should represent the full range of viewpoints both within and outside of the industry. In particular, scenario development should take into account the viewpoints of creative and innovative thinkers. In addition, in order for scenarios to be useful, they need to be internally consistent. One should make sure that the main trends within a scenario are mutually consistent with each other and that the key uncertainties within a scenario are compatible. For example, it is unlikely that the near future will include a situation where there is full employment and zero inflation. Similarly, when postulating possible actions of major stakeholders, one should make sure that these actions are consistent with their interests. One way to help in the development of a realistic scenario is to try to understand the underlying problems and factors that can affect the future rather than merely brainstorming a wide-ranging list of possible symptoms.

By its very nature, a good scenario will often fly in the face of the conventional wisdom of the organization. Although organizational management may have legitimate political, emotional, and other concerns, the development of the good scenario must be predicated on intellectual honesty and an objective look at all the relevant factors that may affect the organization's future.

However, a good scenario is not merely a snapshot of what the future might hold. Rather, it is a roadmap showing how the situation may develop from its current state to the projected future state.

Lack of Decision-Maker Input

Finally, good scenarios need to be relevant to the key decision makers within the organization. It is the responsibility of those who develop the scenarios to make sure that decision-makers understand its relevance. For example, the implications of the rising cost of a barrel of oil may not be immediately apparent to widget manufacturer. However, if that manufacturer is involved in the global economy, the rising cost of a barrel of oil will translate into rising transportation cost both upstream and downstream in the supply chain that could potentially price the organization out of competition. Similarly, even if the widgets are only sold locally, rising fuel costs could translate into a situation where fewer potential customers are willing to pay for the fuel necessary to go to the widget store to purchase a widget. However, if the decision makers do not understand such facts, they may dismiss a realistic scenario out of hand.

CONCLUSION

Scenario planning is an approach to strategic planning helps the organization better understand the nature and impact of forces driving its future. Scenarios are based on the insights of experienced stakeholders as they attempt to consolidate and express their observations of past experience and future trends. Scenario planning has been successfully used by many Fortune 1000 companies. However, it is often not used more widely because scenario planning requires decision makers to think "out of the box" and envision possible likely futures that may run counter to current corporate plans and philosophies. In addition, scenario planning is not universally successful due to a number of potential pitfalls stemming from both the process used for developing the scenarios as well as the quality of the content of the scenarios themselves.

Bibliography

Chakraborty, A., Kaza, N., Knaap, G., & Deal, B. (2011). Robust plans and contingent plans. *Journal of the American Planning Association, 77*(3), 251–266. Retrieved November 20, 2013 from EBSCO online database Business Source Premier. http://search.ebscohost.com/login.aspx?direct=true&db=buh&AN=63000186

Courtney, H., Lovallo, D., & Clarke, C. (2013). Deciding how to decide. *Harvard Business Review, 91*(11), 62–70. Retrieved November 20, 2013 from EBSCO online database Business Source Premier. http://search.ebscohost.com/login.aspx?direct=true&db=buh&AN=91571432

Rasmus, D. W. (2011). Scenario planning the future. *Chief Learning Officer, 10*(2), 28–31. Retrieved November 20, 2013 from EBSCO online database Business Source Premier. http://search.ebscohost.com/login.aspx?direct=true&db=buh&AN=57636393

Shell International. (2003). *Scenarios: An explorer's guide.* Retrieved January 3, 2008, from Shell International website. http://www.shell.com/static/aboutshell-en/downloads/our%5fstrategy/shell%5fglobal%5fscenarios/scenario%5fexplorersguide.pdf

Shoemaker, P. J. H. (1990). Twenty common pitfalls in scenario planning. In L. Fahey & R. M. Randall (Eds.). *Learning from the future: Competitive foresight scenarios* (pp. 422–431). New York, NY: John Wiley and Sons.

Stauffer, D. (2002). Five reasons why you still need scenario planning. *Harvard Management Update, 7*(6), 3–7. Retrieved January 2, 2008, from EBSCO Online Database Business Source Complete. http://search.ebscohost.com/login.aspx?direct=true&db=bth&AN=6756894&site=ehost-live

Tips for strategic scenario planning. (2013). *Controller's Report, 2013*(7), 2–3. Retrieved November 20, 2013 from EBSCO online database Business Source Premier. http://search.ebscohost.com/login.aspx?direct=true&db=buh&AN=88426965

Verity, J. (2003) Scenario planning as a strategy technique. *European Business Journal, 15*(4), 185–195. Retrieved January 2, 2008, from EBSCO Online Database Business Source Complete. http://search.ebscohost.com/login.aspx?direct=true&db=bth&AN=12548913&site=ehost-live

Wilkinson, A., & Kupers, R. (2013). Living in the futures. *Harvard Business Review, 91*(5), 118–127. Retrieved November 20, 2013 from EBSCO online database Business Source Premier. http://search.ebscohost.com/login.aspx?direct=true&db=buh&AN=87039876

Suggested Reading

Axson, D. J. (2011). Scenario planning: Navigating through today's uncertain world. *Journal of Accountancy, 211*(3), 22–27. Retrieved November 20, 2013 from EBSCO online database Business Source Premier. http://search.ebscohost.com/login.aspx?direct=true&db=buh&AN=58704579

Chermack, T. J. (2011). *Scenario planning in organizations: How to create, use, and assess scenarios.* San Francisco, CA: Berrett-Koehler. Retrieved November 20, 2013 from EBSCO online database eBook Academic Collection (EBSCOhost). http://search.ebscohost.com/login.aspx?direct=true&db=e000xna&AN=354488&site=ehost-live

Goodwin, P., & Wright, G. (2001). Enhancing strategy evaluation in scenario planning: A role for decision analysis. *Journal of Management Studies, 38*(1), 1–16. Retrieved January 2, 2008, from EBSCO Online Database Business Source Complete. http://search.ebscohost.com/login.aspx?direct=true&db=bth&AN=4110445&site=ehost-live

Hindle, T. (2003). Scenario planning. In *Guide to management ideas*(2nd ed.). New York, NY: Bloomberg Press, 191–193. Retrieved January 2, 2008, from EBSCO Online Database Business Source Complete. http://search.ebscohost.com/login.aspx?direct=true&db=bth&AN=26023622&site=ehost-live

More, H. (2003). Scenario planning or does your organisation rain dance? *New Zealand Management, 50*(4), 32–34. Retrieved January 2, 2008, from EBSCO Online Database Business Source Complete. http://search.ebscohost.com/login.aspx?direct=true&db=bth&AN=9819185&site=ehost-live

Shell International. (2005). *Shell global scenarios to 2025: The future business environment—Trends, trade-offs and choices.* Hague, Netherlands: Author.

Shell International. (2007). *Signposts: Supplement to 'Global scenarios to 2025.'* Hague, Netherlands: Author. Retrieved November 20, 2013, from: http://s06.static-shell.com/content/dam/shell/static/aboutshell/downloads/our-strategy/shell-global-scenarios/supp-glo-sc.pdf

Ruth A. Wienclaw, Ph.D.

SERVICE OPERATIONS MANAGEMENT

ABSTRACT

An increasing number of businesses are offering services rather than tangible goods. Although customers' opinions of service quality are directly related to a company's profitability, many organizations fail to control and improve their customer service processes. These processes tend to be difficult and costly to control because of their intangibility, heterogeneity, and inseparability. However, operations management principles can be applied to service industries in an effort to improve quality. One must first understand what the customer wants from the customer service process and then identify fail points in the process where it is likely to go wrong. No matter how well the customer service process is designed and implemented, problems are unavoidable. Customer dissatisfaction as a result of errors, however, is not. There are a number of ways to recover from customer service problems and maintain customer loyalty.

OVERVIEW

As the state-of-the-art 21st century technology continues to expand and high tech solutions proliferate, more and more businesses offer services instead of, or in addition to, tangible products. In fact, the service industry is the largest and fastest growing business sector in the United States. Despite the opportunities offered by this growing sector, however, businesses are faced with the problem of determining how to manage operations where the products are intangible. As a result, research has found that most consumers are dissatisfied with the customer service they receive from these businesses. This fact, combined with the increasing service competition that arises out of the growing trend toward globalization, means that increased emphasis needs to be placed on operations management in service organizations just as it is in manufacturing organizations.

Operations Management & the Service Sector

Operations management comprises those areas of management that are concerned with productivity, quality, and cost in the operations function (i.e., those activities necessary to transform inputs such as business transactions and information into outputs such as completed transactions) as well as strategic planning for the organization. The service sector has been described in many ways. In its essence, the service sector includes those industries and businesses that provide services rather than tangible products for individual consumers, businesses, or a combination of the two. These can include physical, mental, or aesthetic activities (e.g., legal services, entertainment, auto repair) or the transformation of something through such an activity (e.g., hair cutting, education, management consulting).

Like defining the service sector itself, defining operations management for the service sector is more problematic than defining operations management for other sectors (i.e., transportation, communications, and utilities; wholesale or retail trade; finance, insurance, and real estate; public administration). It is relatively easy to determine when a widget is not of acceptable quality. The manufacturer will have a manufacturing specification that describes what the tolerances are for the product and quality control will accept or reject the product based on whether or not it is within the specifications. Similarly, a manufacturing process can be evaluated to see where there is waste in the process or where efficiencies can be introduced. However, it is not so obvious where to improve quality or cost-effectiveness for service industries. For example, how does one specify the quality of a new hairstyle? Although in some cases a bad haircut can be obvious to all, a new hairstyle may be a matter of aesthetics: What looked good in the magazine on the 20 year-old model may not look so good on the middle-aged customer with a different bone structure. Similarly, how does one evaluate the cost of creating a new work of art or the training of a hotel employee? Yet, the quality of customer service must be operationally defined in order for the organization to be consistently effective.

Quality Improvement & Control

Despite the fact that research has shown that customers' opinions of service quality are directly related to company profitability, many service organizations do not try to control and improve quality. This is due in part to the fact that service quality is often difficult and costly to control and improve. It is also due to the differences between the activities and products of the service industry and those of the manufacturing industry. In manufacturing, results are tangible and can be quantified. This fact makes it easier to control quality than in the service industry where the "product" is intangible. Further, in manufacturing, statistical quality control methods can be built into the process so that quality is monitored and corrected at several key points in the process. In most manufacturing processes, there are typically several points at which the product can be quality tested so that substandard parts or products can be rejected or the process can be rectified as necessary before the products reach the consumer. This approach, however, is not possible in the service industry: One cannot do a quality control check on services before they reach the customer.

Three Reasons for Control Difficulties

There are three reasons that services are difficult to control: intangibility, heterogeneity, and inseparability. The quality of customer service is not based on a product that one can touch. Characteristics of good customer service more often have to do with speed of delivery of the service, the competence with which the service is delivered, and the courtesy with which it is offered. Such factors are difficult to quantify for a number of reasons, not the least of which is the perceptions and expectations of the customer. It can be difficult to operationally define good customer service. For example, does walking the customer through a troubleshooting procedure step-by-step in an attempt to be thorough constitute good customer service, or does listening to the customer in an attempt to find out what s/he has already tried constitute good customer service? The former situation is apt to antagonize someone who is knowledgeable about the process while the latter approach is likely to miss important steps with a customer who only thinks s/he is knowledgeable. In some situations, there are, of course, some aspects of customer service that are tangible (e.g., receiving starter checks when opening a new bank account). However, these tend to be much poorer predictors of customer satisfaction than are the intangible factors.

Factors that Affect Quality of Service

In addition to being intangible, services tend to be heterogeneous in nature, and not consistently performed. Quality of service depends on a number of factors, including the personalities and expectations of each of the parties involved. For example, when a technophobe calls a technical support help line to troubleshoot what is wrong with his computer, he expects and needs to be treated with a step-by-step, hand-holding approach that will allow him to trust the person on the other end to walk him through the steps. If an experienced computer programmer calls the technical help line, however, the same step-by-step approach based on the assumption that the customer is clueless is more apt to be irritating than helpful. Similarly, the retail assistant who greets the customer at the door and follows her throughout the shopping experience may be perceived as helpful to some customers and intrusive by other customers. Human nature makes customer service a complicated process. What works with a given customer today (e.g., when the customer wants help) may not work with the same customer tomorrow (e.g., when the customer is in a hurry and does not want to linger over the process).

A third characteristic of customer service is inseparability. Customer service is performed in the presence of the customer and becomes inseparable in the customer's mind from the organization as a whole. So, for example, if a software manufacturing company provides poor customer service to someone logging on to the support database or calling the technical help line, in the customer's mind, the service will be inseparable from the product. Most customers do not differentiate between the quality of the product and the quality of the service. An overview of the dimensions of customer service is given in Table 1.

Firm					Soft
Framework of Time	***Fault-Freeness***	***Flexibility***	***Style***	***Steering***	***Safety***
• Availability of service (i.e., hours/day)	• Physical items of the service bundle	• To customize the service	• Appropriateness of attitudes	• Perceived importance	• Trust
• Availability of all aspects of the service package	•	• To cope with mistakes	• Accessibility (to people and location)	• Feelings of being in control	• Confidence
• Responsiveness (i.e., how long to react to customer)	• Correctness of information/ advice	• To introduce new services (to complete a service package)	• Perceived value	• Clarity of service (e.g., where to go, what to do, whom to see)	• Honesty of advice/ information
• Queue time			• Ambience (e.g., decoration, lighting, temperature, cleanliness, dress)	• Consistency	• Security
• Process time				• Psychological timing (how long the service seems to take)	
• Dependability/ repeatability of service time					

Table 1: Dimensions of Customer Service
(Adapted from Armistead, 1989, p. 249)

Steps to Improving Customer Service

Despite the more nebulous nature of service versus manufacturing, operations management principles can be applied to service industries in an effort to improve quality. The first step in improving customer service is to ascertain whether or not one is offering the service that the customer wants. For example, no matter how good an automated troubleshooting system is, if the customer wants the personalized service of talking to a live person, the automated system will never be sufficient. Another action taken to improve customer service is to improve the service system itself. Various program management techniques including PERT charts and Six Sigma programs can be used in an attempt to regularly assess and ensure quality. However, when dealing with the service industry, these tools tend to miss one of the major components of the system: The customer's interaction with the service.

The Blueprint Method

Once the service for which the customer is looking has been determined, one can next determine how to better provide that service for the customer. One of the ways to overcome this omission is through the "blueprint" method. The various steps part of this method are:

Flowcharting

The first step in the blueprint method is to specify the complete service process in a flow chart. This schematic should distinguish between those operations or activities that are seen by the customer and those that are not. Even though part of the process is not seen by the customer, it still can affect overall customer satisfaction with the service. For example, the computer software used by a credit card company will probably never be seen by the customer. However, if the software prints out credit card statements in a format that the customer finds difficult to decipher, the software will negatively impact customer satisfaction. Similarly, many grocery stores use software to help design the store layout in order to give customers easier access to certain items or to give designated stock a place of prominence for promotional purposes. Although the customer will probably never see that software, either, if s/he has to search for the Nutty Crunchy cereal for the third time in two months, s/he is not likely to be satisfied with the store's customer service.

Determining Fail Points

Once the service process has been flowcharted, the next step in the blueprint method is to analyze it to determine where there are fail points — the critical points in the process where the provider has the opportunity to make a serious mistake that can negatively impact the customer's satisfaction with the process or his/her perception of quality. This allows the provider the opportunity to design fail-safe subprocesses that can be integrated into the overall service process so that potential missteps are caught before they affect the customer's perceptions of the service or the process. The determination and elimination of fail points is one of the most difficult steps in the blueprint process. One of the reasons for this is that it is important to determine the time frame of the fail points since time is an important factor in service cost. However, the more complex the service process, the more difficult it is to pinpoint time frames.

Determining Time Frame

To do this part of the analysis, it can be helpful to first determine how long it takes to perform the process when all aspects of the situation are normal. From a customer's point of view, satisfaction with the process or service decreases in direct relations to the degree to which the process or service takes longer than expected. Once this "ideal" time frame is developed, time frames can be developed for various foreseeable deviations from the normal case. For example, a grocery store could determine the amount of time it should take a checkout clerk to ring up an order with a given number of items. From there, it could be determined how long it would take if one of the items were not marked with the price or the SKU had not been entered into the system. This process could be performed for other deviations from the "ideal" checkout situation such as the use of coupons, the customer not having picked up sufficient items to qualify for a sale price, and so forth.

Profitability Check

Once the ideal and deviation time frames have been determined, the blueprint should next be checked for profitability. This activity involves quantifying the cost of various deviations on profitability. For example, the situation where an item is not entered into the computer means that the transaction needs to be stopped while someone is sent to look for the correct price on the shelves or in the sales flyer. This person needs to return to the checkout line or call the checker with the correct price. This deviation not only affects the time frame for service of the person's order with the undocumented item, but also affects the time frame for service for the people standing in line behind that person.

Use of Technology

In some instances, there are ways to speed up processes or increase efficiency through the use of technology. For example, to help get the customer through to the correct person on a telephone help line, many businesses use an automated telephone answering system. From the organization's point of view, the use of this technology can get customers help in a more timely manner while reducing the number of employees that the organization needs to hire to answer the phones. The automated system can even offer the customer answers to frequently asked questions while they are waiting on hold. However, if from the customer's point of view the answering system is too impersonal or cumbersome, then customer satisfaction decreases and counteracts the efficiencies gained by implementing the system. When dealing with customer service issues, the object of the exercise is not only to increase the efficiency of the process, but to do so while not decreasing the customer's perception of quality.

APPLICATIONS

No matter how well the customer service process is designed and implemented, errors and problems are unavoidable. Customer dissatisfaction as a result of these things, however, is not. It may be tempting to consider the one complaining customer as an outlier who does not represent customers in general or whose opinion does not reflect badly on the organization's service process. However, such customers should not be dismissed. Such customers typically represent a silent number of other customers who did not bother to complain. In addition, according to industry experts, it costs five times more to replace a customer than to retain one. Therefore, customer satisfaction is important to the success of the business.

At virtually every fail point, there is a concomitant opportunity for recovery. To take advantage of these opportunities, however, appropriate mechanisms need to be in place. The best way to recover from problems with customer service is to empower front-line employees to handle them as they arise. Being told that the problem is not the fault of the employee and that s/he can do nothing about it is not going to soothe the customer. The customer sees the front-line employee as a representative of the organization at large; if the front-line employee is powerless or incompetent, the customer is more likely to take the same view of the business in general. Therefore, although it is important to manage service operations well, it is equally important to be able to manage service recovery well for those inevitable situations where problems arise.

There are several ways to do this. First, management needs to understand the costs associated with mismanaged customer service as well as the costs to recover from the situation. For example, at Club Med, a satisfied customer typically visits the resort chain four more times after the initial visit whereas a dissatisfied customer does not. On average, for every customer who does not return, Club Med loses $2400 in income. This loss is in addition to the expenses of marketing to find replacement customers.

Another way to improve customer service is to listen closely to what the customer has to say. One way to do this, of course, is to listen to customer complaints and take them seriously. These are opportunities to learn how to improve the service process. However, although some customers freely complain to the organization about poor service, most do not, and just slip quietly away. To help overcome this problem, the business should make it easy for customers to complain. Asking customers how the service was is one way to do this, as are toll-free 24-hour complaint hot lines. However, no matter the medium, it is important to really listen to the customer so that the complaint and the underlying problem are well understood and appropriate action can be taken. It is also important that this action be taken quickly before the customer's negative reaction to the business becomes solidified.

Although management is sometimes required to intervene in order to solve a customer service problem, the best way to handle problems quickly and to minimize negative impact is to train employees to identify problems and empower them to respond to them. Training can help employees know where the fail points in the process are and help them learn to detect when a problem occurs. In addition, employees who deal with customers need to be given both the authority and responsibility to react to customer service problems and rectify the situation appropriately. To further encourage trained, empowered employees to give excellent service, it is helpful to put incentives in place to encourage good customer service and to recognize those who rectify problems quickly, quietly, and well. Through this combination of actions, the impact of inevitable customer service problems can be minimized and the business can keep and expand its customer base.

BIBLIOGRAPHY

Armistead, C. G. (1989). Customer service operations management in service businesses. *Service Industries Journal, 9*(2), 247-260. Retrieved May 29, 2007, from EBSCO Online Database Business Source Complete. http://search.cbscohost.com/login.aspx?direct=true&db=bth&AN=6421930&site=ehost-live

Hart, C. W. L., Heskett, J. L., & Sasser, W. E. Jr. (1990). The profitable art of service recovery. *Harvard Business Review, 68*(4), 148-156. Retrieved May 29, 2007, from EBSCO Online Database Business Source Complete. http://search.ebscohost.com/login.aspx?direct=true&db=bth&AN=9008131633&site=ehost-live

Idris, F. (2012). Achieving flexibility in service operations using the rigid flexibility framework: an exploratory study. *International Journal of Business & Society, 13*(3), 279-292. Retrieved November 15, 2013, from EBSCO Online Database Business Source Complete. http://search.ebscohost.com/login.aspx?direct=true&db=bth&AN=85407023&site=ehost-live

Liu, X., & Donalds, K. (2013). Stimulating reflective learning in teaching a service operations management course. *Proceedings for the Northeast Region Decision Sciences Institute (NEDSI),* 792-797. Retrieved

November 15, 2013, from EBSCO Online Database Business Source Complete. http://search.ebscohost.com/login.aspx?direct=true&db=bth&AN=88837750&site=ehost-live

Montoya, M. M., Massey, A. P., & Khatri, V. (2010). Connecting IT services operations to services marketing practices. *Journal of Management Information Systems, 26*(4), 65-85. Retrieved November 15, 2013, from EBSCO Online Database Business Source Complete. http://search.ebscohost.com/login.aspx?direct=true&db=bth&AN=49164622&site=ehost-live

Tinkham, M. A. & Kleiner, B. H. (1992). New developments in service operations management. *Industrial Management, 34*(6), 20-22. Retrieved May 29, 2007, from EBSCO Online Database Business Source Complete. http://search.ebscohost.com/login.aspx?direct=true&db=bth&AN=4983050&site=ehost-live

SUGGESTED READING

Craighead, C. W., Karwan, K. R., & Miller, J. L. (2004). The effects of severity of failure and customer loyalty on service recovery strategies. *Production & Operations Management, 13*(4), 307-321. Retrieved May 29, 2007, from EBSCO Online Database Business Source Complete. http://search.ebscohost.com/login.aspx?direct=true&db=bth&AN=15753580&site=ehost-live

Harvey, J. (1989). Designing efficient and manageable public professional service processes. *International Journal of Operations & Production Management, 9*(1), 35-44. Retrieved May 29, 2007, from EBSCO Online Database Business Source Complete. http://search.ebscohost.com/login.aspx?direct=true&db=bth&AN=5118145&site=ehost-live

Johnston, R. (1999). Service operations management: Return to roots. *International Journal of Operations & Production Management, 19*(2), 104-124. Retrieved May 29, 2007, from EBSCO Online Database Business Source Complete. http://search.ebscohost.com/login.aspx?direct=true&db=bth&AN=19525930&site=ehost-live

Killeya, J. C. & Armistead, C. G. (1983). The transfer of concepts and techniques between manufacturing and service systems. *International Journal of Operations & Production Management, 3*(3), 22-28. Retrieved May 29, 2007, from EBSCO Online Database Business Source Complete. http://search.ebscohost.com/login.aspx?direct=true&db=bth&AN=5131551&site=ehost-live

Morris, B. & Johnston, R. (1987). Dealing with inherent variability: The difference between manufacturing and service? *International Journal of Operations & Production Management, 7*(4), 13-22. Retrieved May 29, 2007, from EBSCO Online Database Business Source Complete. http://search.ebscohost.com/login.aspx?direct=true&db=bth&AN=5118875&site=ehost-live

Ruth A. Wienclaw, Ph.D.

SPECIAL TOPICS IN MANAGEMENT

ABSTRACT

This article will focus on special topics in management that cut across management fields and areas of expertise. The special topics of this article, which include human-resource management, information management, crisis management, and issues management within organizations, will be of special interest to students, scholars, and practitioners of management. An overview of the field of management, including the history of management, management careers, and management roles and skills, will be provided and serve as the foundation for the discussion of special topics in management.

OVERVIEW

Management refers to the work or act of directing and controlling a group of people within an organization for the purpose of accomplishing shared goals or objectives. People in management positions control and coordinate organizational activities, employees, processes, resources, goals, and objectives in every field and industry. Managers of all kinds work within organizations. The structures of organizations, from financial investment firms to industrial production facilities to colleges and universities to hospitals and medical facilities, have similarities in areas such as established work flow, clear leadership, and shared objectives. The study of management reveals that managers in all industries must handle employees, information, change, crisis, and ethical issues. Special topics in the study of management reveal what unites managers in their work and what issues unite the field of management studies.

The following sections — history of management, management careers, and management roles and functions — will serve as the foundation for a discussion of the management issues of human-resource management, information management, crisis management, and issues management that cut across all fields and industries. These special topics may be of critical interest to all those concerned with the effective management of people, information, material resources, time, and money.

The History of Management

The focused study of management began during the late 19th century in an effort to increase the efficiency of the labor force. The Industrial Revolution, a period characterized by the adoption of large-scale factory production, changed labor practices throughout the world. The creation of large-scale production facilities necessitated the creation of the role of manager to coordinate the efforts and labors of large groups of people.

The study of management during the late 19th to mid-20th century was conceived of as an applied science intended to increase worker and organizational efficiency. Classics in the study of management include Frederick Taylor's scientific management, Henri Fayol's theories of administration and labor, Max Weber's classical organization theory and bureaucracy model, the Hawthorne studies' human-relations model, Douglas McGregor's Theory X and Theory Y, and Abraham Maslow's model of hierarchy of human needs.

Management, as defined and understood by classical management theorists such as Fayol and Taylor, leads, enforces, and plans in the interest of efficiency and profit. Fayol, along with Taylor and other classical management theorists, developed a deeply entrenched theory, approach, and practice of management appropriate for hierarchical and bureaucratic organizations. Classic management, as defined by Fayol, consists of five main functions, roles, or actions:

- Planning: forecasting, strategizing, and deciding what needs to happen in the future.
- Organizing: making efficient use of human and material resources.
- Leading: motivating, commanding, and exhibiting skills to inspire and lead employees.
- Coordinating: unifying and harmonizing all organizational activity and effort.
- Controlling: monitoring and checking employee performance for conformity and uniformity.

The study and practice of management from 1960 to 1990 was characterized by psychologically focused management strategies such as the management grid and job-enrichment programs. Management theory, practice, and scholarship since 1990 has been characterized by a focus on issues of leadership, group dynamics, and employee motivation. Managers in modern organizations must respond to new technologies, new organizational models, the economic forces of globalization, and increased diversity in the workforce (Zuidema, 1994).

Management: Functions, Roles, & Skills

The field of management includes numerous areas of expertise and influence. Managers work in business, industry, education, and social-service organizations. Examples of management occupations, as described by the US Department of Labor, include the following:

- Administrative services managers
- Advertising, marketing, promotions, public relations, and sales managers
- Computer and information systems managers
- Construction managers
- Education administrators
- Farmers, ranchers, and agricultural managers
- Financial managers
- Food service managers
- Human resources managers
- Industrial production managers
- Lodging managers
- Medical and health services managers
- Property, real estate, and community association managers
- Social and Community Service Managers

- Top executives (Occupational Outlook Handbook, 2014)

What is a manager's job? While the exact skill set required of a manager varies by industry, there are similarities in designated managerial functions, roles, and skills. Management theory, as described in the previous section, was first defined in the early 1900s. Classic theories and approaches to management continue to influence both management curriculum and practice.

As described by Henri Fayol's 14 principles of management, first published in *General and Industrial Management* (1917), classical management theory of the 20th century was characterized by proscribed rules, expectations, demeanor, and values as described below:

- Division of work: specialization of work and labor will increase personal and organizational productivity.
- Authority: management has the right to give orders and the power to expect obedience.
- Discipline: employees must obey, and management must provide good leadership.
- Unity of command: each employee has only one boss, with no challenges to lines of reporting and command.
- Unity of direction: workers engaged in the same activities must receive the same direction and objectives.
- Subordination of individual interests: workers and managers must work for and toward the goals of the organization.
- Remuneration: payment for services is required for reasons of ethics and motivation.
- Centralization: management functions are generally centralized and consolidated at one level of the organization.
- Chain of authority: a formal and hierarchical chain of command should structure the organization.
- Order: formal organization of material and human (or personnel) resources is required.
- Equity: employees of an organization should receive equitable treatment.
- Personnel tenure: stability of employment and limited turnover of personnel strengthen an organization.
- Initiative: employees should be allowed opportunities to demonstrate initiative within the organization.
- Esprit de corps: morale, harmony, and cohesion should be facilitated and encouraged within the organization.

While modern approaches to management still include these 14 principles, they also require the ability to manage change, information, and organizational values. Modern management, particularly in information technology (IT) and service sector fields, is characterized by adaptability, flexibility, and responsiveness.

Modern business organizations, responding to new technology, increased competition, and changes in trade regulations around the world, are transitioning from hierarchical and centralized forms to group-model and decentralized organizations. In response to the new forms of business organizations, such as high-tech companies and multinational corporations, managers and management theory have evolved their skill sets to include greater facility for managing change, information, and human differences.

Ultimately, the job of management includes planning, organizing, staffing, directing, controlling, motivating, communicating, coaching, problem solving, decision making, and leading. In any of the common modern branches of management, including clinical management, financial management, facility management, operations management, human-resource management, information management, information systems management, and general retail, business, and industry management, managers will be challenged by the special issues described in the following section (Wartenberg, 1996).

ISSUES

Managing Employees, Information, Crises, & Ethical Issues

There are numerous topics and issues that cut across management fields and careers. In particular, managers in all industries encounter issues associated with managing employees, information, crises, and ethical issues. These management challenges belong to established fields of management study:

- Human-resource management
- Information management
- Crisis management
- Issues management

The following sections analyze these special topics in management.

Human-Resource Management

Human-resource management (HRM), also called personnel management, refers to how organizations manage the valuable resource of human capital. HRM is considered to be a source of competitive advantage for organizations and is linked to increased productivity and employee performance. Organizations that explicitly value employees as a source of competitive advantage have been found to have better performance than other firms.

Organizations may choose between traditional and high-involvement human-resource strategies. High-involvement HRM strategy emphasizes the value of employees as a source of competitive advantage in the marketplace. HRM strategies are employed by multinational corporations and local firms alike in organizations around the world. The field of strategic human-resource management (SHRM) focuses on the relationship between motivation and employee performance (Bae & Lawler, 2000).

The management of employee performance centers on the organizational gains created from extrinsic and intrinsic motivation. Employees vary in their inclination and ability to be satisfied from extrinsic and intrinsic motivation. Savvy human-resource managers match the motivation and reward to the employee's temperament and disposition. Extrinsic motivation occurs when employees are able to satisfy their needs indirectly from rewards such as monetary compensation. Organizations that link employees' monetary motivation to the goals and objectives of the organization are said to have achieved extrinsically motivated coordination. Intrinsic motivation occurs when an activity is undertaken for the sole purpose of satisfying one's needs. Intrinsic motivation is self-sustaining and generated by commitment to work itself. Human-resource managers who wish to generate intrinsic motivation in employees will match employee intellect and abilities to appropriately challenging and structured work opportunities.

Employee motivation must be managed in order to create the necessary and desirable balance between intrinsic and extrinsic motivation. Intrinsic motivation, if not monitored and nurtured, risks being obscured and squashed by strong monitoring and incentives such as piece rates and bonuses. Complex jobs require intrinsic motivation to allow the creative and intellectual leaps that produce invention, ingenuity, and growth in organizations (Osterloh, 2003).

Human-resource managers shape the organizational culture in ways that promote pro-social behavior by employees. They work to promote organizational citizenship behavior (OCB) as a means of facilitating organizational effectiveness. OCB, also known as pro-social organizational behavior (POB), refers to the helpful, cooperative behaviors that are not explicitly required of employees. Examples of pro-social behaviors in the workplace include assisting new employees and self-limiting sick days. There are three key management issues related to OCB:

- Perceptions of fairness and trust in the workplace
- Norms of helpfulness and cooperation in the workplace
- Fair reward systems based on broad contributions. (Schneider, 1994)

In addition to the focus on employee motivation and pro-social behavior, HRM acknowledges and incorporates differences in employee values, ethics, and perceptions. In all fields and industries, HRM works within a given organizational set of values. Managers have the job of mediating the relationship between these organizational values and diverse and sometimes opposing employee values.

Information Management

Managers in all fields and industries are responsible for information and knowledge management. What do managers do with company information or knowledge such as data, company history, production processes, and financial reports? Information management, or knowledge management (KM), is a relatively new area of study about an age-old process and need. KM refers to the systematic and explicit management of vital information. The work of KM includes the creation, organization, diffusion, and use of information within an organization. Knowledge sharing is vital to the operation of the self-directed work-group models that characterize many modern organizations.

Managers in modern organizations are increasingly applying information technologies (IT) to the problems and challenges of KM. IT helps organizations create knowledge-management systems (KMS) that structure information storage, use, and distribution within an organization. Organizational KMSes include elements such as data mining, learning tools, intranets, e-mail, telecommunication and video-conferencing technologies, knowledge directories, decision support tools, expert systems, workflow systems, social network analysis tools, and knowledge codification tools. KMSes create searchable digital storage to facilitate the retrieval and distribution of an organization's information.

KM tools must be matched to the technological interests and abilities of the organization. The primary difficulty of using IT to create KMSes may be the multiplicity of knowledge. Much contemporary research in IT and KM focuses on developing a core set of KM tools for use across organizations, fields, and industries (Butler & Murphy, 2007).

Crisis Management

Organizational crises and vulnerabilities, such as extortion, hostile takeovers, product tampering, copyright infringement, security breaches, bribery, information sabotage, sexual harassment, plant explosions, counterfeiting, boycotts, or natural disasters that destroy production facilities, affect all types of organizations. An organizational crisis is an unlikely yet possible event that would threaten the viability of the organization. It is characterized by uncertainty of cause, effect, and method of solution as well as by the certainty that decisions must be made expeditiously to save the organization.

Organizational crisis management refers to an attempt by organizational members with external stakeholders to both avoid crises and effectively solve any crises that do happen. An organization's crisis-management framework or model for analyzing often includes the 4C frame of causes, consequences, caution, and coping:

- Causes: the immediate failures that triggered the crisis.
- Consequences: the immediate and long-term results.
- Caution: the procedures taken to avoid or curtail the impact of a possible crisis.
- Coping: the responding actions to a crisis that has happened.

Criteria for evaluating crisis-management effectiveness centers on evaluating the perceptions of key stakeholders. The effectiveness of organizational crisis management is demonstrated when potential crises are averted or when the major stakeholders of an organization believe that the success outcomes of short-term impacts outweigh the failure outcomes. Crisis-management outcomes are often evaluated on a success-failure continuum based on the idea that all organizational crises result in degrees of success and failure.

The predominant trend in developing crisis-management models for organizations is a multidisciplinary approach that incorporates psychological, socio-political, and techno-structural perspectives. Multidisciplinary models of crisis management explicitly recognize the objective, subjective, and perceptual components of organizational crises and acknowledge the complexity of crisis outcomes (Pearson & Clair, 1998).

Issues Management

Managers in all fields and industries must handle ethical issues that arise in the workings of an organization. Issues managers are responsible for integrating business decisions and ethical decisions. The field of issues management, which is based loosely on Emmanuel Kant's (1724–1804) philosophy of ethics, refers to the "executive function of strategic public relations that deals with problem solving, organizational policy, long-range planning, and management strategy as well as communication of that strategy internally and externally" (Bowen, 2005). Strategies for handling ethical dilemmas in organizations involve the identification of issues, research, analysis, and the creation of responsive organization-wide policies. Issues management provides a framework for analysis of ethical dilemmas and situations that arise in the workplace. Managers committed to ethical issues management operate with a working definition of Kantian concepts such as ethics, autonomy, principle of reversibility, duty, intention, respect for others, and symmetrical communication.

One of the main challenges of ethical issues management involves the practical implementation of strategies and policies. Issues managers must match the degree of ethics formality to the style of organization. They may strengthen their ethical issues-management process by adopting a formal code of ethics for the organization and conducting issues-management meetings. Ethics statements articulate the values with which employees should make work-related decisions. In addition to an ethics code, issues managers may work with employees to evaluate work-related decisions prior to making definitive and final decisions. This decision-making model is a less formal approach to ethical decision making than an ethics code (Bowen, 2005).

CONCLUSION

The relevance of the special topics introduced in this article extends to managers in almost every field and industry. Managers who work in a variety of roles, such as operations managers, sales managers, financial managers, merchandising managers, management analysts, corporate planners, human-resource managers, and small-business operators, have common challenges and similar concerns. What unites them is the need to handle and embrace organizational change. The economic climate is shifting. The competition created by the globalization of economic markets challenges business organizations to produce rapid product innovation, cost efficiency, and increased customer responsiveness.

In response to new market demands, old models of hierarchical organizations are being replaced by new forms of organizations, such as self-managed teams, cross-functional teams, and self-directed work groups. These new team-based work groups are increasingly restructuring and distributing management responsibilities, such as production schedules, budgeting, and problem solving, throughout the work group and organization. Examining special topics in management that cut across industry differences and apply to all types of managers may provide a competitive advantage for modern managers in the global marketplace.

BIBLIOGRAPHY

Bae, J., & Lawler, J. (2000). Organizational and HRM strategies in Korea: Impact on firm performance in an emerging economy. *Academy of Management Journal, 43,* 502–517. Retrieved March 22, 2007, from EBSCO Online Database Business Source Complete. http://search.ebscohost.com/login.aspx?direct=true&db=bth&AN=3269709&site=ehost-live

Bowen, S. (2005). A practical model for ethical decision making in issues management and public relations. *Journal of Public Relations Research, 17,* 191–216. Retrieved March 22, 2007, from EBSCO Online Database Business Source Complete. http://search.ebscohost.com/login.aspx?direct=true&db=bth&AN=17408195&site=ehost-live

Brown, S. A., Dennis, A. R., Burley, D., & Arling, P. (2013). Knowledge sharing and knowledge management system avoidance: The role of knowledge type and the social network in bypassing an organizational knowledge management system. *Journal of the American Society for Information Science & Technology, 64,* 2013–2023. Retrieved November 21, 2013, from EBSCO Online Database Business Source Complete. http://search.ebscohost.com/login.aspx?direct=true&db=bth&AN=90167661&site=ehost-live

Butler, T., & Murphy, C. (2007). Understanding the design of information technologies for knowledge management in organizations: a pragmatic perspective. *Information Systems Journal, 17,* 143–163. Retrieved March 22, 2007, from EBSCO Online Database Business Source Complete. http://search.ebscohost.com/login.aspx?direct=true&db=bth&AN=23983454&site=ehost-live

Greve, H. R. (2013). Microfoundations of management: Behavioral strategies and levels of rationality in organizational action. *Academy of Management Perspectives, 27,* 103–119. Retrieved November 21, 2013, from EBSCO Online Database Business Source Complete. http://search.ebscohost.com/login.aspx?direct=true&db=bth&AN=88419316&site=ehost-live

Kachgal, J. A. (2015). The synergy needed for business resilience. *Journal of Business Continuity & Emergency Planning, 9*(1), 10–17. Retrieved December 4, 2015, from EBSCO Online Database Business Source Complete. http://search.ebscohost.com/login.aspx?direct=true&db=bth&AN=110394504&site=ehost-live&scope=site

Kahn, W. A., Barton, M. A., & Fellows, S. (2013). Organizational crises and the disturbance of relational systems. *Academy of Management Review, 38,* 377–396. Retrieved November 21, 2013, from EBSCO Online Database Business Source Complete. http://search.ebscohost.com/login.aspx?direct=true&db=bth&AN=88424236&site=ehost-live

Krausert, A. (2014). HRM Systems for Knowledge Workers: Differences among Top Managers, Middle Managers, and Professional Employees. *Human Resource Management, 53,* 67–87. Retrieved

December 3, 2014, from EBSCO Online Database Business Source Complete. http://search.ebscohost.com/login.aspx?direct=true&db=bth&AN=94063591

Lopez, R. (2014). The Relationship between Leadership and Management: Instructional Approaches and Its Connections to Organizational Growth. *Journal of Business Studies Quarterly, 6,* 98–112. Retrieved December 3, 2014, from EBSCO Online Database Business Source Complete. http://search.ebscohost.com/login.aspx?direct=true&db=bth&AN=98181431

Osterloh, M., Frost, J., & Frey, B. (2002). The dynamics of motivation in new organizational forms. *International Journal of the Economics of Business, 9* , 61–77. Retrieved March 22, 2007, from EBSCO Online Database Business Source Complete. http://search.ebscohost.com/login.aspx?direct=true&db=bth&AN=6428886&site=ehost-live

Pearson, C., & Clair, J. (1998). Reframing crisis management. *Academy of Management Review, 23,* 59–76. Retrieved March 22, 2007, from the EBSCO Online Database Business Source Complete. http://search.ebscohost.com/login.aspx?direct=true&db=bth&AN=192960&site=ehost-live

Pender, J. (2007). Management as a regulated profession. *Journal of Management Inquiry, 16,* 32–42. Retrieved March 22, 2007, from EBSCO Online Database Business Source Complete. http://search.ebscohost.com/login.aspx?direct=true&db=bth&AN=24229009&site=ehost-live

Schneider, B., Gunnarson, S., & Niles-Jolly, K. (1994). Creating the climate and culture of success. *Organizational Dynamics, 23,* 17-29. Retrieved March 22, 2007, from EBSCO Online Database Business Source Complete. http://search.ebscohost.com/login.aspx?direct=true&db=bth&AN=9408183850&site=ehost-live

US Department of Labor. (2006). *Occupational outlook handbook.* The Bulletin 2600. Retrieved March 22, 2007, from http://www.bls.gov/oco/oco1001.htm

Wartenberg, M. (1996). Management fads or management basics? *Management Review, 85,* 62. Retrieved March 22, 2007, from EBSCO Online Database Business Source Complete. http://search.ebscohost.com/login.aspx?direct=true&db=bth&AN=9603130337&site=ehost-live

Zuidema, K., & Kleiner, B. (1994). New developments in developing self-directed work groups. *Management Decision, 32,* 57. Retrieved March 22, 2007, from EBSCO Online Database Business Source Complete. http://search.ebscohost.com/login.aspx?direct=true&db=bth&AN=9606030969&site=ehost-live

Suggested Reading

Atkinson, S. (2014). *The business book.* New York, NY: Dorling Kindersley, 2014.

Cooke, B., Mills, A., & Kelley, E. (2005). Situating Maslow in cold war America: a recontextualization of management theory. *Group & Organization Management, 30,* 129–152. Retrieved March 22, 2007, from EBSCO Online Database Business Source Complete. http://search.ebscohost.com/login.aspx?direct=true&db=bth&AN=16462436&site=ehost-live

Gerhart, B. (2005). Human resources and business performance: findings, unanswered questions, and an alternative approach. *Management Revue, 16,* 174–185. Retrieved March 22, 2007, from EBSCO Online Database Business Source Complete. http://search.ebscohost.com/login.aspx?direct=true&db=bth&AN=17110699&site=ehost-live

Gherardi, S., & Murgia, A. (2014). What Makes a "Good Manager"? Positioning Gender and Management in Students' Narratives. *Equality, Diversity & Inclusion, 33,* 690–707. Retrieved December 3, 2014. Retrieved December 3, 2014, from EBSCO Online Database Business Source Complete. http://search.ebscohost.com/login.aspx?direct=true&db=bth&AN=99410366

Giannoccaro, I. (2013). *Behavioral issues in operations management: New trends in design, management, and methodologies.* London: Springer. Retrieved November 21, 2013, from EBSCO Online Database eBook Collection. http://search.ebscohost.com/login.aspx?direct=true&db=nlebk&AN=564874&site=ehost-live

Harari, O. (1995). The missing link in performance. *Management Review, 84,* 21. Retrieved March 22, 2007, from EBSCO Online Database Business Source Complete. http://search.ebscohost.com/login.aspx?direct=true&db=bth&AN=9503153033&site=ehost-live

Simone I. Flynn, Ph.D.

STATISTICAL PRINCIPLES FOR PROBLEM SOLVING

ABSTRACT

Problem solving and decision making are important aspects of running a business. One of the tools that can help in solving real world problems is statistics. Descriptive statistics include graphical techniques to organize and summarize data so that they are more easily comprehensible and simple processes to summarize basic parameters of distributions. Inferential statistics helps decision makers solve problems in more complex situations and to draw conclusions about what the data signify rather than merely describing what they look like. Statistics can also be of help in business problem solving through the development of mathematical models. To meaningfully apply statistics to real world data, the researcher needs to do two things: Control the situation so that the research is only measuring what it is supposed to measure and include as many of the relevant factors as possible so that the research fairly emulates the real world experience.

OVERVIEW

Just as in the rest of life, problem solving and decision making are important aspects of running a business. Changes in the economy, innovations by one's competitors, and new demands and expectations of the marketplace all mean that the organization needs to constantly adjust how it does business in order to stay competitive and gain or maintain its market share. For example, implementation of new technology to become more competitive may require an investment, and the savvy organization needs to determine whether or not the benefits of the investment will exceed its costs. Similarly, if a long-standing business process cannot keep up with expanding customer demands, management must determine whether to try to repair the existing process or develop and implement an entirely new one. If the engineering department proposes a new widget to be added to the product line, it must be determined whether or not potential customers are likely to buy the product as well as whether or not the addition will compete with the existing product line or enhance it.

Many times, decisions such as these are made subjectively based on the insights of experienced managers and other decision makers. This is not necessarily a bad idea: veteran managers can take advantage of years of experience to extrapolate trends in ways that are still not possible through the use of quantitative techniques alone. In addition, in some situations there may be insufficient data to use quantitative techniques, necessitating the use of qualitative forecasting methods. However, not every manager or decision maker has the skills or experience to make such decisions unaided. In addition, real world problems are complex, and insightful managers use every tool at their command to make the best decisions possible. One of these tools is statistics.

Statistics is a branch of mathematics that deals with the analysis and interpretation of data. Mathematical statistics provides the theoretical underpinnings for various applied statistical disciplines, including business statistics, in which data are analyzed to find answers to quantifiable questions. Applied statistics uses these techniques to solve real world problems. In general, there are two types of statistical tools:

- Descriptive statistics helps one describe and summarize data so that they can be more easily understood.
- Inferential statistics is used in the analysis and interpretation of data to make inferences from the data and help in the processes of problem solving and decision making.

Descriptive Techniques: Graphing Techniques

Descriptive statistics helps describe data through graphical techniques that organize and summarize them so that they are more easily comprehensible. Descriptive statistics also include various processes to simply summarize basic parameters of distributions including various techniques to find the "average" or mathematically describe the shape of the distribution. There are many graphing techniques available.

Frequency Distribution

One of the most frequently used methods is the frequency distribution. In this type of graph, data are divided into intervals of typically equal length, thereby decreasing the number of data points on the graph and organizing the data to make them easier

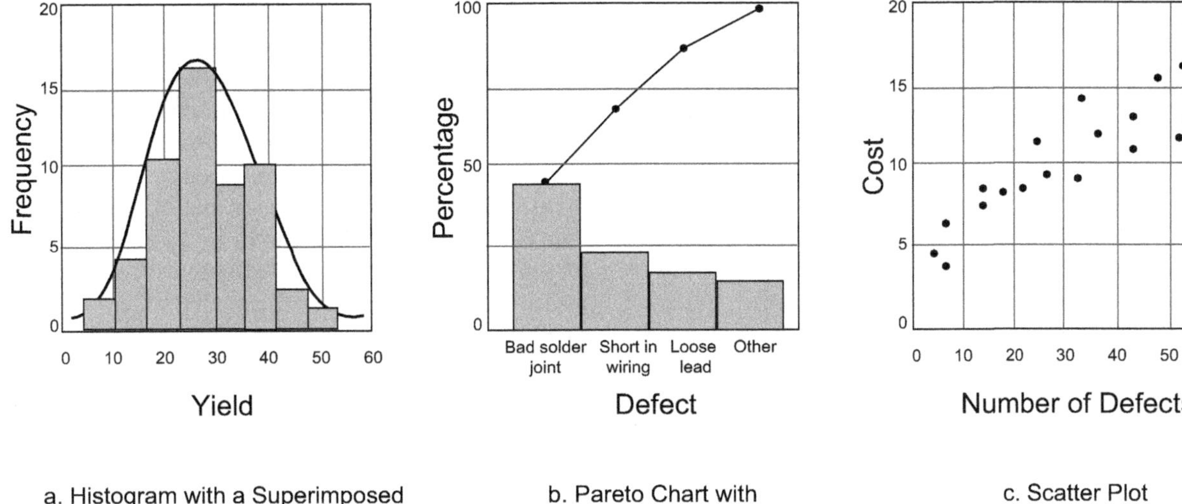

Figure 1: Examples of Some Commonly Used Graphing Techniques

to comprehend. Other types of graphing techniques used in descriptive statistics include histograms, Pareto diagrams, scatter plots, and graphs.

Histograms

Histograms are vertical bar charts that graph frequencies of objects within various classes on the *y* axis against the classes on the *x* axis.

Pareto Diagrams

Pareto diagrams are vertical bar charts that graph the number and types of defects for a product or service against the order of magnitude (from greatest to least). Pareto charts are often shown with cumulative percentage line graphs to more easily show the total percentage of errors accounted for by various defects.

Scatter Plots

Scatter plots graphically depict two-variable numerical data so that the relationship between the variables can be examined. For example, of one wanted to know the relationship between number of defects observed in a given month and the cost of the loss of quality to the company, these two values (number of defects and concomitant cost) could be graphed on a two-dimensional graph so that one could better understand the relationship.

Examples of a histogram (with frequency distribution), Pareto chart (with cumulative percentage line graph) and scatter plot are shown in Figure 1.

Descriptive Techniques: Central Tendency

In addition to graphing techniques, descriptive statistics can be used to describe the central tendency and the variability of a sample. Measures of central tendency estimate the midpoint of a distribution. These measures include the median (the number in the middle of the distribution when the data points are arranged in order), the mode (the number occurring most often in the distribution), and the mean (a mathematically derived measure in which the sum of all data in the distribution is divided by the number of data points in the distribution). For example, as shown in Figure 2, for the distribution 2, 3, 3, 7, 9, 14, 17, the mode is 3 (there are two 3s in the distribution, but only one of each of the other numbers), the median is 7 (when the seven numbers in the distribution are arranged numerically, 7 is the number that occurs in the middle), and the mean (or arithmetic mean) is 7.857 (the sum of the seven numbers is 55; 55 / 7 = 7.857).

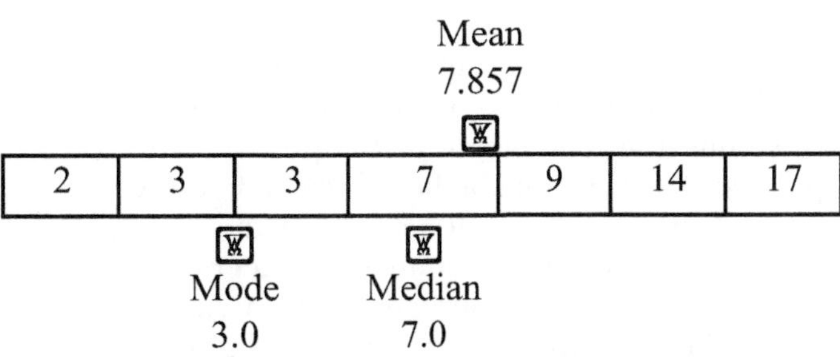

Figure 2: Measures of Central Tendency for a Simple Distribution

Descriptive Techniques: Variability

In addition to measures of central tendency, descriptive statistics include measures of variability that summarize how widely dispersed the data are over the distribution. The first of these statistics is the range, which is the difference between the highest and lowest scores. By knowing the range in addition to one of the measures of central tendency, one can better understand the data. For example, two distributions with a mean of 10 would be quite different if the range of one was between 1 and 100 and the range of the other was between 9 and 11. However, although the range does help one better understand the data, it is not a very refined statistic. To better understand the shape of the distribution, one can calculate the standard deviation. This is a mathematically derived index of the degree to which scores differ from the mean of the distribution and describes how far the typical score in a distribution is from the mean of the distribution. The standard deviation is obtained by determining the deviation of each score from the mean (i.e., subtracting the mean from the score), squaring the deviations (i.e., multiplying them by themselves), adding the squared deviations, and dividing this number by the total number of scores. The larger the standard deviation, the farther away it is from the midpoint of the distribution.

Shewhart Control Charts

These two types of descriptive statistics can be combined into a technique called Shewhart control charts that help quality control engineers and managers solve problems regarding quality of a product and whether or not a process is under control. An example of this kind of chart is the *X*-bar chart (so named for *X*¾, the mathematical symbol for the arithmetic mean). This is a chart of the means of some characteristic of the product (e.g., acceptability of solder joints) of small random samples taken from the production line over time. As shown in Figure 3, the means are plotted over time on a chart that contains a center line (i.e., the mean for the process) and upper and lower control limits that are three standard deviations on either side of this line. *X*-bar charts help quality control engineers and managers determine where problem areas lie in a production process. If all the points plotted on the chart fall between the upper and lower control limits, the process is considered to be in control. However, if sample means fall outside the control limits, the process is considered to be out of control and the process is stopped so that an assignable cause can be determined. In addition to *X*-bar charts that keep track of processes by examining the means of samples, quality control charts include *R* charts that keep track of the range, *p* charts track the proportion of defective products, *c* charts track the number of defects, and *s* charts that examine sample variance.

Inferential Statistics

Although descriptive statistics are useful in helping one better understand data, inferential statistics help decision makers to problem solve based on data for more complex situations.

Inferential statistics helps decision makers to draw conclusions about what the data signify rather than merely describing what they look like. Through the use of inferential statistics, one can analyze various characteristics of a random sample to determine whether or not any observed differences are due to chance or because of a real difference in the sample from the population. Inferential statistics includes a wide range of tests of statistical significance to help solve problems and make decisions by estimating the degree to which it is probable that the observed results occurred by chance alone or are due to an experimental manipulation or other predetermined factor.

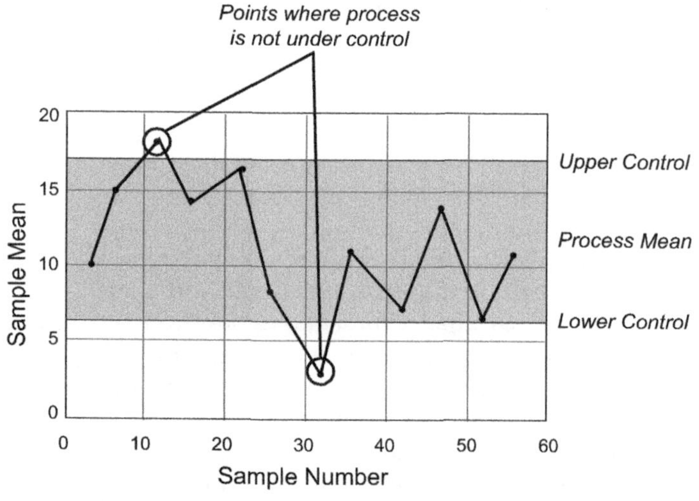

Figure 3: Simplified X Bar

Correlation

Another frequently used statistical tool with real world applications is correlation. This tool allows one to determine the degree to which two events or variables are related. For example, a market researcher may want to know if people with greater disposable income are more likely to buy luxury items. The correlation coefficient is the statistical method for determining this relationship. Correlation may be positive (i.e., as the value of one variable increases the value of the other variable increases), negative (i.e., as the value of one variable increases the value of the other variable decreases), or zero (i.e., the values of the two variables are unrelated). Correlation does not imply causation, however: Just because two variables are related does not mean that one caused the other. Both may be caused by a third, unknown factor.

Mathematical Models

Another way that statistics can be of help in business problem solving is through the development of mathematical models. Regression is a statistical technique used to develop a mathematical model for use in predicting one variable from the knowledge of another variable. There are a number of regression techniques available for models to be used in problem solving ranging from simple linear regression to more advanced techniques that allow the analyst to use both multiple independent and dependent variables. No matter the technique, the resulting regression equation is a mathematical model of a real world situation. This can be invaluable for forecasting and learning more about the interaction of variables in the real world. The use of models is particularly helpful for problem solving in complex situations that cannot be solved intuitively. Models are very useful tools that create a representation that can be examined and manipulated to include relevant variables and relationships in the decision making process to reflect various alternate solutions to a problem. However, models need to be validated at each step and consequently adjusted as necessary and revalidated in order to optimize their use in decision making. This process is illustrated in Figure 4.

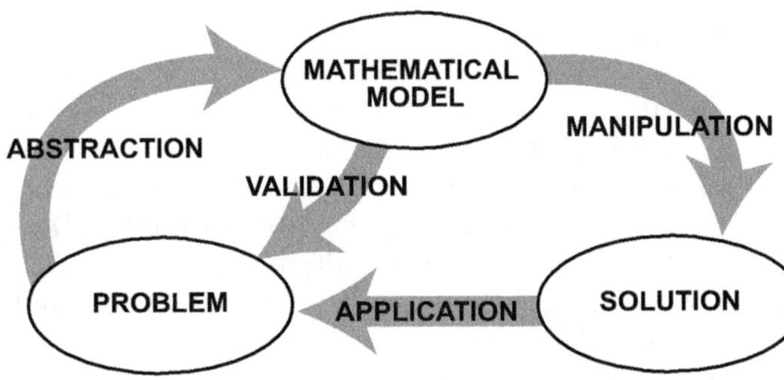

(from Plane & Kochenberger, p. 14)

Figure 4: Problem Solving Flow

APPLICATIONS

Inferential statistics allow one to problem solve by determining the answers to real world questions. The goal of research is to describe, explain, and predict behavior. For example, the marketing department may need solve the problem of which of two proposed new company logos will be most memorable and will have the most positive image in the minds of prospective customers, or the engineering department may need to determine which of two graphical user interfaces is more user friendly. Inferential statistics can help answer such questions.

Research Requirements

To solve these or other real world problems, the researcher needs to do two things: Control the situation so that the research is only measuring what it is supposed to measure and include as many of the relevant factors as possible so that the research fairly emulates the real world experience. As shown in Figure 5, in experimental research, a stimulus (e.g., a new graphical user interface) is presented to the research subjects (e.g., potential customers) and a response is observed and recorded (e.g., which interface they liked better). Researchers look at the independent variable (i.e., the stimulus or experimental condition that is hypothesized to affect behavior — such as the type of graphical user interface) and the dependent variable (i.e., the observed effect on behavior caused by the independent variable — such as the user's response to the interfaces). However, real world problems are rarely this clean, and one must also consider extraneous variables — variables that affect the outcome of the experiment (i.e., whether or not the people questioned like the new interface) that have nothing to do with the independent variable itself. For example, if a person is in a hurry to get somewhere else or has something else on

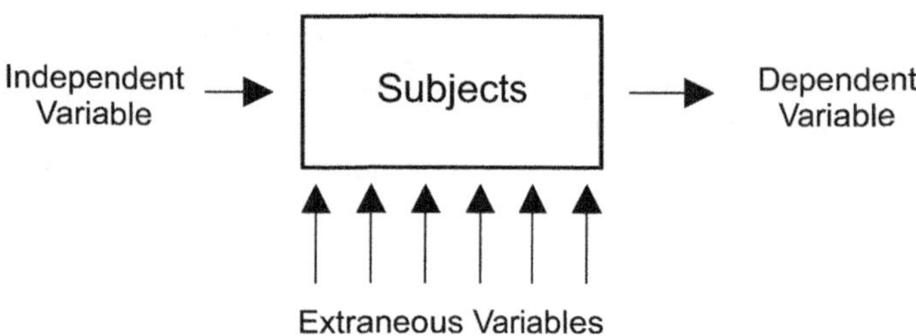

Figure 5: Research Variables

his or her mind, he or she may not give the alternative interfaces all the consideration that is needed to tell which is better. Although it is impossible to control for every possible extraneous variable, a well-designed experiment controls for as many of the extraneous variables as possible.

Laboratory Research

Laboratory research allows one the most control over variables. However, it often is far-removed from real life and the actual problems that need to be solved. Although controlling variables is important, it is just as important to conduct research in a setting as close to the real world as possible. For example, users will typically use a user interface in less than ideal conditions, such as when they are tired or distracted, not just when they are at their best. In order to be able to extrapolate research results to the real world and have them be meaningful, it is important to design an experiment that not only controls extraneous variables, but is as realistic as possible.

Field Simulation & Experimentation

In addition to laboratory research, there are several research techniques that can be used to investigate real world business problems. A more realistic approach to real world research is offered by simulation. This technique allows the researcher to bring in more real world variables while still controlling many of the extraneous variables. For example, people could be asked to do a set number of tasks with the new graphical user interface in an environment that simulates they way will actually would use it in the real world (e.g., while doing other tasks or being exposed to various distractions). Another approach to real world research is the field experiment in which people are given the product to try at work under the actual conditions in which they would use it. However, although this approach has the advantage of being more realistic, it has the concomitant disadvantage of giving the researcher less control over extraneous variables.

Field Study & Survey Research

The laboratory experiment, field experiment, and simulation give the experimenter some control over the variables. However, it is not always possible to do research in such settings. There are other approaches to studying business problems that trade more realism for less control. One of these approaches is the field study. This approach examines how people behave in the real world. For example, if both interface designs are already on the market, the researcher could observe what type of people bought each design and use this information to determine how to target the marketing of the product. The field study can also be combined with another research technique called survey research. Subjects could be interviewed by a member of the research team or asked to fill out a questionnaire regarding their preferences, reactions, habits, or other questions of interest to the researcher. Although it is possible in theory to develop a very detailed research instrument that could be used to collect all the data that the researcher needed for analysis, in practice, such detailed instruments are often more lengthy than the potential research subject's attention span. Survey research and interview techniques have the additional drawback of not being based on observation. Because of this fact, there is no way to know whether or not the subject is telling the truth for any number of reasons (e.g., s/he did not have much time to answer the questionnaire, was not really interested in helping in the research, did not like the company, wanted to please the researcher).

Bibliography

Aliev, R. A., PedrycZ, W. W., & Huseynov, O. H. (2012). Decision theory with imprecise probabilities. *International Journal of Information Technology & Decision Making, 11*(2), 271-306. Retrieved November 27, 2013 from EBSCO Online Database Business Source Premier. http://search.ebscohost.com/login.aspx?direct=true&db=buh&AN=75255353

Black, K. (2006). *Business statistics for contemporary decision making* (4th ed.). New York: John Wiley & Sons.

Carmeli, A., Gelbard, R., & Reiter-Palmon, R. (2013). Leadership, creative problem-solving capacity, and creative performance: The importance of knowledge sharing. *Human Resource Management, 52*(1), 95-121. Retrieved November 27, 2013 from EBSCO Online Database Business Source Premier. http://search.ebscohost.com/login.aspx?direct=true&db=buh&AN=85103177

Perla, R. J., Provost, L. P., & Parry, G. J. (2013). Seven propositions of the science of improvement: Exploring foundations. *Quality Management in Health Care, 22*(3), 170-186. Retrieved November 27, 2013 from EBSCO Online Database Business Source Premier. http://search.ebscohost.com/login.aspx?direct=true&db=buh&AN=89445306

Plane, D. R. & Kochenberger, G. A. (1972). *Operations research for managerial decisions* Homewood, IL: Richard D. Irwin.

Witte, R. S. (1980). *Statistics.* New York: Holt, Rinehart and Winston.

Suggested Reading

Aparisi, F., Avendaño, G., & Sanz, J. (2006). Techniques to interpret T2 control chart signals. *IIE Transactions, 38*(8), 647-657. Retrieved August 28, 2007, from EBSCO Online Database Business Source Complete. http://search.ebscohost.com/login.aspx?direct=true&db=bth&AN=20917671&site=ehost-live

Bardia, S. C., Shweta, K., & Garima, B. (2011). Inferential statistics as a measure of judging the short-term solvency: An empirical study of five pharmaceutical companies in India. *IUP Journal Of Accounting Research & Audit Practices, 10*(1), 69-80. Retrieved November 27, 2013 from EBSCO Online Database Business Source Premier. http://search.ebscohost.com/login.aspx?direct=true&db=buh&AN=57489825

Bowerman, B. L. & O'Connel, R. T. (2005). *Business statistics in practice* (4th ed.). Columbus, OH: Irwin/McGraw-Hill.

Groebner, D. F., Shannon, P. W., Fry, P. C., & and Smith, K. D. (2003). *Business statistics: A decision-making approach* (6th ed.). Upper Saddle River, NJ: Prentice Hall.

Levine, D. M., Krehbiel, T. C., & Berenson, M. L. (2005). *Business statistics: First course* (4th ed.). Upper Saddle River, NJ: Prentice Hall.

Ormerod, T., MacGregor, J., Chronicle, E., Dewald, A., & Chu, Y. (2013). Act first, think later: The presence and absence of inferential planning in problem solving. *Memory & Cognition, 41*(7), 1096-1108. Retrieved November 27, 2013 from EBSCO Online Database Business Source Premier. http://search.ebscohost.com/login.aspx?direct=true&db=buh&AN=90290452

Taplin, R. (2007). Enhancing statistical education by using role-plays of consultations. *Journal of the Royal Statistical Society, 170*(2), 267-300. Retrieved August 28, 2007, from EBSCO Online Database Business Source Complete. http://search.ebscohost.com/login.aspx?direct=true&db=bth&AN=24651036&site=ehost-live

Ruth A. Wienclaw, Ph.D.

T

Team Management

ABSTRACT

This article will focus on the complexities of managing teams in today's contemporary organizations. With organizations shifting from tall hierarchical functional structures to flatter team and network structures, managers are faced with some new challenges. These challenges include how to manage team types, team stages, communication strategies, and team leadership strategies and styles. The manager is faced with juggling between advocating change and controlling/evaluating team performance. It appears that the new manager should emphasize transformation rather than transaction when managing a team environment.

OVERVIEW

Role of Teams in Contemporary Organizations

Many environmental forces, such as information, technology, and new decision-making strategies, have caused organizations to move towards integrating employee work teams into their structural makeup. One such environmental force has been the shift from the industrial worker to the knowledge worker as a result of the information boom (Drucker, as cited in LaRue, Childs, & Larson, 2004). With the speed, availability, and accessibility of information, a need to share knowledge within organizations has been a prime driving force for creating an atmosphere of teamwork. Technology advancements make it possible for social capital to be as strategically important to organizations as intellectual capital. Never in history has the technological infrastructure made it so easy to implement collaborative strategies such as cross-functional teams, self-managed teams, committees, and virtual work groups. The way decisions are made transformed from a top management activity to a responsibility of all employees (LaRue et al., 2004). These forces, among others, have created a need for employees to work together, formally or informally, in order to share information and employ interdependency as a means for accomplishing organizational objectives. The use of teams, groups, committees, and other collaborative work structures are gaining in use as organizations attempt to adjust to these environmental changes. As such, leaders and managers must consider their approach to teams (their style, behaviors, strategies, role, and their disposition towards the team structure) as part of their leadership and management framework.

Team Formation Decision Factors for Managers

The decision to implement a team within the confines of an organization should not be taken lightly. Creating work teams is an investment in people, time, energy, resources, and workspace. As such, the conditions that favor the creation of organizational teams should be well understood before making the risky leap into team implementation. Steps should be taken to ensure that the conditions are right; the decision to implement a team structure is often considered a crucial strategic decision.

Several conditions should exist before creating a team. First, a clear and concise team vision and mission should be defined and closely aligned with the overall organizational strategy (Caplan et al., 1992). Second, the business needs goals and objectives that are complex and require high quality decisions (Pitman, 1994). Third, the benefits of pooling knowledge must outweigh the efficiency lost because of group engagement (MacNeil, 2003). Fourth, mutual commitment by those recruited to the team is possible and desired (Pitman, 1994). Fifth, the organization must have a trusting environment that allows for mutually effective collaboration between team members (Politis, 2003). Finally, the team needs to have the full support from the management and leaders of the organization (Jones & Schilling, 2000). Organizational managers and leaders need to engage in a research phase to ensure that these conditions exist. Otherwise, the organization may simply be setting the team up for subsequent and unanticipated failure.

Management & Leadership in Teams

In a team environment, an organizational manager/ leader should consider two things; (1) the type of team, and (2) the stage of development in which the team resides.

Team Type

Different team types include cross-functional teams, self-managed teams, virtual teams, task forces, committees, ad hoc groups, quality circles, and process improvement teams, among others. Managers should consider team type as part of their management style. For example, the management required for a cross-functional product development team, for example, would likely be more directive than the leadership and management required for a virtual self-managed team, where the leadership roles are shared between the members. Using the wrong leadership or management behavior while interacting in a particular team type can be catastrophic — such as the manager recruited to participate in a self-managed team who behaves in a directive and authoritarian manner. Understanding the team stage is also important. Beck and Yeager (1996) described four team stages: team orientation, clarifying roles and responsibilities, doing the actual work or project, and solving problems. Depending on the stage that the team is in, the leader should be directing, delegating, empowering, or developing, or some combination thereof.

Team Stage

In addition to leadership/management behaviors and style, a manager's communication strategy should also be based on team stage. The most widely recognized model for organizational team stages was developed by Tuckman (Kinicki, 2003), and consisted of five stages; (1) forming, (2)storming, (3) norming, (4) performing, and (5) adjourning. The forming stage is the initial break-in stage of the team members. Members try to determine where they fit in, what the team focus is, and what their individual role will be. In the storming stage, the power within the group is ironed out, and individuals start to understand what their roles and influences on the team will be. In the norming stage, teams begin to come together as a cohesive group. Cooperative group discussions replace bids for power. In the performing stage, the group has matured, and is operating in a tight-knit committed group that holds each other mutually accountable. The project goal becomes the main task at hand, rather than relationships and leadership concerns. Once complete, the team adjourns, where an evaluation and "post mortem" analysis can often lead to the dismantling of the team.

Ranney and Deck (1995) developed a useful matrix for a communication strategy when leading teams — a strategy that is dependent on the team stage. Their examples included (1) being a coach and promoter in the forming stage, (2) being a coach, giving frequent feedback, reinforcing vision, and reviewing boundaries in the storming stage, (3) managing team membership and coaching in the performing stage, (4) being encouraging, recognizing achievement, and being supportive in the high performance stage, and (5) expressing appreciation in the completing stage. Successful management and leadership approaches often emphasize the importance of being conscious of team type and process stage in order to apply the most effective leadership/ management methodology.

Leadership Strengths & Weaknesses

A manager's strengths and weaknesses should also be considered when managing teams. For example, a manager's strengths might be his or her ability to be rational, pragmatic, logical, practical, and emotionally stabile. His or her weaknesses might be a need for perfection, micromanaging, and lack of delegation. Strengths and weaknesses such as these take on an entirely new meaning when evaluating management and leadership from a team perspective. As such, there are additional considerations that should be modified and included in this plan.

Team Member Perspective

A manager who is pragmatic and focused on logic can easily conflict with a fellow team member's style on a self-managed team. A team member who is creative, works at a quick pace and is outgoing, may have difficulty with the aforementioned behavior. The manager's need for perfection might be an excellent style to use in a quality circle, but is likely very ineffective in a new product think tank. A manager should create a process in which he or she is always conscious of the team type, team stage, and his or her own leadership strengths and weaknesses and how they match with the team needs.

Team Leader Perspective

Conger (1999) presented nine leadership styles that portray a convergence of three main leadership theories. The leadership dimensions were: Creating vision, providing inspiration, role modeling, intellectual stimulation, meaning -making, appealing to higher-order needs, empowering, setting high expectations, and fostering collective identity. These particular dimensions of leadership seem even more appropriate for the team environment. In particular, creating vision and fostering collective identity will be extremely beneficial to a team leader. In creating and implementing an organizational team, a clear and concise team vision and mission should be defined and closely aligned with the overall organizational strategy (Caplan et al., 1992). High performance teams require mutual commitment and accountability (Pitman, 1994). This will result in the desired collective identity. In addition, the other dimensions will also help lead a team, especially when creating change or transformation. The nine dimensions identified by Conger help team managers and leaders determine their approach and style.

Leading Change within a Team

Using the wrong leadership style at the wrong time can be a roadblock to team success. Some research suggests that team leadership is one of the major reasons why teams fail within organizations (Katzenbach, as cited in Sivasubramaniam, Murry, Avolio, & Jung, 2002). Some researchers suggest that leaders use a style that was less transactional and more transformational (Kinicki, 2003), based on the leader-follower relationship. In the team context, especially when driving change through a team effort, the leadership style and behaviors should emphasize the transformational leadership style as much as possible. Another word for change is to transform. This is the essence of transformational leadership — to drive continuous change through the organization. In a team environment, once the team has become familiar with their roles and mission, an effective team leader will focus on transformational behavior, and only use transactional behavior when an adjustment to the team is required, or when the results are not acceptable.

Yukl opened that transformational leaders "formulate a vision, develop a commitment to it among internal and external stakeholders, implement strategies to accomplish the mission, and imbed the new values and assumptions in the culture of the organization" (as cited in Strang, 2005, p.76). Formulating the vision is the first and likely the most important step in driving change through the implementation of teams. Nanus (2003) described what vision is and what vision is not. He defined vision as a perspective that is appropriate for the organization, clarifies purpose and direction, sets standards of excellence, inspires enthusiasm and commitment, is easily articulated and understood, is different, and ambitious. He opined that vision was not a prophecy, not a mission, not factual, not true or false, not static and not a constraint. Kouzes and Posner (2003) discussed *finding your voice* as a key leadership behavior in creating vision and inspiring and motivating others. Other research suggests that employing a transformational leadership style will result in a team that trusts leader judgment, comprehends their mission, supports team values, and has strong emotional ties (Avolio, Waldman, & Einstein, 1988). This certainly appears to be a formula for success in driving organizational change through teams, and is the framework that managers and leaders can embrace in creating an effective vision for leading change within a team.

Evaluation & Control

Performance evaluation is often considered a management function, rather than a leadership function. One of the major differences between management and leadership in Kotter's (2001) model is that managers control and problem solve while leaders motivate and inspire. Evaluating performance and making adjustments to improve performance would seem to fall under the management function of controlling. Popular management textbooks continue to emphasize controlling as a managerial function. However, part of the leadership construct in the team environment is to do exactly that—evaluate and control performance.

The element that links evaluation and control to leadership is trust. Bennis (1991) suggested that developing trust is one of the key ingredients for achieving personal growth in others. The team evaluation process builds this trust. Jones and Schilling (2000) stated, "The team-performance measurement process shows management the results of team performance, so management can trust that teams are doing the right things" (p.2). Even in self-managed teams, evaluating performance is critical for maintaining the support of the management team, which is an important component to team success. Mintzberg opined that the leadership and management components of one's job cannot be separated from a behavioral standpoint. The model suggested that leadership is simply a component of the management framework. In this context, there is little difference between team management and team leadership.

Managing Performance in Self-managed Virtual Teams

There are three main areas that relate to leadership performance in a self-managed virtual team. The first evaluation area relates to the type of leadership that the team uses within the virtual team environment. The second area relates to shared accountability for individual contributions and overall team results. The last area relates to the decision-making methods employed by the team to complete work assignments.

Management and leadership in a self-managed, self-directed, virtual learning team is quite different from the traditional management/leadership role in workplace teams. Traditional teams in the workplace had one leader/manager who would act as the director, facilitator, coach, guide and conduit to the rest of the organization. Self-managed, self-directed, virtual learning teams are a "different animal." In general, leadership is a shared responsibility in a self-managed team. In a shared leadership environment, the first priority of team leadership is the task itself (Bell and Kozlowski, as cited in Carte, Chidambaram, & Becker, 2006). Carte, et al. (2006) posited that there are two primary modes of leadership in a self-managed team environment. The first is expertise leadership, where team members tend to adopt leadership roles in their areas of expertise. The second is collective participatory management. The study indicated that in addition to individual leadership that stems from respective expertise, the team members need to collectively move the team towards the goal in a participatory way.

Mutual Accountability

Part of the shared leadership in a self-managed virtual team is mutual accountability. Team members have the task of holding each other accountable for his or her role and expected deliverables and members are expected to manage any resulting conflict effectively within the team. In academia, for example, Hackman (1990) asserted that academic teams have the challenge of managing differing work styles and work pace. This team phenomenon leads to the team having to "fit an indeterminate amount of work into a fixed amount of time" (Hackman, 1990, p.110). One effective way to manage this challenge in a virtual self-managed team is to hold each other accountable for individual tasks and expected content, timely submission of individual contributions, and involvement in the integration of individual ideas into a team product. High expectations of accountability in this team environment leads to each member trying to go above and beyond expectations in order to please and support their fellow team members.

Decision-Making

One of the major challenges that a self-managed team faces is the desire by team members to have an environment of conformity, consensus, and cohesiveness. As such, oftentimes self-managed teams find themselves engaged in the phenomenon of groupthink (Kinicki, 2003), where team members make decisions that they do not believe in, simply to be agreeable and pleasing to others on the team. The team might also engage in making satisficing decisions, where team members agree to decisions that satisfy a problem need without evaluating all the alternatives from which the best solution or decision may evolve. Part of the shared leadership in a self-managed virtual team is to ensure that the team consciously engages in constructive decision-making methods.

Creating an environment for effective decision-making is essential for the success of self-managed virtual teams. Manz and Neck (1995) created a decision-making model that can prevent groupthink and satisficing decision-making called Teamthink. The model presented 8 steps in the decision-making process. These included: "encouragement of divergent views, open expression of concerns/ideas, awareness of limitations/threats, recognition of each member's unique value, recognition of views outside of the group, discussion of collective doubts, adoption/utilization of non-stereotypical views, and recognition of ethical and moral consequences of decisions" (Manz, et al. 1995, p.7). An effective self-managed team will adopt these behaviors and expectations. During the brainstorming, each team member should be encouraged to provide critical input regarding approach, content, and project interpretation. All team members should accept constructive criticism gracefully and should be open to new ideas that conflict with their own beliefs and assumptions. One area that can proactively improve the process is to actually formalize these steps. Such an approach might make sense if the team were to remain together for a long time — more than just a few weeks.

APPLICATION

The discussion concerning team management and leadership revolved around four areas. First, an acute understanding of team type and team stage has a direct impact on the leadership style, behaviors, and communication strategies that one should employ in a team environment, both as a team manager/leader and as a team participant. Second, the manager should consider development areas that relate to his or her strengths and weaknesses and how these fit within an organizational team. Third, it would seem that the mix of transformational and transactional leadership behaviors needs to emphasize transformational leadership in a team environment, more so than in a traditional leader/constituent relationship. Finally, a new paradigm emerges; one in which the leadership falls under the management umbrella, rather than a separate entity. This paradigm shift was the result of analysis regarding how evaluation and control of team performance is critical to team success and critical to developing organizational trust.

As organizations have moved from employing a traditional mechanistic form into a more modern and contemporary form, formal organizational hierarchies and centralized decision-making structures have been replaced by hybrid, matrix and network forms that include the incorporation of high performance work teams. Modern day managers and leaders need to be prepared to understand the nature of teams, including when to implement teams, how to set teams up for success, and how to make teams integrated as an organizational cultural norm. The author of this paper presented ideas to facilitate the understanding of managing teams, including organizational context, framework and processes. Team creation and implementation within an organization is complex, as there are social, behavioral and process dynamics. The discussion helps the reader understand this complexity, making the decision to implement a team less risky.

BIBLIOGRAPHY

Avolio, B., Waldman, D., & Einstein, W. (1988). Transformational leadership in a management game simulation. *Group & Organization Studies, 13*(1), 59-80. Retrieved on March 14, 2007, from EBSCO Online Database Business Source Complete. http://search.ebscohost.com/login.aspx?direct=true&db=bth&AN=6537840&site=ehost-live

Beck, J. D. W., & Yeager, N. M. (1996). How to prevent teams from failing. *Quality Progress, 29*(3), 27.

Bennis, W. (1991). Leading followers, following leaders. *Executive Excellence, 8*(6), 5.

Caplan, D. W., Givens, D., Luff, G., Kowel, E. P., Sturrock, J. L., & Worden, D. D. (1992). A practical roadmap for high performing natural teams. *The Journal for Quality and Participation, 15*(3), 60.

Carte, T., A. , Chidambaram, L., & Becker, A. (2006). Emergent leadership in self-managed virtual teams. *Group Decision and Negotiation, 15*(4), 323-343. Retrieved May 1, 2007, from EBSCO Online Database Business Source Complete. http://search.ebscohost.com/login.aspx?direct=true&db=bth&AN=21587995&site=ehost-live

Conger, J. A. (1999). Charismatic and transformational leadership in organizations: An insider's perspective on these developing streams of research. *Leadership Quarterly, 10*(2), 145. Retrieved on May 1, 2007, from EBSCO Online Database Business Source Complete. http://search.ebscohost.com/login.aspx?direct=true&db=bth&AN=2406535&site=ehost-live

Hackman, J. R. (1990). *Groups that work (and those that don't)* (1st ed.). San Francisco: Jossey-Bass.

Hall, J. L. (2013). Managing teams with diverse compositions: Implications for managers from research on the faultline model. *SAM Advanced Management Journal, 78*(1), 4–10. Retrieved November 19, 2014, from EBSCO Online Database Business Source Complete. http://search.ebscohost.com/login.aspx?direct=true&db=bth&AN=88038524&site=bsi-live

Hoch, J. E., & Kozlowski, S. J. (2014). Leading virtual teams: Hierarchical leadership, structural supports, and shared team leadership. *Journal of Applied Psychology, 99*(3), 390–403. Retrieved November 19, 2014, from EBSCO Online Database Business Source Complete. http://search.ebscohost.com/login.aspx?direct=true&db=bth&AN=96070382&site=bsi-live

Hodes, B. (2013). Stupid games. *Sales & Service Excellence, 14*(9), 21. Retrieved November 15, 2013, from EBSCO Online Database Business Source Complete. http://search.ebscohost.com/login.aspx?direct=true&db=bth&AN=90416913&site=ehost-live

Jones, S. D., & Schilling, D. J. (2000). *Measuring team performance: A step-by-step customizable approach for managers, facilitators, and team leaders* (1st ed.). San Francisco, CA.: Jossey Bass.

Kinicki, A., & Williams, B. (2003). *Management: A practical introduction* (2nd ed.). New York, N.Y.: McGraw-Hill.

Kotter, J., P. (2001). What leaders really do. *Harvard Business Review, 79*(11), 85-96. Retrieved March 14, 2007, from EBSCO Online Database Business Source Complete. http://search.ebscohost.com/login.aspx?direct=true&db=bth&AN=5634852&site=ehost-live

Kouzes, J., & Posner, B. (2003). *The Leadership Challenge* (3rd ed.). San Francisco, CA.: Jossey-Bass.

LaRue, B., Childs, P., & Larson, K. (2004). *Leading organizations from the inside out: Unleashing the collaborative genius of Action-Learning Teams* (2nd ed.). New York: John Wiley and Sons.

Lorinkova, N.M., Pearsall, M.J., & Sims Jr., H.P. (2013). Examining the differential longitudinal performance of directive versus empowering leadership in teams. *Academy of Management Journal, 56*(2), 573-596. Retrieved November 15, 2013, from EBSCO Online Database Business Source Complete. http://search.ebscohost.com/login.aspx?direct=true&db=bth&AN=87563907&site=ehost-live

MacNeil, C. (2003). Line managers: Facilitators of knowledge sharing in teams. *Employee Relations, 25*(3), 294–307. Retrieved May 1, 2007, from EBSCO Online Database Business Source Complete. http://search.ebscohost.com/login.aspx?direct=true&db=bth&AN=11949390&site=ehost-live

Manz, C. C., & Neck, C. P. (1995). Teamthink: Beyond the groupthink syndrome in self-managing work teams. *Journal of Managerial Psychology, 10*(1), 7–15. Retrieved on May 1, 2007, from EBSCO Online Database Business Source Complete. http://search.ebscohost.com/login.aspx?direct=true&db=bth&AN=3926617&site=ehost-live

Mintzberg, H., Lampel, J., Quinn, J. B., & Ghoshal, S. (2003). *The strategy process* (4th ed.). Saddle River, N.J: Prentice Hall.

Nanus, B. (Ed.). (2003). *Business leadership* (1st ed.). San Francisco, Ca.: Jossey-Bass.

Nielsen, B., & Nielsen, S. (2013). Top management team nationality diversity and firm performance: A multilevel study. *Strategic Management Journal, 34*(3), 373–382. Retrieved November 15, 2013, from EBSCO Online Database Business Source Complete. http://search.ebscohost.com/login.aspx?direct=true&db=bth&AN=85018754&site=ehost-live

Politis, J.D. (2003). The connection between trust and knowledge management: What are its implications for team performance. *Journal of Knowledge Management, 7*(5), 55.

Pitman, B. (1994). Get a G.R.I.P.—On building high-performance teams. *Journal of Systems Management, 45*(8), 26.

Ranney, J., & Deck, K. (1995). Making teams work: Lessons from the leaders in new product development. *Planning Review, 23*(4), 6–13. Retrieved May 1, 2007, from EBSCO Online Database Business Source Complete. http://search.ebscohost.com/login.aspx?direct=true&db=bth&AN=9507311608&site=ehost-live

Sivasubramaniam, N., Murry, W., Avolio, B., J., & Jung, D. I. (2002). A longitudinal model of the effects of team leadership and group potency on group performance. *Group & Organization Management, 27*(1), 66–96. Retrieved May 1, 2007, from EBSCO Online Database Business Source Complete. http://search.ebscohost.com/login.aspx?direct=true&db=bth&AN=6300972&site=ehost-live

Strang, K. D. (2005). Examining effective and ineffective transformational project leadership. *Team Performance Management, 11*(3/4), 68.

Suggested Reading

Gibson, C., Vermulen, F. (2003). A healthy divide: Subgroups as a stimulus for team learning behavior. *Administrative Science Quarterly, 48*(2), 202–239. Retrieved May 1, 2007, from EBSCO Online Database Business Source Complete. http://search.ebscohost.com/login.aspx?direct=true&db=bth&AN=11542797&site=ehost-live

McLean, J. (2007). Prepare for the future. It's happening fast! *British Journal of Administrative Management,* (58), 17. Retrieved May 1, 2007, from EBSCO Online Database Business Source Complete. http://search.ebscohost.com/login.aspx?direct=true&db=bth&AN=24789661&site=ehost-live

Rosen, B., Furst, S., Blackburn, R. (2006). Training for virtual teams: An investigation of current practices and future needs. *Human Resource Management, 45*(2), 229–247. Retrieved May 1, 2007, from EBSCO Online Database Business Source Complete. http://search.ebscohost.com/login.aspx?direct=true&db=bth&AN=20917041&site=ehost-live

Yang, I. (2013). When team members meet in a new team: An exploration of team development. *Human Systems Management, 32*(3), 181–197. Retrieved November 19, 2014, from EBSCO Online Database Business Source Complete. http://search.ebscohost.com/login.aspx?direct=true&db=bth&AN=91895716&site=bsi-live

John D. Benson, M.B.A.

TEAMS & TEAM BUILDING

ABSTRACT

Increasingly, teams are the foundation of the 21st century workplace. The philosophy behind this widespread use of teams is that their use can create an environment in which synergy is achieved and the final outcome is greater than that which would have been achieved by individuals alone. Team development comprises several stages. However, this process is not always linear, and teams may experience multiple stages simultaneously or revert to previous stages. Team building efforts conducted by an outside party can help teams acquire the knowledge, skills, and abilities necessary for functional teamwork and achieving synergy, and to avoid pitfalls of team situations such as group-think. Team building efforts usually focus on defining the roles of team members, setting team goals, problem solving, and interpersonal processes.

OVERVIEW

Groups vs. Teams

At one time or another, most people in the twenty-first-century workplace will find themselves working as part of a team. Teams in an organizational setting can be as simple as two people working together to write a white paper or technical document or as complex as multiple businesses working together to bid a proposal or build the next-generation destroyer for the navy. However, not every group of people who work together can be considered a team. In general, groups in the workplace comprise two or more individuals who are interdependent and who interact over time. So, for example, the sales staff of a retail store might be considered a group. They interact with each other, ask each other for help (e.g., ring up a customer, find an item in stock or inventory), and support each other in accomplishing the tasks necessary for running a successful retail store. Groups work toward a common goal, are accountable to a manager, and may (ideally) accomplish their goals. Leadership of a group is held by a single individual. However, groups do not have a clear, stable culture, so conflict may be frequent.

Teams, on the other hand, are a special type of group. In a team, there is a differentiation of skills where one individual does a specific part of the task and other individuals do other specific parts of the task. Another way teams are differentiated from groups is that the members of a team perform their work in the context of a common fate. For example, although the members of the retail staff may help each other in the context of doing their jobs, they also all tend to do the same job. For the most part, dealing with one salesperson in a retail store should be the same as dealing with another person in the retail store. Further, members of a sales group typically do not share a common fate. For example, if Harvey does not do his job adequately, it will be Harvey—and not the rest of the sales staff—who will be reprimanded or fired.

On the other hand, some sales and marketing staffs are truly teams where there is differentiation of skill among the team members. For example, when trying to sell a learning management system for a computer-based training system, one member of the marketing team may specialize in comparing the business's system with that of the competition, while another team member might specialize in answering technical questions regarding the programmability of the system. If the remuneration of the team members is based in part on commission for making the sale, then the fate of the individual members of the team depends on the fate of the team as a whole (i.e., whether or not they sell the system). Leadership of a team is shared, and members are mutually accountable to each other. Because of these team characteristics, team members are committed to the goal and mission of the team, trust each other, and have a more collaborative culture than groups in general. As a result, teamwork often leads to a situation of synergy (Nahavandi, 2000).

Types of Teams

In general, four types of teams can be found in the workplace:

- Manager-led teams,
- Self-managing teams,
- Self-designing teams, and
- Self-governing teams (Hackman, 1987).

In manager-led teams, the design of the organizational context, the design of the team as a performing unit, and the monitoring and managing of the performance processes of the team is all a responsibility of the team manager. In self-managing teams, the design of the organizational context in which the team works as well as the design of the group as a performing unit are both done by management. However, the self-managing team not only executes the task, but also monitors and manages the performance processes used in the performance of the task. In a self-designing team, the organizational context in which the team operates is designed by management. However, all other aspects of the team functioning (i.e., design of the group as a performing unit, monitoring and managing of performance processes, and executing the task) are the responsibility of the team. In self-governing teams, all aspects of the team – including its design within the context of the organization – are the responsibility of the team.

FURTHER INSIGHTS

Team Development

Although organizations sometimes act as though teams can be created by fiat, team development is in fact a multistage process (Robbins, 1996). As illustrated in Figure 1, before a team is formed, it is a collection of individual entities. They may be part of a group (e.g., a sales staff), or they may not even know each other (e.g., individuals from two or more business who will write a proposal together). Once it is decided that a team will be formed (Stage 1), the team members still have a great deal of uncertainty concerning the nature of the team such as its mission and purpose, the capabilities of the other team members, what processes will best result in synergy, and the leadership of the team. During the forming stage of team development, members of the team try to determine the answers to these and other questions. Members learn to know each other better, determine each other's areas of expertise and experience, and try to determine what types of behavior is acceptable within the group. The forming stage is completed once the members no longer consider themselves to

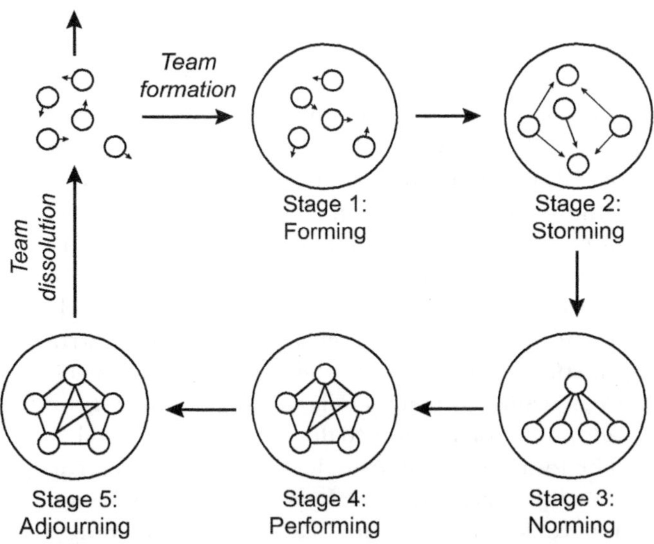

Figure 1: Stages in Team Development (Adapted from Robbins, 1996)

be a random collection of individuals, but as part of a team.

According to this theory, the second stage in team development is storming. This is often a stage of conflict within the team as members struggle with the constraints placed on them as individuals. For example, every semester, a teacher requires her students to do a team research project. Within these broad parameters, they are allowed to divide the tasks of the group in any way they want, are able to establish individual or team leadership, and, in general, perform the tasks of the team in whatever way they determine will best allow them to develop a project that will earn them a good grade. Every semester, at least one of these teams rebels and announces unequivocally that it is unfair to require them to depend on each other for a grade on the project. However, since satisfactory completion of the project is necessary to pass the course, these teams must use their conflict management skills in order to come to some level of mutual understanding about the leadership hierarchy within the group. This situation mimics that of the real-world workplace in which team members must learn to relinquish some of their individuality in favor of the potential that can be gained through teamwork and establish an acceptable leadership hierarchy in order to accomplish its tasks.

During the norming stage, the team develops norms—standards or patterns of behavior that are accepted as normal within the team—so that the team can accomplish its tasks. During this stage of team development, the team members bond with each other within the context of the team and its tasks and become a cohesive team. Another characteristic of this stage of team development is the development and assimilation of a set of common assumptions and expectations about what defines acceptable behavior within the group. For example, a project team in one class might decide that all members are expected to complete and submit their portion of the project on time according to a mutually agreed upon schedule and that each of the members is responsible for writing a specific part of the final report. In the workplace, a team may make similar arrangements for the development of a technical document or proposal.

The fourth stage of team development is performing. By this phase, the members of a functional team will have learned to know each other (forming), worked through the initial conflicts (storming), and determined how the team will operate (norming). It is time for the team to actually do the work for which it was brought together: conduct the research project, write the proposal, build a working model, etc. In some cases, teams are set up on a permanent basis to perform a certain kind of task. For example, an engineering team might be established to develop prototypes of new products. After the completion of one prototype, the team is then assigned to develop the prototype for another product. For such permanent teams, team development ends at this point.

However, a great many teams are established on a temporary basis. Once the project (or the class) is over, members (or students) are unlikely to continue to work together on other projects. Similarly, in the workplace, there are temporary teams such as Red Teams, task forces, and temporary committees. When the work of such teams has been accomplished, they move into the final stage of team development: adjourning. The team no longer needs to focus on accomplishing its task and, instead, focuses on the tasks necessary to wrap up the project and disband the group (e.g., final reports, distribution of products). As the work of the team winds down, the bonds between the members dissolve as the team disbands and members go back to other activities that do not involve the entire team. At this point, the team members once again become unassociated individuals.

Team Building

Although there is always the potential for teams to be dysfunctional and produce a lower-quality outcome than an individual, the concept of synergy resulting from teamwork is an attractive one, and many organizations use teams in order to foster this synergy and produce a superior outcome. Similarly, it is virtually impossible for many single organizations to be successful in meeting the needs of large contracts (e.g., development of a new destroyer), so the establishment of functional teams is essential. The question, then, becomes how to best help a team to work together harmoniously while reducing the likelihood of group-think and increasing the likelihood of synergy.

Team building is the process of turning a group of individuals who work together from a collection of individuals doing related tasks to a cohesive unit where the efforts of the team members act synergistically to yield results that could not have been done by the individuals alone. Typically, team-building efforts focus on defining the roles of team members, setting goals for the team, problem solving, and interpersonal processes (McShane & Von Glinow, 2003). Team building often comprises such activities as physical exercises that force team members to depend on each other in order to achieve a desired goal, communication exercises to teach team members to be better communicators, and small group sessions in which team members get to know each other in a nonthreatening situation.

Knowledge, Skills & Abilities (KSA)

Team-building efforts can take the form of many different types of activities targeted toward helping team members to manage conflict, avoid groupthink, and become synergistic. Although the methods used may differ, in general there are certain interpersonal and self-management knowledge, skills, and abilities (KSAs) that need to be present in a team – or taught through team building – that can help achieve these goals. According to Stevens & Campion (1994), from an interpersonal perspective, team members need to have strong conflict management KSAs, collaborative problem-solving KSAs, and communication KSAs. For conflict management, team members need "to be able to recognize and encourage desirable, but discourage undesirable, team conflict." In addition, team members need to be able "to recognize the type and source of conflict confronting the team and to implement an appropriate conflict resolution strategy." Finally, team members need to be able to "employ an integrative (win-win) negotiation strategy rather than the traditional distributive (win-lose) strategy" (Stevens & Campion, 1994, p. 505).

In addition to conflict management KSAs, team members also need the KSAs to collaboratively solve problems in order for the team to be functional. Specifically, team members need to be able to identify situations requiring "participative group problem solving and to utilize the proper degree and type of participation" (p. 505) and recognize the obstacles to collaborative group problem solving and implement appropriate corrective actions.

Further, team members need the KSAs necessary for clear communication. This means that team members need to be able to understand communication networks and to utilize decentralized networks to enhance communication where possible; communicate openly and supportively (i.e., send messages that are behavior- or event-oriented, congruent, validating, conjunctive, and owned); listen nonjudgmentally and appropriately use active listening techniques; maximize consonance between nonverbal and verbal messages; recognize and interpret the nonverbal messages of others; and engage in ritual greetings and small talk, with a recognition of their importance (Stevens & Campion, 1994, p. 505).

High functioning teams need to not only possess the interpersonal KSAs discussed above, but must also have the appropriate KSAs for self-management of the team. Specifically, team members need to be able to set goals and manage performance within the team. KSAs necessary for this aspect of team functionality include the KSAs to help establish specific, challenging, and accepted team goals and to monitor, evaluate, and provide feedback on both overall team performance and individual team member performance. In addition, team members need to possess the KSAs to plan and coordinate the tasks of the team. These include the abilities to "synchronize activities, information, and task interdependencies between team members and to help establish task and role expectations of individual team members, and to ensure proper balancing of workload in the team" (Stevens & Campion, 1994).

VIEWPOINTS

The five-stage model of team development described by Robbins has been popular since the 1960s. However, although it does describe the general progression of team development, it does so at a simplistic level. For example, it is unlikely that all conflict will be permanently resolved at the conclusion of the storming stage. In fact, many experts believe that conflict is necessary to accomplish the synergy desired from teamwork. Otherwise, a situation of groupthink can arise in which group members tend to have the same opinion as each other in order avoid conflict, reduce interpersonal pressure, or maintain an illusion of unity or cohesiveness without thoroughly thinking through the problem. This condition works against the process of good decision making and can result in a poorer product from a group effort rather than the synergy desired from teamwork. Similarly, the five-stage model presents team development as a linear process, proceeding neatly from one stage to another. In actuality, many teams return to previous stages or even exist in multiple stages at the same time (e.g., storming and performing simultaneously).

For most of us, teams are a reality of the twenty-first-century workplace. The goal of teams is typically to develop a physical, written, or conceptual product that is better than that which any one individual could have developed alone. However, the development of a functional team takes work and each team must go through several stages before it becomes optimally functional. External team-building efforts can help teams become more functional, avoid potential pitfalls such as groupthink, and work together synergistically to produce a better product. Research continues into the dynamics and performance of teams and other groups, with companies and other organizations continually looking for ways to improve teamwork and therefore overall efficiency, productivity, and satisfaction. For example, psychological tests may be used to evaluate employees or contractors in an effort to identify the best members for an ideal team.

BIBLIOGRAPHY

Hackman, J. R. (1987). The design of work teams. In J. W. Lorsch (Ed.), *Handbook of Organizational Behavior*. Upper Saddle River, NJ: Prentice Hall.

Hillier, J., & Dunn-Jensen, L. M. (2013). Groups meet ... teams improve: Building teams that learn. *Journal of Management Education, 37*(5), 704–733. Retrieved November 27, 2013 from EBSCO online database Business Source Premier. http://search.ebscohost.com/login.aspx?direct=true&db=buh&AN=89989968

McShane, S. L., & Von Glinow, M. A. (2003). *Organizational behavior: Emerging realities for the workplace revolution* (2nd ed.). Boston, MA: McGraw-Hill/Irwin.

Nahavandi, A. (2000). *The art and science of leadership* (2nd ed.). Upper Saddle River, NJ: Prentice Hall.

Pentland, A. (2012). The new science of building great teams. *Harvard Business Review, 90*(4), 60–70. Retrieved November 27, 2013 from EBSCO online database Business Source Premier. http://search.ebscohost.com/login.aspx?direct=true&db=buh&AN=73561030

Radomes, A. A., Jr. (2013). The whole can be worse than the sum of its parts: Counterintuitive consequences of group facilitation. *Advances in Management, 6*(5), 11–23. Retrieved November 27, 2013 from EBSCO online database Business Source Premier. http://search.ebscohost.com/login.aspx?direct=true&db=buh&AN=87502396

Rahman, M., & Kumaraswamy, M. M. (2012). Multicountry perspectives of relational contracting and integrated project teams. *Journal of Construction Engineering & Management, 138*(4), 469–480. Retrieved November 27, 2013 from EBSCO online database Business Source Premier. http://search.ebscohost.com/login.aspx?direct=true&db=buh&AN=74299796

Rentsch, J. R., Delise, L. A., Mello, A. L., & Staniewicz, M. J. (2014). The integrative team knowledge building training strategy in distributed problem-solving teams. *Small Group Research, 45*(5), 568–591. Retrieved from EBSCO Online Database Business Source Complete. http://search.ebscohost.com/login.aspx?direct=true&db=bth&AN=98397418&site=ehost-live&scope=site

Robbins, S. P. (1996). *Organizational behavior: Concepts, controversies, and applications*. Upper Saddle River, NJ: Prentice Hall.

Stevens, M. J., & Campion, M. A. (1994). The knowledge, skill, and ability requirements for teamwork: Implications for human resource management. *Journal of Management, 20*(2), 503. Retrieved April 28, 2010 from EBSCO Online Database Business Source Complete http://search.ebscohost.com/login.aspx?direct=true&db=bth&AN=9512136558&site=ehost-livee

Wilsher, S. (2015). Behavior profiling: implications for recruitment and team building. *Strategic Direction, 31*(9), 1–5. Retrieved Dec. 4, 2015, from EBSCO Online Database Business Source Complete. http://search.ebscohost.com/login.aspx?direct=true&db=bth&AN=109959523&site=ehost-live&scope=site

SUGGESTED READING

Aldag, R. J., & Kuzuhara, L. W. (2015). *Creating high performance teams: Applied strategies and tools for managers and team members*. New York, NY: Routledge.

Aritzeta, A., Swailes, S., & Senior, B. (2007). Belbin's team role model: Development, validity and applications for team building. *Journal of Management Studies, 44*(1), 96–118. Retrieved April 28, 2010 from EBSCO Online Database Business Source Complete http://search.ebscohost.com/login.

aspx?direct=true&db=bth&AN=23615479&site=ehost-live

Boss, R. W. (2000). Is the leader really necessary? The longitudinal results of leader absence in team building. *Public Administration Quarterly, 23*(4) 471–486. Retrieved April 28, 2010 from EBSCO Online Database Business Source Complete http://search.ebscohost.com/login.aspx?direct=true&db=bth&AN=3709683&site=ehost-live

Bottom, W. P., & Baloff, N. (1994). A diagnostic model for team building with an illustrative application. *Human Resource Development Quarterly, 5*(4), 317–336. Retrieved April 28, 2010 from EBSCO Online Database Business Source Complete http://search.ebscohost.com/login.aspx?direct=true&db=bth&AN=14858754&site=ehost-live

Buller, P. F., & Bell, C. H., Jr. (1986). Effects of team building and goal setting on productivity: A field experiment. *Academy of Management Journal, 29*(2), 305–328. Retrieved April 28, 2010 from EBSCO Online Database Business Source Complete http://search.ebscohost.com/login.aspx?direct=true&db=bth&AN=4394892&site=ehost-live

Chen, Y.-C., Che, Y.-C., & Tsao, Y.-L. (2009). Multiple dimensions to the application for the effectiveness of team building in ROTC. *Education, 129*(4), 742–754. Retrieved April 28, 2010 from EBSCO Online Database Academic Search Complete http://search.ebscohost.com/login.aspx?direct=true&db=a9h&AN=40310243&site=ehost-live

Darling, J. R. (1990). Team building in the small business firm. *Journal of Small Business Management, 28*(3), 86–91. Retrieved April 28, 2010 from EBSCO Online Database Business Source Complete http://search.ebscohost.com/login.aspx?direct=true&db=bth&AN=9604164295&site=ehost-live

Horak, B. J., Hicks, K., Pellicciotti, S., & Duncan, A. (2006). Create cultural change and team building. *Nursing Management, 37*(12), 12–14. Retrieved April 28, 2010 from EBSCO Online Database Academic Search Complete http://search.ebscohost.com/login.aspx?direct=true&db=a9h&AN=23316551&site=ehost-live

Jones, M. C. (2008). Large scale project team building: Beyond the basics. *Communications of the ACM, 51*(10), 113–116. Retrieved April 28, 2010 from EBSCO Online Database Academic Search Complete http://search.ebscohost.com/login.aspx?direct=true&db=a9h&AN=34540767&site=ehost-live

McCune, W. B. (1989). Internal communications and participatory management: An experiment in team building. *Public Relations Quarterly, 34*(3), 14–18. Retrieved April 28, 2010 from EBSCO Online Database Business Source Complete http://search.ebscohost.com/login.aspx?direct=true&db=bth&AN=4466000&site=ehost-live

McSherry, M., & Taylor, P. (1994). Supervisory support for the transfer of team-building training. *International Journal of Human Resource Management, 5*(1), 107–119. Retrieved April 28, 2010 from EBSCO Online Database Business Source Complete http://search.ebscohost.com/login.aspx?direct=true&db=bth&AN=5801828&site=ehost-live

Page, D., & Donelan, J. G. (2003). Team-building tools for students. *Journal of Education for Business, 78*(3), 125–128. Retrieved April 28, 2010 from EBSCO Online Database Academic Search Complete http://search.ebscohost.com/login.aspx?direct=true&db=a9h&AN=9944602&site=ehost-live

Scarfino, D., & Roever, C. (2009). Team-building success: It's in the cards. *Business Communication Quarterly, 72*(1), 90–95. Retrieved April 28, 2010 from EBSCO Online Database Business Source Complete http://search.ebscohost.com/login.aspx?direct=true&db=bth&AN=36366002&site=ehost-live

Staggers, J., Garcia, S., & Nagelhout, E. (2008). Teamwork through team building: Face-to-face to online. *Business Communication Quarterly, 71*(4), 472–487. Retrieved April 28, 2010 from EBSCO Online Database Business Source Complete http://search.ebscohost.com/login.aspx?direct=true&db=bth&AN=35344498&site=ehost-live

Svyantek, D. J., Goodman, S. A., Benz, L. L., & Gard, J. A. (1999). The relationship between organizational characteristics and team building success. *Journal of Business and Psychology, 14*(2), 265–283. Retrieved April 28, 2010 from EBSCO Online Database Academic Search Complete http://search.ebscohost.com/login.aspx?direct=true&db=a9h&AN=12428251&site=ehost-live

Thomas, M., Jacques, P. H., Adams, J. R., & Kihneman-Wooten, J. (2008). Developing an effective project: Planning and team building combined. *Project Management Journal, 39*(4), 105–113. Retrieved April 28, 2010 from EBSCO Online Database Business Source Complete http://search.ebscohost.

com/login.aspx?direct=true&db=bth&AN=43852407&site=ehost-live

Turaga, R. (2013). Building trust in teams: A leader's role. *IUP Journal of Soft Skills, 7*(2), 13–31. Retrieved November 27, 2013 from EBSCO online database Business Source Premier. http://search.ebscohost.com/login.aspx?direct=true&db=buh&AN=89521619

Wigtil, J. V., & Kelsey, R. C. (1978). Team building as a consulting intervention for influencing learning environments. *Personnel and Guidance Journal, 56*(7), 412–416. Retrieved 28 April 2010 from EBSCO Online Database Academic Search Complete http://search.ebscohost.com/login.aspx?direct=true&db=a9h&AN=6475526&site=ehost-live

Ruth A. Wienclaw, Ph.D.

TYPES OF BUSINESS ORGANIZATIONS

ABSTRACT

This article will focus on different forms of business. There are a number of ways to structure a business—these include sole proprietorships, different types of partnerships, limited liability companies, and corporations. Each form of business organization has advantages and disadvantages and these are largely influenced by the purpose of the enterprise as well as a number of other factors. Each type of organization poses different legal ramifications and income tax considerations. This article will provide an analysis of the different types of business organization as well as a brief discussion of the advantages and disadvantages of each structure.

OVERVIEW

There are a number of ways to structure a business, and the factors involved in choosing the appropriate legal structure include: the purpose of the organization; the size of the entity; the costs involved in starting the entity; state, federal and local laws and rules governing the business; and tax considerations. Essentially, there are four types of legal structures for business:

- Sole Proprietorship
- Partnership
- Limited Liability Company
- Corporation

There are advantages and disadvantages to each type of business organization and these are driven by a number of factors. The following is an analysis of the four legal structures.

Sole Proprietorship

A sole proprietorship is the most basic business form and is frequently utilized by a single person owning or running a business on his or her own. Such business enterprises are often run from the person's home. Owners pay taxes on the business profits and this is reflected on individual tax returns (Form 1040 and Schedules C and E). In some states, the costs of a business that is being operated from an individual's home may be deducted from income taxes. However, at the same time, certain counties and states may require a sole proprietor to pay property taxes on the value of any office equipment used for the business. In addition to tax liabilities, sole proprietors are also responsible for the debts of the business (Butow 2004).

Partnership

A partnership is the legal structure for a business enterprise when two or more people start a business. There are different types of partnerships, and these include general partnerships, limited partnerships and limited liability partnerships. In order to set forth how the business will operate, the partners should enter into a partnership agreement. The partnership agreement should specify who the partners are, what their roles and responsibilities are, and most importantly spell out how the profits will be divided between or among the partners.

A general partnership is a business structure where each partner is liable beyond what he or she has invested in the enterprise. Also, each partner can take actions that may bind the entire partnership. A general partnership is not a taxable entity because the income and losses pass to each partner who, in turn, reports the profit and loss on individual tax returns. Because the income and losses pass to each partner, these entities are also referred to as "pass-through" enterprises. In a general partnership, the profits and losses are normally distributed equally between or among the partners. At the same time, each partner is jointly and severally liable for all the obligations of the partnership. That means a person suing the partnership can choose to collect from any partner and does not have to collect an equal amount from each partner. (Rianda, 2011).

On the other hand, a limited partnership (LP) is one where two or more partners agree to operate a business jointly. In this structure, each partner is liable only to the extent of the amount each has invested in the business. This entity is also pass-through enterprise. A limited partnership can also include both general and limited partners. In these cases, the general partners usually are responsible for running the operations of the business while the limited partners are essentially investors. Further, each partner shares the profits and losses according to the partnership agreement (Butow 2004).

Another type of partnership is a limited liability partnership or LLP. These structures are normally used by professional organizations such as law firms and accounting companies. An LLP has similar features to a partnership, but the partnership as a business entity is responsible for any debts and the individual partners are shielded from these liabilities. Some US states also recognize limited liability limited partnerships (LLLPs), which mix features of limited partnerships and limited liability partnerships.

Limited Liability Companies (LLC)

A limited liability company is a cross between a corporation and a partnership. This type of business organization offers more protection from creditors' claims than a partnership. In this way, it is similar to a corporation, but it is also a pass-through entity so it shares the features of a partnership. However, LLCs have distinct features and requirements. In an LLC, the owners are called members. Members, in turn, can be individuals or corporations. However, unlike a partnership where profits and losses are evenly distributed according to the partnership agreement, there is greater flexibility in this regard for a limited liability company.

Further, in order to establish an LLC, it is necessary to file articles of organization with the secretary of state. Another way that LLCs are similar to partnerships is that a limited liability company is required to have an operating agreement. The operating agreement should specify who the members are, what the role and responsibility of each member will be and how profits will be shared between or among the members. The operating agreement should also contemplate changes in ownership if other members are invited to join the enterprise or if an existing member decides to sell his or her interest. Finally, because this is also a pass-through structure, members report income and losses on personal income tax returns.

Some states require that certain types of professionals that provide special types of services, such as doctors, lawyers, or architects, do not form normal LLCs; this ensures that their liability for their services is not limited in way that could potentially harm consumers. Instead, these professionals may register as a professional limited liability company (PLLC), which restricts the limitations on liability to business matters.

Corporations

A corporation is essentially an entity that exists separate and apart from its owners. Corporations are required to have at least one owner, and owners are called shareholders or stockholders; ownership interests are referred to as stock. Because a corporation exists separate and apart from the owners, the owners are protected from debts and liabilities. The corporation itself assumes liability for the debts and obligations of the business, putting aside the issue of personal guarantees (Rianda, 2011).

A corporation is established when articles of incorporation are filed with the secretary of state. This document establishes the reason for the enterprise and in some states it is referred to as a certificate of incorporation or a company's charter. The articles should clearly state the business purpose, but at the same time that description should also allow the business flexibility to grow and evolve. The basic information that should be stated in the articles includes the business' name and address, the name of the incorporators, the intended duration of the business entity (either perpetual or of limited duration) and the purpose of the business (Arend 1999).

An incorporator is the responsible individual for filing the articles with the secretary of state. In many states, the incorporator cannot be an owner, officer or director of the business entity. A legal agent is a third party who is not affiliated with the business entity who will be responsible for accepting any legal process papers filed against the business. A legal agent can be a law firm, but there are also professional organizations that perform these duties.

Corporations are also required to have written by-laws. This is the governing document of the business and it establishes the operating procedures for the entity. By-laws describe the management structure and what the roles and responsibilities of the officers and directors will be. Generally, directors are senior executives or managers who are responsible for the day-to-day operations of the business while officers are the individuals appointed to implement the policies and procedures established by the directors. Officers report to the directors who are ultimately accountable to the owners, that is, the shareholders. By-laws should also specify the voting procedures, notice requirements, proxy, and the minimum number of people who must be present for a vote to be effective—this is referred to as a quorum.

Corporations are required to have an annual meeting, but meetings can also be held once every quarter, once a month, or at any time an action is taken that affects the operations of the business. Such action includes mergers, establishing new business ventures and promoting or terminating officers and directors. Minutes, or a written record of the meeting, must be prepared and the actions taken during these meetings are often memorialized in a written resolution. Resolutions, minutes and notices are required to be maintained with the company's books and records along with the articles of incorporation and by-laws.

There are two types of corporations: "C" corporations and "S" corporations. The former refers to a business that meets the minimum requirements for the definition of a corporation established by the Internal Revenue Service tax code while the latter is a designation for a business that is established pursuant to subchapter "S" of the code. A subchapter "S" designation allows a business to be taxed like a partnership where the profits and losses are passed through to the shareholders. At the same time, owners are provided with protection from debt liability. Finally to qualify as an "S" corporation there must be one or more, but fewer than seventy-five owners.

On the other hand, a "C" corporation does not have a limit to the number of owners; however, these businesses are not pass-through entities and the corporation's profits are taxed. Because of this, "C" corporations are subject to what has been termed "double taxation." In addition to the profits being taxed, shareholders are taxed on the dividends that are paid on the stock that they own. Further, shareholders are also taxed on any profits they receive on shares of stock that they sell. This is known as a capital gains tax. Corporations are required to pay salaries to the directors, officers and employees, who are also required to pay taxes on that income (Barney 1997). Finally, unlike pass-through entities, C corporations do not separately state income or loss items. These are instead taken together to arrive at total taxable income, with the same tax rates applying to ordinary income and capital gains. Since income does not retain its original character in a corporation, many of the benefits available at the individual level are unavailable when the corporate form is chosen (Wong & Zambrano, 2012).

Corporations may also be subdivided, combined, and controlled in various ways. Holding companies are often formed as the owner of a corporation's stock in order to reduce ownership risk. Corporations may merge into one larger entity, sometimes requiring government approval due to antitrust measures. Corporations may also be considered conglomerates, in that they own and run many smaller, often seemingly unrelated businesses.

APPLICATIONS

The type of legal structure that is appropriate for individuals starting a business depends on a number of factors. The following is a comparative analysis of the advantages and disadvantages of each form of business organization.

The most basic form of business, the sole proprietorship, is the best option for a single owner of a business. These entities are relatively easy to establish since they do not require extensive documents to be filed. At the same time, some states require certain business enterprises to be licensed. This includes, but is not limited to, electricians, plumbers, home-improvement contractors, real estate brokers, mortgage brokers, financial planners and even hairdressers. Some of the advantages of a sole proprietorship are that individuals can start these businesses without significant initial costs. Further, taxes are not paid by the business, but rather by the owner, and any profits are reported on individual tax returns. Therefore there is no need for extensive financial statements to be prepared.

The main disadvantage to this form of business organization is that the individual is responsible for any debts incurred by the business as well as other legal claims that can be initiated in the courts. This is especially relevant if the sole proprietor is a homeowner or owns other residential property. If the individual running the business does not pay debts or if a lawsuit is commenced against the business, a judgment can subsequently attach these debts to the person's dwelling. In short, a sole proprietor exposes their real property and other assets to debt and legal liabilities.

Another form of business organization that has been discussed is the partnership. This legal structure is frequently used by family businesses. Other than the possible licensing requirements, there is no need for extensive documentation and filings. Moreover, the profits of the business are not taxed since these are passed through to the individual partners. One disadvantage to this type of legal structure is that each partner is subject to a certain amount of liability for debts. Further, unless the partnership agreement states what should occur in the event of the death of a partner, partnerships do not provide for continuity of life. So if one of the partners dies, the partnership agreement may need to be renegotiated, and the surviving partner can find him- or herself doing business with people who were not originally part of the business.

A hybrid of partnerships and corporations is what is commonly known as a limited liability company, and this type of business draws on the advantages of partnerships and corporations. The main advantage is that the operating agreement can establish a flexible means for the members to share the profits and losses. Some of the factors in making this determination include the financial investment of each member as well as his or her role and responsibilities. Like a corporation, members of limited liability companies are protected from debts. Thus members can protect their assets from claims arising from creditors or lawsuits. However, this legal structure does not provide the flexibility that is available to a corporation with respect to arranging for financing the business operations.

Finally, there are a number of advantages for establishing a corporation. An "S" corporation is probably the best option for a business with one owner or where few people are involved in the business. The main benefit is that the profits are not subject to double taxation. More importantly, an "S" corporation enables owners to protect their private property and other assets. This designation is well suited for a small business, and as stated above, is only available to business entities that have seventy-five or fewer owners. A "C" corporation has a great deal of flexibility to finance its operations. Corporations can sell more stock, issue debt, and obtain lines of credit from a variety of financial institutions. Another benefit of such corporations is that they provide continuity of life. This means that the business entity will continue in the event of the death of an owner or if an owner decides to sell his or her ownership interest (Barney 1997).

As mentioned above, however, the main disadvantage of a corporate structure is that the entity is subject to double taxation. At the same time, corporations have a number of means at their disposal to mitigate tax consequences. Many of the expenses associated with running the business can be deducted from income taxes, and an array of financial and accounting mechanisms enable corporations to mitigate tax liabilities. Further, many states offer corporations tax relief in order to attract these entities to do business in the state. If a corporation is large, generates sufficient revenue, and offers employment opportunities to a number of people, such incentives ultimately benefit a state's economy. Oklahoma, for example, offers a tax incentive that exempts horizontally drilled oil and gas wells from the state's 7% production tax for a limited period of time (Watts, 2013).

Another way for a corporation to mitigate its tax liability is to incorporate in a state in which it is not actually located. For instance, many Fortune 500 companies incorporate in the state of Delaware. This is so because this state has procedures in place that enable business entities to establish themselves quickly. Further, Delaware does not tax the profits of the corporation if business is not actually conducted in the state (Vinzant 1999). Such states, or even other countries, with favorable tax laws that attract many businesses are often referred to as corporate havens. Some regulators see these and other tax loopholes as unfair, however, and some jurisdictions have penalties for businesses that seek to exploit them.

CONCLUSION

In the final analysis, the type of legal structure business people choose depends on a number of variables that have been discussed herein. There are numerous legal and tax implications to consider, as well as federal, state and local laws that may apply to a particular business. This is an important point because some types of business are subject to a great deal of oversight. Moreover, for corporations that are also publicly traded entities, that is, a company whose shares of stock are bought and sold on one of the stock exchanges or other trading outlet, there are substantial financial and reporting requirements that stem from the Sarbanes-Oxley Act of 2002. Further if deficiencies are discovered in a corporation's financial statements, the business and the responsible individuals (chief executives and the like) are subject to felony prosecution.

Another matter to consider is the potential for lawsuits. Sole proprietors who fail to fulfill their obligations in a business transaction expose themselves to legal actions and if the person suing them prevails, the business person's real property and other assets will not be protected. In this regard, business enterprises can also be exposed to product liability lawsuits. A partnership or small business that makes toys for children, for example, can be sued if those toys cause harm or injury to a consumer. While the owners of corporations can protect their real property and assets from such legal claims, large corporations that generate a lot of profit are invariably the targets of class action lawsuits — and whether or not these lawsuits have merit, such legal actions can be costly.

Ultimately, the appropriate form of business organization depends on the purpose of the business, the number of people who will have an ownership interest, the amount of profit or revenue that will be generated, and finally the number of people that the business will employ. At the end of the day, the final factor that needs to be considered is that any type of business consists of people and the success of the enterprise will be significantly affected by the roles and responsibilities of these individuals, and the relationships that they create. In short, business people should carefully consider all of these variables and, moreover, rely on the advice of financial advisers and legal counsel. In this regard, the matters discussed in this article are for informational purposes only and should not be construed as financial or legal advice.

Bibliography

Aghina, W., Smet, A. D., & Heywood, S. (2014). The past and future of global organizations. *Mckinsey Quarterly*, (3), 97–106. Retrieved Dec. 4, 2015, from EBSCO Online Database Business Source Complete. http://search.ebscohost.com/login.aspx?direct=true&db=bth&AN=102111153&site=ehost-live&scope=site

Anderson, B.L. (2004). Benefit issues regarding Partnerships, S Corporations, and Sole Proprietorships. *Journal of Pension Benefits, 11*, 26–31. Retrieved January 2, 2007, from EBSCO Online Database Business Source Premier. http://search.ebscohost.com/login.aspx?direct=true&db=buh&AN=13143807&site=ehost-live

Arend, T.E. Jacobs, J.A. (1999). Drafting proper governance documents. *Association Management, 51*, 111–113. Retrieved January 2, 2007, from EBSCO Online Database Business Source Premier. http://search.ebscohost.com/login.aspx?direct=true&db=buh&AN=1763040&site=ehost-live

Barney, D.K. (1997). Understanding the appropriate business form. *National Public Accountant, 42*, 9–16. Retrieved January 2, 2007, from EBSCO Online Database Business Source Premier. http://search.ebscohost.com/login.aspx?direct=true&db=buh&AN=54358&site=ehost-live

Butow, E.E. (2004). Starting your own business: Costs, structures, and pitfalls. *Intercom, 51*, 20–23. Retrieved January 2, 2007, from EBSCO Online Database Business Source Premier. http://search.ebscohost.com/login.aspx?direct=true&db=buh&AN=15213690&site=ehost-live

Haigh, N., Walker, J., Bacq, S., & Kickul, J. (2015). Hybrid organizations: Origins, strategies, impacts, and implications. *California Management Review, 57*(3), 5–12. Retrieved Dec 4, 2015, from

EBSCO Online Database Business Source Complete. http://search.ebscohost.com/login.aspx?direct=true&db=bth&AN=103146032&site=ehost-live&scope=site

Rianda, P.A. (2011). Those letters at the end of company name say a lot. *ISO & Agent, 7,* 17. Retrieved November 3, 2013, from EBSCO Online Database Business Source Complete. http://search.ebscohost.com/login.aspx?direct=true&db=bth&AN=72320108&site=ehost-live

Vinzant, C. (1999). Why do corporations love Delaware so much? *Fortune, 139,* 32. Retrieved January 2, 2007, from EBSCO Online Database Business Source Premier. http://search.ebscohost.com/login.aspx?direct=true&db=buh&AN=1454114&site=ehost-live

Watts, J. (2013). Oklahoma: Tax reform cuts both ways. *Bond Buyer, 385*(33949), 9. Retrieved November 3, 2013, from EBSCO Online Database Business Source Complete. http://search.ebscohost.com/login.aspx?direct=true&db=bth&AN=89374490&site=ehost-live

Wong, A., & Zambrano, J.M. (2012). How changes in corporate tax rate can affect choice of C vs. S corp. *Tax Adviser, 43,* 646–647. Retrieved November 3, 2013, from EBSCO Online Database Business Source Complete. http://search.ebscohost.com/login.aspx?direct=true&db=bth&AN=82350805&site=ehost-live

Suggested Reading

Hillman, R. W., & Loewenstein, M. J. *Research handbook on partnerships, LLCs and alternative forms of business organizations.* Cheltenham, UK: Edward Elgar Publishing.

McCahery, J.A. (2001). Comparative perspectives on the evolution of the unincorporated firm: An introduction. *Journal of Corporation Law, 26,* 803–818. Retrieved January 2, 2007, from EBSCO Online Database Business Source Premier. http://search.ebscohost.com/login.aspx?direct=true&db=buh&AN=6093915&site=ehost-live

Olson, E.G. (2005). Strategically managing risk in the information age: A holistic approach. *Journal of Business Strategy, 26,* 45–54. Retrieved January 2, 2007, from EBSCO Online Database Business Source Premier. http://search.ebscohost.com/login.aspx?direct=true&db=buh&AN=19329863&site=ehost-live

Slemrod, J.L. (2005). What corporations say they do and what they really do: Implications for tax policy and tax research. *Journal of American Taxation Association, 27,* 91–99. Retrieved January 2, 2007, from EBSCO Online Database Business Source Premier. http://search.ebscohost.com/login.aspx?direct=true&db=buh&AN=17041924&site=ehost-live

Yu, X. (2013). Securities fraud and corporate finance: recent developments. *Managerial & Decision Economics, 34*(7/8), 439–450. Retrieved November 3, 2013, from EBSCO Online Database Business Source Complete. http://search.ebscohost.com/login.aspx?direct=true&db=bth&AN=90469319&site=ehost-live

Richa S. Tiwary, Ph.D., M.L.S.

GLOSSARY

360-Degree Feedback: An approach to giving employees feedback on their job performance in which representatives of the major groups working with a person provide feedback on his or her performance. In 360-degree feedback, employees receive feedback not only from their supervisors, as in the traditional performance-appraisal paradigm, but also from their subordinates, coworkers, customers, and other groups with whom they work.

3PL Management: The process of choosing and managing relationships between the firm and any third-party logistics management providers.

5G Workplace: This is a shorthand phrase referring to the fact that the labor force has members of five different generations working side by side: traditionalists, baby boomers, generation X, generation Y, and generation Z.

Accommodation: An approach to conflict management in which one party completely gives in to the position of the other party or acts with little or no attention to its own interests. Accommodation can be a functional conflict management approach if the opposing party has substantially more power or if the issue is not as important to the first party as it is to the opposing party.

Acquisition: The process in which one company purchases another and incorporates its human and capital resources.

Active Listening: An approach to improving communication in which the receiver of the message attempts to better understand the message being transmitted, formulates a response based on this understanding, and responds in a way that clarifies the message.

Activity-Based Costing: An accounting or finance-based management tool used in management accounting.

Actuarial Science: Branch of knowledge dealing with the mathematics of insurance, including probabilities. It is used in ensuring that risks are carefully evaluated, that adequate premiums are charged for risks underwritten, and that adequate provision is made for future payments of benefits.

Adjuster: (or Claims Adjuster) A person who investigates the extent of damage or injury to determine the insurance company's liability and propose a settlement.

Administrative Agency: A governmental entity created by legislation to enforce the law and develop rules and regulations to that end. Administrative agencies are generally part of the executive branch of government.

Administrative Law: Administrative law is the branch of public law created by administrative agencies. It is important that we look at Administrative law, since Administrative agencies create rules, regulations, orders, and act as the primary interpreters and enforcers of business regulatory schemes.

Affective Organizational Commitment: Affective organizational commitment is the degree to which a member of the organization is dedicated to the organization's success, not just at an intellectual or practical level, but also at an emotional level. Studies suggest that leaders who use an inclusive leadership style tend to produce higher levels of affective organizational commitment among their followers.

Alliance: A contractual grouping together of people or entities based on some common interest in which all parties will invest. A strategic alliance is a business collaboration that satisfies some strategic goal of the business entities such as increased sales, greater efficiencies, reduced cost, etc.

Analysis of Variance (ANOVA): A family of statistical techniques that analyze the joint and separate effects of multiple independent variables on a single dependent variable and determine the statistical significance of the effect.

Analytics: The tools and data used by a business to enable managers to control business processes and optimize business resources and opportunities.

Application Software: A software program that helps users perform tasks not directly related to the running of the actual computer. Application software includes desktop publishing, electronic spreadsheets, graphic design , media players, and presentation software among others.

Applications Software (Customized): Computer programs that are custom developed by in-house management information staff (or by contract programmers) to perform tasks specific to the environment for which they were developed.

Applications Software (Vendor Produced): Computer programs available from software companies designed to perform specific tasks such as word processing, database management, or computer security.

Appreciative Inquiry: A method for organizational transformation that focuses on the successes rather than the failures in order to pinpoint areas in which to change.

Arbitration: The involvement of a neutral third party in the negotiation process who has the authority to decide an agreement.

Architecture: The structure of a communications network, including how the various components are linked, interact, and cooperate. Network architectures may be centralized, distributed, or a combination of the two. An emerging architecture, software-defined networking (SDN), gives more control of these functions to the programmer.

Articles of Incorporation: Governing document of a corporation that establishes the reason for a corporation's existence; must be filed with the secretary of state.

Artificial Intelligence (AI): The branch of computer science concerned with development of software that allows computers to perform activities normally considered to require human intelligence. Artificial intelligence applications include the development of expert systems that allow computers to make complex, real world decisions; programming computers to understand natural human languages; development of neural networks that reproduce the physical connections occurring in animal brains; and development of computers that react to visual, auditory, and other sensory stimuli (i.e., robotics).

Assertiveness: In conflict management, the motivation to satisfy one's own interests (cf. cooperativeness).

Asset-Liability Management: A risk management practice used to make investment or disinvestment decisions and maintain a credit service ratio.

Autocorrelation: (also called serial correlation): A problem occurring over time in regression analysis when the error terms of the forecasting model are correlated.

Autoregressive Integrated Moving Average (ARIMA): An integrated tool for understanding and forecasting using time series data. The ARIMA model has both an autoregressive and a moving average component. The ARIMA model is also referred to as the Box-Jenkins model.

Avoidance: An approach to conflict management in which the parties attempt to manage their differences by smoothing them over or avoiding or minimizing the situations in which conflict might arise. Although avoidance is not a functional long-term solution to conflict situations, it can be useful in the shortterm as a way to temporarily cool down heated disputes or for situations where the issue causing conflict is trivial. Avoidance approaches are low in both assertiveness and cooperativeness.

Baby Boomers: Baby Boomers are members of the generation born between 1946 and approximately 1964. When soldiers returned home from World War II, they were anxious to get married and start a family, so an unusually large number of children were born in the years after the war ended in 1945. This earned the children the name baby boomers because they were part of a boom (a large increase in number) of babies.

Backward Vertical Integration: A manufacturer assuming the supply function for their respective value chain.

Bandwidth: The data transfer rate, or the amount of data that can be transmitted within a given time period. The higher the bandwidth of a transmission, the higher the transfer rate. Bandwidth is expressed in thousands of bits of information per second (kbps), millions of bits per second (mbps), or billions of bits per second (gbps).

Bank-Firm Relationships: The prolonged close interaction between a firm and a bank that can provide lenders with more information about, and influnce in, firm affairs.

Banking Industry: Traditional banks that provide residential (home) loans to consumers.

Bayes' Decision Rule: A decision making strategy in which one chooses the option with the largest expected payoff. This is determined by multiplying the consequences of each act by the probability of the several occurrences and then adding the products together.

BCG Matrix: A portfolio analysis tool to assess business unit strength, determined by relative market growth rate and relative market share.

Behavioral Approach: A way of defining competencies that concentrate on behaviors, motivations and knowledge relevant to a job – i.e. job-relevant behavior.

Behavioral Competencies: Behaviors a person exhibits that result in good performance.

Benefits and Services: Non-financial components of an employee's remuneration package. These may include medical care, loans, travel, accommodation and catering.

Body Language: The communication of thoughts or feelings through physical expression such as posture, gesture, facial expression, or other movements. Body language may reinforce or contradict the verbal message being given by the person.

Borrowed & Tailored Approach: A competency modeling approach which borrows a competency framework from an existing organization while tailoring the model to the new organization.

Borrowed Approach: A competency modeling approach that borrows from an existing organization, without taking into consideration the uniqueness of the adopting organization.

Bottom Line: Net profit or loss on a project for a specific period of time.

Brainstorming: A group process used to generate ideas in a face-to-face group problem-solving situation. In brainstorming, team members generate as many ideas as possible, piggybacking on other ideas where possible. The goal of a brainstorming session is to generate ideas, so suggestions are not evaluated during the process.

Breakthrough Innovation: Innovation based on technologies previously new to the world; also referred to as disruptive, radical, or discontinuous innovation.

Business Continuity Plan: A logistical plan that details how an organization will recover and reestablish interrupted critical function(s) after an extended disruption due to disaster or other causes. Business continuity plans are written to address the possibility of loss of an organization's facility or access to it, loss of information technology, loss of people, or loss of supply chain. Business continuity plans are also known as disaster recovery plans or business process contingency plans.

Business Cycle: A continually recurring variation in total economic activity. Such expansions or contractions of economic activity tend to occur across most sectors of the economy at the same time.

Business Data Mining: The process of using large amounts of historical transaction data from an organization's databases to analyze business issues and opportunities such as relationships between customer characteristics and their purchasing patterns and forecast future behavior.

Business Ethics: Company code or standard that governs one's behavior on the job. Usually communicated and demonstrated for employees through training, company manuals and company leadership.

Business Impact Analysis: The process of identifying the risk of exposure to specific threats to the organization and assessing the impact of these threats should they occur.

Business Intelligence: Accurate information regarding a businesses market.

Business Intelligence: Technology and systems used to gather and analyze business information for decision-making.

Business Model: The paradigm under which an organization operates and does business in order to accomplish its goals. Business models include consideration of what the business offers of value to the marketplace, building and maintaining customer relationships, an infrastructure that allows the organization to produce its offering, and the income, cash flow, and cost structure of the organization.

Business Organization: The legal structure of a business enterprise — sole proprietorship, partnership, limited liability company and corporation.

Business Process Reengineering (BPR): A management approach that strives to improve the effectiveness and efficiency of the various processes within an organization.

Business Process: Any of a number of linked activities that transforms an input into the organization into an output that is delivered to the customer. Business processes include management processes, operational processes (e.g., purchasing, manufacturing, marketing), and supporting processes, (accounting, human resources).

Business Strategy: Also known as competitive strategy, it is that strategy developed by the firm's strategic business units that gives the firm its competitive advantage.

Business-to-Business (B2B) Applications: Applications software that supports interaction and transactions between businesses including supply chain systems, order entry and processing, and collaboration on design or fulfillment requirements.

Business-to-Consumer (B2C) Applications: Applications software that supports interaction and transactions between business and the end consumer including order entry and processing, order tracking, and customer service.

By-Laws: Governing document of a corporation that spells out the operating procedures and describes the role and responsibilities of the officers and directors.

Capacity: The combinations of material flows, production capabilities, and human resources that enables a company to achieve strategies and maintain a competitive ability.

Capital Deepening: The increase in capital services per hour worked.

Capital Gains Tax: Tax paid on the profit generated from the sale of an asset such as stock, or from dividends paid to stockholders by a corporation.

Capital Structure: The various long-term debt and equity money used to finance a business endeavor. These finances can include long-term debt, common stock, preferred stock, warrants, pensions, and lease liabilities. The more leveraged a capital structure is, the more debt it has relative to its equity.

Capture: The process of collecting various types of data and information for later processing and transmission.

Career Planning and Development: The assistance given to employees, to help them plan for, execute and manage their career development within an organization.

Case Law: The collection of reported cases that create the body of law within a certain jurisdiction.

Centralization: The degree to which formal power in the organization is consolidated or distributed throughout the organization. In a centralized organization, the power is held by a small group of people, usually at the top of the organization. In a decentralized organization, power is distributed throughout the organization so that decisions can be made by those who best understand the situation.

CFRR: Collaborative Planning Forecasting and Replenishment.

Change Agent: A person who guides an organization through a change effort. To be effective, change agents need to have knowledge of how to conduct a change effort, an understanding of the organization, and sufficient power to be able to able to implement the change.

Change Management: Methods designed to help organizations successfully implement and sustain significant organizational transformation.

Charismatic Leadership: A charismatic leadership style differs from an inclusive style in the fact that charismatic leadership does not require any particular action on the part of the leader to enact it. Charismatic leadership occurs when a leader's personality inspires confidence and trust in followers, who feel naturally inclined to follow the leader. Inclusive leadership and most other styles are about what the leader does, while charismatic leadership is mainly about who the leader is.

Clayton Act: The 1914 Act in which Congress barred anticompetitive stock acquisitions.

Clinical Approach: A means of defining competencies by identifying underlying personal characteristics of the individual, independent of any job connection.

Cold Site: A facility that can be readily equipped with data processing capabilities and other services necessary to maintain business operations.

Cold War: The period of conflict, tension, and competition between the United States and the Soviet Union and their allies from the mid-1940s to the early 1990s.

Collaboration: A conflict management style in which the parties attempt to resolve their conflict by finding a mutually beneficial solution through problem solving. Collaborative solutions are high in both cooperativeness and assertiveness. Collaboration is the preferred method for conflict management when the parties do not have perfectly opposing interests and when there is sufficient trust and openness between the parties so that information can be shared.

Collective Bargaining Agreement: An employment agreement concerning wages, hours, working conditions, and benefits that is reached by bargaining between authorized union representatives on behalf of members of the labor force.

Combined Ratio: A number used to reflect and report the degree of profit or loss with respect to underwriting profit of an insurance company; does not take into account investment income.

Commerce Clause: US Constitution Article I, §8, cl. 3, which gives Congress the exclusive power to oversee commerce between states.

Commercial Banks: Financial institutions that provide services to small and large businesses as well as individual clients.

Commodity Risk: A form of market risk resulting from change in commodity prices.

Common Law: The body of law derived from judicial decisions rather than from statutes or the Constitution.

Communication Barriers: Anything that hinders the unambiguous transmission and reception of a message between two persons trying to communicate. Communication barriers include different perceptions of a situation, filtering, language, jargon, and ambiguity.

Communication: The transmission and receipt of data and information over a linked set of hardware and software at multiple locations.

Communications Channel: A communications channel (sometimes called a communications medium) can be a physical or cableless medium that links the components of a network.

Communications Hardware: The technology that enables computers to communicate with each other and which supports the communications between employees within the organization as well as workers in supplier or customer organizations.

Communications Network: Sets of locations (or nodes) with concomitant hardware, software, and information that are linked together to form a system that transmits and receives information and data.

Company Leaders: Senior leadership, directors, and officers of a company with the power to make decisions that have a major and direct impact on the success or failure of the company.

Comparative Management: The study of management practices in different countries.

Compensation and Incentives: Compensation includes the whole range of rewards and incentives that are applied in relation to employees. Incentives are those offerings that have a tendency to motivate employees to will or to act as the organization desires.

Competencies: Abilities shown to predict and measure superior performance.

Competition: An approach to conflict management in which one party attempts to "win" at the other party's expense. Competition tends to be a winlose situation with high assertiveness and low cooperativeness. Competitive solutions to conflict situations can be appropriate if the party knows that its solution is correct and a quick solution is needed or where the other party would take advantage of a more cooperative approach.

Competitivc Advantage: This refers to one organization having the upper hand over its rivals, through sources and means such as capital, technology, location, and increasingly, human resources.

Competitiveness: The set of institutions, policies, and conditions that decide productivity levels.

Compromise: An approach to conflict management in which one party attempts to reach a middle ground with the opposing party. Compromise positions tend to have moderate levels of assertiveness and cooperativeness. When attempting to compromise, parties typically look for solutions in which losses are offset by equally valued gains. Compromise tends to work best in situations in which there is little possibility of mutual gain through problem solving, both parties have equal power, and there are time pressures to settle the conflict.

Computer Systems: The integrated configuration of central processing chips, memory, storage devices (hard drives), communications interfaces, and operating systems software that provide the hardware platform for management information systems.

Concentration Strategies: Growth strategies whereby a firm maintains a competitive focus within their particular industry.

Concentric Diversification: The development or acquisition of business-lines *related* to the firm's existing corporate portfolio.

Conflict Management: The process of altering the severity and form of conflict in order to maximize its benefits and minimize its negative consequences. Between parties, conflict can be resolved through collaboration, accommodation, competition, compromise, or avoidance. Conflict management can also refer to interventions performed by an objective outside party in the attempt to de-escalate conflict between parties.

Conflict Resolution: The use of techniques to create civility, harmony, or consensus between both sides of a conflict.

Conflict Stimulation: The creation of conflict in an organization to promote change and growth.

Conflict: A situation in which one party believes that its interests are negatively affected by another party.

Conglomerate Diversification: The addition of *unrelated* lines of business to the corporate portfolio.

Conglomerate Merger: All non-vertical and non-horizontal mergers and acquisitions.

Constituent: Refers to the follower in the leadership/follower relationship.

Contingency Approach: A foundational concept in organizational behavior theory in which it is recognized that the consequences of an action may differ depending on the given situation in which it is performed.

Cooperativeness: In conflict management, the motivation to satisfy the interests of the other party (cf. assertiveness).

Core Competency: The collection of a firm's internal strengths that are sources of competitive advantage.

Core Values: The fundamental beliefs and purpose of an organization and its management.

Corporate Consolidation: A process through which two corporations join and form a new corporation.

Corporate Development: The activities that companies undertake to grow through inorganic means such as mergers and acquisitions, strategic alliances, and joint ventures.

Corporate Responsibility: The actions taken by an organization to meet various needs concerning socially relevant issues in the community at large.

Corporate Strategy: The *game-plan* developed by top management for how a corporation intends to compete within its respective industry.

Corporation: A legal business entity that is created under and governed by the laws of the state of incorporation.

Correlation: The degree to which two events or variables are consistently related. Correlation may be positive (i.e., as the value of one variable increases the value of the other variable increases), negative (i.e., as the value of one variable increases the value of the other variable decreases), or zero (i.e., the values of the two variables are unrelated). Correlation does not imply causation.

Cost of Conformance: The investment made to ensure that processes are done correctly including quality initiatives, training and inspection (Keck, 2006).

Cost of Nonconformance: The money an organization wastes when processes are not done correctly the first time (Keck, 2006).

Cost-Plus Fixed-Fee Contract: A type of cost-reimbursement contract in which the contractor receives a negotiated fee at the beginning of the contract. This fee may be adjusted if the work to be performed under the contract changes. This type of contract is often used to lessen the contractor's risk on projects that might otherwise be too risky.

Cost-Plus Incentive Fee Contract: A type of cost-reimbursement contract in which the fee negotiated before the start of the contract is later adjust by a formula that considers the relationship of total allowable costs to total target costs.

Creativity: The ability to produce novel and useful ideas.

Credit Unions: A non-profit financial institution which is owned and operated by its members and provides financial services such as savings and lending.

Crisis Management: A systematic attempt by organizational members with external stakeholders to avert crises or effectively manage those that do occur.

Crisis: This is the first of three stages of a turnaround, where a company is close to bankruptcy or liquidation, and where cash outflows exceed cash inflows. This stage calls for financial action, and preferably, changes in the top management team.

Criterion: A dependent or predicted measure that is used to judge the effectiveness of persons, organizations, treatments, or predictors. The ultimate criterion measures effectiveness after all the data are in. Intermediate criteria estimate this value earlier in the process. Immediate criteria estimate this value based on current values.

Critical Path Method (CPM): A method for project management that defines a set of tasks — each of which is dependent on the performance of the previous task — that together takes the longest time to complete.

Critical thinking: An ability to evaluate information and opinions in a systematic, purposeful, efficient manner.

Cross-Cultural Training: A training program designed to help employees to deal effectively with persons from another culture by familiarizing them with various cultural differences including values, assumptions, and communication styles. One of the purposes of cross-cultural training is to increase intercultural sensitivity.

Cross-functional Teams: An organizational team composed of employees from different functional departments, such as a team that consists of someone from sales, someone from manufacturing, and someone from operations.

Culture Shock: The psychological toll experienced by expatriates after approximately four to six months living in another country. Symptoms of culture shock include homesickness, irritability, hostility toward local nationals and ineffectiveness at work.

Culture: The basic shared assumptions, beliefs, norms, and values held by a group of people. These may be either consciously or unconsciously held.

Currency Risk: A form of market risk resulting from changes in foreign exchange rates.

Current Population Survey: AA household survey conducted monthly by the Census Bureau to obtain data on the labor force, employment, unemployment, and those not in the labor force. This data is then used by the Bureau of Labor Statistics.

Customer Relations Management Systems (CRM): An integrated suite of applications software modules that help organizations manage relations with customers, sales efforts, and customer service.

Customer Relationship Management: The process of identifying prospective customers, acquiring data concerning these prospective and current customers, building relationships with customers, and influencing their perceptions of the organization and its products or services.

Cyber-risk Management Insurance: Internet based insurance coverage that protects companies from theft of trade secrets, destructions of hardware, software, data and extortion of hackers. Third-party coverage protects against forwarded computer viruses, loss of productivity due to hacker violations, unauthorized data on websites and theft of credit card records.

D&O Liability Insurance: Liability insurance that provides coverage for directors and officers of a company. It provides protection for directors' and officers' individual assets, defense costs and settlement payouts.

Data Analysis: The process of extracting or compiling data from business data management systems that can help guide managers in making decisions or planning strategies.

Data Communications: The sending and receiving of facts, figures, details, and other information over a communications network.

Data Dictionary (DD): A DD is a database of descriptors for each piece of data used in an organization's data management activities.

Data Mining: The process of analyzing large collections of data to establish patterns and determine previously unknown relationships. The results of data mining efforts are used to predict future behavior.

Data Processing: Is a systematic approach of bringing order and meaning to data created in every-day business processes.

Data Storage: The process of managing the software and hardware necessary to store and allow access to data created in business operations.

Data Warehouse: Systems designed to manage the storage and access of a wide variety of types of data generated by the different applications software packages used by an organization.

Data: (sing. datum) In statistics, data are quantifiable observations or measurements that are used as the basis of scientific research.

Database: A collection of data items used for multiple purposes that is stored on a computer.

Decision Analysis: A collection of procedures, methods, and tools used to identify, represent, and assess the important aspects of a decision being considered in a decision making process.

Decision Making: The process employed by a business enterprise that establishes its goals and the strategy to achieve those goals.

Decision Processes: Steps taken in the decision making process, usually requiring gathering and analysis of information related to specific decision areas.

Decision Support Systems (DSS): Applications software packages designed to provide assistance for specific decision-making tasks. While DSSs can be developed for and used by personnel throughout an organization and middle and lower managers most commonly employ them.

Decision Theory: A body of knowledge and related analytical techniques designed to give a decision maker information about a situation or system and the consequences of alternative actions in order to help choose among the set of alternatives.

Decision Tree: An analytical tool used by businesses to determine the best course of action among a number of alternatives.

Decision-Making: The process of deciding from among alternatives to drive action.

Decline: This is a period of sustained poor performance that a company goes through prior to a turnaround.

Decomposition: The process of breaking down time series data into the component factors of trends, business cycles, seasonal fluctuations, and irregular or random fluctuations.

Deductible: The amount of money an insured is required to pay before the insurance company becomes liable for damages.

Defensive Strategies: Those strategies a firm employs when experiencing financial trouble.

Delayering: The process of removing layers of middle management to 'flatten' an organizational hierarchy and streamline decision making, communications, and operations.

Dependent Variable: The outcome variable or resulting behavior that changes depending on whether the subject receives the control or experimental condition (e.g., a consumer's reaction to a new cereal).

Descriptive Statistics: A subset of mathematical statistics that describes and summarizes data.

Design Review: Any of a number of reviews of the product design, usually held between the customer and the contractor to determine the completeness and feasibility of the design at a given time in the contract. Two of the most common design reviews are the preliminary design review (PDR) — held after the completion of the preliminary design but before the start of the detail design — and the critical design review — held before the design is released for production.

Deterministic Variables: Variables for which there are specific causes or determiners. These include trends, business cycles, and seasonal fluctuations.

Disaster: Any event that prevents the continuation of normal functioning of the organization's business processes and functions.

Disputants: Parties involved in a disagreement.

Distributive Negotiation: Negotiation that seeks to divide up a fixed amount of resources.

Diversification Strategy: Adding related or unrelated products/ services to the firm's core business.

Diversity Training: A training program designed to help employees to deal with persons from a different culture more effectively through an understanding of their values, assumptions, and communication styles. Diversity training can be used to help employees preparing to work with a different culture or for employees within a culturally diverse workplace to better understand each other.

Divestiture: Spin-offs of a firm's business assets because of unprofitability or because it does not represent a good strategic fit with the firm's core business.

Division of Labor: The way in which work is divided into separate jobs assigned to different people within an organization.

Divisional Structure: An approach to organization design that groups employees together based on clients, products or services, or geographic location.

Dysfunctional Conflict: Conflict that hurts or sabotages group performance.

E-Commerce: E-commerce (i.e., electronic commerce) is the process of buying and selling goods or services—including information products and information retrieval services—electronically rather than through conventional means. E-commerce is typically conducted over the Internet.

Earned Premium: The amount of premium that corresponds to the elapsed period of time the insurer was exposed to risk. That portion of the premium represents the coverage already provided.

Economic Growth: The quantitative change or increase in development in a country's economy.

Effectiveness: The degree to which an organization achieves its goals, satisfies its purpose, and/or meets external demands.

Efficacy: The act of being efficient and effective.

Efficiency: The extent to which an organization minimizes its average costs, expands worker output holding costs constant, or simplifies tasks or decisions and makes them routine.

Emotional Intelligence: The ability of a person to manage their emotions and recognize the emotions in others.

Empirical: A type of theory or evidence that is derived from or based on observation or experiment.

Employee Acquisition: Internal and external selection and recruitment of employees to jobs. It includes the hiring of temporary work assistance and the use of external consultants.

Employee Exit and Separation Management: The planning, facilitation and management of the departure of employees from an organization.

Employee Relations: The manner in which an organization treats its employees. Ideally, employees should be treated with concern through effective internal communication flows; enhancement of the quality of work life; good labor relations; and health, welfare and safety programs.

Employee Retention Strategies: The measures put in place to keep employees in an organization, thus reducing the labor turnover rate.

Employee Work Engagement: Employee work engagement is a measurement of an employee's level of interest in the work he or she has been assigned to complete. Generally, employee work engagement is higher when employees are assigned tasks they know how to do and have the proper authority to perform. One role of leadership is to align the right employees with the right tasks so that employee work engagement remains high.

Empowering: The act of sharing power or giving subordinates ultimate decision-making authority.

End-to-End Process: The end-to-end principle in the context of ERP or enterprise-wide systems requires a business to look at its processes across the entire business spectrum (from sourcing to sales to customer satisfaction).

Enterprise Resource Planning (ERP) Software: An integrated suite of applications software modules that help organizations manage procurement, logistics, production planning, and manufacturing.

Enterprise: A business entity. Although this term is often applied to large organizations, the term can be applied to both small and large organizations.

Equity Index Risk: A form of market risk resulting from changes in index prices.

Equity Risk: A form of market risk resulting from changes in stock process.

Equity Theory: Refers to an employee requiring fairness in the employee/employer relationship. Based on the work by Adams.

Ethical Conduct: The actions and behavior of managers rooted in their values and the values of the organization.

Executive Information Systems (EIS): Applications software packages designed to provide assistance for executives in making high-level management decisions.

Executive Leadership: Occurs when the joint actions of a chief executive and the organization's board members lead to successful resource acquisitions, mission accomplishments, and external affairs.

Expatriate: A person who is not a citizen of the country in which s/he is working.

Expectancy Theory: Refers to how an employee is motivated to do a task by means of effort, outcome and reward. Based on Vroom's work.

Experience Curve: The experience curve is an idea that emerged in the 1960s. It describes a theoretical model that explains the tendency for overall production costs to decrease as the volume of production increases.

Expert System: A decision support system that utilizes artificial intelligence technology to evaluate a situation and suggest an appropriate course of action.

Explicit Knowledge: Explicit knowledge is clearly articulated by the organization and is part of the organization's official image and purpose; an example of this might be the organization's mission statement or corporate charter, both of which are on record and available to anyone who wishes to consult them.

Extended ERP: (ERP technology as defined after 2000). The next generation of ERP that typically includes e-business solutions such as CRM (customer relations management) and SCM (supply chain management).

External Consultant: Individual hired from outside an organization to provide expert advice to that organization as concerns its operations.

External Risk: The risk of events that may strike individuals unexpectedly (from the outside, as it were) but that happen regularly enough and often enough in a whole population of people to be broadly predictable, and so insurable.

Fail Point: Those critical points in the service process where the provider has the opportunity to make a serious mistake that can negatively impact the customer's satisfaction with the process or the perception of quality.

Family-Friendly Benefits: An employment benefit approach and package that allows workers to accommodate their family needs while still achieving their job responsibilities.

Federal Reserve: The Federal agency charged with regulatory oversight and monetary policy for banks and other financial institutions.

Feedback: Information a person receives about his or her behavior or its consequences.

Filtering: The process of eliminating or reducing the amount of certain types of information (negative or emotionally-charged information) from a communication.

Financial Institutions: Institutions that provide financial services.

Financial Services: The products and services offered by financial institutions to facilitate loans, insurance, commerce, investment, money management, and stock transactions.

Firewall: A special-purpose software program or piece of computer hardware that is designed to prevent authorized access to or from a private network. Firewalls are often used to prevent unauthorized access to a private network from the Internet.

Firm Fixed-Price Contract: A contract in which the price is not subject to adjustment on the basis of the contractor's expenses in performing the contract. Firm fixed-price contracts maximize the contractors' risk and give them full responsibility for all costs and resultant profit or loss.

Firm: A business that is owned by stockholders and operated by professional managers.

Fixed-Price Incentive Contract: A type of fixed-price contract that allows profit and final contract price to be adjusted on the basis of a pre-established formula calculating the relationship of total negotiated cost to total target cost. This final price is subject to a ceiling negotiated at the beginning of the contract.

Fixed-Price with Redetermination Contract: A contract that provides a firm fixed-price for the initial delivery or contract period with prospective redetermination of price for later periods of performance.

Flextime: A work schedule that allows employees to work combinations of hours and at times that helps them balance their personal life with their professional life.

Float: The accumulated premiums paid before losses are incurred.

Flow Chart: A schematic representation of a process that specifies the order and relationship of operations or activities.

Forecasting: In business, forecasting is the science of estimating or predicting future trends. Forecasts are used to support managers in making decisions about many aspects of the business including buying, selling, production, and hiring.

Form 1040: Individual tax form that must be filed by a sole proprietor or partners who receive profits.

Formal Organization: The goals, structure, skills, technology, and other resources of the organization that are readily observable to others.

Formalization: The degree to which an organization standardizes behavior through the imposition of rules, polices, practices, procedures, or formal training.

Forward Vertical Integration Strategy: A manufacturer taking over the distribution function for their particular product.

Fourth-Party Logistics Providers (4PLs): Organizations who manage the 3PL provider relationships of a firm.

Framing: In behavioral economic terms, the manner by which a rational choice problem is presented.

Full Vertical Integration: A firm taking over the entire value chain of supplying the inputs of production (i.e., raw materials or component parts), manufacturing the product, and distribution of the product.

Functional Conflict: Conflict that improves the performance of the group.

Functional Job Analysis: A job system analysis that examines jobs based on data, people, and things.

Functional Strategy: Strategy flowing from organizations' functional areas, developed in furtherance of the corporate and business-level strategies.

Functional Structure: An approach to organization design that groups employees together based on their specific knowledge, skills, or other resources.

Functionality: Activity for which a person or department is specifically fitted or used.

Gaming: An activity in which two or more independent parties attempt to achieve objectives within a limiting context. In business, gaming involves the use of mathematics to determine optimal strategies and make the best possible decisions in context.

Gap/Glut: Gap is a shortage of resources required to produce a product or deliver a service and glut is an over supply of resources that are not necessary to meet current demands for products or services.

GE Business Screen Matrix: A more comprehensive derivation of the BCG Matrix, which considers portfolio analysis on low, medium, and high dimensions, based on industry attractiveness and competitive position.

General Partnership: A business partnership with two or more partners who are each liable for any debts and who also share in the administration, profits and losses of the operation.

Generation Z: Members of Generation Z were born after 1996. There is as yet relatively little hard data available about the characteristics of Generation Z, but indications are that they are at least as comfortable with technology as millennials and may have similar attitudes about the value of education and the need to make a positive contribution to society.

Geopolitical Risk: Any peril that arises from geographic, historic, and societal variables related to international politics.

Glass-Steagall Act: Post-Depression law (repealed in 1999) that separated commercial bank activities from those of investment banks.

Global Market: The way that all markets around the world affect one another.

Globalization: Globalization is the process of businesses or technologies spreading across the world. This creates an interconnected, global marketplace operating outside constraints of time zone or national boundary. Although globalization means an expanded marketplace, products are typically adapted to fit the specific needs of each locality or culture to which they are marketed.

Goal Setting: A motivating technique that allows employees to have a sense of ownership in their work, making them more committed to the organizational objectives.

Government Oversight: The process of the government regulating or monitoring commercial and industrial activities.

Grand Strategy: The grand strategy, or master strategy, is a result of an analysis of the environment in which the company operates. The grand strategy is the mechanism by which the separate entities within the firm develop their strategies and operational plans and determine their resources requirements.

The Great Man Theory: Refers to one of the first formal leadership theories that asserts that leadership is exclusively a function of one's traits and characteristics.

Group Decision Support Systems: Systems supporting group collaboration on complex problems.

Group: Two or more interdependent individuals who interact over time. Groups work toward a common goal, are accountable to a manager, and may accomplish their goals. Leadership of a group is by a single individual. Groups do not have a clear, stable culture, so conflict is frequent.

Groupthink: The tendency to have the same opinion as the other members of the group as a way to avoid conflict, reduce interpersonal pressure, or maintain an illusion of unity or cohesiveness without thoroughly thinking through the problem. Groupthink interferes with effective decision making.

Groupthink: When groups or teams members collectively disagree with a decision, but decide not to speak out before the decision is made.

Groupware: Application software that provides tools to help workgroups communicate, coordinate, and organize their activities. Groupware capabilities include scheduling, resource allocation, e-mail, password protection, and file distribution.

Growth: Economic expansion as measured by any number of indicators such as increased revenue, staffing, and market share.

Health Maintenance Organizations (HMO): An organization that provides healthcare services for it members in exchange for monthly premiums. The members of the HMO are usually required to receive those services from specific providers affiliated with the HMO.

Helicopter Parents: Millennials and post-millennials are known for having been raised by extremely attentive parents, in contrast to members of generation X, who were much more independent as children. Some parents have been so attentive that observers have said they practically hover over their children at all times, like helicopters—hence the name. This behavior occasionally continues through college and even beyond, extending into the millennial child's entry into the workforce. Stories are told of angry parents calling college professors or work supervisors to complain about how their children are being treated unfairly.

Heuristics: Psychological method used to rapidly come to a conclusion based on the probability of an optimal solution.

Hierarchy of Needs: A theory of motivation developed by Abraham Maslow. According to Maslow, there are five levels of need: physiological, safety, belongingness, esteem, and self-actualization. The theory posits that people's behavior is motivated by where they are in the hierarchy. People can move up and down the hierarchy and can also experience needs from several levels at once.

Hierarchy: Refers to the pyramidal structure of the organization, usually presented in an organization chart format.

High Performing Organization: Businesses that consistently out-perform their competitors.

Horizontal Integration: When a firm acquires competitors in the same industry.

Horizontal Merger: The business act in which a firm acquires another firm in the same industrial and geographical area that sells a similar product. Horizontal mergers are a way companies eliminate competition.

Hot Site: A facility already equipped with data processing capabilities and other services necessary to maintain business operations.

Human Capital: The value of an organization's employees, including knowledge, skills, abilities, training and education.

Human Performance Technologists: A person who is an expert in the field of HPT and practices the concept when assisting an organization with resolving problems.

Human Performance Technology: The recognition and amelioration of those elements within an organization that prohibit it and its employees from finding success; performed with and through technological systems.

Human Relations: School of thought that is based on a cooperative relationship between the organization and the employees.

Human Resource Management: The set of activities focused on the effective management and development of the organization's work force.

Human Resource Planning: Predicting future business and environmental costs and generating the personnel requirements determined by those future conditions. Human resource planning may be done in response to the organization business planning process or as an integral part of the business planning process.

Human Resource Strategy: This is the set of decisions or factors that shape and guide the management of human resources in an organizational context. It is also a set of strategic processes communally shared by human resources and line managers to resolve people-related business issues. It is directly related to the business strategy and focuses on the formulation and alignment of human resource activities to achieve organizational competitive objectives.

Human Resources: In general, human resources are any personnel employed by an organization or, the field of study related to recruiting and managing the organization's personnel. Human resources systems need to consider human resource planning; recruitment, hiring, and placement; training and development; wages, compensation, perquisites ("perks"); and employee relations.

Hygiene Theory: Herzberg's theory that motivation is a two-step process; first, eliminating the things that dissatisfy (usually context and environment related), and second, creating motivators or the things that satisfy (promotion, achievement, recognition, etc).

Hypothesis: An empirically-testable declaration that certain variables and their corresponding measure are related in a specific way proposed by a theory.

Identity Management: Identity management (IdM) is related to data security and refers to the management of a user's credentials and how users might log into an online system.

Inbound Logistics: Materials handling, transportation, receipt and warehousing of raw materials, parts, and supplies, and their distribution to manufacturing as they are needed in the production process.

Incorporator: Responsible individual who files articles of incorporation with the secretary of state.

Incremental Innovation: Improvement of technology performance or product feature enhancement.

Independent Variable: The variable in an experiment or research study that is intentionally manipulated in order to determine its effect on the dependent variable (e.g., the independent variable of type of cereal might affect the dependent variable of the consumer's reaction to it).

Industrial Relations: A precursor to present-day human resource management, 'industrial relations' is a term that was popular from the mid-1950s to the late 1960s, during the period when trade unions were particularly dominant.

Inferential Statistics: A subset of mathematical statistics used in the analysis and interpretation of data. Inferential statistics are used to make inferences such as drawing conclusions about a population from a sample and in decision making.

Informal Organization: The attitudes, values, feelings, interactions, and group norms that affect organizational functioning and effectiveness.

Information Management: The systematic and explicit management of vital information in an organization.

Information System Development Life Cycle (ISDLC): The multi step structured process in which an information system is developed and maintained.

Information System: A system that improves the flow of information and data between people or departments.

Information Systems: Interrelated components working together to collect, process, store and disseminate information to support decision making, coordination, control, analysis, and visualization in an organization (Laudon & Laudon, 2001).

Information Technology: The use of computers, communications networks, and knowledge in the creation, storage, and dispersal of data and information. Information technology comprises a wide range of items and abilities for use in the creation, storage, and distribution of information.

Information: The data that is available to a business enterprise about its market and products.

Innovation: The use of a new product, service, or method in business practice immediately subsequent to its discovery.

Inquiry Process: A decision making process that encourages cognitive conflict in order to bring about the best ideas.

Insolvency: A financial condition when assets are inadequate to pay obligations.

Insured: A person or entity covered by a policy of insurance.

Insurer: The entity contractually bound to reimburse or compensate an insured party upon the happening of a covered event.

Integrative Negotiation: Negotiation that seeks a settlement in which both sides of the conflict win or profit.

Intercultural Sensitivity: The ability to interpret situations and events in the same way as persons native to the culture in which they take place.

Interest Rate Risk: A form of market risk resulting from changes in interest rates.

Intermediate-term Loan: A 1-3-year commercial bank loan businesses use for capital, equipment purchases and other short-term needs.

Internal Consultant: Organizational development professionals who work exclusively for one organization and are direct reports to a designated level of management.

International Human Resource Management: The discipline and occupational function involved with employee issues such as expatriate management, cross-cultural awareness, cross-cultural sensitivity, diversity management, and understanding of the daily operations of international business.

International Organization for Standardization (ISO): The organization that compiles, develops, and promotes global standards for performance and quality.

Internet: Also known as the "information highway." This tool houses a seemingly unlimited amount of information (online banking, email, map directions, news, etc).

Intranet: A private network similar to the Internet, but which is intended for use only by a single enterprise and authorized outside parties (e.g., customers, suppliers, partners). Intranets typically contain proprietary information and are protected by a firewall. The part of an intranet that is made available to outside parties is referred to as an extranet.

Issues Management: The executive function of strategic public relations that deals with problem solving, organizational policy, long-range planning, and management strategy as well as communication of that strategy internally and externally.

Jargon: Technical language, acronyms, specialized language, or other words or phrases that are unique — or uniquely interpreted — to a given group or organization that are not in wide acceptance outside that group.

Job Analysis: The systematic, empirical process of determining the exact nature of a job, including the tasks and duties to be done; the knowledge, skills and abilities necessary to adequately perform these; and the criteria that distinguish between acceptable and unacceptable performance. The results of a job analysis are typically used in writing job descriptions and setting standards for use in performance appraisals.

Job Description: A document that lists the duties and tasks related to a job. Job descriptions may also specify the knowledge, skills, and abilities necessary to do the job as well as the performance standards that differentiate acceptable from unacceptable performance.

Job Evaluation: The method of determining how much a job is worth to an organization.

Job/Role Competencies: Skills and behaviors that someone must demonstrate to achieve superior performance in a specific job, role, function, task, duty, organizational level, or entire organization.

Johari Window: A model of interpersonal communication that encourages the use of disclosure and feedback to decrease communication barriers and increase open communication.

Joint Ventures: Temporary partnerships between two firms, used when both firms wish to capitalize on a mutually beneficial opportunity.

Just-in-Time Manufacturing (JIT): A manufacturing philosophy that strives to eliminate waste and continually improve productivity. The primary characteristics of JIT include having the required inventory only when it is needed for manufacturing and reducing lead times and set up times. Also called "lean manufacturing."

Knowledge Competency: An individual's professional knowledge regarding a profession, job, or organization.

Knowledge Management System (KMS): A system for structuring information storage, use, and distribution within an organization.

Knowledge Management: Knowledge management is an umbrella term used to describe all of the different ways that an organization manipulates knowledge, from acquiring it and organizing it to distributing and storing it. Generally speaking, the more adept an organization is at knowledge management, the greater will be that organization's aptitude for organizational learning.

Labor Productivity: The measurement of output quantity relative to the measurement of a certain quantity of labor used, such as total hours worked.

Labor Quality: The labor input per hour worked.

Leaders: Persons who focus on doing the right thing above all else.

Leadership Style: The way in which a leader supervises his/her employees. Different leadership styles (e.g., coercive, permissive, persuasive) are appropriate depending on the ability and needs of the workers, the situation in which they are working, and the personality of the leader.

Leadership Theory: Models of the ways in which to influence others while helping them to achieve the goals of the team or organization.

Leadership Traits: The traits or characteristics of a manager's personality that will enable him or her to become a leader. The traits include integrity, pride, sincerity, curiosity, passion and courage.

Leadership: The process of intentionally influencing others and providing an environment that facilitates them in the achievement of team and organizational objectives.

Lean Manufacturing: A set of tools and techniques used to eliminate all waste from production processes.

Learning Curve: A learning curve is a visual representation of the relationship of acquiring experience to acquiring skill, and it is used with both individuals and organizations. As the amount of experience with a new task or process increases, the subject's aptitude at performing the task also increases. In other words, both people and organizations get better at doing things as they get more practice. This even applies, somewhat recursively, to the process of learning itself. The more an individual or an organization engages in learning, the better it becomes at learning—it learns how to learn.

Leveraged Buyout: One company buys out another to take it over using limited funds of its own and borrowing the rest.

Limited Liability Company: A business organization that has features of a partnership and a corporation.

Limited Liability Partnership: A form of business partnership normally utilized by law firms and accounting companies. The partners are shielded from the debts incurred by the partnership.

Limited Partnership: A business partnership consisting of one or more partners who manage the business and are liable for its debts.

Liquidation: Selling off a company's assets for their tangible net worth; signals the end of the firm's existence.

Local Area Network (LAN): Multiple computers that are located near each other and linked into a network that allows the users to share files and peripheral devices such as printers, fax machines, and storage devices.

Logistics Management: Management of the movement of goods and information.

Logistics Network Design: The design of information management systems to aid in the seamless integration of the various logistics management activities.

Major Medical Insurance: An insurance policy that provides benefits only for extraordinary major illnesses and injuries which most people would be unable to pay without great hardship. This type of insurance is typically a supplement to a more comprehensive healthcare plan. These Major Medical Insurance plans usually have high benefit limits and deductibles.

Management by Objectives (MBO): An approach to performance appraisal in which the employee and his or her manager jointly set performance objectives for the coming appraisal period and then review the progress made toward accomplishing these objectives at predefined times. The employee's performance is evaluated in terms of how well he or she met the objectives previously determined.

Management Competencies: Those job/role competencies which define exemplary management performance.

Management Consultant: A management consultant is a qualified professional who works with upper level management in an organization to analyze the organization's health and effectiveness, identify problem areas, make recommendations, and assist in implementing the recommendations. Management consultants' activities include diagnosing and making recommendations for existing business problems or in the development of future plans.

Management Development: A range of policies and programs to assist managers in developing leadership, supervision and control.

Management Information Systems: Comprised of computing and communications hardware, operating and systems software, applications software to support business functions, and specialized staff; designed to achieve business goals and objectives.

Management of Human Resources: A wide variety of policies and procedures which are strategically significant for the organization and are typically used to promote employee commitment, flexibility, good quality of work life as well as to realize overall business goals such as organizational values, structure, productivity, and production techniques.

Management Style: The way in which a manager supervises his/her employees. Different management styles (coercive, permissive, persuasive) are appropriate depending on the ability and needs of the workers, the situation in which they are working and the personality of the manager.

Management: The process of efficiently and effectively accomplishing work through the coordination and supervision of others.

Managerial Leadership: The ability of managers to master the main functions of management and to lead an organization or group by adhering to core values and ensuring that their actions and behaviors are ethical.

Managers: Persons who focus doing things right above all else.

Manufactured Risk: Risk that is created by organizations through the selection of technologies or business practices.

Market Risk: The potential for an investor to experience loss from fluctuations in securities prices.

Market Share: The proportion of total sales of a given type of product or service that are earned by a particular business or organization.

Market Structures: The pattern formed by the number, size, and distribution of buyers and sellers in a market.

Markov Chain: A random process comprising discrete events in which the future development of each event is either independent of past events or dependent only on the immediately preceding event. Markov chains are often used in marketing to model subsequent purchases of products (i.e., the probability of the customer making a purchase from a particular business or brand is dependent only on his/her last purchase of that brand or independent of the brand).

Material Requirements Planning (MRP): The process of determining resources necessary to fill current and future orders for products or services.

Mathematical Statistics: A branch of mathematics that deals with the analysis and interpretation of data. Mathematical statistics provide the theoretical underpinnings for various applied statistical disciplines, including business statistics, in which data are analyzed to find answers to quantifiable questions.

Matrix Structure: An approach to organization design in which employees report both to a functional or departmental supervisor and a project supervisor.

Mediation: The use of a third-party in the negotiation process to facilitate a resolution through persuasion or alternative ideas.

Members: The owners in a limited liability company.

Mentoring: A common method of transferring knowledge and understanding within an organization which provides staff development, transmission of corporate culture, and socialization.

Merger: A situation where two companies come together and they no longer exist as separate entities.

Metadata: Refers to anything that defines a data warehouse object, such as a table, a column, a query, a report, a business rule, or a transformation algorithm.

Metrics: A related set of business performance measurements that enable managers to develop strategies and plan and organize business activities.

Metropolitan Area Network (MAN): Computer networks that transmit data and information citywide and at greater speeds than a local area network.

Middleware: Computer software that connects applications. These applications can be within a company or from a company to a partner's application.

Millennials: The generation born in the early 1980s and reaching adulthood around the year 2000. Millennials are sometimes referred to as generation Y. They have the reputation of being comfortable with technology and with diversity, and have the highest rate of education.

Mitigation: Efforts taken to reduce either the probability or consequences of a threat.

Model: A representation of a situation, system, or subsystem. Conceptual models are mental images that describe the situation or system. Mathematical or computer models are mathematical representations of the system or situation being studied.

Monopolistic Competition: A market structure where a number of different sellers each produce similar yet slightly different products. Each seller sets its own price and quantity without having an affect on the marketplace as a whole.

Monopoly: A market structure where one company owns all or almost all of the market for a certain type of product or service. This situation arises when there is an entry barrier into the industry that allows the monopolistic company to produce without the threat of competition. Possible entry barriers can include vast economies of scale or governmental regulation. In this type of market structure the single producer will often produce an amount of the product that is less than market demand because then prices can be raised and revenue increased.

Motivation: An internal process that gives direction to, energizes, and sustains an organism's behavior. Motivation can be internal (e.g., I am hungry so I eat lunch) or external (e.g., the advertisement for the ice cream cone is attractive so I buy one).

Motivational Competencies: An individual's feeling about their job, organization, or geographic location which may impact upon performance.

Moving Average: A method used in forecasting in which the average value from previous time periods is used to forecast future time periods. The average is updated in each ensuing time period by including the new values not available in the previous average and dropping out the date from the earliest time periods.

Multifactor Productivity: The measurement of a certain input quantity which can be used to estimate total inputs.

Mutual Company: A form of private company common in the insurance industry that is owned by customers who receive distribution based on their exposure to the business.

Need: A condition in which an organism experiences the deprivation of something necessary for physiological or psychological fulfillment.

Needs Theories: Motivational theories based on the individual's needs.

Negotiation: An interactive process between two or more conflicting parties in which the parties attempt to reach a mutually acceptable agreement about an issue or issues of mutual interest.

Neoclassical Growth Theory: A growth model, also referred to as the exogenous growth model, which focuses on productivity growth.

Network Structure: A loosely aligned group of organizations that work together to provide a service or develop a product.

Network: A set of computers that are electronically linked together. A local area network (LAN) comprises multiple linked computers that are located near each other and that allow users to share files and peripheral devices such as printers, fax machines, and storage devices. A metropolitan area network (MAN) is a computer network that transmits data and information citywide and at greater speeds than a local area network. A wide area network (WAN) comprises multiple computers that are widely dispersed and that are linked into a network. Wide area networks typically use high speed, long distance communications networks or satellites to connect the computers within the network.

New Growth Theory: A growth model, also referred to as the endogenous growth theory, which developed in the 1980s in response to criticism of the neoclassical growth theory.

Non-Integration: The use of contractual arrangements, i.e., long-term agreements between the firm and its suppliers and/or distributors to provide services over a specified time period.

Nondisclosure Agreement: A legal agreement to prevent individuals or entities from taking a company's internal secrets and using them for profit.

Nonverbal Communication: Communication that does not use words (i.e., is not written or spoken). Nonverbal communication includes gestures, facial expression, tone of voice, body language, posture, dress, and spatial distance from the other person.

Norms: Standards or patterns of behavior that are accepted as normal within the culture.

Null Hypothesis (H0): The statement that the findings of the experiment will show no statistical difference between the current condition (control condition) and the experimental condition.

Offshoring: The practice of relocating part of an organization's business to another country with lower costs. Off-shore work is performed by local employees in the new country and was previously performed by domestic employees.

Oligopoly: A market controlled by a small number of participants who together are able to dominate product supply and market prices.

Operating System Software: The programs that enable the different parts of a computer system to function together in order to run applications software.

Operational Decisions: Decisions that concern the day to day functions of a business.

Operational Definition: A definition that is stated in terms that can be observed and measured.

Operational Risk: Operational risk refers to the financial losses that could potentially result from either internal procedural failures or external affairs.

Operational Velocity: The point at which the business has sufficient speed in delivering products or services to market, while simultaneously meeting all customer expectations in a timely manner, and obtaining a positive revenue stream from each activity. If addressed appropriately, maximization of operational velocity will drive the enterprise to achieve greater market share and revenue as operational efficiencies are instituted.

Operations Management: Those areas of management that are concerned with productivity, quality, and cost in the operations function (i.e., activities necessary to transform inputs such as business transactions and information into outputs such as completed transactions) as well as strategic planning for the organization.

Organization Development (OD): A long-range effort to improve the organization's problem-solving and renewal processes. OD involves the application of behavior science knowledge to the problems of the workplace.

Organization: A formal arrangement of people committed to shared goals and objectives.

Organizational Behavior: The study of organizational dynamics, including individuals, groups and teams.

Organizational Change: An organization-wide transformation due to factors such as a change in mission, restructuring operations, new technologies, mergers, major collaborations, rightsizing, or re-engineering.

Organizational Competencies: Those unique competitive forces which form the basis upon which organizations compete – sometimes referred to as core competencies.

Organizational Consultants: Experts who specialize in developing planned approaches for implementing changes that will assist the organization in achieving its vision, mission and goals.

Organizational Crisis: An unlikely yet possible event that would threaten the viability of the organization, characterized by uncertainty of cause, effect, and method of solution as well as by the certainty that decisions must be made expeditiously to save the organization.

Organizational Culture: The set of basic shared assumptions, values, and beliefs that affect the way employees act within an organization.

Organizational Innovation: The process of changing the organization by introducing different methods of production or administration.

Organizational Metacognition: This idea describes how an organization thinks about its own learning process. Many organizations that prioritize learning try to find organizational learning methods that are more effective than others, so they can give themselves an advantage over competitors. This type of reflective thinking about how one learns and what resources would be the best fit with one's learning style, is typical of metacognition at the organizational level.

Organizational Purpose: The reason that a business or any organization exists, whether to provide goods or services, and the way in which that purpose is achieved.

Organizational Structure: The design of an organization including its division of labor, delegation of authority, and span of control.

Outbound Logistics: Activities involving materials handling, order fulfillment, packaging, transportation, warehousing, and distribution of finished products to the ultimate consumer.

Outcomes: Changes, results or impacts that generally focus on employees, but could be a program or institutional change.

Outsourcing: Work that could be done by an organization that is instead performed by another company on a contract basis. Outsourcing can include support (e.g., cleaning and janitorial services), production (e.g., the manufacture of parts needed to make a product), or services (e.g., customer service provided by a contract organization).

Owners: In the context of a corporation, the stock holders or shareholders.

Participatory Management: Including employees in the process of making important organizational or departmental decisions.

Partnership Agreement: The governing document of the partnership that spells out the roles and responsibilities for the partners.

Partnership: A business enterprise where two or more partners are each liable for any debts and share in the administration, profits and losses of the operation.

Pass-Through: In the context of partnerships, profits and losses are passed to each partner who then files this income on individual tax returns.

Pay for Performance: An incentive plan in which employees are rewarded financially for high performance and contributing to the organization's goals. Pay for performance plans are applicable to all levels within the organization.

Perfect Competition: A market structure characterized by a free exchange of information, no entry barriers, and a large number of buyers and sellers. These characteristics create a market in which no individual participant can dominate or influence prices or supply.

Performance Appraisal: A performance management tool, often in interview form, used to evaluate employees at work. Performance appraisals are used for goal setting, rewards, coaching, and aspects of career development.

Performance Gap: The comparison between the current performance of project and work level tasks and the desired performance of project and work level tasks.

Performance Management: Management that encourages a setting and situation in which employees are capable of performing to their highest ability.

Performance: The measured results of organizational or investment activities over a certain time period.

Perquisites ("perks"): Something given to the employee in return for work over and above regular pay or compensation. Perks may include such things as health insurance, a company car, or a private office.

Personal Competencies: An individual display of characteristics representing general standards for acceptable performance (level of achievement or output) in a given role.

Personnel Administration/Personnel Management: A precursor to present-day human resource management, 'personnel administration' and 'personnel management' were popular terms that emerged in the late 1960s, and 1970s.

Persuasion: The process of convincing someone to take a particular course of action or hold a particular point of view by argument, reasoning, or entreaty.

Population: The entire group of subjects belonging to a certain category (e.g., all women between the ages of 18 and 27; all dry cleaning businesses; all college students).

POS-D-CORB: An abbreviation that summarizes Barnard's executive functions, which are: Planning, organizing, staffing, directing, coordinating, and budgeting.

Potential Development: A company-wide management development program that seeks to cultivate performance and leadership at the top of the organization, through the provision of the necessary training, support and opportunities.

Principle of Reversibility: An ethical principle based on whether or not a decision maker would approve and support a decision if he or she were on the receiving end of the decision.

Principles of Risk Management: Three key steps to identify a potential problem, options to correct problems and consequences of action or inaction. Important exercise for all businesses to go through in order to determine risks and to take the necessary steps to resolve them.

Private Sector: All enterprises that are outside of government control including micro, small, medium, and large enterprises.

Probability: A branch of mathematics that deals with estimating the likelihood of an event occurring. Probability is expressed as a value between 0 and 1.0, which is the mathematical expression of the number of actual occurrences to the number of possible occurrences of the event. A probability of 0 signifies that there is no chance that the event will occur and 1.0 signifies that the event is certain to occur.

Procedural Law: Defines the steps which allow for a right or duty to be judicially enforced; in conrast to law which defines the rights and duties themselves.

Process Improvement Teams: An organizational team composed of employees dedicated towards improving organizational processes; usually pertaining to manufacturing goods or products.

Process Theories: Motivational theories based on the process of completing job tasks.

Process: Steps taken to achieve some end.

Processing: The activities of computer programs that convert, analyze, compute, and synthesize data to increase its usefulness.

Product Recall: The process of removing tainted or defective products from the market or offering to replace or repair major consumer items because of manufacturing defects or safety issues.

Productivity: A measurement of economic efficiency demonstrating whether or not economic inputs are effectively turned into into outputs.

Profit Maximization: A hypothesis that the goal of a firm is to maximize its profit.

Profitability Analysis: An analytical tool which compares the inner workings and profitability of a financial institution.

Program Evaluation and Review Technique (PERT): A form of the critical path method that organizes project task and activity information in a way that allows project managers and other team members to understand which tasks are critical to keeping the project on track and how the other tasks feed into these.

Property and Casualty Insurance: Insurance policies written to cover losses related to property and legal liability to third parties arising from injury related to the property.

Prospect Theory: 1979 theory serving as a critique of the inability of mainstream economic analysis to accurately account for consumer decision-making behavior.

Proxy: In the context of corporations, the assignment of a voting right by one owner, officer or director to another.

Public Sector: The economic and administrative enterprises of a local, regional, or national government.

Pure Risk: A category of risk that results exclusively in loss and failure.

Qualitative Results: Results that are measured by values, ethical behavior, organizational purpose, and learning.

Quality Assurance: Actions and processes to ensure products and services meet quality standards.

Quality Circles: An organizational team composed of employees dedicated to correcting problems that lead directly to an improvement in quality of products or processes.

Quality Control: Systems to control quality in product design and manufacture.

Quality: Fitness for use often defined by the customer.

Quantitative Results: Results that can be measured or reflected by numbers such as sales figures, profits and percentages.

Quasi-Integration: An arrangement whereby a company does not make any supplies or distribute any of its products, but owns a partial interest in a supplier or distributor to guarantee access to supplies or distribution channels.

Quorum: The minimum number of people who must be available to have a valid corporate meeting.

Rain Hedges: Type of weather derivative that compensates businesses from loss due to rain shortage and/or increases.

Reciprocal Agreement: An agreement that allows two organizations to back up each other by providing the facilities, technology, or personnel necessary to maintain business operations.

Recovery Time Objective (RTO): The time goal for reestablishing and recovering a business's functions and resources.

Recovery: Also known as 'expansion,' this is the third stage of the turnaround process. Recovery calls for strategic action to bring about a return to normal profits and growth.

Regression: A statistical technique used to develop a mathematical model for use in predicting one variable from the knowledge of another variable.

Reinforcement Theory: A motivational theory based on behavior and outcomes, consisting of positive reinforcement, negative reinforcement, extinction, and punishment.

Reinsurance: A practice common in the insurance industry whereby one insurance company assumes part or all of a risk underwritten by another insurance company.

Reliability: The consistency of measurement data.

Reporting Hierarchy: A chart organizing a company into orders or ranks; each subordinate to the one above it.

Representativeness: Judgments of conditional probabilities that are based on how well the data or sample represents the existing hypothesis or classification.

Reputation Management: The process of protecting the reputation of a company and minimizing the negative impact of events or circumstances on its reputation.

Resolutions: Document prepared by an officer or director of a company that memorializes action taken at a meeting.

Resource Loading: The process of examining the project to determine which resources are most critical to the success of the project, and proportioning them among the various activities.

Resource Planning: The process or planning resources necessary to implement functional support and grand strategies and assures that the acquisition of resources are planned in a manner that facilities efficient work flow across functions.

Retention: To remain and keep employed in the pay of the company.

Retrenchment: This refers to the reduction of expenditures by a company in order to achieve financial stability.

Retroceding: The practice whereby a reinsurer lays-off a risk assumed from the primary insurer.

Return on Investment (ROI): A measure of the organization's profitability or how effectively it uses its capital to produce profit. In general terms, return on investment is the income that is produced by a financial investment within a given time period (usually a year). There are a number of formulas that can be used in calculating ROI. One frequently used formula for determining ROI is (profits — costs) / (costs) x 100. The higher the ROI, the more profitable the organization.

Reverse Logistics: The reverse flow of goods and information along the supply chain due to products returned because of defects, obsolescence, product recalls, etc.

Rewards and Recognition: Tangible and intangible means of encouraging and motivating employees based on performance.

Risk Assessment: The process of determining the potential loss and probability of loss of the organization's objectives. Risk assessment is one step in risk management.

Risk Management: The process of evaluating, classifying, and reducing risks to a level acceptable by stakeholders.

Role-Based Access Control (RBAC): Defines roles and grants certain access rights for users to access databases.

Safety Stocks: Those items which are needed to assure the production required to meet orders and maintain optimal velocity and efficient use of capacity.

Sample: A subset of a population. A random sample is a sample that is chosen at random from the larger population with the assumption that such samples tend to reflect the characteristics of the larger population.

Sampling Error: An error that occurs in statistical analysis when the sample does not represent the population.

Sarbanes-Oxley Act: A law, enacted in 2002, which introduced highly significant legislative changes to financial practice and corporate governance regulations.

Scenario Planning: An approach to strategic planning in which a limited number of possible scenarios are drawn to describe possible alternative futures that may affect the functioning of the organization. Scenario planning helps the organization to better understand the nature and impact of the forces driving its future. Scenario planning emphasizes the open exchange of knowledge from all involved parties and a mutual understanding of issues that are central to the healthy functioning of the organization.

Scenario: A description of a possible future that identifies some significant events, the major parties involved in that future, and the assumed motivations of those parties for their actions in that future.

Schedule: A planning and tracking document that specifies the project tasks, how long each takes, and the order in which they must be accomplished in order to meet the project goals. Tools for scheduling include the PERT technique, Gantt chart, and CPM.

Scientific Management: The process in early American industry whereby production workers were managed in a way that optimized their productivity through time and motion studies.

Scientific Method: A cornerstone of organizational behavior theory in which a systematic approach is used to understand some aspect of behavior in the workplace by individuals, teams, or organizations. The scientific method is based on controlled and systematic data collection, interpretation, and verification in a search for reproducible results. In organizational behavior theory, the goal is to be able to apply these results to real world applications.

Seasonal Fluctuation: Changes in economic activity that occur in a fairly regular annual pattern. Seasonal fluctuations may be related to seasons of the year, the calendar, or holidays.

Securities Act of 1933: Federal law which requires public disclosure of financial and similarly vital organizational information with regard to public security offerings.

Securities Act of 1934: TThe federal law regulating the public trading of securities. This law provides for the registration and supervision of securities exchanges and brokers, and regulates exchanges and brokers, and regulates proxy solicitations.

Securities Act: A federal or state law protecting the public by regulating the registration, offering, and trading of securities.

Self-Actualization: The need to live up to one's full and unique potential. Associated with self-actualization are such concepts as wholeness, perfection, or completion; a divestiture of "things" in preference to simplicity, aliveness, goodness, and beauty; and a search for meaning in life. In Maslow's hierarchy of needs, this is the ultimate level of behavior motivation.

Self-Managed Teams: An organizational team that does not have a designated leader or manager for the majority of the team activity and decision-making process.

Servant Leadership: A perspective emphasizing service and originating with Greenleaf in which servant-leaders are those who place the interests of followers ahead of their own.

Server: The computer that hosts a network and provides services to the other computers in the network (e.g., a web serve serves up web pages). The term server is also used to refer to the software running on the server computer.

Service Learning: A form of community service in which students learn some leadership skills.

Service Oriented Architecture (SOA): Service-orientation describes an architecture that uses loosely coupled services to support the requirements of business processes and users. Resources on a network in an SOA environment are made available as independent services that can be accessed without knowledge of their underlying platform implementation (Wikipedia, 2007).

Service Sector: In its essence, the service sector includes those industries and businesses that provide services rather than tangible products for individual consumers, businesses, or a combination of the two. These can include physical, mental, or aesthetic activities (e.g., legal services, entertainment, auto repair) or the transformation of something through such activity (e.g., hair cutting, education, management consulting).

Sherman Act: The federal government's first antitrust statute.

Single Factor Productivity: The measurement of output quantity in relation to a single input.

Situation Leadership: A leadership school of thought which asserts that leaders should adapt their style depending on the situation and maturity of their employees.

Six Sigma (6s): An approach to improving quality. The term "six sigma" is a statistical term referring to the degree to which a product reaches its quality goal. At six sigma, a product is reaching its quality goal 99.9999997 percent of the time, or has only 3.4 defects per million. The six sigma system was originally developed by Motorola.

Social Capital: The advantages created by having social networks, such as organizational teams and interpersonal relationships.

Social Exchange Theory: Social exchange theory is a set of ideas that seeks to describe the ways that people in organizations interact with one another as they attempt to complete the tasks that have been assigned to them. The theory states that if one person performs a task for another, then the person who benefitted from having that task will be more likely to reciprocate. Modern leadership theories rely heavily on ideas around social exchange, the idea being that people follow their leaders because the leaders provide them with something in exchange for their cooperation.

Sole Proprietorship: Business organization usually formed when one person operates the business.

Span of Control: The number of people who directly work for a person on the next level of the organizational hierarchy.

Speculative Risk: Risky action that results in an uncertain degree of gain or loss.

Spreadsheet: A table of values arranged in rows and columns in which the values have predefined relationships. Spreadsheet application software allows users to create and manipulate spreadsheets electronically.

Stabilization: Also known as 'renewal,' this is the second stage of the turnaround process, beginning when cash flows equal or exceed cash outflows. This stage calls for operational action to bring about profits.

Stakeholder: A person or group that can affect or be affected by a decision or action. In marketing, stakeholders may include the organization's employees, suppliers, distributors, and stockholders.

Standard Deviation: A measure of variability that describes how far the typical score in a distribution is from the mean of the distribution. The standard deviation is obtained by determining the deviation of each score from the mean (i.e., subtracting the mean from the score), squaring the deviations (i.e., multiplying them by themselves), adding the squared deviations, and dividing by the total number of scores. The larger the standard deviation, the farther away it is from the midpoint of the distribution.

Statistical Significance: The degree to which an observed outcome is unlikely to have occurred due to chance.

Statistics: A branch of mathematics that deals with the analysis and interpretation of data. Mathematical statistics provide the theoretical underpinnings for various applied statistical disciplines, including business statistics, in which data are analyzed to find answers to quantifiable questions. Applied statistics uses these techniques to solve real world problems.

Statute: A law passed by a legislature; either state or federal.

Statutory Law: Collection of laws created through statute rather than from the constitution or judicial rulings.

Stochastic: Involving chancc or probability. Stochastic variables are random or have an element of chance or probability associated with their occurrence.

Stock Holders: Owners of a corporation.

Stock: A unit of ownership interest in a corporation.

Storage Area Network (SAN): A specialized, high-speed network attaching servers and storage devices. A SAN allows any-to-any connection across the network, using interconnect devices such as routers, gateways, hubs, and switches (Tate, et al., 2004).

Strategic Business Units: Divisions and subsidiaries within a multi-business firm.

Strategic Decisions: Decisions that establish long-term goals and policies of a business.

Strategic Plan: A document based on the process of determining the long-term goals of an organization and developing a plan to use the company's resources — including materials and personnel — in reaching these goals.

Strategy: In business, a strategy is a plan of action to help the organization reach its goals and objectives. A good business strategy is based on the rigorous analysis of empirical data, including market needs and trends, competitor capabilities and offerings, and the organization's resources and abilities.

Subject Matter Experts (SMEs): An individual who understands a business process or area well enough to answer questions form people in other groups who are typing to help.

Substantive Law: Law concerning personal power, rights and duties.

Succession Planning: A management development program aimed at filling specific positions with one of two potential candidates.

Supply Chain Management (SCM): The term SCM was coined in the 1980s to refer to the necessary business requirement of integrating key business processes from the end user back to original suppliers. Companies and corporations partake in a supply chain through the exchange of information with partners and customers to facilitate efficient business operations.

Supply Chain Management Systems: Applications software that is integrated into a communications network that enables organizations to communicate about and support their purchasing, sales, and shipping needs.

Supply Chain: A network of organizations involved in production, delivery, and sale of a product. The supply chain may include suppliers, manufacturers, storage facilities, transporters, and retailers. Each organization in the network provides a value-added activity to the product or service. The supply chain includes the flow of tangible goods and materials, funds, and information between the organizations in the network.

Support Strategies: Those strategies such as accounting, finance, legal, and research and development strategies that are necessary to execute functional strategies.

Survey Research: A type of research in which data about the opinions, attitudes, or reactions of the members of a sample are gathered using a survey instrument. The phases of survey research are goal setting, planning, implementation, evaluation, and feedback. As opposed to experimental research, survey research does not allow for the manipulation of an independent variable.

Survey: (a) A data collection instrument used to acquire information on the opinions, attitudes, or reactions of people; (b) a research study in which members of a selected sample are asked questions concerning their opinions, attitudes, or reactions are gathered using a survey instrument or questionnaire for purposes of scientific analysis; typically the results of this analysis are used to extrapolate the findings from the sample to the underlying population; (c) to conduct a survey on a sample.

Symmetrical Communication: A strategy used by issues-management practitioners to bring about symbiotic changes in the ideas, attitudes, and behaviors of both their organizations and the public.

Synergy: The process by which the combined product resulting from the work of a team of individuals is greater than the results of their individual efforts.

System Dynamics: A method for studying and managing complex feedback systems in a business environment.

Systematic Approach: The measured and defined method for designing, developing, managing and evaluating learning resources and processes.

Systems Development Life Cycle: Five phase process of developing information systems.

Systems Development: Creating or modifying existing business systems.

Systems Theory: A cornerstone of organizational behavior theory that assumes that the organization comprises multiple subsystems and that the functioning of each affects both the functioning of the others and the organization as a whole.

Tacit Knowledge: Tacit knowledge is that organizational knowledge which is unspoken but known to all. An example of tacit knowledge could be seen at a company where there is an unspoken rule that no one is promoted to vice president without serving at least six months at the company's London office. This is not an official rule that is inscribed somewhere, but it is an unwritten requirement that everyone in the company knows about.

Tactical Decisions: Decisions that are aimed at bringing a company closer to its goals and implementing its policies.

Tailored Approach: A competency modeling approach tailored to the meet the unique needs of an organization.

Taper Integration: A firm relies on outside firms for: 1) supplying only a portion of production inputs or 2) distributing a portion of its products.

Task Interdependence: "The degree to which team members must share common inputs, interact in the process of executing their work, and receive outcomes determined partly by their mutual performance" (McShane & Von Glinow, 2003).

Team Building: The process of turning a group of individuals who work together from a collection of individuals doing related tasks to a cohesive unit where the efforts of the team members act synergistically to yield results that could be achieved by the individuals alone.

Team-Based Structure: An approach to organizational structure based on self-directed work teams.

Team: A type of group within which there is skill differentiation among team members and the entire team works within the context of a common mission. Unlike groups in general, team members are committed to the goal and mission of the team and have a collaborative culture in which the members trust each other. Leadership of a team is shared, and members are mutually accountable to each other. Teamwork often leads to a situation of synergy.

Teamthink: A decision-making model that is intended to eliminate groupthink.

Technical Training: Training for specific competence on the job, with regard to technology and/or business process change.

Technological Innovation: The process by which industry generates new and improved products and production processes

Technological Risks: Risks caused or created by technologies which can include trains wrecking, bridges falling, and planes crashing.

Technology: The application of scientific methods and knowledge to the attainment of industrial or commercial objectives. Technology includes products, processes, and knowledge.

Telecommunication: The transmission and receipt of data and information over a linked set of hardware and software at multiple locations.

Temperature Risks: Type of weather derivative that compensates businesses from loss due to weather related issues like a shortage of snow or prolonged cold temperatures in a normally warm climate, etc.

Third-Party Logistics Providers (3PLs): Third-party firms who contract to manage a firm's logistics function.

Thrifts: Savings and loan associations, credit unions, or savings banks.

Tier-1 Supplier: A direct supplier to a firm.

Tier-2 Supplier: A supplier of inputs to a given firm's tier-1 supplier.

Time and Materials Contract: A type of contract in which the customer pays for actual direct labor at fixed hourly rates (including wages, overhead, general and administrative expenses, and profit) and the actual cost of materials used in the project. This type of contract places the least risk on the contractor and the most risk on the customer.

Time Series Data: Data gathered on a specific characteristic over a period of time. Time series data are used in business forecasting. To be useful, time series data must be collected at intervals of regular length.

Total Cost of Quality: A metric made up of two types of costs: The cost of nonconformance and the cost of nonconformance.

Total Factor Productivity: The measurement of total output quantity in relation to a measurement of the total input quantity.

Total Quality Management (TQM): A management strategy that attempts to continually increase the quality of goods and services as well as customer satisfaction through raising awareness of quality concerns across the organization.

Traditionalists: This is one of several names used to describe those born prior to 1946. They are also known as the Greatest Generation because of their sacrifices during World War II and the Great Depression. They tend to have more challenges using technology because they have lived most of their lives without having to learn it or rely upon it.

Trait Theories: Refers to leadership theories that are based on an individual's traits.

Transactional Leadership: Transactional leadership is a leadership style in which the leader's role is simply to manage exchanges between different people and/or departments. It does not place a high value on leader behaviors such as persuasion, inspiration, or collaboration. Instead, transactional leadership relies on leaders issuing orders which subordinates follow. If subordinates do not comply with the orders, then the leader is responsible for punishing the failure to comply.

Transformational Leadership: Transformational leadership is a style that seeks to inspire the members of an organization to work together in order to create a system that is greater than the sum of its parts, and to cooperate on efforts that have the potential to change the world. Transformational leaders inspire their followers to discover new parts of themselves and to share these with one another for the benefit of all.

Transmission: The process of distributing data or information over a communications network.

Transportation Management: Determining the most efficient and cost-effective way to execute the movement of goods, via various modes of transportation.

Trend: The persistent, underlying direction in which something is moving in either the short, intermediate, or long term. Identification of a trend allows one to better plan to meet future needs.

Turnaround Environment: This is the social, technological, economic and political environment in which an ailing company functions.

Turnaround Investing: A high-risk, potentially high-return form of investment, where investors are given the chance to acquire underperforming companies at low prices, and create value by bringing the companies to a position of substantial and sustained positive performance.

Turnaround Manager: This is a consultant who specializes in reviving failing businesses.

Turnaround Strategies: These are the key set of activities employed to halt decline and stimulate the upturn cycle of a company.

Turnaround: A turnaround is a process whereby a company that has been experiencing an extended period of poor performance, is led to experience substantial and sustained positive performance.

Turnover Rates: The rate at which employees leave an organization and must be replaced.

Turnover: The number of new employees that an organization must hire in order to replace those who have left the company in a given period of time.

Underwriting: In the context of insurance, means to assume liability for certain events. In the context of investment banking, refers to guaranteeing the sale of certain securities.

Underwriting/Insurance Cycle: Generally refers to the fluctuations in the profitability of the insurance industry.

Uniform Commercial Code (U.C.C.): Country-wide law concerning the sale of goods, secured transaction and negotiable instruments.

UNIX: A 1960's computer operating system developed at Bell Labs.

Utility: Value derived from choice.

Validity: The ability of a method to measure what it intends to measure.

Value-at-Risk Analysis: A measure of which direction and how far the market value of an asset or of a portfolio of assets is going to move during a given time period assuming regular conditions.

Variable: An object in a research study that can have more than one value. Independent variables are stimuli that are manipulated in order to determine their effect on the dependent variables (response). Extraneous variables are variables that affect the response but that are not related to the question under investigation in the study.

Vertical Merger: The business act in which one firm acquires either a customer or a supplier.

Virtual Organization: An association of multiple independent organizations that are allied for the purpose of product development or serving a client.

Virtual Team: A team in which the members are geographically or organizationally dispersed. Virtual team members interact primarily through communication technology and may never meet face-to-face.

Virtual Work Groups: Work groups or teams that do not meet face-to-face.

Warehouse Management: Also known as warehousing, warehouse management is the management of the movement and storage of materials throughout the warehouse.

Wealth Maximization: In an efficient market, it is the maximization of the current share price.

Weather Derivatives: Financial instrument that can be customized to the company's needs to determine weather related risks.

Wellness Program: Company sponsored programs which emphasize the good health of employees.

Wide Area Network (WAN): Multiple computers that are widely dispersed and that are linked into a network. Wide area networks typically use high speed, long distance communications networks or satellites to connect the computers within the network.

Win-Lose Orientation: The belief in a conflict situation that there is a fixed pool of resources that are to be divided among all parties so that the more one side receives, the less the other side receives.

Win-Win Orientation: The belief that it is possible to arrive at a mutually agreeable solution for all parties in a conflict situation.

Wireless Communications System: A communication system that transmits data using radio signals over the air or through space as opposed to through wire or optical cables.

Work Breakdown Structure (WBS): A hierarchical outline of tasks and activities necessary to complete a project. In addition to the major tasks to be accomplished, the WBS specifies the substeps necessary for each task. See Figure 1.

Workstation: A desktop computer that is connected to a network. Workstations are also sometimes referred to as clients or nodes.

INDEX

E

M